Footprint **Rajasthan**

Matt Barrett
2nd edition

*"Such is Rajasthan, the land of Rajput warriors – bold and beauteous,
simple and yet difficult, welcoming and yet self-conscious,
full of valor and full of romance."*

Suniti Chandra Mishra

Rajasthan Highlights

See colour maps at back of book

The Government of India state that "the external boundaries of India are neither correct nor authenticated"

❶ Balaji Temple
Exorcism at first hand, not for the faint-hearted

❷ Karauli
A little-visited town with a fantastically quirky heritage hotel

❸ Ranthambore National Park
Go tiger-spotting in stunning surroundings

❹ Bundi
The massive fort here towers over an authentic and hugely atmospheric town

❺ Juna Mahal, Dungarpur
A fascinating glimpse of how life in a royal palace was lived 200 years ago

❻ Ranakpur
Incredibly intricate temples and remarkably untouristy

❼ Meherangarh Fort Rajasthan's most imperious fort, fantastically restored

❽ First sight of Jaisalmer
An incredible fort which rises so majestically from flat desert plain you'll think it's a mirage

9 Osian
An extraordinary variety of temples surrounded by desert

10 Nagaur
An authentic cattle fair and fascinating fort

11 Kakoo
An unspoilt desert village surrounded by high sand dunes

12 Sunset over Pushkar Lake
Enjoy the view, often to the sound of beating drums

13 Nasiyan Jain Temple Ajmer
Jain vision of the universe, rendered in pure gold

14 Maharaja Palaces
Any maharaja who was anyone in Rajasthan had a palace in Jaipur, and many are now beautiful hotels – your chance to live like a king

15 Malji ka Kamra Haveli, Churu
One of the best preserved painted *havelis* in Shekhawati, but crumbling fast so get there quick

16 Apani Dhani
A friendly, well-run eco-farm and hotel

In the shadows
Parts of the Rajasthan landscape are characterised by shifting sands and sky-high dunes; best experienced aloft a ship of the desert.

A foot in the door

Rajasthan is a land of unending variety, in parts painfully touristy, in others completely untouched. Its people range from suave, polo-playing Rajputs and their elegant, jewellery-draped wives to tall, incandescently turbaned camel drivers, a gold hoop in each ear almost bridged by a luxuriant moustache, their hard-working women often hidden behind a swathe of brilliantly bright fabrics, an inverse camouflage against the surrounding sand.

Its history is one of fierce pride, unflinching chivalry and unequivocal independence until the arrival of the British, who granted the Maharajas huge wealth but very little power. As a result, the period under their rule was characterized by consumption and extravagant consumerism. This varied past has left behind a veritable feast of unparalleled riches: a collection of forts, palaces, temples and treasures which no other state can begin to equal.

In recent years, however, Rajasthan has been struggling to find a place in today's increasingly high-tech India. Rooted in its past but with little identity other than as a tourist destination, it is regarded as backward and parochial by a large number of Indians. Many of the major sites have done little to preserve their valuable heritage, controlled as they have been by well-meaning maharajahs with little professional experience. A much needed transition is now under way, however, with Meherangarh Fort in Jodphur a superb example for the rest to follow. Whereas tourists were perhaps once seen as an entertaining diversion, their role as the mainstay of the local economy is now being taken far more seriously, with the standards of facilities on offer improving dramatically as a result.

1 Some of the most skilfully weaved saris are made in Rajasthan. Kota is home to a village where hundreds of weavers work towards making some of the best. ►► See page 178.

2 The Adinath Temple at Ranakpur has no less than 1,444 engraved pillars each one individually carved. ►► See page 160.

3 Mandawa isn't the prettiest of towns but it is home to some little-visited havelis with frescos adorning the walls. ►► See page 259.

4 The ancient feudal village of Bijaipur has one of the oldest forts in Rajasthan. ►► See page 176.

5 The friendly village of Dungarpur is also one of Rajasthan's most alluring, with an exquisitely decorated palace and surrounded by Lake Gaibsagar. ►► See page 154.

6 During Diwali, the festival of lights, even the sacred cow is encouraged to get involved. ►► See page 48.

7 Udaipur is thought by many to be one of India's romantic cities. Here, women wash clothes on the bank of its centrepiece, Lake Pichola. ►► See page 140.

8 Hawa Mahal, 'Palace of the Winds', was built for ladies of the harem; the façade enabled them to look down on the street below without being seen. ►► See page 115.

9 The atmospheric, unspoilt city of Bundi is fascinating to wander around. ►► See page 178.

10 In the region of Shekhawati are some of the finest havelis. ►► See page 256.

11 Pushkar Camel Fair is a sight to be seen. Seemingly every camel owner in the state descends on the village for a week of selling, buying and celebrating. ►► See page 238.

12 Surrounded by sand dunes, Osian's eighth- to tenth-century temple complex is amazingly well sited. ►► See page 198.

8 Wonder walls

Rajasthan's cities traditionally consisted of a central fort surrounded by a dense forest of housing, narrowly separated by a jumble of alleyways, and surrounded by a thick defensive wall. Many of the original structures remain, with the evocative old cities still wonderfully atmospheric, their tight lanes a defence against the advance of modernity. The forts of Amber, Bikaner, Chittaurgarh and Bundi are all impressive, but it is those of Jaisalmer and Jodhpur that really stand out, as much for the sheer dominance of their positions as their indisputable architectural prowess; the views from both are stunning.

Golden days

There was a time when Rajasthan's maharajas had little more to concern themselves with than the opulence of their surroundings, their personal appearance, and making sure that the two were captured on camera! Testimony to this can be seen in the shape of Rajasthan's magnificent palaces and the photograph-lined walls within. Samode, Deogarh, Udaipur's City Palace and, perhaps the most authentic of them all, Dungarpur's untouched Juna Mahal are all well worth a visit. The finest of Shekawati's havelis, ornately decorated mansions built by local merchants during the boom period of the 18th and 19th centuries, come close to matching these royal residences, their crumbling condition somehow adding to their charm.

The approach to the city of Jaisalmer is enough to make you weep. Within the fortified desert settlement are tight, dusty alleys lined with sandstone buildings, some crumbling away and some beautifully carved.

Diverse deities

Many of India's major religions are represented in Rajasthan resulting in the extraordinarily intricate Jain temple complexes in Mount Abu and Ranakpur, as well as the pure gold presentation of the Jain vision of the universe in Ajmer, also home to one of Indian Islam's holiest shrines, the Dargah. Of the many Hindu temples and towns, Deshnoke's infamous 'rat temple' and the sacred lake in Pushkar are perhaps the most impressive, but it's often the time of day, people present and any number of less tangible factors which can bring these places to life; all can be special when the timing's right.

Stars and sands

As well as its people and places, Rajasthan's landscapes also leave a lasting impression from the endless expanses of desert sand to forests of tiger-concealing trees and green, rolling hills. The desert is best seen from a camel's lofty back, or experienced at night when stars – almost too bright to believe – perforate the ink black sky. Get yourself within earshot of a talented player of the twin desert flute and the magic is complete. While Jaisalmer has long been the centre for safaris, other options such as Bikaner, Pushkar and Kakoo have emerged as interesting alternatives in recent years.

Close encounters

Away from the desert, it's the wildlife which takes centre stage. Pride of place must go to the tigers of Ranthambore, where the chances of spotting one of these magnificent creatures in their natural habitat are as good as anywhere in the world. Don't get too caught up in the tiger hunt however; all manner of monkeys, deer, leopards and hyenas also compete for attention, watched over by the imperious blue bull. There's also an exceptional array of birdlife, particularly at Keoladeo National Park, where pedal power is the only permitted mode of transport, making this a peaceful escape from the rigours of life on the road. Man's traditionally close proximity to beast is reflected in the myriad cattle and camel fairs for which the state is so justifiably famed.

Contents

Introducing
Rajasthan highlights 2
A foot in the door 5

Essentials
Planning your trip 12
Before you travel 19
Money 22
Getting there 24
Touching down 26
Getting around 31
Sleeping 40
Eating 42
Entertainment 45
Festivals and events 46
Shopping 49
Sport and activities 50
Health 53
Keeping in touch 59

Guide

Delhi & Agra
Delhi 64
  Sights 65
  Listings 88
Agra 101
  The Taj Mahal 101
  Agra Fort (Red Fort) 103
  I'timad-ud-Daulah 106
  Sikandra 107
  Listings 107

Jaipur & around
Jaipur 114
  Listings 123
Around Jaipur 131
  Amber 131
  Jaigarh Fort 133
  Jal Mahal and Gaitore 133
  Sanganer 133
  Choki Dhani 134
  Sisodia Rani-ka and
    Vidyadhar baghs 134
  Ramgarh Lake and
    Jamwa Sanctuary 134
  Bagru 134
  Madhogarh 135

Samode 135
Listings 135

Southern Rajasthan
Udaipur 140
  Listings 146
Around Udaipur 153
  Listings 156
**Kumbhalgarh,
Ranakpur and
around** 158
  Kumbhalgarh 158
  Ghanerao and Rawla
    Narlai 159
  Ranakpur 160
  Listings 160
**Mount Abu and
around** 162
  Listings 168
**Chittaurgarh and
around** 173
  Chittaurgarh 173
  Chittaurgarh to Kota 176
  Kota 176
  Bundi 178
  Listings 181

Western Rajasthan
Jodhpur 187
  Listings 193
Around Jodhpur 197
  Listings 200
Jaisalmer 201
  Listings 206
Around Jaisalmer 210
  Listings 212

Eastern Rajasthan
**Alwar, Sariska
and around** 216
  Delhi Jaipur Road 217
  Alwar 217
  Sariska Tiger Reserve 218
  Listings 219
**Deeg, Bharatpur and
around** 220
  Bhandarej to
    Bharatpur 222

Bharatpur 222
Keoladeo Ghana
  National Park 223
Listings 225
**Ranthambhore
National Park** 227
  Listings 230
Ajmer and Pushkar 232
  From Jaipur to Ajmer 233
  Ajmer 234
  Pushkar 238
  Listings 239

Northern Rajasthan
Bikaner and around 248
  Listings 252
Shekhawati 256
  Listings 262

Background
History 266
Modern Rajasthan 277
Economy 279
Culture 280
Religion 292
**Land and
environment** 305
Books 316

Footnotes
Language 320
Eating and drinking 323
Glossary 328
Index 336
Map index 339
Ad index 339
Acknowledgements 340
Credits 341
Complete listings 340
Map symbols 343
Colour maps 344

Inside front cover
Sleeping and eating price
  codes

Inside back cover
Author biography

Planning your trip   12
Before you travel   19
Money   22
Getting there   24
Touching down   26
Getting around   31
Sleeping   40
Eating   42
Entertainment   45
Festivals and events   46
Shopping   49
Sport and activities   50
Health   53
Keeping in touch   59

⁝ Footprint features

Money matters   23
Exchange rates   24
Touching down   27
Great expectations   28
Riding the rails   33
The hazards of the road   37
Hotel price codes explained   41
A cup of chai   44
Two masala dosai
    and a pot of tea   43
Fighter pilots   47

Planning your trip

Where to go

Rajasthan offers an almost daunting range of possibilities for travellers. You could travel for weeks without seeing it all. Here we suggest some possible tours ranging from one-week to one-month trips. Travel networks of road, rail and air are so interconnected that you can combine parts of the routes given below in a range of different ways. Travel agencies are listed through the book, who can make the necessary arrangements for a relatively small fee, saving you time and bother, but remember that air tickets can be difficult to get at short notice for some trips, especially during the winter peak season. Allow a little more time if you are planning to travel entirely by road and rail. However, if you use overnight trains for longer journeys you can cover almost as much ground in the same time as flying.

One week

You'll probably need a night or two in Delhi to recover from the flight and adjust to both the time zone and being in India! Most people have the Taj Mahal as a top priority even on a flying visit; if you're keen to see it you could either head to Agra first, or follow these suggestions in reverse and leave it until the end. Wherever you go from Agra it's probably worth stopping off at Fatehpur Sikri for at least a couple of hours on the way. From there you could head to Bharatpur if you fancy some birdspotting in tranquil Keoladeo National Park, or if tigers are more your thing make for Ranthambore, possibly stopping off for a night at the wonderfully wacky Bhanwar Vilas Palace in Karauli along the way. Most tourists head to Jaipur from Agra, or vice versa, on the ever-popular 'Golden Triangle' route. Jaipur is not everyone's cup of tea, however; many feel that the hustle and bustle is not outweighed by the city's attractions. Other options include staying at one of the heritage hotels nearby, at Kanota and Bhandarej, for example, and then heading back towards Delhi on the quieter Alwar road if you're travelling by car, perhaps stopping for the night at Sariska Palace or Kesroli Hill Fort.

   If this is a bit more relaxed than you'd like, but don't fancy spending long in Jaipur, it's perfectly possible to get the train in to Jaipur and then continue on elsewhere from there, Ajmer/Pushkar for example. From there you could get as far as Jodhpur or even Udaipur, and then take fly back to Delhi.

Two weeks

The extra week could be spent travelling further in one direction; to Bikaner and then Jaisalmer in the west if you felt like taking in some authentic desert scenery and culture; Mount Abu, Ranakpur and Kumbhalgarh to the south if you'd like to see stunning Jain temples, an amazing fort and experience Rajasthan's coolest climate; or Bundi, Kota and Chittaurgarh in the east if you felt like getting off the beaten track and witnessing the Rajasthan of yesteryear.

One month

One month is enough time to complete an entire loop of Rajasthan, or at a more leisurely pace, either an eastern or western loop and taking in most of the sights of north and south. Opting for the latter, this would mean either leaving Delhi for Agra, and then on to places such as Bharatpur, Ranthambore, Bundi, Kota, Chittaurgarh, Dungarpur and then Udaipur. From there you could head back to Delhi, probably taking in Jodhpur and Jaipur on your way, giving an interesting mix of historical sights, major cities and varied wildlife. Alternatively, you could head through the Shekawati region from Delhi, perhaps stopping at Neemrana along the way. From there you could head to Bikaner, Jaisalmer, Jodhpur, and then on through the Ranakpur/ Kumbhalgarh region to Udaipur. After a couple of days there you could start heading north, stopping at Ajmer/Pushkar and Jaipur en route, meaning you'd have seen a fascinating blend of desert landscapes and culture, religious sites and major cities. Travelling by plane and/or hiring a car with driver with free up more time for sightseeing making an entire loop at a reasonably leisurely place possible.

When to go

Late-October to early March is the most pleasant period to visit Rajasthan and Gujarat, especially the desert districts of Jaisalmer, Jodhpur, and Bikaner, but also the busiest time of year, with much of the best accommodation being booked up months in advance. The summer months of April to June get extremely hot while the southwest monsoon (July to September), in addition to being very humid, brings other hazards. Road surfaces are often damaged by heavy rain, most national parks are closed and some remote places become inaccessible. Travelling slightly outside the peak season often means cheaper accommodation and fewer crowds, advantages which can outweigh the less predictable climate.

If you'd like to time your trip to coincide with a festival or two, it's worth noting that while Rajasthan's most famous fair, the Pushkar Camel Fair, takes place in November, January and February see the highest concentration of events. Highlights include the camel fair in Bikaner in January, the boisterous but authentic cattle fair in Nagaur in January/February and the Elephant Festival in Jaipur in March, or else the highly regarded Desert Festival in Jaisalmer in February. Remember, however, that prices tend to sky rocket around these events, so try to book well in advance if possible.

Tour operators

You may choose to try an inclusive package holiday or let a specialist operator quote for a tailor-made tour. Out of season these can be worth exploring. The lowest prices quoted in early 2004 from the UK vary from about US$550 for a week (flights, hotel and breakfast) in the low season, to over US$3,000 for three weeks during the peak season. Most will chalk out individual itineraries and cover the major sights with small groups. The following tour companies are based in the UK, USA, Australia and India. Many arrange anything from general tours to wildlife safaris to meditation courses, to train tickets, hotel bookings and so on.

Ace, T01223-835055, ace@studytours.org. Cultural study tours, expert led.
Adventures Abroad, T0114-2473400 (USA & Canada, T800 665 3998, Australia, T800 890 790), info@adventures-abroad.org. Outward bound.
Andrew Brock (Coromandel), T01572-821330, abrock@aol.com. Special interest: crafts, textiles, botany etc.
Asian Journeys, T01604-234401, www.asianjourneys.com. Fairs, festivals, culture, religion.

Banyan Tours, T01672-564090, www. india -traveldirect.com. Tailored tours, local contact.
Cox & Kings (Taj Group), T020-78735001, F6306038. Palaces, forts, tourist high spots.
Discovery Initiatives, T020-79786341, www.discoveryinitiatives.com. Wildlife safaris.
Dragoman, T01728-86113, www.dragoman. co.uk. Overland, adventure, camping.
Exodus Travels, T020-87723822, sales@exodustravels.co.uk.

Explore, T0870-333 4002, www.explore.co.uk. An overland group tours specialist.

Forts & Palaces Tours, Jaipur, T+91-141-235 4508, www.palaces-tours.com. A friendly outfit offering sightseeing tours, hotel reservations, ticketing, etc.

Gateway to India, T0870-4423204, www.gateway-to-india.com. Tailor-made, off-the-beaten-track, local reps.

Greaves Tours, T020-74879111, sbriggs@greavesuk.com. Railways, cities, heritage.

Ibex Expeditions, Delhi, T+91-11-26912641, www.ibexexpeditions.com. Trains, palaces, forts, safaris and eco tours.

Indian Magic, T020-84274848, sales@indiamagic.co.uk. Homestays, small-scale, pulse of India.

Indo Asian Tours, Delhi, T+91-11-4691733, www.indoasia-tours.com. Professional tour operators.

Mountain Adventures, Delhi, T+91-2622 2216, www.mountainindia.com. Trekking, cycling, motorbiking, jeep safaris and cultural tours.

Myths & Mountains, 976 Tee Court, Incline Village, Nevada 89451, T0800-670 6984, www.mythsandmountains.com.

Paradise Holidays, Delhi, T+91-11-51644534, www.paradiseholidays.com. Wide range of tours, experienced.

Parul Tours & Travels, 20 Lal Ghat, Udaipur, T0294-2421697, www.travel-with-comfort.com. Tours, travel arrangements, hotel bookings, help with itineraries, etc.

Pettitts, T01892-515966, pettitts@centrenet.co.uk. Unusual locations, activities, wildlife.

Royal Expeditions, Delhi, T+91-11- 2623 8545, www.royalexpeditions.com. Tailor-made tours, walking, wildlife, culture.

Spirit of India, USA T888-3676147, inquire@spirit-of-india.com. Focused, local experts.

Steppes East, 51 Castle St, Cirencester, GL7 1QD, T01285 651010, www.steppeseast.co.uk Well run outfit offering tailor-made tours.

Trans Indus, T020-8566 2729, www.transindus.co.uk. Activities, wildlife.

Wanderlust, Delhi, T+91-11-30920231, www.wanderlustindia. com. Safaris, wildlife, cultural tours, etc.

Western & Oriental, T020-73136611, enquiries@westernoriental.com. Upmarket, unique heritage hotels.

Finding out more

Tourist offices

There are state tourist offices in the major cities of Rajasthan. They produce their own tourist literature and supply lists of hotels. The quality of material is improving though maps handed out are often inadequate. The Tourism Development Corporations run modest hotels and mid-way motels with restaurants which are adequate (though rarely efficiently run). They also offer tours of the city, neighbouring sights and overnight and regional packages and have a list of approved guides. The officers can put you in touch with car rental firms but their advice may not always be unbiased.

> ✱ *Don't take advice from unofficial Tourist Offices at airports or railway stations.*

Essentials Planning your trip

Tourist offices overseas

Australia Level 1, 2 Picadilly, 210 Pitt St, Sydney, NSW 2000, T612-292644855, gitosyd@nextcentury.com.au.
Canada 60 Bloor St, West Suite No 1003, Toronto, Ontario, T416-9623787, indiatourism@bellnet.ca.
France 11-13 Bis Boulevard Hausmann, F75 009, Paris T45233045, indtourparis@aol.com.

Germany Baserler St 48, 60329, Frankfurt AM-Main 1, T069-2429490, info@india tourism.com.
Italy Via Albricci 9, Milan 20122, T8053506, info@indiatourismmilan.com.
Japan Pearl Building, 9-18 Chome Ginza, Chuo Ku, Tokyo 104, T33-5715062, indiatourt@smile.ocn.ne.jp.
The Netherlands Rokin 9-15, 1012 Amsterdam, T020-6208991,

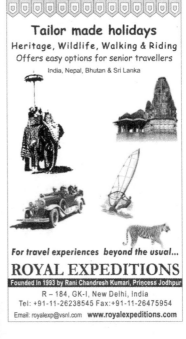

info.nl@indiatourism.com.

Singapore 20 Kramat Lane, 01-01A United House, Singapore 0922, T62353800, indtour.sing@pacific.net.sg.

Sweden Sveavagen 9-11 1st floor, S-III 57 Stockholm 11157, T468-101187, F210186.

Switzerland 1-3 rue de Chantepoulet, 1201 Geneva, T41-227321813, F7315660.

Thailand 3rd floor, KFC Bldg, 62/5 Thaniya

Rd, Bangkok 10500, T662-2352585.

UK 7 Cork St, London W1X 2AB, T020-74373677, T08700-102183, info@indiatouristoffice.org.

USA 3550 Wilshire Blvd, Room 204, Los Angeles, California 90010, T213-3808855; Suite 1808, 1270 Avenue of Americas, New York, NY 10020, T212-5864901, ny@itonyc.com.

More and more Rajasthan-specific websites are being put together, some very commercially-minded and short on objective information, others which add useful insights into certain aspects of the state. Travel and accommodation are widely covered, with historical/cultural content being a little harder to track down.

www.rajasthantourismindia.com The official state government website, less commercial than most if a little chaotically put together.

www.umaidbhawan.com A hotel website, but click on the travel guide for a comprehensive listing of tour/travel options, as well as some useful tips.

www.apanidhani.com Environmentally friendly and socially aware tours and information on the Shekawati region.

www.mapsofindia.com/maps/rajasthan Exhaustive collection of high quality maps.

www.rajasthantravelguide.com Good range of information, tour packages etc.

www,rajasthanunlimited.com Quirky collection of features and travel advice.

www.irctc.co.in Comprehensive train timetable and online booking service.

www.tourindia.com The official government promotional site with useful information but no objective evaluation of problems and difficulties. Has separate state entries within it. 'India Travel Online' is informative and issued fortnightly.

www.indiacurrentaffairs.com/ Regularly updated cuttings from Indian national dailies.

www.fco.gov Advice from the Foreign Office, London.

www.india.org The sites on India section contains excellent information on the structure of Indian government. Tourism Information is less useful.

www.123india.com Wide-ranging current affairs and general India site.

www.tourismindia.com Yellow pages for major cities.

www.wunderground.com An excellent weather site, world wide, city specific and fast.

Language

Hindi, spoken as a mother tongue by over 400 million people, is India's official language. The use of English is also enshrined in the Constitution for a wide range of official purposes, notably communication between Hindi and non-Hindi speaking states. Most of the regional languages have their own scripts. In all there are 15 major and several hundred minor languages and dialects.

It takes little effort to learn and use common gestures of courtesy but they are greatly appreciated by Indians. For a list of useful words and phrases, see page 280. Many people speak English to varying degrees. People working in the tourist industry are more likely to have a good grasp of English than an agricultural worker for example.

Disabled travellers

India is not geared up specially for making provisions for the physically handicapped or wheelchair bound traveller. Access to buildings, toilets (sometimes 'squat' type), pavements, kerbs and public transport can prove frustrating, but it is easy to find people to give a hand with lifting and carrying. Provided there is an able-bodied companion to scout around and arrange help, and so long as you are prepared to pay for at least mid-price hotels or guest houses, private car-hire and taxis, India should be perfectly rewarding, even if in a somewhat limited way.

● *Whilst it is true that India adopted the English language, the English also adopted some*
● *Indian words; pajama, shampoo and nincompoop to name a few.*

Some travel companies specialize in exciting holidays, tailor-made for individuals depending on their level of disability. For those with access to the internet, a Global Access – Disabled Travel Network Site is www.geocities.com/Paris/1502. It is dedicated to providing travel information for 'disabled adventurers' and includes a number of reviews and tips from members of the public. You might also want to read *Nothing Ventured*, edited by Alison Walsh (Harper Collins), which gives personal accounts of worldwide journeys by disabled travellers, plus advice and listings.

Gay and lesbian travellers

Indian law forbids homosexual acts for men (but not women) and carries a maximum sentence of life imprisonment. Although it is common to see young males holding hands in public, it doesn't necessarily indicate a gay relationship and is usually an expression of friendship. Overt displays of affection between homosexuals and hetrosexuals give offence and should be avoided.

Student travellers

Full-time students qualify for an ISIC (International Student Identity Card) which is issued by student travel and specialist agencies (eg **Trailfinders, STA**) at home. A card allows certain travel benefits (eg reduced prices) and acts as proof of student status within India which may allow ticket concessions into a few sites. For details contact **STIC** in Imperial Hotel, Janpath, New Delhi, T011-2332 7582. Those intending to study in India may get a one year student visa, see below.

Travelling with children

Children of all ages are widely welcomed, being greeted with a warmth in their own right which is often then extended to those accompanying them. However, care should be taken when travelling to remote areas where health services are primitive since children can become more rapidly ill than adults. It is best to visit India in the cooler months since you need to protect children from the sun, heat, dehydration and mosquito bites. Cool showers or baths help and of course avoiding being out during the hottest part of the day. Diarrhoea and vomiting are the most common problems, so take the usual precautions, but more intensively. See health page 54. Breastfeeding is best and most convenient for babies. In the big cities you can get safe baby foods and formula milk, although they are much sweeter than their Western equivalents. It doesn't harm a baby to eat an unvaried and limited diet of familiar food carried in packets for a few weeks if the local dishes are not acceptable, but it may be an idea to give vitamin and mineral supplements. Many restaurant kitchens are happy to prepare a simple, unseasoned dish for children along with their parent's meal, and also to boil water for them to drink. Wet wipes, always useful, are sometimes difficult to find in India as are disposable nappies. The biggest hotels provide babysitting.

Women travellers

Although it is relatively safe for women to travel around Rajasthan most people find it an advantage to travel with a companion. Even so, privacy is rarely respected and there can be a lot of hassle, pressure and intrusion on your personal space, as well as outright harassment. Backpackers setting out alone often meet like-minded travelling companions at budget hotels. If you are blonde, you are quite naturally likely to attract more attention. Some seasoned travellers find that dyeing their hair dark helps. One way of dealing with people who hassle you on the street is to simply say 'thank you', smile and walk away. If you show annoyance, it may result in more pestering or abusive language. See also page 30.

Working in the country

It is best to arrange voluntary work well in advance with organizations in India (addresses are given in some towns); alternatively, contact an organization abroad. In the UK: **International Voluntary Service** ① *7 Upper Bow, Edinburgh EH1 2JN, T0131-2266722, www.ivs-gb.org.uk.* Alternatively, students may spend part of their 'year off' helping in a school through 'GAP', teach English or help with a conservation project through **'i to i' International Projects** ① *Woodside House, 261 Low Lane, 5NY, T0870-332332, www.i-to-i.com.* In the USA: **Council for International Programs** ① *1101 Wilson Blvd St 1708, Arlington, VA 22209, www.cipusa.org.*

Before you travel

Visas

Virtually all foreign nationals require a visa to enter India. Nationals of Bhutan and Nepal only require a suitable means of identification. The rules regarding visas change frequently and arrangements for application and collection also vary from town to town so it is essential to check details and costs with the relevant office. These remain closed on Indian national holidays. In London, applications are efficiently processed in an hour or two (0800-1200). Visitors from countries which do not have an Indian representation may apply to the resident British representative, or enquire at the **Air India** office. An application on the prescribed form should be accompanied by three passport photographs and your passport which should be valid for at least three months beyond the period of the visit.

Visa extensions applications should be made to the Foreigners' Regional Registration Offices at New Delhi, Mumbai, Kolkata or Chennai, or an office of the Superintendent of Police in the District Headquarters. After six months, those with a tourist visa must leave India and apply for a new visa – the Nepal office is known to be difficult. Anyone staying in India for a period of longer than 180 days (six months) must register at a convenient Foreigners' Registration Office, see Registration below.

Visa fees vary according to nationality. In mid-2004 the following rules applied:
Transit For passengers en route to another country (valid for three to five days).
Tourist Six-month visa from the date of issue with multiple entry. Most common.
Business Up to one year from the date of issue. A letter from company giving the nature of business is required.
Five year For those of Indian origin only, who have held Indian passports.
Student Valid up to one year from the date of issue. Attach a letter of acceptance from Indian institution, and an AIDS test certificate. Allow up to three months for approval.

Embassies overseas

Australia 3-5 Moonah Place, Yarralumla, Canberra T26273-3999; Level 2, 210 Pitt St, Sydney T9223-9500; Melbourne T93846-0141.
Canada 10 Springfield Rd, Ottawa, Ontario K1M 1C9, T613-7443751. Toronto T416-9600751, Vancouver T604-6628811.

France 15 Rue Alfred Dehodencq, Paris, T40507070.

Germany Tiergartenstrasse 17,10785 Berlin,T00-49-30-257950 Consulates: Bonn T0228-540132; Frankfurt T069-271040, Hamburg T040-338036, Munich T089-92562067, Stuttgart T0711-1530050.

Ireland 6 Lesson Park, Dublin 6, T01-4970843.

UK India House, Aldwych, London WC2B 4NA, T020-78368484 (0930-1300, 1400-1730; visas 0800-1200), www.Hcilondon.org. Consulates: The Spencers, 19 Augusta St, Birmingham, B18 6DS, T0121-2122782; 6th floor, 134 Renfrew St, Glasgow 3 7ST, T0141-3310777, F331-0666.

USA 2107 Massachusetts Ave, Washington DC 20008, T202-9397000. Consulates: New York T212- 8797800, San Francisco T415-6680662, Chicago T312-5950405.

Customs and duty free

Duty free

Some airports have duty-free shops though the range of goods is very limited. Tourists are allowed to bring in all personal effects 'which may reasonably be required' without charge. The official customs allowance includes 200 cigarettes or 50 cigars, 0.95 litres of alcohol, a camera with five rolls of film and a pair of binoculars. Valuable personal effects or professional equipment must be registered on a **Tourist Baggage Re-Export Form** (TBRE), including jewellery, special camera equipment and lenses, lap-top computers, sound and video recorders. These forms require the serial numbers of such equipment. It saves considerable frustration if you know the numbers in advance. In addition to the forms, details of imported equipment may be entered into your passport. Save time by completing the formalities while waiting for your baggage. It is essential to keep these forms for showing to the customs when leaving India, otherwise considerable delays are very likely at the time of departure.

Currency regulations

There are no restrictions on the amount of foreign currency or TCs a tourist may bring into India. If you were carrying more than US$10,000 or its equivalent in cash or TCs you need to fill in a currency declaration form.

Prohibited items

The import of dangerous drugs, live plants, gold coins, gold and silver bullion and silver coins not in current use are either banned or subject to strict regulation. It is illegal to import firearms into India without special permission. Enquire at consular offices abroad for details.

Export restrictions

Export of gold jewellery purchased in India is allowed up to a value of Rs 2,000 and other jewellery (including settings with precious stones) up to a value of Rs 10,000. Export of antiquities and art objects over 100 years old is restricted. Ivory, skins of all animals, *toosh* wool, snake skin and articles made from them are banned, unless you get permission for export. For further information enquire at the Indian High Commission or consulate, or access the Government of India at www.indiagov.org, or the customs at www.konark.ncst.ernet.in/customs/.

Other formalities

Restricted and protected areas

Rajasthan does not require special permits. The only place where this is likely for most visitors is on camel safari from Jaisalmer, where the permits can be obtained locally.

No foreigner needs to register within the 180 day period of their tourist visa. All foreign visitors who stay in India for more than 180 days are required to register at the nearest Foreigners' Registration Office and get an **income tax clearance** exemption certificate from the Foreign Section of the Income Tax Department in Delhi, Mumbai, Kolkata or Chennai.

Permits

Foreigners should apply to the Indian representative in their country of origin for the latest information about work permits. Periodically some Indian states have introduced prohibition, but not Rajasthan. When applying for your visa you can ask for an **All India Liquor Permit**. You can also get the permit from any Government of India Tourist Office in Delhi or the state capitals.

What to take

Here are some items you might find particularly helpful in India: Loose-fitting, light cotton **clothes** are good for travelling almost anywhere at any time of year, being cool and comfortable with the added advantage of being quick drying. Pale colours may give some protection against mosquitoes. Sarongs are useful – they can be used as a skirt, scarf, towel etc. Women should dress modestly. Brief shorts and tight vest tops are best avoided, though on the beach 'modest' swim wear is fine. Locally bought, inexpensive and cool *kurta pyjama* for men, and *shalwar kameez* for women are excellent options on the plains but it can be cold in the desert and on the hills between December and February, where

> ‼ *Travel light. Many essentials are available in the cities, items are cheap and laundry services are generally speedy.*

some heavier clothing is essential. Comfortable shoes, sandals or trainers are essential and can be difficult to replace outside the bigger cities. Take high-factor sun screen and a sun hat.

It is best to take a sufficient supply of personal **medicines** from home, including inhalers and anti-malarial drugs (Proguanil is not available from pharmacists). For protection against mosquitoes, take *Mosiguard* repellent, recommended by MASTA. Most **toiletries**, contact lens cleaners, tampons and barrier contraceptives are available in the larger cities. Contact lens wearers can be affected by the high level of pollution in some large cities so carry your specs as well (plus your prescription).

As for **photography**, given the dusty conditions, a UV filter is best left on the lens permanently and a polarising filter can often give you stronger colours, better contrast and a bluer sky. Although good quality films are available in all major cities and tourist centres, including increasingly APS film, it is best to take rolls from home and certainly any specialist camera batteries. Only buy films from a reputable shop since hawkers and roadside stalls may not be reliable and check the carton carefully as well as the expiry date. Photocopies of essential **documents**, passport identification and visa pages, and spare photos are useful when applying for permits or in case of loss or theft.

Budget travellers Nets are rarely provided in cheap hotels so try to take an impregnated mosquito net. Earplugs come in handy especially during festivals when loudspeakers playing Hindi film music tend to work overtime all the time. On overnight journeys, blocking out the perpetual light is effective with eye-shades (given away by some airlines). A good padlock to secure your budget room (secret combination number recommended). A cotton, sheet sleeping bag which can cover a pillow, makes all the difference when you can't be sure of clean linen. Toilet paper, soap, towel and the washbasin plug may all be missing so be prepared.

Money

Prices in the handbook are quoted in Rupees, although top hotels often quote rates in US$. Very few people are familiar with international currencies apart from currency touts on city street corners. You do best to think in Rupee terms.

Currency

Indian currency is the Indian Rupee (Re/Rs). It is **not** possible to purchase these before you leave. If you want cash on arrival it is best to get it at the airport bank, or from the ATM in the arrivals hall. Rupee notes are printed in denominations of Rs 500, 100, 50, 20, 10 and 5. The Rupee is divided into 100 paise. Coins are minted in denominations of Rs 5, 2, 1, and 50, 25, 20, 10 and 5 paise, though coins below 50 paise are rarely seen. Carry money, mostly as TCs, in a money belt worn under clothing, although bear in mind that international ATMs are becoming increasingly widespread. Have enough for daily requirements in an easily accessible place. The new Rs 500 note is difficult to change outside of the big cities, but it has also encouraged a wave of convincing forged copies. Always check the security features carefully and avoid changing with unlicensed dealers.

Exchange

Travellers' cheques (TCs) issued by Thomas Cook and American Express are accepted without difficulty in the major towns and tourist centres. Most banks, but not all, will accept US$ or £ sterling TCs, so it is a good idea to carry some of each. The introduction of the Euro in 2002 may not be universally adopted in Indian banking for some time, so do not rely on the new currency for the foreseeable future. TCs can be exchanged in banks, hotels, or a growing number of private dealers, the latter often offering a faster service at a higher rate. They can be used directly for payment in the more expensive hotels and souvenir shops, as well as for purchasing airline tickets and foreign quota train tickets. Otherwise, ensure that you have enough cash to cover your needs. Your passport and visa must be shown. In banks, encashing any form of currency nearly always takes up to 30 minutes or longer, so it is worth taking larger denomination TCs and changing enough money to last for some days. If you are travelling to remote areas it can be worth buying Indian Rupee TCs from a major bank, as these are more widely accepted than foreign currency ones. If stolen, you must get a police report and be prepared to contact the issuing company with the numbers of the stolen checks, your receipt and a plausible story! For some, the wait for replacement checks can take weeks, so take great care of them.

Credit cards Major credit cards are increasingly acceptable in the main centres, though in smaller cities and towns it is still rare to be able to pay by credit card. Payment by credit card can sometimes be more expensive than payment by cash, whilst some credit card companies charge a premium on cash withdrawals **Visa** and **Mastercard** have a growing number of ATMs in major cities, but many ATMs only deal with local account holders. It is however straightforward to obtain a cash advance against a credit card. Railway Reservation centres in 17 major cities are now taking payment for train tickets by Visa card which can be very quick as the queue is very short, although they cannot generally be used for Tourist Quota tickets!

Banks/authorised money changers When changing money request some Rs 100 and 50 notes. Rs 500 (which can be mistaken for Rs 100) notes can reduce 'wallet bulge' but can be difficult to change. The **State Bank of India** and several others in major towns are authorized to deal in foreign exchange. Some give cash against

⁝ Money matters

It can be difficult to use torn or very worn currency notes. Check notes carefully when you are given them and refuse any that are damaged. A good supply of small denomination notes always comes in handy for bus tickets, cheap meals and tipping. Remember that if offered a large note the recipient will never have any change! It can be worth carrying a few clean, new sterling or dollar notes for use where travellers' cheques and credit cards are not accepted.

Visa/Master cards (eg **Standard Chartered, Grindlays, Bank of Baroda** who print a list of their participating branches, **Andhra Bank**). **American Express** cardholders can use their cards to get either cash or TCs in the four major cities. They also have offices in Ahmadabad and Vadodara.

The larger cities and tourist centres have **licensed money changers** with offices usually in the commercial sector. Changing money through unauthorized dealers is illegal. Liberalisation of the currency market introduced by the then prime minister, Narasimha Rao, in the mid-1990s effectively destroyed the currency black market overnight. Consequently, premiums on the street corner are very small and highly risky, especially with the influx of fake Rs 500 notes. Large **hotels** change money 24 hours a day for guests, but banks often give a substantially better rate of exchange than hotels. It is best to get exchange on

⁝ *If you cash sterling, always make certain that you have been given Rupees at the sterling and not at the dollar rate.*

arrival at the airport bank or the Thomas Cook counter. **Thomas Cook** has a high reputation for excellent service and has branches across the country. Many international flights arrive during the night, and it is generally far easier and less time consuming to change money at the airport than in the city.

You should be given a foreign currency **encashment certificate** when you change money through a bank or authorized dealer, ask for one if it is not automatically given. It allows you to change Indian Rupees back to your own currency on departure, so ensure that you have a valid one at this time. It also enables you to use Rupees to pay hotel bills or buy air tickets for which payment in foreign exchange may be required although in practice, those using mid-range or cheaper hotels rarely have to produce them. The certificates are only valid for three months.

Transferring money to India HSBC, Barclays and **Standard Chartered Grindlays** and others can make 'instant' transfers to their offices in India but charge a high fee (about US$30). **Standard Chartered Grindlays** issues US$ TCs. **Western Union** have a growing number of agents throughout the country. Sending a bank draft (up to US$1,000) by post (four to seven days by **Speedpost**) is the cheapest option.

Cost of living

The cost of living remains well below that in the West. The average wage is about Rs 10,000 per month (US$220) for government employees according to government statistics – manual workers, unskilled labourers (women are often paid less than men), farmers and others in rural areas earn considerably less.

Cost of travelling

Most food, accommodation and public transport, especially rail and bus, are exceptionally cheap. There is a widening range of moderately priced but clean hotels and restaurants outside the big cities, making it possible to get a great deal for your money. Budget travellers sharing a room, eating in local restaurants, and using the

Exchange rates

Nov 2004	Rs
Australian $	32.65
Euro €	57.2
Japanese Yen	42.1
New Zealand $	28.85
UK £	82.5
US $	45.8

cheapest means of travel can expect to spend around Rs 420-500 (about US$10-12) a day, although this will vary according to the size of the place you're visiting and the time of year that you're there; food and accommodation is generally more expensive in the bigger, more touristy cities, but rates come down significantly over the summer. Those looking for the comfort of the occasional night in a simple a/c room, and using reserved seats on trains and luxury buses, should budget for about US$25-30 a day. However, if you travel alone and are looking for reasonably comfortable a/c rooms, use taxis and second-class a/c train berths, expect to spend US$70-75 a day. When shopping or hiring an unmetered vehicle, bargaining is expected, and essential. Many visitors hire a car with driver in Delhi to take them around Rajasthan, often with hotels also arranged as part of the deal. Be sure to shop around before agreeing a price, the more unscrupulous operators have been known to take advantage of new arrivals in Delhi by grossly overcharging them.

Getting there

Air

India is accessible by air from virtually every continent. Most international flights arrive in Delhi or Mumbai from which you can fly to some cities in Rajasthan. Some international carriers permit 'open-jaw' travel, arriving in, and departing from, different cities in India. Some (eg **Air India, British Airways**) have convenient non-stop flights from London taking only nine hours.

The cheapest fares from Europe tend to be with Central European, Central Asian or Middle Eastern airlines (see below). With such airlines it pays to confirm your return flight as early as possible. You can also get good discounts from Australasia, Southeast Asia and Japan. If you plan to visit two or more South Asian countries within three weeks, you may qualify for a 30 per cent discount on your international tickets. Ask your National Tourist office. International air tickets can be bought in India though payment must be made in foreign exchange.

Stop-overs and Round-the-World tickets

You can arrange several stop-overs in India on Round-the-World and long-distance tickets. Round-the-World tickets allow you to fly in to one and out from another international airport. You may be able to arrange some internal flights using international carriers eg **Air India**, www.airindia.com, sometimes allows stop-overs within India for a small extra charge.

Airline security

International airlines vary in their arrangements and requirements for security, in particular the carrying of equipment like radios, tape-recorders, lap-top computers and batteries. It is advisable to ring the airline in advance to confirm what their current regulations are. Internal airlines often have different rules from the international carriers. You are strongly advised not to pack valuables in your luggage.

From the UK, Continental Europe and the Middle East

Flights cost anything from £600-700 direct and £500 indirect in the high season, falling to £450-500 direct, £350 indirect in the low season. Availability can be particularly low around September and Christmas. The flight from London to Delhi takes on average eight hours.

Airlines

Air India, www.airindia.com, T020 8560 9996, offers direct flights to Mumbai and Delhi, easily the best value business class.
British Airways, www.ba.com, T0870 850 9 850.
Lufthansa, www.lufthansa.com, T0870 8377747, for flights via Frankfurt.
KLM, www.klm.com, T08705 074074, via Amsterdam.
Austrian Airlines, www.aua.com, T020 7766 0300.
Virgin Atlantic, www.virgin-atlantic.com, T01293 747 747.
Emirates, www.emirates.com, T0870 2432222, probably the pick of the Middle Eastern airlines. Other options include **Royal Jordanian** and **Gulf Air**.
Aeroflot, www.aeroflot.co.uk, T020 7355 2233, more reliable, if slightly more expensive than the Central Asian options such as **Uzbek Airways**.

Agents

Companies dealing in volume and taking reduced commissions for ticket sales can offer better deals than the airlines themselves. The national press carry their advertisements. The best deals are offered from the UK.
www.cheapflights.com. Online provider.
www.ebookers.com. Online provider.
Flight Centre, T0870 499 5520. Relative new- comer offering good prices.
Flightbookers, T0870 010 7000. Another big player offering good deals.
North South Travel, T01245 608291, profits to charity, good concessions.
STA, T0870 160 6070, www.statravel.co.uk, has offices nationwide offering special deals for under-26s.
Trailfinders, T0870 814 6614, has agencies nationwide.
Travelbag, T01420 80828, www.travelbag. adventures.co.uk. Quotes competitive fares.

From Australasia

Flights cost anything from AS$1500-2500 in the high season, falling to AS$1000 in the low season. Availability can be particularly low around September and Christmas.

Airlines

Air India, www.airindia.com, Sydney T61- 2- 92834020.
British Airways, www.ba.com, T1300 767 177.
Lufthansa, www.lufthansa.com, Sydney T1300 365 727.
KLM, www.klm.com, T1300 303 747 via Seoul.
Emirates, www.emirates.com, T02-92909700, probably the pick of the Middle Eastern airlines, other options include **Royal Jordanian** and **Gulf Air**.
Qantas, www.qantas.com, T131313, to Mumbai only.

Agents

STA and **Flight Centres** offer discounted tickets from their branches in major cities in Australia and New Zealand.

From North America and Canada

Flights cost anything form US$1300 in the high season, falling to US$1000 in the low season from New York, and US$1500/US$1200 from LA. Availability can be particularly low around September and Christmas. From the east coast, it is best to fly direct to India from New York via London by Air India (18 hours).

Airlines

Air India, www.airindia.com, LA
T310-3388485, NY T718-632-0121.
British Airways, www.ba.com,
T1-800-AIRWAYS.
Lufthansa, www.lufthansa.com, NY T212
479-8800.
KLM, www.klm.com, T1-800-225-2525.
Austrian Airlines, www.aua.com,
T1-800-843-0002.
Virgin Atlantic, www.virgin-atlantic.com,
Conneticut, T203 750 2000.
Emirates, www.emirates.com, T1800 777
3999, probably the pick of the Middle
Eastern airlines, other options include **Royal
Jordanian** and **Gulf Air**.
Aeroflot, www.aeroflot.com, NY T888
340-6400, LA T310 281 5300, more reliable, if
slightly more expensive than the rock

bottom Central Asian options such as
Uzbekistan or **Turkmenistan Airways**.

Agents

Discounted tickets on **British Airways**, **KLM**,
Lufthansa, **Gulf Air** and **Kuwait Airways** are
sold through agents although they will
invariably fly via their country's capital cities.
From the west coast, it is best to fly via Hong
Kong, Singapore or Bangkok to Delhi, Kolkata
or Mumbai using one of those countries'
national carriers.
Hari World Travels, www.hariworld.com,
and **STA**, www.sta-travel.co.uk, have offices
in New York, Toronto and Ontario.
Student fares are also available from **Council
Travel**, www.counciltravel.com, with several
offices in the USA and **Travel Cuts**,
www.travelcuts.com, in Canada.

Overland

Crossings between India and its neighbours are affected by the political
relations between them. Several road border crossings are open periodically,
but permission to cross cannot be guaranteed. The reopening of Iran to travellers of
most nationalities has reinstated the Istanbul-Teheran-Quetta route. We highly
recommend *Footprint Pakistan*, which is invaluable for anyone contemplating the
journey. Make sure that you acquire your Indian visa in advance, before arriving at
the border.

Touching down

Airport information

Documentation

The formalities on arrival in India have been increasingly streamlined during the last
five years and the facilities at the major international airports greatly improved.
However, arrival can still be a slow process. Disembarkation cards, with an attached
customs declaration, are handed out to passengers during the inward flight. The
immigration form should be handed in at the immigration counter on arrival. The
customs slip will be returned, for handing over to the customs on leaving the baggage
collection hall. The immigration formalities can be very slow. You may well find that
there are delays of over an hour in processing passengers passing through
immigration who need help with filling forms.

Departure tax

Rs 500 is payable for all international departures other than those to neighbouring
SAARC countries, when the tax is Rs 250 (not reciprocated by Sri Lanka). This must be
paid in Rupees in India but it is normally included in your international ticket; check

Touching down

Electricity 220-240 volts AC. Some top hotels have transformers. There may be pronounced variations in the voltage, and power cuts are common. Socket sizes vary so you are advised to take a universal adaptor; low quality items are available locally. Many hotels, even in the higher categories, don't have electric razor sockets. During power cuts, diesel generators are often used in the medium and higher category hotels to provide power for essential equipment but this does not always cover air conditioning.

Hours of business Banks: 1030-1430, Monday-Friday; 1030-1230, Saturday. Top hotels sometimes have a 24-hour service. Post offices: usually 1000-1700, Monday-Friday; Saturday mornings. Government offices: 0930-1700, Monday-Friday; 0930-1300, Saturday (some open on alternate Saturday only). Shops: 0930-1800, Monday-Saturday. Bazars keep longer hours.

Telephone IDD 91. A double ring repeated regularly means it is ringing. Equal tones with equal pauses means engaged.

Official time GMT +5½ hours throughout the year (USA, EST +10½ hours).

Weights and measures The metric system has come into universal use in the cities. In remote rural areas local measures are sometimes used.

when buying. Look for 'FT' in the tax column of your ticket 'Security Check' your baggage before checking-in at Departure.

Local customs and laws

Most travellers experience great warmth and hospitality in India. You may however, be surprised that with the warm welcome comes an open curiosity about personal matters. Total strangers on a train, for example, may ask for details about your job, income and family circumstances, or discuss politics and religion.

Conduct

Respect for the foreign visitor should be reciprocated by a sensitivity towards local customs and culture. How you dress is mostly how people judge you. Clean, modest clothes and a smile go a long way. Scanty, tight clothing draws unwanted attention. Nudity is not permitted on beaches in India and although there are some places where this ban is ignored, it causes widespread offence. Displays of intimacy are not considered suitable in public.

You may at times be justifiably frustrated by delays, bureaucracy and inefficiency, but displays of anger and rudeness will not achieve anything positive, and may in fact make things worse. We suggest you remain patient and polite. The concept of time and punctuality is also rather vague so be prepared to be kept waiting.

Hands and eating

Traditionally, Indians use the right hand for eating, cutlery being alien at the table except for serving spoons. In rural India, don't expect table knives and forks though you might find small spoons. Use your right hand for giving, receiving, eating or shaking hands as the left is considered to be unclean since it is associated with washing after using the toilet.

Great expectations

The exciting images of an ancient and richly diverse culture which draw many visitors to India can be completely overwhelmed by the immediate sensations which first greet you. These can all be daunting and make early adjustment to India difficult. Even on a short visit you need to give yourself time and space to adjust! Be prepared for:

1 Pollution. In some of the major towns and cities, particularly in the winter, the air can be incredibly thick with pollution. Take a hankerchief.

2 Noise. Many people find India incredibly noisy, as radios, videos and loudspeakers seem to blare in unlikely places at all times of day and night.

3 Smells. India has an almost baffling mixture of smells, from the richly pungent and unpleasant to the delicately subtle.

4 Pressure. From stepping out of the airport or hotel everybody seems to clamour to sell you their services. Taxi and rickshaw drivers are always there when you don't want them, much less often when you do. There often seems to be no sense of personal space or privacy. Young women are often stared at and sometimes touched.

5 Public hygiene. Or lack of it. It is common to see people urinating in public places (eg roadside), and defecating in the open countryside.

Women

Indian women in urban and rural areas differ in their social interactions with men. Certainly, to the westerner, Indian women may seem to remain in the background and appear shy when approached, often hiding their face and avoiding eye contact, especially in the more rural areas of Rajasthan. Yet you will see them working in public, often in jobs traditionally associated with men in the West, in the fields, in construction sites or in the market place. Even from a distance, men should not photograph women without their consent.

Women do not, in general, shake hands with men since physical contact is not traditionally acceptable between acquaintances of the opposite sex. A westernized city woman, however, may feel free to shake hands with a foreign visitor. In traditional rural circles, it is still the custom for men to be offered food first, separately, so don't be surprised if you, as foreign guest (man or woman), are awarded this special status when invited to an Indian home, and never set eyes on your hostess.

Visiting religious sites

Visitors to all religious places should be dressed in clean, modest clothes; shorts and vests are inappropriate. Always remove shoes before entering (and all leather items in Jain temples). Take thick socks for protection when walking on sun-baked stone floors.

Non-Hindus are sometimes excluded from the inner sanctum of **Hindu** temples and occasionally even from the temple itself. Look for signs or ask. In certain temples, and on special occasions, you may only enter if you wear unstitched clothing such as a *dhoti*.

In **Muslim** mosques, visitors should only have their face, hands and feet exposed; women should also cover their heads. Mosques may be closed to non-Muslims shortly before formal prayers.

Some temples have a register or a receipt book for **donations** which works like an obligatory entry fee. The money is normally used for the upkeep and services of the temple or monastery. In some pilgrimage centres, as at Pushkar, priests can become unpleasantly persistent. In general, if you wish to leave a donation, put money in the donation box. Some priests do not handle money. It is also not customary to shake

Begging

Beggars are often found in busy street corners, as well as at bus and train stations where they often target foreigners for special attention. Visitors usually find this very distressing, especially the sight of severely undernourished children or those displaying physical deformity. You may be particularly affected when some persist on making physical contact. You might find a firm '*Jaao*' (go away) works. In some of the larger cities, beggars are often exploited by syndicates which cream off most of their takings. Yet those seeking alms near religious sites are another matter, and you may see Indian worshippers giving freely to those less fortunate than themselves, since this is tied up with gaining 'merit'. Young children sometimes offer to do 'jobs' such as call a taxi, carry shopping or pose for a photo. You may want to give a coin in exchange. However, it is not helpful to hand out sweets, 'school pens' and money indiscriminately to open-palmed children who tag on to any foreigner. Some prefer to give fruit, tea and biscuits to beggars.

Charitable giving

A pledge to donate a part of one's holiday budget to a local charity would be an effective formula for 'giving'. Some visitors like to support self-help co-operatives, orphanages, refugee centres, disabled or disadvantaged groups, or international charities which work with local partners, by either making a donation or by buying their products. Some of these are listed under the appropriate towns. A few (which also welcome volunteers) are listed here: www//Indiacharitynet.com, is useful.

Recommended charities include: **Novartis** ① *T0044-616977200, novartis.found ations@group.novartis.com*, sustainable development, leprosy; **Oxfam** ① *Sushil Bhawan, 210 Shahpur Jat, New Delhi 110049, T011-6491774*, and *274 Banbury Rd, Oxford OX2 7D2, UK, oxindia@giasdlo1.vsnl.net.in*, 400 grassroots projects; **SOS Children's Villages** ① *A-7 Nizamuddin (W), New Delhi 110013, T011-4647835, www.pw2.netcom/sanjayd/sos.html*, over 30 poor and orphaned children's projects in India (eg opposite Pital Factory, Jhotwara Road, Jaipur 302016, T0141-322393); and **Urmul Trust** ① *Urmul Dairy, Ganganagar Rd, Bikaner, Rajasthan, T0151-2522 139*, health care, education and rural crafts in Rajasthani villages.

Tipping

A tip of Rs 10 to a bell-boy carrying luggage in a modest hotel (Rs 20 in a higher category) would be appropriate. In upmarket restaurants, a 10 per cent tip is acceptable when 'Service' is not already included, while in places serving very cheap meals, round off the bill with small change. Indians don't normally tip taxi drivers but a small extra amount over the fare is welcomed. Porters at airports and railway stations often have a fixed rate displayed but will usually press for more. Ask fellow passengers what the fair rate is (about Rs 20 per piece) – they will nearly always advise.

Photography

Many monuments now charge a camera fee ranging from Rs 20-50 for still cameras, and as much as Rs 500 for video cameras (more for professionals). Special permits are needed from the Archaeological Survey of India, New Delhi for using tripods and artificial lights. When photographing people, it is polite to first ask – they will usually respond warmly with smiles, although the 'moment' may have been lost as they line up, military style! Visitors often promise to send copies of the photos – don't unless you really mean to do so. Photography of airports, military installations, bridges and in tribal and 'sensitive border areas', is not permitted.

Safety

Personal security

In general the threats to personal security for travellers are remarkably small. In most areas it is possible to travel either individually or in groups without any risk of personal violence. However, care should be taken.

Theft

Theft is not uncommon. It is best to keep travellers' cheques, passports and valuables with you at all times since you can't regard hotel rooms as automatically safe; even hotel safes don't guarantee secure storage. Avoid leaving valuables near open windows even when you are in the room. Use your own padlock in a budget hotel when you go out. **Pickpockets** and other thieves operate in the big cities. Crowded areas are particularly high risk. **Confidence tricksters** are particularly common where people are on the move, notably around railway stations or places where budget tourists gather. A common plea is some sudden and desperate calamity; sometimes a letter will be produced in English to back up the claim. The demands are likely to increase sharply if sympathy is shown. Never accept food or drink from casual acquaintances. Travellers have reported being drugged and then robbed.

Take special care of your belongings when getting on or off **public transport**. It can be difficult to keep an eye on your belongings when travelling. Nothing of value should be left close to open train windows. First-class a/c compartments are self-contained and normally completely secure. Second-class a/c compartments are larger, allowing more movement of passengers but are not so secure. Attendants may take little notice of what is going on, so luggage should be chained to a seat for security overnight. Locks and chains are easily available at main stations and bazars. Some travellers prefer to reserve upper berths which offer some added protection against theft and also have the benefit of allowing daytime sleeping.

Police

If you have items stolen, they should be reported to the police as soon as possible. Keep a separate record of vital documents, including passport details and travellers' cheques numbers. Larger hotels will be able to assist in contacting and dealing with the police. Dealings with the police can be very difficult. The paperwork involved in reporting losses can be time consuming and irritating, and your own documentation (eg passport and visas) may be demanded. In some places the police themselves sometimes demand bribes, though tourists should not assume, however, that if procedures move slowly they are automatically being expected to offer a bribe. If you have to go to a police station, try to take someone with you. If you face really serious problems, for example in connection with a driving accident, you should contact your consular office as quickly as possible. Some towns have introduced special Tourist Police to help the foreign traveller.

Drugs

Certain areas have become associated with foreigners taking drugs. The government takes the misuse of drugs very seriously. Anyone charged with the illegal possession of drugs risks facing a fine of Rs 100,000 and a minimum 10 years imprisonment. Several foreigners have been imprisoned for drugs related offences in the last decade.

Women travelling alone

There are some problems to watch out for and some simple precautions to take to avoid both personal harassment and giving offence. Modest dress is always advisable: loose-fitting non-see-through clothes, covering the shoulders, and skirts, dresses or shorts of a decent length. Many find the *shalwar-kameez*-scarf ideal. In mosques women should be covered from head to ankle. Unaccompanied women are most vulnerable in major cities, crowded bazars, beach resorts and tourist centres where men may follow them and touch them. 'Eve teasing' is the euphemism for physical harassment; some buses have seats reserved for women. If you are harassed, it can be effective to make a scene. Be firm and clear if you don't wish to speak to someone. Many railway booking offices have separate women's ticket queues or ask women to go to the head of the general queue. It is best to be accompanied at night, especially when travelling by rickshaw or taxi in towns. Be prepared to raise an alarm if anything unpleasant threatens. Women have reported that they have been molested while being measured for clothing in tailors' shops. If possible, take a friend with you.

Advice

It is better to seek advice on security from your own embassy than from travel agencies. Before you travel you can contact **British Foreign & Commonwealth Office** ⓘ *Travel Advice Unit, Consular Division, 1 Palace St, London SW1E 5HE, UK, T020-72384503, www.fco.gov.uk/travel*. **US State Department's Bureau of Consular Affairs** ⓘ *Overseas Citizens Services, Room 4800, Department of State, Washington, DC 20520-4818, USA, T0202-6474225, www.travel.state.gov/travel_warnings.html*. **Australian Department of Foreign Affairs** ⓘ *Canberra, Australia, T06-62613305, www.dfat.gov.au/consular/advice.html*. Canadian official advice is on *www.dfait-maeci.gc.ca/travelreport/menu_e.htm*.

Getting around

Air

India has a comprehensive network linking the major cities of the different states. In addition to **Indian Airlines** (the nationalized carrier) www.indian-airlines.comand its subsidiary **Alliance Air,** which has the poorest safety record, there are several private airlines such as **Jet Airways** and **Sahara,** www.airsahara.net and the new no-frills **Air Deccan,** www.airdeccan.net which provide supplementary flights on several routes as well as filling gaps in a particular area, as with **Jagson.** Ask your travel agent for details of their services. Competition from the efficiently run private sector has, in general, improved the quality of services provided by the nationalized airlines. The airports authorities too have made efforts to improve handling on the ground. A recent price war has seen the airlines start to compete with the price of first-, and sometimes even second-class train travel. They tend to advertise sensationally cheap rates, Rs500 Delhi-Mumbai for example, but in reality sell very few seats at this price. However, it is now possible to fly Delhi-Mumbai for around Rs3,500 one way if you book far enough in advance.

> ‡ *Indian Airlines don't permit batteries in cabin baggage, and once confiscated, you may never see them again.*

Although flying is expensive, for covering vast distances or awkward links on a route it is an option worth considering (though delays and re-routing can be irritating). However, for short distances, and on some routes (eg Delhi-Agra-Delhi) it makes more sense to travel by train.

All the major airlines are connected to the central reservation system and there are local travel agents who will book your tickets for a fee if you don't want to spend precious time waiting in a queue. Remember that tickets are in great demand in the peak season on some sectors particularly between Rajasthan and Delhi (eg Udaipur-

Delhi) so it is essential to get them months ahead. If you are able to pre-plan your trip, it is even possible to ask if the internal flights can be booked at the time you buy your international air ticket at home through an agent (eg **Trailfinders**, SD Enterprises, London) or direct (eg **Jet Airways**).

Foreign passport holders buying air tickets in India must pay the 'US dollar rate' (higher than published Rupee rates) and pay in foreign exchange (major credit cards, travellers' cheques accepted), or in rupees against an encashment certificate which will be endorsed accordingly. There is very little difference in prices quoted by competing airlines.

Rail

Trains can still be the cheapest and most comfortable means of travelling long distances saving you hotel expenses on overnight journeys. Above all, you have an ideal opportunity to meet local travellers and catch a glimpse of life on the ground although the dark glass fitted on a/c coaches does restrict vision. See the colour maps at the back of the guide for the layout of the railway network.

High-speed trains

There are over 170 air-conditioned 'high-speed' *Shatabdi* (or 'Century') for day travel, and *Rajdhani Express* ('Capital City') for overnight journeys. These cover large sections of the network but as they are in high demand you need to book them up to 60 days ahead. Meals and drinks are usually included.

Royal trains

You can travel like a maharaja on the *New Palace on Wheels* which gives visitors an opportunity to see some of the 'royal' cities in Rajasthan during the winter months for around US$250 a day. The diesel *Palace on Wheels* has been widely publicized. Weekly departures (Wednesday) from Delhi from October to April. The itinerary includes Jaipur and Amber Fort, followed by overnight travel to Chittaurgarh, Udaipur (**Lake Palace Hotel**), Jaisalmer, Jodhpur (**Umaid Bhawan Palace**) and Bharatpur ending with trips to Fatehpur Sikri, Agra and Delhi. It is a well packaged but rather compressed for some of the key sites. Travelling by night means that you don't see much of the countryside.

The oldest working steam engine, *Fairy Queen* built in 1855, has been commissioned to run a weekend tour for 50, twice a month in the winter. It starts in Delhi, then to Sariska Tiger Sanctuary with a transfer by road from Alwar, Rs 8,000. There is a contact at the National Rail Museum in New Delhi ① *To11 2688 1816, www.icindia.com/fairy*.

Riding the rails

High-class, comfortable, and by Indian standards quick, new express trains, known as *Shatabdis*, have brought many journeys within daytime reach. But while they offer an increasingly functional means of covering long distances in comfort, it is the overnight trips which still retain something of the early feel of Indian train travel. The bedding carefully prepared – and now available on a/c Second Class trains – the early morning light illuminating another stretch of hazy Indian landscape, the conversations with fellow travellers – these are still on offer, giving a value far beyond the still modest prices. Furthermore, India still has a complete guide to its rail timetables. *The Trains at a Glance* available at stations (Rs 25) lists all important trains.

Essentials Getting around

Classes

A/c First Class is available only on main routes and cheaper than flying, is very comfortable with bedding being provided. It will also be possible for tourists to reserve special coaches (some a/c) which are normally allocated to senior railway officials only. **A/c Sleeper**, two and three-tier, are clean and comfortable and good value. **A/c Executive Class**, with wide reclining seats are available on many *Shatabdi* trains at double the price of the ordinary **a/c Chair Car** which are equally comfortable. **Second Class** (non-a/c) two and three-tier, provides exceptionally cheap travel but can be crowded and uncomfortable, and toilet facilities can be unpleasant. It is nearly always better to use the Indian style toilets as they are better maintained.

Indrail passes

These allow travel across the network without having to pay extra reservation fees and sleeper charges but you have to spend a high proportion of your time on the train to make it worthwhile. A two-week Green Pass bought from the UK for example costs £112. However, the advantages of pre-arranged reservations and automatic access to 'Tourist Quotas' can tip the balance in their favour for some travellers.

Tourists (foreigners and Indians resident abroad) may buy these passes for periods ranging from seven to 90 days from the tourist sections of principal railway booking offices, and pay in foreign currency, major credit cards, travellers' cheques or Rupees with encashment certificates. Indrail passes can also conveniently be bought abroad from special agents. For most people contemplating a single long journey soon after arriving in India, the Half or One Day Pass with a confirmed reservation is worth the peace of mind; Two or Four Day Passes are also sold. Contact the below.

Agents

UK SD Enterprises Ltd, 103, Wembley Park Dr, Wembley, Middlesex HA9 8HG, UK, T020-89033411, dandpani@dircon.co.uk.
Australia Adventure World, PO Box 480, North Sydney NSW 2060, T9587766.
Canada Hari World Travels, 1 Financial Pl, 1 Adelaide St East, Concou Level, Toronto, T0416-3662000.

France Le Monde de L'Inde et de L'Asie, 15 Rue Des Ecoles, Paris 75005.
Germany Asra-Orient, Kaiserstrasse 50, D-6000 Frankfurt/M, T069253098, asra-orient@t-online-d.
Israel Teshet, 32 Ben Yehuda St, Tel Aviv 63805, T6290972.
USA Hari World Travels, 25W 45th St, 1003, New York, NY 10036, T9573000.

A White Pass allows first-class a/c travel; a Green, a/c two-tier Sleepers and Chair Cars; and the Yellow, only second-class travel. Passes up to four days' duration are only sold abroad.

Cost

A/c first class costs about double the rate for two-tier shown below, and non a/c second class about half. Children (5-12) travel at half the adult fare. The young (12-30) and senior citizens (65+) are allowed a 30 per cent discount on journeys over 500 km.

Period	A/c 2-tier US$	Period	A/c 2-tier US$
½ day	26	21 days	198
1 day	43	30 days	248
7 days	135	60 days	400
15 days	185	90 days	530

Fares for individual journeys are based on distance covered and reflect both the class and the type of train. Higher rates apply on the Mail and Express trains and the air-conditioned *Shatabdi* and *Rajdhani Expresses*.

Rail travel tips

Food and drink It is best to carry some though tea and snacks are sold on the platforms (through the windows). Carry plenty of small notes and coins on long journeys. Rs 50 and Rs 100 notes can be difficult to change when purchasing small food items. On long-distance trains, the restaurant car is often near the upper-class bogies (carriages).

Timetables Regional timetables are available cheaply from station bookstalls; the monthly 'Indian Bradshaw' is sold in principal stations, while the handy 'Trains at a Glance' (Rs 25) lists popular trains likely to be used by most foreign travellers. The latter is available from reservation offices in the larger cities (ask at the tourist counter first). For those planning extensive travel by train it is recommended that a copy is purchased at the earliest opportunity.

Delays Always allow plenty of time for booking and connections. Delays are common on all types of transport. The special *Shatabdi and Rajdhani Express* are generally quite reliable. Ordinary Express and Mail trains have priority over local services and occasionally surprise by being punctual, but generally the longer the journey time, the greater the delay. Delays on the rail network are cumulative, so arrivals and departures from mid-stations are often several hours behind schedule. Allow at least two hours for connections, more if the first part of the journey is long distance.

Tickets You can save a lot of time and effort by asking a travel agent to get yours for a small fee, usually around Rs 25-50. Non-Indrail Pass tickets can be bought over the counter. It is always best to book as far in advance as possible (usually up to 60 days). Avoid touts at the station offering tickets, hotels or money changing.

Ladies' queues Separate (much shorter) ticket queues may be available for women.

Quotas A large number of seats are technically reserved as 'quotas' for various groups of travellers (civil servants, military personnel, foreign tourists etc). In addition, many stations have their own quota for particular trains so that a train may be 'fully booked' when there are still some tickets available from the special quota of other stations. These are only sold on the day of departure so wait-listed passengers are often able to travel at the last minute. Ask the Superintendent on duty to try the 'Special' or 'VIP Quota'. The 'Tatkal' system realeases a small percentage of seats at 0800 on the day before a train departs; you pay an extra Rs 50 to get on an otherwise heavily booked train.

Reservations Ask for the separate Tourist Quota counter at main stations, and while queuing fill up the Reservation Form which requires the number, name, departure time of the train, and the passenger's name, age and sex; you can use one form for up to four passengers. If you don't have a reservation for a particular train but carry an Indrail Pass, you may get one by arriving about three hours early. Remember that Tourist Quota tickets must be paid for in foreign currency, so have an exchange certificate (and your passport) handy. It is possible to buy tickets for trains on most routes countrywide at many of the 520 computerised reservation centres across India.

Porters Carry prodigious amounts of luggage. Rates vary from station to station but are usually around Rs 5 per item of luggage (board on the station platform). They can be quite aggressive particularly on the main tourist routes: be firm but polite and remember that they will always leave the train when it pulls out of the station!

Getting a seat It is usually impossible to make seat reservations at small 'intermediate' stations as they don't have an allocation. You can sometimes use a porter to get you a seat in a second class carriage. For about Rs 20 he will take the luggage and ensure that you get a seat!

Berths It is worth asking for upper berths, especially in second-class three-tier sleepers, as they can also be used during the day time when the lower berths are used as seats, and which may only be used for lying down after 2100.

Overbooking Passengers with valid tickets but no berth reservations are sometimes permitted to travel overnight, causing great discomfort to travellers occupying lower berths. Wait-listed passengers should confirm the status of their ticket in advance by calling enquiries at the nearest computerised reservation office. At the station, check the reservation charts (usually on the relevant platform) and contact the Station Manager or Ticket Collector.

Ladies' compartments A woman travelling alone, overnight, on an unreserved second-class train can ask if there is one of these.

Left-luggage Bags left in station cloakrooms must be lockable. Don't leave any food in them. These are especially useful when there is time to sightsee before an evening train, although luggage can be left for up to 30 days.

Road

Road travel is often the only choice for reaching many of the places of outstanding interest in which India is so rich. For the uninitiated, travel by road can also be a worrying experience because of the apparent absence of conventional traffic regulations. Vehicles drive on the left – in theory. Routes around the major cities are usually crowded with lorry traffic (especially at night), and the main roads are often poor and slow. There are several motorway-style expressways but most main roads are single carriageway. Some district roads are quiet, and although they are not fast they can be a good way of seeing the country and village life if you have the time.

The roads of Rajasthan have been much improved over recent years, with smooth surfaces the morm between most towns. Rural roads are less reliable.

Bus

Buses now reach virtually every part of India, offering a cheap, if often uncomfortable means of visiting places off the rail network. Very few villages are now more than 2 or

3 km from a bus stop. Services are run by the State Corporation from the State Bus Stand (and private companies which often have offices nearby). The latter allow advance reservation and though tickets prices are a little higher, they have fewer stops and are a bit more comfortable.

There are three categories: **A/c luxury coaches**, though comfortable for sight-seeing trips, apart from the very best 'sleeper coaches' can be very uncomfortable for really long journeys. Often the air conditioning is very cold, so wrap up warm! Journeys over 10 hours can be extremely tiring so it is better to go by train if there is a choice. **Express buses** run over long distances (frequently overnight). These are often called 'video coaches' and can be an appalling experience unless you appreciate loud film music blasting through the night. Ear plugs and eye masks may ease the pain. They rarely average more than 45 km per hour. Some companies are now offering Volvo buses, which are a big improvement. **Local buses** are often very crowded, quite bumpy and slow and usually poorly maintained. However, over short distances, they can be a very cheap, friendly and easy way of getting about. Even where signboards are not in English someone will usually give you directions. Many larger towns have minibus services which charge a little more than the buses and pick up and drop passengers on request. Again very crowded, and with restricted headroom, they are the fastest way of getting about many of the larger towns.

Tips Some towns have different bus stations for different destinations. Booking on major long-distance routes is now computerized. Book in advance where possible and avoid the back of the bus where it can be very bumpy. If your destination is only served by a local bus you may do better to take the Express bus and 'persuade' the driver, with a tip in advance, to stop where you want to get off. You will have to pay the full fare to the first stop beyond your destination but you will get there faster and more comfortably. When an unreserved bus pulls into a bus station, there is usually an unholy scramble for seats, whilst those arriving have to struggle to get off! In many areas there is an unwritten 'rule of reservation' using handkerchiefs or bags thrust through the windows to reserve seats. Some visitors may feel a more justified right to a seat having fought their way through the crowd, but it is generally best to do as the local people do and be prepared with a handkerchief or 'sarong'. As soon as it touches the seat, it is yours!

Car

A car provides a chance to travel off the beaten track, and gives unrivalled opportunities for seeing something of Rajasthan's great variety of villages and small towns. Until recently the most widely used hire car was the Hindustan Ambassador. However, it is often very unreliable, and although they still have their devotees, many find them uncomfortable for long journeys. For a similar price, Maruti cars and vans (Omni) are much more reliable and comfortable, and are now the preferred choice in many areas. Gypsy 4WDs and Jeeps are also available, especially in the national parks and the desert. Maruti Esteems are comfortable and have optional reliable a/c, so are recommended in the hot weather. A specialist operator can be very helpful in arranging itineraries and car hire in advance.

Car hire, with a driver, is generally cheaper than in the West. A car shared by three or four can be very good value. Two or three-day trips from main towns can also give excellent opportunities for sightseeing off the beaten track in reasonable comfort. Local drivers often know their way much better than drivers from other states, so where possible it is a good idea to get a local driver who speaks the state language, in addition to being able to communicate with you. Drivers may sleep in the car overnight, though hotels sometimes provide a bed for them. You are responsible for all their expenses, including their meals. A tip at the end of the tour of Rs 100 per day

⋮ The hazards of the road

On most routes it is impossible to average more than 50-60 kph in a car. Journeys are often very long, and can seem an endless succession of horn blowing, unexpected dangers and unforeseen delays. Villages are often congested – beware of the concealed spine-breaking speed bumps – and pedestrians, cyclists, cattle, sheep and goats may wander at will across the road. Directions can also be difficult to find. Drivers frequently don't know the way, maps are often hopelessly inaccurate and map reading is an almost entirely unknown skill. Training in driving is negligible and the test often a farce. You will note a characteristic side-saddle posture, one hand constantly on the horn, but there can be real dangers from poor judgement, irresponsible overtaking and a general philosophy of 'might is right'. Travelling at night should be avoided wherever possible.

in addition to their daily allowance is perfectly acceptable. Check beforehand if fuel and inter-state taxes are included in the hire charge. Be sure to check carefully the mileage at the beginning and end of the trip.

Cars can be hired through private companies. International companies such as **Hertz, Europcar** and **Budget** operate in some major cities and offer reliable cars; their rates are generally higher than those of local firms, eg **Sai Service, Wheels**). The price of an imported car can be three times that of the Ambassador.

Car hire rates

Economy car with driver	Regular a/c Maruti 800 Ambassador	Premium a/c Maruti 800 Ambassador	Luxury a/c Maruti 1000 Contessa	Esteem Opel etc
8 hrs/80 km	Rs 800	Rs 1,000	Rs 1,400	Rs 1,800+
Extra km	Rs 4-7	Rs 9	Rs 13	Rs 18
Extra hour	Rs 40	Rs 50	Rs 70	Rs 100
Out of town				
Per km	Rs 7	Rs 9	Rs 13	Rs 18
Night halt	Rs 100	Rs 200	Rs 250	Rs 250

Self-drive Car hire is still in its infancy and many visitors may find the road conditions difficult and sometimes dangerous. If you drive yourself it is essential to take great care. Pedestrians, cattle and a wide range of other animals roam at will. This can be particularly dangerous when driving after dark especially as even other vehicles often carry no lights. If you do dare the roads, bear in mind the following. When booking emphasize the importance of good tyres and general roadworthiness. On main roads across India petrol stations are reasonably frequent, but some areas are poorly served. Some service stations only have diesel pumps though they may have small reserves of petrol. Always carry a spare can. Diesel is widely available and normally much cheaper than petrol. Petrol is rarely above 92 octane. Drivers must have third party insurance. This may have to be with an Indian insurer, or with a foreign insurer who has a national guarantor. You must also be in possession of an 'International Driving Permit', issued by a recognised driving authority in your home country (eg the AA in the UK, apply at least six weeks before leaving). Asking the way can be very frustrating as you are likely to get widely conflicting advice each time you stop to ask. Accidents often produce large and angry crowds very quickly. It is best to leave the scene of the accident and report it to the police as quickly as possible thereafter. Ensure that you have adequate food and drink, and a basic tool set in the car.

The **Automobile Association** offers a range of services to members. In New Delhi, AA of Upper India, Lilaram Building, 14F Connaught Place. In Mumbai, Western India AA, Lalji Narainji Memorial Building, 76, Vir Nariman Road.

Taxi

'Yellow-top' taxis in cities and large towns are metered although tariffs change frequently. These changes are shown on a fare chart which should be read in conjunction with the meter reading. Increased night time rates apply in some cities, and there is a small charge for luggage, insist on the taxi meter being 'flagged' in your presence. If the driver refuses, the official advice is to call the police. This may not work, but it is worth trying. When a taxi doesn't have a meter, you will need to fix the fare before starting the journey. Ask at the hotel desk for a guide price.

At stations and airports it is often possible to share taxis to a central point. It is worth looking for fellow passengers who may be travelling in your direction and get a pre-paid taxi. At night, always have a clear idea of where you want to go and insist on being taken there. Taxi drivers may try to convince you that the hotel you have chosen 'closed three years ago', is 'completely full' or is an 'unsafe den'. You may have to say that you have an advance reservation. See individual city entries for more details.

Rickshaws

Auto-rickshaws ('autos') are almost universally available in towns across India and are the cheapest convenient way of getting about. In addition to using them for short journeys it is often possible to hire them by the hour, or for a half or full day's sight-seeing. In some areas younger drivers who speak some English and know their local area well, may want to show you around. However, rickshaw drivers are often paid a commission by hotels, restaurants and gift shops, so advice is not always impartial. Drivers sometimes refuse to use a meter, quote a ridiculous price or attempt to stop short of your destination. If you have real problems it can help to threaten to go to the police.

> ❖ It is best to walk a short distance away from a hotel gate before picking up an auto to avoid paying an inflated rate.

Cycle-rickshaws and horse-drawn tongas These are more common in the more rustic setting of a small town or the outskirts of a large one. You will need to fix a price by bargaining. The animal attached to a tonga usually looks too undernourished to have the strength to pull the driver, leave alone passengers.

Cycling

Cycling is an excellent way of seeing the quiet by-ways of Rajasthan and is particularly enjoyable if you travel with a companion. It is easy to hire bikes in most small towns from about Rs 20 per day. Indian bikes are heavy and without gears, but on the flat they offer a good way of exploring comparatively short distances outside towns. In the more prosperous tourist resorts, mountain bikes are now becoming available, but at a higher hire charge. It is also quite possible to tour more extensively and you may then want to buy a cycle.

Buying a bicycle There are shops in every town and the local Hero are considered the best, with Atlas and BSA good alternatives; expect to pay around Rs 1,200-1,500 for a second-hand Indian bike but remember to bargain. At the end of your trip you can usually sell it quite easily at half that price. Imported bikes have the advantage of lighter weight and gears, but are more difficult to get repaired, and carry the much greater risk of being stolen or damaged. If you wish to take your own, it is quite easy if you dismantle it and pack it in its original shipping carton. Be sure to take all essential spares including a pump. All cyclists should take bungy cords (to strap down a backpack) and good lights from home, although cycling at night is not recommended; take care not to leave your machine parked anywhere with your belongings though. Bike repair shops are universal and charges are nominal. You are usually not far from a 'puncture wallah' who can make minor repairs cheaply.

It is possible to cover 50 to 80 km a day quite comfortably. Should you wish to take your bike on the train, allow plenty of time for booking it in on the brake van at the Parcels office, and for filling in forms. It is best to start a journey early in the morning, stop at midday and resume cycling in the late afternoon. Try to avoid the major highways as far as possible. Fortunately foreign cyclists are usually greeted with cheers, waves and smiles and truck drivers are sometimes happy to give lifts to cyclists (and their bikes).

Motorcycling

Motorcycling across India is particularly attractive for bike enthusiasts. It is easy to buy new Indian-made motorcycles including the Enfield Bullet and several 100cc Japanese models, including Suzukis and Hondas made in collaboration with Indian firms. Buying new ensures greater reliability and fixed price – (Indian Rajdoots are less expensive but have a poor reputation for reliability). Buying second hand in Rupees takes more time but is quite possible; expect to get a 30-40 per cent discount. You can get a broker to help with the paper-work involved (certificate of ownership, insurance etc) for a fee. They charge about Rs 5,000 for a 'No Objection Certificate' (NOC) which is essential for reselling; it is easier to have the bike in your name.

When selling, don't be in a hurry, and only negotiate with 'ready cash' buyers. A black bike is easier to sell than a coloured one! Repairs are usually easy to arrange and quite cheap. Bring your own helmet and an International Driving Permit.

Peter and Friends Classic Adventures ① *based in Goa at Casa Tres Amigos, Socol Vado 425, Assagao (4 km west on Anjuna road), T0832-273351*, an Indo-German company, includes organized motorbike tours in Rajasthan, ranging from four days to three weeks. In Delhi try **Mountain Adventures** ① *T2622 2216, www.mountain india.com*, for motorbike and cycling tours in Rajasthan and elsewhere **Chandertal Tours & Himalayan Folkways**, based in the UK, includes Royal Enfield tours of Rajasthan. ① *Contact 20 The Fridays, East Dean, Eastbourne, East Sussex BN20 0DH, UK, T00-911323422213, www.steali.co.uk/India.*

Hitchhiking

Hitchhiking is uncommon in India, partly because public transport is so cheap. If you try, you are likely to spend a very long time on the roadside. However, getting a lift on motorbikes/scooters and on trucks in areas with little public transport can be worthwhile. It is not recommended for women on their own.

Maps

For anyone interested in the geography of India, or even simply getting around, trying to buy good maps is a depressing experience. For security reasons it is illegal to sell large scale maps of any areas within 80-km of the coast or national borders. The export of large-scale maps from India is also prohibited.

The **Bartholomew** 1:4 m map sheet of India is the most authoritative, detailed and easy to use map available. It can be bought worldwide. **GeoCenter** World Map 1:2 m, covers India in three regional sections and are clearly printed. Sources of maps in the UK include **Blackwell's**, www.bookshop.blackwell.co.uk, and **Stanfords**, www.stanfords.co.uk. In the USA, **Michael Chessler**, PO Box 2436, Evergreen, CO 80439, T800-6548502.

Sleeping

There is an enormously wide range of accommodation in Rajasthan. In the larger towns and cities, there are high-quality hotels, offering a full range of personal and business facilities. In small centres even the best hotels are far more variable. In the peak season – October to April – bookings can be extremely heavy in popular destinations. It is sometimes possible to book in advance by telephone, fax or email either from abroad or in India itself. However, double check your reservation, and always try to arrive as early as possible in the day.

Hotels

These fall in to two categories; those aimed at foreign tourists, and those targeting domestic guests. The former vary enormously, but tend to offer Western niceties such as soap, towels and toilet paper, and a continental section on their restaurant menus, usually with room service also on offer. The staff will generally have a reasonable level of English and some experience of dealing with Western expectations. This type of hotel is generally found closer to the areas of tourist, rather than commercial, interest.

Indian-style hotels, catering for Indian tourists and businessmen, are springing up fast in or on the outskirts of many small- and medium-sized towns. Most have some air-conditioned rooms and attached showers. They are variable in quality but it is increasingly possible to find excellent value accommodation even in remote areas, though the staff may be less used to dealing with foreigners than in more touristy areas.

Palaces, forts and havelis

To allow you to experience something different, several old maharajas' palaces and forts have been privately converted into comfortable and unusual hotels. They retain the inherent character, ambience and interiors of the property but have modernized bathrooms and amenities (eg TV, fridge). Many of these are individual homes where former ruling families still reside. They treat guests as if they were part of a house party. Others are managed by well-known chains while a few (eg Neemrana Fort on the Jaipur-Delhi road) are run by private entrepreneurs. Many merchants' *havelis* (see page 258) and mansions belonging to the *rawals* and *thakurs*, too, have been converted to atmospheric hotels with a lot of character. It must be said that although many are wonderful, some of them fall short of the idyllic experience. For example, while some rooms may have excellent views others have little or none. Especially in more remote rural areas, you may find facilities remain very simple (eg hot water may come in buckets). Also, despite efforts at their control, pests like rats are sometimes found.

The **Heritage Hotels Association** ① *306, Anukampa Tower, Church Rd, Jaipur, T0141-2372 084*, can supply a list of member hotels which are particularly attractive. For **Historic Resort Hotels** (HRH) in former palaces ① *City Palace, Udaipur, T0294-528016, www.hrhindia.com*. These are in Udaipur, Kumbhalgarh, Jodhpur, Jaisalmer, Gajner, Bikaner, Kolayat and Jaipur. **WelcomHeritage** ① *C-7, J Block, Saket, T112686 8992, www.welcomheritage.com*, has properties in Jodhpur, Bal Samand, Kota, Ranakpur, Mount Abu, Sardar Samand, Khimsar, Nagaur and Jaisalmer. The **Taj Group**, too, owns some former royal lodges, www.tajhotels.com.

Jungle lodges and camps

Accommodation in the national parks and wildlife sanctuaries varies from comfortable royal hunting lodges in some (eg **Sawai Madhopur Lodge**, Ranthambore and **Ramgarh Lodge** facing Jamwa Ramgarh Lake) and 'Palaces' (eg Gajner, Sariska) to very spartan rooms often lacking hot water and electricity (eg **Bagha ke Bagh**, Ghanerao, Forestry Department Rest Houses).

Hotel price codes explained

LL (US$250+) and **L** (US$150-250) These are exceptional hotels. They are in the metropolitan cities or in exclusive locations such as a commanding coastal promontory, a lake island or a scenic hilltop, with virtually nothing to fault them. They have high-class business facilities, specialist restaurants and well-stocked bars, several pools, sports.

AL US$100-150) and **A** (US$50-100) Most major towns have at least some in these categories which too reach high international standards but are less exclusive. Many quote an inflated 'dollar price' to foreigners.

B (US$25-50) Comfortable but not plush, choice of restaurants, pool, some have a gym. These are often aimed at the business client.

C (US$15-25) and **D** (Rs 400-750) In many small towns the best hotel is in the **C** category, but they are not necessarily the best value. Some charge higher prices for a flash reception area, usually central a/c, restaurant, satellite TV, foreign exchange and travel desk. **D** hotels often offer very good value though quality and cleanliness can vary

widely. Most have some a/c rooms with bath, satellite TV, restaurants. **D** hotels may have some rooms in the **E** price range, so if you are looking for good but cheap accommodation, start here!

E (Rs 200-400) Simple room with fan (occasionally air-cooler or a/c), often shared toilet and shower. May not have a restaurant or provide bed linen, towel etc.

F (under Rs 200) Very basic, shared toilet (often 'squat'), bucket and tap, variable cleanliness and hygiene.

E and **F** category hotels are often in busy parts of town. They may have some rooms for under Rs 100, and dormitory beds for under Rs 50. Some only have four or six beds.

Most hotel rooms rated at Rs 1,000 or above (above a **D**) are subject to an expenditure tax of 10 per cent. There may also be a luxury tax. Some hotels additionally add a service charge of 10 per cent! Taxes are not payable on meals, so it is worth settling the meals bill separately from the room bill. Check the situation before booking.

Tent resorts and camps are popular in Rajasthan. Some are permanent or semi-permanent camps, self-contained with attached showers, which are situated in orchards or farms and charge about US$100 on full board for two. **The Maharajah of Jodhpur Royal Camp** imitates hunting tents used by them in the 1930s which are pitched inside forts like Nagaur or near their palace properties, and have showers and flush toilets. Temporary camps are set up for fairs and festivals by Rajasthan and Gujarat Tourism and private hoteliers, as at Pushkar.

Guesthouses

Guest houses in towns and cities usually provide basic accommodation, generally with Indian squat toilets and running cold water with hot water brought in buckets, but there are exceptions. Bedding is not always provided; there will always be a sheet on the mattress, and usually a pillow, but that may be all. Towels and soap are unlikely to be provided. Those aimed at the backpacker market might have internet facilities on offer, however, as well as basic travel desks.

● *Large reductions are made by hotels in all categories out-of-season in many resorts.*
● *Always ask if any is available.*

Essentials Sleeping

Paying guest accommodation

Paying guest accommodation varies from rooms in a family home to small hotels. This option can provide a great opportunity to gain an insight into Indian family life. A list is available from the Tourist Reception Centres. Contact Ramesh Jangid at **Alternative Travels** ⓘ *Nawalgarh, Rajasthan, T01594-222 239, www.apanidhani.com*, if you want to experience rural life with home-stays in villages.

Railway and airport retiring rooms

Railway stations often have 'Retiring Rooms' or 'Rest Rooms' which may be hired for periods of between one and 24 hours by anyone holding an onward train ticket. They are cheap and simple though some stations have a couple of a/c rooms, which are often heavily booked. They are convenient for short stops, though some can be very noisy. Some major airports (eg Delhi, Mumbai) have similar facilities.

Government rest houses

In many areas there are government guest houses, ranging from 'Dak Bungalows' to 'Circuit Houses', often in attractive locations. The latter are now reserved almost exclusively for travelling government officers, but Dak Bungalows may sometimes be available for overnight stays, particularly in remote areas. They are usually extremely basic, with a caretaker who can sometimes provide a simple meal, given sufficient notice. Travelling officials always take precedence, even over booked guests. Check the room rate in advance as foreigners are sometimes overcharged.

Hostels

The Department of Tourism runs 16 hostels, each with about 50 beds, usually organized into dormitory accommodation. The YHA also have a few sites all over India. Travellers may also stay in religious hostels (*dharamshalas*) for up to three days. These are primarily intended for pilgrims and are sometimes free of charge though voluntary offerings are always welcome. Usually only vegetarian food is permitted; smoking and alcohol are not.

Eating

Food

When travelling through Rajasthan you will encounter a huge variety of delicous dishes from all over India. Combinations of spices and local produce give each region its distinctive flavour. Rajasthani food varies regionally between the arid desert districts and the greener eastern areas. Typical dishes are *Daal-Bhatti-Choorma*, little breads full of clarified butter roasted over hot coals served with a dry, flaky sweet made of gram flour, and *Ker-Sangri* made with a desert fruit and beans. Millets, lentils and beans are basic ingredients. *Sogra* (thick and rather heavy millet *chapatis*) and *makkai ka roti* (maize flour *chapatis*) are very popular, served with *ghee*. Game (wild boar, fowl) feature in local non-vegetarian dishes. *Sohita* (mutton cooked with millet), *sulla* (mutton *kebabs* which have been marinated in piquant vegetables and cooked over charcoal), *Khud kharghosh* (rabbit), *Ker kumidai saliria* (beans with cumin and chillies) are also favourites. *Mawa-ki-kachori* is a particularly rich dessert consisting of pastry stuffed with nuts and coconut and smothered in syrup. *Halwas* and *kheer* (made with thickened milk) are other favourite sweets.

In many of the tourist centres, European options such as toasted sandwiches, stuffed pancakes, apple pies, crumbles and cheese cakes are readily available.

⁑ Two masala dosai and a pot of tea

A traveller reported that a hotel bar prohibition has had some unexpected results. One traveller to Ooty reported that the hotel bar had closed, apparently permanently. He found however that it was still possible to obtain alcoholic drinks from the restaurant. Having ordered and been served a beer, he was intrigued that when the bill came it was made out for "2 masala dosai". The price was, of course, correct for the beer!

Another traveller found that a well-known hotel in the heart of New Delhi also appeared to have been forced to adapt its attitude to serving alcohol to the prevailing laws. Asked in the early evening for a double whisky the barman was very happy to comply until he was asked to serve it in the garden. On being told that he could only drink it in the bar the visitor expressed great disappoint- ment, on which the barman relented, whispering that if the visitor really wanted to drink it outside he would serve it to him in a tea pot!

If you are thirsting for alcohol in a prohibitionist area perhaps you need to order two masala dosai and a pot of tea.

Italian favourites (pizzas, pastas) can be very different from what you are used to. Western confectionery, in general, is disappointing. Ice creams, on the other hand, can be exceptionally good. There are excellent Indian ones as well as international brands such as Cadbury's and Walls.

For many visitors, with the prevalance of Indian cuisine in the West, eating out in Rajasthan is unlikely to present your first encounter with Indian food. However, if you are unused to spicy food, go slow. Stick to Western or mild Chinese meals in good restaurants, and try the odd Indian dish to test your reaction. Popular local restaurants are obvious from the number of people eating in them. Try a traditional *thali*, which is a complete meal served on a large stainless steel plate (or very occasionally on a banana leaf). Several preparations, placed in small bowls, surround the central serving of wholewheat *chapati* and rice. A vegetarian *thali* would include *daal* (lentils), two or three curries (which can be quite hot), and crisp poppadums, although there are regional variations. A variety of pickles are offered – mango and lime are two of the most popular. These can be exceptionally hot, and are designed to be taken in minute quantities alongside the main dishes. Plain *dahi* (yoghurt), or *raita*, usually acts as a bland 'cooler'.

India has many delicious tropical fruits. Some are highly seasonal (eg mangoes, pineapples and lychees), while others (eg bananas, grapes, oranges) are available throughout the year. It is safe to eat the ones you can wash and peel.

Drink

Drinking water Water from the tap or a well should never be considered safe to drink since public water supplies are often polluted. Bottled water is now widely available although most bottled water is not mineral water, but simply purified water from an urban supply. Buy from a shop or stall, check the seal carefully (some companies now add a second clear plastic seal around the bottle top) and avoid street hawkers; when disposing bottles puncture the neck which prevents misuse but allows recycling for storage. There is growing concern over the mountains of plastic bottles that are collecting and the waste of resources to produce them, so travellers are encouraged to use alternative methods of getting safe drinking water. You may

! A cup of chai

Not long ago, when you stopped at a roadside tea stall nearly anywhere in India and asked for a cup of chai, the steaming hot sweet tea would be poured out into your very own, finely handthrown, beautifully shaped clay cup! Similarly, whenever a train drew into a railway station, almost any time of day or night, and you heard the familiar loud call of "chai garam, garam chai!" go past your window, you could have the tea served to you in your own porous clay cup.

True, it made the tea taste rather earthy but it added to the romance of travelling. Best of all, when you had done with it, you threw it away and it would shatter to bits on the road side (or down on the railway track) – returning 'earth to earth'. It was the eco-friendly 'disposable' cup of old – no question of an unwashed cup which someone else had drunk out of, hence unpolluted and 'clean'. And, of course, it was good business for the potter.

But, time had moved on, and we had advanced to tea stalls that preferred thick glass tumblers (which leave you anxious when you glance down at the murky rinsing water). A step ahead – those catering for the transient customer now offered the welcome hot chai in an understandably convenient, light, hygienic, easy-to-stack, thin plastic cup which one gets the world over, sadly lacking the biodegradability of the earthen pot. With the fast disappearing terracotta cup we were in danger of losing a bit of the magic of travelling in India. However, the Congress party's rise to power after the 2004 general elections led to a new Railways Minister taking office, his primary objective to bring back the clay cup!

wish to purify water yourselves. A portable water filter is a good option, carrying the drinking water in a plastic bottle in an insulated carrier. Always carry enough drinking water with you when travelling. It is important to use pure water for cleaning teeth.

Hot drinks Tea and coffee are safe and widely available. Both are normally served sweet and with milk. If you wish, say 'no sugar' (*chini nahin*), 'no milk' (*dudh nahin*) when ordering. Alternatively, ask for a pot of tea, and milk and sugar to be brought separately. Freshly brewed coffee is a common drink in South India, but in the North, ordinary city restaurants will usually serve the instant variety. Even in aspiring smart cafés, *Espresso* or *Capuccino* may not turn out quite as one would expect in the West.

Soft drinks Bottled carbonated drinks such as 'Coke', 'Pepsi', 'Teem' and 'Gold Spot' are universally available but always check the seal when you buy from a street stall. There are now also several brands of fruit juice sold in cartons, including mango, pineapple and apple. Don't add ice cubes as the water source may be contaminated. Take care with fresh fruit juices or *lassis* as ice is often added (partly to reduce the amount of liquid given and thus increase profits!). Juice stalls often charge an extra rupee for drinks without ice.

Alcohol Indians rarely drink alcohol with a meal, water being on hand. In the past, wines and spirits were generally either imported and extremely expensive, or local and of poor quality. Now, the best Indian whisky, rum and brandy (IMFL or 'Indian Made Foreign Liquor') are widely accepted, as are good Champagneoise and other wines from Maharashtra. If you hanker after a bottle of imported wine, you will only find it in the top restaurants and have to pay Rs 800-1,000 at least. For the urban elite, cooling Indian beers are popular when eating out and so are widely available, though you may need to check the 'chill' value. The 'English Pub' has appeared in the major cities, where the foreign traveller too would feel comfortable. Seedy, all male drinking dens in the larger cities are perhaps best avoided. Head for the better hotel bar instead. In rural India, local rice, palm, cashew or date juice *toddy* and *arak* should be treated with great caution!

Because of increased rates of bar licences in Rajasthan, many hotels and restaurants have stopped serving alcohol and there are few bars outside the upmarket hotels. You can however buy alcoholic drinks from shops in a city and have them in your hotel room. In some heritage hotels, owners 'invite' guests to join them for drinks. Some others will serve beer even if it is not listed and bill you for soft drinks at the price of the beer consumed! For liquor permits, see page 21.

Eating out

Rajasthan offers a huge variety of eating experiences, from local specialities dished out on street corners – often delicious but care should be taken to ensure freshness – to full blown luxury restaurants replete with a wine list. Standards of service vary just as widely, with a common complaint being the failure to produce the component parts of a dish at the same time, your toast arriving 5 minutes after your scrambled eggs for example! Street stalls or 'dhabas', local restaurants, can be good places for breakfast, with an 'aloo parantha', flat bread stuffed with potato and chilli, washed down with coffee often the favourite choice. South Indian cuisine is less heavy than its Northern, and Rajasthani counterparts, and so is a good choice for lunch, with 'masala dosa' a perennial favourite. Rajasthani or Punjabi dishes are quite rich, so make a satisfying dinner experience. Some Western, usually Italian, dishes are usually offered, but can be a bit of a gamble, especially away from the major tourist centres. It's probably best to stick to what the chef knows best! The smarter restaurants can often appear overstaffed, with a different waiter to take your order, serve food, drinks etc. There's sometimes even someone standing at your table while you eat; this is not considered intrusive by Indian diners, but rather a sign of attentive service. The larger hotels, open to non-residents, often offer buffet lunches with Indian, Western and sometimes Chinese dishes. These can be good value (Rs 250-300; but around Rs 450 in the top grades) and can provide a welcome, comfortable break in the cool, as well as a good chance to have a look at some stunning interiors without the cost of spending a night. The health risks, however, of food kept warm for long periods in metal containers are considerable, especially if turnover at the buffet is slow. We have received several complaints of stomach trouble following a buffet meal, even in five- star hotels.

It is essential to be very careful since food hygiene may be poor, flies abound and refrigeration in the hot weather may be inadequate and intermittent because of power cuts. It is best to eat only freshly prepared food by ordering from the menu (especially meat and fish dishes); avoid salads and cut fruit.

Entertainment

Despite an economic boom in cities like Delhi and Mumbai and the rapid growth of a young business class, India's night life has been slow to respond.Until now focused on club discos in the biggest hotels, more and more private clubs and 'lounge bars' are opening up in the bigger cities. More traditional, popular entertainment is widespread across Indian villages in the form of folk drama, dance and music, each region having its own styles, and open-air village performances are common. The hugely popular Hindi film industry comes largely out of this tradition. It's always easy to find a cinema, but prepare for a long sitting with a standard story line and set of characters and lots of action. See also page 52 for spectator sports.

Festivals and events

India has an extraordinary wealth of festivals with many celebrated nationwide, while others are specific to a particular state or community or even a particular temple. Many festivals fall on different dates each year depending on the Hindu lunar calendar so check with the tourist office.

The Hindu Calendar → See also page 300.

Some major regional festivals are listed below. A few count as national holidays: **26 January**: *Republic Day*; **15 August**: *Independence Day*; **2 October**: *Mahatma Gandhi's Birthday*; **25 December**: *Christmas Day*.

January

New Year's Day (1 Jan) is accepted officially when following the Gregorian calendar but there are regional variations which fall on different dates, often coinciding with spring/harvest time in Mar and Apr.
Makar Sankranti or **Uttarayana**, marks the end of winter and the beginning of the spring harvest, to 'welcome the sun to the northern tropic'. The occasion is celebrated with special fervour in Jaipur. (14-15 Jan).
Camel Festival, at Bikaner, organized by Rajasthan Tourism, features camel polo, races, dancing camels and camel obedience competitions. The fire dances of the Siddh Naths are another attraction. (24-25 Jan 2005, 13-14 Jan 2006).

February

Nagaur Fair is one of the best known camel and cattle marts in Rajasthan. (15-18 Feb 2005, 4-7 Feb 2006).
Desert Festival at Jaisalmer is a jamboree of classical and folk performances, desert musicians, folk crafts, camel polo, 'Mr Desert' competition and desert sports. (21-23 Feb 2005, 10-12 Feb 2006).
Baneshwar Fair is one of Rajasthan's largest tribal fairs. **Vagad Festival**, nearby, offers an insight into tribal culture of Dungarpur and Bhenswada districts. (19-23 Feb 2005, 8-12 Feb 2006).
Shekhawati Festival highlights rural dances, rural games, *havelis* and agriculture of the four districts of Shekhawati.

March

Sivaratri marks the night when Siva danced his celestial dance of destruction (*Tandava*) celebrated with feasting and fairs at Siva temples, but preceded by a night of devotional readings and hymn singing. Orthodox Saivites fast during the day and offer prayers every three hours. Devotees who remain awake through the night believe they will win the Puranic promise of prosperity and salvation.

March-April

Holi, the festival of colours, marks the climax of spring. The previous night bonfires are lit in parts of North India symbolizing the end of winter (and conquering of evil). People have fun throwing coloured powder and water at each other and in the evening some gamble with friends. If you don't mind

● *Purnima means full moon. Many religious festivals depend on the phases of the moon.*
● *Full-moon days are particularly significant and can mean extra crowding and merrymaking in temple towns throughout India. They are sometimes public holidays.*

Fighter pilots

The sky over Rajasthan is a riot of colour each year at Makar Sankranti (14-15 January). It is the time for kite flying and kite fights in which the idea is to bring down the opponents' kites by severing their kite strings. There are two methods of doing this – *dheel*, during which the strings are slackened rapidly, and *ghaseti*, which involves skilful manoeuvring to slice the opponent's kite string. The kites generally flown are the 'Indian fighters' and the skill of the kite flyer, the strength of the string and the balance of the kite are key factors that decide the victory in these 'fights' (kites from Bareily made with boiled bamboo are highly rated for their ability to balance themselves in the breeze). The kites come in a variety of colours and are often quite decorative, some even taking the shape of eagles or film stars! After dark, larger and stronger kites are flown, their strings carrying lanterns lit by candles.

The 'fight' itself is called a *pench*, the special kite string sharpened by using glass powder and rice paste is called *manjah*, the bamboo and wood reels are called *phirkis*. The days before Makar Sankranti are a flurry of activity, as work begins on making manjah and winding the string on phirkis. Kites in bright colours are turned out by thousands, and ephemeral markets are set up around town. Beside local artisans, kite and string makers from other parts of India come to sell their products. Umaid Bhawan Palace in Jodhpur arranges a desert kite festival.

getting covered in colours, you can risk going out but celebrations can sometimes get rowdy. Some link the festival to worship of Kama the god of pleasure; some worship Krishna who defeated the demon Putana. Holi is particularly colourful at Jaipur, Jodhpur (where the royal family often celebrates it with guests), Jaisalmer, Udaipur and Bikaner. In rural areas like Daspan it is more subdued with folk dancing and music. The **Tilwara Fair** near Balotra is one of Rajasthan's largest camel and cattle fairs. **Gangaur**, at Jaipur, Udaipur and other cities features colourful processions. At Udaipur, the procession arrives on foot at the Pichola Lake, and continues on boats. In Jodhpur colourfully dressed women carry pots of water to Girdikot. (11-12 Apr 2005, 1-2 Apr 2006).

April-June

Mewar Festival, Udaipur, features cultural programs of the region. (11-12 Apr 2005, 1-2 Apr 2006).
Mahavir Jayanti celebrates the birth of the founder of the Jain religion.
Mahaveerji Fair near Sawai Madhopur is an important Jain event with prayers.
A **Summer festival**, which includes traditional music, dance and crafts, is held at Mt Abu. (1-3 Jun every year).

July-August

Raksha Bandhan (literally 'protection bond') commemorates the wars between *Indra* (the king of heaven) and the demons, when Indra's wife tied a silk amulet around his wrist to protect him from harm. The full-moon festival symbolizes the bond between brother and sister. A sister says special prayers and ties coloured threads around her brother's wrist while he in turn gives her a gift and promises to protect and care for her.
Teej, a fertility festival, celebrates the reunion of Siva and Parvati at the onset of the monsoon. There is a big procession with ornately dressed elephants. In the villages women wear bright clothes and green striped veils, and sit on swings decorated with flowers, singing songs to welcome the rains. (8-9 Aug 2005, 28-29 Jul 2006).
Independence Day is a national secular holiday. In cities it is marked by special events, and in Delhi there is an impressive

flag hoisting ceremony at the Red Fort. (15 Aug).

August-September

Janmashtami, the birth of Krishna, is celebrated at midnight at Krishna temples. **Ganesh Chaturthi**, unlike most Hindu festivals, has a known origin. It was established just over 100 years ago by the Indian nationalist leader Tilak. The elephant-headed god of good omen (also called Ganpati) is shown special reverence. On the last of the five-day festival after harvest, clay images of the god are taken in procession with dancers and musicians, which are then immersed in the sea, river or pond. The Ganesh temple in Ranthambore receives a large influx of pilgrims on this day.

October-November

Gandhi Jayanti, Mahatma Gandhi's birthday, is remembered with prayer meetings and devotional singing. (2 Oct). **Navratri** in parts of Rajasthan is a colourful 9-night event featuring music and dancing. It is marked by Garba, Dandia-ras and other dances as well as fasting, feasting and religious rites. Shakti temples at Ambaji and Pawagadh are visited by pilgrims in this period as it celebrates nine goddesses. Navratri culminates in **Dasara**.

Various episodes of the Ramayana story or *Ramlila* (see p281), are enacted and recited, with particular reference to the battle between the forces of good and evil as in *Rama*'s victory over the demon king *Ravana* of Lanka with the help of loyal *Hanuman* (Monkey). Huge effigies of *Ravana* made of bamboo and paper are burnt on the 10th day of *Dasara* in public parks. Kota is well known for its Dasara fair. (10-12 Oct 2005, 30-2 Sep 2006).
Marwar Festival features folk music and dances of the region at Jodhpur (6-7 Oct 2005, 16-17 Oct 2006).
Diwali/Deepavali (from the Sanskrit *dipa* lamp) is the festival of lights. Some Hindus celebrate Diwali as Krishna's victory over the demon Narakasura, some Rama's return after his 14 years' exile in the forest when citizens lit his way with earthen oil lamps (see also p302). *Rangolis* are painted on the floor as a sign of welcome. Fireworks have become an integral part of the celebration. Equally, Lakshmi, the Goddess of Wealth (as well as Ganesh) is worshipped by merchants and the business community who start the accounting year on the day. Most people wear new clothes; some play games of chance.
Kartik Poornima is one of the most important dates in the Hindu calendar. Pushkar, Chandrabhaga and Kolayat hold cattle and camel fairs.

Muslim holy days

These are celebrated in cities with a significant Muslim population like Ajmer in Rajasthan. The dates are fixed according to the lunar calendar, see page 302. According to the Gregorian calendar, they tend to fall 11 days earlier each year, dependent on the sighting of the new moon.

Ramadan, the ninth month of the Islamic year, is a month of fasting. It is a period of atonement and recalls the "sending down of the Quran as a guidance for the people". All Muslims (except young children, the very elderly, the sick, pregnant women and travellers) must abstain from food and drink, from sunrise to sunset. **Id-ul-Fitr** is the three-day festival marks the end of Ramadan.

Id-ul-Zuha/Bakr-Id is when Muslims commemorate Ibrahim's sacrifice of his son according to God's commandment; the main time of pilgrimage to Mecca (the Hajj). It is marked by the sacrifice of a goat, feasting and alms giving.

Muharram is when the killing of the Prophet's grandson, Hussain, is commemorated by Shi'a Muslims. Decorated *tazias* (replicas of the martyr's tomb) are carried in procession by devout wailing followers who beat their chests to express their grief. Shi'as fast for the 10 days.

Shopping

India excels in producing fine crafts at affordable prices through the tradition of passing down ancestral skills. You can get handicrafts of different states from the government emporia in the major cities which guarantee quality at fixed prices (no bargaining), but many are poorly displayed, not helped by reluctant and unenthusiastic staff. Private upmarket shops and top hotel arcades offer better quality, choice and service but at a price. Vibrant and colourful local bazars (markets) are often a great experience but you must be prepared to bargain.

Bargaining can be fun and quite satisfying. It is best to get an idea of prices being asked by different stalls for items you are interested in, before taking the plunge. Some shopkeepers will happily quote twice the actual price to a foreigner showing interest, so you might well start by halving the asking price. On the other hand it would be inappropriate to do the same in an established shop with price-tags, though a plea for the 'best price' or a 'special discount' might reap results even here. Remain good humoured throughout. Walking away slowly might be the test to ascertain whether your custom is sought and you are called back!

The country is a vast market place but there are regional specializations. The larger cities give you the opportunity to see a good selection from all over India. If you are planning to travel widely, wait to find the best places to buy specific items. Export of certain items is controlled or banned, see page 20.

Carpets and dhurries
Rajasthan has had a tradition of carpet and dhurrie weaving using camel wool and cotton. Weaving of traditional woollen dhurries became associated with prisoners in Bikaner, Jaipur and Ahmadabad jails but today attractive dhurries in pastel colours are produced in small commercial units as a cottage industry. The pile carpets made near Jaipur based on floral and geometrical patterns are of medium quality with around 80 knots per square inch. These are good buys.

Jewellery
Rajasthan is famed for cut and uncut gemstones (emeralds. sapphires, rubies and diamonds). *Kundan* work specializes in setting stones in gold; sometimes *meenakari* (enamelling) complements the setting on the reverse side of the pendant, locket or earring. Whether it is chunky tribal silver jewellery or precious gems set in gold, or semi-precious stones in silver, the visitor is drawn to the arcade shop window as much as the way-side stall. It is best to buy from reputable shops (and if in Jaipur, get expensive purchases checked by the Gem Testing Laboratory). Make sure your knowledge is up to scratch if considering investing in gems or jewellery, and never be persuaded to buy for an unknown third-party.

Paintings
Miniature paintings on old paper (they are not real antiques) and new silk, sometimes using natural colours derived from minerals, rocks and vegetables, following old techniques are produced in varying degrees of quality. Sadly the industry is reaching mass production levels in Rajasthan's back alleys though fine examples can still be found in good crafts shops. Coveted contemporary Indian art is exhibited in modern galleries in the state capitals often at a fraction of London or New York prices.

Stoneware
Ornamental pieces of perforated marble *jali* work are produced in Rajasthan. Artisans in Agra inspired by the Taj Mahal continue the tradition of inlaying tiny pieces of gem

stones on fine white marble, to produce something for every pocket, from a small coaster to a large table top. Softer soap stone is cheaper.

Pitfalls

Taxi and rickshaw drivers and tour guides sometimes insist on recommending certain shops where they expect a commission, but prices there are invariably inflated. Some shops offer to pack and post your purchases but small private shops can't always be trusted. Unless you have a specific recommendation from a person that you know, only make such arrangements in government emporia or a large store. Don't enter into any arrangement to help 'export' marble items, jewellery etc which a shopkeeper may propose by making tempting promises of passing on some of the profits to you. Several visitors have been cheated through misuse of their credit card accounts, and have been left with unwanted purchases. Make sure that credit cards are not run off more than once when making a purchase.

Sport and activities

Participation activities

Camel safaris

Today's camel safaris try to recreate something of the atmosphere of the early merchant camel trains that travelled through the desert. The Thar desert, in Rajasthan, with its vast stretches of sand, dotted with dunes and its own specially adapted shrubs and wildlife is ideal territory. The guides are expert navigators and the villages on the way add colour to an unforgettable experience, if you are prepared to sit out the somewhat uncomfortable ride, see page 205.

Jaisalmer has regular camel safaris ranging from short rides on the dunes to long hauls of six or seven days visiting villages, towns, dunes, wildlife areas and scenic places. Facilities vary: simple safaris allow you to spend the night on the dunes, in tents or village huts supplied with bed-rolls, and you get simple Rajasthani food; deluxe ('royal') safaris provide luxury self-contained tents, multi-cuisine meals and camel carts to transport your baggage. Jaisalmer is the easiest place to organize a camel safari. Bikaner and Jodhpur have fewer tour operators and hotels offering safaris but these are often preferable as they are much less commercialized though they could be more pricey than those of Jaisalmer. If you want something more exclusive, and traverse areas where you do not keep bumping into tourists these could be a better options. Hotels in Manvar, Osian, Gajner also arrange camel safaris. Others coincide with colourful fairs like those at Pushkar and Tilwara.

Horse safaris

These are similar to camel safaris, with grooms (and often the horse owner) accompanying. The best months are November to March when it is cooler in the day (and often cold at night). The trails chosen usually enable you to visit small villages, old forts and temples, and take you through a variety of terrain and vegetation including scrub covered arid plains to forested hills. The charges can be a lot higher than for a camel safari but the night stays are often in comfortable palaces, forts or *havelis*.

The popular areas for horse safaris are the desert plains and Aravalli hills of Shekhawati, the Marwar plains south from Jodhpur to the hills of Ranakpur, and the Aravalli passes of the Mewar triangle and the Vindhya hills of southeastern Rajasthan. Heritage hotels of Dundlod and Nawalgarh (in Shekhawati), Udaipur, Bijaipur near Chittaurgarh, and Rohet near Jodhpur, are known for their horse safaris.

The safaris are only recommended for those who are reasonably adept at horse back riding for the trips can be long and tiring, the horses are quite spirited and require good handling. Most routes are planned to include interesting sight seeing destinations within a week or ten day horseback tour.

Jeep safaris

Besides game drives by jeep in sanctuaries and national parks, some hotels and tour operators now arrange jeep safaris, with accommodation in heritage hotels and camps along the way along lesser roads and cross-country trails.

Bird watching

The country's diverse and rich natural habitats harbour over 1,200 species of birds of which around 150 are endemic. Visitors to all parts of the country can enjoy spotting Oriental species whether it is in towns and cities, in the country side or more abundantly in the national parks and sanctuaries. On the plains, the cooler months (November to March) are the most comfortable for a chance to see migratory birds from the hills. Water bodies large and small draw visiting water fowl from other continents during the winter. It is quite easy to get to some parks from the important tourist centres, for example Keoladeo Ghana, in Rajasthan, or Nal Sarovar, in Gujarat. *A Birdwatcher's Guide to India* by Krys Kazmierczak and Raj Singh, published by Prion Ltd, Sandy, Bedfordshire, UK, 1998, is well researched and comprehensive with helpful practical information and maps. Useful websites include www.oriental birdclub.org and biks@giasdlo1.vsnl.net.in, for **Bird Link**, concerned with conservation of birds and their habitat. **The Salim Ali Centre for Ornithology and Natural History** is at centre@sacon.ernet.in.

Yoga and meditation

There has been a growing Western interest in the ancient life-disciplines in search of physical and spiritual wellbeing, as practised in ancient India. Yoga is supposed to regulate the nervous system and aims to attain perfect equilibrium through the practice of *asanas* (body postures), breath control, discipline, cleansing, contemplation and awareness. It seeks to achieve moral purification through abstinence and restraint (dietary and sexual). Meditation which complements yoga to relieve stress, increase awareness and bring inner peace, prescribes *dhyana* (purposeful concentration) by withdrawing oneself from external distractions and focusing ones attention to consciousness itself. This leads ultimately to *samadhi* (release from worldly bonds). At the practical level *Hatha Yoga* has captured the Western imagination as it promises good health through postural exercises, while the search for inner peace and calm drive others to learn meditation techniques.

Centres across the country offer courses for beginners and practitioners. Some are at special resort hotels which offer all inclusive packages in idyllic locations, some advocate simple communal living in an ashram while others may require rigorous discipline in austere monastic surroundings. In Rajasthan, hotels in Pushkar such as **White House** can arrange lessons. Alternatively, enquire at the **Vipasana Buddhist Meditation Centre** at Dhamma Giri, PO Box 6, Igatpuri, Nasik, Maharashtra for their branch in Jaipur, which also has a **Yoga and Naturopathy Centre** at 'C Scheme' opposite Rajasthan University. You can contact **Om Shanti Bhavan** run by the Brahma Kumaris in Mount Abu, see page 167. **Sariska Palace**, see page 220, provides courses in luxurious surroundings.

Cycling

Cycling offers a peaceful – not to mention healthy – alternative to cars, buses or trains. Touring on locally hired bicycles is ideal if you want to see village life in Rajasthan. As cycles are an important means of transport, it is easy to find repairers for punctures and other problems in towns and cities. These cycles are simple and do not have gears. If you bring mountain bikes and multi-geared cycles for touring with you, be warned that cycle thefts are not uncommon. Delhi based tour operators arrange deluxe cycle tours of Rajasthan with guide, back-up vehicles and accommodation in good hotels on the way. Mopeds are an alternative to cycling and these can be bought or hired in popular tourist destinations like Jaipur and Udaipur.

Motorbiking

For those keen on moving faster along the road, discover the joys of travelling on the two wheels of a motorbike. The 350 cc Enfield Bullets are particularly attractive. Vespa, Kinetic Honda and other makes of scooters in India are slower than motorbikes but comfortable for short hauls of less than 100 km and have the advantage of a 'dicky' (small, lockable box) for spares, and a spare tyre. Scooters can be hired at Jaipur, Udaipur, Bikaner et cetera, to tour areas in and around the cities. See page 39.

Trekking

Heritage hotels, resorts and tour operators offer treks in the Aravalli and Vindhya hills of Rajasthan. As the altitudes here are much lower than the Himalayas and the Western Ghats, the focus is on visiting tribal villages and seeing wildlife and birds along the trail, and perhaps a fort or a temple.

The easily accessible parts of the national parks, wildlife sanctuaries and reserved forests provide ample opportunity for walking but if you want to venture deeper you'll need to take a local guide as paths can soon become indistinct and confusing. Some areas require a permit to visit since the authorities wish to keep disturbance to wildlife and tribal communities to a minimum. The government Wildlife and Forestry Departments and private tour operators will be able to set you on the right path but you need to enquire, sometimes as much as a month, in advance. There are simple lodges and guest houses in most areas including tribal villages, but more comfortable jungle camps and luxury safari lodges also exist in the national parks, which can be used as a base for day treks.

Spectator sports

Soccer

India's greatest popular entertainment has become sport, soccer being one. It is played from professional level to kick-about in any open space. Professional matches are played in large stadia attracting vast crowds.

Cricket

Cricket has almost a fanatical following across the country. Reinforced by satellite TV and radio, and a national side that enjoys high world rankings and much outstanding individual talent, cricket has become a national obsession. Stars have cult status, and you can see children trying to model themselves on their game on any and every open space. The national side's greatest moment was, arguably, winning the 1983 World Cup. The low point in Indian cricket is the attention now focused on the role of 'Bombay bookmakers' in the sport's current corruption enquiry, and the implication of leading players in match-fixing. When foreign national sides tour India, tickets are remarkably easy to come by (for Test matches at least), and are considerably cheaper than for corresponding fixtures back home. Tickets are often sold through local bank branches.

● *The best precaution against a snake bite is not to walk in snake territory with bare feet,*
● *sandals or shorts and not to touch snakes even if assured they are harmless. Make noise (with a stick) to scare snakes away in advance.*

Health

Travellers to India are exposed to health risks not encountered in Western Europe or North America. Because much of the area is economically underdeveloped, serious infectious diseases are common, as they were in the West some decades ago. Obviously, business travellers staying in international hotels and tourists on organized tours face different health risks to travellers backpacking through rural areas. There are no absolute rules to follow; you will often have to make your own judgement on the healthiness of your surroundings. With suitable precautions you should stay healthy.

There are many well qualified doctors in India, most of whom speak English, but the quality and range of medical care diminishes rapidly as you leave the major cities. If you are in a major city, your embassy may be able to recommend a list of doctors. If you are a long way from medical help, some self-treatment may be needed. You are more than likely to find many drugs with familiar names on sale. Always buy from a reputable source, and check date stamping. Vaccines in particular have a much reduced shelf-life if not stored properly. Locally produced drugs may be unreliable because of poor quality control and the substitution of inert ingredients for active drugs.

Before you go

Insurance and other preparations
Take out good medical insurance. Check exactly what the level of cover is for specific eventualities, in particular whether a flight home is covered in case of an emergency, whether the insurance company will pay any medical expenses directly or whether you have to pay and then claim them back, and whether specific activities such as trekking or climbing are covered. If visiting for a while have a dental check up. Take spare glasses (or at least a glasses prescription) and/or lenses, if you wear them. If you have a long-standing medical problem such as diabetes, heart trouble, chest trouble or high blood pressure, get advice from your doctor, and carry sufficient medication to last the full duration of your trip. You may want to ask your doctor for a letter explaining your condition.

What to take
Self-medication may be forced on you by circumstances so the following text contains the names of drugs and medicines which you may find useful in an emergency or in out-of-the-way places. You may like to take some of the following items with you from home: **anti-infective ointment** eg cetrimide; **dusting powder** for feet, containing fungicide; **antacid tablets**; **antibiotics** (ask your GP); **anti-malarial tablets**; **painkillers** (paracetamol or aspirin); **rehydration salts** packets plus anti-diarrhoea preparations; **travel sickness tablets**; **first aid kit** including a couple of sterile syringes and needles and disposable gloves (available from camping shops) in case of an emergency.

Vaccination and immunization
If you require travel vaccinations see your doctor well in advance of your travel. Most courses must be completed in a minimum of four weeks. Travel clinics may provide rapid courses of vaccination but are likely to be more expensive. The following vaccinations are recommended:

Typhoid This disease is spread by the insanitary preparation of food. A single dose injection is now available (*Typhim Vi*) that provides protection for up to three years. A vaccine taken by mouth in three doses is also available, but the timing of doses can be a problem and protection only lasts for one year.

Polio Protection is by a live vaccine generally given orally, and a full course consists of three doses with a booster every five years.

Tetanus If you have not been vaccinated before, one dose of vaccine should be given with a booster at six weeks and another at six months. Ten yearly boosters are strongly recommended. Children should, in addition, be properly protected against diphtheria, mumps and measles.

Infectious hepatitis If you are not immune to hepatitis A already, the best protection is vaccination with *Havrix*. A single dose gives protection for at least a year, while a booster taken six months after the initial injection extends immunity to at least 10 years. If you are not immune to hepatitis B, the vaccine Energix is highly effective. It consists of three injections over six months before travelling. A combined hepatitis A & B vaccine is now licensed and available.

Malaria For details of malaria prevention, see below.

The following vaccinations may also be considered:

Tuberculosis The disease is still common in the region. Consult your doctor for advice on BCG inoculation.

Meningococcal Meningitis and Diphtheria If you are staying in the country for a long time, vaccination should be considered.

Japanese B Encephalitis (JBE) Immunization (effective in 10 days) gives protection for around three years. There is an extremely small risk in India, though it varies seasonally and from region to region. Consult a travel clinic or your family doctor.

Rabies Vaccination before travel gives anyone bitten more time to get treatment (so particularly helpful for those visiting remote areas), and also prepares the body to produce antibodies quickly. The cost of the vaccine can be shared by three persons receiving vaccination together.

Travelling with children

Children get dehydrated very quickly in hot countries and can become drowsy and uncooperative unless cajoled to drink water or juice plus salts. The treatment of diarrhoea is the same for adults, except that it should start earlier for children and be continued with more persistence. Colds, catarrh and ear infections are also common so take suitable antibiotics. To help young children to take anti-malarial tablets, one suggestion is to crush them between spoons and mix with a teaspoon of dessert chocolate (for cake-making) bought in a tube.

An A-Z of health risks

AIDS

In India, AIDS is increasing in prevalence with a pattern typical of developing societies. Thus, it is not wholly confined to the well known high-risk sections of the population ie, homosexual men, intravenous drug abusers, prostitutes and the children of infected mothers. Heterosexual transmission is now the dominant mode and so the main risk to travellers is from casual unprotected sex. The same precautions should be taken as when encountering any sexually transmitted disease. The AIDS virus (HIV) can be passed via unsterile needles which have previously been used to inject a HIV positive patient, but the risk of this is very small. It would, however, be sensible to check that needles have been properly sterilized, or better still, disposable needles used. The chance of picking up hepatitis B in this way is much more of a danger. The risk of receiving a blood transfusion with blood infected with the HIV virus is greater than from dirty needles because of the amount of fluid exchanged. Supplies of blood for transfusion are now usually screened for HIV in reputable hospitals, so the risk may be small. Catching the AIDS virus does not necessarily produce an illness in itself; the only way to be sure if you feel you have been at risk is to have a blood test for HIV antibodies on your return to a place where there are reliable laboratory facilities.

Bites and stings

If you are unlucky enough to be bitten by a venomous snake, spider, scorpion, centipede or sea creature, try (within limits) to catch the animal for identification. Failing this, an accurate description will aid treatment. See the information on rabies (below) for other animal bites. The reactions to be expected are fright, swelling, pain and bruising around the bite, soreness of the regional lymph glands (eg armpits for bites to hands and arms), nausea, vomiting and fever. If, in addition, any of the following symptoms supervene get the victim to a doctor without delay: numbness, tingling of face, muscular spasm, convulsions, shortness of breath or haemorrhage. Commercial snake bile or scorpion sting kits may be available but are only useful for the specific type of snake or scorpion for which they are designed. The serum has to be given by injection into a vein, so it is not much good unless you have some practice in making and giving such injections. If the bite is on a limb, immobilize the limb and apply a tight bandage (not a tourniquet) between the bite and the body. Be sure to release it for 90 seconds every 15 minutes. Do not try to slash the bite and suck out the poison because this will do more harm than good. Reassurance of the bitten person is important. Death from snake-bite is extremely rare. Hospitals usually hold stocks of snake-bite serum, though it is important to have a good description of the snake, or where possible, the creature itself.

Avoid spiders and scorpions by keeping your bed away from the wall, look under lavatory seats and inside your shoes in the morning. Dark dusty rooms are popular with scorpions. In the event of being bitten or stung, consult a doctor quickly.

Dengue fever

Dengue fever is present in India. It is a viral disease, transmitted by mosquito bites, presenting severe headache, fevers and body pains. Complicated types of dengue known as haemorrhagic fevers occur throughout Asia, but usually in persons who have caught the disease a second time. Thus, although it is a very serious type, it is rarely caught by visitors. There is no treatment; you must just avoid mosquito bites as much as possible.

Heat and cold

Full acclimatization to high temperatures takes about two weeks. During this period it is normal to feel relatively apathetic, especially if the relative humidity is high. Drink plenty of water and avoid extreme exertion. When you are acclimatized you will feel more comfortable but your need for plenty of water will continue. Tepid showers are more cooling than hot or cold ones. Remember that especially in the mountains, deserts and the highlands, there can be a large and sudden drop between temperatures in the sun and shade and between night and day. Large hats do not cool you down but do prevent sunburn. Warm jackets or woollens are essential after dark at high altitude. Loose cotton is still the best material when the weather is hot.

The burning power of the tropical sun is phenomenal, especially at altitude. Always wear a wide brimmed hat and use some form of sun cream or lotion. Normal temperate suntan lotions (up to factor seven) are not much good. You will need to use the types designed specifically for the tropics or for mountaineers/skiers, with a protection factor between seven and 25 (dependent on skin type). Glare from the sun can cause conjunctivitis, so wear good quality UV protection sunglasses on beaches and snowy areas. There are several variations of 'heat stroke'. The most common cause is severe dehydration, so drink plenty of non-alcoholic fluid. Sun-block and cream is not widely available in India, so you should bring adequate supplies with you.

Infectious hepatitis (jaundice)

Medically speaking there are two types. The less serious but more common is **hepatitis A**, a disease frequently caught by travellers, and common in India. The main symptoms are yellowness of eyes and skin, lack of appetite, nausea, tiredness and stomach pains. The best protection is careful preparation of food, the avoidance of contaminated drinking water and scrupulous attention to toilet hygiene.

The other, more serious version is **hepatitis B**, which is acquired as a sexually transmitted disease, from blood transfusions or injection with an unclean needle, or possibly by insect bites. The symptoms are the same as hepatitis A, but the incubation period is much longer.

You may have had jaundice before or you may have had hepatitis of either type without becoming jaundiced, in which case it is possible that you could be immune to either form. This immunity can be tested for before you travel. There are various other kinds of viral hepatitis (C, E etc) which are fairly similar to A and B, but currently vaccines do not exist for these.

Insects

These can be a great nuisance. Some of course are carriers of serious disease. The best way to keep mosquitoes away at night is to sleep off the ground with a mosquito net and to burn mosquito coils containing Pyrethrum (available in India). Aerosol sprays or a 'flit' gun may be effective, as are insecticidal tablets which are heated on a mat which is plugged into a wall socket. These devices, and the refills, are not widely available in India, so if you are taking your own make sure it is of suitable voltage with the right adaptor plug. Bear in mind also that there are regular power cuts in many parts of India.

A better option is to use a personal insect repellent of which the best contain a high concentration of Diethyltoluamide (DEET). Liquid is best for arms, ankles and face (take care around eyes and make sure you do not dissolve the plastic of your spectacles). These are available in India (eg Mospel, Repel), although it is recommended that you bring your own supply. Aerosol spray on clothes and ankles deter mites and ticks. Liquid DEET suspended in water can be used to impregnate cotton clothes and mosquito nets. MASTA recommends Mosiguard which does not contain DEET as an insect repellent.

If you are bitten, itching may be relieved by cool baths and anti-histamine tablets (care with alcohol or driving), corticosteroid creams (great care and never use if hint of infection or on the face) or by judicious rubbing or scratching. Calamine lotion and cream are of no real use, and anti-histamine creams may sometimes cause skin allergies so use with caution. Bites which do become infected (common in India) should be treated with a local antiseptic or antibiotic cream such as Cetrimide, as should infected scratches. Skin infestations with body lice, crabs and scabies are easy to pick up, particularly by those travelling cheaply. Use Gamma benzene hexachloride for lice and Benzylbenzoate for scabies. Crotamiton cream alleviates itching and also kills a number of skin parasites. Malathion 5% is good for lice, but avoid the highly toxic full strength Malathion used as an agricultural insecticide.

Intestinal upsets

Intestinal upsets are due, most of the time, to the insanitary preparation of food. Do not eat uncooked fish, vegetables or meat (especially pork, though this is highly unlikely in India), fruit with the skin on (always peel fruit yourself), or food that is exposed to flies (particularly salads). **Shellfish** eaten raw are risky and at certain times of the year some fish and shellfish concentrate toxins from their environment and cause various kinds of food poisoning. **Tap water** should be assumed to be unsafe, especially in the monsoon; the same goes for stream or well water. Bottled mineral water is now widely available, although not all bottled water is mineral water; some is simply purified water from an urban supply. If your hotel has a central hot water supply, this is generally safe to drink after cooling. Ice for drinks should be made from boiled water but rarely is, so stand your drink on the ice cubes rather than putting them in your drink. For details on water purification, see box. Heat treated **milk** is widely available, as is ice cream produced by the same methods. Unpasteurized milk products, including cheese, are sources of tuberculosis, brucellosis, listeria and other food poisoning germs. You can render fresh milk safe by heating it to 62°C for 30 minutes, followed by rapid cooling or by boiling. Matured or processed cheeses are safer than fresh varieties.

Diarrhoea is usually the result of food poisoning, occasionally from contaminated water. There are various causes: viruses, bacteria or protozoa (like amoeba and giardia). It may take one of several forms, coming on suddenly, or rather slowly. It may be accompanied by vomiting or by severe abdominal pain and the passage of blood or mucus with stools. How do you know which type you have and how do you treat them? All kinds of diarrhoea, whether or not accompanied by vomiting, respond favourably to the replacement of water and salts taken as frequent small sips of some kind of rehydration solution. Proprietary preparations, consisting of sachets of powder which you dissolve in water (ORS, or Oral Rehydration Solution) are widely available, although it is recommended that you bring some of your own. They can also be made by adding half a teaspoonful of salt (3½ g) and four tablespoonfuls of sugar (40 g) to a litre of safe drinking water. If you can time the onset of diarrhoea to the minute, then it is probably viral or bacterial, and/or the onset of dysentery. The treatment, in addition to rehydration, is Ciprofloxacin (500 mg every 12 hours). The drug is now widely available. If the diarrhoea has come on slowly or intermittently, then it is more likely to be protozoal (ie caused by amoeba or giardia). These cases are best treated by a doctor, as should any diarrhoea continuing for more than three days. If medical facilities are remote a short course of high dose Metronidazole (Flagyl) may provide relief. This drug is widely available in India, although it is best to bring a course with you after discussion with your family doctor. If there are severe stomach cramps, the following drugs may sometimes help: Loperamide (Imodium, Arret) and Diphenoxylate with Atropine (Lomotil). Thus, the lynch pins of treatment for diarrhoea are rest, fluid and salt replacement, antibiotics such as Ciprofloxacin for some bacterial types and special diagnostic tests and medical treatment for amoeba and giardia infections.

Salmonella infections and **cholera** can be devastating diseases and it would be wise to get to a hospital as soon as possible if these were suspected. Fasting, peculiar diets and the consumption of large quantities of yoghurt have not been found to be useful in calming travellers' diarrhoea or in rehabilitating inflamed bowels. As there is some evidence that alcohol and milk might prolong diarrhoea, they should probably be avoided during and immediately after an attack. Antibiotics to prevent diarrhoea are probably ineffective and some, such as Entero-vioform, can have serious side effects if taken for long periods.

Malaria

In India malaria was once theoretically confined to coastal and jungle zones, but is now on the increase again. It remains a serious disease and you are strongly advised to protect yourself against mosquito bites and to take prophylactic (preventive) drugs. Certain areas are badly affected particularly by the highly dangerous falciparum strain. Mosquitoes do not thrive above 2,500 m, so you are safe at altitude. Recommendations on prevention change, so consult your family doctor or see the further information at the end of this section. However, the current combination of anti-malarial drugs for use in India requires a daily dosage of Proguanil (brands such as Paludrine) and a weekly dosage of Chloroquine (various brands). Start taking the tablets one week before exposure and continue to take them for four weeks after leaving the malarial zone. For those unable to use these particular drugs, your doctor may suggest Mefloquine, although this tends to be more expensive, less well tried, and may cause more serious side effects so it is best to try two doses before leaving.

The subject of malaria prevention is becoming more complex as the malaria parasite becomes immune to some of the older drugs. In particular, there has been an increase in the proportion of cases of falciparum malaria which is particularly dangerous. Some of the preventive drugs can cause side effects, especially if taken for long periods of time, so before you travel you must check with a reputable agency the likelihood and type of malaria in the areas you intend to visit. Take their advice on prophylaxis, but be prepared to receive conflicting advice. Do not use the possibility of side effects as an excuse not to take drugs.

You can catch malaria even when taking prophylactic drugs, although it is unlikely. If you do develop symptoms (high fever, shivering, severe headache, sometimes diarrhoea) seek medical advice immediately. The risk of disease is obviously greater the further you move from the cities into rural areas with primitive facilities and standing water.

Prickly heat

Prickly heat is a very common itchy rash, and can be avoided by frequent washing and by wearing loose clothing. It is helped by the use of talcum powder to allow the skin to dry thoroughly after washing.

Rabies

Rabies is endemic in India. If you are bitten by a domestic or wild animal, do not leave things to chance. Scrub the wound immediately with soap and water/disinfectant. Try to capture the animal (within limits). Treatment depends on whether you have already been vaccinated against rabies. If you have (and this is worthwhile if you are spending lengths of time in developing countries) then some further doses of vaccine are all that is needed. Human diploid cell vaccine is best, but expensive; other, older types of vaccine such as that made of duck embryos may be the only type available. These are effective, much cheaper and interchangeable generally with the human derived types. If not already vaccinated then anti-rabies serum (immunoglobulin) may be required in addition. It is wise to finish the course of treatment whether the animal survives or not.

Returning home

It is important to take your anti-malaria tablets for four weeks after you return. Malaria can develop up to one year after leaving a malaria area. If you do become ill with fever or the other symptoms listed above, make sure your doctor knows about your trip. If you have had attacks of diarrhoea, it may be worth having a stool specimen tested in case you have picked up amoebic dysentery, giardiaisis or other protozoal infections.

Further information

Further information on medical problems abroad can be obtained from: *Travellers' Health: How To Stay Healthy Abroad*, edited by Richard Dawood (Oxford University Press), recently updated. A new edition of the HMSO publication *Health Information*

Keeping in touch

Communications

Internet

Access is becoming increasingly available in major cities and tourist centres as cyber cafés mushroom and PCOs (Public Call Office) are beginning to offer the service, but in small towns the machines can be woefully slow. Internet access is spreading wider to reach remote areas, and is becoming faster year by year. As access improves, surfing charges fall, ranging from Rs 100 per hour (US$2.50) in remote places and some hotels to as little as Rs 25 (US$0.50) in big towns.

Post

The post is frequently unreliable and delays are common. It is advisable to use a post office where it is possible to hand over mail for franking across the counter, or a top hotel post box. Valuable items should only be sent by **Registered Mail**. Government Emporia or shops in the larger hotels will send purchases home if the items are difficult to carry. **Airmail** service to Europe, Africa and Australia takes at least a week and a little longer for the Americas. **Speed post** (which takes about four days to the UK) is available from major towns. Specialist shippers deal with larger items, normally approximately US$150 per cubic metre. **Courier services** (eg DHL) are available in the larger towns. At some main post offices you can send small packages under 2 kg as Letter Post (rather than parcel post) which is much cheaper at Rs 220. 'Book Post' (for printed paper) is cheaper still, approximately Rs 170 for 5 kg. Book parcels must be sewn in cloth (best over see-through plastic) with a small open 'window' slit for contents to be seen. The process can take up to two hours!

Parcels Check that the post office holds necessary customs declaration forms (two/three copies needed). Write 'No commercial value' if returning used clothes, books etc. Air mail is expensive; sea mail slow but reasonable (10 kg, Rs 800). 'Packers' outside post offices will do all necessary cloth covering, sealing etc for Rs 20-50; you address the parcel, obtain stamps from a separate counter; stick stamps and one customs form to the parcel with glue available (the other form/s must be partially sewn on). Post at the Parcels Counter and obtain a Registration slip. **Maximum dimensions**: Height 1 m, width 0.8 m, circumference 1.8 m. **Cost**: Sea mail Rs 775 for first kilogram, Rs 70 each extra kilogram. Air mail also Rs 775 first kilogram, Rs 200 each subsequent kilogram.

Warning Many people complain that private shops offering a postal service actually send cheap substitutes. It is usually too late to complain when the buyer finds out. It is best to buy your item and then get it packed and posted yourself.

Poste restante facilities Widely available in even quite small towns at the GPO where mail is held for one month. Ask for mail to be addressed to you with your surname in capitals and underlined. When asking for mail at Poste Restante check under surname as well as Christian name. Any special issue foreign stamps are likely to be stolen from envelopes in the Indian postal service and letters may be thrown away.

Advise people who are sending you mail to India to use only definitive stamps (without pictures).

Telephone → *International code: 00 91.*

International Direct Dialling is now widely available in privately run call 'booths', usually labelled on yellow boards with the letters 'PCO-STD-ISD'. You dial the call yourself, and the time and cost are displayed on a computer screen. They are by far the best places from which to telephone abroad. Cheap rate (2100-0600) means long queues may form outside booths. Telephone calls from hotels are usually much more expensive (check price before calling). One disadvantage of the tremendous pace of the telecommunications revolution is the fact that millions of telephone numbers go out of date every year. Current telephone directories themselves are often out of date and some of the numbers given in the Handbook will have been changed even as we go to press. Directory enquiries, **197**, can be helpful but works only for the local area code. **Ringing tone:** Double ring, repeated regularly. **Engaged:** Equal length, on and off. Both are similar to UK ringing and engaged tones.

Media

Newspapers

International newspapers (mainly English language) are sold in the bookshops of top hotels in major cities, and occasionally by booksellers elsewhere. India has a large English language press. They all have extensive analysis of contemporary Indian and some international issues. The major papers now have internet sites which are excellent for keeping daily track on events, news and weather. The best known are: **The Hindu,** www.hinduonline.com/today/, **The Hindustan Times,** www.hindustan times.com, **The Independent, The Times of India,** www.timesofindia.com/, and **The Statesman,** www.thestatesman.org/. **The Economic Times** is possibly the best for independent reporting and world coverage. **The Telegraph,** published in Kolkata, www.telegraphindia.com/, has good foreign coverage. **The Indian Express,** www.expressindia.com/, has stood out as being consistently critical of the Congress Party and Government. **The Asian Age** is now published in the UK and India simultaneously and gives good coverage of Indian and international affairs. Of the fortnightly magazines, some of the most widely read are **Sunday, India Today** and **Frontline,** all of which are current affairs journals on the model of Time or Newsweek. To check weather conditions, try www.wunderground.com.

Television and radio

India's national radio and television network, *Doordarshan*, broadcasts in national and regional languages but things have moved on. The advent of satellite TV has hit even remote rural areas. The 'Dish' can help travellers keep in touch through Star TV from Hong Kong (accessing BBC World, CNN etc), VTV (music) and Sport, now available even in some modest hotels in the smallest of towns. The decision by the government to issue more licences to satellite broadcasters in 2001 has resulted in up to 50 available channels, from MTV to Maharishi Veda Vision!

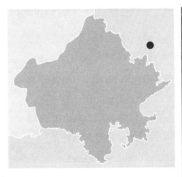

Delhi & Agra

Delhi	64
Ins and outs	64
History	65
Sights	65
Old Delhi	66
New Delhi	73
South Delhi	78
Listings	88
Sleeping	88
Eating	88
Bars and clubs	91
Entertainment	91
Festivals and events	91
Shopping	92
Activities and tours	95
Transport	96
Directory	100
Agra	101
The Taj Mahal	101
Agra Fort (Red Fort)	103
I'timad-ud-Daulah	106
Sikandra	107
Listings	107

Introduction

Delhi is not so much a city to see as to experience. You'll smell fragrances too exotic to place, odours too familiar to ignore, hear blaring Bhangra and Bryan Adams, taste rich curries and scented sweets. You'll see destiny-driven Hindus, demure Muslims and exuberant Sikhs against a million different backdrops. The multiple-mobile toting, upper-class youth rub gym-honed shoulders with the rag-clad slum dwellers that make up a third of the city's 14 million people. Exclusive housing areas, where hawkers bring every last convenience to door's answered by suppliant servants, lie a stone's throw from the regularly-razed slums which line the Yamuna River, a great waterway upon which the city has largely turned its back.

The city's history, a study in instability, is reflected in its myriad world-class monuments, temples and mosques. Broad, tree-lined avenues lead directly into teeming alleyways; elegant whitewashed bungalows, surrounded by impossibly green lawns, give way to precarious piles of mismatched masonry. Radical anti-pollution laws mean that all forms of public transport now run on gas, but still compete for ever-diminishing road space with family-packed cars, rickshaws and bicycles, watched over with unbending benevolence by the city's true ruling class, its sacrosanct cows.

Like Delhi, Agra stands on the right bank of the Yamuna River. The bustle of modern day city only serves to accentuate the serenity of the incomparable Taj Mahal, one of man's most magnificent monuments. The lightness of the Taj's white marble contrasts starkly with the imposing, heavyweight presence of the Red Fort, the transition from defensive solidity to material heartbreak eased by the intervening river.

★ Don't miss...

❶ Jama Masjid The view from the minaret of sprawling Delhi is jaw dropping, page 71.

❷ India Gate at sunset Crowds of Delhites come here to mill around, have an ice cream or go boating on the lakes, page 72.

❸ Gurudwara Bangla Sahib A great chance to experience the serenity and hospitality of the Sikh religion, page 77.

❹ Lodi Gardens Dotted with Moghul monuments and impeccably maintained, there's no better place to escape the mid-city madness, page 78.

❺ Taj Mahal from opposite riverbank As good a view as any, and definitely the best bet if you're in town on a Friday, page 101.

❻ Sikandra Notable as much for its monkey and deer-filled gardens as its magnificent architecture, page 106.

Delhi & Agra

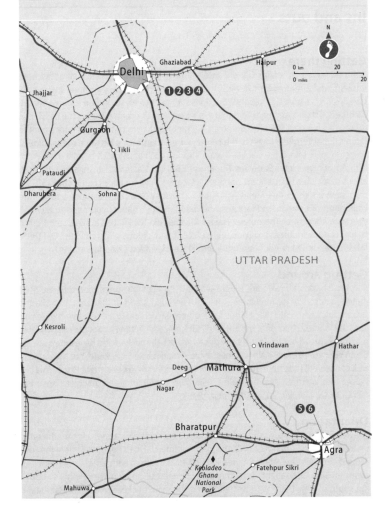

Delhi

Todays Delhi spreads over the remains of nearly a dozen earlier centres which once occupied this vital strategic site. Old Delhi or Shah Jahanabad ('city of the ruler of the world') was built by the Mughal Emperor Shah Jahan in the first half of the 17th century. Focusing on his great Red Fort and Jama Masjid, this walled city is still a dense network of narrow alleys and tightly packed markets and houses, with Muslims, Sikhs and Hindus living side by side, but separated in their own defined quarters. The thriving commercial district is centred on Chandni Chowk. Immediately to the south is the British-built capital of New Delhi, a self-conscious attempt to match the imperial grandeur of the Mughal capital, while post-Independence Delhi has dramatically accelerated its suburban expansion. There is also a 'third city', often scarcely seen, its squatter settlements which provide the only shelter for at least one-third of Delhi's total population. ▸▸ *For Sleeping, Eating and other listings, see pages 83-101.*

Ins and outs → *Phone code: 011. Dial 1952, then old number, to get new phone number.*

Colour map 3, grid B2. Population: 12.8 million. Area: 434 sq km.

Getting there

Delhi is served by **Indira Gandhi International (IGI) Airport**, which handles both international and domestic traffic. The Domestic Terminal 1, 15 km from the centre, handles flights from two separate sections: 'A', exclusively for **Indian Airlines** and 'B' for others. The International Terminal 2 is 23 km from the centre. During the day, it can take 30-45 minutes from the Domestic Terminal and 45 minutes to an hour from the International Terminal to get to the centre. A free shuttle runs between the terminals. To get to town take a pre-paid taxi or an airport coach or ask your hotel to collect.

The principal **Inter State Bus Terminus (ISBT)** is at Kashmir Gate, near the Red Fort, about 30 minutes by bus from Connaught Place. Services connect it to the other ISBTs.

There are three main railway stations. The busy **New Delhi** station, a 10-minute walk north of Connaught Place, can be maddeningly chaotic; you need to have all your wits about you. The quieter **Hazrat Nizamuddin** (which has some south-bound trains) is 5 km southeast of Connaught Place. The overpoweringly crowded **Old Delhi (Main) Station** (2 km north of Connaught Place) has a few important trains.

Getting around

Auto-rickshaws and taxis are widely available, though few are prepared to use their meters, especially for foreigners – use the pre-paid stand at the junction of Radial Road 1 and Connaught Place if possible, otherwise be sure to agree a fare before you start the journey. They offer the only realistic choice for getting about the city, which is much too spread out to walk, as city buses are usually packed and have long queues. Be on your guard around New Delhi station. A road (State Entry Road, but the name is well concealed) runs from the southern end of platform 1 to Connaught Place. This is a hassle-free alternative to the main Chelmsford Road during the day (gate closed at night). ▸▸ *See Transport, page 96, for further details.*

Orientation

The Red Fort and Jama Masjid are the focal point of Old Delhi, about 2 km northeast of Connaught Place. Chandi Chowk, the main commercial area heads east from the Fort. Around this area are narrow lanes packed to the rafters with all different types of wares for sale. Connaught Place, the main commercial centre of New Delhi, is about 1 km south of New Delhi railway station and the main backpackers' area, Paharganj.

Running due south of Connaught Place is Janpath with small shops selling a variety of craft products and hotels like **Imperial** and **Le Meridien**. Running east west across Janpath is Rajpath with all the major state buildings at its western end. Immediately beyond them is the diplomatic enclave, Chanakyapuri. Most of the upmarket hotels are scattered across the wide area between Connaught Place and the airport to the southwest. As Delhi has spread southwards a series of new markets has grown up to serve extensive housing colonies such as South Extension, Greater Kailash and Safdarjang Enclave. This development has brought one of the major historic sites, the Qutb Minar, within the limits of the southern city, about half an hour by taxi from Connaught Place.

Best time to visit

October-March are the best months, but December and January can get quite cold and foggy at night. Pollution can affect asthma sufferers. Monsoon lasts from the end of June to mid-September. May and June are very hot and dry.

History

Delhi's present position as capital was only confirmed on 12 December 1911, when King George V announced at the Delhi Durbar that the capital of India was to move from Calcutta to Delhi. The new city, New Delhi, planned under the leadership of British architect Edwin Lutyens with the assistance of his friend Herbert Baker, was inaugurated on 9 February 1931.

The city was to accommodate 70,000 people and have boundless possibilities for future expansion. The King favoured something in form and flavour similar to the Mughal masterpieces but fretted over the horrendous expense that this would incur. A petition signed by eminent public figures such as Bernard Shaw and Thomas Hardy advocated an Indian style and an Indian master builder. Herbert Baker had made known his own views even before his appointment when he wrote "first and foremost it is the spirit of British sovereignty which must be imprisoned in its stone and bronze". Lutyéns himself despised Indian architecture. "Even before he had seen any examples of it", writes Tillotson (architectural historian), "he pronounced Mughal architecture to be 'piffle', and seeing it did not disturb that conviction". Yet in the end, Lutyens was forced to settle for the compromise.

The Viceroy's House, the centrepiece of imperial proportions, was 1 km around the foundations, bigger than Louis XIV's palace at Versailles. It had a colossal dome surmounting a long colonnade and 340 rooms in all. It took nearly 20 years to complete, similar to the time it took to build the Taj Mahal. In the busiest year, 29,000 people were working on the site and buildings began to take shape. The project was surrounded by controversy from beginning to end. Opting for a fundamentally classical structure, both Baker and Lutyens sought to incorporate Indian motifs, many entirely superficial. While some claim that Lutyens achieved a unique synthesis of the two traditions, Tillotson asks whether "the sprinkling of a few simplified and classicized Indian details (especially *chhattris*) over a classical palace" could be called a synthesis.

Sights

The sites of interest are grouped in three main areas. In the centre is the British built capital of **New Delhi**, with its government buildings and wide avenues. The heart of **Shah Jahanabad** (Old Delhi) is about 2 km north of Connaught Circus. Ten kilometres to the south is the **Qutb Minar** complex, with the old fortress city of **Tughluqabad**, 8 km to its east. You can visit each separately, or link routes together into a day-tour to include the most interesting sites. See page 99 for tour details.

Old Delhi

Shah Jahan (ruled 1628-1658) decided to move back from Agra to Delhi in 1638. Within 10 years the huge city of **Shahjahanabad**, now known as Old Delhi, was built. The plan of Shah Jahan's new city symbolized the link between religious authority enshrined in the Jama Masjid to the west, and political authority represented by the Diwan-i-Am in the Fort, joined by Chandni Chowk, the route used by the Emperor. The city was protected by rubble-built walls, some of which still survive. These walls were pierced by 14 main gates. The **Ajmeri Gate, Turkman Gate** (often referred to by auto-rickshaw wallahs as 'Truckman Gate'!), **Kashmir Gate** and **Delhi Gate** still survive.

Chandi Chowk

Shahjahanabad was laid out in blocks with wide roads, residential quarters, bazars and mosques. Its principal street, Chandni Chowk, had a tree-lined canal flowing down its centre which quickly became renowned throughout Asia. The jumble of shops, labyrinthine alleys running off a main thoroughfare with craftsmen's workshops, hotels, mosques and temples, cause it to retain some of its magic, although the canal is long gone. A cycle rickshaw ride gives you a good feel of the place.

The impressive red sandstone façade of the **Diagambar Jain Mandir** (temple) standing at the eastern end of Chandni Chowk, faces the Red Fort. Built in 1656, it contains an image of Adinath. The bird hospital within this compound releases the birds on recovery (instead of returning them to their owners); many remain within the temple precincts.

The Red Fort (Lal Qila)

ⓘ *Closed Mon, daily sunrise to sunset, US$2 foreigners, Rs 10 Indians, allow 1 hour. The entrance is through the Lahore Gate (nearest the car park) with the admission kiosk opposite. Keep your ticket as you will need to show it at the Drum House. The toilets are in Chatta Chowk and near Asad Burj but are best avoided.*

Between the new city and the river Yamuna, Shah Jahan built a fort. Most of it was built out of red (*lal*) sandstone, hence the name **Lal Qila** (Red Fort), the same as that at Agra on which the Delhi fort is modelled. Begun in 1639 and completed in 1648, it is said to have cost Rs 10 million, much of which was spent on the opulent marble palaces within. Visitors may be saddened by the neglected state of the once imposing fort – coloured marble-inlay is missing and the gardens are bare. However, despite the modern development of roads and shops and the never-ending traffic, that dominating impression is still immensely powerful.

The approach The entrance is by the Lahore Gate (make this clear to the rickshaw driver). The defensive barbican that juts out in front of the Lahore Gate was built by Aurangzeb, see page 272. A common story suggests that Aurangzeb built the curtain wall at the entrance to save his nobles and visiting dignitaries from having to walk – and bow – the whole length of Chandni Chowk, for no one was allowed to ride in the presence of the Emperor. When the Emperor sat in the Diwan-i-Am he could see all the way down the Chowk, so the addition must have been greatly welcomed by his courtiers. The new entrance arrangement also made an attacking army more vulnerable to the defenders on the walls.

Chatta Chowk Inside is the 'Covered Bazar', quite exceptional in the 17th century. In Shah Jahan's time there were shops on both upper and lower levels. Originally they catered for the Imperial household and carried stocks of silks, brocades, velvets, gold and silverware, jewellery and gems. There were coffee shops too for nobles and courtiers. Walk through the left-hand archway and you will see a small building on your right near the Art Corner shop.

The Naubat Khana (Naqqar Khana) The Naubat Khana (**Drum House** or music gallery), marked the entrance to the inner apartments of the fort. Here everyone except the princes of the royal family had to dismount and leave their horses or elephants (*hathi*), hence its other name of **Hathi Pol** (Elephant Gate). Five times a day ceremonial music was played on the kettle drum, shahnais (a kind of oboe) and cymbals, glorifying the emperor. In 1754 the Emperor Ahmad Shah was murdered here. The gateway with four floors is decorated with floral designs. You can still see traces of the original panels painted in gold or other colours on the interior of the gateway.

Diwan-i-Am Between the first inner court and the royal palaces at the heart of the fort, stood the Diwan-i-Am (Hall of Public Audience), the farthest point the normal visitor would reach. It has seen many dramatic events – the destructive whirlwind of the Persian Nadir Shah in 1739 and of Ahmad Shah the Afghan in 1756, and the trial of the last 'King of Delhi', **Bahadur Shah II** in 1858.

The well-proportioned hall was both a functional building and a showpiece intended to hint at the opulence of the palace itself. In Shah Jahan's time the sandstone was hidden behind a very thin layer of white polished plaster, *chunam*. This was decorated with floral motifs in many colours, especially gilt. Silk carpets and heavy curtains hung from the canopy rings outside the building, such interiors reminders of the Mughals' nomadic origins in Central Asia, where royal durbars were held in tents.

The throne surround At the back of the hall is a platform for the emperor's throne. Around this was a gold railing, within which stood the princes and great nobles separated from the lesser nobles (inside the hall) and minor officials from the general public in the courtyard (now the lawn). Behind the throne canopy are 12 marble inlaid panels. Figurative workmanship is very unusual in Islamic buildings, and this one panel is the only example in the Red Fort. Wherever you stand in the hall (everyone except the Emperor's favourite son had to stand), there is an uninterrupted view of the throne – a powerful psychological effect.

The business comprised official and domestic administration, reports from the provinces, tax and revenue matters and official appointments. On the personal side, Shah Jahan would listen to accounts of illness, dream interpretations and anecdotes from his ministers and nobles. He usually retired to bed at around 2200 and liked to be read to, his particular favourite being the *Babur-i-nama*, the autobiography of his great-great-grandfather.

Wednesday was the day of judgement. Sentences were often brutal but swift and sometimes the punishment of dismemberment, beating or death was carried out on the spot. The executioners were close at hand with axes and whips. On Friday, the Muslim holy day, there would be no business.

Inner palace buildings Behind the Diwan-i-Am is the private enclosure of the fort. Along the east wall, overlooking the River Yamuna, Shah Jahan set six small palaces

Shah Jahan used to spend about two hours a day in the Diwan-i-Am. According to Bernier, the French traveller, the emperor would enter to a fanfare and mount the throne by a flight of movable steps.

Delhi & Agra Delhi *Sights*

(five survive). Also within this compound are the Harem, the Life-Bestowing Garden and the Nahr-i-Bihisht (Stream of Paradise). Leave the throne canopy area by the steps to your left, follow the path and carry on until you reach the white marble garden pavilion.

Life-Bestowing Gardens (Hayat Baksh Bagh) The original gardens were landscaped according to the Islamic principles of the Persian *char bagh*, with

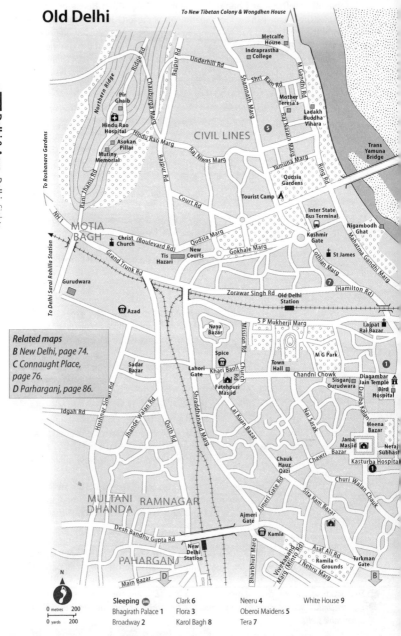

Old Delhi

Delhi & Agra Delhi Sights

Related maps
B New Delhi, page 74.
C Connaught Place, page 76.
D Parharganj, page 86.

Sleeping		Neeru 4	White House 9
Bhagirath Palace 1	Clark 6	Oberoi Maidens 5	
Broadway 2	Flora 3	Tera 7	
	Karol Bagh 8		

0 metres 200
0 yards 200

pavilions, fountains and water courses dividing the garden into various but regular beds. The two pavilions **Sawan** and **Bhadon**, named after the first two months of the rainy season (July-August), reveal something of the character of the garden. The garden used to create the effect of the monsoon and contemporary accounts tell us that in the pavilions, some of which were especially erected for the *Teej* festival which marks the arrival of the monsoon, the royal ladies would sit in silver swings and watch the rains. Water flowed from the back wall of the pavilion through a slit above the marble shelf and over the niches in the wall. Gold and silver pots of flowers were placed in these alcoves during the day whilst at night candles were lit to create a glistening and colourful effect. To the west is **Mehtab Bagh** which has a *baoli* (step well) to its northwest.

Shahi Burj From the pavilion next to the Shahi Burj ('Royal Tower') the canal known as the **Nahr-i-Bihisht** (Stream of Paradise) began its journey along the Royal Terrace. The three-storey octagonal Tower, seriously damaged in 1857, is still unsafe. The lower storey contained a tank from which water was raised to flow into the garden. In Shah Jahan's time the Yamuna lapped the walls. Shah Jahan used the tower as his most private office and only his sons and a few senior ministers were allowed with him.

Moti Masjid To the right are the three marble domes of Aurangzeb's 'Pearl Mosque' (shoes must be removed). Bar the cupolas, it is completely hidden behind a wall of red sandstone, now painted white. Built in 1662 of polished white marble, it has some exquisite decoration. All the surfaces are highly decorated in a fashion similar to rococo, which was developed at the same time in Europe. Unusually the prayer hall is on a raised platform with inlaid outlines of individual 'prayer mats' (*musallas*) in black marble. While the outer walls were aligned to the cardinal points like all the other fort buildings, the inner walls were positioned so that the mosque would correctly face Mecca.

Hammam The Royal Baths have three apartments separated by corridors with canals to carry water to each room. The two flanking the entrance, for the royal

Yamuna River

Grand Trunk Rd

Poste Restante

Red Fort

Ring Rd

P

P

Vijay Ghat

Shanti Vana

Netaji Subhash Marg

Park Marg

Kasturba

DARYAGANJ

Netaji Subhash Marg

Bazar Chitli Kabar

Ansari Rd

Mahatma Gandhi Rd

Delhi Gate

Ansari Rd

Raj Ghat

Eating 🍴
Apki Pasand **4**
Chor Bizarre **5**
Karim's **1**
Motimahal **2**
Peshawari **3**

Delhi & Agra Delhi Sights

children, had hot and cold baths. The room furthest away from the door has three basins for rose water fountains.

Diwan-i-Khas Beyond is the single-storeyed 'Hall of Private Audience', topped by four Hindu-style *chhattris* and built completely of white marble. The *dado* (lower part of the wall) on the interior was richly decorated with inlaid precious and semi-precious stones. The ceiling was silver but was removed by the Marathas in 1760. Outside, the hall used to have a marble pavement and an arcaded court. Both have gone.

This was the Mughal office of state. Shah Jahan spent two hours here before retiring for a meal, siesta and prayers. In the evening he would return to the Hall for more work before going to the harem. The hall's splendour moved the 14th-century poet **Amir Khusrau** to write the lines inscribed above the corner arches of the north and south walls: "*Agar Firdaus bar rue Zamin-ast/Hamin ast o Hamin ast o Hamin ast*" (If there be a paradise on earth, it is here, it is here, it is here).

Royal palaces Next to the Diwan-i-Khas is the three-roomed **Khas Mahal** (Private Palace). Nearest the Diwan-i-Khas is the **Tasbih Khana** (Chamber for the Telling of Rosaries) where the emperor would worship privately with his rosary of 99 beads, one for each of the mystical names of Allah. In the centre is the Khwabgah ('*Palace of Dreams'*) which gives on to the octagonal **Mussaman Burj** tower. Here Shah Jahan would be seen each morning. A balcony was added to the tower in 1809 and here George V and Queen Mary appeared in their Coronation Durbar of 1911. The **Tosh Khana** (*Robe Room*), to the south, has a beautiful marble screen at its north end, carved with the scales of justice above the filigree grille. If you are standing with your back to the Diwan-i-Khas you will see a host of circulating suns (a symbol of royalty), but if your back is to the next building (the Rang Mahal), you will see moons surrounding the scales. All these rooms were sumptuously decorated with fine silk carpets, rich silk brocade curtains and lavishly decorated walls. After 1857 the British used the Khas Mahal as an officer's mess and sadly it was defaced.

Beneath the Khas Mahal is the **Khirzi Gate**. This is neglected now, but was an important and convenient private entrance for the Emperor and his most senior nobles.

The **Rang Mahal** (Palace of Colours), the residence of the chief *sultana*, was also the place where the Emperor ate most of his meals. To protect the rich carpets, calico-covered leather sheets were spread out. It was divided into six apartments. Privacy and coolness were ensured by the use of marble *jali* screens. Like the other palaces it was beautifully decorated with a silver ceiling ornamented with golden flowers to reflect the water in the channel running through the building. The north and south apartments were both known as **Sheesh Mahal** (Palace of Mirrors) since into the ceiling were set hundreds of small mirrors. In the evening when candles were lit a starlit effect would be produced. This type of decoration was a favourite in Rajasthan before the Mughals arrived (see page 132 – Amber Fort). In the summer the ladies went to the water-cooled cellars underground (not accessible now).

Through the palace ran the **Life-bestowing Stream** and at its centre is a lotus shaped marble basin which had an ivory fountain. As might be expected in such a cloistered and cossetted environment, the ladies sometimes got bored. In the 18th century the **Empress of Jahandar Shah** sat gazing out at the river and remarked that she had never seen a boat sink. Shortly afterwards a boat was deliberately capsized so that she could be entertained by the sight of people bobbing up and down in the water crying for help.

The southernmost of the palaces, the **Mumtaz Mahal** (Palace of Jewels) ① *0900-1700, closed Fri*, was also used by the harem. The lower half of its walls are of marble and it contains six apartments. After the Mutiny of 1857 it was used as a guardroom and since 1912 it has been a museum with exhibits of textiles, weapons, carpets, jade and metalwork as well as works depicting life in the court. It should not be missed.

Outside of the Red Fort, cycle rickshaws offer a trip to the Spice Market, Jama Masjid and back through the bazar. You travel slowly westwards down Chandni Chowk passing the town hall. Dismount at Church Road and follow your guide into the heart of the market on Khari Baoli where wholesalers sell every conceivable spice. Ask to go to the roof for an excellent view over the market and back towards the Red Fort. The ride back through the bazar is equally fascinating – look up at the amazing electricity system. The final excitement is getting back across Netaji Subhash Marg. Panic not, the rickshaw wallahs know what they are doing. Negotiate for one hour and expect to pay about Rs 50. The spice laden air may irritate your throat.

Jama Masjid (The Friday Mosque)

ⓘ *Visitors welcome from 30 mins after sunrise until 1200; and from 1345 until 30 mins before sunset, free, still or video cameras Rs 100, tower entry Rs 10.*

The magnificent Jama Masjid is the largest mosque in India and the last great architectural work of Shah Jahan, intended to dwarf all mosques that had gone before it. With the fort, it dominates Old Delhi. The mosque is much simpler in its ornamentation than Shah Jahan's secular buildings – a judicious blend of red sandstone and white marble, which are interspersed in the domes, minarets and cusped arches.

❖ The general public enter by the north gate. You must remove shoes and cover all exposed flesh from your shoulders to your legs.

The gateways Symbolizing the separation of the sacred and the secular, the threshold is a place of great importance where the worshipper steps to a higher plane. There are three huge gateways, the largest being to the east. This was reserved for the royal family who gathered in a private gallery in its upper storey. Today, the faithful enter through the east gate on Fridays and for *Id-ul-Fitr* and *Id-ul-Adha*. The latter commemorates Abraham's (Ibrahim's) sacrificial offering of his son Ishmael (Ismail). Islam (unlike the Jewish and Christian tradition) believes that Abraham offered to sacrifice Ishmael, Isaac's brother.

The courtyard The façade has the main arch (*iwan*), five smaller arches on each side with two flanking minarets and three bulbous domes behind, all perfectly proportioned. The *iwan* draws the worshippers' attention into the building. The minarets have great views from the top; well worth the climb for Rs 10 (woman may not be allowed to climb alone). The **hauz**, in the centre of the courtyard, is an ablution tank placed as usual between the inner and outer parts of the building to remind the worshipper that it is through the ritual of baptism that one first enters the community of believers. The **Dikka**, in front of the ablution tank, is a raised platform. Muslim communities grew so rapidly that by the eighth century it sometimes became necessary to introduce a second *muballigh* (prayer leader) who stood on this platform and copied the postures and chants of the *imam* inside to relay them to a much larger congregation. With the introduction of the loudspeaker and amplification, the *dikka* and the *muballigh* became redundant. In the northwest corner of the masjid there is a small shed. For a small fee, the faithful are shown a hair from the beard of the prophet, as well as his sandal and his footprint in rock.

The Kawthar Inscription Set up in 1766, the inscription commemorates the place where a worshipper had a vision of the Prophet standing by the celestial tank in paradise. It is here that the Prophet will stand on Judgment Day. In most Islamic buildings, the inscriptions are passages from the Koran or Sayings of the Prophet. Shah Jahan, however, preferred to have sayings extolling the virtues of the builder and architect as well. The 10 detailed panels on the façade indicate the date of construction (1650-1656), the cost (10 lakhs – one million rupees), the history of the building, the architect (Ustad Khalil) and the builder (Nur Allah Ahmed, probably the son of the man who did most of the work on the Taj Mahal).

New Delhi

India Gate and around

A tour of New Delhi will usually start with a visit to India Gate. This war memorial is situated at the eastern end of **Rajpath**. Designed by Lutyens, it commemorates more than 70,000 Indian soldiers who died in the First World War. Some 13,516 names of British and Indian soldiers killed on the Northwest Frontier and in the Afghan War of 1919 are engraved on the arch and foundations. Under the arch is the Amar Jawan Jyoti, commemorating Indian armed forces' losses in the Indo-Pakistan War of 1971. The arch (43 m high) stands on a base of Bharatpur stone and rises in stages. Similar to the Hindu *chhattri* signifying regality, it is decorated with nautilus shells symbolizing British maritime power.

To the northwest of India Gate are two impressive buildings, **Hyderabad House** and **Baroda House**, built as residences for the Nizam of Hyderabad and the Gaekwar of Baroda. Now used as offices, both were carefully placed to indicate the paramountcy of the British Raj over the Princely States. The *Nizam*, reputed to be the richest man in the world, ruled over an area equal to that of France. The *Gaekwar* belonged to the top level of Indian Princes and both, along with the Maharajas of Mysore, Jammu and Kashmir and Gwalior were entitled to receive 21-gun salutes.

Rajpath leads west from India Gate towards **Janpath**. To the north are the **National Archives**. Formerly the Imperial Record Office, and designed by Lutyens, this was intended to be a part of a much more ambitious complex of public buildings. To the south is the National Museum (see below).

National Gallery of Modern Art

① *Jaipur House, near India Gate, T23384640, closed Mon, 1000-1700, Rs 10, foreigners Rs 150.*

The excellent collection is housed in a former residence of the Maharaja of Jaipur. Some of the best exhibits are on the ground floor which is devoted to post-1930 works. To view the collections chronologically, begin on the first floor. Artists include: Amrita Shergil (ground floor): over 100 exhibits, synthesizing the flat treatment of Indian painting with a realistic tone; Rabindranath Tagore (ground floor): examples from a brief but intense spell in the 1930s; The Bombay School or Company School (first floor): includes Western painters who documented their visits to India. Realism is reflected in Indian painting of the early 19th century represented by the schools of Avadh, Patna, Sikkim and Thanjavur; The Bengal School (the late 19th-century Revivalist Movement): artists such as Abanindranath Tagore and Nandalal Bose have their works exhibited here. Western influence was discarded in response to the nationalist movement. Inspiration derived from Indian folk art is evident in the works of Jamini Roy and YD Shukla.

National Museum

① *Janpath, T23019272, closed Mon, 1000-1700, Rs 10, foreigners Rs 150 (students Rs 1), camera Rs 300; free guided tours 1030, 1130, 1200, 1400, films are screened every day (1430), marble squat toilets, but dirty.*

The collection was formed from the nucleus of the Exhibition of Indian Art, London (1947). Now merged with the Asian Antiquities Museum it displays a rich collection of the artistic treasure of Central Asia and India including ethnological objects from prehistoric archaeological finds to the late Medieval period. Replicas of exhibits and books on Indian culture and art are on sale. There is a research library.

Ground floor Prehistoric: seals, figurines, toy animals and jewellery from the Harappan civilization (2400-1500 BC). Maurya Period: terracottas and stone heads from the Sunga period (third century BC) include the *chaturmukha* (four-faced) *lingam*. Gandhara School: stucco heads showing the Graeco Roman influence. Gupta terracottas (circa AD 400): include two life-size images of the river goddesses Ganga and Yamuna and the four-armed bust of Vishnu from a temple near Lal Kot. South Indian sculpture: from Pallava and early Chola temples and relief panels from Mysore. Tenth-century AD sculptures. Bronzes from the Buddhist monastery at Nalanda. Some of Buddha's relics were placed in the Thai pavilion in 1997.

First floor Illustrated manuscripts: include the *Babur-i-nama* in the Emperor's own handwriting and an autographed copy of Jahangir's memoirs. Miniature paintings: Include the 16th-century Jain School, the 18th-century Rajasthani School and the Pahari Schools of Garhwal, Basoli and Kangra. The Aurel Stein Collection consists of antiquities recovered by him during his explorations of Central Asia and the western borders of China at the turn of the century.

Second floor Pre-Columbian and Mayan artefacts: anthropological section devoted to tribal artefacts and folk arts. Sharad Rani Bakkiwal Gallery of Musical Instruments: displays over 300 instruments collected by the famous *sarod* player.

The Secretariats
At the Secretariat and Rashtrapati Bhavan gates, the mounted and unmounted troops parade in full uniform on Saturdays at 1030 and are worth attending. Standing on either side of Raisina Hill, **North Block** houses the Home and Finance Ministries, **South Block** the Ministry of Foreign Affairs. These long classical buildings, topped by Baroque domes, designed by Baker, are similar to his Government Buildings of Pretoria, and were derived from Wren's Royal Naval College at Greenwich. The towers were originally designed to be twice the height of the buildings and to act as beacons guarding the way to the inner sanctum. Their height was reduced and with it their impact. The domes are decorated with lotus motifs and elephants, while the north and south gateways are Mughal in design. On the northern Secretariat building is the imperialistic inscription "Liberty will not descend to a people: a people must raise themselves to liberty. It is a blessing which must be earned before it can be enjoyed".

In the **Great Court** between the Secretariats are the four **Dominion Columns**, donated by the governments of Australia, Canada, New Zealand and South Africa – ironically, as it turned out. The resemblance of Baker's domes to his work in Pretoria is also striking and ironic! Each is crowned by a bronze ship sailing east, symbolizing the maritime and mercantile supremacy of the British Empire. In the centre of the court is the Jaipur column of red sandstone topped with a white egg, bronze lotus and six-pointed glass star of India (which has evolved into today's five-pointed star). Across the entrance to the Great Court is a 205 m wrought iron screen.

Rashtrapati Bhavan and Nehru Memorial Museum
Once the Viceroy's House, Rashtrapati Bhavan is the official residence of the President of India. Designed by Lutyens, it combines western and eastern styles. Philip Davies describes it as a masterpiece of symmetry, discipline, silhouette and harmony. The Durbar Hall, 23 m in diameter, has coloured marble from all parts of India.

To the south is Flagstaff House, formerly the residence of the Commander-in-Chief. Renamed Teen Murti Bhawan it now houses the **Nehru Memorial Museum** ① *Teen Murti Bhavan, closed Mon, museum 1000-1500 and planetarium 1130-1500, Library closed Sun, 0900-1900, free, T2301 4504*. Designed by Robert Tor Russell, in 1948 it became the official residence of India's first Prime Minister, Jawaharlal Nehru. Converted after his death (1964) into a national memorial, the reception, study and

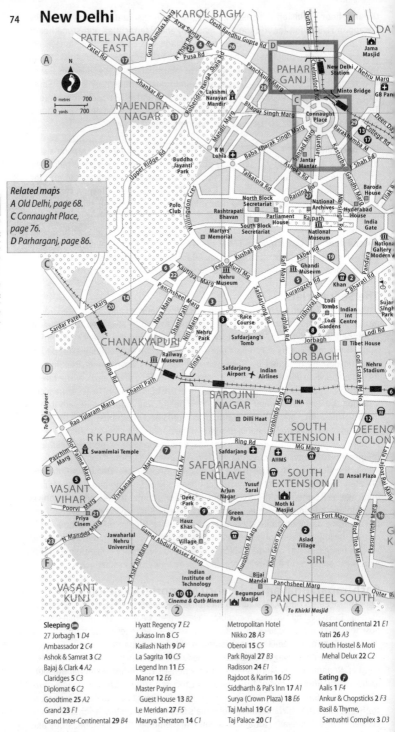

Delhi & Agra Delhi Sights

Related maps
A Old Delhi, page 68.
C Connaught Place, page 76.
D Parharganj, page 86.

Sleeping			
27 Jorbagh 1 D4	Hyatt Regency 7 E2	Metropolitan Hotel	Vasant Continental 21 E1
Ambassador 2 C4	Jukaso Inn 8 C5	Nikko 28 A3	Yatri 26 A3
Ashok & Samrat 3 C2	Kailash Nath 9 D4	Oberoi 15 C5	Youth Hostel & Moti
Bajaj & Clark 4 A2	La Sagrita 10 C5	Park Royal 27 B3	Mehal Delux 22 C2
Claridges 5 C3	Legend Inn 11 E5	Radisson 24 E1	
Diplomat 6 C2	Manor 12 E6	Rajdoot & Karim 16 D5	Eating
Goodtime 25 A2	Master Paying	Siddharth & Pal's Inn 17 A1	Aalis 1 F4
Grand 23 F1	Guest House 13 B2	Surya (Crown Plaza) 18 E6	Ankur & Chopsticks 2 F3
Grand Inter-Continental 29 B4	Le Meridan 27 F5	Taj Mahal 19 C4	Basil & Thyme,
	Maurya Sheraton 14 C1	Taj Palace 20 C1	Santushti Complex 3 D3

bedroom are intact. Note his extensive reading and wide interests. A *Jyoti Jawahar* (torch) symbolizes the eternal values he inspired, and a granite rock is carved with extracts from his historic speech at midnight 14-15 August 1947. A very informative and vivid history of the Independence Movement.

The **Martyr's Memorial**, at the junction of Sardar Patel Marg and Willingdon Crescent, is a magnificent 26-m long, 3-m high bronze sculpture by DP Roy Chowdhury. The 11 statues of national heroes are headed by Mahatma Gandhi.

Gandhi Museum

ⓘ *Birla House, 5 Tees Jan Marg (near Claridges Hotel), closed Mon and 2nd Sat, 0930-1730, free, film at 1500, T2301 2843*, contains photos and memorabilia including his few possessions during his final days in the house. A monument marks where he fell. Definitely worth a visit. Others museums in the city related to Gandhi include **Gandhi Darshan** ⓘ *opposite Raj Ghat, closed Mon, 1000-1700, T2331 1793*, has five pavilions – sculpture, photographs and paintings of Gandhi and the history of the *Satyagraha* movement, the philosophy of non-violence; **Gandhi Smarak Sangrahalaya** ⓘ *Raj Ghat, T3011480, closed Thu, 0930-1730*, displays some of Gandhi's personal belongings and a small library includes recordings of speeches; **Indira Gandhi Museum** ⓘ *1 Safdarjang Rd, T3010094, 0930-1700, closed Mon, free*, charts the phases of her life from childhood up to the moment of her death.

Parliament House and around

Northeast of the Viceroy's House is the **Council House**, now **Sansad Bhavan**. Baker designed this and Lutyens suggested that it be circular (173 m diameter). Inside is the library and chambers for the Council of State, Chamber of Princes and Legislative Assembly – the **Lok Sabha**. Just opposite the Council House is the **Rakabganj Gurudwara** in Pandit Pant Marg. This 20th-century white marble shrine, which

Big Chill **4** *E5*
Diva **14** *F5*
Imperial Garden **7** *F5*
Lodi **8** *D4*
Massid Moth **15** *F5*
Mini Mahal &
  Golden Dragon **5** *E1*
Nathu's **13** *B4*
Nirula's **6** *D4*
Olive **10** *F2*

Park Baluch & Bistro **9** *E2*
Sagar's & Colonel's
  Kebabs **12** *E4*
Thai Wok **11** *F2*
Triveni Café
  & Galley **17** *B4*

Bars & clubs
Bohemia, Shalom &
  Fabindia **16** *F4*

integrates the late Mughal and Rajasthani styles, marks the spot where the headless body of **Guru Tegh Bahadur**, the ninth Sikh Guru, was cremated in 1657. West of the Council House is the Cathedral **Church of the Redemption** (1927-1935) and to its north the Italianate Roman Catholic **Church of the Sacred Heart** (1930-1934), both conceived by Henry Medd whose designs won architectural competitions.

Connaught Place and Connaught Circus

Connaught Place and its outer ring, Connaught Circus, comprise two-storey arcaded buildings, arranged radially. In 1995 they were re-named **Rajiv Chowk** and **Indira Chowk** respectively, but are still widely known by their original names. Designed by **Robert Tor Russell**, they have become the main commercial centre of Delhi. Sadly, the

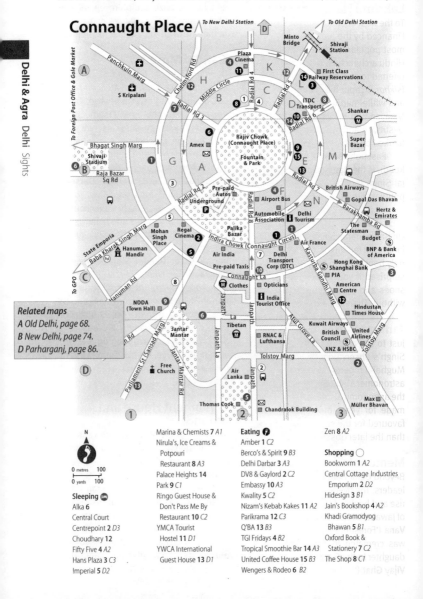

Connaught Place

Related maps
A Old Delhi, page 68.
B New Delhi, page 74.
D Parharganj, page 86.

N

0 metres 100
0 yards 100

Sleeping
Alka 6
Central Court
Centrepoint 2 D3
Choudhary 12
Fifty Five 4 A2
Hans Plaza 3 C3
Imperial 5 D2

Marina & Chemists 7 A1
Nirula's, Ice Creams &
  Potpouri
  Restaurant 8 A3
Palace Heights 14
Park 9 C1
Ringo Guest House &
  Don't Pass Me By
  Restaurant 10 C2
YMCA Tourist
  Hostel 11 D1
YWCA International
  Guest House 13 D1

Eating
Amber 1 C2
Berco's & Spirit 9 B3
Delhi Darbar 3 A3
DV8 & Gaylord 2 C2
Embassy 10 A3
Kwality 5 C2
Nizam's Kebab Kakes 11 A2
Parikrama 12 C3
Q'BA 13 B3
TGI Fridays 4 B2
Tropical Smoothie Bar 14 A3
United Coffee House 15 B3
Wengers & Rodeo 6 B2

Zen 8 A2

Shopping
Bookworm 1 A2
Central Cottage Industries
  Emporium 2 D2
Hidesign 3 B1
Jain's Bookshop 4 A2
Khadi Gramodyog
  Bhawan 5 B1
Oxford Book &
  Stationery 7 C2
The Shop 8 C1

area also attracts bands of aggressive touts ready to take advantage of the unwary traveller by getting them into spurious 'official' or 'government' shops and travel agencies. The area (and Palika Bazar) is renowned for its shoe-shine tricksters. Large wadges of slime appear mysteriously on shoes and are then pointed out eagerly by attendant boys or men who offer to clean them off at a price. This can just be the start of 'necessary repairs' to the shoes for which bills of over Rs 300 are not unknown. If caught, insist politely but firmly that the dirt is cleaned off free of charge.

To the south in **Janpath** (the People's Way), the east and west Courts were hostels for the members of the newly convened Legislative Assembly. With their long colonnaded verandahs, these are Tuscan in character.

Lakshmi Narayan Mandir

To the west of Connaught Circus is the Lakshmi Narayan **Birla Temple** in Mandir Marg. Financed by the prominent industrialist **Raja Baldeo Birla** in 1938, this is one of the most popular Hindu shrines in the city and one of Delhi's few striking examples of Hindu architecture. Dedicated to Lakshmi, the goddess of well-being, it is commonly referred to as **Birla Mandir**. The design is in the Orissan style with tall curved towers (*sikhara*) capped by large *amalakas*. The exterior is faced with red and ochre stone and white marble. Built around a central courtyard, the main shrine has images of Narayan and his consort Lakshmi while two separate cells have icons of Siva (the Destroyer) and his consort Durga (the 10-armed destroyer of demons). The temple is flanked by a *dharamshala* (rest house) and a Buddhist *vihara* (monastery).

East from the Birla Temple, down Kali Bari Marg to Baba Kharak Singh Marg (Irwin Road), is the **Hanuman Mandir**. This small temple (circa 1724) was built by Maharaja Jai Singh II of Jaipur. Of no great architectural interest, the temple is increasingly popular with devotees. **Mangal haat** (Tuesday Fair) is a popular market.

Gurudwara Bangla Sahib

On Baba Kharak Singh Road is a fine example of Sikh temple architecture, featuring a large pool reminiscent of Amritsar's Golden Temple. The 24-hour reciting of the faith's holy book adds to the atmosphere, and there's free food on offer, although don't be surprised if you're asked to help out with the washing up! You must remove your shoes and cover your head to enter – suitable scarves are provided if you arrive without. There is no charge to enter.

Jantar Mantar

Just to the east of the Hanuman Mandir in Sansad Marg (Parliament Street) is Jai Singh's observatory ('Jantar Mantar') ① *sunrise-sunset, Rs 5, foreigners US$2*. The Mughal Emperor Mohammad Shah (ruled 1719-1748) entrusted the renowned astronomer Maharaja Jai Singh II with the task of revising the calendar and correcting the astronomical tables used by contemporary priests. Daily astral observations were made for years before construction began and plastered brick structures were favoured for the site instead of brass instruments. Built in 1725 it is slightly smaller than the later observatory at Jaipur.

Memorial Ghats

Beyond Delhi Gate lies the **River Yamuna**, marked by a series of memorials to India's leaders. The river itself, a kilometre away, is invisible from the road, protected by a low rise and banks of trees. The most prominent memorial, immediately opposite the end of Jawaharlal Nehru Road, is that of Mahatma Gandhi at **Raj Ghat**. To its north is **Shanti Vana** ('Forest of Peace'), landscaped gardens where Prime Minister Jawaharlal Nehru was cremated in 1964, and subsequently his grandson Sanjay Gandhi in 1980, daughter **Indira Gandhi** in 1984 and elder grandson, Rajiv, in 1991. To the north again is **Vijay Ghat** ('Victory Bank') where Prime Minister Lal Bahadur Shastri was cremated.

South Delhi

The spacious layout of New Delhi has been preserved despite the building on empty sites and the sub-division of previously large gardens. Still close to the centre, there are several attractive high-class residential areas such as Jor Bagh near the Lodi Gardens, while beyond the Ring Road are sprawling estates of flats and larger apartments and huge shopping and commercial centres.

The Lodi Gardens

These beautiful gardens, with mellow stone tombs of the 15th- and 16th-century Lodi rulers, are popular for gentle strolls as much as for jogging. In the middle of the garden facing the east entrance from Max Mueller Rd is **Bara Gumbad** (Big Dome), a mosque built in 1494. The raised courtyard is provided with an imposing gateway and *mehman khana* (guest rooms). The platform in the centre appears to have had a tank for ritual ablutions.

The Sheesh (Shish) **Gumbad** (Glass Dome, late 15th-century) is built on a raised incline a few metres north of the Bara Gumbad and was once decorated with glazed blue tiles, painted floral designs and Koranic inscriptions. The façade gives the impression of a two-storeyed building, typical of Lodi architecture. **Mohammad Shah's tomb** (1450) is that of the third Sayyid ruler. It has sloping buttresses, an octagonal plan, projecting eaves and lotus patterns on the ceiling. **Sikander Lodi's tomb**, built by his son in 1517, is also an octagonal structure decorated with Hindu motifs. A structural innovation is the double dome which was later refined under the Mughals. The 16th-century **Athpula** (Bridge of Eight Piers) nearby, near the northeastern entrance, is attributed to Nawab Bahadur, a nobleman at Akbar's court.

Safdarjang's tomb

ⓘ *Sunrise to sunset, Rs 5, foreigners Rs 100.*

Relatively little visited, Safdarjang's tomb was built by Nawab Shuja-ud-Daulah for his father Mirza Mukhim Abdul Khan, entitled Safdarjang, who was Governor of Oudh (1719-1748), and Wazir of his successor (1748-1754). Safdarjang died in 1754. With its high enclosure walls, *char bagh* layout of gardens, fountain and central domed mausoleum, it follows the tradition of Humayun's tomb. Typically, the real tomb is just below ground level. Flanking the mausoleum are pavilions used by Shuja-ud-Daulah as his family residence. Immediately to its south is the battlefield where Timur and his Mongol horde crushed Mahmud Shah Tughluq on 12 December 1398.

Hazrat Nizamuddin

ⓘ *Dress ultra-modestly if you don't want to feel uncomfortable or cause offence.*

At the east end of the Lodi Road is Hazrat Nizamuddin Dargah. Nizamuddin 'village', now tucked away behind the residential suburb of Nizamuddin West, off Mathura Road, grew up around the shrine of Sheikh Nizamuddin Aulia (1236-1325), a Chishti saint. *Qawwalis* are sung at sunset after *namaaz* (prayers), and are particularly impressive on Thursdays.

West of the central shrine is the **Jama-at-khana Mosque** (1325). Its decorated arches are typical of the Khalji design also seen at the Ala'i Darwaza at the Qutb Minar. South of the main tomb and behind finely crafted screens is the grave of princess Jahanara, Shah Jahan's eldest and favourite daughter. She shared the emperor's last years when he was imprisoned at Agra Fort. The grave, open to the sky, is in accordance with the epitaph written by her "Let naught cover my grave save the green grass, for grass suffices as the covering of the lowly". Pilgrims congregate at the shrine twice a year for the *Urs* (fair) held to mark the anniversaries of Hazrat Nizamuddin Aulia and his disciple **Amir Khusrau**, whose tomb is nearby.

ⓘ *Sunrise to sunset, Rs 10, Rs 250 foreigners, video cameras Rs 25, located in Nizamuddin, 15 mins by taxi from Connaught Circus, allow 45 mins.*

Eclipsed later by the Taj Mahal and the Jama Masjid, Humayun's tomb is the best example in Delhi of the early Mughal style of tomb. Superbly maintained, it is well worth a visit, preferably before visiting the Taj Mahal in Agra. **Humayun**, the second Mughal Emperor, was forced into exile in Persia after being heavily defeated by the Afghan Sher Shah in 1540. He returned to India in 1545, finally recapturing Delhi in 1555. The tomb was designed and built by his senior widow and mother of his son Akbar, Hamida Begum. A Persian from Khurasan, after her pilgrimage to Mecca she was known as **Haji Begum**. She supervised the entire construction of the tomb (1564-1573), camping on the site.

The plan The tomb has an octagonal plan, lofty arches, pillared kiosks and the double dome of Central Asian origin, which appears here for the first time in India. Outside Gujarat, Hindu temples make no use of the dome, but the Indian Muslim dome had until now, been of a flatter shape as opposed to the tall Persian dome rising on a more slender neck. Here also is the first standard example of the garden tomb concept: the **char bagh** (garden divided into quadrants), water channels and fountains. This form culminated in the gardens of the Taj Mahal. However, the tomb also shows a number of distinctively Hindu motifs. Tillotson has pointed out that in Humayun's tomb, Hindu *chhattris* (small domed kiosks), complete with temple columns and *chajjas* (broad eaves), surround the central dome. The bulbous finial on top of the dome and the star motif in the spandrels of the main arches are also Hindu, the latter being a solar symbol.

The approach The tomb enclosure has two high double-storeyed gateways: the entrance to the west and the other to the south. A *baradari* occupies the centre of the east wall, and a bath chamber that of the north wall. Several Moghul princes, princesses and Haji Begum herself lie buried here. During the 1857 Mutiny **Bahadur Shah II**, the last Moghul Emperor of Delhi, took shelter here with his three sons. Over 80, he was seen as a figurehead by Muslims opposing the British. When captured he was transported to Yangon (Rangoon) for the remaining four years of his life. The tomb to the right of the approach is that of Isa Khan, Humayun's barber.

The dome (38-m high) does not have the swell of the Taj Mahal and the decoration of the whole edifice is much simpler. It is of red sandstone with some white marble to highlight the lines of the building. There is some attractive inlay work, and some *jalis* in the balcony fence and on some of the recessed keel arch windows. **The interior** is austere and consists of three storeys of arches rising up to the dome. The Emperor's tomb is of white marble and quite plain without any inscription. The overall impression is that of a much bulkier, more squat building than the Taj Mahal. The cavernous space under the main tombs is an ideal home for great colonies of bats.

Hauz Khas

ⓘ *1- hour cultural show, 1845, Rs 100 (check with Delhi Tourism).*

Immediately to the north again, and entered off either Aurobindo Marg on the east side or Africa Avenue on the west side, is Hauz Khas. Ala-ud-din Khalji (ruled 1296-1313) created a large tank here for the use of the inhabitants of **Siri**, the second capital city of Delhi founded by him. Fifty years later **Firoz Shah Tughluq** cleaned up the silted tank and raised several buildings on its east and south banks which are known as Hauz Khas or Royal Tank.

Firoz Shah's austere tomb is found here. The multi-storeyed wings, on the north and west of Firoz Shah's tomb, were built by him in 1354 as a *madrasa* (college). The octagonal and square *chhattris* were built as tombs, possibly to the teachers at the college. Hauz Khas is now widely used as a park for early morning recreation – walking, running and yoga exercises. Classical music concerts, dance performances and a *son et lumière* show are held in the evenings when monuments are illuminated by thousands of earthen lamps and torches.

The Qutb Minar Complex

① *Sunrise-sunset, US$5 foreigners, Rs 10 Indians. Bus 505 from New Delhi Railway station (Ajmeri Gate), Super Bazar (east of Connaught Circus) and Cottage Industries Emporium, Janpath. Auto Rs 100, though drivers may be reluctant to take you.*

Muhammad Ghuri conquered northwest India at the very end of the 12th century. The conquest of the Gangetic plain down to Benares (Varanasi) was undertaken by Muhammad's Turkish slave and chief general, **Qutb-ud-din-Aibak**, whilst another general took Bihar and Bengal. In the process, temples were reduced to rubble, the remaining Buddhist centres were dealt their death blow and their monks slaughtered. When Muhammad was assassinated in 1206, his gains passed to the loyal Qutb-ud-din-Aibak. Thus the first sultans or Muslim kings of Delhi became known as the **Slave Dynasty** (1026-1290). For the next three centuries the Slave Dynasty and the succeeding Khalji (1290-1320), Tughluq (1320-1414), Sayyid (1414-1445) and Lodi (1451-1526) dynasties provided Delhi with fluctuating authority. The legacy of their ambitions survives in the tombs, forts and palaces that litter Delhi Ridge and the surrounding plain. **Qutb-ud-din-Aibak** died after only four years in power, but he left his mark with the **Qutb Minar** and his **citadel**. Qutb Minar, built to proclaim the victory of Islam over the infidel (unbeliever), dominates the countryside for miles around. Visit the Minar first.

Qutb Minar In 1199 work began on what was intended to be the most glorious tower of victory in the world and was to be the prototype of all *minars* (towers) in India. Qutb-ud-din-Aibak had probably seen and been influenced by the brick victory pillars in Ghazni in Afghanistan, but this one was also intended to serve as the minaret attached to the Might of Islam Mosque. From here the muezzin could call the faithful to prayer. Later every mosque would incorporate its minaret.

As a mighty reminder of the importance of the ruler as Allah's representative on earth, the Qutb Minar (literally 'axis minaret') stood at the centre of the community. A pivot of Faith, Justice and Righteousness, its name also carried the message of Qutb-ud-din's ('Axis of the Faith') own achievements. The inscriptions carved in Kufi script tell that "the tower was erected to cast the shadow of God over both east and west". For Qutb-ud-din-Aibak it marked the eastern limit of the empire of the One God. Its western counterpart is the **Giralda Tower** built by Yusuf in Seville.

The Qutb Minar is 73 m high and consists of five storeys. The diameter of the base is 14.4 m and 2.7 m at the top. Qutb-ud-din built the first three and his son-in-law Iltutmish embellished these and added a fourth. This is indicated in some of the Persian and Nagari (North Indian) inscriptions which also record that it was twice damaged by lightning in 1326 and 1368. While repairing the damage caused by the second, Firoz Shah Tughluq added a fifth storey and used marble to face the red and buff sandstone. This was the first time contrasting colours were used decoratively, later to become such a feature of Mughal buildings. Firoz's fifth storey was topped by a graceful cupola but this fell down during an earthquake in 1803. A new one was added by a Major Robert Smith in 1829 but was so out of keeping that it was removed in 1848 and now stands in the gardens.

The original storeys are heavily indented with different styles of fluting, alternately round and angular on the bottom, round on the second and angular on the third. The beautifully carved honeycomb detail beneath the balconies is reminiscent of the Alhambra Palace in Spain. The calligraphy bands are verses from the Koran and praises to its patron builder.

Quwwat-ul-Islam Mosque The Quwwat-ul-Islam Mosque (The Might of Islam Mosque), the earliest surviving mosque in India, is to the northwest of the Qutb Minar. It was begun in 1192, immediately after Qutb-ud-din's conquest of Delhi and completed in 1198, using the remains of no fewer than 27 local Hindu and Jain temples.

The architectural style contained elements that Muslims brought from Arabia, including buildings made of mud and brick and decorated with glazed tiles, *squinches* (arches set diagonally across the corners of a square chamber to facilitate the raising of a dome and to effect a transition from a square to a round structure), the pointed arch and the true dome. Finally, Muslim buildings came alive through ornamental calligraphy and geometric patterning. This was in marked contrast to indigenous Indian styles of architecture. Hindu, Buddhist and Jain buildings relied on the post-and-beam system in which spaces were traversed by corbelling, ie shaping flat-laid stones to create an arch. The arched screen that runs along the western end of the courtyard beautifully illustrates the fact that it was Hindu methods that still prevailed at this stage, for the 16-m high arch uses Indian corbelling, the corners being smoothed off to form the curved line.

Screens Qutb-ud-din's screen formed the façade of the mosque and, facing in the direction of Mecca, became the focal point. The sandstone screen is carved in the Indo-Islamic style, lotuses mingling with Koranic calligraphy. The later screenwork and other extensions (1230) are fundamentally Islamic in style, the flowers and leaves having been replaced by more arabesque patterns.

Indian builders mainly used stone, which from the fourth century AD had been intricately carved with representations of the gods. In their first buildings in India the Muslim architects designed the buildings and local Indian craftsmen built them and decorated them with typical motifs such as the vase and foliage, tasselled ropes, bells and cows.

Iltutmish's extension The mosque was enlarged twice. In 1230 Qutb-ud-din's son-in-law and successor **Shamsuddin Iltutmish** doubled its size by extending the colonnades and prayer hall – 'Iltutmish's extension'. This accommodated a larger congregation, and in the more stable conditions of Iltutmish's reign, Islam was obviously gaining ground. The arches of the extension are nearer to the true arch and are similar to the Gothic arch that appeared in Europe at this time. The decoration is Islamic.

Almost 100 years after Iltutmish's death, the mosque was enlarged again, by **Ala-ud-din Khalji**. The conductor of tireless and bloody military campaigns, Ala-ud-din proclaimed himself 'God's representative on earth'. His architectural ambitions, however, were not fully realized, because on his death in 1316 only part of the north and east extensions were completed.

Ala'i Minar and the Ala'i Darwaza To the north of the Qutb complex is the 26-m **Ala'i Minar**, intended to surpass the tower of the Qutb, but not completed beyond the first storey. Ala-ud-din did complete the south gateway to the building, the **Ala'i Darwaza**; inscriptions testify that it was built in 1311 (Muslim 710 AH). He benefited from events in Central Asia. Since the early 13th century, Mongol hordes from Central Asia fanned out east and west, destroying the civilization of the Seljuk Turks in West Asia, and refugee artists, architects, craftsmen and poets fled east. They brought to India features and techniques that had developed in Byzantine Turkey, some of which can be seen in the Ala'i Darwaza.

The gate-house is a large sandstone cuboid, into which are set small cusped arches with carved *jali* screens. The lavish ornamentation of geometric and floral designs in red sandstone and white marble produced a dramatic effect when viewed against the surrounding buildings.

The inner chamber, 11 sq m has doorways and, for the first time in India, true arches. Above each doorway is an Arabic inscription with its creator's name and one of his self-assumed titles – 'The Second Alexander'. The north doorway, which is the main entrance, is the most elaborately carved. The dome, raised on squinched arches, is flat and shallow. Of the effects employed, the arches with their 'lotus-bud' fringes are Seljuk, as is the dome with the rounded finial and the façade. These now became trademarks of the **Khalji style**, remaining virtually unchanged until their further development in Humayun's tomb.

Iltutmish's Tomb Built in 1235, Iltutmish's Tomb lies in the northwest of the compound, midway along the west wall of the mosque. It is the first surviving tomb of a Muslim ruler in India. Two other tombs also stand within the extended Might of Islam Mosque.

The idea of a tomb was quite alien to Hindus, who had been practising cremation since around 400 BC. Blending Hindu and Muslim styles, the outside is relatively plain with three arched and decorated doorways. The interior carries reminders of the nomadic origins of the first Muslim rulers. Like a Central Asian *yurt* (tent) in its decoration, it combines the familiar Indian motifs of the wheel, bell, chain and lotus with the equally familiar geometric arabesque patterning. The west wall is inset with three *mihrabs* that indicate the direction of Mecca.

The tomb originally supported a dome resting on *squinches* which you can still see. The dome collapsed (witness the slabs of stone lying around) suggesting that the technique was as yet unrefined. From the corbelled squinches it may be assumed that the dome was corbelled too, as found in contemporary Gujarat and Rajput temples. The blocks of masonry were fixed together using the Indian technology of iron dowels. In later Indo-Islamic buildings lime plaster was used for bonding.

Other tombs To the southwest of the uncompleted Quwwat-ul-Islam mosque, an L-shaped ruin marks the site of **Ala-ud-din Khalji's tomb** within the confines of a **madrasa** (college). This is the first time in India that a tomb and *madrasa* are found together, another custom inherited from the Seljuks.

Immediately to the east of the Ala'i Darwaza stands the **tomb of Imam Zamin**, an early 16th-century *sufi* 'saint' from Turkestan. It is an octagonal structure with a plastered sandstone dome and has *jali* screens, a characteristic of the Lodi style of decoration.

Tughluqabad
ⓘ *Sunrise-sunset, Rs 5, foreigners Rs 200, video camera Rs 25, allow 1 hr, very deserted so don't go alone, take plenty of water, for return rickshaws, turn right at entrance and walk 200 m.*

Tughluqabad's ruins, 7½ km east from Qutb Minar, still convey a sense of the power and energy of the newly arrived Muslims in India. From the walls you get a magnificent impression of the strategic advantages of the site. **Ghiyas'ud-Din Tughluq** (ruled 1321-1325), after ascending the throne of Delhi, selected this site for his capital. He built a massive fort around his capital city which stands high on a rocky outcrop of the Delhi Ridge. The fort is roughly octagonal in plan with a circumference of 6½ km. The vast size, strength and obvious solidity of the whole give it an air of massive grandeur. It was not until Babur (ruled 1526-1530) that dynamite was used in warfare, so this is a very defensible site.

● *The Baha'i faith was founded by a Persian, Baha'u'llah (meaning 'glory of God';*
● *1817-1892), who is believed to be the manifestation of God for this age. His teachings were directed towards the unification of the human race, the establishment of a permanent universal peace.*

East of the main entrance is the rectangular **citadel**. A wider area immediately to the west and bounded by walls contained the **palaces**. Beyond this to the north lay the **city**. Now marked by the ruins of houses, the streets were laid out in a grid fashion. Inside the citadel enclosure is the **Vijay Mandal** tower and the remains of several halls including a long underground passage. The fort also contained seven tanks.

A causeway connects the fort with the tomb of Ghiyas'ud-Din Tughluq, while a wide embankment near its southeast corner gave access to the fortresses of **Adilabad** about 1 km away, built a little later by Ghiyas'ud-Din's son Muhammad. The tomb is very well preserved and has red sandstone walls with a pronounced slope (the first Muslim building in India to have sloping walls), crowned with a white marble dome. This dome, like that of the Ala'i Darwaza at the Qutb, is crowned by an *amalaka*, a feature of Hindu architecture. Also Hindu is the trabeate arch at the tomb's fortress wall entrance. Inside are three cenotaphs belonging to Ghiyas'ud-Din, his wife and son Muhammad.

Ghiyas'ud-Din Tughluq quickly found that military victories were no guarantee of lengthy rule. When he returned home after a victorious campaign the welcoming pavilion erected by his son and successor, **Muhammad-bin Tughluq**, was deliberately collapsed over him. Tughluqabad was abandoned shortly afterwards and was thus only inhabited for five years. The Tughluq dynasty continued to hold Delhi until Timur sacked it and slaughtered its inhabitants. For a brief period Tughluq power shifted to Jaunpur near Varanasi, where the Tughluq architectural traditions were carried forward in some superb mosques.

Baha'i Temple (Lotus Temple)

ⓘ *1 Apr-30 Sep 0900-1900, 1 Oct-31 Mar 0930-1730, closed Mon, free entry and parking, visitors are welcome to services, and at other times the temple is open for silent meditation and prayer. Audio visual presentations about the faith in English are at 1100, 1200, 1400 and 1530, remove your shoes before entering. Taxi or auto-rickshaw though Bus 433 from the centre (Jantar Mantar) goes to Nehru Pl, within walking distance (1½ km) of the temple at Kalkaji.*

Architecturally the Baha'i Temple is a remarkably striking building. Constructed in 1980-1981, it is built out of white marble and in the characteristic Baha'i temple shape of a lotus flower – 45 lotus petals form the walls – which internally creates a feeling of light and space (34 m high, 70 m in diameter). It is a simple design, brilliantly executed and very elegant in form. All Baha'i temples are nine sided, symbolizing 'comprehensiveness, oneness and unity'. The Delhi temple, which seats 1,300, is surrounded by nine pools, an attractive feature also helping to keep the building cool. It is particularly attractive when flood-lit. Baha'i temples are "dedicated to the worship of God, for peoples of all races, religions or castes. Only the Holy Scriptures of the Baha'i Faith and earlier revelations are read or recited".

🛏 Sleeping

Avoid hotel touts. Airport taxis may pretend not to know the location of your chosen hotel so give full details and insist to be taken there. Hotel prices in Delhi are significantly higher than in most other parts of the country. Smaller **C**, **D** guesthouses away from the centre in South Delhi (eg Kailash, Safdarjang) or in Sunder Nagar, are quieter and often good value but may not provide food. Cheaper **E**, **F** accommodation is concentrated around Janpath and Paharganj (New Delhi), and Chandni Chowk (Old Delhi) – well patronized but basic and usually cramped yet good for meeting other backpackers. Some have dormitory beds for under Rs 100. Some city centre hotel rooms are windowless. Signs in some hotels warn against taking drugs as this is becoming a serious cause for concern. Police raids are frequent.

Old Delhi *p66, map p68*

L-AL Oberoi Maidens, 7 Sham Nath Marg, T2397 5464, www.oberoihotels.com. 54 large well-appointed rooms, restaurant (slow), barbecue nights are excellent, coffee shop, old-style bar, attractive colonial style in quiet area, spacious gardens with excellent pool, friendly welcome, personal attention. Recommended.

B Broadway, 4/15A Asaf Ali Rd, T2327 3821, www.oldworldhospitality.com. 32 clean but slightly underwhelming rooms in an interestingly quirky hotel. **Chor Bizarre** restaurant and bar (see below) is highly regarded, as is the 'Thugs' pub – easily one of the best options in Old Delhi.

C Flora, Dayanand Rd, Daryaganj, T2327 3634, F2328 0887. 24 small but clean a/c rooms centre 2 km, good restaurant.

C-E Wongdhen House, 15A New Tibetan Colony, Manju-ka-Tilla, T2381 6689, wongdhenhouse@hotmail.com. Very clean rooms, some with a/c and TV, safe, homely, good breakfast and Tibetan meals, an insight into Tibetan culture, peacefully located by the Yamuna River yet 15 mins by auto-rickshaw north from Old Delhi station, recommended.

D Bhagirath Palace, opposite Red Fort, Chandni Chowk, T2386 6223, hotbha@del3. vsnl.net.in. 12 rooms, some a/c, 1 km Old Delhi Railway, bar.

E Tera, 2802a Bazar, Kashmir Gate, T2391 1532. 42 rooms, some a/c, 500 m Old Delhi Railway, restaurant, coffee shop, TV.

E-F Noor, 421 Matia Mahal, Jama Masjid (1st left after **Flora's Restaurant**, then 3rd left), T2326 7791. 34 clean, quiet rooms, shared facilities (Indian WC), fans, rooftop views of Jama Masjid and fort, experience of Old Delhi.

New Delhi *p72*

Connaught Place *p76, map p76*

LL-L Park, 15 Sansad Marg, T2374 3000, www.theparkhotels.com. 224 of the best contemporary-styled rooms in town, good views, friendly, award-winning Indian restaurant and funky, modern bar, recommended.

LL-AL Imperial, Janpath, T2334 1234, www.theimperialindia.com. 263 rooms in supremely elegant Lutyens-designed 1933

hotel. Unparalleled location, great bar, gardens and secluded pool, slightly disappointing restaurants and service a bit fierce, but still quite an experience, highly recommended, check website for offers.

L The Hans Plaza, 15 Barakhamba Rd (16th-20th floor), T2331 6868, www.hanshotels. com. 67 slightly uninspired rooms, not a 'boutique hotel' as advertised but clean and quiet with superb views from the roomy rooftop restaurant.

A Hotel Alka, P Block, Connaught Circus, T2334 4328, hotelalka@vsnl.com. 21 well-appointed rooms in glitzy surroundings, including two spotless restaurants and a distinctively decorated bar.

A Centrepoint, 13 Kasturba Gandhi Marg, T2335 4304, www.thecentrepoint.com. Well-located, charming old building, although starting to show its age. 52 large, plainclean rooms, some with cramped bathrooms, smarter road side rooms can be noisy, restaurant lacks variety but reasonable breakfasts (included), reception 'willing but pushed', good exchange rate.

A Marina, G-59 Connaught Circus, T2332 4658, marina@nde.vsnl.net.in. 93 slightly old-fashioned but clean rooms (**A** suites), bath with tubs, some large, others cramped but refurbished, attractive marble reception, good coffee shop, travel agent recommended, pleasant.

A Nirula's, L-Block, Connaught Circus, T2341 7419, www.nirulas.com. 31 small, plain, well-appointed rooms, good Potpourri restaurant, ice cream and pastry shops, internet, very central, clean, peaceful suites, efficient but not especially good value.

B Fifty Five, H-55 Connaught Pl, T2332 1244, bookings@hotel55.com. 15 small, clean, well-maintained rooms, darkish decor, central a/c, road can be a bit noisy, roof terrace for breakfast, helpful, very friendly staff, recommended.

B-C Central Court, N-Block, T23315013, F23317582. Simple hotel with basic 60s furniture, clean, very large doubles/suites with bath (small singles), windows in doors only, coffee shop, friendly staff, but no restaurant.

B-C YWCA International Guest House, Sansad Marg (near Jantar Mantar), T2336 1561, www.ywcaindia.org. 24 clean, cozy, upgraded a/c rooms, centre 1 km, open to both sexes, restaurant (see below), handy internet in foyer, peaceful garden, convenient location, good value.

B-C YMCA Tourist Hostel, Jai Singh Rd, T2336 1915, www.delhiymca.com. 120 rooms, for both sexes, a/c rooms with bath (B-Block, non a/c and shared bath), some reported dirty, restaurant (breakfast included but disappointing), travel, peaceful gardens, tennis, good pool (Rs 100 extra), luggage stored (Rs 5 per day), pay in advance but check bill, reserve ahead, very professional.

C Choudhary, H 35/3 Connaught Circus, T2332 2043, harsh@del3.vsnl.net.in. Tucked away but worth seeking out; 8 very clean rooms in a central location with a friendly manager who knows his stuff.

C-D Hotel Palace Heights, D Block, Connaught Pl, T2341 5419. 18 passable rooms, 6 with attached bathrooms and a/c on top floor with terrace and friendly staff.

E-F Ringo Guest House, 17 Scindia House (upstairs), off Kasturba Gandhi Marg, T2331 0605. Tiny rooms (some windowless) but no bugs, cheap crowded dorm (beds 15 cm apart) or beds on rooftop, hot showers, basic toilets, lockers, good restaurant (0700-2300), courtyard, friendly staff, backpackers' haunt (other hotel touts waylay travellers), superior to nearby **Sunny**, recommended at the price.

Paharganj *p72, map p86*

Rooms tend to be cheap, usually with shared baths, and the street-side rooms can be noisy. Though the packed bazars and crowded lanes can be dirty, Parharganj is where backpackers congregate. Sandwiched between the main sights and near the main railway station, it is convenient and on hand are plenty of shops selling souvenirs, travel agents, cheap hotels and cafés catering for Western tastes. For a more sedate, 'authentic' experience, you might like to try elsewhere. Avoid **Hotel Bright**.

B-C Gold Regency, 4350 Main Bazar, T2356 2101, www.goldregency.com. 40 good, clean, smallish a/c rooms, plus a moderately priced restaurant, disco and Cyber Café. Good facilities but some power problems.

B-C Hotel Ajanta, 36 Arakashan Rd, T5154 1995, www.tourism-india.com/hotelajanta.

60 reasonably well-maintained rooms, most with a/c, good service and decent restaurant.

B-C Tourist Deluxe, 7361 Qutb Rd, Ramnnagar, T2367 0985, touristdeluxe@ vsnl.net. 40 comfortable a/c rooms plus a few suites with tubs, vegetarian restaurant, on busy main road.

C Tourist, T2361 0334, tourist@schand.com. 65 rooms, 30 a/c, cleaner than Tourist Deluxe (and uncarpeted), vegetarian restaurant, rooms at rear quieter.

C-D Rail Yatri Nivas, behind New Delhi Railway Station (3-min walk from Ajmeri Gate, 8-storey building), T2323 3561. Only for transit train passengers holding a valid ticket. 36 cleanish rooms plus a dorm (rs135), all rates include breakfast. Phone ahead to book, very convenient location.

C-D Shelton, 5043 Main Bazar, T2358 0575. 36 clean, light rooms in a slightly grander hotel than its neighbours – it even has a lift!

D Baba Deluxe, 7795 Arakashan Rd, Ramnagar, T2354 8334, F3559858. 52 clean rooms, friendly staff, generator.

D Rak International, 820 Main Bazar, Chowk Bowli, T2358 6508. 27 basic but clean rooms in professionally run, quiet hotel with a rooftop restaurant and water feature and a friendly manager, recommended.

D Royal Guest House, 4464 Main Bazar, T2358 6176, royalguesthouse@yahoo.com. 17 spotless rooms, some a/c, in an exceptionally well-maintained, friendly hotel.

D-E Bless Inn, 2339-41, Rajguru Rd, Chuna Mandi, T2368 8400, narang_kelson@hotmail. com. 20 surprisingly smart rooms given unprepossessing exterior, but no character.

D-E Hare Rama Guest House, 298 Main Bazar, T2356 1301, harerama_2000@hotmail. com. 65 clean, tiled rooms, 24-hr hot water, many facilities, staff protective of female guests on their own, recommended.

D-E Heritage Inn, 2374 Raj Guru Rd, Chuna Mandi, T2358 8222. 20 simple, spotless rooms in brand new building with friendly staff.

D-E Railway Retiring Rooms, New (and Old) Delhi Railway Station. For 12 and 24 hrs, dorm beds (10 rooms, 6 a/c are usually pre booked), only for train ticket-holders, basic, noisy, but convenient.

D-E Star Palace, 4590 Dal Mandi, off Main Bazar (lane opposite Khalsa Boots), T2358 4849, www.stargroupofhotels.com. 31 clean, well kept rooms (some a/c) with "fantastic showers", quiet, friendly, safe.

D-E Starview, 5136 Main Bazar, T2358 6810, www.stargroupofhotels.com. 23 small but adequate rooms, some with a/c, some triples.

D-E Vivek, 1534-1550, Main Bazar, T5154 1435, www.vivekhotel.com. 50 adequate rooms which are outshone by this hotel's impressive communal areas and a/c café. Plenty of facilities and friendly staff, good value, recommended.

E Ajay's, 5084a Main Bazar, T2358 3125, www.anupamhoteliersltd.com. 48 fairly clean (windowless) rooms with bath, dorm, good bakery, restaurant, friendly, popular backpackers' hangout.

E Anoop, 1566 Main Bazar, T5154 1390, www.anupamhoteliersltd.com. 43 rooms with bath, some with air-cooler, very clean though basic, noisy at times, safe, good 24-hr rooftop restaurant shared with **Hare Krishna** (waiters can 'forget' to give change).

E Hare Krishna, 1572 Main Bazar, T2352 9188, www.anupamhoteliersltd.com. 24 cleanish rooms with bath (some windowless, stuffy), friendly, travel, good rooftop restaurant.

E-F Namaskar, 917 Chandiwalan, Main Bazar, T2362 1234, namaskarhotel@ yahoo.com. 32 small basic rooms (2-4 beds) with bath (bucket hot water), clean but some windowless, newer **D** a/c rooms (Rs 450) in extension, generator, safe, friendly service, good atmosphere, quiet at night, stores luggage, reserve ahead, unreliable travel information.

Elsewhere in New Delhi *p72, map p74*
LL Grand Inter-Continental, Barakhamba Ave, T2341 1001, www.intercontinental.com. 444 elegant, modern rooms in 28-storey hotel some find impersonal, others among

Paharganj

Related maps
A Old Delhi, page 68.
B New Delhi, page 74.
C Connaught Place, page 76.

0 metres 100
0 yards 100

Sleeping
Ajanta **8**
Ajay's & Bholenath Travel **1**
Anoop & Hare Krishna **2**
Baba Deluxe **7**

Bless Inn **4**
Clark **20**
Gold Regency **5**
Hare Rama & Rooftop
 Restaurant **6**
Heritage Inn **3**
Karol Bagh **21**
Namaskar & Rak
 International **10**

Rail Yatri Nivas **12**
Royal Guest House **11**
Shelton **14**
Star Palace &
 Everest Cafe **17**
Star Paradise **18**
Starview **19**
Tourist Deluxe
 & Tourist **9**

Vivek **13**
White House **22**

Eating
Appetite **4**
Madan's **1**
Malhotra **2**
Temptations **3**

best in its class, good patisserie, great views from rooftop restaurants.

LL Le Meridien, Windsor Pl, Janpath, T2371 0101, www.lemeridien-newdelhi.com. 355 rooms, visually striking space station interior, but otherwise disappointing, "too American, no soul".

LL-L Metropolitan Hotel Nikko, Bangla Sahib Rd, T5250 0200, www.nikkohotels. com. 167 classy, modern rooms (great bathrooms) in ultra-smart Japanese chain hotel. Excellent Japanese restaurant, highly professional staff, recommended.

Outer New Delhi *p72, map p74*
Avoid **Singh Palace**, Karol Bagh.
LL Oberoi, Dr Zakir Hussain Marg, T2436 3030, www.oberoihotels.com. 300 rooms, overlooking golf club, immaculate, quietly efficient, excellent all round but expensive Chinese restaurant disappointing.

LL Park Royal Intercontinental, Nehru Pl, T2622 3344, www.newdelhi.intercontinental. com. 224 light, modern and well-appointed rooms in a high class hotel, although location is not the best.

LL Taj Mahal, 1 Mansingh Rd, T2302 6162, www.tajhotels.com. 300 attractive, comfortable rooms, excellent restaurants and service (**Haveli** offers wide choice and explanations for the newcomer, **Ming House's** spicing varies), coffee shop pokey and disappointing, good Khazana shop, lavishly finished, friendly bar, good city views but lacks atmosphere.

LL-L Maurya Sheraton Hotel and **Towers**, Sardar Patel Marg, T2611 2233, www.wel comegroup.com. 516 rooms, those in premium block outstanding, excellent decor and service, splendid pool (solar heated), disco (noisy late at night, so avoid rooms nearby), good restaurants (see p94).

LL-L Taj Palace, 2 Sardar Patel Marg, T2611 0202, www.tajhotels.com. 421 rooms, slightly dated bathrooms, standard 5-star facilities but well done, purpose-built for business travellers, generally excellent, **Orient Express** restaurant highly recommended (haute French), "service outstanding, food superb", 'Masala Art' Indian restaurant also good.

L Claridges, 12 Aurangzeb Rd, T2301 0211, www.claridges.com. 138 recently refurbished, classy rooms, art deco style interiors, colonial atmosphere, attractive restaurants (good **Jade Garden** Chinese), impeccable service, more atmosphere than most, recommended.

AL Ambassador (Taj), Sujan Singh Park, T2463 2600, www.tajhotels.com. 81 rooms in period property, no pool but pleasant garden, quirky bar and coffee shop, calm atmosphere, quiet and convenient location.

AL Ashok (ITDC), 50-B Chanakyapuri, T2611 0101, www.theashok.com. 571 large rooms (some upgraded) in huge property, sunny coffee shop, 24-hr bank, smart new Lebanese restaurant, trendy **Ssteels** bar, quiet but overpriced.

AL Diplomat, 9 Sardar Patel Marg, T2301 0204, www.thehoteldiplomat.com. 25 rooms, all different, pleasant garden but no pool, quietly located, very popular.

A Jukaso Inn, 50 Sunder Nagar, T2435 0308, www.indiamart.com/jukasoinn. 50 a/c rooms, restaurant, room service, garden, pleasant, quiet, friendly staff, recommended.

A Nirula's, C-135 Sector 2, NOIDA, 15 km east of centre, T0120-2526512, www.nirulas. com (also Connaught Circus). Comfortable, friendly and helpful, pleasant atmosphere, good **Potpourri** restaurant and bar.

A-B La Sagrita, 14 Sunder Nagar, T2435 8572, www.lasagrita.com. 24 recently refurbished a/c rooms, modern bathrooms, phone, restaurant, helpful staff, quiet location.

B Bajaj Indian Homestay, 8A/34 WEA, Karol Bagh, T2573 6509, www.indianhomestay. com. Newish, Indian decor, all rooms different, mod cons, breakfast included, homely.

B Rajdoot, Mathura Rd, T2431 6666, F2464 7442. 55 rooms, convenient location for Nizammuddin Railway, pool.

B-C Good Times, 8/7 WEA Karol Bagh, off Pusa Rd, T5100 5140, www.goodtimeshotel. com. 27 clean, modern rooms, friendly staff and a good rooftop restaurant.

B-C Pal's Inn, E Patel Nagar, Karol Bagh, T2578 5310, palsinn@del3vsnl.net. 16 rooms in new guest house, marble baths, clean, well kept, lobby café facing park (full break- fast included), good car hire (Rs 600 for 8 hrs), friendly and caring owner, attentive staff.

C-D Master Paying Guesthouse, R-500 New Rajendra Nagar (Shankar & GR Hospital Rds crossing), T2874 1089, www.master-guest

house.com. 5 clean rooms (some **B** a/c), spotless shared facilities, rooftop for breakfast, evening *thalis*, warm welcome, personal attention, secure, recommended. Very knowledgeable owner also runs tours of 'hidden Delhi', which are recommended.

C-D Yatri Paying Guest House, corner of Panchkuin and Mandir Margs, T2362 5563, yatri@vsnl.com. 6 large clean rooms (some a/c) in family home, cold in winter, garden, mosquito problem, quiet, peaceful oasis, friendly, welcoming but can't stay long, discount during summer.

Youth hostels

D-F Youth Hostel, 5 Naya Marg, Chanakya-puri, T2611 6285, www.yhaindia.org. Wide range of room from a/c doubles at Rs 700 to a basic dorm (Rs 50), breakfast, prefer International YHA members, popular, great location.

South Delhi *p78*

LL-L Hyatt Regency, Bhikaiji Cama Pl, Ring Rd, T2679 1234, www.delhi.hyatt.com. 518 rooms, smart but tiny for price, restaurants good but expensive, glitzy but a little stuffy.

LL-L Surya, Crown Plaza, New Friends Colony, T2683 5070, www.suryadelhi.crowne plaza.com. 195 rooms, slightly isolated, good views, good service, renowned Chinese rooftop restaurant.

LL-L Vasant Continental, Vasant Vihar, T2614 8800, www.jaypeehotels.com. 110 rooms in recently renovated, contemporary styled hotel, convenient for airports (free transfer), large pool and gardens near Basant Lok Market, good service, interesting range of restaurants, all with 'live' kitchens, recommended.

LL-AL The Grand (formerly Hyatt), Nelson Mandela Rd, Vasant Kunj Phase II, T2677 1234, www.thegrandnewdelhi.com. 390 rooms, 25 suites in new, contemporary styled luxury hotel, choice of good restaurants, great pool, health club, tennis, golf (20 mins drive). Recommended.

L Manor, 77 Friends Colony, T2692 5151, www.themanordelhi.com. Contemporary styledboutique hotel with 10 stylish rooms, heavenly beds, polished stone surfaces and chrome, relaxing garden, a haven.

B '27' Jorbagh, 27 Jorbagh (2 mins from Lodi tombs), T2682 2763, www.jorbagh 27.com. 20 a/c rooms, car hire, not plush but very quiet (Western food nearby), hassle free, book ahead. Highly recommended.

B Kailash Nath, 39 Prithviraj Rd, T2469 4523, F4635706. 15 a/c rooms in private guest-house in a bungalow, free airport pick-up/drop, full services, used by NGOs and foreign consultants.

B Legend Inn, E-4 East of Kailash, T2621 6111, www.thelegendinn.com. Comfortable a/c rooms, no restaurant but it does have a 40-ft climbing wall and adventure museum!

🍴 Eating

The larger hotel restaurants are often the best for cuisine, decor and ambience. Buffets (lunch or dinner) cost Rs 500 or more. Others may only open around 1930 for dinner; some close on Sun. Alcohol is served in most top hotels, but only in some non-hotel restaurants eg **Amber**, **Ginza**, **Kwality**.

Old Delhi *p66, map p68*

🍴🍴🍴 **Chor Bizarre**, Broadway Hotel, Asaf Ali Rd, T2327 3821. Noted *tandoori* and Kash-*miri* cuisine (Wazwan, Rs 500). Comfortable if quirky decor, including salad bar that was vintage car.

🍴 **Flora**, Daryaganj. North Indian, excellent kalmi chicken kebab, biryani and breads, dark and gloomy but good food, very popular.

🍴 **Karim's**, Gali Kababiyan (south of Jama Masjid). Mughlai. Authentic, busy, plenty of local colour. The experience, as much as the food, makes this a must. Not much to tempt the vegetarian though.

🍴 **Peshawari**, 3707 Subhash Marg, Daryaganj. Tiny, with tiled walls, serves delicious chicken, closed Tue.

New Delhi *p72*

Connaught Place *p76, map p76*
🍴🍴🍴 **Rodeo**, 12a, T2371 3780. Excellent Mexican (3-course and beer, Rs 350), Italian, continental. "Heavenly", fast service, fully-stocked bar, wild west decor.

¶¶ **Zen**, B-25, T2335 7444. Stylish, impersonal but popular, generous portions for Chinese, more expensive Japanese and seafood.

¶¶ **Amber**, N-Block, T3312092. High-class decor and lightly spiced Mughlai cuisine, reasonable beer.

¶¶ **Berco's**, L-Block, T2331 8134. Chinese, Japanese. Generous helpings, fast service, very popular, quieter for dinner.

¶¶ **DV8**, 13 Regal Building, T5150 0693, with smart and cosy pub below. Round the world meals, good buffet (Rs 250), á la carte (Rs 150+), good music, great Espresso coffee.

¶¶ **Embassy**, D-11, T2341 6434. International. Mirrored, very popular, good food, long standing local favourite.

¶¶ **Gaylord**, B16 Regal Building, T2374 4677. Multi cuisine menu takes back seat to original 1949 decor and old world ambience. Separate bar equally charming.

¶¶ **Kwality**, Parliament St. International. Try spicy Punjabi dishes with various breads.

¶¶ **Potpourri**, Nirula's, L-Block, T2331 6694. Indian and continental. Bright, clean and very popular – tasty light meals, snacks, ice creams, salad bar (safe!) Rs 143, beers, several branches including N-Block.

¶¶ **Q'BA**, E-42 Connaught Pl, T5151 2888. Mystifying name but super-stylish decor and attractive menu should make this new venture a run away success.

¶¶ **Spirit**, E-34 Connaught Pl, T5100 6603. Very chic Lebanese\Italian restaurant and bar, service and food outstanding.

¶¶ **TGI Fridays**, F-16, T2371 1991. Western meals, Texmex, Americana style decor with 50s objects on walls, TV, Western music, 'Happy Hour' (1700-1930).

¶¶ **United Coffee House**, E-15 Connaught Pl, T2341 1697. Recommended as much for the colonial-era cake-icing decor as for the fairly average food. Always attracts a mixed crowd, well worth a visit.

¶ **Don't Pass Me By**, by Ringos, 17 Scindia House. Chinese. Bit dingy, but good basic food and plenty of it, prompt, cooler upstairs.

¶ **Kake's**, H-block, Plaza Building, T2341 1580. Famous Punjabi dhaba. Handi dishes and delicious green masala fish, very cheap.

¶ **Nathu's**, Bengali Market (east of Connaught Place), T2371 7313. Sweet shops serving mainly vegetarian food. Good dosa, idli, utthapam and North Indian chana bathura, clean, functional canteen.

¶ **Nizam's Kathi Kebabs**, H-5 Plaza, T2371 3078. Very good, tasty filled parathas, good value, clean, excellent '3-D toilets' (note emergency button!).

¶ **Tropical Smoothie**, L-13 Connaught Pl Outer Circle, T5151 7021. Another great place for an escape to the West – fantastic smoothies, tasty wraps and a wonderfully cool interior.

Paharganj *p72, map p86*

The rooftop restaurants here are great locations.

¶¶-¶ **Appetite**, 1575 Main Bazar, T2753 2079. Chinese, Nepali, Italian. Mouth-watering bakery, good lassis.

¶¶-¶ **Everest Bakery Cave**, Dal Mandi, near Star Palace Hotel. Fantastic momos, cakes and pies with an ambience to match. Highly recommended.

¶¶-¶ **Madan's**, 1601 Main Bazar. International. Egg and chips to *thalis*, not special but friendly, popular, good value.

¶¶-¶ **Malhotra's**, 1833 Laxmi Narayan St, T2358 9371. Good Indian and Chinese, wide choice, a/c section; also takeaway.

¶¶-¶ **Temptation**, at Chanakya, 4350 Main Bazar. Pleasant. Good western (veg burgers, cakes), internet, disco and bar.

Elsewhere in New Delhi *p72, map p74*

¶¶¶ **Bukhara**, Maurya Sheraton, T2611 2233. Stylish Northwest Frontier cuisine. Amidst rugged walls draped with rich rugs (but uncomfortable seating), outstanding meat dishes but not much for the vegetarian.

¶¶¶ **Chinese**, does great soups, "waiters treat beer bottles as fine wines!".

¶¶¶ **Corbett's**, Claridge's Hotel, T2301 0211. Authentic North Indian. Animal park theme outdoor, straw huts, jungle soundtrack, hidden animals delight children, good value.

¶¶¶ **Dum Phukt**, Maurya Sheraton, T2611 2233. North Indian. Slowly steam-cooked in sealed *handis* produces excellent melt-in-

🍵 *The old-fashioned 'tea on the lawns' is still served at the Imperial and in the Claridges.*
● *Aapki Pasand, on 15 Netaji Subhash Marg, is another unique tea-tasting, in high-class, extremely professional surroundings, quite an experience.*

the-mouth Nawabi dishes. High quality service and decor. Expensive and a bit pretentious.

La Rouchelle, Oberoi, T2436 4084. High class French cuisine.

Lodi, Lodi Gardens, T4655054. Excellent lunchtime continental, dinner Indian in pleasant, Mediterranean style surroundings.

Parikrama, Kasturba Gandhi Marg, T2372 1616. International. Savour the rich food and the views as the restaurant slowly revolves – a quiet and relaxing way to see Delhi!

Spice Route, Imperial Hotel. Slightly disappointing, and definitely overpriced, Kerala, Thai, Vietnamese cuisines in extraordinary surroundings.

Basil and Thyme, Santushti Complex, Chanakyapuri, T2467 3322. Continental. Pleasant setting, simple decor, a/c, modestly priced Western snacks at lunch, fashionable meeting place (busy 1300-1400).

Moti Mahal Deluxe, Malcha Marg, Chanakyapuri (near *Diplomat*), T2611 8698. Excellent Mughlai, closed Tue, short on ambience but food makes up for it.

Ten (YWCA International GH), Sansad Marg. Indian, Western. Good meals and snacks. New management, clean, modern, well run, recommended

Andhra Bhavan, near India Gate. South Indian (Chettinad).

Karim's Nemat Kada, Nizamuddin West. Mughlai. Good value.

South Delhi *p88*

Bistro, Hauz Khas Village, a complex of restaurants, the pick of which is the open-air Mughlai on the rooftop, which boasts fantastic views over old ruins, hugely atmospheric by night.

La Piazza, Hyatt Regency, Bhikaji Cama Place, T2618 1234. Authentic Italian. Mon-Sat lunch buffet Rs 550. Try pizzas from wood-fired oven, good atmosphere.

Olive, Kalika Dass Marg, Mehrauli, T2664 5500. The city's best attempt at an upmarket Mediterranean restaurant, set in a lovely whitewashed building. Authentic menu and reliable, the bar is a great place to unwind.

Orient Express, Taj Palace Hotel, T2611 0202. Continental. Recreated luxury of the famous train carriages, formal dress code, expensive but different.

Park Baluch, inside Deer Park, Hauz Khas Village, T2685 9369. Highly praised cuisine in peaceful, understated surroundings.

Thai Wok, 1091/1 Ambavata Complex, Mehrauli, T2664 4289. Interesting Thai menu and outstanding views over the Qutab minar from the large terrace.

Ankur, Siri Fort Marg, Asiad Village. Mexican. Good food, especially the fajitas, agreeable bar and staff.

The Big Chill, F-38 East of Kailash (off Lala Lajpat Rai Path near Spring Meadows Hospital), also in Khan Market, 1230 till late. A bright, new café with a difference. A wide range of carefully prepared, wholesome light meals of grills, bakes, fresh pasta and salads, spectacularly successful homemade desserts. Great atmosphere (choose your own music.

Chopsticks, Siri Fort Marg, T2649 2348. Chinese, Thai. Good value, pleasant ambience, bar, weekend buffet lunches.

Golden Dragon, C Block, Vasant Vihar, T2614 1849. Very reliable Chinese, reasonably priced, long happy hours.

Imperial Garden, E3 Masjid Moth, Gt Kailash II, T2647 7798. Excellent Oriental, unusual menu, one of the best in town.

Mini Mahal, C-25A Vasant Vihar. North Indian. Popular with diplomats.

Punjabi by Nature, 11 Basant Lok, T5151 6666, for outstanding and very popular Punjabi dishes.

O'Briens, 32 Basant Lok, T5166 9166. An Irish sandwich bar franchise offering an unusual range of freshly-produced variations on the sandwich.

Colonelz Kebabz, Defence Colony Market. Tandoori. Excellent tikkas and kebabs. Several others, including RK Puram. and delicious, safe 'street food' 1000-2200.

Keraleeyam, Yusuf Sarai, next to Indian Oil. Malabar. Spicy unusual non-vegetarian dishes.

Moti Mahal, South Extn II (branch at M-13 GKI). Tandoori. Noisy and now very average food, more pleasant tented section outside.

Naivedyam, Haus Khas Village, T2696 0426. Very good south Indian, clean and cheap.

Sagar, 18 Defence Colony Market, T2433 3110. Excellent South Indian. Cheap and 'amazing!' *thalis* and coffee, very hectic (frequent queues). (Others in Vasant Kunj, Malviya Nagar and NOIDA).

Sona Rupa, 46 Janpath. Recommended for snacks (1030-2400).

♠ Bars and clubs

Many national holidays are 'dry' days. Normally hotel restaurants, bars and clubs serve alcohol. All top hotels have bars. Delhi's 'in' crowd is notoriously fickle, meaning that the hip place to be seen changes almost weekly; below is a selection of places which were popular in Sep 2004, but may not be for long!
1911, at **Imperial Hotel**, elegantly styled colonial bar, good snacks.
Bohemia, opposite **Shalom**, T2622 3328. Relaxed, contemporary bar, friendly staff plus a good Indian restaurant upstairs.
Dublin at the Sheraton, classic repro Irish bar, everything but Guiness.
F Bar, MG Rd. Trendy fashion bar cum club, but not a bad place for a boogie.

Pegasus, at **Nirula's**, N-Connaught Circus. English-style pub, very friendly.
Pluto's, Vasant Kunj. Proper nightclub, full of whistle-blowing, hands in the air teenagers, raving Delhi-style.
RG's, opposite Qutab Minar. One of the few nightclubs outside the 5 stars, expensive (Rs 2000 per couple) but drinks are included.
Shalom, 'N' Block Market, Greater Kailash 1, T98101 48084. Comfortable, stylish lounge bar serving Lebanese cuisine while the resident DJ plays ambient music at a pleasantly low volume.
Ssteels, at **Ashok Hotel**. Trendy, industrial decor, very crowded at weekends, good range of cocktails.

♠ Entertainment

First City monthly (Rs 20) with reviews, the free fortnightly weekly *Delhi City Info*, and the weekly *Delhi Diary*.

Cinemas
PVR Anupam, Community Centre, Saket, T2686 5999. Good choice, phone reservations before 2000.
Priya, the 'young spot', Vasant Vihar, T2614 0048. Usual action movies.
Satyam, Patel Nagar, T2589 3322.
Regal, PVR Plaza, Connaught Place, usually screen Hindi movies.

Clubs
Delhi Gymkhana Club, 2 Safdarjang Rd, T2301 5533. Mostly for government and defence personnel, squash, tennis, swimming, bar and restaurant.
Habitat Centre, Lodi Rd, T2468 2222, with good programme of lectures, exhibitions, excellent restaurant.

Son et Lumière
Red Fort: Apr-Nov 1800-1900 (Hindi), 1930-2030 (English). Entry Rs 50. Tickets available after 1700. Take mosquito cream.

☸ Festivals and events

Consult the weekly *Delhi Diary* available at hotels and many shops and offices around town for exact dates. The following list gives an approximate indication of the dates.

January

Lohri (**13th**), the climax of winter is celebrated with bonfires and singing.
Republic Day Parade (**26th**), Rajpath. A spectacular fly-past and military march-past, with colourful pageants and tableaux from every state, dances and music. Tickets through travel agents and most hotels, Rs 100. You can see the full dress preview free, usually 2 days before; week-long celebrations during which government buildings are illuminated.
Beating the Retreat (**29th**), Vijay Chowk, a stirring display by the armed forces' bands marks the end of the Republic Day celebrations.**Martyr's Day** (**30th**), marks Mahatma Gandhi's death anniversary; devotional *bhajans* and Guard of Honour at Raj Ghat. **Kite Flying Festival** on

Makar Sankranti above Palika Bazar, Connaught Pl.

February

Vasant Panchami (**2nd**), celebrates the first-day of spring. The Mughal Gardens are opened to the public for a month. **Delhi Flower Show**, Purana Qila. **Thyagaraja Festival**, South Indian music and dance, Vaikunthnath Temple.

March

Basant Ritu Sammelan, North Indian music.

April

Amir Khusrau's Birth Anniversary, a fair in Nizamuddin celebrates this with prayers and *qawwali* singing.

May

Buddha Jayanti, the **first full moon night** in May marks the birth of the Buddha and prayer meetings are held at Ladakh Buddha Vihara, Ring Rd and Buddha Vihara, Mandir Marg.

August

Janmashtami celebrates the birth of the Hindu god Krishna. Special *puja*, Lakshmi Narayan Mandir. **Independence Day (15th)**, impressive flag hoisting ceremony and Prime Ministerial address at the Red Fort. **Vishnu Digambar Sammelan**, North Indian music and dance festival.

October-November

Gandhi Jayanti (**2nd**), Mahatma Gandhi's birthday; devotional singing at Raj Ghat. **Dasara**, with over 200 Ramlila performances all over the city recounting the Ramayana story (see p281). **The Ramlila Ballet** at Delhi Gate (south of Red Fort) and Ramlila Ground, is performed for a month and is most spectacular. Huge effigies of Ravana are burnt on the **9th night**; noisy and flamboyant. **National Drama Festival**, Shri Ram Centre. **Diwali**, the festival of lights; lighting of earthen lamps, candles and firework displays. **National Drama Festival**, Rabindra Bhavan.

December

Christmas (**25th**). Special Christmas Eve entertainments at all major hotels and restaurants; midnight mass and services at all churches. **Ayyappa Temple Festival**, Ayyappa Swami Temple, Ramakrishnapuram; South Indian music. **New Year's Eve (31st)**, celebrated in most hotels and restaurants offering special food and entertainment. Muslim festivals of.**Ramadan**, **Id-ul-Fitr**, **Id-ul-Zuha** and **Muharram** celebrated according to lunar calendar.

✪ Shopping

There are several state emporia around Delhi including the Cottage Industries Emporium (CIE), a huge department store of Indian handicrafts, and those along Baba Kharak Singh Marg. It is a convenient way of shopping; the choice being huge, as the shelves are packed with goods that are made all over India and everything has a fixed price. You may have to pay a little more for this.

Shops generally open from 1000-1930 (winter 1000-1900). Food stores, chemists stay open later. Most shopping areas are closed on Sun. Banks tend to follow the same pattern. Weekly *Free Ads* (Rs 5, Thu) lists 2nd-hand cameras, binoculars, etc.

Art galleries

Galleries exhibiting contemporary art are listed in *Delhi Diary*.
Delhi Art Gallery, Hauz Khas Village. A newly expanded gallery with a good range of moderately priced contemporary art. **Espace**, 16 Community Centre, New Friends Colony, T2683 0499. Group and solo shows by artists from all over India.

Bookshops

Hotel booksellers often carry a good selection of imported books about India, though

some charge inflated prices. Among those with specialist academic and art books focusing on India are: **Jainson's**, Janpath Hotel; **Krishan**, Claridges; **Khazana**, Taj Mahal and **Taj Palace** hotels (0900-2000).
Bahri & Sons, opposite Main Gate, Khan Market. Has a wide choice.
The Bookshop, Khan Market. Has a wide choice (also at Jor Bagh Market).
Bookworm, B-29, Connaught Place. Wide selection, including art, Indology, fiction.
Central News Agency, P 23/90, Connaught Place. Carries national and foreign newspapers and journals.
ED Galgotia, 17B, Connaught Place. Highly recommended.
Jacksons, 5106, Main Bazar, Paharganj, T5535 1083. Selection in many languages.
Jain's Bookshop C-Block, Connaught Place, the government book agency.
New Book Depot, 18B, Connaught Place. Highly recommended.
Oxford Book and Stationery, Scindia House, Connaught Place. Wide selection, including art, Indology, fiction.
Manohar, 4753/23 Ansar Rd, Daryaganj, Old Delhi. A real treasure trove for books on South Asia and India especially, most helpful, knowledgeable staff. Highly recommended.
MI, 15a, Khan Market. Has a wide choice.
Motilal Banarsidass, Nai Sarak, Chandni Chowk. Have books on Indology.
Munshiram Manoharlal, Nai Sarak, Chandni Chowk. Have books on Indology.
People Tree, 8 Regal Building, Parliament St, Connaught Place. Ecology oriented.
Prabhu & Sons, Hauz Khas Village, well-hidden on 1st floor balcony down side street, for antiquarian/second-hand books.
Timeless, 46 The Housing Society, 3rd floor and basement, Part 1, South extensions, full of coffee tables, art books and novels.
Vintage, next door to **Prabhu & Sons**, again selling antiquarian/second-hand books.

Clothing shops

For inexpensive (Western and Indian) clothes, try shops along Janpath and between Sansad Marg and Janpath; you can bargain down 50 per cent. Top quality clothes in the latest Western styles and fashionable fabrics are almost unobtainable. Having said that **Hauz Khas Village** and **Sunder Nagar Market** have some designer wear many for export to the West.
Archana, Gt Kailash I, has several boutiques.
Central Cottage Industries Emporium, good selection, also sells fabrics.
Fab India, 14N-Gt Kailash I (4 outlets in N Block and also in Vasant Kunj). Excellent shirts, Nehru jackets, *salwar kameez*, linen, furnishing fabrics and now furniture.
Khadi shop, near the Regal building, Janpath, for Indian wares.
Main Bazar, Paharganj, often passes off very poor quality items.
Palika Bazar, Connaught Circus, underground, a/c, can be a hassle but has decent salwar kameez, leather jackets and trousers (bargain very hard).
The Shop, Regal Building, Connaught Pl. Modest selection.

Tailoring at small shops charge around Rs 70-100 to copy a dress or shirt; trousers Rs 100-150. Nearly all big hotels have upmarket boutiques and also fabric/tailor's shops (some may allow fabric purchased elsewhere); allow 24 hrs for stitching.
Delhi Cloth House, fabric.
Grover, fabric.
Khan Market, several tailors and cloth stores.
Shankar Market, near Connaught Pl, has good suiting, corduroys, denim etc, and will suggest tailors.

Food

Assam, excellent Indian teas.
Bhim Sen's, Bengali Market, end of Tansen Marg, near Connaught Pl. For ome of the best, freshest (hence safest) Indian sweets.
Central Cottage Industries Emporium, Janpath. Excellent Indian teas.
Darjeeling Tea Bureau, Kaka Nagar Market (opposite Delhi Golf Club), T4622442, F6843737, nathmulls@goldentipstea.com. Charming, reliable and good selection. Highly recommended.
Evergreen, Green Park. Fresh *jelabies*.
Khari Baoli, Chandni Chowk, lined with colourful shops. Spices and dried fruit etc.
Modern Bazar, Vasant Vihar Market. Cold meats, cheeses, yoghurts, tea.
Steak House, Jorbagh Market. Cold meats, cheeses, yoghurts.
W Bengal Emporia, excellent Indian teas.

Handicrafts

Carpets

Carpets can be found in shops in most top hotels and a number round Connaught Pl, not necessarily fixed-price. If you are visiting Agra, check out the prices here first.

Earthenware

Unglazed earthenware *khumba matkas* (water pots) are sold round New Delhi Rly Station (workshops behind the main road).

Emporia

Most open 1000-1800 (close for lunch, 1330-1400).

Central Cottage Industries Emporium, corner of Janpath and Tolstoy Marg, offers hassle-free shopping, exchange counter (spend at least 50 per cent of amount to be cashed, take bills to till and use TCs/ credit card to pay and get exchange), gift wrapping, will pack and post overseas; the best one if you are short of time.

Dilli Haat, opposite INA Market, is a well-designed open-air complex with rows of brick alcoves for craft stalls from different states, changed periodically; local craftsmen's outlets (bargaining possible), occasional fairs (tribal art, textiles etc). (Also good regional food – hygienic, safe 'street food'!) Very pleasant, quiet, clean (no smoking) and uncrowded, no hassle. Entry Rs 10, open 1000-2230.

Khadi Gramodyog Bhawan, Regal Building, for inexpensive homespun cotton *kurta pajama* (loose shirt and trousers), cotton/silk waistcoats, fabrics and Jaipuri paintings.

Khazana, Taj Mahal and Taj Palace hotels (0900-2000; daily) is high class.

Santushti, Chanakyapuri, opposite **Hotel Samrat** has attractive a/c units in a garden setting, hassle free. Shops sell good quality clothes, crafts, linen, saris, silver etc (1000-1800, except Sun, some close for lunch), **Basil and Thyme** serves trendy western snacks (busy 1300-1400); **Anokhi**, near the entrance, has good household gifts and clothes; **IK** sells high quality silver gifts, jewellery and paintings.

Jewellery

Traditional silver and goldsmiths in Dariba Kalan, off Chandni Chowk (north of Jama Masjid). Cheap bangles and along Janpath; also at Hanuman Mandir, Gt Kailash I, N-Block, where you can get *henna* painted on the hand.

Jewel Mine, 12A Palika Bazar. Has silver, beads, semi-precious stones and fair prices.

Silverline, 18 Babar Rd, Bengali Market, T2335 0454. Contemporary silver jewellery at wholesale prices.

Sundar Nagar market (see below).

Leather

Cheap sandals from Janpath (Rs 100).

Baluja, Connaught Pl. Shoes.

Bata, Connaught Pl. Shoes and bags.

Bharat, Connaught Pl, opposite **Nirula's**.

Hidesign, G49, Connaught Pl, high class.

Khan Market, goods and shoes.

South Extension, goods and shoes.

Markets and malls

Beware of pickpockets in markets and malls.

Ansal Plaza, HUDCO, Khelgaon Marg (south of South Extension) is Delhi's first European style shopping mall. Very smart, lots of chains.

Basant Lok, Vasant Vihar, has a few upmarket shops attracting the young.

Hauz Khas village authentic, old village houses converted into designer shops selling handicrafts, ceramics, antiques and furniture in addition to luxury wear. Many shops are expensive, but some are good value. You will also find art galleries and restaurants.

Jorbagh, Gt Kailash Pt I-M, Western travellers hankering for the familiar, and prepared to pay the price, will find a good range of eatables and toiletries.

Khan Market, good for books, food, clothes.

Main Bazar, Paharganj, again a good range of food and toiletries for Westerners with enough cash.

Santushti, Chanakyapuri, see Handicrafts.

Sarojini Nagar sells daily necessities as well as cheap fabric and clothing.

South Extension is good for clothes, shoes, jewellery, music etc.

Sunder Nagar has a few shops selling Indian handicrafts and jewellery (precious and semi-precious); some quite original.

Tibetan Market stalls along Janpath have plenty of curios – most are new but rapidly aged to look authentic.

▲▲ Activities and tours

Guided sightseeing tours can be arranged through approved travel agents and tour operators. For approved tourist guides/agencies contact India Tourist Office and travel agents. There are many small agents, eg opposite New Delhi Railway Station, seemingly offer unusual itineraries, but their standards can't be guaranteed and their rates are not significantly lower. Rates: Delhi only, half day Rs 90, full day Rs 160. **India Tourism Development Corporation** (ITDC) and **Delhi Tourism** both run city sightseeing tours. Combining Old and New Delhi tours on the same day can be very tiring. A/c coaches are particularly recommended during the summer months. The price includes transport and guide services, but all are whistle-stop tours. Check whether the recently raised entrance fees to many sights are still included in the price of the tour. A group of 3 or 4 people could

consider hiring a car and doing the tour at their own pace. Another alternative is to hire an auto-rickshaw for the day (around Rs 200). It will entail visiting gift shops for the driver to get a commission, but you don't have to buy.

Delhi Tourism Tours

Check time, T3314229. Book day in advance. Departure point: Delhi Tourism, Bombay Life Building, N-Block, Connaught Pl.
New Delhi Tour (0800-1400): Jantar Mantar, Qutb Minar, Lakshmi Narayan Temple, Safdarjang's Tomb, Diplomatic Enclave, India Gate.
Old Delhi Tour (1400-1700): Jama Masjid, Red Fort, Shanit Vana, Raj Ghat, Kotla Firoz Shah.
Evening Tour (1800-2200): Lakshmi Narayan Temple (evening prayer), India Gate, Purana Qila, son et lumière (Red Fort), Jama Masjid (dinner at a Mughlai restaurant). Both Rs 150.
Museum Tour (Sun only, check time): Air Force, Rail and Transport, and National Museums, Indira Gandhi Memorial, Nehru Planetarium, Museum of Natural History and Dolls Museum.

ITDC Tours

Guides are generally good but tours are rushed, T2332 0331. Tickets can be booked from **Hotel Indraprastha**, T2334 4511.
New Delhi Tour: departs from L-1 Connaught Circus and **Hotel Indraprastha** (0800-1330), Rs 125 (a/c coach): Jantar Mantar, Lakshmi Narayan Temple, India Gate, Nehru Pavilion, Pragati Maidan (closed Monday), Humayun's Tomb, Qutb Minar.
Old Delhi Tour: departs from **Hotel Indraprastha**. (1400-1700), Rs 100: Kotla Firoz Shah, Raj Ghat, Shantivana, Jama Masjid and Red Fort.

Taj Mahal tours

Many companies offer coach tours to Agra (eg **ITDC**, from L1 Connaught Circus, 0630-2200 except Fri, Rs 600, a/c coach). However, travelling by road is slow and uncomfortable; by car, allow at least 4 hrs each way. Train is a better option; take either the *Shatabdi*, or *Taj Express*, but book early.

Walking tours

Chor Bizarre, Hotel Broadway, T2327 3821 see p94, offers special walking tours of Old Delhi, with good lunch, 0930-1330, 1300-1630, Rs 350 each, Rs 400 for both.

Master Paying Guest House (see Sleeping p83) offers walking tours twice a week which are highly recommended for a more intimate experience of Old Delhi.

🚌 Transport

Air

International flights arrive at Indira Gandhi International Terminal. Enquiries T2565 2010; pre-recorded arrivals and departures, T144/5; reservations, T146. Watch out for inflated prices for food and drink. Palam Domestic Terminal; enquiries T2567 5181; pre- recorded arrivals and departures, T142/3, private air- lines, T149, **Indian Airlines** reservations, T141.

Delhi has daily connections (many direct) with the following domestic destinations. The number of flights, if more than 1, is shown in brackets. The codes are as follows: IC = Indian Airlines, CD Alliance, JA = Jagson, 9W = Jet Air. Daily flights to **Agra** (IC); **Jaipur** (9W); **Udaipur** (IC, 9W); and non-daily flights to **Jaipur** (CD, IC); **Jaisalmer** (CD, JA); **Jodhpur** (CD, JA); **Udaipur** (CD).

To and from the airport

Buses run by Ex-Servicemen's Airlink Transport Service (EATS) , F Block Connaught Pl, T3316530, **Delhi Transport Corp (DTC)** and **Airports Authority of India (AAI)** from the 2 terminals go to Connaught Pl, New Delhi Railway Station and ISBT (Kashmir Gate) via some hotels. One leaves from IA office, Connaught Pl, goes to the Domestic and then the International terminal, 0400, 0530, 0730, 1000, 1400, 1530, 1800, 1900, 2200, 2330; Rs 50; Rs 10 luggage. There is a booth just outside 'Arrivals' at the International and Domestic terminals. A bus is a safe, economical option, particularly for the first-time visitor on a budget. At night, take a pre-paid taxi to a pre-booked hotel (see below). There is a Travellers' Lounge above the Arrival Hall, Rs 25 per seat.

There is a free shuttle between the 2 terminals every 30 mins during the day. Some hotel buses leave from the Domestic terminal. **Bus 780** runs between the **airport** and **New Delhi Railway station**.

The International and Domestic terminals have pre-paid taxi counters outside the baggage hall (3 price categories) which ensure that you pay the right amount (give your name, exact destination and number of all items of luggage). Most expensive are white 'DLZ' limousines and then white 'DLY' luxury taxis. Cheapest are 'DLT' ordinary Delhi taxis (black with yellow top Ambassador/Fiat cars, note that this desk is outside the terminal building – turn right out of the arrivals hall and it's immediately on your right). 'DLY' taxis charge 3 times the DLT price. A 'Welcome' desk by the baggage reclamation offers expensive taxis only. Take your receipt to the ticket counter outside to find your taxi and give it to the driver when you reach the destination; you don't need to tip (although they will ask!). From the International terminal DLT taxis charge about Rs 200 for the town centre (Connaught Place area); night charges, double, 2300-0500. Rates from the Domestic terminal are slightly lower.

The Government **Tourist Information** desk is usually very helpful and efficient. They will book a hotel but not in the 'budget' category. **Indian Railways Counter**, beyond pre-paid taxi kiosks. Helpful computerized booking; easier and quicker than at a station.

Airlines

Abbreviations used: A = Airport phone no. KG Marg = Kasturba Gandhi Marg

Domestic Check in for all **Indian Airlines** flights at terminal 1-A. For J class Tele Check-in T2566 5166. Check in for all other domestic airlines Terminal 1-B. Arrivals for all domestic flights Terminal 1-C.

Private Jagson Airways, 12 E Vandana Building, 11 Tolstoy Marg, T2332 8580, A 2566 5375. Jet Airways, 13 Community Centre, Yusuf Sarai, T2685 3700, A 2567 5404; G-12 Connaught Pl, T23320961, A 2566 5404, Tele Check-in T2656 2266.

International Aeroflot, 1517 Tolstoy Marg, off Janpath, T2331 2843. **Air Canada**, Janpath, T2372 0014, A 2565 2850. **Air France**, 6 Scindia House, KG Marg, T2373

8004, A 5652294. **Air India**, Jeevan Bharati Building T2373 6446, A 25652050**Alitalia**, 3rd floor, 16 Barakhamba Rd, T2372 1006, A 2565 2349. **Biman**, WTC, Up Gr Fl, Babar Rd, T2341 4401, A 2565 2943. **British Airways**, DLF Plaza Tower, Gurgaon, T95124-5120747; Gopal Das Building, Barakhamba Rd, T2332 7139, A 25652077. **Cathay Pacific**, 809 Ashoka Estate, Barakhamba Rd, T2332 1286. **Delta**, DLF Centre, Gurgaon T916-388977; Sansad Marg, T2373 0197. **Druk Air**, Ansal Bhawan, KG Marg, T2335 7703, A 25653207. **El-Al**, 911 Prakash Deep, 7 Tolstoy Marg, T2335 7965. **Emirates**, 18 Barakhamba Rd, 5531 4444, A 25696861. **Gulf Air**, G-12 Connaught Circus, T2335 1353, A 25652065. **Japan Airlines**, Chandralok Building, Janpath, T2332 7104, A 25653942. **KLM**, 7 Tolstoy Marg, T23357747, A 2565 2715. **Kuwait**, Ansal Bhawan, KG Marg, T23354373. **Lufthansa**, 56 Janpath, T2372 4222, A 5652064. **Malaysian**, Ashoka Building, 24 Barakhamba Rd, 10th floor, T2335 9711, A 2565 2395. **Nepal Airlines**, 44 Janpath, T2332 1164, A 2569 6876. **PIA**, 26 KG Marg, T23737791, A 25652841. **Philippine**, N-40 Connaught Circus, T2331 4978. **Qantas**, 13 Tolstoy Marg, T2335 5284. **Royal Jordanian** G-56 Connaught Circus, T2331 9890. **Saudia**, 16 Barakhamba Rd, T2331 0464. **SAS**, 14 KG Marg, T2335 2299. **Singapore Airlines**, Ashoka Estate, 24 Barakhamba Rd, T2335 6283, A 2565 3072. **Sri Lanka**, Janpath Hotel, Janpath, T2373 1473, A 2565 2349. **Swissair**, Gurgaon T916-388911; World Trade Tower, Barakhamba Lane, T2341 5000, A 25652531. **Thai**, Park Royal Hotel, Nehru Pl, T5149 7777, A 2565 2796. **United Airlines**, 14 KG Marg, T2335 3377, A 2565 3910. **US Air**, 24 Barakhamba Rd, T3311362. **Virgin**, DLF Centre, Parliament St, 5150 1300.

Auto-rickshaw

Local

Widely available at about half the cost of taxis (Rs 4 per km). Normal capacity for foreigners is 2 people! (3rd person extra); insist on using the metre or agree fare in advance. Expect to pay Rs 10 for the shortest journeys. Pre-paid auto kiosks at Palika Bazar and New Delhi station give you an idea of a fair charge. Allow Rs 50 for 2 hrs' sight-seeing /shopping. It is best to walk away from tourist centres to look for an auto. When using the meter, you pay 2½ times the reading plus Rs 3; another 100 per cent from 2300 to 0500. Ask to see tariff card and follow a map.

Cycle-rickshaws and tongas (horse-drawn traps) are available in the Old City. Be prepared to bargain, remembering that it should be cheaper than motorized transport, eg New Delhi station to Jama Masjid Rs 15-20. Not allowed into Connaught Pl.

Bicycle

Cycle hire in the shops near Minto Bridge, off Connaught Pl, on Mohan Singh Pl near Rivoli cinema and in Paharganj; about Rs 5 per hr to Rs 25 per day plus a refundable deposit.

Bus

Local
The city bus service run by the **Delhi Transport Corporation (DTC)** connects all important points in the city. There are over 300 routes. Information is available at DTC assistance booths and at all major bus stops. Don't be afraid to ask conductors or fellow passengers. Buses are usually hopelessly overcrowded so only use at off-peak.

Long distance
Delhi is linked to most major centres in Rajasthan. Services are provided by Delhi Transport Corp (DTC) and State Roadways of neighbouring states from various **Inter-State Bus Termini (ISBT)**; these have bus services between them. Allow at least 30 mins for buying a ticket and finding the right bus.

The main bus terminals for Agra or Rajasthan are **Kingsway Camp** with services run by **Haryana Roadways**, T2296 1262; daily to **Agra** (5-6 hrs, Rs 80, quicker by rail), **Jaipur** (Rs 150, 6½ hrs). Also **Rajpur Rd** with services run by **Rajasthan Roadways**, T2296 1246, for **Agra**, 5-6 hrs (quicker by rail), Rs 58; via **Mathura** and **Vrindavan**, **Ajmer**, **Alwar**, **Bharatpur** (5 hrs), **Bikaner** (11 hrs), **Gwalior**, Jodhpur, Pushkar (10 hrs), Udaipur etc. From **Bikaner House**, Pandara Rd, south of India Gate,

T2338 3469, several 'Deluxe' buses leave for **Jaipur**, 6 hrs, Rs 230 (a/c); ask for 'direct' bus (some buses stop at **Amber** for a tour of the fort). To **Udaipur** (via **Ajmer**), 1900; to **Jodhpur** (2120, 2200).

Car

All road journeys in India are slow. Main roads out of Delhi are very heavily congested. Best time to leave is very early morning. Delhi is well connected by road with major cities: by NH2 to **Agra** (200 km), **Ajmer** (399 km); by NH8 to **Jaipur** (261 km), **Jodhpur** (604 km), and **Udaipur** (635 km).

Car hire
An excellent way of getting about town if you have several journeys to make during the day is by hiring a car with driver. This is also a great way of travelling around Rajasthan. See also p31.

Full day local use with driver (non a/c) is about Rs 700-800, 80 km/8 hrs, driver overnight *bata* Rs 150 per day; self-drive 24 hrs/150 km Rs 1,200. Airport to city centre Rs 400-500. To Jaipur, about Rs 3,000; return Rs 5,400. The Tourist Office, 88 Janpath, has a list of approved agents.
Cozy Travels, N1 BMC House, Middle Circle, Connaught Place, T2331 1593, F23711 3869, cozytravels@vsnl.net.com, for Ambassador or similar, Rs 650 non-a/c, Rs 850 a/c.
Ex-Soldiers Tourist Taxis, opposite 16 Dr Rajendra Prasad Marg.
Metropole Tourist Service, 244 Defence Flyover Market, T2431 2212, F2431 1819, metropole@vsnl.com, car/jeep (US$30-40 per day), reliable and recommended.
Mohindra Tourist Taxis, corner of Poorvi/Paschimi Margs, Vasant Vihar, T2614 3188, "excellent service, safe driving".
Western Court Tourist Taxis, 36 Janpath, outside **Hotel Imperial**, T2332 1236. Helpful.

International companies charge higher prices but provide dependable service:
Budget, 78/3 Janpath, T2371 5657, F2373 9182; G3 Arunachal Building, Barakhamba Rd, T3318600; 82 Nehru Pl, T2645 2634.
Europcar, 14 Basant Lok, Vasant Vihar, T2614 0373; M-3 Connaught Circus, T2686 2248.
Hertz, Barakhamba Rd, T2331 8695; GF29 Ansal Chamber, Bhikaji Cama Pl, T2619 7188, F2619 7206.

Motorcycle

Karol Bagh has specialist shops.

Chawla Motorcycles, 1770, Shri Kissan Dass Marg, Naiwali Gali, is very reliable, trustworthy, highly recommended for restoring classic bikes.

Ess Aar Motors, Jhandewalan Extn, west of Paharganj. Recommended for buying Enfields, very helpful.

Inder Motors, 1744 Hari Singh Nalwa Gali, Abdul Aziz Rd, T2572 5879. The most expensive, but also the most professional.

Nanna Motors, 112 Press Rd, east of Connaught Circus, T2335 1769. Recommended for buying Enfields, very helpful.

Taxi

Environment friendly taxis and autos with a green stripe run on compressed natural gas. Yellow-top taxis are easily available at taxi stands or you can hail one on the road. Meter: multiply the final reading by 6 and add Rs 3.50 (eg Rs 4 will be Rs 27.50). You can ask for the conversion card. Add 25 per cent night charge (2300-0500) plus 50p for each piece of heavy luggage (over 20 kg). These extras apply to auto-rickshaws as well. For complaints, ring police line, T3737300.

Private: 1629. Ring for a taxi, anywhere in Delhi. Reliable but expensive, Rs 15 per km.

Train

'Trains at a glance' (Rs 25) lists important trains across India and is invaluable if you intend to do a lot of train travel on your trip. **Delhi Tourism**, Connaught Circus, issues tickets on the spot.

Local
The Delhi suburban railway is neither very popular nor convenient. A ring route operates 3 times a day – 0755, 1625, 1725, starting from Hazrat Nizamuddin station.

Long distance
New Delhi Railway Station and Hazrat Nizamuddin Station (just north and 5 km southeast of Connaught Place, respectively) connect Delhi with most major places. The latter has many important south-bound trains.

of the centre, has broad and metre gauge trains. **Delhi Sarai Rohilla**, serves Rajasthan.

Enquiries T131, T2336 6177. Waiting Rooms and Rest Rooms are for those 'in transit' (tickets are likely to be checked). Authorized porters (*coolies*), wear red shirts and white *dhotis;* the number on the brass badge identifies each so it is best to make a note of it, and agree the charge, before engaging one. For left luggage, you need a secure lock and chain.

Reservations T1330, T2334 8686, Old Delhi T3975357, though generally for Northern Railway only (not all-India). Allow time (1-2 hrs) and be prepared to be very patient as it can be a nightmare, but don't be tempted to go to an unauthorized agent (see below). The Central Booking Office has counters for paying by credit cards (although these cannot be used for booking tickets on the tourist quota). Computerized reservation offices (in separate building in Connaught Circus); 0745-2100, Sun 0745-1400; fee Rs 20. May be quicker than ITB, but no advice offered. The Sarojini Nagar office is quick, hassle free (especially the credit card counter) and is well worth the detour. Alternatively, you can use a recommended travel agent for tickets/reservations and pay Rs 30-50 fee.

At **New Delhi Station** International Tourist Bureau (ITB), 1st Floor, Main Building, T2373 4164, for foreigners, Mon-Fri 0930-1630; Sat 0930-1430; efficient and helpful if slow. You need your passport and visa; pay in US$, or rupees (with an encashment certificate). Those with Indrail passes, should confirm bookings. There is also a counter for foreigners and NRIs at Delhi Tourism, N-36 Connaught Pl, 1000-1700, Mon-Sat. The Airport counter (when open) is quick and efficient for air tickets and reservations. The pre-paid taxi and auto-rickshaw kiosks are next to the taxi rank as you come out of the station. Queue at the appropriate window, give your name, exact destination (hotel/street), number of pieces of luggage over 20 kg; collect your slip on payment and go to the head of the taxi/auto-rickshaw rank (you are not supposed to hire one 'privately'). Hand the slip to the driver at your destination; you don't need to tip. An auto to Connaught Place costs around Rs 15, Old Delhi Station Rs 25. Rickshaw drivers/touts may say the ITB is closed/has moved and then offer fake Rail Passes, or falsely insist that you need a hotel reservation slip before leaving the station; you don't. Some take you to a travel agent, others insist that you need a rickshaw to Paharganj. Avoid **Kashmir Holiday Tours and Travels**, opposite the station. Arriving very early or late can be an added problem.

Stations from which trains originate have codes: **OD** – Old Delhi, **ND** – New Delhi, **HN** – Hazrat Nizamuddin, **DSR** – Delhi Sarai

Rohilla. **Agra**: *Shatabdi Exp*, *2002*, ND 0600, 2 hrs; *Taj Exp*, *2180*, HN, 0715, 2¾ hrs. **Jaipur**: *Shatabdi Exp*, *2015*, daily except Sun, ND, 0615, 4¾ hrs; *Delhi-Jodhpur Exp*, *4859*, OD, 1655, 5½ hrs. **Jodhpur**: *Mandore Exp*, *2461*, OD, 2100, 11 hrs. **Udaipur**: *Chetak Exp*, *9615*, DSR, 1410, 20¼ hrs; *Ahamadabad Exp*, *9943*, DSR, 2100, 21 hrs.

For special steam *Fairy Queen* and the diesel *Palace on Wheels* tours, see p32. The latter departs from Delhi Cantonment every Wed Sep-Apr, US$270-325 each per night with 2 sharing a cabin.

⊙ Directory

Banks

Open Mon-Fri 1000-1400, Sat 1000-1200. Cash against Visa can take up to 1 hr; it is usually quicker to change foreign cash and TCs at hotels, though the rate may be slightly poorer. ATMs for International Visa/Plus card-holders using PIN at **HDFC**, **HSBC**, **Standard Chartered** and **Citibanks** all over Delhi. Foreign banks and money changers include: **American Express**, A-Block Connaught Pl, excellent (closed Sun); small branch in Paharganj; **Standard Chartered Grindlays**, 15 KG Marg; **Thomas Cook**, Hotel Imperial, Janpath; New Delhi Railway station (24 hrs).

Indian banks (dealing in foreign exchange) open 24 hrs: **Central Bank of India**, Ashok Hotel, **State Bank of India**, Palam Airport.

Swift transfers from overseas through **Western Union**, SITA, F-12, Connaught Pl.

Chemists

Many hospitals have 24-hr services: **Hindu Rao Hospital**, Sabzi Mandi; **Ram Manohar Lohia Hospital**, Willingdon Crescent; **S Kripalani Hospital**, Panchkuin Rd. In Connaught Pl: **Nath Brothers**, G-2, off Marina Arcade; **Chemico**, H-45

Embassies

Visas are easy (photo needed), collect passport next day.
Australia, 1/50-G Shantipath, T5139 9900.
Canada, 7-8 Shantipath, T5178 2000.
France, 2/50-E Shantipath, T2611 8790.
Ireland, 13 Jor Bagh, T2462 6733.
UK, Shantipath, T2687 2161.
USA, Shantipath, T2419 8000.

Hospitals

Embassies and High Commissions have lists of recommended doctors and dentists. Doctors approved by IAMAT (International Association for Medical Assistance to Travellers) are listed in a directory. Casualty and emergency wards in both private and government hospitals are open 24 hrs.
Ram Manohar Lohia, Willingdon Crescent, T2336 5525, 24 hr A&E.
Hindu Rao, Sabzi Mandi, T2251 3355.
JP Narain, J Nehru Marg, Delhi Gate, T2331 1621.
Safdarjang General, Sri Aurobindo Marg, T2616 5060.
S Kripalani, Panchkuin Rd, T2336 3788.

Post

Stamps are often available from the reception in the larger hotels. **Speedpost** from 36 centres. Head post offices at **Sansad Marg**, 1000-1830 Mon-Sat, **Eastern Court**, Janpath, 24 hrs, **Connaught Place**, A-Block, 1000-1700 Mon-Sat (parcel packing service outside). New Delhi GPO at **Ashoka Place**, southwest of Connaught Pl, 24 hrs.

Poste restante is available; make sure senders specify 'New Delhi 110001'; collect from counter behind sorting office, 0900-1700, until 1300, Sat. Don't forget to take your passport.

Useful addresses

Ambulance (24 hrs): T102. **Fire**: T101. **Foreigners' Registration Office**: 1st floor, Hans Bhawan, Tilak Bridge, T2331 9489. **Police**: T100.

Agra → *Phone code: 0562. Colour map 3, grid C3. Population: 956,000.*

The romance of the world's most famous building still astonishes in its power. In addition to the Taj, Agra also houses the great monuments of the Red Fort and the I'timad-ud-Daulah, but to experience their beauty you have to endure the less attractive sides of one of India's least prepossessing towns. A big industrial city, the monuments are often covered in a haze of all too polluted air, while visitors may be subjected to a barrage of high power selling. Despite it all, the experience is still unmissable. The city is also the convenient gateway to the wonderful, abandoned capital of Fatehpur Sikri. ⟫ *For Sleeping, Eating and other listings, see pages 107-110.*

Ins and outs

Getting there By far the best way to arrive is by using the *Shatabdi Express* train. Considering waiting time and delays, it is usually faster than flying, and infinitely more comfortable than bus or car. There are frequent 'express' buses from Delhi and Jaipur, but it can take up to five tiring hours by bus or car.

Getting around Buses run a regular service between the station, bus stands and the main sites. See Entrances page 102. Cycle-rickshaws and taxis can be hired to go further afield, or a bike if it's not too hot. ⟫ *See Transport, page 110, for further details.*

Climate Best time to visit is between November and March.

Delhi & Agra Agra Sights

The Taj Mahal

ⓘ *Daily except Fri, 0600-1900, Rs 20, foreigners Rs750, includes still camera (video cameras not allowed). No photos inside the tomb (instant fines). Allow at least 1 hr.*

It is not only the exquisite, breathtaking beauty of the Taj Mahal, but also the heart-rending romance of the story behind its construction, which make it so extraordinarily special. When Shah Jahan's wife, Mumtaz Mahal, died during the birth or their 14th child in 1631, the great emperor was utterly griefstricken, and set about building a mausoleum which would adequately reflect the immensity of his love for her. The staggering result was 22 years in the making, and employed an estimated 20,000 workers from as far afield as France, Italy and Iran.

> ⚎ *Visit at sunrise an sunset to avoid crowds and take photographs in peace (early morning can be misty). Hiring a guide isn't necessary.*

Sadly, this poignant love story was to have an unhappy ending. Shah Jahan was imprisoned in Agra Fort by his son Aurangzeb for the last eight years of his life, a punishment for his profligate overspending of State funds. Legend has it that this great Mughal emperor spent his final years gazing wistfully across the river at his greatest creation continuing to mourn for his beloved queen until his dying day. He had planned for an exact replica of the Taj Mahal to be built in black marble on the opposite bank of the river to house his own tomb, but instead Aurangzeb put him next to his wife, the only flaw in the otherwise perfect symmetry of the Taj Mahal.

Viewing

The white marble of the Taj is extraordinarily luminescent and even on dull days seems bright. The whole building appears to change its hue according to the light in the sky. In winter (December-February), it is worth being there at sunrise. Then the mists that often lie over the river Yamuna lift as the sun rises and casts its golden rays over the pearl white tomb. Beautifully lit in the soft light, the Taj appears to float on air. At sunset, the view from across the river is equally wonderful. The Archaeological Survey of India explicitly asks visitors not to make donations to anyone including the custodians in the tomb who often ask for money.

Entrances

To reduce damage to the marble by the polluted atmosphere, local industries are having to comply with strict rules now and vehicles emitting noxious fumes are not allowed within 2 km of the monument. People are increasingly using horse drawn carriages or walking. You can approach the Taj from three directions. The western entrance is usually used by those arriving from the fort. At the Eastern entrance, rickshaws and camel drivers offer to take visitors to the gate for up to Rs 100 each; however, an official battery bus ferries visitors from the car park to the gate for Rs 2 each.

The approach

In the unique beauty of the Taj, sudbtlety is blended with grandeur and a massive overall design is matched with immaculately intricate execution. You will already have seen the dome of the tomb in the distance, looking almost like a miniature, but as you go into the open square the Taj itself is so well hidden that you almost wonder where it can be. The glorious surprise is kept until the last moment, for wholly concealing it is the massive red sandstone gateway of the entrance, symbolizing the divide between the secular world and paradise.

The gateway was completed in 1648, though the huge brass door is recent. The original doors (plundered by the Jats) were solid silver and decorated with 1,100 nails whose heads were contemporary silver coins. Although the gateway is remarkable in itself, one of its functions is to prevent you getting any glimpse of the tomb inside until you are right in the doorway itself. From here only the tomb is visible, stunning in its nearness, but as you move forward the minarets come into view.

The garden

The Taj garden, well kept though it is nowadays, is nothing compared with its former glory. The guiding principle is one of symmetry. The *char bagh*, separated by the watercourses (rivers of heaven) originating from the central, raised pool, were divided into 16 flower beds, making a total of 64. The trees, all carefully planted to maintain the symmetry, were either cypress (signifying death) or fruit trees (life). The channels were stocked with colourful fish and the gardens with beautiful birds. It is well worth wandering along the side avenues for not only is it much more peaceful but also good for framing photos of the tomb with foliage. You may see bullocks pulling the lawnmowers around!

The mosque and its jawab

On the east and west sides of the tomb are identical red sandstone buildings. On the west (left-hand side) is a mosque. It is common in Islam to build one next to a tomb. It sanctifies the area and provides a place for worship. The replica on the other side is known as the **Jawab** (answer). This cannot be used for prayer as it faces away from Mecca.

The tomb

There is only one point of access to the **plinth** and tomb where, shoes must be removed (socks can be kept on; remember the white marble gets very hot) or cloth overshoes worn (Rs 2, though strictly free).

The **tomb** is square with bevelled corners. At each corner smaller domes rise while in the centre is the main dome topped by a brass finial. The dome is actually a double dome and this device, Central Asian in origin, was used to gain height. The

● *The four minarets at each corner of the plinth provide balance to the tomb – see how each*
● *slants outwards. Familiar with the disastrous effects of earthquakes on mosques in Gujarat to the south, the architects deliberately designed the minarets so they would fall away from the tomb, not onto it.*

resemblance of the dome to a huge pearl is not coincidental. The exterior ornamentation is calligraphy (verses of the Koran), beautifully carved panels in bas relief and superb inlay work.

The **interior** of the mausoleum comprises a lofty central chamber, a crypt (*maqbara*) immediately below this, and four octagonal corner rooms. The central chamber contains replica tombs, the real ones being in the crypt. The public tomb was originally surrounded by a jewel encrusted silver screen. Aurangzeb removed this, fearing it might be stolen, and replaced it with an octagonal screen of marble carved from one block of marble and inlaid with precious stones. It is an incredible piece of workmanship. This chamber is open at sunrise, but may close during the day.

Above the tombs is a **Cairene lamp** whose flame is supposed to never go out. This one was given by Lord Curzon, Governor General of India (1899-1905), to replace the original which was stolen by Jats. The tomb of Mumtaz with the 'female' slate, rests immediately beneath the dome. If you look from behind it, you can see how it lines up centrally with the main entrance. Shah Jahan's tomb is larger and to the side, marked by a 'male' pen-box, the sign of a cultured or noble person. Not originally intended to be placed there but squeezed in by Aurangzeb, this flaws the otherwise perfect symmetry of the whole complex. Finally, the acoustics of the building are superb', the domed ceiling being designed to echo chants from the Koran and musicians' melodies.

The **museum** ① *1000-1700, closed Fri*, above the entrance has a small collection of Mughal memorabilia, photographs and miniatures of the Taj through the ages but has no textual information. Sadly, lights do not always work.

Jami Masjid (1648), near the Fort railway, is attributed to Shah Jahan's dutiful elder daughter Jahanara. The fine marble steps and bold geometric patterns on the domes are quite striking. The large gardens have deer, black buck and monkeys.

Agra Fort (Red Fort)

① *0600-1830. Rs 15, Foreigners Rs 300 (or Rs 50 if you've already been to the Taj), video Rs25. Allow a minimum of 1½ hrs for a visit.*

On the west bank of the Yamuna River, Akbar's magnificent fort dominates the centre of the city. Many visitors who come to Agra expecting to see nothing but the Taj Mahal, are taken aback by the this magnificent building, and the views of the Taj it affords. You can only enter now from the hugely imposing Amar Singh gate in the south. Although only the southern third of the fort is open to the public, this includes nearly all the buildings of interest.

These buildings retain some distinctively Islamic Persian features – the geometrical planning of the pavilions and the formal layout of the gardens, for example. Tillotson points out that here 'Hindu motifs are treated in a new manner. The temple columns and corbel capitals have been stripped of their rich carving and turned into simpler, smoother forms. The *chhattris* have Islamic domes, the indigenous motifs are bound with Islamic components into a new style. The unity is assisted by the use of the cusped arch and the *Bangladar* roof'.

> ‼ *The best route round is to start with the building on your right before going through the gate at the top of the broad 100 m ramp; the gentle incline made it suitable for elephants.*

Jahangiri Mahal Despite its name, this was built by Akbar (circa 1570) as women's quarters. It is all that survives of his original palace buildings. In front is a large **stone bowl** with steps both inside and outside, which was probably filled with fragrant rose water for bathing. The presence of distinctively Hindu features in the exterior does not indicate a synthesis of architectural styles at this early stage of Mughal architecture, as can be seen much more clearly from inside the **Jahangiri Mahal Jodha Bai's Palace**, on the south side, is named after one of Jahangir's wives.

Turn left through to **Shah Jahan's Khas Mahal** (1636) The open tower allows you to view the walls and see to your left the decorated Mussaman Burj tower.

Anguri Bagh (Vine Garden) The formal, geometric gardens are on the left. In the middle of the white marble platform wall in front is a decorative water slide. The surface was scalloped to produce a rippling waterfall, or inlaid to create a shimmering stream bed. Behind vertical water drops, there are little cusped arch niches into

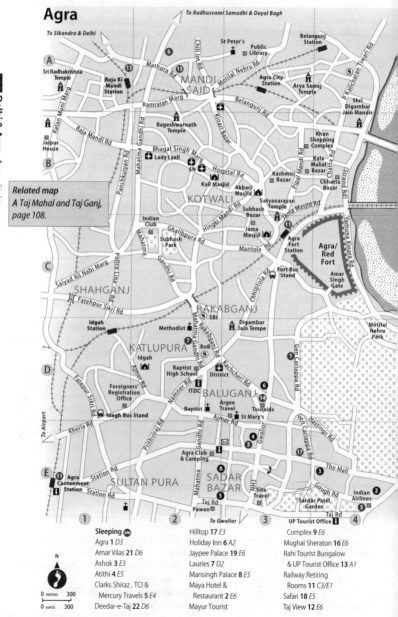

Agra

Related map
A Taj Mahal and Taj Ganj,
page 108.

Sleeping
Agra **1** D3
Amar Vilas **21** D6
Ashok **3** E3
Atithi **4** E5
Clarks Shiraz , TCI &
  Mercury Travels **5** E4
Deedar-e-Taj **22** D6

Hilltop **17** E3
Holiday Inn **6** A2
Jaypee Palace **19** E6
Lauries **7** D2
Mansingh Palace **8** E5
Maya Hotel &
  Restaurant **2** E6
Mayur Tourist

Complex **9** E6
Mughal Sheraton **16** E6
Rahi Tourist Bungalow
  & UP Tourist Office **13** A1
Railway Retiring
  Rooms **11** C3/E1
Safari **18** E5
Taj View **12** E6

0 metres 300
0 yards 300

which flowers would be placed during the day and lamps at night. The open pavilion on your right has a superb view across to the Taj.

Golden Pavilions The curved *chala* roofs of the small pavilions by the Khas Mahal are based on the roof shape of Bengali village huts constructed out of curved bamboo, designed to keep off heavy rain. These were probably ladies' bedrooms, with hiding places for jewellery in the walls.

Khas Mahal The interior decoration of this gives an impression of how splendid the painted ceiling must have been. The metal rings were probably used for *punkhas*. Underneath are cool rooms used to escape the summer heat.

Mussaman Burj On the left of the Khas Mahal is a beautiful octagonal tower with an open pavilion which could well have been used as the Emperor's bedroom. It has been suggested that this is where Shah Jahan lay on his deathbed, gazing at the Taj. The inlay work here is exquisite, especially above the pillars.

Sheesh Mahal (Mirror Palace) Here are further examples of decorative water engineering in the hammams; the water here may have been warmed by lamps. The mirrors, which were more precious than marble, were set into the walls, often specially chiselled to accommodate their crooked shape.

Diwan-i-Khas The Hall of Private Audience (1637) is next to the Mussaman Burj. The interior would have been richly decorated with tapestries and carpets. The double columns in marble inlaid with semi-precious stones in delightful floral patterns in *pietra dura* have finely carved capitals.

In front of the Diwan-i-Khas are two throne 'platforms' on a **terrace (9)**. The **black marble throne** at the rear of the terrace was used by Jahangir when claiming to be Emperor at Allahabad. The Emperor sat on the white marble platform facing the **Machhi Bhavan** or Fish Enclosure, which once contained pools and fountains.

Diwan-i-Am Go down an internal staircase and you enter the Diwan-i-Am

Tourist Rest
House **14** *D3*
Trident **20** *E6*
Youth Hostel **15** *A2*

Eating
Café Coffee Day **5** *E3*
Dasaprakash **4** *E3*

Only **3** *E4*
Priya **6** *D3 & E6*
Riao **2** *E4*
Shani
Dastarkhawan **1** *E5*
Zorba the
Buddha **8** *E2*

from the side. On the back wall of the pavilion are *jali* screens to enable the women of the court to watch without being seen. The throne alcove of richly decorated white marble used to house the Peacock Throne. 'The canopy was carved in enamel work and studded with individual gems, its interior was thickly encrusted with rubies, garnets and diamonds, and it was supported on 12 emerald covered columns' writes Tillot-son. When Shah Jahan moved his capital to Delhi he took the throne with him to the Red Fort, only for it to be taken back to Persia as loot by Nadir Shah in 1739.

Nagina Masjid From the corner opposite the Diwan-i-Khas two doorways lead to a view over the small courtyards of the *zenana* (harem). Further round in the next corner is the Nagina Masjid, the private mosque of the ladies of the court. Beneath it was a *mina* bazar for the ladies to make purchases from the marble balcony above.

Looking out of the Diwan-i-Am you can see the domes of the **Moti Masjid** (Pearl Mosque, 1646-1653), closed to visitors because of structural problems. In the paved area in front of the Diwan-i-Am is a large well and the tomb of **Mr John Russell Colvin**, the Lieutenant Governor of the Northwest Provinces.

I'timad-ud-Daulah

① *0630-1830, Rs 10, foreigners Rs 110, video Rs 25.*
Sometimes called 'Baby Taj' set a startling precedent as the first Mughal building to be faced with white marble inlaid with contrasting stones. Unlike the Taj it is small, intimate and has a gentle serenity, but is just as ornate. The tomb was built for **Ghiyas Beg**, a Persian who had obtained service in Akbar's court, and his wife, see page 271. On Jahangir's succession in 1605 he became *Wazir* (Chief Minister). Jahangir fell in love with his daughter, **Mehrunissa**, who at the time was married to a Persian. When her husband died in 1607, she entered Jahangir's court as a lady-in-waiting. Four years later Jahangir married her. Thereafter she was known first as **Nur Mahal** ('Light of the Palace'), later being promoted to **Nur Jahan** ('Light of the World'), see page 271. Her niece Mumtaz married Shah Jahan

The plan
Nur Jahan built the tomb for her father in the *char bagh* that he himself had laid out. It is beautifully conceived in white marble, mosaic and lattice. There is a good view from the roof of the entrance.

Marble screens of geometric lattice work permit soft lighting of the inner chamber. The yellow marble caskets appear to have been carved out of wood. On the engraved walls of the chamber is the recurring theme of a wine flask with snakes as handles – perhaps a reference by Nur Jahan, the tomb's creator, to her husband Jahangir's excessive drinking. Stylistically, the tomb marks a change from the sturdy and manly buildings of Akbar's reign to softer, more feminine lines. The main chamber, **Pietra dura**, richly decorated with mosaics and semi-precious stones inlaid in the white marble, contains the tomb of I'timad-ud-Daulah ('Pillar of the goverment') and his wife. Some have argued that the concept and skill must have travelled from its European home of 16th-century Florence to India. However,Florentine *pietra dura* is figurative whereas the Indian version is essentially decorative and can be seen as a refinement of its Indian predecessor, the patterned mosaic. See also page 107.

Sikandra

① *Sunrise-sunset. Indians Rs 10, foreigners Rs110, includes still camera, video Rs 25.*
Akbar's tomb Following the Timurid tradition, Akbar (ruled 1556-1605) had started to

completed it in 1613. The result is an impressive, large but architecturally confused tomb. A huge gateway, the **Buland Darwaza**, leads to the great garden enclosure, where spotted deer run free on the immaculate lawns. The decoration on the gateway is strikingly bold, with its large mosaic patterns, a forerunner of the *pietra dura* technique. The white minarets atop the entrance were an innovation which reappear, almost unchanged, at the Taj Mahal. The walled garden enclosure is laid out in the *char bagh* style, with the mausoleum at the centre.

❣ Morning is the best time to visit when few others are likely to be around.

A broad paved path leads to the 22.5-m high tomb with four storeys. The lowest storey, nearly 100 m sq and 9-m high, contains massive cloisters. The entrance on the south side leads to the tomb chamber. Shoes must be removed or cloth overshoes worn; hire Rs 2. In a niche opposite the entrance is an alabaster tablet inscribed with the 99 divine names of Allah. The sepulchre is in the centre of the room, whose velvety darkness is pierced by a single slanting shaft of light from a high window. The custodian, in expectation of a donation, makes 'Akbaaarrrr' echo around the chamber.

Four kilometres south of Sikandra, nearly opposite the high gateway of the ancient **Kach ki Sarai** building, is a sculptured horse, believed to mark the spot where Akbar's favourite horse died. There are also *kos minars* (marking a *kos*, about 4 km) and several other tombs on the way.

● Sleeping

Agra *p101, map p104 and p108*
Most hotels are 5-10 km from the airport and 2-5 km from Agra Cantt Railway.
LL Amar Vilas, Taj East Gate End, T0562-223 1515, www.oberoihotels.com. 105 rooms, all Taj-facing. Absolutely mind-blowing. The modern-day equivalent of the most luxurious of maharaja's palaces, designed in strict adherence to the Mughal style. The most stunning swimming pool, superb rooms, extraordinary ambience. Reports of inattentive service. Prices start at $350.
LL-AL Mughal Sheraton, Fatehabad Rd, T0562-233 1701, www.sheraton.com. 285 rooms in various stages of renovation. Building beautifully designed in the Mughal tradition but is now in need of a face lift. Suites are absolutely stunning. Low-rise construction means only rooftop observatory offers good views of the Taj. Even has a dog kennel!
L-AL Jaypee Palace, Fatehabad Rd, T0562-233 0800, www.jaypeehotels.com. 350 rooms, enormous place, a little soulless. Aimed mainly at conference crowd, it boasts a leisure mall featuring a 2-lane bowling alley.
L-AL Taj View , Fatehabad Rd, T0562-223 2400, www.tajhotels.com. 100 rooms, vastly improved since recent overhaul. Tasteful Mughal-style interiors, good pool and friendly staff. Recommended.

AL Trident (Oberoi), Fatehabad Rd, T0562-233 1818, www.tridenthotels.com. 143 very comfortable rooms, good pool, beautiful gardens, polite, friendly staff. Recommended.
A Ashok, 6B Mall Rd, T0562-236 1223, moonagra@yahoo.com. 58 rooms, extensive renovation to be finished by 2004 end, relaxing atmosphere, good restaurant, large pool, good value. Recommended.
A Clarks Shiraz, 54 Taj Rd, T0562-222 6121, www.hotelclarksshiraz.com. 237 rooms. Opened 42 years ago as Agra's first 5-star, starting to show its age but is set in pleasant grounds and has a good rooftop restaurant.
A Holiday Inn, Sanjay Place, MG Rd, T0562-252 3460, www.holiday-inn.com. 94 rooms (148 by end of 2004). Situated in heart of business district, standard 5-star fare.
A Mansingh Palace, 181/2 Fatehabad Rd, T0562-223 0202, www.mansinghhotels.com. 97 comfortable rooms, 4th floor awaiting refurbishment, rather soulless, attractive bar and pool, slightly stuffy staff.
B Atithi, Fatehabad Rd, T0562-223 0040, hotelatithi@hotmail.com. 44 clean a/c rooms, attractive pool, friendly management, good value.
B Deedar-e-Taj, Fatehabad Rd, T0562-309 0267, www.deedaretaj.net. 51 clean, good-sized rooms in modern, characterless

building. Has Agra's only revolving restaurant, novel but overpriced.

C Lauries, MG Rd, T0562-236 4536, lauries hotel@hotmail.com. 28 rooms in 1880 building rich in history, including a 1961 visit from Queen Elizabeth II. A little rundown these days but retains an elegant air, and is set in beautiful surroundings.

C Mayur Tourist Complex, Fatehabad Rd, T0562-233 2302, mayur268@rediffmail.com. 24 a/c rooms in slightly rundown bunga-lows. Built in 1976, decor unchanged since; funky but dated. Restaurant, beer-only bar, large pool, relaxing garden setting.

C-D Hotel Hilltop, 21 The Mall, T0562-222 6836. 28 rooms undergoing major refurbish-ment, those finished are clean, modern and good value. Also has extensive lawns, great for camping.

D Agra Hotel, 165 F.M. Cariappa Rd, T0562-363 331, agrahotel@yahoo.co.in. 18 rooms in 1926 'British-time' bungalow. Basic, old fashioned, good food, pleasant garden.

D Maya, near Taj West Gate, Fatehabad Rd, T0562-233 2109, magicinmaya@hotmail. com. 6 rooms, 6 more by 2004 end. Exceptionally clean and well-maintained, tastefully decorated, very friendly manager. Highly recommended.

D Rahi Tourist Bungalow (UP Tourism), Station Rd, opposite Raja-ki-Mandi station, T0562-215 0120, uptdc1@sancharnet.in. 35 clean, well-equipped rooms. Friendly staff, good option if location suits.

E Kamal, Taj South Gate, T0562-233 0126, hotelkamal@hotmail.com. 18 clean rooms in unattractive prison-style arrangement, friendly manager and staff plus a good view from rooftop restaurant.

E Hotel Sheela, East Gate, 2 mins walk from Taj, T0562-233 1194, www.hotelsheelaagra. com. 25 decent rooms with bath, pleasant garden, good restaurant, clean, peaceful, reliable laundry, secure (ask for gates to be unlocked for sunrise or else climb over spiked railings!), very helpful manager, excellent value (no commission to rickshaws), reserve ahead. Recommended.

E Tourists Rest House, Kutchery Rd, Balugunj, T0562-236 3961, dontworry chickencurry@hotmail.com. 28 clean rooms, some a/c, vegetarian restaurant, fairly basic, a bit dog-eared but knowledgeable manager runs a good show and knows it, often full. Offers popular 2 week trips to Rajasthan.

E-F Host, West Gate, T0562-233 1010. 15 clean rooms with bath and hot water, rooftop restaurant with great view of Taj, better option than the nearby Siddartha.

E-F Shah Jahan, South Gate T0562-223 1784, shahjahanhotel@yahoo.co.in. 24 clean rooms, 3 of them a/c and very modern. Rooftop restaurant with obscured Taj view.

F Youth Hostel, Sanjay Pl, MG Rd, T0562-65812. 4 double rooms, 2 singles, 6 dorms. Clean if a little drab, good value but long way from Taj. Usual YHA rules apply.

Eating

Agra *p101, map p104 and p108*
Amongst the hotels, the restaurants at the Clarks Shiraz and the Ashok have good reputations, see Sleeping for details. See also Amar Vilas below.

Amar Vilas, see Sleeping, is worth trying to get a table just to see the place, but do ring ahead to reserve.

Only, 45 Taj Rd, T0562-222 6834. Interesting menu, attractive outside seating, popular with tour groups, live entertainment.

Priya, near Trident Hotel, Fatehabad Rd, T0562-309 1957. Indian, Chinese, a/c, aimed

Taj Mahal & Taj Ganj

Yamuna River

Taj Mahal

Jawab

Local
Yamuna Kinara Rd

Shahjahan Park

To UP Tourist Office

Taj Rd

PURANI MANDI

TAJ GANJ

Dr Shyamal Marg

Fatehabad Rd

East & West Design

N

0 metres 200
0 yards 200

Sleeping 🛏
Host 2
Kamal 3
Shah Jahan 4
Sheela 5

Eating 🍴
Honey 1
Joney's Place 4
Shankara
Vegis 3
Yash Café 2

primarily at tour groups, food has good reputation but restaurant lacks atmosphere despite live music, singing and magic shows.
†† Riao, next to **Clarks Shiraz**, 44 Taj Rd, T0562-309 2928. Good North Indian food, great garden and attitude.
†† Shahi Dastarkhawan, Fatehabad Rd, T0562-309 2534. A famous Delhi eaterie. Strictly for meat-lovers, a great range of Mughlai delicacies, ambience less special.
†† Sonam, 51 Taj Rd. Indian, Chinese. A/c, good food, well-stocked bar, large garden, popular with locals.
†† Tin Tin, near Taj. Chinese. Friendly owners.
† Daawat, Fatehabad Rd. Indian. Beer.
† Dasaprakash, Meher Theatre Complex, 1 Gwalior Rd, T0562-236 3535. Comprehensive range of South Indian offerings, *thalis* a speciality. Slightly sterile interior.
† Joney's Place, the original and, despite numerous similarly-named imitators, still the best. Tiny place but the food is consistently good, and Joney's ability to produce Israeli and even Korean specialities is amazing. Recommended.
† Lucky, near Taj, good food, seasoned to your taste, pleasant, friendly.
† Maya, near Taj West Gate, Fatehabad Rd, T0562-233 2109. Varied menu, good Punjabi *thalis*, pasta, 'special tea', friendly, prompt service, hygienic, tasty, Moroccan style decor. Recommended.
† Shankara Vegis, Taj Ganj, vegetarian as name implies, food prepared in reassuringly clean, open kitchen. Rooftop seats have obscured view of Taj, vies with **Joney's Place** for claim to best lassi in Agra.
† Shivam, in **Raj Hotel** near Taj south gate. Quality Indian, clean.
† Yash Café, Indian/Western menu, cheap but freshly prepared, malai kofta very tasty.
† Zorba the Buddha, E-19 Sadar Bazaar, T0562-222 6091, zorbaevergreen@yahoo. com. Run by disciples of Osho, one of India's more popular, and most libidinous, gurus. Unusual menu (in a good way), naan breads a speciality, very clean , undersize furniture gives doll's house feel, an enjoyably quirky experience, opens 1200-1500, 1800-2100.

Cafes
Café Coffee Day, A7 Sadar Bazaar. Part of nationwide chain, good coffee and western snacks, nice escape.

Park, Taj Rd, Sadar Bazaar. Standard North Indian menu, decor and service above average.

O Shopping

Agra *p101, map p104 and p108*
Many rickshaws, taxi drivers and guides earn up to 40 per cent commission by taking tourists to shops. Insist on not being rushed away from sights. To shop, go independently. To get a good price you have to bargain hard anyway.

Agra specializes in jewellery, inlaid and carved marble, carpets and clothes. The main shopping areas are Sadar Bazar (closed Tue), Kinari Bazar, Gwalior Rd, Mahatma Gandhi Rd and Pratap Pura. Beware, you may order a carpet or an inlaid marble piece and have it sent later but it may not be what you ordered. Never agree to any export 'deals' and take great care with credit card slips (fiddles reported).

Carpets
Silk/cotton/wool mix hand knotted carpets and woven *dhurries* are all made in Agra. High quality and cheaper than in Delhi.
Kanu Carpet Factory, Purani Mandi, Fetehabad Rd, T0562-233 1307. A reliable source.
Mughal Arts Emporium, Shamshabad Rd. Also has marble. Artificial silk is sometimes passed off as pure silk.

Handlooms and handicrafts
State Government emporia in arcade at Taj entrance.
UP Handlooms and **UPICA** at Sanjay Place, Hari Parbat.

Marble
Delicately inlaid marble work is a speciality. Sometimes cheaper alabaster and soapstone is used and quality varies.
Akbar International, Fatehabad Rd. Good selection, inlay demonstration, fair prices.
Handicrafts Inn, 3 Gorg Niketan, Fatehabad Rd, Taj Ganj.
Oswal, 30 Munro Rd, Sadar Bazar, T0562-363240. Watch craftsmen working here, or at **Krafts Palace**, 506 The Mall.
UP Handicrafts Palace, 49 Bansal Nagar. Very wide selection from table tops to coasters, high quality and good value.

⊖ Transport

Agra *p101, map p104 and p108*
Air
Kheria airport is 7 km from city centre.
Transport to town: airport bus to/from major
hotels; auto-rickshaws charge about Rs 50;
Taxis, Rs 75. **Indian Airlines**, Clarks Shiraz,
222 6820, airport 230 2274. Daily flights to
Delhi. Long delays in flight departures and
arrivals possible especially in winter when
Agra and Delhi airports close for periods due
to fog.

Auto rickshaw
Point-to-point rates, eg Idgah Bus Stand to
Taj Ganj Rs 40.

Bus
Local City Bus Service covers most areas.
Plenty leave from the Taj Mahal area and the
Fort Bus Stand. Buses also go to main sites.
Long distance Most buses from Jaipur go
on to a second stop near **Hotel Sakura**:
closer to most hotels and where there is less
hassle from touts; auto from first stop to Taj
Ganj, Rs 25. **UPSRTC Roadways**, Bus Stand,
Idgah, enquiry T0562-2363 588; **Fort Bus
Station** (opposite **Power House**), T2360 948;
Ram Bagh Crossing (across river Yamuna).
Deluxe buses from **Hotel Sheetal**, T236 9420.
Delhi from tourist office, 0700, 1445, Deluxe,
4 hrs. Most long distance services leave from
the **Idgah Bus Stand** including daily Express
buses to: **Fatehpur Sikri** (40 km away, about
an hour). Others hourly, (1 hr), very bumpy.

Cycle rickshaw
Negotiate (pay more to avoid visiting shops);
Taj Ganj to fort Rs 10; Rs 75-100 for visiting
sights, PO, bank etc; Rs 150 for 10 hrs.

Motorbike/bicycle hire
Firoz Motorcycle House, Cariappa Rd,
Enfield Bullets Rs 500 per day. Bike hire from
Sadar Bazar, near Police station and near
Tourist Rest House, Rs 20 per day.

Taxi/car hire
Tourist taxis from travel agents, remarkably
good value for visiting nearby sights.
Non-a/c car Rs 3 per km, full day Rs 400
(100 km), half day Rs 200 (45 km); a/c rates
approximately double; to Fatehpur Sikri
about Rs 650 return). **Budget** Rent-a-car,
T0562-361771; **UP Tours**, T0562-351720.

Train
Train travel from Delhi is quicker and more
reliable. Information and reservations: **Agra
Cantt Railway Station**, enquiries T131,
reservations T0562-236 4244, open
0800-2000. Foreigners' queue at Window 1.
Pre-paid taxi/auto rickshaw kiosk outside
the station. Railway Stations: **Agra Cantt**,
T131, T0562-236 4516; **Agra Fort**, T132,
T0562-236 9590.Trains mentioned arrive and
depart from Agra Cantt southwest of the
city, about 5 km from the Taj Mahal. From
New Delhi: best is *Shatabdi Exp, 2002*, 0600,
2¼ hrs (meals included); *Punjab Mail, 2138*,
0530, 3 hrs; *Kerala Exp, 2626*, 1130, 2¾ hrs;
from **New Delhi (HN)**: *Taj Exp, 2180*, 0715,
2½ hrs; *Lakshadweep Exp, 2618*, 0955, 2½ hrs;
Gondwana Exp, 2412, 1430, 2½ hrs; *Goa Exp,
2780*, 1500, 2½ hrs; *Mahakoshal Exp, 1450*,
1620, 3 hrs. To **New Delhi**: *Shatabdi Exp,
2001*, 2018, 2½ hrs; to **New Delhi (HN)**:
Intercity Exp, 1103, 0600, 3½ hrs (2nd class
only); *Taj Exp, 2179*, 1835, 3¼ hrs (CC/II). To
Jaipur *Howrah-Jodhpur/Bikaner Exp, 2307*,
2000, 8 hrs (from Fort); *Marudhar Exp,
4853/63*, 0715, 6¾ hrs. *Mumbai (CST)*: *Punjab
Mail, 2138*, 0830, 23¼ hrs. **Sawai Madho-
pore** (for Ranthambore) at 0600, 0900, 1800.

⊕ Directory

Agra *p101, map p104 and p108*
Banks Andhra Bank, Taj Rd, opposite
Kwality's gives cash against card. **Canara**,
Sadar Bazar and Sanjay Place, and others.
Internet The Mall (24 hrs). At Taj Mahal
and elsewhere, 1000-1700, closed Sun.
Khurana Cyber Café, 805 Sadar Bazar,
opposite Cantt Hospital, T0562-291562.
Hospital/Doctor District, Chhipitola
Rd/MG Rd, T0562-236 3043. Dr VN, Kaushal,
opposite Imperial Cinema, T0562-236 3550.
Recommended.
Post office GPO opposite India Tourist
Office, with **Poste Restante**.
Useful addresses Ambulance: T202. **Fire:**
T201. **Police:** T200.

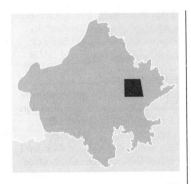

Jaipur	114
Listings	123
Around Jaipur	131
Amber	131
Jaigarh Fort	133
Jal Mahal and Gaitore	133
Sanganer	133
Choki Dhani	134
Sisodia Rani-ka and Vidyadhar baghs	134
Ramgarh Lake and Jamwa Sanctuary	134
Bagru	134
Madhogarh	135
Samode	135
Listings	135

❢ Footprint features

Don't miss	111
Devotion across the seas	119
The Jaipur foot	120
A prayer for a good husband	126

Introduction

The bustle of **Jaipur**, the capital of Rajasthan and the state's most visited city, is at stark contrast to the tranquillity of the area surrounding it. Jaipur has much to offer, but can be something of an assault on your defences; touts prey on new arrivals to make visiting the city's attractions sometimes as much an exercise in refusal as perusal. Having savoured its sights, you might therefore appreciate the opportunity to escape the city, and won't need to go far to find perfect places to unwind. There are hunting lodges, palaces and forts in almost every direction, many set in relaxing rural surroundings and perfectly equipped to refresh and revive the city's sated sightseers.

The fortifications which stride across the arid ridges above Jaipur, including the stunningly situated **Amber Fort**, are a reminder of the fiercely contested political history of northern Rajasthan. Yet alongside its status as a battleground, its dry hills and sometimes fertile valleys have also seen great prosperity, reflected in the palaces and country houses of the maharajas and the remarkable painted houses and *havelis*. The inimitable **Samode Palace** is rich with living reminders of past wealth and culture.

★ Don't miss...

1. **Tiger Fort at sunset** A great place to watch the sun go down over the 'pink city', page 121.

2. **Rambagh Palace, Samode Haveli or Diggi Palace** Any Maharaja who was anyone in Rajasthan had a palace in Jaipur, and many are now beautiful hotels – your chance to live like a king, page 123.

3. **Raj Mandir cinema** Get a taste of Bollywood in this fabulous pink picturehouse, page 127.

4. **Heritage Walk** Take this walk, or simply lose yourself in the bustling backstreets of the Old City, page 129.

5. **Ramgarh Lake** Escape from it all at this tranquil lake, 35 km and another world away from Jaipur, page 134.

6. **Samode Palace** Marvel at the majesty of Samode Palace, one of the world's top hotels, page 135.

7. **Polo** Catch a game of polo, the centre of Jaipur's social scene, page 136.

Jaipur & around

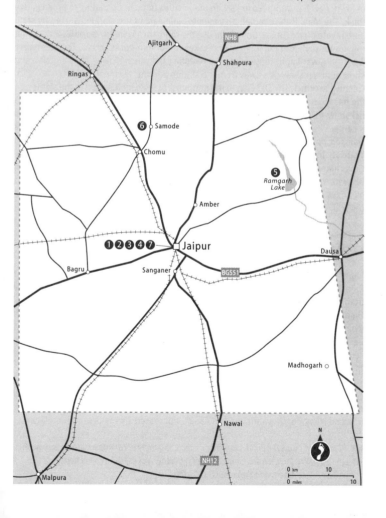

Jaipur → *Phone code: 0141. Colour map 2, grid C6. Population: 2,600,000.*

Jaipur, the 'pink city' and gateway to Rajasthan for many visitors, is home to some of the state's best hotels and services, but also many of its most persistent touts. Its position on the popular 'Golden Triangle' route of Delhi-Agra-Jaipur-Delhi ensures a steady stream of tourists; meaning that the town has to do little to attract visitors. Its historical monuments, although impressive, have been poorly looked after of late and it's not as pink a city as it once was, but still merits a stopover en route to the numerous attractions which surround it. The Old City, with its bazars, palaces and havelis, as well as a couple of forts and the ancient city of Amber nearby, are well worth exploring.
▶▶ *For Sleeping, Eating and other listings, see pages 123-131.*

Ins and outs

Getting there Sanganer Airport, 15 km south of town, has flights from Ahmadabad, Aurangabad, Delhi, Jodhpur, Mumbai, Rajkot and Udaipur. Airport buses, taxis and auto-rickshaws take about 30 minutes to the centre. The railway station, to the west of town, now has improved links with major cities through upgrading to broad gauge track. The Main Bus Terminal, a 15-minute walk east of the station, is used by state and private buses. Buses from Delhi use the dramatically improved NH8, India's first toll 'motorway', and the journey now takes under four hours by car. The alternative Gurgaon-Alwar-Jaipur route is more interesting but much slower. Most hotels are a short auto-rickshaw ride away from the station and bus terminal.

Getting around The Old City, to the northeast of town, holds most of the sights and the bazar within its walls. It's best explored on foot, although you may want to hire a rickshaw to get there. The sprawling new town has spread out dramatically over recent years leaving its few attractions best explored by rickshaw, bus or taxi. ▶▶ *See Transport, page 129, for further details.*

Tourist information Tourist offices are closed on second Sat of month. **Government of India,** To141 511 0591, and **Hotel Khasa Kothi. Rajasthan,** Paryatan Bhavan, **Tourist Hotel,** MI Road, To141 2365256. Counters at railway station, To141 231 5714 and Central Bus Stand. Guides for four to eight hours, about Rs 250-400 (Rs 100 extra for French, German, Japanese, Spanish).

History

Jaipur (City of Victory) was founded in 1727 by **Maharaja Jai Singh II**, a Kachhawaha Rajput, who ruled from 1699-1744. He had inherited a kingdom under threat not only from the last great Mughal Emperor Aurangzeb, but also from the Maratha armies of Gujarat and Maharashtra. Victories over the Marathas and diplomacy with Aurangzeb won back the favour of the ageing Mughal, so that the political stability that Maharaja Jai Singh was instrumental in creating was protected, allowing him to pursue his scientific and cultural interests. Jaipur is very much a product of his intellect and talent. A story relates an encounter between the **Emperor Aurangzeb** and the 10-year-old Rajput prince. When asked what punishment he deserved for his family's hostility and resistance to the Mughals, the boy answered "Your Majesty, when the groom takes the bride's hand, he confers lifelong protection. Now that the Emperor has taken my hand, what have I to fear?". Impressed by his tact and intelligence,

● *In Jai Singh's day, the buildings were painted in a variety of colours, including grey with*
● *white borders. Pink, a traditional colour of welcome, was used in 1853 in honour of the visit by Prince Albert, and the colour is still used.*

Aurangzeb bestowed the title of *Sawai* (one and a quarter) on him, signifying that he would be a leader.

Jai Singh loved mathematics and science. A brilliant Brahmin scholar, Vidyadhar Bhattacharya from Bengal, helped him to design the city. Jai Singh also studied ancient texts on astronomy, had the works of Ptolemy and Euclid translated into Sanskrit, and sent emissaries to Samarkand to inform him on Mirza Beg's 1425 observatory, building masonry observatories at Delhi, Varanasi, Ujjain and Mathura, and most impressively at Jaipur. Work began in 1727 and it took four years to build the main palaces, central square and principal roads. The layout of streets was based on a mathematical grid of nine squares representing the ancient Hindu map of the universe, with the sacred Mount Meru, home of Siva, occupying the central square. In Jaipur the royal palace is at the centre. The three by three square grid was modified by relocating the northwest square in the southeast, allowing the hill fort of Nahargar (Tiger Fort) to overlook and protect the capital. The surrounding hills also provided good defence. At the southeast and southwest corners of the city were squares with pavilions and ornamental fountains. Water for these was provided by an underground aqueduct with outlets for public use along the streets. The main streets are 33-yards wide (33 is auspicious in Hinduism); the lesser ones are graded in width down to 4 m, all being in proportion to one another. The sidewalks were deliberately wide to promote the free flow of pedestrian traffic and the shops were also a standard size. Built with ancient Hindu rules of town planning in mind, Jaipur was advanced for its time. Yet many of its buildings suggest a decline in architectural power and originality. The architectural historian, Giles Tillotson, argues that even in the earliest of them "traditional architectural details lack vigour and depth and are also flattened so that they become relief sculpture on the building's surface, and sometimes they are simply drawn on in white outline".

In addition to its original buildings, Jaipur has a number of examples of late 19th-century public and private buildings which marked an attempt to revive Indian architectural skills. A key figure in this movement was **Sir Samuel Swinton Jacob**, who transferred from the army to the Public Works Department and in 1867 he became Executive Engineer to the Maharaja of Jaipur, living there until 1902. A school of art was founded in 1866 by a group of English officers employed by Maharaja Sawai Madho Singh II (ruled 1880-1922) to encourage an interest in Indian tradition and its development. In February 1876 the Prince of Wales visited Jaipur, and work on the **Albert Hall**, now the Central Museum, was begun to a design of Jacob. It was the first of a number of construction projects in which Indian craftsmen and designers were actively employed in both building and design. This ensured that the Albert Hall was an extremely striking building in its own right, but it was not simply a British Indo-Saracenic building of the type becoming popular elsewhere in India. A number of crafts were revived, a process fostered by the 1883 Jaipur Exhibition which attracted over 250,000 visitors. The opportunities for training provided under Jacob's auspices encouraged a new school of Indian architects and builders. One of the best examples of their work is the **Mubarak Mahal** (1900), now Palace Museum, designed by Lala Chiman Lal.

Sights

Hawa Mahal

ⓘ *Rs 5; cameras Rs 30, video Rs70, 1000-1630, closed Fri, enter from Tripolia Bazar (west of the GPO); for best views accept invitation from shop owners on upper floors across the street.*

The 'Palace of the Winds' (circa 1799) forms part of the east wall of the City Palace complex and is best seen from the street outside. Possibly Jaipur's most famous building, this pink sandstone façade of the palace was built for the ladies of the harem by Sawai Pratap Singh. The five storeys stand on a high podium with an

Jaipur

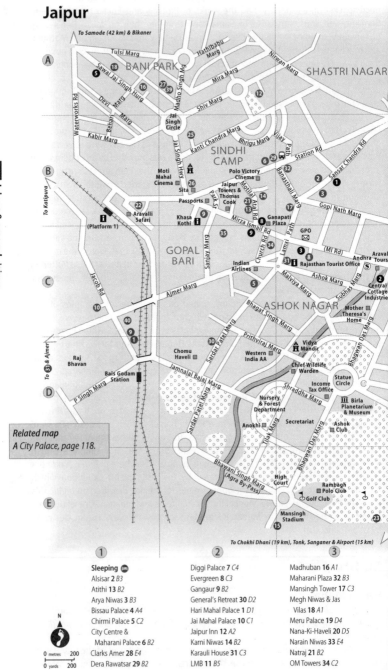

Related map
A City Palace, page 118.

N

0 metres 200
0 yards 200

Sleeping	Diggi Palace **7** *C4*	Madhuban **16** *A1*
Alsisar **2** *B3*	Evergreen **8** *C3*	Maharani Plaza **32** *B3*
Atithi **13** *B2*	Gangaur **9** *B2*	Mansingh Tower **17** *C3*
Arya Niwas **3** *B3*	General's Retreat **30** *D2*	Megh Niwas & Jas
Bissau Palace **4** *A4*	Hari Mahal Palace **1** *D1*	Vilas **18** *A1*
Chirmi Palace **5** *C2*	Jai Mahal Palace **10** *C1*	Meru Palace **19** *D4*
City Centre &	Jaipur Inn **12** *A2*	Nana-Ki-Haveli **20** *D5*
Maharani Palace **6** *B2*	Karni Niwas **14** *B2*	Narain Niwas **33** *E4*
Clarks Amer **28** *E4*	Karauli House **31** *C3*	Natraj **21** *B2*
Dera Rawatsar **29** *B2*	LMB **11** *B5*	OM Towers **34** *C2*

Jaipur & around Jaipur

4

Pearl Palace **35** *C2*
Rajasthan Palace **37** *E5*
Raj Palace **36** *A6*
Rajputana Palace
 Sheraton **22** *B1*
Rajvilas **38** *C6*
Rambagh Palace **23** *E3*
Sajjan Niwas **39** *A2*
Samode Haveli **42** *E6*
Santha Bagh **24** *E4*

5

Shahar Palace **40** *C1*
Shivam **25** *B2*
Teej Tourist Bungalow **26** *B2*
Trident **41** *A6*
Umaid Bhawan **27** *A2*
Youth Hostel **15** *E2*

Eating
Barista **2** *C3*
Chaitanya **1** *B3*

6

Copper Chimney & Handi **3** *C3*
Mehfil **5** *A1*
Niros & Book Corner **7** *C4*
Pizza Hut, Suriya India &
 Rajasthan Travels **8** *B2*
Spice Court **9** *C2*
Surya Mahal, Bookshop
 & Natras **10** *C4*

to circulate and allowed the ladies who were secluded in the *zenana* to watch processions below without being seen. The museum has second-century BC utensils and old sculpture.

The City Palace (1728-1732)

ⓘ *0930-1700 (last entry 1630). Rs 35 (camera Rs50 extra), foreigners Rs180 (includes still camera), includes Sawai Man Singh II Museum and Jaigarh Fort, valid for 2 days. Video (unnecessary) Rs 200; doorkeepers expect tips when photographed. Photography in galleries prohibited, only of façades allowed.*

The City Palace occupies the centre of Jaipur, covers one seventh of its area and is surrounded by a high wall – the *Sarahad*. Its style differs from conventional Rajput fort palaces in its separation of the palace from its fortifications, which in other Rajput buildings are integrated in one massive interconnected structure. In contrast the Jaipur Palace has much more in common with Mughal models, with its main buildings scattered in a fortified campus. To find the main entrance, from the Hawa Mahal go north about 250 m along the Sireh Deori Bazar past the Town Hall (Vidhan Sabha) and turn left through an arch – the *Sireh Deori* (boundary gate). Pass under a second arch – the *Naqqar Darwaza* (drum gate) – into Jaleb Chowk, the courtyard which formerly housed the Palace guard. Today it is where coaches park. This is surrounded by residential quarters which were modified in the 19th century under Sawai Ram Singh II. A gateway to the south leads to the Jantar Mantar, the main palace buildings and museum and the Hawa Mahal.

Mubarak Mahal The main entrance leads into a large courtyard at the centre of which is the Mubarak Mahal, faced in white marble. Built in 1890, originally as a guest house for the Maharaja, the Mubarak Mahal is a small but immaculately conceived two-storeyed building, designed on the same cosmological plan in miniature as the city itself – a square divided into a 3 x 3 square grid, see page 115.

The **Textile and Costume Museum** on the first floor has fine examples of fabrics and costumes from all over India, including some spectacular wedding outfits, as well as musical instruments and toys from the royal nursery. In the northwest corner of the courtyard is the **Armoury Museum** containing an impressive array of weaponry – pistols, blunderbusses, flintlocks, swords, rifles and daggers, as well as some fascinating paintings on the way in. This was originally the common room of the

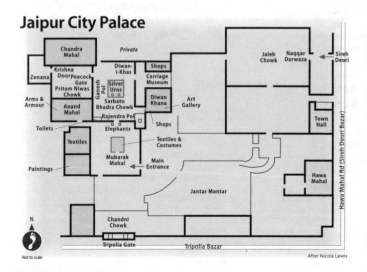

Jaipur City Palace

Not to scale

After Nicola Lewis

Devotion across the seas

The present maharaja's grandfather was an extremely devout Hindu. Any physical contact with a non-Hindu was deemed to be ritually defiling, so contact with the British carried awkward ritual problems. Whenever required to meet a British official, including the Viceroy, the maharaja would wear white gloves, and after any meeting would ritually purify himself in a bath of Ganga water and have the clothes he wore burnt. When he went to England to celebrate Queen Victoria's Diamond Jubilee Sawai Madho Singh had a P&O liner refitted to include a Krishna temple and carried sufficient Ganga water with him in two 309 kg silver urns, the largest in the world and currently on display in Jaipur's City Palace, to last the trip.

harem. From the north facing first floor windows you can get a view of the Chandra Mahal (see below). Just outside the Armoury Museum is **Rajendra Pol**, a gate flanked by two elephants, each carved from a single block of marble, which leads to the inner courtyard. There are beautifully carved alcoves with delicate arches and *jali* screens and a fine pair of patterned brass doors.

Diwan-i-Khas (Sarbato Bhadra) The gateway leads to the courtyard known variously as the Diwan-i-Am, the Sarbato Bhadra or the Diwan-i-Khas Chowk. Today, the building in its centre is known as the Diwan-i-Khas (circa 1730). Originally the Diwan-i-Am, it was reduced to the hall of private audience (Diwan-i-Khas) when the new Diwan-i-Am was built to its southeast at the end of the 18th century. The courtyard itself reflects the overwhelming influence of Mughal style, despite the presence of some Hindu designs, a result of the movement of Mughal-trained craftsmen from further north in search of opportunities to practise their skills. In the Diwan-i-Khas (now known by the Sanskrit name Sarbato Bhadra) are two huge silver urns, ratified by Guiness as being the largest pieces of silver in the world, used by Sawai Madho Singh for carrying Ganga water to England, see box.

Diwan-i-Am (Diwan Khana) Art Gallery Entered in the southeast corner of the Diwan-i-Am courtyard, the 'new' Hall of Public Audience built by Maharaja Sawai Pratap Singh (1778-1803) today houses a fine collection of Persian and Indian miniatures, some of the carpets the maharajas had made for them and an equally fine collection of manuscripts. To its north is the Carriage Museum, housed in a modern building. In the middle of the west wall of the Diwan-i-Am courtyard, opposite the art gallery, is the **Ganesh Pol**, which leads via a narrow passage and the Peacock Gate into **Pritam Niwas Chowk**. This courtyard has the original palace building 'Chandra Mahal' to its north, the *zenana* on its northwest, and the Anand Mahal to its south. Several extremely attractive doors, rich and vivid in their peacock blue, aquamarine and amber colours, have small marble Hindu gods watching over them.

Chandra Mahal Built between 1727 and 1734 the Moon Palace is the earliest building of the palace complex. Externally it appears to have seven storeys, though inside the first and second floors are actually one high-ceilinged hall. The two top floor storeys give superb views of the city and Tiger Fort. On the ground floor (north) a wide verandah – the **Pritam Niwas** (House of the beloved) – with Italian wall paintings, faces the formal Jai Niwas garden. The main section of the ground floor is an Audience Hall. The place is not always open to visitors.

The Jaipur foot

The 'Jaipur foot' may sound like an affliction, but for thousands it represents a miraculous cure to the problems of living with an amputated leg. Artificial feet were available long before orthopaedic surgeons in Jaipur began to work on a local solution to a specifically Indian problem. For while the surgeons had been fitting high quality western-designed artificial feet for some time, they found that patients would frequently give them up and return to crutches. They couldn't use the rigid wooden foot supplied, which had been designed to fit inside shoes and failed to meet the needs for flexibility essential for sitting cross-legged or for walking across fields and village tracks. The answer was to adapt the foot with local skills and technology and a highly resilient, flexible and lightweight foot was developed. The work has been one of the many social service projects undertaken by the Bhagwan Mahaveer Viklang Sahayata Samiti voluntary body to help people irrespective of caste, religion or politics. (Those interested may contact SMS Hospital, Jaipur.) Patients arrive at Jaipur from all over India, but the society now organizes camps in many parts of the country. The Rotary Jaipur Limb Project, started in UK in 1984 raises money to help establish Limb Camps in India and elsewhere.

The hall on the first (and second) floors, the **Sukh Niwas** (House of pleasure), underwent a Victorian reconstruction, above which are the **Rang Mandir** and the **Sobha Niwas**, built to the same plan. The two top storeys are much smaller, with the mirror palace of the **Chavi Niwas** succeeded by the small open marble pavilion which crowns the structure, the **Mukat Niwas**.

In the northeast corner of the Pritam Niwas Chowk, leading into the *zenana*, is the **Krishna door**, its surface embossed with scenes of the deity's life. The door is sealed in the traditional way with a rope sealed with wax over the lock.

Govind Deo Temple and beyond North of the Chandra Mahal, the early 18th-century Govind Deo Temple, which was probably built as a residence, has been restored by an ancient technique using molasses, curd, coconut water, fenugreek, rope fibres and lime, but is again not always open to visitors. The furniture is European – Bohemian glass chandeliers – the decoration Indian. Following the steps around you will see a *mandala* (circular diagram of the cosmos), made from rifles around the royal crest of Jaipur. The ceiling of this hall is in finely worked gold. Further on are the beautiful Mughal style fountains and the **Jai Niwas gardens** (1727), laid out as a *char bagh*, the **Badal Mahal** (circa 1750) and the **Tal Katora** tank. The view extends across to the maharaja's private Krishna temple and beyond the compound walls to the Nahargarh (Tiger Fort) on the hills beyond.

Jantar Mantar (Observatory)
ⓘ *1000-1630, Rs 10 (Mon free), camera Rs 50, video Rs 100 (stills better).*

Literally 'Instruments for measuring the harmony of the heavens', the Jantar Mantar was built between 1728 and 1734. Jai Singh wanted things on a grand scale and chose stone with a marble facing on the important planes. Each instrument serves a particular function and each gives an accurate reading. Hindus believe that their fated souls move to the rhythms of the universe, and the matching of horoscopes is still an essential part in the selection of partners for marriage. Astrologers occupy an important place in daily life and are consulted for all important occasions and decision-making. The

the instruments. There is little shade so avoid the middle of the day.

Moving clockwise you will see the following instruments or **yantras**:

1 Small 'Samrat' is a large sundial (the triangular structure) with flanking quadrants marked off in hours and minutes. The arc on your left shows the time from sunrise to midday, the one on the right midday to sundown. Read the time where the shadow is sharpest. The dial gives solar time, so to adjust it to Indian Standard Timebetween one minute 15 seconds and 32 minutes must be added according to the time of year and solar position as shown on the board.

2 'Dhruva' locates the position of the Pole Star at night and those of the 12 zodiac signs. The graduation and lettering in Hindi follows the traditional unit of measurement based on the human breath calculated to last six seconds. Thus: four breaths = one *pala* (24 seconds), 60 palas = one *gati* (24 minutes), 60 gatis = one day (24 hours).

3 'Narivalya' has two dials: south facing for when the sun is in the southern hemisphere (21 September-21 March) and north facing for the rest of the year. At noon the sun falls on the north-south line.

4 The Observer's Seat was intended for Jai Singh.

5 Small 'Kranti' is used to measure the longitude and latitude of celestial bodies.

6 'Raj' (King of Instruments) is used once a year to calculate the Hindu calendar, which is based on the Jaipur Standard as it has been for 270 years. A telescope is attached over the central hole. The bar at the back is used for sighting, while the plain disk is used as a blackboard to record observations.

7 'Unnathamsa' is used for finding the altitudes of the celestial bodies. Round-the-clock observations can be made and the sunken steps allow any part of the dial to be read.

8 'Disha' points to the north.

9 'Dakshina', a wall aligned north-south, is used for observing the position and movement of heavenly bodies when passing over the meridian.

10 Large 'Samrat' is similar to the small one (1) but ten times larger and thus accurate to two seconds instead of 20 seconds. The sundial is 27.4-m high. It is used on a particularly holy full moon in July/August, to predict the length and heaviness of the monsoon for the local area.

11 'Rashivalayas' has 12 sundials for the signs of the zodiac and is similar to the Samrat yantras. The five at the back (north to south), are Gemini, Taurus, Cancer, Virgo and Leo. In front of them are Aries and Libra, and then in the front, again (north-south), Aquarius, Pisces, Capricorn, Scorpio and Sagittarius. The instruments enable readings to be made at the instant each zodiacal sign crosses the meridian.

12 'Jai Prakash' acts as a double check on all the other instruments. It measures the rotation of the sun, and the two hemispheres together form a map of the heavens. The small iron plate strung between crosswires shows the sun's longitude and latitude and which zodiacal sign it is passing through.

13 Small 'Ram' is a smaller version of the Jai Prakash Yantra (12).

14 Large 'Ram Yantra' Similarly, this finds the altitude and the azimuth (arc of the celestial circle from Zenith to horizon).

15 'Diganta' also measures the azimuth of any celestial body.

16 Large 'Kranti'is similar to the smaller Kranti (5).

Nahargarh (Tiger Fort)

ⓘ *1000-1630, Rs 5, camera Rs 30, video Rs70.*

The small fort with its immense walls and bastions stands on a sheer rock face. The city at its foot was designed to give access to the fort in case of attack. To get there on foot you have to first walk through some quiet and attractive streets at the base of the hill, then 2 km up a steep, rough winding path to reach the top. Alternatively, it can also be reached by road via Jaigarh Fort. Beautifully floodlit at night, it dominates the skyline by day. Much of the original fort (1734) is in ruins but the walls and 19th-century additions survive, including rooms furnished for maharajas. This is a 'real fort', quiet and unrushed, and well worth visiting for the breathtaking views, to look inside the buildings and to walk around the battlements. Women alone may feel vulnerable here. If you fancy a snack **Durg Café** has good views and sells quite reasonable snacks, drinks and chilled beer but service is slow for meals. **Padco Café**, on a terrace at the end of the ruins, has great views, not much in the way of food and drink but is one of the best spot's in Jaipur for a beer at sunset.

You can combine this visit with Jaigarh Fort, see page 133, 7 km away (part of the same defensive network), along the flat-topped hill. A good road, originally a military one, connects the two. A covered aqueduct brought water to Jaigarh over the same distance. Taxis are available or you can walk. It is also a pleasant rickshaw journey from Amber. Tell the auto-rickshaw driver if you want to go to the bottom of the footpath or to take the road to the top (much further and more expensive).

Central Museum and Modern Art Gallery
① *The museum is in the Albert Hall, 1000-1630, closed Fri, Rs 30 (Mon free); the gallery, Ravindra Rang Manch, 1000-1700, free, closed 2nd Sat of month and Sun; Zoological Garden 0900-1700, Rs100 foreigners, Rs10 Indians.*
Within the Ram Niwas Gardens you can visit the museum, gallery and a zoological garden. Housed in the beautiful Albert Hall is the **Central Museum**, displaying mainly excellent decorative metalware, miniature portraits and other art pieces. It also features Rajasthani village life – including some gruesome torture techniques – displayed through costumes, pottery, woodwork, brassware etc. The first floor displays are covered in dust and poorly labelled. The **Modern Art Gallery** has an interesting collection of contemporary Rajasthani art. Finally, in the gardens is the **Zoological Garden** containing lions, tigers, panthers, bears, crocodiles and deer, plus a bird park opposite.

SRC Museum of Indology
① *24 Gangwal Park, 0800-1800, Rs 35 (groups of 10, Rs 10 each).*
Further south, along J Nehru Marg, is the extraordinarily eclectic, and not a little quirky, SRC Museum of Indology. It houses a collection of folk and tantric art including all manner of manuscripts, textiles, paintings, Hindi written on a grain of rice, Sanskrit on a rabbit hair, fossils, medals, weapons and so on.

Birla Mandir
Something of an architectural curiosity, the modern temple built by the Birla family in the southeast of the city is impressive in scale and in the eclecticism of its religious art. The quality of the marble used can be seen in its near transparency.

Surya Mandir
① *Galta Pol can be reached by taking a bus, or by walking the 2 km from the Hawa Mahal. From there it is about 600 m uphill and then downhill.*
From Galta Pol take a walk to the 'Valley of the Monkeys', east of Jaipur, to get a view of the city from the Surya Mandir (Sun Temple). Walk down the steps from the top of the ridge to the five old temples dedicated to Rama-Sita and Radha-Krishna, which have some nice impressive wall paintings. You can watch hundreds of monkeys playing in the water tank below.

⬤ *For an explanation of sleeping and eating price codes used in this guide, see inside the front cover. Other relevant information is found in Essentials, see pages 40-45.*

⏺ Sleeping

Jaipur *p114, map p116*

If you are in need of a break from the pace and pollution of a large Indian city, see p135 for details of hotels around the city. That said there are some old, atmospheric options in Jaipur. The city's popularity has meant that foreigners are being targeted by hotel and shop touts, so you need to be on your guard. Auto-rickshaw drivers often get commission as hotel touts. MG Rd is Mahatma Gandhi Rd, MI Rd is Mirza Ismail Rd.

LL Rajvilas (Oberoi), slightly inconveniently situated 8 km from town on Goner Rd, T0141-268 0101, www.oberoihotels.com. This award-winning hotel is housed in a low-lying re-created fort-palace building situated within large, exquisitely landscaped gardens with orchards, pools and fountains. There are 71 rooms including 13 'tents' and 3 private villas with their own swimming pools! Room interiors are not especially imaginative, the 'tents' however are delightful. Bathrooms are particularly impressive throughout. There is also an ayurvedic spa in a restored *haveli*. The overall feel is of fantastic indulgence but slightly lacking in atmosphere.

LL-L Jai Mahal Palace (Taj), Jacob Rd, Civil Lines, T0141-222 3636, www.tajhotels.com. 100 rooms in 250-year old palace which has managed to maintain a real sense of authenticity. Bathrooms not as good as some but rooms are tastefully decorated and set in very attractive gardens. Swimming pool is particularly lovely.

LL-L Rambagh Palace (Taj), Bhawani Singh Rd, T0141-238 1919, www.tajhotels.com. 90 luxuriously appointed rooms arranged around a central courtyard in a former maharaja's palace, still feels like the real thing. Set in 47 acres of beautifully maintained garden, larger groups are invited to participate in elephant polo on the back lawn! Stunning indoor pool, but the real piece de resistance is the spectacular dining hall, reminiscent of Buckingham Palace. Pleasant, relaxed atmosphere, good food and friendly staff. Recommended.

L Rajputana Palace Sheraton (Welcom-group), Palace Rd, T0141-510 0100, www.welcomgroup.com. 216 rooms in low-rise, modern '*haveli*'-stylebuilding, starting to look a little worn. Rooms unexceptional, excellent bookshop, rather impersonal overall.

L Trident (Hilton), Amber Rd, opposite Jal Mahal, T0141-267 0101, www.trident-hilton.com. 138 modern, attractive rooms, overlooking lake or hills, fully equipped, excellent service. European feel to restaurant. Recommended.

LA Raj Palace (GKV Heritage), **Chomu Haveli**, Zorawar Singh Gate, Amer Rd, T0141-263 4077, www.rajpalace.com. 25 spacious suites with modern baths (extra bed US$15), 5-storeyed *haveli* (1728) with character carefully restored, traditional courtyard, Darbar Hall, garden, well managed, friendly service.

LA Mansingh Tower and **A Hotel Mansingh**, Sansar Chandra Rd, T0141-237 8771, www.mansinghhotels.com. Adjacent hotels owned by same group. Tower (45 rooms) modern, tastefully and imaginatively designed, **Hotel Mansingh** (95 rooms) older and less appealing. Reports of noise from top floor restaurant/nightclub.

A Clarks Amer, JL Nehru Marg, 8 km from centre, T0141-255 0616-19, www.hotelclarks.com. 197 rooms, , friendly, good shops, garden, food occasionally inspired. Rooftop bar very original and entirely unexpected, a real treat.

A Meru Palace, Sawai Ram Singh Rd, T0141-237 1111, merupalace@hotmail.com. Business hotel, 48 rooms, good veg restaurant, bar, exchange, marble building, friendly staff, not a palace but pleasant.

A Samode Haveli, Gangapol, Old City, T0141-263 2407, www.samode.com. 21 lovely rooms in charming, beautifully decorated 19th-century *haveli*. Magnificent dining room, great pool, friendly atmosphere, good rooftop views over city at dawn and sunset. Highly recommended, reservations essential.

B Alsisar Haveli, Sansar Chandra Rd, T0141-236 8290, www.alsisarhaveli.com. 36 intricately painted a/c rooms, modern frescoes, excellent conversion of 1890s character home, attractive courtyards, average food (try **Chaitanya** nearby, listed below), beautiful pool, village safaris, 'super-quiet', service variable.

B Bissau Palace, outside Chandpol Gate,

T0141-230 4371, www.bissaupalace.com. 45 a/c rooms, some charming, in the home of the Rawal of Bissau (built 1919) with library and royal museum, interesting 'memorabilia' and antiques, bookshop, pleasant front garden, good views from terrace of city and nearby forts, tours, excellent camel safaris, exchange etc from **Karwan Tours**, but temple music may irritate.

B Hari Mahal Palace (formerly **Achrol Lodge**), Jacob Rd, Civil Lines, T0141-222 6920, www.harimahalpalace.com. 11 large, quirky rooms with big bath tubs, period furniture in old mansion, large lawn, old world feel.

B Jas Vilas, next to Megh Niwas, C-9 Sawai Jai Singh Highway, Bani Park, T0141 2204638, www.jasvilas.com. An excellent family-run hotel. 9 a/c rooms with bath (tub, power shower), internet, delicious home-cooked meals, pool surrounded by a lawn, friendly family. Recommended.

B Karauli House, New Sanganer Rd, Sodala (towards the airport), T0141-221 1532, www.karauli.com. 6 rooms in a family 'retreat', large garden, pool, personal attention, home-cooked meals.

B LMB, JohariBazar, Old City, T0141-256 5844, info@lmbhotel.com. 33 centrally a/c rooms, currently undergoing wholesale renovation. New rooms are equipped with all mod cons and very comfy beds. Location convenient but can be noisy.

B Maharani Plaza, opposite Sindhi Camp Bus Stand, T0141-237 1717, www.maharani hotels.com. Better bet than nearby **Maharani Palace**. 53 modern rooms, clean and quiet, friendly management, small pool.

B Narain Niwas, Kanota Bagh, Narain Singh Rd, T0141-256 1291, www.hotelnarain niwas.com. 36 well presented rooms in characterful old mansion, great dining room and lounge, clean pool in beautiful gardens, patchy reports on food and service.

B Om Towers (Best Western), Church Rd, off MI Rd, T0141-236 6683, ommljaipur@yahoo. com. 58 ultra modern, international style rooms. Main draw is the revolving restaurant.

C Chirmi Palace Dhuleshwar Garden, Sardar Patel Marg, T0141-236 5063, www.chirmi. com. 23 spacious but variable a/c rooms in 150-year-old *haveli* conversion. Traditional Rajasthani decor, attractive dining room, lawns, pool (summer only), e-mail, gentle

staff, slightly run down but has a pleasant feel overall.

C Dera Rawatsar, D-194/C, Vijay Path, behind Sindhi Camp Bus Station, T0141-236 0717, www.derarawatsar.com. 7 rooms (more planned) in smart new premises, all done to a high standard. Family-run, has a homely feel and pleasant location.

C General's Retreat, 9 Sardar Patel Rd, T0141-237 7134. 8 rooms with bath, some with kitchenettes, attractive bungalow of a retired general, pleasant gardens, restaurant.

C Madhuban, D237 Behari Marg, Bani Park, T0141-220 0033, www.madhuban.net. Classy, characterful hotel, 25 beautifully furnished rooms, small pool, pleasant garden, helpful staff, good food. Recommended.

C Megh Niwas, C-9 Jai Singh Hwy, Bani Park, T0141-220 2034, www.meghniwas.com. 27 tastefully decorated,comfortable rooms, run by charming, knowledgeable family, good pool, excellent food, very soothing feel. Recommended.

C Nana-ki-Haveli, Fateh Tiba, Moti Dungri Rd, near Old City, T0141-261 5502, nanakihavelijaipur@yahoo.com. 12 spacious a/c rooms in a modernized 1918 garden house, very hospitable, friendly family, excellent home cooking. Recommended.

C Natraj, 20 Motilal Rd, T0141-236 1348, www.hotelnatraj.com. 20 large, clean, quirkily decorated rooms, good veg restaurant, piped muzak throughout.

C Santha Bagh, Kalyan Path, Narain Singh Rd, T0141-256 6790. 12 simple, comfortable rooms (a/c or air-cooled), very friendly, helpful and charming staff, excellent meals, lawn, quiet location. Recommended.

C Shahar Palace, Barwada Colony, Civil Lines, T0141-222 1861, www.shaharpalace.com. 6 rooms in a separate annexe of a relaxing residential home. Well maintained gardens, home-cooked food and friendly but discreet attention make this a soothing retreat. Recommended.

C Umaid Bhawan, D1-2A Bani Park, T0141-231 6184, www.umaidbhawan.com. 28 beautifully decorated and ornately furnished rooms, many with balconies, plus a lovely pool and friendly, knowledgeable owners. Recommended.

C-D Diggi Palace, SMS Hospital Rd, T0141-237 3091, www.hoteldiggipalace.com. 43

attractive rooms in charming 125 year old building. Large range of rooms for every budget, rs 500 category particularly good value.Lovely open restaurant, great homegrown food, peaceful garden, enthusiastic, helpful owners, calming atmosphere. Highly recommended.

C-D Rajasthan Palace, 3 Peelwa Gardens, 1 km from Sanganeri Gate, Moti Dungri Rd, T0141-261 1542, rajasthanmotel@yahoo.co.in. Not a palace, 40 rooms, some old-fashioned and wacky, others modern and clean plus budget rooms with shared WC, around pleasant gardens and small pool.

D Arya Niwas, Sansar Chandra Rd (behind Amber Tower), T0141-237 2456, www.aryaniwas.com. 95 very clean, simple rooms but not always quiet, modernized and smart, good very cheap veg food, pleasant lounge, book shop, good travel desk, tranquil lawn, a clean oasis, friendly, helpful, impressivemanagement, book ahead (arrive by 1800), great value. Highly recommended.

D Atithi, 1 Park House Scheme,T0141-237 8679, atithijaipur@hotmail.com. 24 very clean rooms, wonderful hot showers, relaxing roof terrace, internet, good veg food, helpful, friendly staff. Highly recommended.

D Gangaur (RTDC), MI Rd, T0141-237 1641, F0141-237 1647. 63 rooms, some a/c, restaurant, coffee shop, a little neglected, convenient for bus and railway.

D Mundia House, A- 110, Bhan Nagar, T2351117. Situated in residential colony with three comfortable deluxe rooms, own kitchenet, excellent city view, peaceful, free transfers. Recommended.

D Tiger Fort, T236 0238, for an atmospheric stay. Here, you'll find 2 simple rooms with bath. Enquire at **Durg Café**.

D-E Jaipur Inn, B17 Shiv Marg, Bani Park, T0141-220 1121, www.jaipurinn.net. 16 very clean rooms with attached WC, 6 basic rooms with shared facilities plus 12 dorm beds and camping space (**F**). Delightful owners will bend over backwards to help. Pleasant open café downstairs plus a rooftop restaurant offering excellent views of Jaipur. 27 years experience and it shows, great value. Highly recommended.

D-E Karni Niwas, C-5 Motilal Rd, T0141-236 5433, karniniwas@hotmail.com. 13 clean rooms (15 more planned) with hot shower,

some large a/c, some with balconies, breakfast and snacks, internet, feels like a homestay very friendly and helpful owners. Recommended.

D-E Pearl Palace, Hathroi Fort, Ajmer Rd, T0141-237 3700, www.hotelpearlpalace.com. 25 spotless, modern rooms, with or without a/c in quiet location. Run by enthusiastic, innovative owners, personal touches everywhere, stunning rooftop restaurant. Delicious, hygienically prepared food, remarkably good value. Highly recommended.

E City Centre, near Central Bus Stand, T368320. Good sized, clean rooms, western toilet, hot showers, good value, rickshaws reluctant (no commission).

E Evergreen, Keshav Path, Ashok Marg, C-Scheme, T0141-236 2415, evergreen34@ hotmail.com. 97 rooms but standard and prices vary, try to see first) long-established haunt of backpackers, buyers and long-termers, good restaurant, good travel desk, peaceful garden, small pleasant pool, cyber café, often full.

E Sajjan Niwas, D-1/2-B, Via Bank Rd. Behind Collectorate, Bani Park, T0141-231 1544, www.sajjanniwas.com. A pale imitation of **Umaid Bhawan** next door but 22 rooms are not bad value and owners are eager to please. Top floor rooms with balconies are the best bet. Food recommended.

E Shakuntala, D-157 Durga Marg, Bani Park, T0141-220 3225. 16 adequate rooms, family run, attentive service, meals available.

E Tourist Hotel (RTDC), MI Rd, same building as tourist office, T0141-2360238. 47 simple rooms with bath, dorm (Rs 50), little atmosphere, beer bar, tours, well located.

F Shivam, A26, C1, Bharatia Path, Kanti Chandra Rd, Bani Park (behind **Ashok**), T201008. 5 rooms, some with hot shower, dorm in converted garage (Rs 60), mosquito menace, hop over fence and use **Ashok's** pool for Rs 100! Nothing special but one of Jaipur's few cheap options.

F Youth Hostel, T0141-274 1130, near the SMS Stadium, out of town. 8 clean double rooms plus 3 dorms (Rs 40), renovated, good value. Discounts for YHA members.

Paying guests

The tourist office has a list of families. Good home-cooked meals are a bonus.

⦂ A prayer for a good husband

Ishar and Gangaur are the mythical man and wife who embody marital harmony. During the Gangaur Fair colourfully dressed young women carrying brass pitchers on their heads make their way through the streets to the temple of Gauri (another name for Parvati). Here they ceremonially bathe the deity who is then decked with flowers. Young women pray for good husbands, and the long life of their husbands (if they are already married). It ends with singing and rejoicing as it is believed that if a woman is unhappy while she sings she will be landed with an ill-tempered husband! The festivities end when Siva arrives, accompanied by elephants, to escort his bride Gauri home.

E Mandap Homestays, 1 Bhilwa Garden, Moti Dungri Rd, T0141-261 4389. 10 rooms, more under construction, in friendly home of former ruling family.

E Shri Sai Nath, 1233 Mali Colony, outside Chandpol Gate, T0141-230 4975, shree sainath@indya.com. 10 clean, quiet rooms, meals on request, very hospitable family, warm welcome, 'a real delight and very helpful'.

🍴 Eating

Jaipur *p114, map p116*
Watch out for deliberate 'food-poisoning' scams in cheap restaurants involving touts and unscrupulous private 'hospitals'. Fine dining is available in many of the top hotels. There are several very good value pure vegetarian restaurants on Station Rd (near the Bus Station) which though may look a bit grubby so serve lovely freshly cooked food for Rs 30. On the Gaitor road towards Amber, restaurants serve large helpings for Rs 60.
₩₩₩ Jaimahal Palace, see Sleeping, for international cuisine in beautiful surroundings, buffet breakfast and dinner recommended; but snack bar inadequate.
₩₩₩ Rambagh Palace, see Sleeping, for international cuisine in a beautiful restaurant, attractive decor in coffee shop, popular for lunch, pricey but generous.
₩₩₩ Spice Court, Hari Bhawan, Achrol House, Jacob Rd, Civil Lines, T0141-222 0202. Newly opened multicuisine restaurant with distinctive, relaxed 'clubhouse' ambience, superb range of food and drink and outstanding management. Recommended.
₩ Chaitanya, Sansar Ch Rd, 100 m from

Alsisar, in shopping complex on opposite side of road. Excellent vegetarian in civilized surroundings. Extensive menu includes Rajasthani, Italian and Mexican specialities.
₩ Copper Chimney, MI Rd. International. A/c, open for lunch and dinner only, quality food, large non-veg selection including seafood from Sep to Mar. Incessant muzak.
₩ Evergreen, see Sleeping. Good Western, also cyber café. Full of backpackers. Watch bill.
₩ Handi, back of Maya Mansion. Indian. Partly open-air, simple canteen style.
₩ Laxmi, Johari Bazar. Indian vegetarian. Good food and sweets.
₩ LMB, Johari Bazar. Rajasthani vegetarian in slightly confused contemporary interior matched by upbeat dance tunes. Tasty (if a little overpriced) *thalis*; (panchmela saag particularly good).
₩ Mehfil, sweets and *kulfis* outside. New location in tower block basement. Good range of quality Indian, Chinese and Western dishes dishes, friendly service, live music, beer.
₩ Natraj, M1 Rd. Rajasthani, some Chinese, veg only. A/c, much smarter inside than out. Good range of *thalis* and sweets, western classical on stereo.
₩ Niros, MI Rd, T374493. International. A/c, with its bland decor you could be anywhere but there's a good choice of Indian, Chinese and Continental dishes, all set to popzak.
₩ Shiv Sagar, 2nd floor, Mall 21, opposite Raj Mandir Cinema. Strong South Indian selection in fun, modern surroundings.
₩ Sun City, Gangapol. Good value meals in an eccentric environment.
₩ Suriya India, (formerly Swaad), B Ganpati

Plaza, Motilal Atal Rd, T360749. Good selection of pure veg North Indian, live music every evening.

♥♥ **Surya Mahal**, MI Rd. East meets west in chaotic clash of interiors. Wide variety including Mexican and pizzas, food far superior to music.

♥♥ **Temptations**, New Colony. Vegetarian. A/c, varied menu.

Cafés and fast food

BBs, Bhandari Chambers, MI Rd. Western. A/c, clean, swanky, main courses Rs 50.

Barista, Mall 21, opposite Raj Mandir Cinema. National coffee shop chain, good coffee, sandwiches and cakes in a luxuriously hassle-free, a/c environment.

Pizza Hut, 109 Ganpati Plaza, MI Rd, T360749. Italian. A/c, great pizzas.

Royal Fast Food, Johari Bazar. South Indian. Air-cooled, good snacks.

● Entertainment

Jaipur *p114, map p116*
Ayurvedic treatments
Many of the top hotels offer Ayurvedic treatments to non-residents.

Cinema

Raj Mandir Cinema, 'experience' a Hindi film in shell pink interior.

Ravindra Rang Manch, Ram Niwas Garden. Sometimes hosts cultural programmes and music shows.
Also 'shows' at Theme Villages on the outskirts – see below.

Meditation

Vipasana Centre, Dhammathali, Galta, T0141-268 0220 (3 km east of centre). Runs courses for new and experienced students.

● Festivals and events

Jaipur *p114, map p116*
See also p46 for nationwide festivals.
14 Jan Makar Sankranti The kite flying festival is spectacular. Everything closes down in the afternoon and kites are flown from every rooftop, street and even from bicycles! The object is to bring down other kites, attempted to the deafening cheers of huge crowds.

Mar Elephant Festival (25 Mar 2005; 14 Mar 2006, 3 Mar 2007) at Chaugan Stadium, procession, elephant polo etc.

Apr Gangaur Fair (11-12 Apr 2005, 1-2 Apr 2007) about a fortnight after *Holi*, when a colourful procession of women start from the City Palace with the idol of Goddess Gauri. They travel from the Tripolia gate to Talkatora, and these areas of the city are closed to traffic during the festival. See box.

Jul/Aug Teej (8-9 Aug 2005, 28-29 Jul 2006, 15-16 Aug 2007). The special celebrations in Jaipur have elephants, camels and dancers joining in the processions.

● Shopping

Jaipur *p114, map p116*
Jaipur specializes in printed cotton, handicrafts, carpets and *durries* (thick handloomed rug); also embroidered leather footwear and blue pottery. You may find better bargains in other cities in Rajasthan, especially Jodhpur.

Antiques and art

Art Palace, in Chomu Haveli. Specializes in 'ageing' newly crafted items – alternatives to antiques. Also found around Hawa Mahal.

Manglam Arts, Amer Rd. Sells modern miniature paintings and silver.

Mohan Yadav, 9 Khandela House, behind Amber Gauer, SC Rd, T378009. Visit the workshop to see high quality miniatures produced by the family.

Bazars

Traditional bazars and small shops in the Old City are well worth a visit; cheaper than MI Rd shops but may not accept credit cards. Most open 1030-1930; closed on Sun.

Bapu Bazar specializes in printed cloth.

Chaupar and **Nehru Bazars** for textiles.

Johari Bazar for jewellery.

Khajanewalon-ka-Rasta, off Chandpol bazar, for marble and stoneware.

Maniharon-ka-Rasta for lac bangles which the city is famous for.

Ramganj Bazar has leather footwear while opposite Hawa Mahal you will find the famous featherweight Jaipuri *rezais* (quilts).

Tripolia Bazar (3 gates) for inexpensive jewellery.

Blue pottery
Blue Pottery Art Centre, Amer Rd,
near Jain Mandir. For unusual pots.
Recommended.
Kripal Kumbha, B-18, Shiv Marg,
Bani Park.

Books
Book Corner, MI Rd by Niro's Restaurant.
Good selection, largest at the University on
Nehru Marg near Birla Temple.
Bookwise, Rajputana Sheraton Hotel, also
in Mall 21 opposite Rajmandir Cinema. Vast
range, excellent service, fair price, safe
posting. Recommended.

Carpets
Art Age, Plot 2, Bhawani Singh Rd. Watch
durrie weavers.
Channi Carpets and Textiles, Mount Rd
opposite Ramgarh Rd. Factory shop, watch
carpets being handknotted, then washed,
cut and quality checked with a blow lamp!
Kashmiri Carpet Museum, 327 Old Amer
Rd, near Zorawar Singh Gate. Excellent stock.
Maharaja, Chandpol (near Samode Haveli).
Watch carpet weavers and craftsmen, good
value carpets and printed cotton.
The Reject Shop, Bhawani Singh Rd. For
'Shyam Ahuja' durrie collections.

Fabrics
Chirag International, 771 Khawasji ka Rasta,
Hawa Mahal Rd. Wholesale warehouse, with
a corresponding vast selection.
Ridhi Sidhi Textiles, 9 East Govind Nagar,
Amber Rd.

Handicrafts
Anokhi, 2 Yudhistra Marg, opposite
Udyog Bhawan. Well-crafted, attractive
block-printed clothing, linen etc.
Recommended.
Gems & Silver Palace, G11 Amber Tower,
Sansar Ch Rd. Good choice of 'old' textiles,
reasonable prices, helpful owners.
Handloom Haveli, Lalpura House,
Sansar Ch Rd.
Handloom House, Rituraj Building, MI Rd
(near Tourist Hostel).
Rajasthali, Government Handicrafts, MI Rd,
500 m west of Ajmeri Gate.
Rajasthan Fabrics & Arts, near City Palace
gate. Exquisite textiles.

Jewellery
Jaipur is famous for gold, jewellery and gem
stones (particularly emeralds, rubies,
sapphires and diamonds, but the last
requires special certification for export).
Semi-precious stones set in silver is more
affordable (but check for loose settings,
catches and cracked stones); sterling silver
items are rare in India and the content varies
widely. Bargaining is easier on your own so
avoid being taken by a 'guide'. For about Rs
40 you can have gems valued. Do not use
credit cards to buy these goods.

Never agree to 'help to export' jewellery.
Report of misuse of credit card accounts at
Monopoli Gems, opposite Sarga Sooli, Kish-
ore Niwas (1st floor) Tripolia Bazar, Apache
Indian Jewellers (also operating as Krishna
Gems or Ashirwad Gems & Art) opposite
Samodia Complex, Loha Mandi, SC Rd.
Bhuramal Rajmal Surana, 1st floor,
between nos 264 and 268, Haldiyon-ka-
Rasta. Highly recommended.
Beg Gems, Mehdi-ka-Chowk, near Hawa
Mahal.
Dwarka's, H20 Bhagat Singh Marg. Crafts
high-quality gemstones in silver, gold and
platinum in modern and traditional designs.
Gem Testing Laboratory, off MI Rd near
New Gate (reputable jewellers should not
object). Check for members of 'Gems and
Jewellery Association of Rajasthan'.
Johari Bazar, you may be able to see
craftsmen at work especially in
Gopalji-ki-Rasta.
NK Meghraj, 239-240 Johari Bazar.
Ornaments, 32 Sudharma Arcade,
Chameliwala Market, opposite GPO (turn left,
first right and right again), T365051.
Recommended for stones and silver
(wholesale prices; made up in 24 hrs).

Photography
Shops on MI Rd and Chaura Rasta.

Silverware
Amrapali Silver Shop, Chameliwala Market,
opposite GPO, MI Rd.
Arun's Emporium, MI Rd.
Balaji's, Sireh Deori Bazar (off Johari Bazar).
Mona Lisa, Hawa Mahal Rd.
Nawalgarh Haveli, near Amber Fort
Bus Stop.
Silver and Art Palace, Amer Rd.

▲ Activities and tours

Jaipur *p114, map p116*

Some hotels will arrange golf, tennis, squash. **Ashok Club**, Bhagwandas Rd, T381690. Has a squash court (mediocre); temporary membership, Rs 350 per month. Has interesting memorabilia.

City tours

RTDC City Sightseeing, half day: 0800-1300, 1130-1630, 1330-1830, Rs 100; Central Museum, City Palace, Amber Fort and Palace, Gaitore, Nawab ki Haveli, Jantar Mantar, Jal Mahal, Hawa Mahal; City Sightseeing, full day: 0900-1800, Rs 150; including places above plus Nahargarh Fort, Indology Museum, Dolls Museum, Galta, Sisodia Rani Garden. Jaigarh Fort. Nahargarh evening tour, 1800-2200, includes non-veg meal, folk dances. Call T0141-237 5466 or book at Railway station, the hotels, **Gangaur** or **Tourist Hotel** (see Sleeping for details). Other operators also offer city sightseeing: half/full day, Rs 100-150. The tours are worthwhile, but may miss out promised sights claiming they are closed. Some may find the guides' English difficult to follow and the obligatory trip to shops, tedious.

Walking tour

An excellent new initiative is the Heritage Walk of Jaipur, a guided walking tour of some of the lesser known parts of the old city. It leaves from Albert Hall at 0830 every Sat and lasts 2 hrs, covering a distance of 2½ km. There is no charge as such, but donations towards the upkeep of Jaipur's heritage buildings are appreciated. Call T0141-236 7678 for more information.

General tours

Aravalli Safari, opposite Rajputana Palace Hotel, Palace Rd, T0141-237 3124, aravalli2@datainfosys.net. Very professional. **Chetan**, 17 Muktanand Nagar, Gopalpura Bypass, Tonk Rd, T0141-254 5302. Experienced, reliable, car tours. **Forts & Palaces Tours**, S-1, Prabhkar Apartment, Vaishali Nagar, T0141-235 4508, www.palaces-tours.com. A friendly outfit offering camel safaris, hotel reservations, etc. **Karwan Tours**, Bissau Palace Hotel, Chandpol Gate, T0141-230 8103, karwantours@mailcity.com. For camel safaris, tours, taxis, ticketing, exchange, very helpful. **Marudhar Tours**, H-20 Bhagat Singh Marg, C-scheme, T0141-237 1768, marudhar@datainfosys.net.in, car hire, air/train tickets. **Rajasthan Travel**, 52 Ganpati Plaza, MI Rd, T0141-236 5408, rtsjaipur@bhaskarmail.com. Ticketing, reliable guides. Recommended.

● Transport

Jaipur *p114, map p116*
Air

Sanganer airport has good facilities. Transport to town: taxi, 30 mins, Rs 250; auto rickshaw Rs 120. **Indian Airlines**, Nehru Pl, Tonk Rd, T274 3500; airport, T272 1519, flies to **Aurangabad**, **Delhi**, **Jaisalmer**, **Jodhpur**, **Mumbai**, **Udaipur**, **Ahmedabad**, **Kolkata**, **Dubai**, **Bangkok** and **Singapore**. Jet Airways, T360763, airport T551352, flies to **Delhi**, **Mumbai** and **Udaipur**. Sahara Airlines, T237 7637, flies to **Delhi** and **Kolkata**. **Airlines offices** Air India, Ganpati Plaza, MI Rd (opposite All India Rd), T236 8569. **Lufthansa**, T256 1360; others at Jaipur Tower, MI Rd, T237 7051.

Auto rickshaw

Avoid hotel touts and use the pre-paid
auto-rickshaw counter to get to your hotel.
Station to city centre hotel, about Rs 25;
sightseeing (3-4 hrs) Rs 200, 6-7 hrs, Rs 300.
From railway and bus stations, drivers (who
expect to take you to shops for commission)
offer whole day hire including Amber for
Rs 150; have your list of sights planned and
refuse to go to shops.

Bus

Local To get around the city, unless you
have plenty of time or a very limited budget,
an auto is recommended. To **Amber** buses
originate from Ajmeri Gate, junction with MI
Rd so get on there if you want a seat.
Long distance Central Bus Stand, Sindhi
Camp, Station Rd. Enquiries: Deluxe, T511
6031, Express, T511 6044 (24 hrs), Narain
Singh Circle, T256 4016. State and private
'Deluxe' buses are very popular so book 2
days in advance. Deluxe buses depart from
Platform 3 which has the reservation
counter. Journeys can be very bumpy and
tiring. Left luggage, Rs 10 per item per day.
To **Agra** about hourly from bus station 6½
hrs with 1 hr lunch stop, Rs 135/227a/c, pay
when seat number is written on ticket; (230
km, 5 hrs, via Bharatpur) – you can get off at
the 2nd (last) stop to avoid being hassled by
rickshaw drivers; **Ajmer** (131 km, ½ hourly, 3
hrs, rs67/87a/c); **Bharatpur** Rs 90; **Delhi** (261
km, ½ hourly, 5½ hrs, Rs 240/375a/c/425a/c
Volvo); **Jaisalmer** (654 km, 2145, 13 hrs via
Jodhpur, Rs 235). **Jodhpur** (332 km,
frequent, 7 hrs, Rs 154); **Udaipur** (374 km, 12
hrs, Rs 202/252a/c/282a/csleeper 282).

Cycle rickshaw

(Often rickety) station to central hotels, Rs 15;
full day Rs 100.

Taxi

Unmetered taxis; 4 hrs Rs 350 (40 km), 8 hrs
Rs 550 (city and Amber). Out of city Rs 5 per
km; **Marudhar Tours** (see Activities and
tours) recommended; or try **RTDC**, T315714.
Also **Pink City Taxis**, T511 5100, excellent
radio cab service.

Train

Enquiry, T131, T133, reservation T135.
Computerized booking office in separate
building to front and left of station; separate
queue for foreigners. Persistent auto-
rickshaw drivers, in addition to being hotel
touts, may quote Rs 10 to anywhere in town,
then overcharge for city tour. Use pre-paid
rickshaw counter. **Abu Rd (for Mount Abu)**
Ahmadabad Mail, 9106, 0455, 8½ hrs, *Aravali
Exp (goes on to Mumbai), 9708*, 0840, 9½ hrs;
Agra Cantt: *Marudhar Exp, 4854/4864*, 1310,
7 hrs. **Ahmadabad**: *Aravali Exp, 9708*, 0840,
14 hrs; *Ashram Exp, 2916*, 2050, 11½ hrs.
Rajdhani Exp, 2958, Tue, Thu, Sat, 0045, 9 hrs.
Ajmer: *Aravali Exp, 9708*, 0840, 2½ hrs;
Bikaner: *Bikaner Exp, 4737*, 2100, 10 hrs;
Intercity Exp, 2468, 1500, 7 hrs. **Chittaurgarh**:
Jaipur-Purna Exp, 9769, 1220, 7½ hrs; *Chetak
Exp, 9615*, 2050, 8½ hrs. **Delhi**: Shatabdi
2016, 1745, 4 hrs 25 mins, *Jodhpur Delhi Exp,
4860*, 0600, 5 hrs; *Jaipur Delhi Exp, 2414*, 1620,
5½ hrs; *Ahmadabad Mail, 9105*, 2340, 5½ hrs.
Indore: *Jaipur-Purna Exp, 9769*, 1220, 16½
hrs. *Jaipur Indore Exp 9308*, 1545, 16 hrs;
Jodhpur: *Jodhpur Delhi Exp, 4859*, 2330, 6
hrs. **Mumbai (C)**: *Jaipur Mumbai Exp 2956*,
1330, 18½ hrs. To **Udaipur** *Chetak Exp, 9615*,
2220, 12 hrs. **Varanasi** via **Lucknow**:
Marudhar Exp, 4854/4864, 1325, 20 hrs.

● Directory

Jaipur *p114, map p116*
Banks Several on MI Rd. Open 1030-1430,
1530-1630; most change money. **Andhra
Bank**, MI Rd. For Visa: **Indus Bank**, C-Scheme;
SBBJ, both recommended. **Thomas Cook**,
Jaipur Towers, 1st floor, MI Rd (500 m from
railway station, T236 0801, 0930-1730, open
Sun). No commission on own TCs, Rs 20 for
others. Recommended. Often easier to use
hotels, eg Rambagh Palace (0700-2000).
Karwan Tours, Bissau Palace (sunrise until
late). Jewellery shops opposite Hawa Mahal
often hold exchange licences but travellers
report misuse of credit cards at some.
Hospitals Santokba Durlabhji, Bhawani
Singh Rd, T256 6251. **SMS**, Sawai Ram Singh
Marg, T256 0291.
Internet At Ganpati Plaza basement, Re 1
per min. **Cyber Café**, 15 Nandisha Inn, Sivaji
Rd. Reliable. **Interphase**, C-Scheme, plus
many others scattered around city. At hotels:
Mewar, near Central Bus Stand, T206042.
Jaipur Inn, Rs 3 per min. Also 34 Station Rd
(behind Polo Victory Cinema).

Around Jaipur

Amber Fort is one of Jaipur's biggest draws, with an elephant ride to the top high on many people's 'to do' list. It's still an impressive building but has been poorly maintained in recent years. Sanganer and Bagru offer good opportunities to see handicrafts in production, while Samode is perhaps the last word in elegant living.
➤➤ *For Sleeping, Eating and other listings, see pages 135-136.*

Amber (Amer) → *Colour map 2, grid C6. 11 km north of Jaipur.*

As you take the winding road from modern Jaipur between the barren hills immediately to the north there is little hint of the magnificent fort and palace which once dominated the narrow valley. Today there is no town to speak of in Amber, just the palace clinging to the side of the rocky hill, overlooked by the small fort above, with a small village at its base. In the high season this is one of India's most popular tourist sites, with a continuous train of colourfully decorated elephants walking up and down the ramp to the palace. One penalty of its popularity is the persistence of the vendors.

History
Amber, which takes its name from Ambarisha, a king of the once famous royal city of Ayodhya, was the site of a Hindu temple built by the Mina tribes as early as the 10th century. Two centuries later the Kachhawaha Rajputs made it their capital, which it remained until Sawai Jai Singh II moved to his newly planned city of Jaipur in 1727. Its location made Amber strategically crucial for the Mughal emperors as they moved south, and the Maharajahs of Amber took care to establish close relations with successive Mughal rulers. The building of the fort palace was begun by Raja Man Singh, a noted Rajput General in Akbar's army, in 1600, and Mughal influence was strong in much of the subsequent building.

The approach
① *Rs 400 per elephant carrying four, no need to tip, though the driver will probably ask, takes 10 mins. Jeeps Rs 100 each way, or Rs 10 per seat.*
From the start of the ramp you can either walk or ride by elephant; the walk is quite easy and mainly on a separate path. Elephants carry up to four persons on a padded seat. The ride can be somewhat unnerving when the elephant comes close to the edge of the road, but it is generally perfectly safe. You have to buy a 'return ticket' even if you wish to walk down later. The elephants get bad tempered as the day wears on. If you are interested in finding out more about the welfare of Amber's elephants, or indeed any of Jaipur's street animals, you should contact an organization called **Help in Suffering** ① *T0141-276 0803, www.his-india.com.*

The Palace
① *0900-1630. Worth arriving at 0900. Tickets in the Chowk, below the steps up to Shila Mata. Rs 50; camera Rs 25, video Rs 100. Take the green bus from the Hawa Mahal, Rs 5. Auto-rickshaw Rs 50 (Rs 125 for return, including the wait). Guides are worth hiring, Rs 400 for a half day (group of 4), find one with a government guide licence.*
After passing through a series of five defensive gates, you reach the first courtyard of the **Raj Mahal** built by Man Singh I in 1600, entered through the **Suraj Pol** (Sun Gate).

Here you can get a short ride around the courtyard on an elephant, but bargain very hard. There are some toilets near the dismounting platform. On the south side of this Jaleb Chowk with the flower beds, is a flight of steps leading up to the **Singh Pol** (Lion Gate) entrance to the upper courtyard of the palace.

A separate staircase to the right leads to the green marble-pillared **Shila Mata Temple** (to Kali as Goddess of War) ① *opens at certain times of the day and then, only allows a limited number of visitors at a time so ask before joining the queue*, which contains a black marble image of the goddess that Man Singh I brought back from Jessore (now in Bangladesh; the chief priest has always been Bengali). The silver doors with images of Durga and Saraswati were added by his successor.

In the left-hand corner of the courtyard, the **Diwan-i-Am** (Hall of Public Audience) was built by Raja Jai Singh I in 1639. Originally, it was an open pavilion with cream marble pillars supporting an unusual striped canopy-shaped ceiling, with a portico with double red sandstone columns. The room on the east was added by Sawai Ram Singh II. **Ganesh Pol** (circa 1700-1725), south of the chowk, colourfully painted and with mosaic decoration, takes its name from the prominent figure of Ganesh above the door. It separates the private from the public areas.

This leads onto the **Jai Singh I** court with a formal garden. To the east is the two-storeyed cream coloured marble pavilion – **Jai Mandir** (Diwan-i-Khas or Hall of Private Audience) below and **Jas Mandir** (1635-1640) with a curved Bengali roof, on the terrace above. The former, with its marble columns and painted ceiling, has lovely views across the lake. The latter has colourful mosaics, mirrors and marble *jali* screens which let in cooling breezes. Both have **Shish Mahals** (Mirror Palaces) faced with mirrors, seen to full effect when lit by a match. To the west of the chowk is the **Sukh Niwas**, a pleasure palace with a marble water course to cool the air, and doors inlaid with ivory and sandalwood. The Mughal influence is quite apparent in this chowk.

Above the Ganesh Pol is the **Sohag Mandir**, a rectangular chamber with beautiful latticed windows and octagonal rooms to each side. From the rooftop there are stunning views over the palace across the town of Amber, the long curtain wall surrounding the town and further north, through the 'V' shaped entrance in the hills, to the plains beyond. Beyond this courtyard is the **Palace of Man Singh I**. A high wall separates it from the Jai Singh Palace. In the centre of the chowk which was once open is a **baradari** (12-arched pavilion), comb-ining Mughal and Hindu influences. The surrounding palace, a complex warren of passages and staircases, was turned into *zenana* quarters when the newer palaces were built by Jai Singh. Children find it great fun to explore this part.

Amber Palace

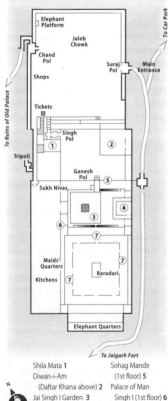

Shila Mata **1**
Diwan-i-Am
  (Daftar Khana above) **2**
Jai Singh I Garden **3**
Jai Mandir
  (Jas Mandir, 1st floor) **4**

Sohag Mandir
  (1st floor) **5**
Palace of Man
  Singh I (1st floor) **6**
Zenana **7**

Not to scale

The Old Palace and nearby temples

Old Palace of Amber (1216) lies at the base of Jaigarh fort. A stone path (currently being restored) from the Chand Pol in the first courtyard of Amber Palace leads to the ruins. Though there is little interest today, nearby are several interesting temples. These include the **Jagatsiromani Temple** dedicated to Krishna, with carvings and paintings; it is associated with **Mira Bai**. Close by is the old temple to Narasinghji and *Panna Mian-ki-Baoli* (step well). Some of the *chhatris* on Delhi Road still retain evidence of paintings.

Jaigarh Fort

① 0900-1630. Rs 20 Indian, Rs35 foreigners including still camera, video Rs150, vehicle entry Rs 50. *To reach the for, from Amber Palace turn right out of the Suraj Pol and follow a stone road past the old elephant quarters. This is the start of the ascent – a steady climb of about 25 mins, or take a taxi. What appears at first to be two adjoining forts is in fact all part of the same structure. There is also a good road from the Jaipur-Amber road which goes straight to Jaigarh Fort and on to Nahargarh.*

Above the palace on the hill top stands the gigantic bulk of Jaigarh, impressively lit at night, its *parkotas* (walls), bastions, gateways and watchtowers a testimony of the power of the Jaipur rulers. It is well worth a visit. The forbidding medieval fort was never captured and so has survived virtually intact which makes it particularly interesting. In the 16th-century well-planned cannon foundry you can see the pit where the barrels were cast, the capstan-powered lathe which bored out the cannon and the iron-workers' drills, taps and dies. The armoury has a large collection of swords and small arms, their use in the many successful campaigns having been carefully logged. There is an interesting photograph collection and a small café outside the armoury. There are gardens, a granary, open and closed reservoirs; the ancient temples of Ram Harihar (10th-century) and Kal Bhairava (12th-century) are within the fort. You can explore a warren of complicated dark passageways among the palaces. Many of the apartments are open and you can see the collections of coins and puppets (shows on demand). The other part of the fort, at a slightly higher elevation, has a tall watch tower. From here there are tremendous views of the surrounding hills. The massive 50 tonne **Jai Ban cannon** stands on top of one tower. Allegedly the largest cannon on wheels in the world, with an 8 m barrel, it had a range of around 20 km, but it was never used. Some 7 km further along the top of the hill is the smaller Nahargarh Fort overlooking Jaipur itself. See page 121.

Jal Mahal and Gaitore → *8 km from Jaipur.*

The **Man Sarobar** lake has the attractive, Rajput style **Jal Mahal** (Water Palace, 1735) at its centre. Though often dry in the summer, during the monsoon the lake is transformed from a huge grassy field into a beautiful water hyacinth-filled lake. Opposite the lake at **Gaitore** are the marble and sandstone *chhatris* of the rulers of Jaipur, built by Jai Singh II and set in landscaped gardens.

Sanganer → *12 km southwest of Jaipur.*

The airport road gives access to this small town through two ruined triple gateways beyond which is the ruined palace and old Jain temples. The main attractions of Sanganer are block-printing and paper-making. The latter uses waste cotton and silk rags which are pulped, sieved, strained and dried. Screen and block-printing is done in Chipa Basti where you can watch the printers in workshops and purchase samples, usually at a fraction of the price asked in Jaipur. **The Village Restaurant** is near the airport. Folk entertainment and a market is planned. There is a **Donkey Fair** at Looniyabas nearby in October where thousands of animals are traded. There are hourly buses from Jaipur.

Chokhi Dhani

ⓘ *Tonk Rd, T0141-277 0555, www.chokhidhani.com. Rs 190 (set against any meal at the restaurants). Buses leave Station Rd, or taxi from Jaipur Rs 300- 400 return.*
On the outskirts of the city, there are various theme villages dotted around offering a chance to sample an authentic Rajasthani meal in pleasant 'rural' surroundings. Chokhi Dhani is one situated 19 km south of Jaipur. Here a typical Rajasthani village has been created and while the concept might sound a little fake, it's been really well done. It is a hugely popular night out amongst Jaipur's residents. The best time to visit is in the evening, when the whole place takes on an ethnic carnival atmosphere, with local artists performing puppetry, acrobatics and folk dancing while skilled artisans demonstrate traditional manufacturing techniques.

Vidyadhar baghs

Vidyadhar Bagh ⓘ *0800-1800, Re 1*, on the Agra Road, is a beautiful garden laid out in honour of Jai Singh's friend and city planner Vidyadhar Bhattacharya. Among the many landscaped gardens laid out by kings and courtiers in the 18th and 19th centuries. Accommodation can be found at **Chokhi Dhani Resort**, see Sleeping below.

Ramgarh Lake and Jamwa Sanctuary → *30 km northeast (45 mins' drive).*

This 15 sq km lake, of Jamwa Ramgarh, which attracts large flocks of waterfowl in winter, lies within a game sanctuary with good boating and bird watching. It was the venue for yachting and other sports in the 1982 Asian Games and is being developed as a water sports resort. Built to supply Jaipur with water it now provides less than one per cent of the city's needs and in years of severe drought it may dry up completely. In the summer of 2000, at the end of a particularly hot dry spell, the lake's crocodiles were reported to be searching the few remaining mud pools in the rapidly drying lake bed. The 300-sq km Jamwa Sanctuary which once provided the Jaipur royal family with game still has some panthers, nilgai and small game. Contact Jaipur Tourist Office for details of public buses.

Bagru → *35 km towards Ajmer on the NH8.*

In this small town *chipa* printers continue the three centuries old tradition of hand block printing using natural dyes and treating the cotton cloth with 'Fuller's earth' from the riverside. They then soak the cloth in turmeric water to produce the traditional cream-coloured background before using hand carved wooden blocks for printing floral patterns. The dyes are specially prepared and fixed with gum – molasses and iron for black; red ochre and alum for red; indigo for blue. The very active *chipa mohalla* (printers' quarter), where the three dozen or so families devoted to printing live and work, makes an interesting excursion.

Madhogarh → 45 km southeast of Jaipur, off the Jaipur-Agra Rd.

Madhogarh is a small but impressive fort, with a strong medieval flavour, and a pleasant place to break your journey between Jaipur and Ranthambore if you have your own transport. It is located on a hillock, and has huge walls, bastions, wells and turrets. The Rajput-Maratha battle of Tunga was fought at the nearby village, with the Jaipur army based at Madhogarh, during the mid-18th century.

Samode → Phone code: 01423. Colour map 2, grid C6. 42 km northwest of Jaipur.

At the head of the enclosed valley in the dry rugged hills of the northern Aravallis, Samode stands on a former caravan route. Today, the sleepy village, with its local artisans producing printed cloth and glass bangles, nestles within its old walls. The old painted *havelis* are still full of character. Samode is well worth the visit from Jaipur or en route to the painted towns of Shekhawati, see page 256. Both the palace and the *bagh* are wonderful, peaceful places to spend a night.

The **palace**, which dominates the village, is fabulously decorated with 300-year old wall paintings (hunting scenes, floral motifs etc) which still look almost new. Around the first floor of the Darbar Hall are magnificent alcoves, decorated with mirrors like *shish mahal* and *jali* screens through which the royal ladies would have looked down into the grand jewel-like Darbar Hall.

Towering immediately above the palace is **Samode Fort**, the maharajah's former residence, reached in times of trouble by an underground passage. The old stone zigzag path has been replaced by 300 steps. Though dilapidated, there are excellent views from the ramparts; a caretaker has the keys. The main fort gate is the starting point of some enticing walks into the Aravallis. A paved path leads to a shrine about 3 km away. There are two other powerful forts you can walk to, forming a circular walk ending back in Samode. Allow three hours, wear good shoes, a hat and carry water.

Samode Bagh, a large 400-year old Mughal-style formal garden with fountains and pavilions, has been beautifully restored. It is 3 km southeast of Samode, towards the main Jaipur-Agra road. Within the grounds are modest-sized, but elaborately decorated tents.

Jaipur & around Listings (side margin)

● Sleeping

Chokhi Dhani *p134*
AL-A Chokhi Dhani, as above. 31 attractive standard and 34 'executive' huts (the 'Shekhavati haveli' with carved doors, open courtyard and frescoes, has 8 suites), mud walls but very modern inside with a/c, TV, comfortable beds, marble bathrooms with hot showers/tubs (at odds with the thatched roof and tribal murals outside!), great pool, gym, exchange (for residents), friendly and professional management.

Ramgarh Lake and Jamwa Sanctuary *p134*
A-B Ramgarh Lodge (Taj), overlooking the lake, T01426-252217, www.tajhotels.com. 18 elegant a/c rooms (2 enormous suites) in the former royal hunting lodge with a museum and library, furnished appropriately, hunting trophies, limited restaurant, delightful walks, fishing and boating plus ruins of old Kachhawaha fort nearby.
D Jheel Tourist Village (RTDC), Mandawa Choraha, T01426-252170. 10 not especially well-maintained rustic huts in pleasant surroundings.

Madhogarh *p135*
B Madhogarh, T01429-281 141. Heritage Hotel with 25 quaint rooms (some in the tower) with views of the countryside. Good (though rather spicy) food, interesting temples nearby, family run, recently converted so still finding its feet. Great

atmosphere on the ramparts in the evening when the family and guests enjoy tea.

Samode *p135*
L-A Samode Palace, T01423-240014, www.samode.com. 43 a/c rooms, tastefully modernized without losing any of the charm (but short of hot water), courtyard and modern indoor restaurants (international menu). The dining room serves buffets to groups, gardens, beautiful, secluded pool with plenty of space to lounge, magnificent setting, shop with good textiles, camel rides around village and to Samode Bagh (but some animals are in poor condition), generally friendly, really remark- able for its setting and atmosphere but some- what impersonal, disappointing service (tip- seeking), Rs 100 entry for non-residents, well worth a visit even if not staying. Highly recommended. Half price 1 May to 30 Sep. Samode Haveli T0141 263 2407, reserve and arrange taxi (Rs 950) from Jaipur. Reservations essential.
A Samode Bagh, T01423-240235, 3 km away from palace, www.samode.com. 44 luxury a/c tents decorated in the Mughal style, each with a beautiful modern bath-room and its own verandah. *Darbar* tent, al fresco meals, pool with slide, tennis, volley-ball, badminton, lovely setting in peaceful walled Mughal gardens, plenty of bird-watching, safaris to sand dunes, amazing. Recommended. Reservations essential.
B-C Maharaja Palace, modern hotel. 18 rooms (some a/c) in mock *haveli*, restaurant, garden with village style huts.

❶ Eating

Chokhi Dhani *p134*
There are 2 restaurants within the 'theme' village to choose from:
▮▮▮-▮▮**Bindola**, a high-class a/c multi-cuisine affair, with live ghazals every evening and a pleasant ambience.
▮ **Sangari**, a real village experience, with a set Rajasthani meal served on leaf platters and seating on the floor.

❶ Shopping

Amber *p131*
At Amber near the *baoli* and temples,

you can see demonstrations of block printing and other handicrafts, there is a small cafeteria for drinks and simple snacks, shops selling gems, jewellery, textiles, handicrafts and 'antiques' (objects up to 90 years old; genuine 100-year old antiques may not be exported). Amber is a tax holiday zone, and products manu-factured by industries here are 10-15 per cent cheaper than at Jaipur (though the benefit may not be passed on to the customer). Travellers warn that the privately owned **Rajasthan Small Scale Cottage Industries** on Jagat Shiromani Temple Rd looks like a government fixed price shop but charges very high prices. The RTDC tour guide even recommends the shop.

Samode *p135*
A small artists' colony in the village produces good quality miniature paintings on old paper. Contact Krishan Kumar Khari, often found at the hotel entrance.

▲ Activities and tours

Ramgarh Lake and Jamwa Sanctuary *p134*
Polo can be played at **Ramgarh Resort** (HRH), T0294-252 8016, www.hrhindia.com. An exclusive facility for polo enthusiasts with a full size polo field near the lake, occasional matches and polo training camps run by World Cup Indian captain Lokendra Singh. **A** Deluxe tented accommodation for participants, restaurant, pool and riding stable.

Samode *p135*
See **Samode Bagh**, Sleeping, for activities within and around this Moghul garden/'hotel'. See also **Samode Palace** for camel safaris. Birdwatching around this area is good too.

❶ Transport

Samode *p135*
Samode is a 1 hr drive from Jaipur. Buses from Chandpol Gate go to Chomu where you can pick a local bus to Samode. A taxi costs Rs950.

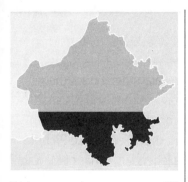

Southern Rajasthan

Udaipur	140
Sights	142
Excursions	146
Listings	146
Around Udaipur	153
South of Udaipur	154
North of Udaipur	155
Listings	156
Kumbhalgarh, Ranakpur and around	158
Kumbhalgarh	158
Ghanerao and Rawla Narlai	159
Ranakpur	160
Listings	160
Mount Abu and around	162
Listings	168
Chittaurgarh and around	173
Chittaurgarh	173
Chittaurgarh to Kota	176
Kota	176
Bundi	178
Listings	181

❗ Footprint features

Don't miss	137
A classic car collection	148
The jauhar - Rajput chivalry	175
Flower power	178

Introduction

Possibly the most varied region in Rajasthan, the southern part of the state boasts a wide array of sights, sounds and experiences. The main draw is incomparable **Udaipur**, with the **Lake Palace** as its shimmering showpiece, **Lake Pichola** and the **City Palace**, home to the legendary Ranas of Mewar, world's oldest ruling dynasty, its unbeatable backdrop. Many regard it as India's most romantic city, and as the sun sets on the lake and the white building soften in the light disappearing sun, it is hard to disagree.

The area around is equally appealing however, from time-warped, untouristy **Bundi** and **Chittorgarh** in the east to the quirky charms of **Mount Abu**, Rajasthan's only hill station and a great escape from the heat of the summer, in the west. To the south lie delightful **Dungarpur** and a range of small heritage hotels dotted around the countryside, perfect places to unwind away from the tourist fray. The area to the north boasts both majestic **Kumbhalgarh Fort**, its mammoth walls so vast they're visible from space, and the exquisite Jain temples at **Ranakpur**, comparable to those in Mount Abu but in a far more tranquil setting.Fascinating drives through the surprisingly green **Aravalli hills** link oneplace to the other, passing through picturesque rural villages and agricultural areas unlike those anywhere else in Rajasthan along the way

Southern Rajasthan

★ Don't miss...

1 Monsoon Palace Not a palace but the view over Udaipur is simply stunning, page 146.

2 Juna Mahal at Dungarpur The most evocative palace in Rajasthan, seemingly untouched for centuries, page 154.

3 Mount Abu Take time out for a trek in the cool climes, and to check out the beaming tourists in the main bazaar, page 162.

4 Chittaurgarh Massive, mysterious and yours to explore, the fort complex is a great place for a wander, page 173.

5 Bundi A stroll through the sleepy streets of this unspoilt town is like taking several steps back in time, page 178.

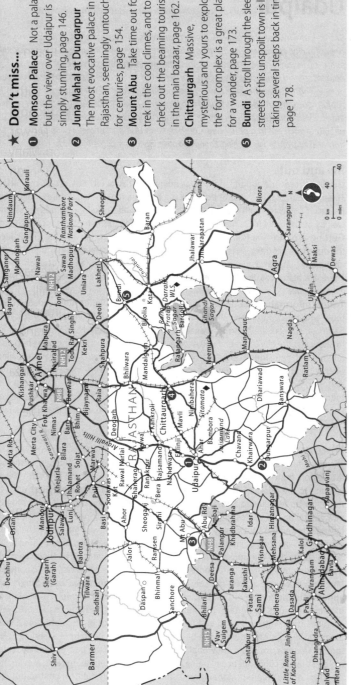

Udaipur → *Phone code: 0294. Colour map 5, grid B1. Population: 500,000.*

Set in the Girwa valley amidst the Aravalli hills of south Rajasthan, Udaipur is a beautiful city, regarded by many as one of the most romantic in India. In contrast to some of its desert neighbours it presents an enchanting image of white marble palaces, placid blue lakes, attractive gardens and green hills that keep the wilderness at bay. High above the lake towers the massive palace of the maharanas. From its rooftop gardens and balconies, you can look over Lake Pichola, at the summer palace, 'adrift like a snowflake' in its centre. Around the lake, the houses and temples of the old city stretch out in a pale honeycomb making Udaipur an oasis of colour in a stark and arid region. ▶▶ For Sleeping, Eating and other listings, see pages 146-153.

Ins and outs

Getting there The airport, about 30-45 minutes by taxi or City Bus, is well connected. The main Bus Stand is east of Udai Pol, 2-3 km from most hotels, while Udaipur City Railway Station is another 1 km south. Both have auto-rickshaw stands outside as well as pushy hotel touts. Remember, Udaipur station to the north, is inconvenient.

Getting around The touristy area around the Jagdish temple and the City Palace, the main focus of interest, is best explored on foot but there are several sights further afield. City buses and unmetered auto-rickshaws cover the city and surrounding area. There are also taxis though some travellers prefer to hire a scooter or bike. ▶▶ *See Transport, page 152, for further details.*

Tourist information Be prepared for crowds, dirt and pollution and persistent hotel touts who descend on new arrivals. It is best to reserve a hotel ahead or ask for a particular street or area of town. Travellers risk being befriended by someone claiming to show you the city for free. If you accept, you run the risk of visiting one shop after another with your 'friend'. *Udaipur, Fabled City of Romance*, 1997, Rs 265, an excellent picture book with well written text is available locally. *Beyond the Palace* by Renee Porte, an American resident of Udaipur, gives an interesting insight into the less touristy side of the city. **Rajasthan** ① *Tourist Reception Centre, Fath Memorial, Suraj Pol, T0294-2411535, 1000-1700, guides 4-8 hrs, Rs 250-400.* Counters at City Railway Station ① *0800-1200*, and at Dabok Airport at flight times.

History

The legendary **Ranas of Mewar** who traced their ancestry back to the Sun, first ruled the region from their seventh-century stronghold Chittaurgarh. The title 'Rana', peculiar to the rulers of **Mewar** (also used in Nepal), was supposedly first used by Hammir who reoccupied Mewar in 1326. In 1568, **Maharana Udai Singh** founded a new capital on the shores of Lake Pichola and named it Udaipur (the city of sunrise) having selected the spot in 1559. On the advice of an ascetic who interrupted his rabbit hunt, Udai Singh had a temple built above the lake and then his palace around it.

In contrast to the house of Jaipur, the rulers of Udaipur prided themselves on being independent from other more powerful regional neighbours, particularly the Mughals. In a piece of local princely one-upmanship, **Maharana Pratap Singh**, heir apparent to the throne of Udaipur, invited Raja Man Singh of Jaipur to a lakeside picnic. Afterwards he had the ground on which his guest had trodden washed with sacred Ganga water and insisted that his generals take purificatory baths. Man Singh reaped appropriate revenge by preventing Pratap Singh from acceding to his throne. Udaipur, for all its individuality, remained one of the poorer princely states in Rajasthan, a consequence of being almost constantly at war. In 1818, Mewar, the Kingdom of the Udaipur Maharanas, came under British political control but still managed to avoid almost all British cultural influence.

Udaipur

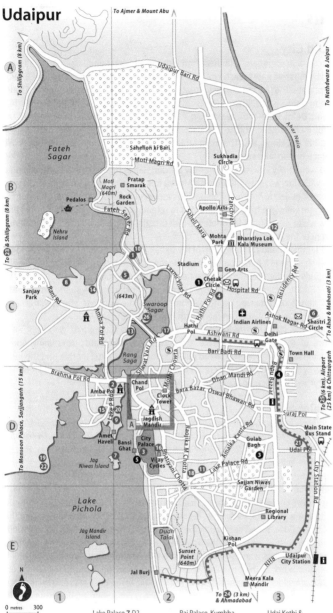

Sleeping 🏨
Anand Bhawan **1** *C2*
Ashish Palace **4** *C2*
Dream Heaven **2** *D2*
Fateh Prakash &
  Shiv Niwas **3** *D2*
Hilltop Palace **5** *C2*
Kajri **6** *C3*
Lakend **8** *C1*

Lake Palace **7** *D2*
Lake Pichola & Sarovar **20** *D2*
Lake Shore, Wonder View
  & Bharti Restaurant **9** *D2*
Laxmi Vilas Palace **10** *C2*
Mahendra Prakash **11** *D2*
Mewar Inn **12** *B3*
Natural **13** *C2*
Pratap Country Inn **25** *D3*
Rajdarshan & Delhi
  Darbar Restaurant **17** *C2*

Raj Palace, Kumbha
  Palace & Mona Lisa **16** *D2*
Rampratap Palace **14** *C1*
Rang Niwas Palace &
  Palace View
  Restaurant **18** *D2*
Rani Village **23** *C1*
Ranjit Niwas **19** *D2*
Shirkarbadi **24** *E3*
Swaroop Vilas **26** *C2*
Trident **19** *D1*

Udai Kothi &
  Queen's Café **15** *D1*
Udai Vilas **22** *D1*
Yatri Guesthouse **21** *D3*

Eating 🍴
Berrys **1** *C2*
Garden Hotel
  & Hariyali **3** *D3*
Park View & Natraj **4** *D3*
Sunset Terrace **5** *D2*

Sights

The Old City

Udaipur is a traditionally planned fortified city. Its bastioned rampart walls are pierced by massive gates, each studded with iron spikes as protection against enemy war elephants. The five remaining gates are: **Hathi Pol** (Elephant Gate – north), **Chand Pol** (Moon Gate – west), **Kishan Pol** (south), the main entrance **Suraj Pol** (Sun Gate – east) and **Delhi Gate** (northeast). On the west side, the City is bounded by the beautiful Pichola Lake and to the east and north, by moats. To the south is the fortified hill of Eklingigarh. The main street leads from the Hathi Pol to the massive City Palace on the lake side.

The walled city is a maze of narrow winding lanes flanked by tall whitewashed houses with doorways decorated with Mewar folk art, windows with stained glass or *jali* screens, majestic *havelis* with spacious inner courtyards and shops. Many of the houses here were given by the Maharana to retainers – barbers, priests, traders and artisans while many rural landholders (titled jagirdars), had a *haveli* conveniently located near the palace.

The **Jagdish Mandir**, 150 m north of the palace (1651), was built by Maharana Jagat Singh. The temple is a fine example of the Nagari style, and contrasts with the serenity of Udaipur's predominantly whitewashed buildings, surrounded as it often is by chanting Sadhus, gamboling monkeys and the smell of incense. A shrine with a brass Garuda stands outside and stone elephants flank the entrance steps; within is a black stone image of Vishnu as Jagannath, the Lord of the Universe.

The lovely 18th-century **Bagore ki Haveli** has 130 rooms and was built as a miniature of the city palace. There are cool shady courtyards containing some peacock mosaic and fretwork, carved pillars made from granite, marble and the local blueish grey stone and lime plastered walls. The museum has a beautiful collection of folk costumes, turbans, hookahs, local art and utensils.

City Palace

ⓘ *From Ganesh Deori Gate: Rs 50 (more from near Lake Palace Ghat). Camera/video Rs 200. 0930-1730, last entry 1630. From 'Maharajah's gallery', you can get a pass for Fateh Prakash Palace, Shiv Niwas and Shambu Niwas, Rs 75. Guided tour, 1 hr, Rs 100 each. A shop sells guidebooks etc (Mewar Paintings recommended). Guides hang around the entrance – if you can't find one you're happy with, ask the staff at the ticket office to recommend somebody – standards vary wildly.*

This impressive complex of several palaces is a blend of Rajput and Mughal influences. Half of it, with a great plaster façade, is still occupied by the royal family. Between the **Bari Pol** (Great Gate, 1608, men traditionally had to cover their heads with a turban from this point on) to the north, and the **Tripolia Gate** (1713), are eight *toranas* (arches), under which the rulers were weighed against gold and silver on their birthdays, which was then distributed to the poor. One of the two domes on top of the Tripolia originally housed a water clock; a glass sphere with a small hole at the base was filled with water and would take exactly one hour to empty, at which point a gong would be struck and the process repeated. The gate has three arches to allow the royal family their private entrance, through the middle, and then a public entry and exit gate to either side. Note the elephant to the far left (eastern) end of the gate structure; they were seen as bringers of good fortune and appear all over the palace complex. The Tripolia leads in to the **Manak Chowk**, originally a large courtyard which was converted in to a garden only

🔵 *The gold cupolas on top of the palace's many domes are the only ones of their kind.*
⚫ *They are taken to denote the proud independence of the Mewar Dynasty, the world's second longest family lineage after the Japanese Samurai.*

66 99 Between the Bari Pol and the Tripolia Gate are eight *toranas* (arches), under which the rulers were weighed against gold and silver on their birthdays, which was then distributed to the poor...

in 1992. The row of lumps in the surface to the left are original, and demarcate elephant parking bays! Claiming descent from Rama, and therefore the sun, the Mewars always insured that there was an image of the sun available for worship even on a cloudy day, thus the beautiful example set in to the exterior wall of the palace. The large step in front of the main entrance was for mounting horses, while those to the left were for elephants. The family crest above the door depicts a Rajput warrior and one of the Bhil tribesmen from the local area who's renowned archery skills were much used in the defence of the Mewar household. The motto translates as 'God protects those who stand firm in upholding righteousness'.

As you enter the main door, a set of stairs to the right leads down to an armoury which includes an impressive selection of swords, some of which incorporate pistols in to their handles. Most people then enter the main museum to the right, although it is possible to access the government museum from here (see below). The entrance is known as **Ganesh Dori**, meaning 'Ganesh's turn'; the image of the elephant God in the wall as the steps start to turn has been there since 1620. Note the tiles underneath which were imported from Japan in the 1930s and give even the Hindu deities an Oriental look to their eyes. The second image is of Laxmi, bringer of good fortune and wealth.

The stairs lead in to **Rai Angan**, 'Royal Court' (1559). The temple to the left is to the sage who first advised that the royal palace be built on this side. Opposite is a display of some of Maharana Pratap Singh's weapons, used in some of his many battles with the Mughals, as well as his legendary horse, Chetak. The Mughals fought on elephants, the Mewars on horses; the elephant trunk fitted to Chetak's nose was to fool the Mughal elephants in to thinking that the Mewar horses were baby elephants, and so not to be attacked. A fuller version of this nosepiece can be seen in one of the paintings on the walls, as indeed can an elephant wielding a sword in its trunk during battle.

The stairs to the left of the temple lead up to **Chandra Mahal**, featuring a large bowl where gold and silver coins were kept for distribution to the needy. Note that the intricately carved walls are made not from marble but a combination of limestone powder, gum Arabic, sugar cane juice and white lentils. From here steps lead up in to **Bari Mahal** (1699-1711), situated on top the hill chosen as the palace site; the design has incorporated the original trees. The cloisters' cusped arches have wide eaves and are raised above the ground to protect the covered spaces from heavy monsoon rain. This was an intimate 'playground' where the royal family amused themselves and were entertained. The painting opposite the entrance is an aerial view of the palace, the effect from the wall facing it is impressive. The chair on display was meant for Maharana Fateh Singh's use at the Delhi Darbar, an event which he famously refused to attend. The chair was sent on and has still never been used.

The picture on the wall of two elephants fighting shows the area that can be seen through the window to the left; there is a low wall running from the Tripolia gate to the main palace building. An elephant was placed either side of the wall, and then each had to try to pull the other until their opponent's legs touched the wall, making them the victor.

The next room is known as **Dil Kushal Mahal**, 'love entertainment room', a kind of mirrored love nest. This leads on to a series of incredibly intricate paintings depicting the story of life in the palace, painted 1782-1828. The **Shiv Vilas Chini ki Chatar Sali** incorporates a large number of Chinese and Dutch tiles in to its decoration, as well as an early petrol-powered fan. Next is the Moti Mahal, the ladies' portion of the mens' palace, featuring a changing room lined with mirrors and two game boards incorporated in to the design of the floor.

Pritam Niwas was last lived in by Maharana Gopal Singh, who died in 1955 having been disabled by polio at a young age. His wheel armchair and even his commode are on display here. This leads on to **Surya Chopar**, which features a beautiful gold leaf image of the sun; note the 3D relief painting below. The attractive **Mor Chowk** court, intended for ceremonial darbars, was added in the mid-17th century, and features beautiful late 19th-century peacock mosaics. The throne room is to its south, the **Surya Chopar**, from which the Rana (who claimed descent from the Sun) paid homage to his divine ancestor. The **Manak Mahal** (Ruby Palace)was filled with figures of porcelain and glass in the mid-19th century. To the north, the **Bari Mahal** or Amar Vilas (1699-1711) was added on top of a low hill. It has a pleasant garden with full grown trees around a square water tank in the central court

A plain, narrow corridor leads in to the **Queen's Palace**, featuring a series of paintings, lithographs and photographs, and leading out in to **Laxmi Chowk**, featuring two cages meant for trapping tigers and leopards.

The entrance to the **government museum** ① *1000-1630, closed Fri, Rs 3*, is from this courtyard. The rather uncared for display includes second century BC inscriptions, fifth- to eighth-century sculpture and 9,000 miniature paintings of 17th- and 19th-century Mewar schools of art but also a stuffed kangaroo and Siamese twin deer.

On the west side of the Tripolia are the **Karan Vilas** (1620-1628) and **Khush Mahal**, a rather grotesque pleasure palace for European guests, whilst to the south lies the **Shambhu Niwas Palace** the present residence of the Maharana.

Maharana Fateh Singh added to this the opulent **Shiv Niwas** with a beautiful courtyard and public rooms, and the **Fateh Prakash Palace**. Here the **Darbar Hall**'s royal portrait gallery displays swords still oiled and sharp. The Bohemian chandeliers (1880s) are reflected by Venetian mirrors, the larger ones made in India of lead crystal. Both, now exclusive hotels (see below), are worth visiting.

The **Crystal Gallery** ① *open to guests only at lunch and dinner, Rs 200 for a guided tour with a talk on the history of Mewar, followed by a cup of tea; cold reception reported by some*, on the first floor has an extensive collection of cut-crystal furniture, vases etc, made in

Jagdish Mandir area

N

0 metres 100
0 yards 100

Sleeping
Badi Haveli & Lehar 1
Caravanserai 2
Evergreen & Lalghat
  Guest House 3
Gangaur Palace 5
Jagat Niwas &
  Kankarwa Haveli 6
Jheel 7

Lake Ghat &
  Rana Castle 8
Mughal Palace 14
Nayee Haveli 4
Nukkad Guesthouse 9
Poonam Haveli 12
Pratap Bhawan 10
Ratan Palace &
  Sai Niwas 11
Udai Niwas 13

Eating
Gokul 4
Heaven 1
King Roof Café 2
Mayur 3

Lake Pichola

Fringed with hills, gardens, *havelis*, ghats and temples, Lake Pichola is the scenic focus of Udaipur though parts get covered periodically with vegetation, and the water level drops considerably during the summer. Set in it are the Jag Niwas (Lake Palace) and the Jag Mandir Palaces.

Jag Mandir, built on an island in the south of the lake, is notable for the Gul Mahal, a domed pavilion started by Karan Singh (1620-1628) and completed by Jagat Singh (1628-1652). It is built of yellow sandstone inlaid with marble around an attractive courtyard. Maharajah Karan Singh gave the young Prince Khurram (later Shah Jahan), refuge here when he was in revolt against his father Jahangir in 1623, cementing a friendly relationship between the Mewar Maharaja and the future Mughal Emperor. Refugee European ladies and children were also given sanctuary here by Maharana Sarap Singh during the Mutiny. There is a lovely pavilion with four stone elephants on each side (some of the broken trunks have been replaced with polystyrene!). You get superb views from the balconies. An enjoyable **boat trip** ① *Apr-Sep 0800-1100, 1500-1800, Oct-Mar 1000-1200, 1400-1700, the 1-hr boat trip, on the hour, Rs 150, landing on Jag Mandir, 30-min boat ride, Rs 75*, around the lake including a visit to Jag Mandir island, operates from Bansi Ghat (City Palace) Jetty. It's especially attractive in the late afternoon light.

The **Jag Niwas** (Lake Palace) ① *for non-residents boat ticket from Bansi Ghat jetty with buffet meal, Rs 500-625 (see Eating); tour operators make block bookings so book in advance or try your luck at the jetty*, island has the Dilaram and Bari Mahal Palaces. They were built by **Maharana Jagat Singh II** in 1746 and cover the whole island. Once the royal summer residences (now a hotel), they seem to float like a dream ship on the blue waters of the lake. The courtly atmosphere, elegance and opulence of princely times, the painted ceilings, antique furniture combined with the truly magical setting make it one of the most romantic in India. There are, of course, superb views.

The **Jal Burj** is on the water's edge, south of the town. A pleasant two-hour walk to the south of the city takes you to the Sunset Point which has excellent views. The path past the café (good for breakfast) leads to the gardens on the wall; a pleasant place to relax. Although it looks steep it is only a 30-minute climb from the café.

From the small **Dudh Talai** (Milk Lake) ① *Rs 5 day time, Rs 10 evening*, nearby, there is an attractive walk to the main lake (especially pleasant in the evening; large fruit bats can also often be seen). A left turn up a new road leads to Manikya Lal Verma Park which has a 'musical fountain' which is switched on in the evening.

Fateh Sagar and around

This lake, north of Lake Pichola, was constructed in 1678 during the reign of Maharana Jai Singh and modified by Maharana Fateh Singh. There is a pleasant lakeside drive along the east bank but, overall, it lacks the charm of the Pichola. Nehru Park on an island (accessible by ferry) has a restaurant.

Overlooking the Fateh Sagar is the **Moti Magri** (Pearl Hill) ① *Rs 10, camera free.* There are several statues of local heroes in the attractive rock gardens including one of Maharana Pratap on his horse Chetak, to which he owed his life. Local guides claim that Chetak jumped an abyss of extraordinary width in the heat of the battle of Haldighati (1576) even after losing one leg. To find out more look at Hero of Haldighati.

Sahelion ki Bari ('Garden of the Maids of Honour') ① *0900-1800. Rs 2, plus Rs 2 for 'fountain show'*, a little northwest from Moti Magri, is an ornamental pleasure garden and it is a great spot; both attractive and restful. In a pavilion in the first courtyard opposite the entrance, a children's museum has curious exhibits including a pickled scorpion, a human skeleton and busts of Einstein and Archimedes! Beautiful black marble kiosks decorate the corners of a square pool. An elegant round lotus pond has four marble elephants spouting water. To the north is a rose garden with over 100 varieties.

At **Ahar** (3 km east) are the remains of the ancient city which has some Jain **chhatris** set on high plinths in the Mahasati (royal cremation ground). A small **museum** ① *1000-1630, closed Fri and holidays, Rs 3*, contains pottery shards and terracotta toys from the first century BC and 10th-century sculptures. Nearby are the temples of Mira Bai (10th century), Adinatha (11th century) and Mahavira (15th century).

Excursions

Monsoon Palace

① *No formal fee but caretaker expects a tip (about Rs 20 per person). It is 15 km west. Taxis minimum Rs 300 (tourist taxis Rs 450 including road toll), auto-rickshaws Rs 200 return, including road toll at the foot of the hill (start from Udaipur by 1700 for sunset). Allow about 3 hrs for the round trip.*

There are good views from this deserted palace on a hilltop. The unfinished building on **Sajjangarh**, at an altitude of 335 m, which looks picturesque from the west facing battlements, was named after Sajjan Singh (1874-1884) and was planned to be high enough to see his ancestral home, Chittaurgarh. Normally, you need a permit from the police in town to enter though many find a tip to the gateman suffices. It offers panoramic views of Udaipur (though the highest roof is spoilt by radio antennas); the windows of the Lake Palace can be seen reflecting the setting sun. The palace itself is very rundown but the views from the hill top are just as good. A visit in the late afternoon is recommended; take binoculars.

Shilipgram 'Crafts Village' and Bari Lake

① *Daily, 1100-1900 in season; some evenings only otherwise. Rs 15, camera Rs10, video Rs50. Some 5 km away, take a taxi or auto-rickshaw. If you cycle, you can have a break and cold drink at the boat jetty on Nehru Island.*

This craft village, near Havala, beyond Fateh Sagar on the Rani Road, has traditional huts from Rajasthan, Gujarat, Maharashtra and Goa faithfully replicated. The collection of colourful folk art, folk music and dancing makes for an interesting outing though it is getting touristy. Crafts demonstrations and sales are held mostly at weekends but it is nearly deserted on weekdays and so can be disappointing. **Shilpi Café and Beer Bar** is good for snacks. The main attraction is the spotless, well-managed swimming pool where you can swim for Rs 100 (loungers, Rs 50). Short camel rides are offered but are not recommended for women alone ("camel driver may climb up behind you and behave most unpleasantly"). Allow two hours for a visit at weekends.

Bari Lake (Tiger Lake), 12 km northwest of Udaipur, past Shilipgram, is a clean lake in a quiet spot. It is good for a swim and a picnic, and strangely reminiscent of the English Lake District.

● Sleeping

Udaipur *p140, map p141 and p144*
Frenzied building work continues to provide more hotels while restaurants compete to offer the best views from the highest rooftop. The area around the lake is undeniably the most romantic place to stay, but also the most congested. The hotels on Lake Palace Road and on the hilltop above Fateh Sagar Lake offer more peaceful surroundings, while Swaroop Sagar offers a good compromise between calmness and convenience. Most hotels can arrange

puppet shows, folk concerts etc if guests are ready to share costs. Paying guest accommodation list at Tourist Reception Centre, Fateh Memorial.

LL Lake Palace (Taj), Pichola Lake, T0294-252 8800, www.tajhotels.com. 84 rooms, most with lake view, in one of the world's most spectacularly located hotels. Standard rooms tasteful but unremarkable, suites outstanding, small pool, quite an experience, service can be slightly abrupt.

LL Udai Vilas (Oberoi), on Pichola Lake, T0294-243 3300, www.oberoihotels.com. The elegant but monochrome exterior of this latter day palace does nothing to prepare you for the opulence within; the stunning entry courtyard sets the scene for the staggeringly beautiful interiors. The 87 rooms are the last word in indulgence; some have one of the hotel's 9 swimming pools running alongside their private balcony. The setting on the lake, overlooking both the lake and city palaces, is superb, as are the food and service. Outstanding.

LL-L Fateh Prakash (HRH), City Palace, T0294-252 8017, www.hrhindia.com. 19 well-appointed, lake-facing rooms in modern 'Dovecote' wing and 7 superb suites in main palace building. Original period furniture, 2 restaurants (see Eating), facilities of Shiv Niwas, good service (residents may ask for a 'Pass' at entrance of City Palace, for a short cut to hotel).

LL-L Shiv Niwas (HRH), City Palace (right after entrance), T0294-252 8018, www.hrh india.com. 19 tasteful rooms, 17 luxurious suites including those stayed in by Queen Elizabeth II and Roger Moore, some with superb lake views, very comfortable, good restaurant, very pleasant outdoor seating for all meals around a lovely marble pool (non-residents pay Rs 300 to swim), tennis, squash, excellent service, beautiful surroundings, reserve ahead in season. Recommended.

LL-L Trident (Oberoi/Hilton), overlooking Lake Pichola, peaceful farside, T0294 243 2200, www.trident-hilton.com. 143 rooms, tastefully decorated, all facilities, good pool, varied restaurants, polite but friendly, lush gardens, unpretentious, relaxing, own ferry to City Palace. Recommended.

LL-AL Laxmi Vilas Palace, on hillock above Fateh Sagar, 5 km station, T0294-252 9711,

www.thegrandhotels.net. 54 rooms are situated in the royal guesthouse (built in 1911), which are still atmospheric, and comfortable, but have less character. Good pool (non-residents, Rs 175), tennis. The suites are in the main palace.

A-B Hilltop Palace, 5 Ambavgarh near Fateh Sagar, T0294-243 2245, hilltop@datainfo sys.net. 62 pleasant rooms (large rooms upstairs with balcony), restaurant (visit for a view from the roof!), bar, exchange, pool, good food, friendly and efficient service.

B Amet Haveli, overlooking Lake Pichola, T0294-243 1085, regiudr@datainfosys.net. 5 rooms maintained to a high standard in fantastic location, question marks over service but views are superb.

B Jagat Niwas, 24-25 Lal Ghat, T0294-242 0133, www.jagatniwaspalace. com. 30 individual, very clean rooms in beautifully restored 17th-century 'fairy tale' *haveli*, very good restaurant, helpful staff, good travel desk, excellent service. Highly recommended.

B Lake Pichola, Hanuman Ghat, overlooking lake, T0294-243 1197. 30 rooms, some a/c, poorly maintained, tired old baths, fantastic views from some rooms, boat rides, friendly, relatively cheap food, jewellery shop sells conservative styles at reasonable prices.

B Rajdarshan, 18 Pannadhai Marg, inside Hathipol against the walls, by Swaroop Sagar lake edge, T0294-252 6601, rdarshan@ sancharnet.in. 52 international standard, central a/c rooms, very good restaurant, bar, exchange, pool, good views from balconies though sacred peepul tree may block out your view! Pleasant service.

B Rampratap Palace, on Fateh Sagar, T0294-243 1701, www.hotelrpp.com. Smart rooms, some a/c, most with lake views in new attractive hotel, lawns, on busy road but friendly.

B Shikarbadi (HRH), Govardhan Vilas, Ahmedabad Rd, 5 km from centre, T0294-258 3201, www.hrhindia.com. 26 good, refurbished a/c rooms, pool, horse riding, attractive 100-year-old royal hunting lodge and stud farm with lake, lovely gardens, deer park, charming and peaceful.

B Udai Kothi, Hanuman Ghat, T0294-243 2810, www.udaikothi.com. 24 attractive rooms, but real piece de resistance is Udaipur's only rooftop pool, a real treat.

☕ A classic car collection

The Garden Hotel was the former royal garage of the Maharanas of Mewar before it was converted into a restaurant. The original fuel pumps can still be seen in the forecourt where 19 cars from the ancestral fleet have been displayed. The impressive collection includes a 1920s Rolls Royce, custom built for a disabled member of the Mewar family, 1930s models of Rolls and Cadillacs, and two 1940s Chevrolet trucks, one of which was used as a school bus to take boys to the Maharana of Mewar's school!

Management reported as uncaring. One guest was forced to sleep on the roof after her room caught fire!

B-C Caravanserai, Jaiwana Haveli, part mid-18th century, 14 Lal Ghat, T0294-252 1252, hotelcaravanserai@yahoo.com. 18 clean, modern rooms, some with great views, particularly good view from rooftop restaurant.

B-C Lakend, Alkapuri, Fateh Sagar, T0294-243 1400, www.lakend.com. 78 average rooms, some a/c and private balconies, poorly maintained pool, large lakeside garden, very peaceful, excellent views.

B-C Rang Niwas Palace, Lake Palace Rd, T0294 252 3980, rangniwas75@hotmail.com. 20 beautifully renovated a/c rooms with bath in 200-year-old building, some in newer annexe, restaurant, very pleasant pool, gardens, very helpful staff, old-world and charming, convenient location. Recommended.

C Ashish Palace, 125 Chetak Marg, T0294-252 5558, ashishpalace@rediffmail. com. 32 good rooms (most a/c) with bath, restaurant, friendly and helpful manager, crowded area but convenient for sightseeing, GPO, Tourist Office.

B-C Sarovar, Hanuman Ghat outside Chandpol, T0294-243 2801, www.hotels arovar.com. 21 slightly musty rooms on 3 floors in a new hotel, 13 with a/c overlook Lake Pichola, rooftop restaurant, sunbathing terrace, free use of good pool near Shilipgram (3 km away).

B-C Swaroop Vilas, 6 Ambavgarh, on Swaroop Sagar Lake, T0294-243 0207, www.swaroopvilas.com. 28 a/c rooms in well-maintained, tastefully decorated hotel, okay views of lake, pleasant gardens and pleasant management.

C Kankarwa Haveli, 26 Lalghat, T0294-241 1457, khaveli@yahoo.com. 3 mins from bazar but quiet, impressive views from terrace, 14 clean, well-maintained rooms, some face lake, in renovated 250-year-old *haveli* on lake shore, breakfast and snacks on the roof terrace, meals on request, family run, lack of common sitting areas a problem in summer.

C Sai Niwas, 75 Navghat, T0294-242 1586. 6 slightly overpriced but characterful rooms in attractive old building, beautiful roof-terrace with good views of lake.

C-D Anand Bhawan (government run), Fateh Sagar Rd, T0294-252 3256. 22 rooms (lake-facing deluxe a/c rooms best), hilltop location with spectacular views, pleasant gardens, 1930s royal guesthouse, but getting increasingly run down with unsatisfactory service, unhelpful management.

C-D Kajri (RTDC), Shastri Circle, T0294-241 0501. 53 rooms, some a/c, and dorm, deluxe overlooking garden best, restaurant (dull, mediocre food), bar, travel, Tourist Reception Centre.

C-D Poonam Haveli, 39 Lal Ghat, T0294-241 0303, poonamhaveli@hotmail.com. 16 modern, attractive, clean rooms plus large roof terrace, although view of Lake Palace is slightly obscured.

C-D Raj Palace, at 103, T0294-241 0364, rajpalaceudr@yahoo.com. 26 clean, comfortable rooms arranged around pleasant courtyard garden, rooftop restaurant, excellent service, good city tour.

C-D Wonder View, 6 Panch Dewari Marg, near **Lake Pichola Hotel**, T0294-243 2494. 8 rooms (6 more coming) on 4 floors, fabulous views especially from rooftop restaurant (food arrives slowly from ground floor kitchen!), very friendly, excellent taxis, peaceful and relaxed part of town.

C-E Mahendra Prakash, Lake Palace Rd, T0294-241 9811, udai99@hotmail.com. 20 large, spotless, well furnished rooms, some a/c, pleasant patio garden, excellent pool, owner/manager of the Maharana's family, friendly, excellent service. Recommended.

D Lake Ghat, 4/13 Lalghat, 150 m behind Jagdish Mandir T0294-252 1636. 13 well-maintained rooms, clean, friendly, great views from terraces, good food.

D Pratap Bhawan, 12 Lal Ghat, T0294-256 0566, pratapbhawan@yahoo.co.in. 10 large, very clean rooms with baths in a lovely guest house, lake-facing terrace restaurant, excellent, home-cooked meals, warm welcome from retired army colonel and his wife. Recommended.

D Pratap Country Inn, Airport Rd, Titadhia Village, T0294-258 3138. 20 rooms, few a/c, restaurant, horse and camel safaris, riding, pool (sometimes empty), old royal country house in attractive grounds, 6 km centre (free transfer from railway station).

D-E Jheel Guest House, 56 Gangor Ghat (behind temple), T0294-421 352. 6 pleasant rooms in new extension with bath and hot water, 8 in older part, good rooftop restaurant, friendly owner, fantastic views.

D-E Yatri Guest House, 3/4 Panchkuin Rd, Udaipol, near the bus stand, T0294-241 7251. 13 simple rooms, helpful, know-ledgeable owner, best option in area.

E Dream Heaven, just over Chandpol, on the edge of the lake, T0294-243 1038, deep_Rg@yahoo.co.uk. 6 clean, simple rooms with bath, family run, no frills but excellent rooftop restaurant.

E Minerwa, 5/13 Gadiya Devra, Chandpole, T0294-252 3471, minerwa66@hotmail.com. 16 plain but clean rooms in a modern, marble building, good restaurant (see Eating).

E Udai Niwas, near Jagdish Temple, Gangaur Marg, T0294-512 0789, hoteludainiwas@yahoo.co.in. 14 renovated rooms in friendly hotel with a pleasant rooftop and good views of the city.

E-F Badi Haveli, near Jagdish Temple, T0294-241 2588, hotelbadahaveli@hotmail.com. 8 rooms with bath, some good, restaurant, travel services, terraces with lake view, pleasant atmosphere, very friendly owner.

E-F Gangaur Palace, 339 Ghadiya Devra Marg, T0294-242 2303. 17 rooms, some in old part of 250-year-old *haveli*, good standard, rooftop restaurant has 2 screens showing Octopussy plus one other film every night, friendly, if slightly slick, management.

E-F Kumbha Palace, 104 Bhatiyani Chotta, T0294-242 2702. 9 rooms, clean, good linen, quiet, very good rooftop restaurant (see below), atmospheric, good views, attractive. Recommended.

E-F Lake Shore, on Lake Pichola, near Lake Palace Rd, T0294-243 2480. 7 funkily decorated rooms, superb terrace, garden, very relaxing, good views of ghats, friendly owner.

E-F Lalghat Guest House, 33 Lal Ghat, T0294-252 5301. 24 rooms, best with great lake views, best dorm in town (Rs 50), good clean beds with curtains (!), spotless baths, breakfast, snacks, drinks, good views from terraces, very relaxed, good travel desk. Recommended.

E-F Mewar Inn, 42 Residency Rd, (pleasantly away from centre), T0294-252 2090, mewarinn@hotmail.com. 20 spotless rooms, some with (brief!) hot shower, street side incredibly noisy, no commission to rickshaws (if they refuse to go; try a horse carriage!), Osho veg restaurant, good cheap bike hire, rickshaw to town Rs 10-20, very friendly, YHA discounts. Recommended.

E-F Mughal Palace, tucked away behind Lal Ghat, T0294-241 7954, mughalpalace2001@hotmail.com. 9 clean, smallish rooms, some with bath, Indian terrace restaurant, individually decorated home, solar power, internet, good value.

E-F Natural, 55 Rang Sagar (between New and Chandelle bridges), T0294-243 1979, hotelnatural@hotmail.com. 16 clean, basic rooms with hot showers, sunny balconies facing lake, good restaurant (see below), peaceful, family-run, "a home from home".

F Lehar, T0294-241 7651. 5 rooms with bath, best with lake view. Not as cute but less crowded than **Badi Haveli**, run by charming lady.

F Mona Lisa, 104 Bhatiyani Chotta, T0294-256 1562. 8 rooms, some air-cooled, with bath, good breakfast, garden,

For an explanation of sleeping and eating price codes used in this guide, see inside the front cover. Other relevant information is found in Essentials, see pages 40-45.

F Nayee Haveli, 55 Gangor Marg, T0294-512 0611, nayeehaveli@yahoo.co.uk. 5 clean, basic rooms in friendly family home, home-cooked food. Recommended.

F Nukkad Guest House, 56 Ganesh Ghat (signposted from Jagdish Temple). 10 small, simple rooms, some with bath, in typical family house, home cooked meals, rooftop, very friendly and helpful, clean. Recommended.

F Rana Castle, 4, Lal Ghat, T0294-241 3666, singh_bhagwat1@yahoo.com. 8 well-maintained rooms, particularly charming lower down. Pleasant rooftop restaurant.

F Queens Café, 14 Bajrang Marg (from Jagdish Temple, cross Chand Pol, then 1st left, continue for a few minutes to find the hotel on your right), T0294-243 0875. 2 decent rooms, shared bath, roof terrace with good views, home cooked meals (including continental Swiss), informal, welcoming family. Meenu teaches cooking and hindi. Highly recommended. See below.

❷ Eating

Udaipur *p140, map p141 and p144*
Try the local *daal, bhati, choorma*. The larger hotels have bars. Plush Heritage hotels (see Sleeping) have expensive menus. These are worth it just for the visit but the non-vegetarian buffet food can be kept warm for long periods and so can be risky. Below are a mix of restaurants within hotels and just restaurants. Many of the budget places are in the Lal Ghat area. The usual fare includes pancakes, macaroni etc for the homesick westerner; some still show the locally shot Octopussy! Those near Jagdish Mandir do not serve alcohol.

TTT Lake Palace, see Sleeping, buffet lunch 1230-1430, dinner 1930-2030 often preceded by puppet show at 1800, expensive drinks (check bill), best way for non-residents to experience this unique palace Fateh Prakash's beautiful Gallery Restaurant. Superb views but pretty tasteless continental food, English cream teas. Tea also at Darbar Hall (see above).

TTT Shiv Niwas, see Sleeping, wonderful buffet followed by disappointing desserts, eat in the bar, or dine in luxury by the pool

listening to live Indian classical music (Rs 1,000); bar expensive but the grand surroundings are worth a drink.

TTT Sunset Terrace, Bansi Ghat, Lake Pichola. Very pleasant, superb views of City Palace Complex and lake, good à la carte selection.

TT Bagore-ki-Haveli, Gangaur Ghat, T0294-309 0686. Multi-cuisine menu including some local specialities in fantastic setting by lake. Recommended.

TT Berrys, near Chetak Circle. International. Standard menu, comfortable, friendly, beer available, open 0900-2300.

TT Jagat Niwas, see Sleeping. Mainly Indian. Jarokha rooftop restaurant with fabulous lake views, excellent meals, breakfast, teas, ices.

TT Kumbha Palace, see Sleeping, T0294-242 2702. Excellent Indian and western food. Rooftop, simple seating under awning (chocolate cake, baked potato, pizzas, milk shakes), friendly, helpful service, closed 1500-1800.

TT Natural, 55 Rang Sagar,. International including Tibetan, Italian and Mexican. Good buffet breakfasts, home-baking, peaceful rooftop. Recommended.

TT Park View, opposite Town Hall, City Station Rd. Good North Indian. Comfortable.

TT Sai Niwas, see Sleeping, 75 Nav Ghat. International. Excellent views from roof terrace, good evening meal, freshly cooked, attentive service.

TT Sankalp, outside Suraj Pol, City Station Rd, T0294-510 2686. Upmarket South Indian in modern surroundings, great range of chutneys.

T Delhi Darbar, Hathipol. Good Mughlai.

T Dream Haven, 22 Bhim Parmeshver Marg, across Chandpol. Excellent, never ending *thalis* (Rs 25) on rooftop "watch the sun go down over the lake listening to the drums from the Jagdish Mandir".

T Garden Hotel, opposite Gulab Bagh, Gujarati/Rajasthani. Air-cooled, excellent veg *thalis*, Rs 45 (try khadhi, khaman, makkhan buda), busy at lunch but not for dinner, interesting building, elderly waiters (will show you around kitchen). Recommended.

T Gokul, Gadiya Devra. Good range, great location, well-maintained. Recommended

T Hariyali, near Gulab Bagh. Has good North Indian in a pleasant garden setting.

T Heaven, street corner near Lal Ghat.

International. A long climb up to rooftop, stunning uninterrupted lake views, usual fare (also cheap rooms).

† **King Roof Café**, Gangor Ghat. North Indian. Delicious spicy dishes, comfy chairs, usual rickety bamboo and matting for shade, most hospitable owner.

† **Maxim's**, nearby, is part art gallery (silk paintings). Slow service but good food.

† **Mayur**, Mothi Chowtha, opposite Jagdish Temple. Mainly Indian. Pleasant for veg *thali* (Rs 45) snacks and Octopussy, but slow service, also exchange after hours (good rate if you walk away!), internet.

† **Natraj**, near Town Hall. Rajasthani. Excellent *thalis* in family run simple dining hall, very welcoming.

† **Natural View**, on rooftop with good lake views.

† **Neelam**, City Station Rd. Average Indian. A/c, a good place to relax while waiting.

† **Purohit**, Anand Plaza. Good dosas.

† **4 Seasons**, near City Palace, and **Green Rose Café**. Western and Indian (mild). Very good food (but irregular hours). Both recommended.

† **Queens Café**, 14 Bajrang Marg (see Sleeping for directions). Fantastic collection of unusual dishes including mango curries and irresistible chocolate balls. Highly recommended. Also cooking lessons, see below.

† **Samore Garden**, opposite *Rang Niwas Hotel*, Lake Palace Rd, has a wide international menu, open later than most, no beer.

☻ Entertainment

Udaipur *p140, map p141 and p144*
Bagore-ki-Haveli, T0294-242 3610 after 1700. Daily cultural shows 1900-2000, enjoyable music and dance performances, reservations unnecessary.
Bharatiya Lok Kala Museum, T0294-252 9296. The 20-min puppet demonstrations during the day are good fun. Evening puppet show and folk dancing, 1800-1900, Sep-Mar, Rs 30, camera Rs 50. Recommended.
Meera Kala Mandir, south of railway station, T0294-258 3176. Daily except Sun, 1900-2000, Rs 60; cultural programme, a bit touristy and amateurish. See Shilpgram in the sights section above.

✺ Festivals and events

Udaipur *p140, map p141 and p144*
Mewar Festival (**11-12 Apr 2005**, 1-2 Apr 2006, 21-22 Mar 2007). See also p46 for statewide festivals.

☯ Shopping

Udaipur *p140, map p141 and p144*
The local handicrafts are wooden toys, colourful portable temples (*kavad*), Bandhani tie-and-dye fabrics, embroidery and Pichchwai paintings. Paintings are of 3 types: miniatures in the classical style of courtly Mewar; phads or folk art; and pichchwais or religious art (see Nathdwara, p156). The more expensive ones are 'old' – 20-30 years – and are in beautiful dusky colours; the cheaper ones are brighter.

The main shopping centres are Chetak Circle, Bapu Bazar, Hathipol, Palace Rd, Clock Tower, Nehru Bazar, Shastri Circle, Delhi Gate, Sindhi Bazar, Bada Bazar.

Books
Mewar International, 35 Lalghat. 'One-Stop-Shop' for wide selection of English books, exchange, films.
Pustak Sadan (Hindi sign), Bapu Bazar, near Town Hall. Good for Rajasthani history. Clothing Good in Hathipol but shop around; prices vary.
Sai, 168 City Palace Rd, 100 m from palace gate. Good English books (new and second-hand), internet, exchange, travel services.
Suresh, Hospital Rd, good fiction, non-fiction and academic books.

Fabric
Ashoka, opposite entrance to Shiv Niwas. Good quality but very expensive.
Monsoon Collection, 55 Bhatiyani Chotta. Quick, quality, tailoring. Recommended.
Shree Ji Saree Centre, Mothi Chowtha, 200 m from Temple. Good value, very helpful owner. Recommended.
Udaipur New Tailors, inside Hathipol. Gents tailoring, reasonably priced, excellent service.

Handicrafts and paintings
Some shops sell old pieces of embroidery turned into bags, cushion covers etc. Others

may pass off recent work as antique.
Ashoka Arts, **Uday Arts**, Lake Palace Rd, **Apollo Arts**, 28 Panchwati. Paintings on marble paper and 'silk', bargain hard. Hathipol shop has good silk scarves (watch batik work in progress).
Gallery Pristine, T0294-242 3916, Kalapi House, Bhatiyani Chotta, Palace Rd. Good collection of contemporary art, including original 'white on brown' paintings, pleasant ambience. Recommended.
Gangour, Mothi Chowtha. Quality miniature paintings.
Gem-arts, near Chetak Circle.
Jagdish Emporium, City Palace Rd. For traditional Udaipur and Gujarati embroideries.
KK Kasara, opposite Nami Gali, 139 Mothi Chowtha. Good religious statues, jewellery.
Shivam Ayurvedic, Lake Palace Rd. Also art store, interesting, knowledgeable owner.
Sisodia Handicrafts, entrance of Shiv Niwas Palace. Miniature 'needle paintings' of high quality – see artist at work, no hard sell.

Photography

Shops on City Station Rd and Bapu Bazar.
Deluxe Camera, 109 Bapu Bazar, 3rd floor. Good repairs.

▲▲ Activities and tours

Udaipur *p140, map p141 and p144*
Art, cooking and hindi classes
Hare Krishna Arts, City Palace Rd, T0294-242 0304. Rs 450 per 2-hrart lesson, miniature techniques a speciality. Cooking classes too.
Queens Café, 14 Bajrang Marg, T0294-243 0875. Rs900 for 5-hr introductory class in basics of Indian cooking. Also Hindi lesson. Both are highly recommended.

Massage
Bharti Guesthouse, Lake Pichola Rd, T0294-243 3469. Indian, Swiss and Mexican styles at reasonable prices.

Riding
On elephant, camel or horse: travel agencies (eg **Namaskar**, **Parul** in Lalghat) arrange elephant and camel rides, Rs 200 per hr but need sufficient notice. Horse riding through hotels (**Shikarbadi**, **Pratap Country Inn** and some castles around Udaipur).

Sightseeing tours
Offered by RTDC Fath Memorial, Suraj Pol. City sightseeing: half day (0800-1230) Rs 75(reported as poor). Excursion: half day (1400-1900), Haldighati, Nathdwara, Eklingji, Rs 105. Chittaurgarh (0800-1800), Rs 230 (with lunch); Ranakpur, Kumbhalgarh (0800-1900) Rs 230; Jagat-Jaisamand- Chavand-Rishabdeo (0800-1900) Rs 230 (with lunch).
Some of the following tour operators offer, as well as sightseeing tours, accommodation bookings and travel tickets.
Aravalli Safari, 1 Sheetla Marg, Lake Palace Rd, T0294-2420282, F2420121. Very professional. Recommended.
Forts & Palaces, 34-35 Shrimal Bhawan, Garden Rd, T0294-417359, jaipur@palaces-tours.com.
Parul, Jagat Niwas Hotel, Lalghat, T0294-242 1697, parul_tour@rediffmail.com. Air/train, palace hotels, car hire, exchange. Highly recommended.
Rajasthan Travels, excellent service.
Srinath Travel, T0294-252 9391. Direct buses to Mount Abu, Mumbai etc. Recommended.
Tourist Assistance Centre, 3 Paneri House, Bhatiyani Chotta, T0294-252 8169. Guides.

Swimming
Some hotel pools are open to non-residents: **Lakshmi Vilas** (Rs 175); **Rang Niwas** (Rs 100); **Shiv Niwas** (Rs 300). Also at Shilipgram Craft Village, Rs 100.

☉ Transport

Udaipur *p140, map p141 and p144*
Air
Dabok airport is 25 km east, T0294-265 5453. Security check is thorough; no batteries or knives allowed in hand luggage. Transport to town: taxis, Rs 190. **Indian Airlines**, Delhi Gate, T0294-241 0999, 1000-1315, 1400-1700. Airport, T0294-265 5453, enquiry T142. Reserve well ahead. **Indian Airlines** flights to **Aurangabad**; **Delhi**, US$90; **Jaipur**, **Jaisalmer**, **Jodhpur**, **Mumbai**. Jet Airways, T0294-256 5105, airport T0294-265 6288: **Delhi** via **Jaipur**, **Mumbai**. UP Air, daily to **Delhi**, **Jaipur**, **Mumbai**, **Rajkot**.

Auto-rickshaw
Rs 5, then Rs 3 per km; about Rs 50 per hr.

Bicycle

Vijay Cycles, half way down Bhatiyani Chotta, charge Rs 25 per day for hire, well- maintained and comfortable. Also shops near **Kajri Hotel**, Lalghat and Gangor Ghat area, which also have scooters (Rs 125 per day).

Bus

Long distance Main State Bus Stand, near railway line opposite Udai Pol, T0294-248 4191; reservations 0700-2100. State RTC buses to **Agra** 15 hrs; **Ahmadabad** 252 km, 7 hrs; **Bhopal** 765 km, 15 hrs; **Bikaner** 13 hrs; **Delhi** 635 km, 17 hrs; **Indore** 635 km; **Jaipur** 405 km, 10 hrs; **Jaisalmer** 14 hrs; **Jodhpur** 8 hrs (uncomfortable, poorly maintained road); **Mount Abu** 270 km, 0800, 1030 and 1500, 7 hrs), Rs 50 (Tourist bus, Rs 75, not much faster); **Mumbai** 802 km, very tiring, 16 hrs; **Pushkar** (Tourist bus, 7 hrs, Rs 90); **Ujjain** (7 hrs). Private buses and Luxury coaches run mostly at night. **Ahmadabad** with **Bonney Travels**, Paldi, Ahmedabad, has a/c coaches with reclining seats (contact **Shobha Travels**, City Station Rd), departs 1400 (6½ hrs), Rs 225, with drink/snack stops every 2 hrs. Highly recommended. **Shrinath** and **Punjab Travels** have non a/c buses to **Ahmedabad** and **Mount Abu. Jaipur**: several 'deluxe' buses (computerized booking) with reclining seats, Rs 200, more expensive but better. **Jaisalmer**: change at Jodhpur, Rs 160. **Jodhpur**: several options but best to book a good seat, a day ahead, RS90. Tour operators have taxis for **Kumbhalgarh** and **Ranakpur**.

Motorbike

Scooters and bikes can be hired from **Heera Tours & Travels** in a small courtyard behind Badi Haveli (Jagdish Temple area), Rs150-300 per day depending on size of machine.

Taxi

RTDC taxis from Fath Memorial, Suraj Pol. Private taxis from airport, railwayy station, bus stands and major hotels; negotiate rates.

Taxi Stand, Chetak Circle, T0294-252 5112. **Tourist Taxi Service**, Lake Palace Rd, T0294-252 4169.

Train

Udaipur City station, 4 km southeast of centre, (0294) 131. **Ahmadabad**: *Ahmadabad Exp, 9943*, 2115, 9½ hrs. **Ajmer**: *Delhi SR Exp, 9944*, 0800, 13 hrs; *Chetak Exp, 9616*, 1810, 8½ hrs. **Delhi (SR)**: *Delhi SR Exp, 9944*, 0800, 23½ hrs; *Chetak Exp, 9616*, 1810, 17½ hrs (best to change at Jaipur at 0715 to faster Intercity for Delhi Junction station). **Jalgaon**: (day and night trains) to visit Ajanta, Aurangabad, Ellora. **Jaipur**: *Delhi SR Exp, 9944*, 0830, 15 hrs; *Chetak Exp, 9616*, 1810, 11½ hrs.

❶ Directory

Udaipur *p140, map p141 and p144*
Banks Foreign exchange at **Andhra Bank**, Shakti Nagar. Cash advance against Visa/ Mastercard, efficient. **Bank of Baroda**, Bapu Bazar. For Amex. **Bank of Bikaner & Jaipur**, Chetak Circle. **Thomas Cook**, inside City Palace. But poor rates. **Trade Wings**, Polo Ground Rd, **Vijaya Bank** at City Palace entrance.
Chemists On Hospital Rd.
Hospitals General Hospital, Chetak Circle. Aravali Hospital (private), 332 Ambamata Main Rd, opposite **Charak Hostel**, T0294-243 0222, very clean, professional. Recommended.
Internet Mayur, Mothi Chowtha. **Mewar**, Raj Palace Hotel, Bhatiyani Chotta, **One Stop Shop**, near Lal Ghat Guest House. **Sai**, 168 City Palace Rd. **Thomas Cook** in City Palace Courtyard. Cyber Café near Jagat Niwas.
Post offices The GPO is at Chetak Circle. Posting a parcel can be a nightmare and mean endless queuing. **Poste Restante**: Shastri Circle Post Office.
Useful addresses Ambulance: T223 333. Fire: T227 111. **Police**: T100.

Around Udaipur

The area around Udaipur is dotted with a wide range of attractions, from some of the grandest of Rajasthan's heritage hotels to some of its cosiest castles, from secluded forest lakes, surrounded by wildlife, to one of the largest reservoirs in Asia. It's also home to some ancient temples and perhaps the most evocative of Rajasthan's plentiful palaces, the Juna Mahal near Dungarpur. ▸▸ *For Sleeping, Eating and other listings, see pages 156-157.*

Ins and outs
Most of the sights in this area are a little isolated and so not well connected by train. However, the quality of the region's roads has greatly improved recently, making travel either by bus or taxi both quick and convenient. ▸▸ *See Transport, page 157, for details.*

South of Udaipur

Jaisamand Lake → *Colour map 5, grid B1/2. 52 km southeast of Udaipur.*
Before the building of huge modern dams in India, Jaisamand was the second largest artificial lake in Asia, 15 km by 10 km. Dating from the late 17th century, it is surrounded by the summer palaces of the Ranis of Udaipur. The highest two of the surrounding hills are topped by the **Hawa Mahal** and **Ruti Rani palaces**, now empty but worth visiting for the architecture and the view. A small sanctuary nearby has deer, antelope and panther. Tribals still inhabit some islands on the lake. Crocodiles, keelback water snakes and turtles bask on other islands.

Bambora → *45-minutes' drive southeast of Udaipur.*
The imposing 18th-century hilltop fortress of Bambora has been converted to a heritage hotel by the royal family of Sodawas at an enormous restoration cost yet retaining its ancient character. The impressive fort is in Mewari style with domes, turrets and arches. To get here from Udaipur, go 12 km east along the airport road and take the right turn towards Jaisamand Lake passing the 11th-century Jagat Temple (38 km) before reaching Bambora.

Sitamata Wildlife Sanctuary → *117 km from Udaipur.*
The reserve of dense deciduous forests covers over 400 sq km and has extensive birdlife (woodpeckers, tree pies, blue jays, jungle fowl). It is one of the few sanctuaries between the Himalayas and the Nilgiris where giant brown flying squirrels have been reported. Visitors have seen hordes of langur monkey, nilgai in groups of six or seven, four-horned antelope, jackal and even panther and hyena, but the thick forests make sighting difficult. There are crocodiles in the reservoirs.

Rishabdeo → *63 km south of Udaipur along the NH8.*
Rishabdeo, off the highway, has a remarkable 14th-century Jain temple with intricate white marble carving and black marble statuary, though these are not as fine as at Dilwara or Ranakpur. Dedicated to the first Jain Tirthankar, Adinath or Rishabdev, Hindus, Bhils as well as Jains worship there. An attractive bazar street leads to the temple which is rarely visited by tourists. Special worship is conducted several times daily when Adinath, regarded as the principal focus of worship, is bathed with saffron water or milk. The priests are friendly; a small donation (Rs 10-20) is appreciated.

Dungarpur → *Phone code: 02964. Colour map 5, grid C1. Population 50,000.*
Dungarpur ('City of Hills') dates from the 13th century. The district is the main home of the Bhil tribal people, see page 290. It is also renowned for its stone masons, who in recent years have been employed to build Hindu temples as far afield as London. The attractive and friendly village has one of the most richly decorated and best preserved palaces in Rajasthan, the Juna Mahal. Surrounded on three sides by Lake Gaibsagar and backed by picturesque hills, the more recent **Udai Bilas Palace** (now a heritage hotel, see Sleeping) was built by Maharawal Udai Singhji in the

from the centre of which rises a four-storeyed pavilion with a beautifully carved wooden chamber.

The **Juna Mahal**, above the village, dates from the 13th century when members of the Mewar clan at Chittaur moved south to found a new kingdom after a family split. It is open to guests staying at Udai Bilas and by ticket for non residents, obtainable at the hotel. The seven-storeyed fortress-like structure with turrets, narrow entrances and tiny windows has colourful and vibrant rooms profusely decorated over several centuries with miniature wall paintings (among the best in Rajasthan),and glass and mirror inlay work. There are some fine *jarokha* balconies and sculpted panels illustrating musicians and dancers in the local green-grey parava stone which are strikingly set against the plain white walls of the palace to great effect.

> ✷ *Dungarpur is a bird-watchers' paradise with lots of ducks, moorhens, waders, ibises at the lake, tropical green pigeons and grey hornbills in the woods.*

The steep narrow staircases lead to a series of seven floors giving access to public halls, supported on decorated columns, and to intimate private chambers. There is a jewel of a Sheesh Mahal and a cupboard in the Maharawal's bedroom on the top floor covered in miniatures illustrating some 50 scenes from the Kama Sutra. Windows and balconies open to the breeze command lovely views over the town below. Perhaps nowhere else in Rajasthan gives as good an impression of how these palaces must have been hundreds of years ago; it is completely unspoilt and hugely impressive.

Rajmata Devendra Kunvar State Museum ① *1000-1630, closed Fri, Rs 3*, has a large gallery of sculptures of sixth-seventh century, 11th-12th century and 16th-18th century periods, excavated from the surrounding region of Vagad. Some interesting temples nearby include the 12th-century Siva temple at **Deo Somnath**, 12 km away, and the splendid complex of temple ruins profusely decorated with stone sculptures.

North of Udaipur

Khempur

This small, attractive village is conveniently located midway between Udaipur and Chittaurgarh. To find it turn off the highway, 9 km south of Mavli and about 50 km from Udaipur. The main reason for visiting is to eat or stay in the charming heritage hotel here, see Sleeping.

Eklingji → *22 km from Udaipur.*

① *0400-0700, 1000-1300 and 1700-1900. No photography.*

The white marble **Eklingji Temple** has a two-storey mandapa to Siva, the family deity of the Mewars. It dates from AD 734 but was rebuilt in the 15th century. There is a silver door and screen and a silver Nandi facing the black marble Siva. The evenings draw crowds of worshippers and few tourists. Many smaller temples surround the main one and are also worth seeing. Nearby is the large but simple **Lakulisa Temple** (972), and other ruined semi-submerged temples. The back street shops sell miniature paintings, see page 286. It is a peaceful spot attracting many waterbirds. Occasional buses go from Udaipur to Eklingji and Nagda which are set in a deep ravine containing the Eklingji Lake. RTDC run tours from Udaipur, 1400-1900.

Nagda

At Nagda, are three temples: the ruined 11th-century Jain temple of **Adbhutji** and the **Vaishnavite Sas-Bahu** ('Mother- in-law'/'Daughter-in-law') temples. The complex, though comparatively small, has some very intricate carving on pillars, ceiling and mandapa walls. You can hire bicycles in Eklingji to visit them.

Nathdwara → *Colour map 5, grid B1. 48 km from Udaipur.*

This is a centre of the Krishna worshipping community of Gujarati merchants who are followers of Vallabhacharya (15th century). Non-Hindus are not allowed inside the temple which contains a black marble Krishna image, but the outside has interesting paintings. The **Shrinathji temple** is one of the richest Hindu temples in India. At one time only high caste Hindus (Brahmins, Kshatriyas) were allowed inside, and the *pichhwais* (temple hangings) were placed outside, for those castes and communities who were not allowed into the sanctum sanctorum, to experience the events in the temple courtyard and learn about the life of lord Krishna. You can watch the 400-year-old tradition of *pichhwai* painting which originated here. The artists had accompanied the Maharana of Mewar, one of the few Rajput princes who still resisted the Mughals, who settled here when seeking refuge from Aurangzeb's attacks. Their carriage carrying the idol of Shrinathji was stuck at Nathdwara in Mewar, 60 km short of the capital Udaipur. Taking this as a sign that this was where God willed to have his home, they developed this into a pilgrim centre for the worship of lord Krishna's manifestation, Shrinathji. Their paintings, *pichhwais*, depict Lord Krishna as Shrinathji in different moods according to the season. The figures of lord Krishna and the gopis (milkmaids) are frozen on a backdrop of lush trees and deep skies. The Bazar sells pichchwais painted on homespun cloth with mineral and organic colour often fixed with starch.

Rajsamand Lake → *Colour map 5, grid B1. 56 km north of Udaipur.*

At **Kankroli**, is the Rajsamand Lake. The **Nauchoki Bund**, the embankment which contains it, is over 335-m long and 13-m high, with ornamental pavilions and *toranas*, all of marble and exquisitely carved. Behind the masonry bund is an 11-m wide earthen embankment, erected in 1660 by Rana Raj Singh who had defeated Aurangzeb on several occasions. Kankroli and its beautiful temple are on the southeast side of the lake.

Deogarh → *Colour map 5, grid B1. 2 km off the NH8. Altitude: 700 m.*

Deogarh (Devgarh) is an excellent place to break journey between Jaipur or Pushkar, and Udaipur to visit sights nearby. It is a very pleasant, little frequented town with a dusty but interesting bazar. Its elevation makes it relatively cool and the countryside and surrounding hills are good for gentle treks. There is an old fort on a hill as well as a magnificent palace on a hillock in the centre with murals illustrating the fine local school of miniature painting. **Raghosagar Lake**, which is very pleasant to walk around, has an island with a romantic ruined temple and tombs (poor monsoons leave the lake dry). It attracts numerous migratory birds and is an attractive setting for the charming 200-year-old palace, **Gokal Vilas**, the home of the present Rawat Saheb Nahar Singhji and the Ranisahiba. Their two sons have opened the renovated 17th-century **Deogarh Mahal Palace** to guests, see Sleeping. The Rawat, a knowledgeable historian and art connoisseur, has a private collection of over 200 paintings which guests may view.

● Sleeping

South of Udaipur *p154*
A Karni Fort (Heritage Hotel), Bambora, T0291-251 2101, www.karnihotels.com. 30 beautifully decorated rooms (circular beds!) in large, imposing fort, marble bathrooms, modern facilities, impressive interiors, enthusiastic and friendly manager, exceptional marble swimming pool, folk concerts, great beer bar, delicious food, hugely enjoyable. Recommended.

● *For an explanation of sleeping and eating price codes used in this guide, see inside the*
● *front cover. Other relevant information is found in Essentials, see pages 40-45.*

A **Udai Bilas Palace**, 2 km from town, Dungarpur, T02964-230 808, www. udaibilas palace.com. 20 unique a/c rooms (including 10 suites of which 3 are vast 'grand suites') mirror mosaics, some dated with art deco furniture, marble bathrooms some with modern furniture in old guest house, all with either a lake or garden view, good food (lunch Rs 380) a 'Country House' style hotel (guests dine together at one table) where Harshvardhan Singh is a charming host, beautiful new swimming pool, boating, TCs and credit cards accepted, idyllic setting, very relaxing. Highly recommended.

B **Jaisamand Island Resort**, Baba Island on Jaisamand Lake, T02906-234 723, www. lakend.com. 40 well equipped a/c rooms, restaurant (international menu), pool, garden, excellent location, great views, mixed reports on food and service.

B-C **Fort Dhariawad**, Sitamata Wildlife Sanctuary, T02950-220050. 14 rooms and 4 suites in restored and converted, mid-16th century fort (founded by one of Maharana Pratap's sons) and some in contemporary cottage cluster, meals (international menu), period decor, medieval flavour, great location by sanctuary (flying squirrels, langur monkeys in garden, crocodiles in reservoir), tribal village tours, jeeps to park, horse safaris, treks.

D **Forest Lodge**, Sitamata Wildlife Sanctuary, Dhariawad. Rather expensive considering lack of amenities, but fantastic location and views, a paradise for birders.

E **Gavri** (RTDC), Rishabdeo, T02907-230145. 8 simple rooms, dorm.

E-F **Vaibhav**, Saghwara Rd, Dungarpur, T02964-230 244. Simple rooms, tea stall style restaurant, owner very friendly and helpful. **Pushpanjali** and **Gayatri** (Pratibha Palace not recommended).

North of Udaipur p155

A-B **Deogarh Mahal**, Deogarh, T02904-252 777, www.deogarhmahal.com. 45 rooms in superb old fort built in 1617, including atmospheric suites furnished in traditional style with good views, best have balconies with private Jacuzzis. Fabulous keyhole-shaped pool, Keralan massage Mewari meals, home grown produce (room service 50 per cent extra), bar, good gift shop, log fires, folk

entertainment, boating, bird watching, jeep safaris, talks on art history, hospitable and delightful hosts. Outstanding hotel. Reserve well ahead. Highly recommended.

B **Heritage Resort**, Eklingji, T0294-440382. Fabulously located by the lake and ringed by hills. 30 excellent a/c rooms, contemporary building in traditional design, good food, pool, jacuzzi, boating, riding, good walking and cycling. Recommended.

B **Ravla Khempur**, Khempur, T02955-237 154, www.ravlakhempur.com. The former home of the village chieftain, this is a charming, small-scale heritage property. The rooms have been sensitively renovated with modern bathrooms, pleasant lawns, horse rides a speciality.

D-E **Gokul** (RTDC), near Lalbagh, 2 km from bus stand, Nathdwara, T02953-230 917. 6 rooms and dorm (Rs 50), restaurant.

D-E **Yatika** (RTDC), Nathdwara, T02953-231 119. 5 rooms and dorm (Rs 50).

😊 Festivals and events

South of Udaipur p154

Baneshwar Fair (19-23 Feb 2005; 8-12 Feb 2006, 29 Jan-2 Feb 2007). The tribal festival at the Baneshwar Temple, 70 km from Dungarpur, is one of Rajasthan's largest tribal fairs when Bhils, see p290, gather to the temple in large numbers for ritual bathing at the confluence of rivers. There are direct buses to Baneshwar during the fair. The temporary camp during the fair is best avoided. **Vagad Festival** in Dungarpur during this period offers an insight into local tribal culture. Both festivals are uncommercialized and authentic. Details from **Udai Bilas**, see Sleeping.

😊 Transport

South of Udaipur p154

From Dungarpur buses travel to/from **Udaipur** (110 km), 2 hrs, **Ahmadabad** (170 km), 4 hrs by car. You will need to hire a taxi to get to the other destinations.

North of Udaipur p155

For **Nathdwara**, several buses from Udaipur from early morning. Buses also go to **Nagda**, **Eklingji** and **Rajsamand**. Private transport only for Khempur and Deogarh.

Kumbhalgarh, Ranakpur and around

Little-known Kumbhalgarh is one of the finest examples of defensive fortification in Rajasthan. You can wander around the palace, the many temples and along the walls – 36-km long in all – to savour the great panoramic views. It is two hours north (63 km) of Udaipur through the attractive Rajasthani countryside. The small fields are well kept, wherever possible irrigated from the streams, and Persian wheels and 'tanks' are dotted across the landscape. In winter, wheat and mustard grow in the fields, and the journey there and back is just as magical and fascinating as the fort itself.

The temples of Ranakpur, while perhaps not quite as exquisite as those in Mount Abu, are still incredibly ornate and amazingly unspoilt by tourism, having preserved a dignified air which is enhanced by the thick green forests that surround them. There are a number of interesting villages and palaces in the nearby area; if time allows this is a great region to explore at leisure, soaking in the unrushed, rural way of life. ▸▸ *For Sleeping, Eating and other listings, see pages 160-162.*

Ins and outs

A round-trip from Udaipur could also take in Eklingji, Nagda and Nathdwara. While most of the places in this section do have bus links, a private car is indispensable and makes the most of the scenic drives on offer. ▸▸ *See Transport, page 162, for details.*

Kumbhalgarh → *Phone code: 02954. Colour map 5, grid B1. 63 km from Udaipur.*

Kumbhalgarh Fort → *Altitude: 1,087m.*

Kumbhalgarh Fort, off the beaten tourist track, was the second most important fort of the Mewar Kingdom after Chittaurgarh. Built mostly by Maharana Kumbha (circa 1485), it is situated on a west facing ridge of the Aravalli hills, commanding a great strategic position on the border between the Rajput kingdoms of Udaipur (Mewar) and Jodhpur (Marwar). It is accessible enough to make a visit practicable and getting there is half the fun. There are superb views over the lower land to the northwest, standing over 200 m above the pass leading via Ghanerao towards Udaipur.

The approach Passing though charming villages and hilly terrain, the route to the fort is very picturesque. The final dramatic approach is across deep ravines and through thick scrub jungle. Seven gates guarded the approaches while seven ramparts were reinforced by semicircular bastions and towers. The 36 km-long black walls with curious bulbous towers exude a feeling of power as they snake their way up and down impossibly steep terrain. They were built to defy scaling and their width enabled rapid deployment of forces – six horses could walk along them side by side. The walls enclose a large plateau containing the smaller Katargarh Fort with the decaying palace of Fateh Singh, a garrison, 365 temples and shrines, and a village. The occupants (reputedly 30,000) could be self-sufficient in food and water, with enough storage to last a year. The fort's dominant location enabled defenders to see aggressors approaching from a great distance. Kumbhalgarh is believed to have been taken only once and that was because the water in the ponds was poisoned by enemy Mughals during the reign of Rana Pratap.

● *The Adinath Temple at Ranakpur has 1,444 engraved pillars. Not two of these pillars are the same, each individually carved.*

The gates The first gate Arait Pol is some distance from the main fort; the area was once thick jungle harbouring tigers and wild boar. Signals would be flashed by mirror in times of emergency. Hulla Pol (Gate of Disturbance) is named after the point reached by invading Mughal armies in 1567. Hanuman Pol contains a shrine and temple. The Bhairava Pol records the 19th-century Chief Minister who was exiled. The fifth gate, the Paghra (Stirrup) Pol is where the cavalry assembled; the Star tower nearby has walls 8-m thick. The Top-Khana (Cannon Gate) is alleged to have a secret escape tunnel. The last, Nimbu (Lemon) Pol has the Chamundi temple beside it.

The palace ① *Rs 5, Rs 100 foreigners.* It is a 30-minute walk (fairly steep in parts) from the car park to the roof of the Maharana's darbar hall. Tiers of inner ramparts rise to the summit like a fairytale castle, up to the appropriately named Badal Mahal (19th century) or Palace in the Clouds, with the interior painted in pastel colours. Most of the empty palace is usually unlocked (a chaukidar holds the keys). The views over the walls to the jungle-covered hillsides (now a wildlife reserve) and across the deserts of Marwar towards Jodhpur, are stunning. The palace rooms are decorated in a 19th-century style and some have attractive coloured friezes, but are unfurnished. After the maze-like palace at Udaipur, this is very compact. The Maharana's palace has a remarkable blue darbar hall with floral motifs on the ceiling. Polished chunar – lime – is used on walls and window sills, but the steel ceiling girders give away its late 19th-century age. A gap separated the mardana (men's) palace from the *zenana* (women's) palace. Some of the rooms in the *zenana* have an attractive painted frieze with elephants, crocodiles and camels. A circular Ganesh temple is in the corner of the *zenana* courtyard. A striking feature of the toilets was the ventilation system which allowed fresh air into the room while the toilet was in use.

Other temples The **Neelkantha, Kumbhaswami temples** and **Raimal's chhatri** nearby, are worth visiting. The **Mahadeva Temple** (1458) in a gorge below contains black marble slabs inscribed with the history of Mewar.

Kumbhalgarh Wildlife Sanctuary
① *Rs 10, Rs 100 foreigner, open sunrise to sunset.*
The sanctuary to the west of the fort covering about 600 sq km has a sizeable wildlife population but you have to be extremely lucky to spot any big game in the thick undergrowth. Some visitors have seen bear, panther, wolf and hyena but most have to be contented with seeing nilgai, sambhar deer, wild boar, jackal, jungle cat, and birds (grey jungle fowl, red spurfowl, painted francolin, quails, flycatchers). Crocodiles and water fowl can be seen at **Thandi Beri Lake**. Jeep and horse safaris can be organized from hotels in the vicinity including **Aodhi, Ranakpur, Ghanerao, Narlai**. The rides can be quite demanding as the tracks are very rough. A small patch of the sanctuary facing the temple has been set aside for deer. There is a four-wheel drive jeep track, and a trekking trail through the safari area can be arranged through **Shivika Lake Hotel**, Ranakpur (see below). Spotted deer and nilgai are easily seen, plus plenty of birdlife. Panthers sometimes trespass in to hunt young animals.

The tribal **Bhils** and **Garasias** (see page 290)– the latter found only in this belt – can be seen here, living in their traditional huts. The Forest Department may permit an overnight stay in their **Rest House** in **Kelwara**, the closest town, 6 km from sanctuary. With steep, narrow streets devoid of cars it is an attractive little place.

Ghanerao and Rawla Narlai → *Colour map 5, grid B1.*

Ghanerao was founded in 1606 by Gopal Das Rathore of the Mertia clan, and has a number of red sandstone *havelis* as well as several old temples, *baolis* and marble chhatris, 5 km beyond the reserve. The village lay at the entrance to one of the few passes through the Aravallis between the territories held by the Rajput princes of Jodhpur and Udaipur. The beautiful 1606 **castle** has marble pavilions, courtyards, faded paintings, wells, elephant stables and walls marked with canon balls. The present Thakur Sajjan Singh, who has opened his castle to guests, see Sleeping, organizes two- to three-day treks to Kumbhalgarh Fort, 18 km (50 km by jeepable road) and Ranakpur temples.

The **Mahavir Jain Temple**, 5 km away, is a beautiful little 10th-century temple. It is a delightful place to experience an unspoiled rural environment.

Rawla Narlai, 25 km from Kumbhalgarh Fort, and an hours drive from Ranakpur, is a Hindu and Jain religious centre. It has a 17th-century fort with interesting architecture, right in the heart of the village, which is ideal for a stop over.

Ranakpur → *Phone code: 02934. Colour map 5, grid B1. 90 km from Udaipur, 25 km from Kumbhalgarh.*

① *Daily; non-Jains may visit the Adinatha only between 1200 and 1700.The head priest helps to show people around. Photos (1200-1700) with permission from Kalyanji Anandji Trust office next to the temple, camera Rs 50, video Rs 150, photography of the principal Adinatha image is prohibited.*

❢ *Shoes and socks must be removed at the entrance. Black clothing is not permitted. No tips though unofficial 'guide' may ask for baksheesh.*

One of five holy Jain sites and a popular pilgrimage centre, it has one of the best known Jain temple complexes in the country. Though not comparable to the Dilwara temples in Mount Abu, it has very fine ornamentation and is in a wonderful setting with peacocks, langurs and numerous birds. The semi-enclosed deer park with spotted deer, nilgai and good birdlife next to the temple, attracts the odd panther! You can approach Ranakpur from Kumbhalgarh through the wildlife reserve in 1½ hours. A visit is highly recommended.

The **Adinatha** (1439), the most noteworthy of the three main temples here, is dedicated to the first Tirthankar. The sanctuary is symmetrically planned around the central shrine and is within a 100-sq m raised terrace enclosed in a high wall with 66 subsidiary shrines lining it, each with a spire; the gateways consist of triple-storey porches. The sanctuary with a clustered centre tower contains a *chaumukha* (four-fold) marble image of Adinatha. The whole complex, including the extraordinary array of engraved pillars, carved ceilings and arches are intricately decorated, often with images of Jain saints, friezes of scenes from their lives and holy sites. The beautiful lace-like interiors of the corbelled domes are a superb example of western Indian temple style. The **Parsvanatha** and **Neminath** are two smaller Jain temples facing this, the former with a black image of Parsvanatha in the sanctuary and erotic carvings outside. The star-shaped **Surya Narayana Temple** (mid-15th century) is nearby.

There is a beautiful 3.7-km trek around the wildlife sanctuary, best attempted from November to March, contact sanctuary office next to temples for information.

● Sleeping

Kumbhalgarh *p158*

A Aodhi (HRH), 2 km from fort gate, T02954-242 341, www.hrhindia.com. Closest place to fort, great location set in to the rock face. 27 roomsin modern stone 'cottages' decorated in colonial style to good effect with attached modern bathrooms. Beautiful restaurant and coffee shop, swimming pool,

relaxing atmosphere, very helpful staff, TCs exchanged, fabulous views, very quiet, superb horse safaris (US$200 per night), trekking, tribal village tours. Highly recommended.

B Kumbhalgarh Fort, on Kelwara-Kumbhalgarh Rd, T02954-242 057, hilltop@bppl.net.in. 21 a/c rooms in attractively designed stone building, superb location with hill, lake and valley views, garden,restaurant, bar, exchange, lovely pool, cycle hire, riding, friendly staff.

B-C Kumbhal Castle, Khelwara Kumbhalgarh Rd, T02954-242 171, hotelkumbhalcastle@yahoo.co.in. 12 simply decorated rooms, some a/c, in new construction which feels a little unfinished. Basic restaurant, good views.

C-D Ratnadeep, Kelwara, in the middle of a bustling village, T02954-242 217, www.hotelsofrajasthan/kumhalgarh/ratnadeep.html. 14 reasonably clean rooms, some deluxe with cooler and marble floors, Western toilets, small lawn, restaurant, camel, horse and jeep safaris, friendly, well-run.

D Forest Department Guest House, near the Parsram Temple, about 3 km by road and 3 km off the road (access by 4WD jeep or trek) from Aodhi. Basic facilities but some fantastic views. Worth a visit for the views over the Kumbalgarh sanctuary towards the drylands of Marwar which rival if not surpass the ones from the fort.

F Government Rest Houses and school hostels nearby may have rooms available.

Ghanerao and Rawla Narlai p159
B Thakur Sajjan Singh castle, see Sights, Ghanerao, call Mumbai for reservations, T022 5555 1101, www.nivalink.com/ghanerao, has suites, a restaurant (simple food), slightly run down but has nostalgic appeal of faded glory, charming hosts, expensive local guide (bargain hard if buying paintings), jeeps and camping arranged.

B-C Fort Rawla Narlai, Rawla Narlai, T02934–282 425, www.ajitbhawan.com. 21 rooms (11 a/c) individually decorated with antiques in the renovated fort, new showers, plus 5 luxurious, well-appointed 'tents', good simple meals under the stars, helpful, friendly staff, attractive garden setting, good riding, overlooked by huge boulder rock; temple on top can be reached via 700 steps.

C Kotri Rawla, Ghanerao, T0294-2560822. 8 rooms, 2 suites in 17th-century royal 'bungalow', excellent horse safaris, run by thakur Mahendra Singh, an expert on

Marwari horses and his son, a well known polo player.

C Royal Castle, Ghanerao, Dist Pali, T02934–284 035, ghanerao@rediffmail.com. Decidedly rustic 'castle', 16 simple rooms with modern bathrooms, pricey

E Bagha-ka-Bagh (Tiger's Den), Ghanerao. Spartan hunting lodge among tall grass jungle near wildlife sanctuary gate. 10 very basic rooms, 5 with bucket hot water, dorm, generator for electricity, breathtaking location, wildlife (including panther, nilgai), rich birdlife, 5-day treks including Kumbhalgarh, Ranakpur. Contact **North West Safaris**, T/F079-6560962, ssibal@ad1.vsnl.net.in.

Ranakpur p160
B Fateh Bagh Palace (HRH), on the highway near the temple, T02934-286 186, www.hrhindia.com. A 200-year-old fort was dismantled in to 65,000 pieces and transported here from it's original site 50km away in order to make this palace. The result is a beautiful property, cleverly combining the old and the new. There are 20 tastefully decorated, well-appointed rooms, 6 more on the way, including 4 suites, best of which have attached Jacuzzis! New restaurant under construction to make space for a small museum, good pool, friendly staff.

B Maharani Bagh (WelcomHeritage), Ranakpur Rd, T02934-285 105, balsamand _1@sify.com. 19 well-furnished modern bungalows with baths in lovely 19th-century walled orchard of Jodhpur royal family full of bougainvillaea and mangos, outdoor Rajasthani restaurant (traditional Marwari meals Rs 300), pool, jeep safaris, horse riding.

B-C Ranakpur Hill Resort, Ranakpur Rd, T02934-286 411, www.ranakpurhillresort. com. 9 good-sized, well-appointed rooms, 5 a/c, in new construction, pleasant dining room, clean pool, friendly owner.

C Shivika Lake Hotel, T02934-286625, www.indiaoverland.com/ranakpur, near the lake in pleasant jungle setting. 9 simple but comfortable rooms (2 a/c) with baths, hot water, 2 tents with shared bath, delicious Rajasthani food, views of lake and wooded

---

● For an explanation of sleeping and eating price codes used in this guide, see inside the
● front cover. Other relevant information is found in Essentials, see pages 40-45.

hills, treks, excellent jeep safaris with spotter guide in Kumbhalgarh sanctuary, camping trips, personal attention, friendly and cheerful hosts.

C-D Roopam, Ranakpur Rd, T02934-285 321, roopaminn@hotmail.com. 12 well-maintained rooms, some a/c, pleasant restaurant, attractive lawns.

D Hotel Castle, T02934-285 133. 20 rather Spartan cottage rooms, some a/c in a pretty jungle setting, not a castle, distant, brackish pool, reasonable restaurant.

D-E Shilpi (RTDC), T02934-285 074. 12 cleanish rooms, best with hot water and a/c, dorm (dirty), veg meals.

F Dharamshala, with some comfortable rooms, simple and extremely cheap veg meals.

❼ Eating

Kumbhalgarh *p158*

❦❦❦ Aodhi is a thatched restaurant with central barbecue area. Good Indian (try *laal maas*, a mutton dish), wide choice, authentic 7-course Mewari meal but service can be very slow.

❦❦ Ratnadeep has an à la carte veg menu.

❦ A shack makes tea and sells chocolates, film rolls, mineral water, biscuits near the fort gate.

Ranakpur *p160*

There are no eateries near the temple, only a tea stall, but the dharamshala serves very good food at lunchtime and again at sunset. Rs20 per meal.

❦❦ Roopam, Ranakpur-Maharani Bagh road, near Shivika. Good Rajasthani food. Pleasant village theme setting, modern facilities, popular.

❦❦ Shivika Lake, part open-air restaurant by lake with hill views. Delicious Rajasthani lunches non-spicy curries possible, barbecued chicken, excellent breakfasts, tea by the lake, family run, shabby but clean.

❸ Transport

Kumbhalgarh *p158*
Bus

For the fort: buses (irregular times) from Chetak Circle, Udaipur go to **Kelwara**, Rs 20, 3 hrs (cars take 2 hrs); from there a local bus (Rs 2) can take you a further 4 km up to a car park; the final 2-km climb is on foot; the return is a pleasant downhill walk of 1 hr. Jeep taxis charge Rs 50-100 from Kelwara to the fort (and say there are no buses). Return buses to Jaipur from Kelwara until 1730.

Taxi

From Udaipur, a taxi for 4, Rs 1,200, can cover the fort and Ranakpur in 11 hrs; very worthwhile.

Ranakpur *p160*
Bus

From Udaipur, 6 daily (0530-1600), slow, 4 hrs from **Jodhpur** (doesn't stop long enough to see the temples so break your journey here) and **Mount Abu**. See Taxi above.

Train

Palna Junction on the Ajmer-Mount Abu line is 39 km away.

Mount Abu and around

Mount Abu, Rajasthan's only hill resort, stretches along a 20-km plateau. Away from the congestion and traffic of the tourist centres on the plains, surrounding the resort there is well-wooded countryside to explore filled with flowering trees, numerous orchids during the monsoon and a good variety of bird and animal life. Many of the rulers from neighbouring princely states had summer houses built here and today, it draws visitors from Rajasthan and neighbouring Gujarat who come to escape the searing heat of summer (and Gujarat's alcohol prohibition!) and also to see the exquisite Dilwara Jain temples. There are also some fabulous heritage hotels in the area, well off the beaten track and unique experiences in themselves. ⟫ *For Sleeping, Eating and other listings, see pages 168-172.*

Mount Abu → *Phone code: 02974. Colour map 4, grid B5. Population: 15,600 . Altitude: 1,720 m.*

Ins and outs

Getting there The nearest railway station is at Abu Road, 27 km away. It is often quicker to take a bus that will go all the way to Mount Abu, instead of going to Abu Road by train and then taking a bus up the hill.

Getting around The compact area by Nakki Lake with several hotels, restaurants and shops, is pedestrianized. Taxis are available at a stand nearby. A form of transport unique to Mount Abu is the *baba gari*, or 'kiddy cart', a small trolley generally used to pull small children up the steepest of Mount Abu's hills, particularly at Sunset Point. Occasionally, however, whole families can be seen being dragged around the high street in these diminutive devices! ▸▸ *See Transport, page 171, for further details.*

Tourist information Rajasthan Tourism ① *opposite bus stand, T02974-235 151. 0800-1100, 1600-2000 (1000-1330, 1400-1700 off-season).* Guides available, four to eight hours, about Rs 250-400.

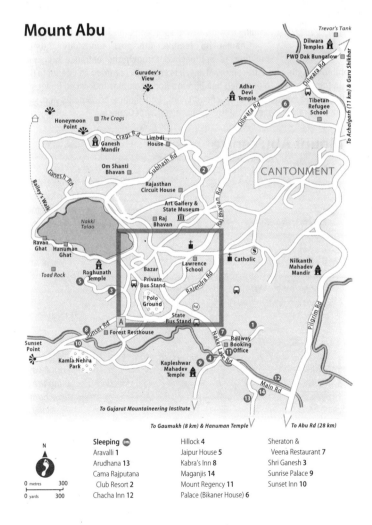

Mount Abu

Southern Rajasthan Mount Abu & Around

Sleeping 🛏
Aravalli **1**
Arudhana **13**
Cama Rajputana
  Club Resort **2**
Chacha Inn **12**

Hillock **4**
Jaipur House **5**
Kabra's Inn **8**
Maganjis **14**
Mount Regency **11**
Palace (Bikaner House) **6**

Sheraton &
  Veena Restaurant **7**
Shri Ganesh **3**
Sunrise Palace **9**
Sunset Inn **10**

Background

Mount Abu was the home of the legendary sage Vasishtha. One day Nandini, his precious wish-fulfilling cow, fell into a great lake. Vasishtha requested the gods in the Himalaya to save her so they sent Arbuda, a cobra, who carried a rock on his head and dropped it into the lake, displacing the water, and so saved Nandini. The place became known as Arbudachala, the 'Hill of Arbuda'. Vasishtha also created the four powerful 'fire-born' Rajput tribes, including the houses of Jaipur and Udaipur at a ritual fire ceremony on the mount. Nakki Talao (Lake), sacred to Hindus, was, in legend, scooped out by fingernails (*nakki*) of gods attempting to escape the wrath of a demon. Abu was leased by the British Government from the Maharao of Sirohi and was used as the HQ for the Resident of Rajputana until 1947, and as a sanatorium for troops.

Dilwara Jain Temples

Set in beautiful surroundings of mango trees and wooded hills, 5 km from the town centre, the temples have superb marble carvings. The complex of five principal temples is surrounded by a high wall, dazzling white in the sunlight. There is a resthouse for pilgrims on the approach road, which is otherwise lined with stalls selling a rare collection of tourist kitsch, lending a carnival atmosphere to the sanctity of the temples.

A notice warns 'Any lady in monthly cycle if enters any of the temples she may suffer'! Leather items not allowed.

Chaumukha temple, the grey sandstone three-storey building, is approached through the entrance on your left. Combining 13th- and 15th-century styles, it is generally regarded as inferior to the two main temples. The colonnaded hall (ground floor) contains four-faced images of the Tirthankar Parsvanatha (hence *chaumukha*), and figures of *dikpalas* and *yakshis*. Along the entrance avenue on the right is a statue of Ganesh.

Mount Abu centre

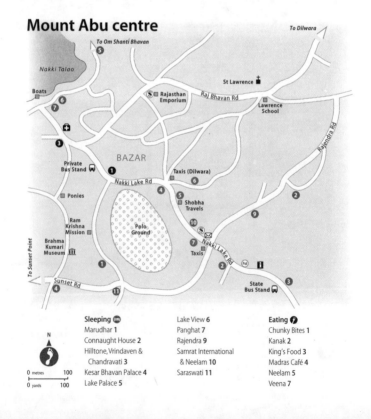

Sleeping	Lake View 6	Eating
Marudhar 1	Panghat 7	Chunky Bites 1
Connaught House 2	Rajendra 9	Kanak 2
Hilltone, Vrindaven &	Samrat International	King's Food 3
Chandravati 3	& Neelam 10	Madras Café 4
Kesar Bhavan Palace 4	Saraswati 11	Neelam 5
Lake Palace 5		Veena 7

N

0 metres 100
0 yards 100

Adinatha Temple (Vimala Shah Temple) lies directly ahead; the oldest and most famous of the Dilwara group. Immediately outside the entrance to the Temple is a small portico known as the Hastishala (elephant hall), built by Prithvipal in 1147-1159 which contains a figure of the patron, Vimala Shah, the Chief Minister of the Solanki King, on horseback. Vimala Shah commissioned the temple, dedicated to Adinatha, in 1031-1032. The riders on the 10 beautifully carved elephants that surround him were removed during Alauddin Khilji's reign. Dilwara belonged to Saivite Hindus who were unwilling to part with it until Vimala Shah could prove that it had once belonged to a Jain community. In a dream, the goddess Ambika (Ambadevi or Durga) instructed him to dig under a champak tree where he found a huge image of Adinatha and so won the land. To the southwest, behind the hall, is a small shrine to Ambika, once the premier deity.

In common with many Jain temples the plain exterior conceals a wonderfully ornately carved interior, remarkably well preserved given its age. It is an early example of the Jain style in West India, set within a rectangular court lined with small shrines and a double colonnade. The white marble of which the entire temple is built was brought not from Makrana, as many guidebooks suggest, but from the relatively nearby marble quarries of Ambaji in Gujarat, 25 km south of Abu Road. Hardly a surface is left unadorned. Makaras guard the entrance, and below them are conches. The cusped arches and ornate capitals are beautifully designed and superbly made.

Lining the walls of the main hall are 57 shrines. Architecturally, it is suggested that these are related to the cells which surround the walls of Buddhist monasteries, but in the Jain temple are reduced in size to house simple images of a seated Jain saint. Although the carving of the images themselves is simple, the ceiling panels in front of the saints' cells are astonishingly ornate. Going clockwise round the cells, some of the more important ceiling sculptures illustrate: Cell 1 lions, dancers and musicians; 2-7 people bringing offerings, birds, music making; 8 Jain teacher preaching; 9 the major auspicious events in the life of the Tirthankars; and 10 Neminath's life, including his marriage, and playing with Krishna and the gopis. In the southeast corner of the temple between cells 22 and 23 is a large black idol of Adinath, reputedly installed by Vimal Shah in 1031.

Dilwara Temples, Mount Abu

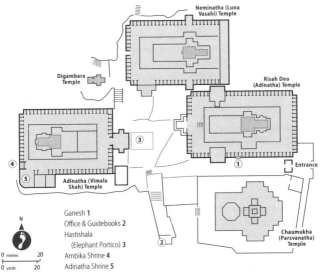

Neminatha (Luna Vasahi) Temple

Digambara Temple

Risah Deo (Adinatha) Temple

Entrance

Adinatha (Vimala Shah) Temple

Chaumukha (Parsvanatha) Temple

N

0 metres 20
0 yards 20

Ganesh **1**
Office & Guidebooks **2**
Hastishala
  (Elephant Portico) **3**
Ambika Shrine **4**
Adinatha Shrine **5**

By cell 32 Krishna is shown subduing Kaliya Nag, half human and half snake, and other Krishna scenes; 38, the 16 armed goddess Vidyadevi (goddess of knowledge); 46-48 16 armed goddesses, including the goddess of smallpox, Shitala Mata; and 49 Narasimha, the 'man-lion' tearing open the stomach of the demon Hiranya-Kashyapa, surrounded by an opening lotus.

As in Gujarati Hindu temples, the main hall focuses on the sanctum which contains the 2½ m image of Adinatha, the first Tirthankar. The sanctum with a pyramidal roof has a vestibule with entrances on three sides. To its east is the Mandapa, a form of octagonal nave nearly 8 m in diameter. Its 6m wide dome is supported by eight slender columns; the exquisite lotus ceiling carved from a single block of marble, rises in eleven concentric circles, carved with elaborately repeated figures. Superimposed across the lower rings are sixteen brackets carved in the form of the goddesses of knowledge.

Risah Deo Temple, opposite the Vimala Visahi, is unfinished. It encloses a huge brass Tirthankar image weighing 4.3 tonnes and made of panchadhatu (five metals) – gold, silver, copper, brass and zinc. The temple was commenced in the late 13th century by Brahma Shah, the Mewari Maharana Pratap's chief minister. Building activity was curtailed by war with Gujarat and never completed.

Luna Vasihi or Neminatha Temple (1231) ⓘ *free (no photography), shoes and cameras, mobile phones, leather items and backpacks (against tokens, Rs 1 per item) are left outside; tip expected, 1200-1800 for non-Jains; some guides are excellent, it's a 1-hr uphill walk from town, or share a jeep, Rs 5 each, good masala chai available nearby*, to the north of the Adinatha Temple, was erected by two wealthy merchants Vastupala and Tejapala, and dedicated to the 22nd Tirthankar; they also built a similar temple at Girnar. The attractive niches on either side of the sanctum's entrance were for their wives. The craftsmanship in this temple is comparable to the Vimala Vasahi; the decorative carving and *jali* work are excellent. The small domes in front of the shrine containing the bejewelled Neminatha figure, the exquisitely carved lotus on the sabhamandapa ceiling and the sculptures on the colonnades are especially noteworthy.

There is a fifth temple for the Digambar ('sky-clad') Jains which is far more austere.

Walks
Trevor's Tank ⓘ *Rs 5, car/jeep taken up to the lake Rs 125*, 50 m beyond the Dilwara Jain temples, is the small wildlife sanctuary covering 289 sq km with the lake which acts as a watering hole for animals including sloth bear, sambhar, wild boar, panther. Most of these are nocturnal but on your walk you are quite likely to see a couple of crocodiles basking on the rocks. The birdlife is extensive with eagles, kites, grey jungle fowl, red spurfowl, francolin, flycatchers, bulbuls etc seen during walks on the trails in the sanctuary. There are superb views from the trails that lead through the park.

Adhar Devi, 3 km from town, is a 15th-century Durga temple carved out of a rock and approached by 220 steep steps. There are steep treks to Anandra point or to a Mahadev temple nearby for great views.

Around **Nakki Lake Honeymoon Point**, and **Sunset Point** to the west, give superb views across the plains. They can both be reached by a pleasant walk from the bus stand (about 2 km). You can continue from Honeymoon Point to **Limbdi House**. If you have another 1½ hours, walk up to **Jai Gurudev's meditation eyrie** – gurus always choose good views! If you want to avoid the crowds at Sunset Point, take the **Bailey's Walk** from the **Hanuman Temple** near Honeymoon Point to **Valley View Point**, which joins up with the Sunset Point walk. You can also walk from the Ganesh temple to the Crags for some great views.

Temple. The **Toad Rock** is here too; the other rock formations (**Nandi** and **Camel**) are not as obvious.

Spiritual University movement

The headquarters of the Spiritual University movement of the Brahma kumaris is **Om Shanti Bhavan** ① *T02974-238 268*, with its ostentatious entrance on Subhash Road. You may notice many residents dressed in white taking a walk around the lake in the evening. It is possible to stay in simple but comfortable rooms with attached baths and attend discourses, meditation sessions, yoga lessons etc; good vegetarian meals are provided. The charitable trust runs several worthy institutions including a really good hospital.

Art Gallery and State Museum and Spiritual Museum

Art Gallery and State Museum ① *1000-1700, closed Fri, free, Raj Bhavan Rd*, has a small collection which includes some textiles and stone sculptures (ninth to 10th centuries). The **Spiritual Museum** ① *0800-2000*, near the pony stand by the lake, has a Disney-like diorama explaining the Brahma Kumari vision of the universe, including a lazer show, and offers courses.

Excursions

The Aravalli hills, part of the subcontinent's oldest mountain range, look more like rocky outcrops, in places quite barren save for date palms and thorny acacias. From Mount Abu it is possible to make day-treks to nearby spots.

Achalgarh, 11 km away, has superb views. The picturesque **Achaleshwar Temple** (ninth century) is believed to have Siva's toeprint, a brass Nandi and a deep hole claimed to reach into the underworld. On the side of **Mandakini tank** near the car park is an image of Adi Pal, the Paramara king and three large stone buffaloes pierced with arrows. A path leads up to a group of carved Jain temples (10-minutes' climb).

Guru Shikhar is the highest peak in the area (1,720 m) with a road almost to the top. It is about 15 km from Mount Abu and taxis take about an hour. To get to the small Vishnu temple you need to climb 300 steps or hire a palanquin. Good views especially at dawn. There is an RTDC Café and chai stalls.

Gaumukh (Cow's Mouth), 8 km southeast, is on the way to Abu Road. A small stream flows from the mouth of a marble cow. There is also a Nandi bull, and the tank is believed to be the site of Vasishtha's fire from which the four great Rajput clans were created. An image of the sage is flanked by ones of Rama and Krishna.

The **Arbuda Devi Temple** carved out of the rocky hillside is also worth walking to for the superb views over the hills.

Around Mount Abu → *Colour map 4, grid B4/5.*

Sheoganj

Sheoganj has a major textile market for Rajasthani bridal dresses, sarees etc. Just south of Sirohi is a large zinc smelting factory, while across to the east the almost camouflaged walls of a fort can be seen, another in the chain which marked the borders of Marwar and Mewar territory. The Sirohi royal family set up Mount Abu and later leased it to the British.

● *In legend, the Mandakini tank at Alchalgarh, was once filled with ghee and the*
● *buffaloes (really demons in disguise), came every night to drink from it until they were shot by Adi Pal.*

Bera → *34 km from Sirohi.*

The large panther population in the surrounding hills of Bera and the Jawai River area draws wildlife photographers. Antelopes and jackals also inhabit the area. Visit the **Jawai Dam**, 150 km from Mount Abu towards Jodhpur, to see historic embankments, numerous birds and basking marsh crocodiles. A bed for the night is provided by **Leopard's Lair** in a colourful Raika village near the lake and jungle, see Sleeping.

Jalor → *160 km north of Mount Abu.*

Jalor is an historic citadel. In the early 14th century, during court intrigues, the Afghani Diwan of Marwar, Alauddin Khilji, took over the town and set up his own kingdom. Later, the Mughal emperor Akbar captured it and returned the principality to his allies, the Rathores of Marwar by means of a peaceful message to the Jalori Nawabs, who moved south to Palanpur in Gujarat. The medieval fort straddles a hill near the main bazaar and encloses Muslim, Hindu and Jain shrines. It is a steep climb up but the views from the fort are rewarding. The old Topkhana at the bottom of the fortified hill has a mosque built by Alauddin Khilji using sculptures from a Hindu temple. Of particular interest are the scores of domes in different shapes and sizes, the symmetry of the columns and the delicate arches. Jalor bazaar is good for handicrafts, silver jewellery and textiles, and is still relatively unaffected by tourist pricing.

Bhenswada → *16 km east of Jalor.*

Bhenswada is a small, colourful village on the Jawai River. It has another Rajput country estate whose 'castle' with a Hawa Mahal, Zenana Chowk and Sirai Mahal, has been converted into an attractive hotel. The jungles and hills nearby have panther, nilgai, chinkara, blackbuck, jungle cat, jackal, porcupines and spiny tailed lizards.

Bhinmal → *95 km northwest of Mount Abu.*

Bhinmal has some important archaeological ruins, notably one of the few shrines in the country to Varaha Vishnu. It is also noted for the quality of its leather embroided mojdis. Nearby at Vandhara is one of the few marble *baolis* (step wells) in India, while the historic **Soondha Mata Temple** is at a picturesque site where the green hills and barren sand dunes meet at a freshwater spring fed by a cascading stream.

Daspan → *25 km north of Bhinmal.*

Daspan is a small village where the restored 19th-century castle built on the ruins of an old fort provides a break between Mount Abu and Jaisalmer.

● Sleeping

Mount Abu *p163, map p163 and p164*
Touts can be a nuisance to budget travellers at the bus stand. Prices shoot up during Diwali, Christmas week and summer (20 Apr-20 Jun) when many **D-F** hotels triple their rates; meals, and ponies and jeeps cost a lot more too. Off-season discounts of between 30 and 50 per cent are usual, sometimes even 70 per cent in mid-winter (when it can get very cold). List of families taking paying guests from the Tourist Information, or ask at **Connaught House** (see below).
A Cama Rajputana Club Resort (Heritage), Adhar Devi Rd, T02974-238 205, cama rajputana@rediffmail.com. Refurbished old club house (1895) for Mount Abu's royal and British residents, guests become temporary members, 42 rooms in split level cottages with views, 2 period suites, lounge with fireplaces and old club furniture, average restaurant (Gujarati flavour to western dishes), eco-friendly (recycled water, alternative energy, drip irrigation), beautifully landscaped gardens, billiards, tennis etc, efficient service, immaculate pool.
A Hillock, opposite petrol pump, T02974-238 463, www.hotelhillock.com. 41 a/c rooms, whole building ostentatiously decorated, swanky restaurant, pleasant

garden and pool (close to road), well presented if slightly anonymous, some staff unhelpful.

A The Jaipur House, above Nakki Lake, T02974-235 176, www.royalfamilyjaipur.com. 9 elegant rooms in the Maharaja of Jaipur's former summer palace, unparalleled location, fantastic views, especially from terrace restaurant, friendly, professional staff. Recommended.

A-B Hilltone, set back from road near petrol pump, T02974-383 913, www.hilltone.com. 66 tastefully decorated rooms (most a/c, heaters), attractive Handi (a style of cooking using baking/steaming in covered pots) restaurant, exchange, pool, garden, quiet,the most stylish of Mt Abu's modern hotels, by some moargin, helpful staff. Recommended.

B Connaught House (WelcomHeritage), Rajendra Marg, uphill from opposite bus stand, T02974-238 560, www.welcomheritage.com. British Resident of Jodhpur's colonial bungalow, 6 pleasantly old fashioned rooms (royal memorabilia), good bathrooms, 8 modern rooms in quieter new cottage, comfortable place to stay, restaurant (average à la carte, good Rajasthani meals), trekking with guide (Rs 2000 plus), beautiful gardens filled with birds, interesting old retainer of the Jodhpur family full of tales, efficient management. Recommended.

B Kesar Bhavan Palace, Sunset Rd, facing polo ground, T02974-235 219, www.mountsabu.com. 19th-century residence of the Sirohi royal family (Mt Abu's oldest royal property), 16 renovated rooms in main palace and 10 attractive rooms with period furniture in stable wing, comfortable, modernized, balconies good views, western breakfast, meals brought in to order, family run, environment friendly.

B Palace Hotel (Heritage), Bikaner House, Dilwara Rd, 3 km from centre, T02974-235 121, bikhouse@sancharnet.in. 38 large renovated rooms with period and reproduction furniture in Swinton Jacob's imposing 1894 hunting lodge, also new annexe, atmospheric public rooms, grand dining hall (good English breakfast, Rajasthani meals with game dishes, memorable à la carte; expensive set menu), tennis etc, distinctively civilized character but

large complex with average service, very quiet, set in sprawling grounds and backdrop of hills (bears come searching for honey combs at night!).

B-C Maganjis, Mount Rd, T02974-238 337, maganjis@datainfoysis.net. 25 well-maintained rooms in modern building, pleasant lawn, welcoming staff.

B-C Sunrise Palace, Bharatpur Kothi, T02974-235 573, www.sunrisepalace-mtabu.co.in. 16 large, sparsely furnished rooms, great bathrooms, in a grand, although slightly unloved, building, good small restaurant, open-air BBQ, converted mansion, elevated with excellent views over town.

B-D Mount Regency, near petrol pump, T02974-235 200, www.mountsabu.com. 20 a/c rooms in high quality modern construction with balconies, lawn, friendly and experienced management.

C Chacha Inn, Main Rd (2 km from centre), T02974-235 374, www.chacha-inn-hotel.com. Attractive though a bit brash, with lots of artefacts on display, 22 good a/c rooms with modern facilities, some with balconies offering hill views, restaurant, bar, garden really good fun; dining lawns with magic and puppet shows, dancing and music.

C Lake Palace, facing lake, T02974-237 154, savshanti@hotmail.com. 13 rooms (some a/c), garden restaurant, beautifully situated with great lake views from terrace, rear access to hill road for Dilwara, well run and maintained. Recommended.

C Sunset Inn, Sunset Rd, 1 km centre, T02974-235 194, thomasg1956@yahoo.com. 40 spacious rooms, some a/c, modern facilities, veg restaurant, outdoor dining, garden, pleasant atmosphere, popular.

C-D Aravalli, Main Rd, T02974-235 316. 40 rooms (12 in cottages, 10 in new wing) on different levels with hill views, good restaurant, very well maintained, landscaped terraced garden, pool, gym, good off-season discount, very helpful staff. Recommended.

C-D Kabra's Inn, Sunset Rd, T02974-238 095. 8 light, clean, modern rooms, small restaurant, relaxed management.

C-D Marudhar, opposite Polo ground near Gurudwara, T02974-238 620. Attractive, modern sandstone exterior conceals 32 standard rooms, lift, okay views.

D Aradhana, St Mary's Rd, T02974-237 227. 8 clean, modern rooms, some a/c, in family home; large terraces, pleasant atmosphere, 10 mins walk from town.

D Maharaja International, near Bus Stand, T02974-235 161, www.hotelmaharajaint abu.com. 51 rooms with hot shower, some a/c, galleries with views, friendly staff, travel ticketing, a bit rough round the edges.

D Samrat International, near bus stand, T02974-235 173, hillock@sancharnet.in. 50 comfortable rooms, Takshila veg restaurant, exchange, travel, pleasant terraces, welcoming staff.

D-E Sheraton, near Bus Stand, T02974-238 366. 40 rooms, modern hotel, clean, characterless, but enthusiastic owner.

E Panghat, overlooking Nakki Lake, T02974-238 886. 10 small but adequate rooms in great location, friendly staff.

E Saraswati, west of Polo Ground, T02974-238 887. 36 rooms (some with balconies), better in annexe, good views from upstairs, simple, clean, large rooms with bath and hot water, smart restaurant (Gujarati *thalis* only), best of many options in area.

E Vrindavan, near bus stand, T02974-235 147. 30 standard rooms set back from busy road, indifferent management but good value.

E-F Lake View, beautiful location on a slope facing the Lake, T02974-238 659. 15 rather shabby rooms with Indian WC, helpful and friendly staff.

E-F Neelam, near Samrat, Main Rd, T02974-235 296, 10 well-maintained, modern rooms in annexe of family home, friendly hosts.

E-F Shri Ganesh, west of the polo ground, uphill behind Brahma Kumari, T02974-237 292, lalit_ganesh@yahoo.co.in. 23 clean, simple rooms, plenty of solar-heated hot water, very quiet, good rooftop café, one of the few places catering specifically for foreign travellers, 16 years' experience shows, recommended. Ring ahead for free pick up.

F Chandravati Palace, 9 Janta Colony, behind Madhuban, T02974-238 219. 4 clean rooms in slightly distant but friendly, quiet location.

F Krishna, Raj Bhawan Rd, T02974-238 045. 12 clean, simple rooms in quiet, homely location.

F Rajendra, Rajendra Rd (from bus stand, turn right at post office), T02974-238 174.

Well designed, clean rooms with bath (bucket hot water), *thalis*, huge balcony, friendly management.

Around Mount Abu *p167*

A Leopard's Lair, in a colourful Raika village, Bera, T02933-43478. 7 a/c rooms in well designed stone cottages, modern amenities, delicious meals included (fresh fish from lake), bar, pool, garden, riding (horse, camel), birdwatching, panther viewing 'safaris' with owner.

C Rawla Bhenswada, Bhenswada, T02978-22080. Reservations from North West Safaris, T079-6302019, ssibal@ad1. vsnl.net.in. 12 comfortable rooms with bath, painted exterior, attractive unique interiors (swings and silver settees for beds), inspired decor ('Badal Mahal' with cloud patterns, 'Hawa Mahal' with breezy terrace etc), breakfast treats of masala cheese toast or vegetarian parathas, delicious Marwari meals ("among the best in Rajasthan"), parakeet-filled orchards, courtyard lawns, pool, interesting visits to Rabari herdsmen and Bhil tribal hamlets, night safaris, hospitable family. Highly recommended.

C-D Woodland Hotel, by the Jawai River (dry except in monsoon) on the highway but with views of Jawai river and rock formations, T 02976 61122, Sheoganj. 21 rooms, most a/c, modern comforts, Indian restaurant (non-vegetarian on request) jeep safari (panthers, nilgai, hyena etc), camel rides, campfires on sand dunes ('for a glimpse of desert scapes'), cultural programmes.

D Castle Durjan Niwas, Daspan, T02969-73523. 11 rooms, pleasant open sitting areas, folk entertainment, very knowledgeable owners, camel rides (Rs 200 per hr; Rs 800 per day).

ⓔ Eating

Mount Abu *p163, map p163 and p164*
Gujaratis visit Mount Abu in large numbers, some come to escape the state's prohibition on alcohol. Small roadside stalls sell tasty local vegetarian food. You can also get good *thalis* (Rs 30-40) at simple restaurants but

For an explanation of sleeping and eating price codes used in this guide, see inside the front cover. Other relevant information is found in Essentials, see pages 40-45.

nightmarish service as they are unused to foreigners.

ᵻᵻᵻ **Handi**, at Hilltone Hotel. Gujarati, Punjabi, Western. Plenty of choice, very comfortable but pricey, open 0900-2300. This (and other large hotels) has a bar.

ᵻᵻ **Neelam**, near bus stand. Indian meals (Rs 50-75), Chinese dishes, Western snacks.

ᵻᵻ **Shere-e-Punjab**, among the best in town for veg/non veg Indian (also some Chinese/ western).

ᵻ **Bhavani**, by the bus stand. Good for daal-bhatti-choorma, Rajasthani snacks and rabri.

ᵻ **Chunky Bites**, on main drag, good selection of Punjabi, pizza, pasta and chaat.

ᵻ **Kanak** and **Purohit**, near Bus Stand. Great Gujarati *thalis* and South Indian snacks (Rs 30-50). Quick service, popular.

ᵻ **King's Food**, near MK, Nakki Lake Rd. Very popular for North Indian veg meal (Rs 40); also Chinese and South Indian, western snacks.

ᵻ **MK**, on the lakeside. Clean tables but a bit musty smelling, non-veg meals (Rs 100), western snacks.

ᵻ **Madras Café**, Nakki Lake Rd. Indian. Veg 'hot dog', *thalis*, juices, real coffee and milk shakes in a garden, meals indoors.

ᵻ **Maharaja**, near bus stand. Gujarati. Simple, clean, produces excellent value *thalis*.

ᵻ **Uncle Fast Food**, Raj Bhawan Rd. Fresh and cheap snacks, immaculately clean.

ᵻ **Veena** near taxi stand. Brews real coffee, serves traditional Indian meals and a few western favourites, very clean, outdoors, loud music, best of many on same strip.

❀ Festivals and events

Mount Abu *p163, map p163 and p164*
An annual **Summer Festival**, **1-3 Jun** every year, features folk music, dancing, fireworks etc. **Diwali** is especially colourful.

Around Mount Abu *p167*
In Bhinmal the **Navratri Festival** is held in **Sep**. Despan also holds special Navratri celebrations.

◘ Shopping

Mount Abu *p163, map p163 and p164*
Shopping is less hassle here than in the tourist towns; most are open 0900-2100 daily.

Readymade Indian clothing and silver jewellery are particularly good value. For Garasia tribal jewellery try stalls near the GPO. **Saurashtra** and **Rajasthan emporia**, Raj Bhavan Rd, opposite the bus stand, sell a good selection.

Chacha Museum, good metal, wood, stone crafts, paintings and odd curios (fixed price but may give a discount).

Khadi Gramudyog, opposite pony hire. Handloom fabric, carved agate boxes, marble figures.

Roopali, near Nakki Lake. Has silver jewellery.

▲ Activities and tours

Mount Abu *p163, map p163 and p164*
Mountain sports
For rock climbing, rapelling, contact **Mountaineering Institute**, near Gujarat Bhawan Hostel. Equipment and guide/ instructors are available. Swimming, tennis, billiards. Non-residents can pay to use facilities at the **Cama Rajputana** and **Bikaner House Palace hotels**.

Pony rides
Short rides from Rs 5.

Tours
Rajasthan Tourism, and **Rajasthan SRTC**, run daily tours to Dilwara, Achalgarh, Guru Shikhar, Nakki Lake, Sunset Point, Adhar Devi and Om Shanti Bhavan, 0830-1300, 1330-1900, Rs 80. **Gujarat**, **Maharajah**, **Shobha** (T02974-238 302) and **Green Travels** also offer similar tours for Rs 40-60; Ambaji-Kumbhairyaji tours Rs 120. A wildlife guide who comes very highly recommended by a large number of readers is **Charles**, T0-94141 54854, mahendradan@ yahoo.com, can be contacted at **Lake Palace Hotel**. Charles offers a wide range of treks through the areas around Mount Abu, from 3-4 hr excursions at Rs150 per person to longer overnight camping trips, and is hugely knowledgeable and enthusiastic.

⊖ Transport

Mount Abu *p163, map p163 and p164*
Toll on entering town, Rs 5 per head. Frequent rockfalls during the monsoon

makes the road from Mount Abu hazardous; avoid night journeys.

Air
The nearest airport is at Udaipur.

Baba garis
To Sunset Point, Rs 50-60.

Bus
Local For **Dilwara** and/or **Achalgarh**; check time.
Long distance State Bus Stand, Main Rd (opposite Tourist Office); Private Bus Stand, north of Polo Ground (towards Lake). To **Abu Rd**: hourly bus (45 mins-1 hr) Rs 10. **Ahmadabad**: several (7 hrs, Rs 100) via Palanpur for Bhuj (3 hrs); **Delhi**: overnight. **Jaipur** (overnight, 9 hrs), **Jodhpur** am and pm (6 hrs). **Mumbai, Pune**: early morning (18 hrs). **Udaipur**: 0830, 1500, 2200 (5-6 hrs, Rs 80). **Vadodara**: 0930, 1930 (5 hrs). Shobha and Gujarat Travels run private buses.

Taxi and jeep
Posted fares for sightseeing in a jeep; about Rs 700 per day; anywhere in town Rs 30; to Sunset Point Rs 50.
Taxi (for sharing) Abu Rd Rs 250; Dilwara stand is near the bazar.

Train
Western Railway Out Agency has a small reservation quota, 0900-1600, Sun 0900-1230. Book well in advance; you may have to wait 2-3 days even in the off-season. Abu Rd is the railhead with frequent buses to Mt Abu. To **Ahmadabad**: *Ashram Exp, 2916*, 0423, 3½ hrs; *Ahmadabad Mail, 9106*, 1305, 4½ hrs; *Aravali Exp, 69708*, 1615, 4½ hrs (continues to Mumbai, further 8½ hrs). **Jaipur**: *Aravalli Exp, 9707*, 1110, 9 hrs; *Ahmadabad-Delhi Mail, 9105*, 1430, 9 hrs. **Jodhpur**: *Ranakpur Exp, 4708*, 0440, 5½ hrs; *Surya Nagri Exp, 4846*, 0150, 5½ hrs. **Delhi**: *Ahmadabad Delhi Mail, 9105*, 1430, 15¾ hrs; *Ashram Exp, 2915*, 2123, 13¾ hrs.

Around Mount Abu *p167*
Trains to **Bera** from **Mumbai** and **Ajmer** via Abu Rd (*Aravalli* and *Ranakpur Exp*) stop at Jawai Dam and Mori Bera. For **Bhenswada**, trains and buses from Abu Rd. From **Bhinmal**, trains from **Jodhpur**, 1530, 2230 (4½ hrs); to **Jodhpur**, 0530, 2030. From **Ahmadabad**, 2130 (12 hrs); to **Ahmadabad**, 1940.

❶ Directory

Mount Abu *p163, map p163 and p164*
Banks State Bank of India, terrible rate.
Post office GPO, on Raj Bhavan Rd.

Chittaurgarh and around

This is a relatively undiscovered corner of Rajasthan but is home to some of the state's oldest and most interesting treasures. Chittaurgarh's 'Tower of Victory' has become well-known in recent years, but the whole of this ancient, historically important city is worth exploring. Kota and the area around Jalawar contain some of the oldest, and most impressive, temples and cave paintings in India, while nowhere takes you back in time as far as Bundi, seemingly untouched for centuries. Limited transport links mean that a visit to this region does require a little more time and effort than to other areas in Rajasthan, but also that the region has remained uncrowded, unspoilt and hugely hospitable. ➤➤ *For Sleeping, Eating and other listings, see pages 181-184.*

Ins and outs
Getting there There are no flights in to this area. All of the region's major towns are served by the railway, but often by branch lines some way off the main routes. Buses starting from all the major cities surrounding the area give quick access to the main towns; Chittaurgarh is 2½ hours from Udaipur for example.

by road a convenient option, especially as many of the highways have been much improved recently. Frequent buses criss-cross the area, but a private taxi might be worth considering as some of the sights, and most interesting places to stay, are somewhat off the beaten track. Most of the towns are small enough to be explored either on foot or by bicycle. ▸▸ *See Transport, page 184, for further details.*

Chittaurgarh → *Phone code: 01472. Colour map 5, grid B2. Population: 100,000.*

The hugely imposing Chittaurgarh Fort stands on a 152 m high rocky hill, rising abruptly above the surrounding plain. The walls, 5-km long, enclose the fascinating ruins of an ancient civilization, while the slopes are covered with scrub jungle. The modern town lies at the foot of the hill with access across a limestone bridge of 10 arches over the Gambheri River.

Ins and outs
Getting there Chittaurgarh is the best connected of the region's main towns, with good bus and train services to both Jaipur and Udaipur. Bottled water at Chittaurgarh station is often tampered with; take extra care.
Getting around The fort is over 6 km from station. Negotiate when hiring an auto or cycle rickshaw. ▸▸ *See Transport, page 184, for futher details.*
Tourist information The tourist office, **Rajasthan** ⓘ *Janta Avas Grih, Station Rd, T01472-241 089.*

History
One of the oldest cities in Rajasthan, Chittaurgarh was founded formally in 728 by Bappu Rawal, who according to legend was reared by the Bhil tribe. However, two sites near the River Berach have shown stone tools dating from half a million years ago and Buddhist relics from a few centuries BC. From the 12th century it became the centre of Mewar. Excavations in the Mahasati area of the fort have shown four shrines with ashes and charred bones, the earliest dating from about the 11th century AD. This is where the young Udai Singh was saved by his nurse Panna Dai; she sacrificed her own son by substituting him for the baby prince when, as heir to the throne, Udai Singh's life was threatened.

Sights
The fort dominates the city. Until 1568 the town was situated within the walls. Today the lower town sprawls to the west of the fort. The winding 1½-km ascent is defended by seven impressive gates: the **Padal Pol** is where Rawat Bagh Singh, the Rajput leader, fell during the second siege; the Bhairon or **Tuta (broken) Pol** where Jaimal, one of the heroes of the third siege, was killed by Akbar in 1567 (chhatris to Jaimal and Patta); the Hanuman Pol and Ganesh Pol; the Jorla (or Joined) Gate whose upper arch is connected to the Lakshman Pol; finally the Ram Pol (1459) which is the main gate. Inside the walls is a village and ruined palaces, towers and temples, most of which are out in the open and so easy to explore.

   Rana Kumbha's Palace, on the right immediately inside the fort, are the ruins of this palace (1433-1468), originally built of dressed stone with a stucco covering. It is approached by two gateways, the large Badi Pol and the three-bay deep Tripolia. Once there were elephant and horse stables, *zenanas* (recognized by the *jali* screen), and a Siva temple. The jauhar committed by Padmini and her followers is believed to have taken place beneath the courtyard. The north frontage of the palace contains an attractive combination of canopied balconies. Across from the palace is the archaeological office and the Nau Lakha Bhandar (The Treasury; nau lakha – 900,000).

The temple to Rana Kumbha's wife **Mira Bai** who was a renowned poetess is visible from the Palace and stands close to the Kumbha Shyama Temple (both circa 1440). The older 11th-century Jain **Sat Bis Deori** with its 27 shrines, is nearby. The **Shringara Chauri Temple** (circa 1456), near the fort entrance, has sculptured panels of musicians, warriors and Jain deities.

Rana Ratan Singh's Palace is to the north by the Ratneshwar Lake. Built in stone around 1530 it too had stucco covering. Originally rectangular in plan and enclosed within a high wall, it was subsequently much altered. The main gate to the south still stands as an example of the style employed.

The early 20th-century **Fateh Prakash Palace** built by Maharana Fateh Singh (died 1930) houses an interesting museum (0800-1630; closed Friday, Rs 3). To the south is the **Vijay Stambha** (1458-1468), one of the most interesting buildings in the fort, built by Rana Kumbha to celebrate his victory over Mahmud Khilji of Malwa in 1440. Visible for miles around, it stands on a base 14 sq m and 3 m high, and rises 37 m. The nine-storeyed sandstone tower has been restored; the upper section retains some of the original sculpture. For Re 0.50 you can climb to the top. Nearby is the Mahasati

Southern Rajasthan Chittaurgarh & around

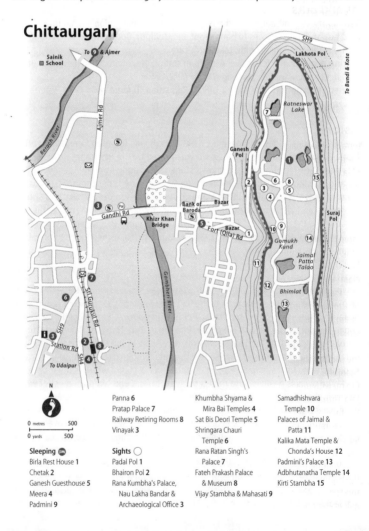

Chittaurgarh

N
0 metres 500
0 yards 500

Sleeping
Birla Rest House 1
Chetak 2
Ganesh Guesthouse 5
Meera 4
Padmini 9
Panna 6
Pratap Palace 7
Railway Retiring Rooms 8
Vinayak 3

Sights
Padal Pol 1
Bhairon Pol 2
Rana Kumbha's Palace,
   Nau Lakha Bandar &
   Archaeological Office 3
Khumbha Shyama &
   Mira Bai Temples 4
Sat Bis Deori Temple 5
Shringara Chauri
   Temple 6
Rana Ratan Singh's
   Palace 7
Fateh Prakash Palace
   & Museum 8
Vijay Stambha & Mahasati 9
Samadhishvara
   Temple 10
Palaces of Jaimal &
   Patta 11
Kalika Mata Temple &
   Chonda's House 12
Padmini's Palace 13
Adbhutanatha Temple 14
Kirti Stambha 15

‡ The jauhar – Rajput chivalry

On three occasions during Chittaurgarh's history its inhabitants preferred death to surrender, the women marching en masse into the flames of a funeral pyre in a form of ritual suicide known as *jauhar* before the men threw open the gates and charged towards an overwhelming enemy and annihilation.

The first was in 1303 when Ala-ud-din Khalji, the King of Delhi, laid claim to the beautiful Padmini, wife of the Rana's uncle. When she refused, he laid siege to the fort. The women committed *jauhar*, Padmini entering last, and over 50,000 men were killed in battle. The fort was retaken in 1313.

In 1535 Bahadur Shah of Gujarat laid claim to Chittaurgarh. Every Rajput clan lost its leader in the battle in which over 32,000 lives were lost, and 13,000 women and children died in the sacred *jauhar* which preceded the final charge.

The third and final sack of Chittaurgarh occurred only 32 years later when Akbar stormed the fort. Again, the women and children committed themselves to the flames, and again all the clans lost their chiefs as 8,000 defenders burst out of the gates. When Akbar entered the city and saw that it had been transformed into a mass grave, he ordered the destruction of the buildings.

In 1567 after this bloody episode in Chittaurgarh's history, it was abandoned and the capital of Mewar was moved to Udaipur. In 1615 Jahangir restored the city to the Rajputs.

terrace where the ranas were cremated when Chittaurgarh was the capital of Mewar. There are also numerous sati stones. Just to the south is the **Samdhishvara Temple** to Siva (11th and 15th centuries), which still attracts many worshippers and has some good sculptured friezes. Steps down lead to the deep Gomukh Kund, where the sacred spring water enters through a stone carved as a cow's mouth (hence its name).

Of the two palaces of **Jaimal and Patta**, renowned for their actions during the siege of 1567, the latter, based on the *zenana* building of Rana Kumbha's Palace, is more interesting. You then pass the Bhimtal before seeing the **Kalika Mata Temple** (originally an eighth century Surya temple, rebuilt mid-16th) with exterior carvings and the ruins of Chonda's House with its three-storey domed tower. Chonda did not claim the title when his father, Rana Lakha, died in 1421.

Padmini's Palace (late 13th century, rebuilt end of the 19th) is sited in the middle of the lake surrounded by pretty gardens. Ala-ud-din Khilji is said to have seen Padmini's beautiful reflection in the water through a mirror on the palace wall. This striking vision convinced him that she had to be his.

You pass the deer park on your way round to the **Suraj Pol** (Sun Gate) and pass the **Adbhutanatha Temple** to Siva before reaching the second tower, the **Kirti Stambha**, a Tower of Fame (13th and 15th centuries). Smaller than the Vijay Stambha (23 m) with only seven storeys, but just as elegant, it is dedicated to Adinath, the first Jain Tirthankar. Naked figures of Tirthankars are repeated several hundred times on the face of the tower. A narrow internal staircase goes to the top.

Of particular interest are the number of tanks and wells in the fort that have survived the centuries. Water, from both natural and artificial sources, was harnessed to provide an uninterrupted supply to the people.

Visiting the fort on foot means a circuit of 7 km; allow four hours. The views from the battlements and towers are worth the effort. The Archaeological Survey Office is in the fort, opposite Rana Kumbha's Palace; guide books are not always available so ask at **Panna Hotel**.

Chittaurgarh to Kota

Bassi

The town, 28 km from Chittaurgarh, is famous for handicrafts and miniature wooden temples painted with scenes from the epics. The **palace**, a massive 16th-century fort, has been opened as a hotel, see Sleeping page 181.

Bijaipur

Bijaipur is a feudal village about 50 km south of Chittaurgarh. The 16th-century **castle**, set among the Vindhya hills and now open as a hotel, see Sleeping page 181, has a splendid location near the **Bassi-Bijaipur wildlife sanctuary** which is home to panther, antelope and other wildlife. The forests are interspersed with lakes, reservoirs, streams and waterfalls with good birdlife in the winter months. The ruined **Pannagarh Fort** facing a lily covered lake is believed to be one of the oldest in Rajasthan.

Kota

Kota's attractive riverside location and relatively wide range of accommodation make it a comfortable place to stay. The town itself is of no special appeal, but makes a good base from which to visit nearby Bundi.

Ins and outs

Getting there Trains link Kota Junction station with Jaipur, Delhi (via Sawai Madhopur) and Mumbai. The station is 4 km north of the bus station at the town centre; shuttle buses run between the two. Regular buses run to Bundi and Jhalawar.
Getting around Autos, cycle rickshaws and fixed-route tempos ferry passengers around town. Parts of the palace in the old fortified town, including the museum, are worth exploring on foot. ▸▸ *See Transport, page 184, for further details.*

History

Cave paintings date the occupation of the area along the Chambal River to prehistoric times. It was ruled by Bhil chieftains until the 13th century, when Jait Singh of Bundi, a Hada Chauhan, usurped their territory. Kota became an independent state from Bundi when Rao Madho Singh was installed as ruler in 1631 with the blessings of the Mughal Emperor Shah Jahan.

Sights

At the south end of the town, near the barrage, is the vast, strongly fortified **City Palace** (1625) which you enter by the south gate having driven through the bustling but quite charming old city. There are some striking buildings with delicate ornamental stonework on the balconies and façade, though parts are decaying. The **Hathi Pol** (Elephant Gate 1625-1648), decorated with more recent murals, shows a royal wedding procession. The **Bhim Mahal**, an early 18th-century Darbar Hall, is covered with Rajput miniatures documenting the town's history and local legends, as well as intricate mirror work and ivory inlaid doors. The best preserved murals and carved marble panels are in the chambers upstairs and in the Arjun Mahal. These murals feature motifs characteristic of the Kota School of art, including portraiture (especially profiles), hunting scenes, festivals and the Krishna Lila. The **Madho Singh Museum** ⓘ *daily except Fri and government holidays, 1000-1630, Rs 50 for foreigners, Rs 10 for Indians, camera Rs 50, video Rs 100*, has an impressive collection of arms and armour, as well as china, silver objects, sculpture and princely relics.

The 15th-century **Kishore Sagar** tank between the station and the palace occasionally has boats for hire. The **Jag Mandir** Island Palace (closed to visitors) is in the centre of the lake. The **Chattra Vilas Park,** near the **Chambal Tourist Bungalow,** has a good view of the lake and the island palace, besides *chhatris* which are attractive though somewhat neglected. The government **Brij Vilas Palace Museum** ① *1000-1700, Fri closed, Rs 3, no photography,* near the park, has architectural fragments and individual sculptures salvaged from the ruins of medieval temples of southeastern Rajasthan (some poorly labelled), besides pre-historic rock inscriptions, coins, weapons, Bundi school miniatures, manuscripts (13th-century *Bhagvad Gita* on one page!) and costumes.

The **Chambal Gardens** by **Amar Niwas,** south of the fort, is a pleasant place for a view of the river, although therare fish-eating gharial crocodiles with which the pond was stocked are rarely seen these days. A variety of birds, occasionally including flamingos, can be seen at the river and in nearby ponds. Upstream at **Bharatiya Kund** is a popular swimming spot whilst the Kota barrage controls the river level and is the headworks for an irrigation system downstream. Photography of the barrage gates is prohibited but you can photograph the view from the bridge. **Boat rides** ① *ask at Tourist Office, Rs 600 per hr (maximum 5 people),* for bird and crocodile watching.

The **Umed Bhawan** (1904), 1 km north of town, was built for the Maharao Umaid Singh II and designed by Sir Samuel Swinton Jacob in collaboration with Indian designers. The buff-coloured stone exterior with a stucco finish has typical Rajput

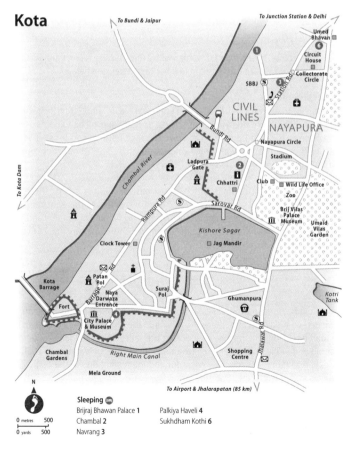

Kota

Sleeping 🛏
Brijraj Bhawan Palace **1**
Chambal **2**
Navrang **3**
Palkiya Haveli **4**
Sukhdham Kothi **6**

0 metres 500
0 yards 500

Southern Rajasthan Chittaurgarh & around

☷ Flower power

Crossing the high plateau between Bundi and Chittaurgarh the landscape is suddenly dotted with tiny patches of papery white flowers. These two Rajasthani districts, along with the neighbouring districts of Madhya Pradesh, are India's opium poppy growing belt, accounting for over 90 per cent of production. As early as the fifteenth century this region produced opium for trade with China. Today the whole process is tightly monitored by the Government. Licences to grow are hard won and easily lost. No farmer can grow more than half a *bigha* of opium poppy (less than one twentieth of a hectare), and each must produce at least 6 kg of opium for sale to the Government. Failure to reach this tough target results in the loss of the licence to grow. Laying out the field, actual cultivation and sale are all government controlled. Between late February and early April the farmers harvest the crop by incising fine lines in one quarter of each poppy head in the evening, and collecting the sap first thing in the morning. The harvesting has to be so precise that each evening a different quarter of the seed head will be cut on a different face - north, south, east or west. Finally the Government announces the collection point for the harvested opium just two or three days in advance, and farmers have to travel miles to the centre selected for weighing and final payment.

detail. The interior, however, is Edwardian with a fine drawing-room, banquet hall and garden. It has now been converted in to a heritage hotel, see below.

Excursions

Khaitoon (pronounced Khetun), about 12 km from Kota, is famous for *Doria* saris with a distinctive checked pattern which are woven on traditional pit handlooms using silk and cotton threads and pure gold *zari*. Prices range from Rs 500 for simple cotton ones, to Rs 25,000 for silk with a high gold content in the zari. About 2000-2500 men and women work at home on weaving Doria saris.

Bardoli (Barolli), 50 km south of Kota, has some of the finest examples of 10th-century Pratihara temples in India, just east of the bus stand. The restored **Ghatesvara Temple** has an elaborately carved *sikhara* over the sanctuary and a columned porch. Inside are sculptures of Siva dancing flanked by Brahma and Vishnu with river goddesses and dancing maidens beneath. One of the sanctuary's five stone lingas resembles an upturned pot or *ghata*.

Bundi → *Phone code: 0747. Colour map 5, grid B3. Population: 100,000.*

Bundi, in a beautiful narrow valley above which towers the Taragarh Fort, can easily be visited on a day trip from Kota. The drive into the town is particularly pleasing as the road runs along the hillside overlooking the valley opposite the fort. Completely unspoilt and rarely visited, it is well worth spending a day or two here to soak in the atmosphere. Bundi is especially colourful and interesting during the festivals, see Festivals and events page 184.

Ins and outs

Getting there Bundi is best reached by bus or car from Kota, Chittaurgarh, Ajmer or Sawai Madhopur.

Getting around The town itself has a compact, if crowded, centre. From the bus stand to the south, a few minutes' walk through the interesting bazar brings you to the start of the climb to the hillside palace and the fort beyond. For visiting sights around Bundi, autos and cycle-rickshaws are available or you can hire a bike from town. ▸▸ *See Transport, page 184, for further details.*

History
Formerly a small state founded in 1342, Bundi's fortunes varied inversely with those of its more powerful neighbours. Neither wealthy nor powerful, it nevertheless ranked high in the Rajput hierarchy since the founding family belonged to the specially blessed Hada Chauhan clan. After Prithviraj Chauhan was defeated by Muhammad Ghuri in 1193, the rulers sought refuge in Mewar. However, adventurous clan members overran the Bhils and Minas in the Chambal valley and established the kingdom of Hadavati or **Hadoti** which covers the area around Bundi, Kota and Jhalawar in southeastern Rajasthan. It prospered under the guidance of the able 19th-century ruler Zalim Singh, but then declined on his death. The British reunited the territory in 1894.

Southern Rajasthan Chittaurgarh & around

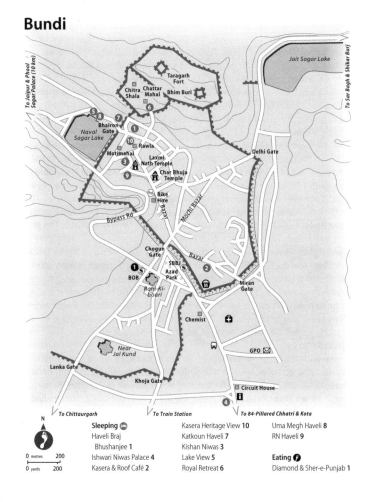

Bundi

To Jaipur & Phool Sagar Palace (10 km)
To Sar Bagh & Shikar Buri

Jait Sagar Lake

Taragarh Fort
Chitra Shala
Chattar Mahal
Bhim Buri

Bhairon Gate
Naval Sagar Lake
Rawla
Motimahal
Laxmi Nath Temple
Char Bhuja Temple
Delhi Gate

Bike Hire
Bypass Rd
Bazar
Mochi Bazar

Chogun Gate
SBBJ
Bazar
BOB
Azad Park
Rani-Ki-boari
Miran Gate

Chemist

Near Jal Kund
GPO

Lanka Gate

Khoja Gate

Circuit House

To Chittaurgarh   *To Train Station*   *To 84-Pillared Chhatri & Kota*

N

0 metres 200
0 yards 200

Sleeping
Haveli Braj Bhushanjee **1**
Ishwari Niwas Palace **4**
Kasera & Roof Café **2**

Kasera Heritage View **10**
Katkoun Haveli **7**
Kishan Niwas **3**
Lake View **5**
Royal Retreat **6**

Uma Megh Haveli **8**
RN Haveli **9**

Eating
Diamond & Sher-e-Punjab **1**

Taragarh Fort ① *0700-1700, foreigner Rs50, Indian Rs20, camera Rs50, video Rs 100*. The fort (1342) stands in sombre contrast to the beauty of the town and the lakes below. There are excellent views but it is a 20-minute difficult climb; good shoes help. The eastern wall is crenellated with high ramparts while the main gate to the west is flanked by octagonal towers. The **Bhim Burj** tower dominates the fort and provided the platform for the Garbh Ganjam, a huge cannon. A pit to the side once provided shelter for the artillery men, and there are several stepped water tanks inside. Cars can go as far as the TV tower then it is 600 m along a rough track.

The palace ① *0900-1700, foreigners Rs50, Indians Rs20*. The palace complex below Taragarh, which was begun around 1600, is at the northern end of the bazaar, and was described by Kipling as "such a palace as men build for themselves in uneasy dreams – the work of goblins rather than of men". The buildings, on various levels, follow the shape of the hill. A steep, rough stone ramp leads up through the **Hazari Darwaza** (Gate of the Thousand) where the garrison lived; you may need to enter through a small door within the *darwaza*. The palace entrance is through the **Hathi Pol** (Elephant Gate, 1607-1631), which has two carved elephants with a water clock. Steps lead up to **Ratan Daulat** above the stables, the unusually small Diwan-i-Am which was intended to accommodate a select few at public audience. A delicate marble balcony overhangs the courtyard giving a view of the throne to the less privileged, who stood below. The **Chattar Mahal** (1660), the newer palace of green serpentine rock, is pure Rajput in style and contains private apartments decorated with wall paintings, glass and mirrors. The **Badal Mahal** bedroom has finely decorated ceilings. Rooms of the Chattar Mahal are kept locked but you may ask for permission at the Rawla office behind the Ayurvedic Hospital below the palace. The **Chitrashali**, a cloistered courtyard (open to the public, free entry) with a gallery running around a garden of fountains, has a splendid collection of miniatures showing scenes from the Radha Krishna story. Turquoise, blues and greens dominate (other pigments may have faded with exposure to sunlight) though the elephant panels on the dado are in a contrasting red. The murals (circa 1800) are some of the finest examples of Rajput art but are not properly maintained. There is supposed to be a labyrinth of catacombs in which the state treasures are believed to have been stored. Each ruler was allowed one visit but when the last guide died in the 1940s the secret of its location was lost! At night, the palace is lit up and the bazar comes alive. To see Badal and Chattar Mahals, ask at Rawla office behind Ayurvedic Hospital.

Other sights There are several 16th-17th-century stepwells and 'tanks' (*kunds*) in town. The 46-m deep **Raniji-ki-baori** ① *closed Sun, 2nd Sat each month, 1000-1700, free, caretaker unlocks the gate*, with beautiful pillars and bas relief sculpture panels of Vishnu's 10 *avatars*, is the most impressive. No longer in use, the water is stagnant.

Sukh Niwas (Mahal), a summer pleasure palace, faces the **Jait Sagar** lake where Kipling spent a night in the original pavilion. Further out are the 66 royal memorials at the rarely visited **Sar Bagh**, some of which have beautiful carvings. The caretaker expects Rs 10 tip.

The square artificial **Naval Sagar** lake has in its centre a half-submerged temple to Varuna, the god of water. The lake surface beautifully reflects the entire town and palace, but tends to dry up in the summer months. West of the Naval Sagar, 10 km away, is **Phool Sagar Palace**, which was started in 1945 but was left unfinished. Prior permission is needed to view.

Excursions

Menal On the road to Chittaurgarh, Menal, 96 km, has a cluster of Siva temples believed to date from the time of the Guptas. They are associated with the Chauhans and other Rajput dynasties. Though neglected the temples have some fine carvings and a panel of erotic sculptures somewhat similar to those at Khajuraho in Madhya Pradesh. Behind is a deep, wooded ravine with a seasonal waterfall.

Jhalawar Jhalawar, 85 km southeast of Kota, was the capital of the princely state of the Jhalas which was separated from Kota by the British in 1838. It lies in a thickly forested area on the edge of the Malwa plateau with some interesting local forts, temples and ancient cave sites nearby.

The **Garh Palace** in the town centre, now housing government offices, has some fine wall paintings which can be seen with permission. The **museum** ① *closed Fri, 1000-1630, Rs 3*, here, established in 1915, has a worthwhile collection of sculptures, paintings and manuscripts. **Bhawani Natyashala** (1921) was known for its performances ranging from Shakespearean plays to Shakuntala dramas. The stage with a subterranean driveway allowed horses and chariots to be brought on stage during performances.

Jhalarapatan The small walled town of Jhalarapatan, 7 km south of Jhalawar, has several fine 11th-century Hindu temples, the **Padmanath Sun Temple** on the main road being the best. The **Shantinath Jain temple** has an entrance flanked by marble elephants. There are some fine carvings on the rear façade and silver polished idols inside the shrines.

About 7 km away, **Chandrawati**, on the banks of the Chandrabhaga River, has the ruins of some seventh-century Hindu temples with fragments of fine sculpture.

● Sleeping

Chittaurgarh *p173, map p174*
B-C Pratap Palace, Sri Gurukul Rd, near Head Post Office, T01472-240 099, hpratapp@hotmail.com. Clean, well-maintained rooms, some a/c, 2 with ornately painted walls good fun, good food in restaurant or in the pleasant garden, jeep and horse safaris visiting villages. Recommended.
C Padmini, Chanderiya Rd, near Sainik School, T01472-241 718, hotel_padmini@rediffmail.com. 46 clean rooms, 30 a/c, Indian style furniture, gloomy restaurant, quiet, airport transfer from Udaipur.
C-D Meera, not far from the railway station, Neemuch Rd, T01472-240934. Modern hotel, 24 a/c and non a/c rooms with TV and phone (watch out for glow in dark stars on ceilings), restaurant (Gujarati/north Indian) and bar, laundry, car rental and travel assistance, internet, generator, accepts credit cards, characterless but efficient.
C-D Vinayak, Collectorate Circle, T01472-245 035. 13 clean rooms in convenient but noisily-located modern block plus good restaurant (see Eating)
D-E Chetak, opposite railway station, T01472-241 679. Modern hotel, 23 clean, fairly pleasant rooms (various categories), only 'deluxe' have Western toilets and hot showers.
D-E Panna (RTDC), Udaipur Rd, near railway station, T01472-241 238. 31 simple rooms, some a/c, best with fort view, dorm (Rs 50), veg dining hall, bar, run down but attentive service. Indian business hotel, popular with those visiting quarries/mines.
E-F Ganesh Guest House, New Fort Rd, opposite Sukhadiya Park, T01472-248 240. 20 basic but well-maintained rooms, Indian toilets only, clean, friendly.
F Birla, near the Kirti Stambh in the fort has been opened by the dharamshala group, T01472-246939. 17-room guesthouse, very basic but only Rs50 per double, great location, water a problem in the summer.

Chittaurgarh to Kota *p176*
B Bassi Fort Palace, Bassi, T01472-225 321, www.bassifortpalace.com. 18 unpretentious rooms in charming, family-run 16th-century fort. Same family has both an abandoned fort on top of the nearby hill, where dinners can be arranged, and a hunting lodge 6km away accessible only by boat or horse. Safaris to this lodge and local tribal villages can be arranged. Refreshingly informal. Recommended.

B Castle Bijaipur (Heritage Hotel), Bijaipur, T01472-240 099, www.castlebijaipur.com. 25 simple rooms decorated in traditional style with comfortable furniture and modern bathrooms in castle and a new wing, lawns and gardens, great hill views from breezy terrace, superb pool, delicious Rajasthani meals, also tea on medieval bastion, jeep/horse safaris with camping, jungle trekking.

Kota *p176, map p177*

Kota has a good selection of mid-range hotels, but very little to suit the budget traveller, who will find a far better choice of accommodation in nearby Bundi.

A-B Brijraj Bhawan Palace, Civil Lines, T0744-450 529, www.indianheritage hotels.com. 7 spacious a/c rooms with verandahs, fixed Indian meals, old British Residency with character, stately drawing and dining rooms (regal memorabilia), superb location overlooking river, immaculate gardens, croquet, tennis, very civilized.

A-B Umed Bhawan (WelcomHeritage), Palace Rd (see above), T0744-232 5262, www.welcomheritage.com. 32 large, comfortable rooms, sympathetic conversion, interesting memorabilia and state rooms, elegant dining room, great beer bar, sunny terraces, behind woods (langurs, deer, parakeets, peacocks), billiards, tennis, attentive staff. Recommended.

C Palkiya Haveli, Mokha Para (in walled city), near Suraj Pol, T0744-2327 375, www.alsisarhaveli.com. 6 traditionally furnished a/c rooms with bath (tubs), well restored, carved wood furniture, exquisite murals at entrance, very good fixed meals, very peaceful courtyard garden (full of birds), family run.

C Sukhdham Kothi, Civil Lines, T0744-232 0081, www.indianheritagehotels.com. 15 elegant rooms (size varies), 10 a/c, in a 19th-century British residence with sandstone balconies and screens, good fixed meals, large, private garden well set back from road, family run, friendly. Recommended.

C-D Navrang, Collectorate Circle, Civil Lines, T0744-232 3294. Much more ornate inside than out, 25 rooms, deluxe much better than standard, aircooled or a/c, TV, **C** suites, new

a/c vegetarian restaurant, well managed. Superior to nearby 'Phul Plaza'.

D Chambal (RTDC), Nayapura, T0744-232 6527. 12 rooms, nothing special but clean, friendly staff, well located close to old city.

C Surpin, Jhalawar Rd, T0744-232 4710. 18 a/c rooms with hot showers, restaurant, popular, fairly modern, long way from old city but convenient if going on to Bundi.

F budget hotels near the bus stand and station can be noisy and dirty.

Bundi *p178, map p179*

B-D Haveli Braj Bhushanjee, below the fort, opposite Ayurvedic Hospital (entrance in alley), T0747-244 2509, www.kiplingsbundi. com. 16 quaint rooms (each different) with clean bath (hot showers), in 19th-century 4-storey *haveli* with plenty of atmosphere and interesting memorabilia, home-cooked Brahmin vegetarian meals (no alcohol), pleasant terrace, good fort views, pick-up from station on request, good craft shop below. Recommended. Also planning to open **E Badi Haveli** next door.

C-D Ishwari Niwas Palace, opposite Circuit House, 1 Civil Lines, T0747-244 2414, www.angelfire.com/amiga/inheritage. 20 simple air-cooled rooms (period furnishings) with bath, around a courtyard, tired looking old Rajput family home, traditional meals (Rs 250), friendly, peaceful, good local tours, "underwhelming".

C-D Royal Retreat, below Fort, T0747-244 4426, jpbundi@yahoo.com. Looks rundown but quite clean and well kept inside, open courts, 5 largish rooms most with bath, family run, good veg restaurant, café, rooftop dining with views, good craft shop, internet, a little overpriced but in a fabulous location.

D Purvaj, centre of Jhalawar, a delightful old *haveli*, owned by an interesting family, delicious and simple homecooked meals.

D-E Katkoun Haveli, near Gopal Mandir, Balchand Para, T0747-244 4311, raghunandansingh@yahoo.com. 6 clean, newly-built rooms with modern bathrooms in pleasant family home, some with small balconies and a view of the fort.

D-E Vrindavati (RTDC), 300 m from Sukh Mahal, on Jait Sagar Lake, T0747-244 2473. 7

● *For an explanation of sleeping and eating price codes used in this guide, see inside the*
● *front cover. Other relevant information is found in Essentials, see pages 40-45.*

rooms in old bungalow in attractive garden with beautiful views, but poorly maintained and a long way from town.
E Menal Motel, Menal, has 1 simple room – handy for a cup of tea or a simple meal.
E-F Kasera, Haveli Dev Baxjiki, Nagadi Bazar (old part of town), T0747-244 6630. 8 simple, clean rooms, some with air-cooler and hot shower, good vegetarian meals in rooftop restaurant, special lassi and cane juice, atmospheric 350-year-old *haveli*, pleasant family.
E-F Kasera Heritage View, below palace, next to Ayurvedic hospital, T0747-244 4679. 11 cute rooms, all with attached bathrooms, plus a rooftop restaurant with good views of the palace and a wide-ranging menu. Same family owns **Kasera** and is soon to open **B-D Kasera Paradise**, which should become Bundi's best hotel, with 10 a/c rooms, marble bathrooms and a rooftop restaurant 5 storeys up in an old *haveli*.
E-F Kishan Niwas, near Laxmi Nath Temple, Nahar ka Chohtta, by Moti Mahal, T0747-244 5807, F443278. 8 spartan, clean rooms with bath (hot water), good home cooking, Mr Singh is very friendly and helpful.
E-F Lake View Paying Guest House, Bohra Meghwan ji ki Haveli, Balchand Para, below the palace, by Nawal Sagar, T0747-244 2326, lakeviewbundi@yahoo.com. 7 simple clean rooms (3 in separate, basic garden annexe with shared bath) in 150-year-old *haveli* with wall paintings, private terrace shared with monkeys and peacocks, lovely views from rooftop, warm welcome, very friendly hosts.
E-F R.N. Haveli, behind Laxmi Nath Temple, next to **Kishan Niwas**, T0-98293 39036, RNHaveli2004@yahoo.co.in. 5 rooms in a friendly family home run exclusively by women, excellent home cooking. Recommended.
E-F Uma Megh Haveli, Balchand Para, T0747-244 2191. 11 unrestored but very atmospheric rooms, 7 with basic attached bathrooms, plus a pleasant garden and restaurant.

ⓕ Eating

Chittaurgarh *p173, map p174*
For the best places to eat, visit the hotels.
� **Pratap Palace**, tasty Indian in pleasant surroundings.
� **Vinayak**, extensive menu including wide range of sweets.

� **Fort View Garden**, Rana Sanga Market, near Chandralok Cinema. Punjabi, Gujurati and Rajasthani, good *thalis*, pleasant lawn.
♀ **RTDC Café**, near the Vijay Stambha is handy for visitors to the fort.

Kota *p176, map p177*
The best, and most expensive, places to eat are the hotels; those listed below offer more reasonable alternatives. Good kulfis and homemade ices in Sindhi shops.
♀♀ **Payal**, Nayapura. Good Indian. Also some Chinese, and Indianized Continental.
♀♀ **Venue**, Civil Lines. A/c, good ,but very spicy Indian, disappointing western.
♀ **Hariyali**, Bundi Rd. Good Punjabi, some Chinese/Continental. Pleasant garden restaurant, outdoors or under a small shelter, very popular but some way out of town so transport can be difficult.
♀ **Jodhpur Sweets**, Ghumanpura Market. Saffron *lassis* and flavoured milks (pista, almonds etc).
♀ **Priya**, Nayapura. Popular for Indian veg.
♀ **Palace View**, outdoor meals/snacks. Handy for visitors to the City Palace.

Bundi *p178, map p179*
Several of the hotels have pleasant rooftop restaurants, see Sleeping above.
♀ **Diamond**, Suryamahal Chowk, in hotel. Very popular locally for cheap vegetarian meals, handy when visiting stepwells.
♀ **Sathi Cold Drinks**, Palace Rd, in hotel. Excellent *lassis* (try saffron, spices, pistachio and fruit), pleasant seating.
♀ **Sher-e-Punjab**, in hotel, near **Diamond**, serves non-vegetarian.

⊛ Festivals and events

Chittaurgarh *p173, map p174*
Mira Utsav is held in Oct/Nov every year, 2 days of cultural evening programmes and religious songs in the fort's Mira temple.

Kota *p176, map p177*
Colourful Gangaur (**11-12 Apr 2005**, 1-2 Apr 2006, 21-22 Mar 2007) and Teej (**8-9 Aug 2005**, 28-29 Jul 2006, 15-16 Aug 2007). Dasara Mela (**10-12 Oct 2005**, **30 Sep-2 Oct 2006**, 19-21 Oct 2007). Great atmosphere, with shows in lit up palace grounds.

Bundi *p178, map p179*
Bundi is especially colourful and interesting during the festivals; **Kajli Teej, 20-21 Aug 2005,** 11-12 Aug 2006, 30-31 Aug 2007, and Bundi Utsav, which takes place 3 days after the Pushkar fair has finished, see box p237. Jhalawar sees the **Chandrabhaga Fair (25-27 Nov 2004)**, a cattle and camel fair with all the colour and authenticity of Pushkar without its commercialization. Animals are traded in large numbers in the fields, pilgrims come to bathe in the river as the temples become the centre of religious activity and the town is abuzz with all manner of vendors.

☻ Transport

Chittaurgarh *p173, map p174*
Bicycle
Bike hire, opposite railway station, Rs 5 per hr.

Bus
Enquiries, T01472-241 177. Daily buses to **Bundi** (4 hrs), **Kota** (5 hrs), **Ajmer** (5 hrs) and **Udaipur** (2½ hrs along a picturesque route passing fields of pink and white poppies, grown legally for opium).

Train
Enquiries, T01472-240 131. A 117 km branch line runs from Chittaurgarh to **Udaipur**. At **Mavli Junction** (72 km) another branch runs down the Aravalli scarp to **Marwar Junction** (150 km). The views along this line are very picturesque indeed. By taking this route you can visit Udaipur, Ajmer and Jodhpur in a circular journey. **Ajmer**: *Purna-Jaipur Exp, 9770,* 0550, 4½ hrs. *Ahmadabad DSR Exp, 9944,* 1500, 6 hrs. **Indore**: *Jaipur-Purna Exp, 9769,* 2015, 7½ hrs; **Jaipur**: *Purna Jaipur Exp, 9770,* 0550, 8½ hrs; *Chetak Exp, 9616,* 2200, 8½ hrs; both continue to **Delhi** 15-16 hrs. **Udaipur**: *Chetak Exp, 9615,* 0650, 3½ hrs; *DSR Ahmadabad Exp, 9943,* 1345, 4½ hrs, (continues to **Ahmadabad**, 17 hrs).

Kota *p176, map p177*
Air
No flights at present.

Bus
At least hourly bus to **Bundi** (45 mins) and a few daily to **Ajmer**, **Chittaurgarh**, **Jhalarapatan** (2½ hrs); also to **Gwalior**, **Sawai Madhopur** and **Ujjain**.

Train
From Kota Junction: **Bharatpur**: *Golden Temple Mail, 2903,* 1130, 4 hrs (and Mathura, 5 hrs). **Mumbai** (Central): *Rajdhani Exp, 2952,* 2050, 11¾ hrs; *Paschim Exp, 2926,* 2355, 15½ hrs; *Golden Temple Mail, 2904,* 1455, 15¼ hrs. **New Delhi**: *Rajdhani Exp, 2951,* 0430, 5½ hrs; *Golden Temple Mail, 2903,* 1130, 7½ hrs; *Dehra Dun Exp, 9019,* 1955, 10½ hrs – all via **Sawai Madhopur**, 1½ hrs.

Bundi *p178, map p179*
Bus
Enquiries: T0747-224 5422. To **Ajmer** (165 km), 5 hrs; **Kota** (37 km), 45 mins; **Chittaurgarh** (157 km), 5 hrs; **Udaipur** (120 km), 3 hrs.

For **Jhalarapatan** catch a bus from **Kota** to **Jhalawar**; then auto-rickshaw or local bus for sights. The Ujjain-Jhalawar road is appalling.

Train
Enquiries: T0747-224 3582. The station south of town has a train each way between **Kota** and **Neemuch** via **Chittaurgarh**.

☻ Directory

Kota *p176, map p177*
Hospitals MBS Hospital, T0744-245 0241. **Internet** Acme, 2nd floor, Kalawati Paliwal Market, Gumantpura. **Police** T0744-245 0066. **Tourist office** Rajasthan, Nayapura Bagh, T0744-232 7695.

Bundi *p, map p*
Banks Exchange can be a problem; try Bank of Baroda, T0747-244 3706. **Hospitals** T0747-244 2833, City, T0747-244 2333. SS Nursing Home, T0747-244 2627. **Internet** At Royal Retreat, and dotted around town. **Tourist office** At Circuit House, T0747-244 3697, has a list of paying guest accommodation.

Jodhpur	187
Sights	188
Excursions	192
Listings	193
Around Jodhpur	197
North from Jodhpur	198
South from Jodhpur	199
Listings	200
Jaisalmer	201
Listings	206
Around Jaisalmer	210
Listings	212

✦ Footprint features

Don't miss	185
True blue	190
The Bishnois	192
Tall stories of Nagaur	199
On a camel's back	205

Introduction

The Rajasthan of most people's imagination is found in this part of the state; camels crossing windswept sand dunes, colourful tribes dancing against a stark desert landscape, and some imperious buildings surveying the scene from on high.

Jaisalmer is perhaps the ultimate expression of these romantic desert images. The amazing, and almost painfully picturesque, fort is surrounded by rolling sand dunes as far as the eye can see. However, perhaps no other fort in Rajasthan exudes the same authority as **Jodhpur**'s Meherangarh, watching over the town with unmatched majesty. There are also some exceptional forts, palaces, towns and villages dotted all over this section of the state from remote desert hamlets to some superb heritage hotels. This is also the place to come for festivals, with something happening most months of the year, providing a great opportunity to see something of the unique desert culture of this fascinating part of the world.

There are also some interesting excursions from both of these cities; the area south of Jodhpur is dotted with some of the state's most secluded heritage hotels, while to the north lie the utterly authentic attractions of **Nagaur** and **Osian**. Jaisalmer serves as a gateway to desert culture, although expect to journey some way to find the 'real thing'.

The strategic importance of this area to the Indian Army means that the roads are exceptionally well maintained so getting around isn't as bumpy as elsewhere. However, to get further afield you'll need to hire some transport; all the usual options are available, but this is the place to try out a camel!

Western Rajasthan

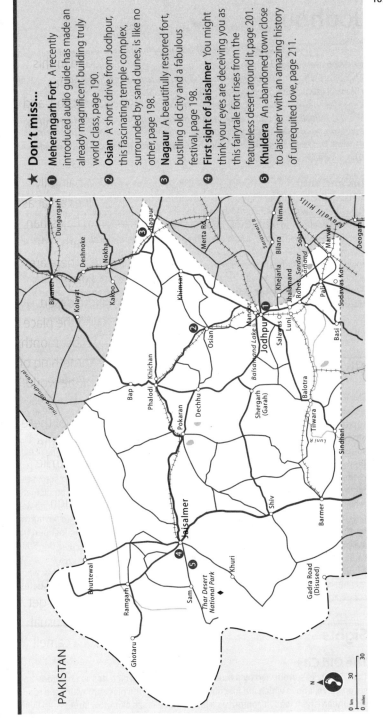

★ Don't miss...

❶ **Meherangarh Fort** A recently introduced audio guide has made an already magnificent building truly world class, page 190.

❷ **Osian** A short drive from Jodhpur, this fascinating temple complex, surrounded by sand dunes, is like no other, page 198.

❸ **Nagaur** A beautifully restored fort, bustling old city and a fabulous festival, page 198.

❹ **First sight of Jaisalmer** You might think your eyes are deceiving you as this fairytale fort rises from the featureless desert around it, page 201.

❺ **Khuldera** An abandoned town close to Jaisalmer with an amazing history of unrequited love, page 211.

Jodhpur → *Phone code: 0291. Colour map 4, grid A6.*

Rajasthan's second largest city, Jodhpur is entirely dominated by its spectacular fort, towering over proceedings below with absolute authority. The fascinating old city is a hive of activity, the colourful bazaars and narrow lanes often frequented by equally colourful tribal people from the surrounding areas. South of the railway line things are altogether more serene, and nowhere more so than the massively impressive Umaid Bhawan Palace, its classic interior belying the art deco extravaganza within. If you can spare no more than a day, try to see Meherangarh Fort and Museum, the nearby Jaswant Thada (cenotaphs) and Umaid Bhavan Palace. ▸▸ *For Sleeping, Eating and other listings, see pages 193-197.*

Ins and outs

Getting there Jodhpur has good air, rail and road links with the other major cities of Rajasthan as well as Delhi and Mumbai. Many visitors stop here either on the way to or from Jaisalmer, or on their way down to Udaipur.

Getting around The train and bus stations are conveniently located close to the old city, with most hotels a Rs 20-30 rickshaw ride away, while the airport is 5 km south of town. The old city is small enough to walk around, although many people find a rented bicycle the best way to get about. ▸▸ *See Transport, page 196, for further details.*

Tourist information The government tourist office is on the grounds of the RTDC Hotel Ghoomar ① *High Court Rd, To291-254 5083.* As well as the usual supply of maps and pamphlets, it also organize half-day city tours and village safaris. Also, International Tourist Bureau ① *Railway station, To291-243 9052.*

History

The **Rathore** Rajputs had moved to **Marwar** – the 'region of death' – in 1211, after their defeat at Kanauj by Muhammad Ghori. In 1459 Rao Jodha, forced to leave the Rathore capital at Mandore, 8 km to the north, chose this place as his capital because of its strategic location on the edge of the Thar Desert. The Rathores subsequently controlled wide areas of Rajasthan. Rao Udai Singh of Jodhpur (died 1581) received the title of Raja from Akbar, and his son, Sawai Raja Sur Singh (died 1595), conquered Gujarat and part of the Deccan for the Emperor. Maharaja Jaswant Singh (died 1678), having supported Shah Jahan in the Mughal struggle for succession in 1658, had a problematic relationship with the subsequent Mughal rule of Aurangzeb, and his son Ajit Singh was only able to succeed him after Aurangzeb's own death in 1707. In addition to driving the Mughals out of Ajmer he added substantially to the Meherangarh Fort in Jodhpur. His successor, Maharaja Abhai Singh (died 1749) captured Ahmedabad, and the State came into treaty relations with the British in 1818.

Jodhpur lies on the once strategic Delhi-Gujarat trading route and the Marwaris managed and benefited from the traffic of opium, copper, silk, sandalwood, dates, coffee and much more besides.

Sights

The Old City

The Old City is surrounded by a huge 9½-km long wall which has 101 bastions and seven gates, above which are inscribed the names of the places to which the roads underneath them lead. It comprises a labyrinthine maze of narrow streets and lively markets, a great place to wander round and get lost. Some of the houses and temples are of richly carved stone, in particular the red sandstone buildings of the Siré (Sardar) Bazar. Here the **Taleti Mahal** (early 17th century), one of three concubines' palaces in Jodhpur, has the unique feature of *jarokhas* decorated with temple columns.

The new city

The new city beyond the walls is also of interest. Overlooking the Umaid Sagar is the **Umaid Bhawan Palace** on Chittar Hill. Building started in 1929 as a famine relief exercise when the monsoon failed for the third year running. Over 3,000 people worked for 14 years, building this vast 347 room palace of sandstone and marble. The

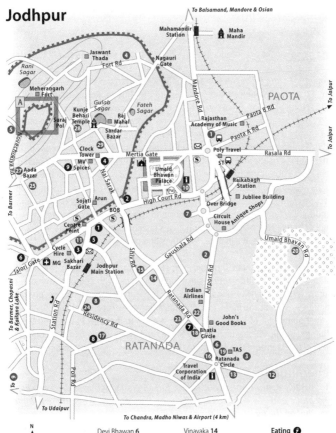

Jodhpur

N

0 metres 300
0 yards 300

Sleeping
Abhay Days 1
Ajit Bhawan, Ranbanka
 & On the Rocks 2
Blue House 27
Chauhan's 4
Cosy Guest House & Yogis 5

Devi Bhawan 6
Durag Niwas
 & Durag Vilas 7
Durjan Niwas 8
Ghoomar 10
Govind & Utsav 11
Guru International 9
Haveli Guest House 28
Haveli Palace Inn 29
Inn Season 17
Karni Bhawan 12
Madho Niwas 3
Newton's Manor 13

Vinayaka 14
Raman Guest House 15
Ratanada Polo Palace 16
Ratan Vilas 24
Royal Palace 18
Singhvi's Haveli 25
Sun City Guesthouse 23
Taj Hari Mahal 19
Umaid Bhawan Palace 20
Youth Hostel 22

Eating
Agra Sweet Home
 & Uttam 1
Gypsy 8
Poonam 2
Kalinga 3
Mishrilal 4
New Jodphur Lodge 9
Rawat Mishtan
 Bhandar 5
Sankalp 7
Shandar 6

Western Rajasthan Jodhpur

⁞ True Blue

As you approach the fort you will notice the predominance of blue houses which are often inaccurately referred to as "Brahmin houses" – the colour being associated with the high caste. In fact they are blue due to termites (white ants). It appears that the white lime-wash used originally did not deter the pests which caused havoc, making unsightly cavities in local homes. The addition of chemicals (eg copper sulphate), which resulted in turning the white lime to a blue-wash, was found to be effective in limiting the pest damage and so was widely used in the area around the fort. This also happens to be a part of town where large numbers of the Brahmin community live.

hand hewn blocks are interlocked into position, and use no mortar. It was designed by HV Lanchester, with the most modern furnishing and facilities in mind, and completed in 1943. The interior decoration was left to the artist JS Norblin, a refugee from Poland; he painted the frescoes in the Throne Room (East Wing). For th architectural historian, Tillotson, it is "the finest example of Indo-Deco. The forms are crisp and precise, and the bland monochrome of the stone makes the eye concentrate on their carved shapes". The royal family still occupy part of the palace. Part is a museum and part a luxury hotel (see Sleeping), and the interior produces a remarkable sensation of separation from the Indian environment in which it is set. There is a subterranean swimming pool decorated with signs of the zodiac; the murals are Norblin's. **Umaid Bhawan Palace Museum** ⓘ *T0291-251 0101, 0900-1700, Rs 10, foreigners Rs 40*, includes the Darbar Hall with its elegantly flaking murals plus a good collection of miniatures, armour and quirky old clocks as well as a bizarre range of household paraphernalia; if it was fashionable in the 1930s, expensive and not available in India, it's in here. The plans and photographs of the rest of the palace are also worth seeing.

    Government Museum ⓘ *Umaid Park, closed Fri, 1000-1630, Rs 3*, is a time-capsule from the British Raj, little added since Independence, with some moth-eaten stuffed animals and featherless birds, images of Jain Tirthankars, miniature portraits and antiquities. A small zoo in the gardens has a few rare exotic species.

    Just southeast of Raikabagh Station are the **Raikabagh Palace** and the **Jubilee Buildings**, public offices designed by Sir Samuel Swinton Jacob in the Indo-Saracenic style. On the Mandore Road, 2 km to the north, is the large **Mahamandir** temple.

Meherangarh

ⓘ *T0291-254 8790, 0900-1700, Rs 20, foreigners Rs 250 including excellent MP3 audio guide and camera fee, video Rs 200, allow at least 2 hrs, there is a pleasant restaurant on the terrace near the ticket office.*

The 'Majestic Fort' sprawls along the top of a steep escarpment with a sheer drop to the south. Originally started by Rao Jodha in 1459, it has walls up to 36 m high and 21 m wide, towering above the plains. Most of what stands today is from the period of Maharajah Jaswant Singh (1638-1678). On his death in 1678, Aurangzeb occupied the fort. However, after Aurangzeb's death Meherangarh returned to Jaswant Singh's son Ajit Singh and remained the royal residence until the Umaid Bhavan was completed in 1943. It is now perhaps the best preserved and presented palace in Rajasthan, an excellent example which the others will hopefully follow.

    The summit has three areas: the palace (northwest), a wide terrace to the east of the palace, and the strongly fortified area to the south. There are extensive views from the top. One approach is by a winding path up the west side, possible by rickshaw,

The gateways There were originally seven gateways. The first, the **Fateh Gate**, is heavily fortified with spikes and a barbican that forces a 45° turn. The smaller **Gopal Gate** is followed by the **Bhairon Gate**, with large guardrooms. The fourth, **Toati Gate**, is now missing but the fifth, **Dodhkangra Gate**, marked with cannon shots, stands over a turn in the path and has loopholed battlements for easy defence. Next is the **Marti Gate**, a long passage flanked by guardrooms. The last, **Loha (Iron) Gate**, controls the final turn into the fort and has handprints (31 on one side and five on the other) of royal *satis*, the wives of maharajas, see page 281. It is said that six queens and 58 concubines became *satis* on Ajit Singh's funeral pyre in 1724. *Satis* carried the Bhagavad Gita with them into the flames and legend has it that the holy book would never perish. The main entrance is through the **Jay (Victory) Pol**.

The palaces From the Loha Gate the ramp leads up to the Suraj (Sun) Pol, which opens onto the Singar Choki Chowk, the main entrance to the museum, see below. Used for royal ceremonies such as the anointing of rajas, the north, west and southwest sides of the Singar Choki Chowk date from the period immediately before the Mughal occupation in 1678. The upper storeys of the chowk were part of the *zenana*, and from the **Jhanki Mahal** ('glimpse palace') on the upper floor of the north wing the women could look down on the activities of the courtyard. Thus the chowk below has the features characteristic of much of the rest of the *zenana*, *jarokhas* surmounted by the distinctive Bengali style eaves, and beautifully ornate *jali* screens. These allowed cooling breezes to ventilate rooms and corridors in the often stiflingly hot desert summers.

    Also typical of Mughal buildings was the use of material hung from rings below the eaves to provide roof covering, as in the columned halls of the **Daulat Khana** and the **Sileh Khana** (armoury), which date from Ajit Singh's reign. The collection of Indian weapons in the armoury is unequalled, with remarkable swords and daggers, often beautifully decorated with calligraphy. Shah Jahan's red silk and velvet tent, lavishly embroidered with gold thread and used in the Imperial Mughal campaign, is in the **Tent Room**. The **Jewel House** has a wonderful collection of jewellery, including diamond eyebrows held by hooks over the ears. There are also palanquins, howdahs and ornate royal cradles, all marvellously well preserved.

    The **Phool Mahal** (Flower Palace), above the Sileh Khana, was built by Abhai Singh (1724-1749) as a hall of private audience. The stone *jali* screens are original and there are striking portraits of former rulers, a lavishly gilded ceiling and the Jodhpur coat of arms displayed above the royal couch; the murals of the 36 musical modes are a late 19th-century addition.

    The **Umaid Vilas**, which houses Rajput miniatures, is linked to the **Sheesh Mahal** (Mirror Palace), built by Ajit Singh between 1707 and 1724. The room has characteristic large and regularly sized mirror work, unlike Mughal 'mirror palaces'. Immediately to its south, and above the Sardar Vilas, is the **Takhat Vilas**. Added by Maharajah Takhat Singh (1843-1873), it has wall murals of dancing girls, love legends and Krishna Lila, while its ceiling has two unusual features: massive wooden beams to provide support and the curious use of colourful Belgian Christmas tree balls.

    The **Ajit Vilas** has a fascinating collection of musical instruments and costumes. On the ground floor of the Takhat Vilas is **Sardar Vilas**, and to its south the **Khabka**

In 1886 the Jodhpur Railway first introduced camel drawn trains until steam engines were acquired. The maharaja's luxurious personal saloons which date from 1926 are beautifully finished with inlaid wood and silver fittings and are on display near the Umaid Bhawan Palace.

The Bishnois

The Bishnois (Vishnois), follow '29' (bish-noi) principles of a non-violent Vaishnava sect, founded in the 15th century by Jambeswarji. They are known for their reverence for wildlife and their careful environmental management, protecting, especially, green vegetation and preserving the blackbuck antelope from extinction. They are a gentle community of potters, weavers, leather embroiderers and camel herders. Some groups are being helped to overcome their addiction to opium.

and **Chandan Mahals** (sleeping quarters). The **Moti Vilas** wings to the north, east and south of the Moti Mahal Chowk, date from Jaswant Singh's reign. The women could watch proceedings in the courtyard below through the *jali* screens of the surrounding wings. Tillotson suggests that the **Moti Mahal** (Pearl Palace) ① *15 mins for Rs 150*, to the west, although placed in the *zenana* of the fort, was such a magnificent building that it could only have served the purpose of a Diwan-i-Am (Hall of Public Audience). The Moti Mahal is fronted by excellently carved 19th-century woodwork, while inside waist-level niches housed oil lamps whose light would have shimmered from the mirrored ceiling. A palmist reads your fortune at Moti Mahal Chowk (museum area).

Mehrangarh Fort Palace Museum is in a series of palaces with beautifully designed and decorated windows and walls. It has a magnificent collection of the maharajas' memorabilia – superbly maintained and presented.

Jaswant Thada ① *off the road leading up to the fort, 0900-1700, Rs 10*, is the cremation ground of the former rulers with distinctive memorials in white marble which commemorate Jaswant Singh II (1899) and successive rulers of Marwar.

Excursions

Bishnoi villages

A village safari visiting a Bishnoi village is recommended, although they have naturally become more touristy over the years. Most tours include the hamlets of **Guda**, famous for wildlife, **Khejarali**, a well-known Bishnoi village, **Raika** cameleers' settlement and **Salawas**, see page 199.

Jhalamand

This small, semi-rural village 12 km south of Jodhpur is a good alternative to staying in the city, particularly if you have your own transport. It works especially well as a base from which to explore the nearby Bishnoi and Raika communities. See Sleeping.

Mandore

Some 8 km north of Jodhpur, the old 14th-century capital of Marwar is set on a plateau. Set around the old cremation ground with the red sandstone *chhatris* of the Rathore rulers, the gardens are usually crowded with Indian tourists at weekends. The **Shrine of the 33 Crore Gods** is a hall containing huge painted rock-cut figures of heroes and gods, although some of the workmanship is a little crude. The largest *deval*, a combination of temple and cenotaph, is Ajit Singh's (died 1724); worth a closer look but is unkempt. A small **museum** ① *closed Fri, 1000-1630*, in the Janana Mahal contains some fine sculpture and miniature paintings. The remains of an eighth-century Hindu temple is on a hilltop nearby.

Bal Samand Lake

The oldest artificial lake in Rajasthan is 5 km north. Dating from 1159, it is surrounded by parkland laid out in 1936 where the 19th-century **Hawa Mahal** was turned into a royal summer palace. Although the interior is European in style, it has entirely traditional red sandstone filigree windows and beautifully carved balconies. The peaceful and well-maintained grounds exude calm and tranquillity, while the views over the lake are simply majestic.

● Sleeping

Jodhpur *p187, map p189*

LL-L Umaid Bhawan Palace, T0291-251 0101, www.amanresorts.com. Was taken over by Aman group in Nov 2003 and has been closed for renovation, opening on 1 Dec 2004. Already an amazing building, it should be very special when it re-opens.

L Taj Hari Mahal, 5 Residency Rd, T0291-243 9700, www.tajhotels.com. 93 plush rooms blending traditional and modern, imaginatively designed, good restaurants, excellent pool, the epitome of comfort.

A Ajit Bhawan, Airport Rd, near Circuit House, T0291-251 1410, www.ajitbhawan. com. 65 a/c rooms, 50 in cottages, best heritage rooms in main building plus 5 attractive tents. Great pool, good Indian buffets, well-kept garden, 'village safari' (see Around Jodhpur p197), group-oriented.

A Bal Samand Palace (WelcomHeritage), is in extensive grounds, on lakeside, see Excursions, T02912-572 321, www.welcomheritage.com. There are 9 attractively furnished suites in the separate atmospheric palace and 26 rooms in the imaginatiively renovated stables, restaurant (mainly buffet), lovely pool, boating, pleasant orchards which attract nilgai, jackals, peacocks, has a calming, tranquil atmosphere, making it an excellent alternative to staying in Jodhpur.

A Ranbanka, next to Ajit Bhawan, Circuit House Rd, T0291-251 2801, www.ranbanka hotels.com. 31 renovated rooms in period property, communal areas a little unloved but staff are charming, small pool, large garden.

B Abhay Days, Mandore Rd, off Paota Circle, T0291-254 2980, www.daysindia.com. 72 a/c rooms in modern hotel with western standards, excellent reasonably priced vegetarian restaurant, good pool and health club, good value.

B Durjan Niwas, Daspan Vihar, off Loco Shed Rd, Ratanada, T0291-264 9546, www. durjanniwas.com.16 comfortable, a/c rooms with balcony, pool, old house of Thakur family in a quiet location, friendly, helpful.

B Jhalamand Garh, Jhalamand, see Excursions, T0291-272 0481, www.heritage hotelsindia.com. 17 comfortable rooms in whitewashed, family-run period property. Good local dishes in atmospheric dining hall, jeep, horse and camel safaris arranged, perhaps not the most professional set up but all the more charming for it.

B Karni Bhawan, Palace Rd, T0291-251 2101, www.karnihotels.com. 30 clean, simple, classy rooms (20 a/c), each with a different theme and period furniture to match, in 1940s sandstone 'colonial bungalow' (on 3 floors!). Village theme restaurant, peaceful lawns, clean pool, unhurried helpful staff.

B Royal Palace, Bhatia Circle, Ratanada, T0291-515429, hrpalaceindia@yahoo.com. 24 a/c rooms, 2 suites, modern 4-storey building, restaurant, helpful family and staff.

B-C Inn Season, PWD Rd, T0291-261 6400, www.innseasonjodhpur.com. 11 classy a/c rooms in smart, well-run hotel, good pool in beautiful gardens, a definite cut above.

B-C Ratan Vilas, Loco Shed Rd, Ratanada, T0291-261 4418. 11 rooms (more on way), some a/c, arranged around beautiful court-yard in elegant period property. Very well maintained, lovely gardens, friendly family.

B-C Ratanada Polo Palace, Residency Rd, T0291-243 1910. Closed for renovation at time of writing, but traditionally one of Jodhpur's better hotels.

C Guru International, 26 Nai Sarak, T0291-263 7152, www.hotelguruinter national.com. The best of the many similar, Indian business class hotels on the same street. 22 a/c rooms, okay value, friendly, helpful staff.

C Utsav, Raibahadur Bazar, MG Rd, T0291-510 5100, hotelutsav@mailinfinity.com. 42 a/c rooms in modern, contemporary style, good views from top floors, discreet staff.

C-D Devi Bhavan, 1 Ratanada Circle, T0291-251 1067, www.devibhawan.com. 10 rooms (2 more on the way) with bath, most with a/c, delightful shady garden, excellent Indian dinner (set timings), Rajput family home. Recommended.

C-D Haveli Palace Inn, behind clock tower, T0291-261 2519, haveliinn@rediffmail.com. 8 atmospheric, spotless rooms (more planned) in authentic 200-year-old *haveli* complete with elaborately decorated drawing room/mini-museum, charming owners, good views from roof. Recommended.

C-D Hotel Ghoomar (RTDC), High Court Rd, T0291-254 4010. Most rooms not worth considering, but 'super-deluxe' a/c rooms have been renovated to a high standard and are good value at Rs900.

C-D Newton's Manor, 86 Jawahar Colony, Central School Rd, T0291-243 0686, www.newtonsmanor.com. 5 quaintly kitsch a/c rooms, touches of Victoriana plus stuffed animals, breakfast and dinner on request, a break from the norm.

C-E Haveli Guest House, Makaran Mohalla, opposite Turji ka Jhalra, T0291-261 4615, www.haveliguesthouse.net. Attractive sandstone building with 7 balconies, 22 simple, clean rooms, cheerful decor, breezy roof terrace with veg restaurant and great views of fort. Reports of poorly prepared food and unscrupulous payments to rickshaw drivers.

C-E Sun City Guest House, 1/C High Court Colony, Ratanada, T0291-262 5880. 8 good-sized, clean, basic rooms run by very enthusiastic and friendly family.

D Vinayaka Guest House, Shiv Rd, Ratanada, T0291-251 4950, vinayaka_td@re diffmail.com. 6 clean, well looked after rooms in tasteful, spacious family home. Pleasant lawn, quiet location, charming hosts.

D-E Blue House, Sumer Bhawan, Moti Chowk, T0291-262 1396, bluehouse36@ hotmail.com. 7 clean rooms, 5 with bath (hot water all day), home cooked meals, great views from roof top restaurant but gets mixed reviews, including reports of aggressive and unkind behaviour by staff. Be wary of trips to cousin's overpriced handicrafts shop.

D-E Govind, Station Rd, opposite GPO, T0291-262 2758, www.govindhotel.com. 12 cleanish rooms, some a/c, good rooftop veg restaurant with fort views but slow service(breakfast from 0530!), camel safaris, bus and rail ticketing, internet, friendly, very helpful owner but noisy location.

D-E Madho Niwas, New Airport Rd, Ratanada, T0291-251 2486, madhoniwas@ satyam.net.in. 16 fairly basic rooms in period bungalow, Marwari meals in garden, pool, safaris, mixed reports on service and cleanliness.

D-E Singhvi's Haveli, Navchokiya, Ramdevji ka Chowk, T0291-262 4293, singhvi15ad haveli@hotmail.com. 7 rooms in charming, 500-year-old *haveli*, tastefully decorated, friendly family. Recommended.

D-F Chauhan's Guest House, Fort Rd, T0291-254 1497. Quirky home- stay offering courses in Hindi, yoga, music, art, relaxing café, family run, shop, book exchange.

D-F Cosy Guest House, Novechokiya Rd (north from Jalori Gate), Brahm Puri, Chuna ki Choki, just west of the fort, T0291-261 2066, cosyguesthouse@yahoo.com. 6 simple clean rooms, good home-cooked meals (other restaurants 15-min walk), bus bookings, rooftop views of fort and old city, quiet, reports of unfriendly behaviour.

D-F Yogi's Guest House, Raj Purohit ji ki Haveli, Manak Chowk, old town, T0291-264 3436, yogiguesthouse@hotmail.com. 12 rooms, most in 500-year-old *haveli*, clean, modern bathrooms, camel/jeep safaris, friendly and experienced management.

E Durag Vilas, 1 Old Public Park, near Circuit House, T0291-251 2298. 10 very clean, quiet, air-cooled rooms with shower, travel bookings, desert safaris, family run, friendly, helpful, free lift from station/airport. Superior to next door **Durag Niwas**.

E Hotel Shiva, Station Rd, T0291-262 4774. 14 clean, well-maintained rooms, peaceful atmosphere, friendly staff.

E-F Hare Krishna Guest House, Killi Khana, Mehron Ka Chowk, old town, T0291-265 4367, panditart1500ad@yahoo.co.in. 7 small, clean, characterful and airy rooms in family home, very welcoming.

E-F Raman Guest House, opposite Keshar Bagh, Shiv Rd, T0291-251 3980. 20 clean

though simply furnished rooms with bath (hot water), 3 with a/c, family atmosphere, traditional meals, quiet area, pleasant rooftop, friendly and efficient owner.
F Youth Hostel, Bhatia Circle, Ratanada, T0291-251 0160. 5 rooms and 6 dorms in attractive, well-located building. Friendly staff, camping lawn.

❼ Eating

Jodhpur *p187, map p189*
The best restaurants are in hotels and you must reserve ahead. For *Daal-bhatti, lassi* and *kachoris* head for Jalori and Sojati gates.
♦♦♦ Ajit Bhawan, T0291-251 1410. Evening buffet, excellent meal in garden on a warm evening with entertainment, but poor atmosphere if eating indoors in winter.
♦♦♦ Umaid Bhavan, T0291-251 0101. Closed for renovation until Dec 2004 but fabulous setting should make it a great place for dinner. **Pillars**, a tiny garden restaurant, can be hired for one couple for Rs 2000, easily the most romantic setting in town.
♦♦ Gypsy, PWD Colony, T510 3888. 1130-1530 and 1900-2300. Good range of Indian, Continental and Mexican dishes, choice of indoor or outdoor seating, swanky place popular with well-off locals.
♦♦ Kalinga, opposite station. Western and Indian. A/c, good food (try butter chicken and aubergine dishes), friendly service, music may not please, breakfast good value Nearby **Midtown** is similar but not quite as smart.
♦♦ On the Rocks, near Ajit Bhavan, T0291-510 2701, good mix of Indian and Continental, plus a relaxing bar, patisserie, ice cream parlour and lovely gardens.
♦♦ Sankalp, Bhati Circle, Ratanada, T0291-510 9192, 1030-2300. Upmarket a/c South Indian, dosas come with a fantastic range of chutneys, good service. Recommended.
♦ Hotel Priya, 181 Nai Sarak. Fantastic special *thalis* for Rs 49 and extra quick service.
♦ Jodhpur Coffee House, Sojati Gate. Good South Indian snacks and *thalis*.
♦ New Jodhpur Lodge, a real challenge to find, ask for Golion ki Haveli in Tripoliya Bazar in the old city, 261 3340. A family home which offers good, basic *thalis* for Rs30 in a shaded courtyard, quite an experience.
♦ Poonam, High Court Rd. Pure veg Indian.

"Gorgeous 4-foot masala dosas".
♦ Shandar, Jalori Gate. Indian vegetarian. Good food and sweets.
♦ Uttam, High Court Rd, near Sojati Gate. Good a/c *thali* restaurant friendly, fast service.

Sweets and drinks
Agra Sweet Home, near Sojati Gate.
Janata, Nai Sarak. Recommended.
Mishrilal, main entrance to Sardar Bazar. Splendid creamy and saffron flavoured *makhania lassi* – the best in town!
Rawat Mishtan Bhandar, near railway station. Tempting Indian sweets and drinks.

❶ Bars and clubs

Jodhpur *p187, map p189*
In **Umaid Palace**, **On the Rocks**, **Ashok** and in **Kalinga Restaurant** (see above).

❀ Festivals and events

Jodhpur *p187, map p189*
Several are special to Rajasthan. See also p.
Jul/Aug, Nag Panchami, when *Naga (naag)*, the cobra, is worshipped. The day is dedicated to *Sesha*, the 1000-headed god or *Anant* ('infinite') *Vishnu*, who is often depicted reclining on a bed of serpents. In Jodhpur, snake charmers gather for a colourful fair in Mandore. **Marwar Festival** (**26-27 Oct 2004**, 16-17 Oct 2005, 6-7 Oct 2006), held at full moon, includes music, puppet shows, turban tying competitions, camel polo and ends with a fire dance on the dunes at Osian.

❍ Shopping

Jodhpur *p187, map p189*
Jodhpur is famous for its once popular *jodhpurs* (riding breeches), tie-and-dye fabrics, lacquer work and leather shoes. Export of items over 100-years-old is prohibited. The main areas are: **Sojati Gate** for gifts; **Station Rd** for jewellery; **Tripolia Bazar** for handicrafts; **Khanda Falsa** for tie-and-dye; **Lakhara Bazar** for lac bangles. Shoes are made in **Mochi Bazar**, **Sardarpura** and **Clock Tower**, *bandhanas* in **Bambamola**, and around **Siwanchi** and **Jalori Gates**. *Durries* are woven at **Salavas** village, 18 km away.

Antiques

Shops on road between Umaid and Ajit Bhawans, flourishing trade though pricey. **Kirti Art Collection**, T0291-512 136. Has a good selection. Recommended.

Books
John's Good Books, Bhati Circle, Circuit House Rd. Small but a good selection. **Khazana**, at Taj Hari Mahal, has books on India, and English fiction.

Handloom and handicrafts
Khadi Sangh, Station Rd. Quality, fair prices. **Marasthaly**, High Court Rd. Quality, fair prices. **Rajasthan Khadi Sangathan**, BK ka Bagh. **Shriganesham**, 1st floor Pal-Haveli, behind clocktower. Wide selection, honest.

Photography
Shops in High Court Rd, Sojati Gate and in Jalori Gate. **Kala Colour Lab**, opposite MG Hospital. Recommended.

Spices
Mohanlal Verhomal Spices, 209B, Kirana Merchant (from Clock Tower enter veg market, then turn right), T0291-615846, www.mvspices. com. Sought after for hand-mixed spices, more expensive than competitors but quality assured.

▲ Activities and tours

Jodhpur *p187, map p189*
Many of the hotels organize village safaris, as does the tourist office, which charges Rs 1,100 for 4 people including car, guide and tips given to villagers. City sightseeing, starts from Tourist Office at **Ghoomar Hotel**,

T0291-254 5083: half day (0830-1300, 1400-1800). Fort and palaces, Jaswant Thada, Mandore Gardens, Government Museum, bazar around Old City clock tower. Tour operators include:
Aravali Safari, 4 Kuchaman House Area, Airport Rd, T0291-2626799.
Forts & Palaces, 15 Old Public Park, T0294-251 1207, www.palaces-tours.com.
Poly Travels, 10D Bus Stand, Paota, T0291-254 5210, poly@nda.vsnl.net.in.
Ayurvedic massages are offered by **Ajit Bhawan**, **Balsamand Palace** and **Khimsar Fort**, see Sleeping.

☺ Transport

Jodhpur *p187, map p189*
Air
Transport to town: by taxi, Rs 200; auto-rickshaw, Rs 120. **Indian Airlines**, near Bhati Cross Roads, T510757. 1000-1300, 1400-1700; airport enquiries T0291-251 2617, reser- vations T0291-251 0757. **Indian Airlines** flies to **Delhi**, **Jaipur**, **Mumbai**, **Udaipur**. Jet Airways, T0291-230 2222, airport T0291-233 1331, **Delhi**.

Bicycle
Bike hire shops on the road opposite the station (near **Kalinga Restaurant**).

Bus
Local Mini-buses cover most of the city except Fort and Umaid Bhavan Palace. For **Mandore**, frequent local/city bus leave Jodhpur, 100 m from the station and Paota Bus Stand.
Long distance Earplugs are recommended on video coaches. Allow time

to find the correct bus; match number on ticket with bus registration plate.

A convenient bus route links Jodhpur with **Ghanerao** and **Ranakpur, Kumbhalgar** and **Udaipur**. RST Bus Stand, near Raikabagh railway station, T0291-254 4989. 1000-1700; bookings also at tourist office. **Ahmadabad**, 11 hrs; **Jaipur**, frequent, 8 hrs; **Mt Abu Rd**, 6½ hrs; **Ajmer**, 4½ hrs; **Jaisalmer**, 0630 (depart Jaisalmer, 1400), 5-6 hrs, Rs 90; faster than train but scenically tedious; **Pali**, 4 hrs, Rs 30; **Udaipur**, 8-9 hrs, best to book a good seat a day ahead. Private operators: **HR Travels, Sun City Tours**, and **Sethi Yatra**, opposite Main Railway Station. For private buses ask at **Govind Hotel**, opposite Railway Station. Deluxe video coaches and Express buses between Jodhpur and **Delhi, Ahmadabad, Bikaner, Bhilwara**: most depart 0600 and 2200. **Jaipur**: 5 hrs; **Jaisalmer**: about hourly from 0600 ('when full'), 4-5 hrs, Rs 100 (tickets from travel agents); comfortable buses on good road, but beware of touts on arrival at Jaisalmer; decide on hotel in advance.

Car
Car hire from tourist office, **Ghoomer Hotel**, whole day about Rs 550; half day Rs 300.

Rickshaw
Railway station to fort should be about Rs 25 (may demand Rs 50; try walking away).

Taxi
T0291-262 0238.

Train
Jodhpur Station enquiries: T131/132. Open 0800-2400. Reservations: T0291-263 6407.

Open 0900-1300, 1330-1600. Advance reservations, next to GPO. Tourist Bureau, T0291-254 5083 (0500-2300). **International Tourist Waiting Room** for passengers in transit (ground floor), with big sofas and showers; clean Indian toilets in 2nd Class Waiting Room on the 1st floor of the Station Foyer. To **Abu Rd (Mount Abu)**: *Ranakpur Exp, 4707*, 1515, 5½ hrs. **Agra**: *Marudhar Exp, 4854/4864*, 0700, 14 hrs *Jodhpur-Howrah Exp, 2308*, 1715, 12¾ hrs. **Ahmadabad**: *Surya Nagri Exp, 4845*, 1855, 9½ hrs. **Barmer**: *Barmer Exp, 4807*, 0805, 4½ hrs. **Delhi** (no 1st class): *Mandore Exp, 2462*, 1930, 11 hrs (OD); *Jodhpur Delhi Exp, 4860*, 2300, 12½ hrs (OD) **Jaipur**: *Inter-City Exp, 2467*, 0545, 6 hrs; *Mandore Exp, 2462*, 1930, 5 hrs; *Marudhar Exp, 4854/4864*, 0700, 5 hrs. **Jaisalmer**: *Jodhpur Jaisalmer Exp*, and *4810 Exp*, 2315, 6½ hrs. **Varanasi** via Lucknow: *Marudhar Exp, 4854/4864*, 0700, 19 hrs (Lucknow), 26 hrs (Varanasi).

❶ Directory

Jodhpur *p187, map p189*
Banks 1030-1400. For Visa. **Punjab National Bank**, Ratanada. For TCs. **State Bank of India**, High Court Rd (inside High Court complex). Currency and Tcs.
Hospital MG Hospital, T636437. Dispensary: Paota, Residency. Open 0800-1200, 1700-1900, Sun 0800-1200.
Internet **Amardeep**, Sardarpura, 3 km southwest of railway station, above Marudhar Jewellers, Ghoomer Hotel.
Post office GPO, south of Jodhpur station, 1000-2000, Sat 1000-1600.
Useful addresses Ambulance: T102. Fire: T101. Police: T100.

Around Jodhpur

The temples of Osian are remarkable as much for their location in the middle of the desert as their architecture, while Nagaur is one of Rajasthan's busiest but most unaffected cities. The area south of Jodhpur is refreshingly green and fertile compared to the desert landscapes of most of Western Rajasthan. Going away from the city, the landscape soon becomes agricultural, punctuated by small, friendly villages, some of which house stunning heritage hotels. ➤➤ *For Sleeping, Eating and other listings, see pages 200-201.*

North from Jodhpur

Osian

Surrounded by sand dunes, this ancient town north of Jodhpur in the Thar desert contains the largest group of eighth- to 10th-century Hindu and Jain temples in Rajasthan. The typical Pratihara Dynasty **temple complex** is set on a terrace whose walls are finely decorated with mouldings and miniatures. The sanctuary walls have central projections with carved panels' and above these rise curved towers. The doorways are usually decorated with river goddesses, serpents and scrollwork. The 23 temples are grouped in several sites north, west and south of the town. The western group contains a mixture of Hindu temples, including the **Surya Temple** (early eighth century) with beautifully carved pillars. The Jain **Mahavira Temple** (eighth to 10th centuries) the best preserved, 200 m further on a hillock, rises above the town, and boasts a fantastically gaudy interior. The 11th- to 12th-century **Sachiya Mata Temple** is a living temple of the Golden Durga. Osian is well worth visiting.

Khimsar

On the edge of the desert, 80 km northeast of Jodhpur and 60 km from Osian, Khimsar was founded by the Jain saint Mahavir 2,500 years ago. The isolated, battle scarred, 16th-century moated castle of which a section remains, had a *zenana* added in the mid-18th century and a regal wing added in the 1940s.

Nagaur

① *Rs10, foreigners Rs50, still camera Rs25, video Rs50.*

Nagaur, 137 km north of Jodhpur, was a centre of Chishti Sufis. It attracts interest as it preserves some fine examples of pre-Mughal and Mughal architecture. The dull stretch of desert is enlivened by Nagaur's fort palace, temples and *havelis*. The city walls are said to date from the 11th- to 12th-century Chauhan period. Akbar built the mosque here and there is a shrine of the disciple of Mu'inuddin Chishti of Ajmer, see page 234. **Ahhichatragarh Fort**, which dominates the city, is absolutely vast, contains palaces of the Mughal emperors and of the Marwars, and is being restored with help from the Paul Getty Foundation. The Akbar Mahal is really stunning, unspeakable elegant and perfectly proportioned. The fort also has excellent wall paintings and interesting ancient systems of rainwater conservation and storage, ably explained by a very knowledgeable curator. It was awarded a UNESCO Heritage Award in 2000.

Khichan

Four kilometres from Phalodi, southwest of Bikaner, just off the NH15, is a lovely, picturesque village with superb red sandstone *havelis* of the Oswal Jains. Beyond the village are sand dunes and mustard fields, and a lake which attracts ducks and other waterfowl. The once small quiet village has grown into a bustling agricultural centre and a prominent bird feeding station. Jain villagers put out grain behind the village for winter visitors; up to 8,000 demoiselle cranes and occasionally Common eastern cranes can be seen in December and January on the feeding grounds.

Pokaran

Pokaran, between Jaisalmer and Jodhpur, stands on the edge of the great desert with dunes stretching 100 km west to the Pakistan border. It provides a mid-way stopover between Bikaner/Jodhpur and Jaisalmer for tourists as it did for royal and merchant caravans in the past. The impressive 16th-century yellow sandstone Pokaran fort, overlooking a confusion of streets in the town below, has a small museum with an interesting collection of medieval weapons, costumes and paintings. There are good views from the ramparts. Pokaran is also well known for its potters who make

⋮ Tall stories of Nagaur

Nagaur and the area around it seem to have an extraordinary preponderance of remarkable phenomenon. First up is none other than the prophet Mohammed's shirt, apparently ensconced in a place called Role, en route to Sikar. Next in a long line is "2½ peg Devi", a deity local to Bawal Matar, on the road to Merta, who physically imbibes 2½ measures of whisky a day. Not to be outdone, there's a place called Ren, where the local speciality is floating bricks, or for the physically disabled, a temple in Butati which will cure any paralysis!

red-and-white pottery and terracotta horses/elephants. **Ramdeora**, the Hindu and Jain pilgrim centre nearby, has Bishnoi hamlets and a preserve for blackbuck antelope, Indian gazelle, bustards and sand grouse. **Ramdeora Fair** is an important religious event (12-13 September 2005, 2-3 September 2006, 21-22 September 2007).

Khetolai, about 25 km northwest of Pokaran, is the site of India's first nuclear test explosion held underground on 18 March 1974, and of further tests in May 1998.

South from Jodhpur

Salawas
Salawas, about 30-minutes' drive south from Jodhpur, is well known for its pit loom weaving. The village produces *durries*, carpets, rugs, bed covers and tents using camel hair, goat hair, wool and cotton in colourful and interesting patterns. You can visit the weavers' co-operative **Roopraj Durrie Udyog**, where you can buy authentic village crafts, but watch out for high prices and pushy salesmen.

Luni
The tiny bustling village of Luni, 40 km from Jodhpur, sits in the shadow of the 19th-century red sandstone Fort Chanwa which has been converted to a hotel. With its complex of courtyards, water wheels, and intricately carved façades, the fort and its village offer an attractive and peaceful alternative to the crowds of Jodhpur. The village of Sanchean, which you will pass through on the way from Jodhpur, is worth exploring.

Rohet and Sardar Samand
Rohet, 50 km north of Jodhpur, was once a picturesque hamlet settled by the Bishnoi community. It is now a busy highway village. At the end of the village a lake attracts numerous winter migrants in addition to resident birds. Rohetgarh, a small 'castle' beside the lake, which has been converted in to a hotel, has a collection of antique hunting weapons.

The lake nearby is a beautiful setting for the royal 1933 art deco hunting lodge, **Sardar Samand Palace**, see page 201. The lake attracts pelicans, flamingos, cranes, egrets and kingfishers and the wildlife sanctuary has blackbuck, gazelle and nilgai, but the water level drops substantially during summer; the lake has actually dried up from April-June in recent years. Sardar Samand is 60 km southeast of Jodhpur.

Nimaj
Nimaj is a small feudal town 110 km east of Jodhpur on the way to the main Jaipur-Udaipur highway. The real attraction here is the artificial lake, **Chhatra Sagar**, 4 km away. The ex-ruling family have recreated a 1920s style tented hunting lodge on the lake's dam, which offers amazing views over the water and a genuine family welcome.

Balotra and around

The small textile town, 100 km southwest of Jodhpur, is known for its traditional weaving using pit looms and block prints. Nearby is the beautiful Jain temple with elephant murals at **Nakoda**, which also hosts a remarkable **camel and cattle fair** which takes place on the riverbed in March/April. **Kanana**, near Balotra, celebrates **Holi** with stage shows and other entertainment. There is a *dharamshala* at Nakoda and guesthouses at Balotra. At **Tilwara**, 127 km from Jodhpur, the Mallinathji **cattle fair** is a major event. Held just after **Holi** every year, over 80,000 animals, including Kapila (Krishna's) cows and Kathiawari horses, are brought making it Rajasthan's largest.

● Sleeping

Osian *p198*

L Camel Camp, on the highest sand dunes, T0291-243 7023, www.camelcamposian.com. A beautiful complex of 50 double bedded luxury tents with modern conveniences (attached baths, hot showers), superb restaurant and bar plus an amazing pool – quite a sight at the top of a sand dune! Tariff inclusive of meals and camel safaris, ask in advance for jeep/camel transfers to avoid a steep climb up the dunes. Recommended. Also some **E** and **F** guesthouses in town.

Khimsar *p198*

A Khimsar Fort, T01585-262 345, www. khimsarfort.com. 48 large, comfortable a/c rooms, good restaurant on breezy roof top with lovely views, fabulous pool, yoga, gym, beautiful large gardens, fire dances at the illuminated medieval fort, award-winning heritage hotel, one of the best in Rajasthan. Highly recommended.
A Khimsar Sand Dunes Village, 6 km from the fort, contact fort as above. 16 ethnically styled luxury huts in the heart of the dunes around a small lake, unbeatable setting.

Nagaur *p198*

A Royal Camp, T0291-257 2321, www.wel comheritage.com. Operates during the camel fair (when the price rises **L**) and Oct-Mar. 20 delightful deluxe 2-bed furnished tents (hot water bottles, heaters etc), flush toilets, hot water in buckets, dining tent for buffets, all inside fort walls, an experience.
C-E Mahaveer International, Vijay Vallabh Chowk, near bus stand, T01582-243 158. 15 okay rooms, 7 a/c, huge dining hall, friendly knowledgeable manager.
D Shree Aditya, Ajmer Rd, near Vyas petrol pump, T01582-245 438. 24 modern rooms, 12 a/c, in brand new building.

Pokaran *p198*

B-C Manwar Desert Camp, 61 km from Pokaran in Manwar, has beautifully designed cottages with attractive interiors, some a/c, restaurant (a good lunch stop), handicrafts.
C Fort Pokaran, T02994-222 274. 14 quaint, quirky rooms with bath (some need improving), old 4-posters, some carved columns, good hot lunches Rs 200-250 (order ahead if passing through town), not family run so service and welcome a little detached.
D Motel Pokaran (RTDC), on NH15, T02994-222 275. 8 sparse rooms in a ramshackle building, plus 5 passable garden cottages.
Tented Resort, 61 km from Pokaran in Man-war, 2½ km on a sand dune, reservations T02928-66137, good 2-bed tents with hot showers, flush toilets, meals, camel, jeep safaris and visits to Bishnoi villages.

Luni *p199*

A-B Fort Chanwa, T02931-284 216, www. fortchanwa.com. 31 good rooms in 200-year-old fort, not large but well furnished, individually designed (best in the keep), excellent Rajasthani meals in impressive dining room, pleasant lawn for drinks, excellent pool, well managed, a bit impersonal but exceptionally maintained. You can visit craft villages, watch good handloom weaving and bargain to buy.

Rohet and Sardar Samand *p199*

A Rohetgarh, Rohet, T02936-268 231, www.rohetgarh.com. 32 pleasant rooms, some cramped, attached baths (avoid rooms near outdoor restaurant), in 1622 fort. Fine Rajasthani food, ordinary architecture but in beautiful environment, pleasant lake view terraces, pool, health club, riding and safaris to Bishnoi, Raika and artisans' villages,

boating on the lake, a relaxing getaway.
A Sardar Samand Palace, Sardar Samand, T02960-245 001, www.welcomheritage.com. 19 colonial style rooms (11 a/c), in a slightly forbidding-looking building, somehow reminiscent of a British lighthouse. Built in 1933 as a hunting lodge, much of the furniture is original, and lends a very unIndian feel. Safaris and boating trips arranged in the season, Nov best time for birdspotting on the lake, good pool and tennis court, isolated but atmospheric.

Nimaj *p199*
L Chhatra Sagar, 4 km from Nimaj, T02939-230 118, www.chhatrasagar.com. 11 beautiful colonial-style tents on the banks of a very picturesque reservoir. The ex-rulers of Nimaj have recreated the hunting lodge of their forefathers to great effect, and still live on the lake themselves, so a very convivial family atmosphere. Safaris arranged, all meals included in the tariff, recommended. Open 1 Oct-31 Mar.

❼ Eating

Pokaran *p198*
Pick up fresh *pakoras* from highway stalls on the outskirts or delicious *gulab jamuns* from the local *halwai* (sweet shop).

❀ Festivals and events

Nagaur *p198*
The popular **Cattle and Camel Fair** (**15-18 Feb 2005**, 4-7 Feb 2006, 25-28 Feb 2007) is held just outside the town during which there are camel races, cock fights, folk dancing and music. The fields become full of encampments of pastoral communities, tribal people and livestock dealers with their cattle, camels, sheep, goat and other animals.

❍ Shopping

Pokaran *p198*
Kashida, just outside town, Jaisalmer-Bikaner Rd, T02994-222 511. Excellent handwoven crafts from the desert region, clean, well laid out, reasonably priced, profits help local self-help projects, part of the URMUL trust, see box p254.

❂ Transport

Buses from Jodhpur travel to **Salawas**. Trains and buses to **Luni** from Jodhpur (40 km). For **Rohet**, frequent buses leave from Jodhpur (50 km north). Jodhpur-Jaisalmer train stops at **Osian**, 4 daily buses from Jodhpur, 2 hrs.

Jaisalmer → *Phone code: 02992. Colour map 1, grid B2. Population: 80,000.*

The approach to Jaisalmer is magical as the city rises out of the barren desert like an approaching ship. With its crenellated sandstone walls and narrow streets lined with exquisitely carved buildings, through which camel carts trundle leisurely, it has an extraordinarily medieval feel and an incredible atmosphere. The fort inside, perched on its hilltop, contains some gems of Jain temple building, while beautifully decorated merchants' havelis are scattered through the town. That said, some travellers find the town is overrated and the people unfriendly. It is true, parts are decaying and wear an air of neglect though efforts are being made; all new structures must now be built out of the local honey-coloured sandstone. ▸▸ *For Sleeping, Eating and other listings see pages 206-210.*

Ins and outs

Getting there The nearest airport is at Jodhpur, 275 km away. Trains from Jodhpur arrive at Jaisalmer railway station, to the east of town. Phone ahead and ask your hotel if they offer a pick-up. Most long-distance buses arrive at the station bus stand and then go to Amar Sagar Pol which is about a 15-minute walk from the fort gate.
Getting around Unmetered jeeps and auto-rickshaws can be hired at the station

(and in the walled town) but they are no help inside the fort so you may have to carry your luggage some distance uphill if you choose a fort hotel. You can hire a bike for the day from Gopa Chowk (Rs 25) though the whole town is really best explored on foot. Most of the hotels and restaurants are clustered around the two chowks and inside the fort. ▸▸ *See Transport, page 210, for further details.*

Tourist offices Rajasthan ① *near TRC, Station Rd, Gadi Sagar Pol, T02992-252 406, 0800-1200, 1500-1800.* Counter at railway station.

Best time to visit Temperature in summer 47°C, minimum 27°C. In winter, maximum 25°C, minimum 15°C. Rainfall is 100 mm during July and August. Best time to visit is November to March.

Background

Founded by Prince Jaisal in 1156, Jaisalmer grew to be a major staging post on the trade route across the forbidding Thar desert from India to the West. The merchants prospered and invested part of their wealth in building beautiful houses and temples with the local sandstone. The growth of maritime trade between India and the West caused a decline in trade across the desert which ceased altogether in 1947. However, the wars with Pakistan (1965 and 1971) resulted in the Indian government developing the transport facilities to the border to improve troop movement. This has also helped visitors to gain access. Today, the army and tourism are mainstays of the local economy; hotel touts and pushy shopkeepers have become a problem in recent years.

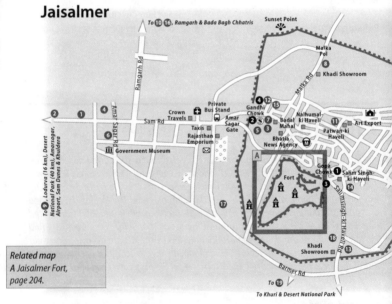

Jaisalmer

Related map
A Jaisalmer Fort,
page 204.

Sleeping	Heritage Inn 2	Moomal 6
Ashoka 23	Himmatgarh Palace 10	Nachana Haveli 7
Dhola Maru 21	Jaisal Palace & Kalpana	Narayan Niwas 8
Fifu Guest House 19	Restaurant 3	Pleasure 12
Fort Rajwada 25	Jawahar Niwas 4	Rajdhani & Residency
Golden City 13	Mahadev Palace 20	Centre Point 11
Gorbandh Palace 1	Mandir Palace 5	Rajwada 22

Sights

The fort

On the roughly triangular-shaped Trikuta Hill, the fort stands 76 m above the town, enclosed by a 9-km wall with 99 bastions (mostly 1633-1647). You enter the fort from the east from Gopa Chowk. The inner, higher fort wall and the old gates up the ramp (Suraj, Ganesh, Hawa and Rang Pols) provided further defences. The Suraj Pol (1594), once an outer gate, is flanked by heavy bastions and has bands of decoration which imitate local textile designs. Take a walk through the narrow streets within the fort,

> ✱ The best light for photography is in the late afternoon.

often blocked by the odd goat or cow, and see how even today about a 1,000 of the town's people live in tiny houses inside the fort often with beautiful carvings on doors and balconies. It is not difficult to get lost.

As with many other Rajput forts, within the massive defences are a series of palaces, the product of successive generations of rulers' flights of fancy. Often called the Golden Fort because of the colour of the sandstone, it dominates the town. The stone is relatively easy to carve and the dry climate has meant that the fineness of detail has been preserved through the centuries. The *jali* work and delicately ornamented balconies and windows with wide eaves break the solidity of the thick walls which gives protection from the heat, while the high plinths of the buildings keep off the sand. **'Sunset Point'**, just north of the fort, is popular at sundown for views over Jaisalmer.

To Mohangarh (NH15)

Kishanghat Pol
21
20

State Bus Stand
23

Gadi Sagar Pol
Barmer Rd

Desert Cultural Centre
Desert National Park Office

Folklore Museum
Tilon-ki Pol

To & Wood Fossil Park (17 km)

To & Jodhpur

Gadi Sagar

	Eating
Rang Mahal **9**	Natraj **1**
Rawal **18**	Ringo Rooftop **4**
Rawal-kot **24**	Sky, Trio, Top Deck
Samrat **14**	& Thar Safari **2**
Shahi Palace **17**	Treat **3**
Suman Motel **16**	
Swastika **15**	

Fort Palace Museum and Heritage Centre ① *0800-1800 summer, 0900-1800 winter, Rs 10, Rs 70 foreigners, camera Rs 50, video Rs 150.* The entire palace has been recently renovated and an interesting series of displays established, including sculpture, weapons, paint ings and well presented cultural information. The view from the roof, the highest point inside the fort, is second to none. The Juna Mahal (circa 1500) of the seven-storey palace with its *jali* screens is one of the oldest Rajasthani palaces. The rather plain *zenana* block to its west, facing the *chauhata* (square) is decorated with false *jalis*. Next to it is the *mardana* (men's quarters) including the Rang Mahal above the Hawa Pol, built during the reign of Mulraj II (1762-1820), which has highly detailed murals and mirror decoration. Sarvotam Vilas built by Akhai Singh (1722-1762) is ornamented with blue tiles and glass mosaics. The adjacent Gaj Vilas (1884) stands on a high plinth. Mulraj II's Moti Mahal has floral decoration and carved doors.

Jain temples (12th-16th centuries) ① *0700-1200, Rs 10, camera Rs 50, video Rs 100, leather shoes not* *permitted*. The open square beyond the gates has a platform reached by climbing some steps; this is where court was held or royal visitors entertained. There are also fascinating Jain temples within the fort. Whilst the Rajputs were devout Hindus they permitted Jainism to be practised. The **Parsvanatha** (1417) has a fine gateway, an ornate porch and 52 subsidiary shrines surrounding the main structure. The brackets are elaborately carved as maidens and dancers. The exterior of the **Rishbhanatha** (1479) has more than 600 images as decoration whilst clusters of towers form the roof of the **Shantinatha** built at the same time. **Ashtapadi** (16th century) incorporates the Hindu deities of Vishnu, Kali and Lakshmi into its decoration. The **Mahavir Temple** ① *view 1000-1100*, has an emerald statue. The **Sambhavanatha** (1431) ① *1000-1100*, has vaults beneath it that were used for document storage. The **Gyan Bhandar** here is famous for its ancient manuscripts.

Havelis

There are many exceptional *havelis* (mansions of rich merchants, see box page 258) both in the fort and the walled town. Many have beautifully carved façades, *jali* screens and oriel windows overhanging the streets below. The ground floor is raised above the dusty streets and each has an inner courtyard surrounded by richly decorated apartments. An unofficial 'guide' will usually show you the way to them for about Rs20.

Inside Amar Sagar Pol, the former ruler's 20th-century palace **Badal Mahal** with a five-storeyed tower, has fine carvings. **Salim Singh-ki Haveli** (17th century) ① *0800-1800, Rs15, good carvings but being poorly restored, over-long guided tour*, near the fort entrance is especially attractive with peacock brackets and because of its distinctive and decorative upper portion is often referred to as the Ship Palace. **Nathumal-ki Haveli** (1885) ① *when the havelis are occupied, you may be allowed in on a polite request, otherwise, your 'guide' will help you gain access for a small fee (though this may just get you as far as the shops in the courtyard!)*, nearer Gandhi Chowk, was built for the Prime Minister. Partly carved out of rock by two craftsmen, each undertaking one half of the house, it has a highly decorative façade with an attractive front door guarded by two elephants. Inside is a wealth of decoration; notice the tiny horse-drawn carriage and a locomotive showing European influence!

Jaisalmer Fort

N

0 metres 100
0 yards 100

Sleeping 🛏
Desert Haveli 9
Fort View & Kanchan
  Shree Restaurant 1
Jaisal Castle 3
Laxmi Niwas (New) 4

Laxmi Niwas &
  Surya Restaurant 5
Paradise 6
Simla & Victoria 8
Suraj 10
Temple View 7

Eating 🍴
8th July 1
La Purezza 3
Little Tibet 2
Vyas 4

Patwon-ki Haveli (1805) ① *best 1030-1700, Rs 2 to view the gold ceilings and enjoy the view from the rooftop, Rs10 for the private museum*, further east, is a group of five built for five brothers. Possibly the finest in town, they have beautiful murals and carved pillars. A profusion of balconies cover the front wall and the inner courtyard is surrounded by richly decorated apartments; parts well-restored. The main courtyard and some roofs are now used as shops.

Desert Cultural Centre

Desert Cultural Centre ① *Gadisar Circle, T02992-252 188, 1000-1700, Rs 10*, was established in 1997 with the aim of preserving the culture of the desert. The museum contains a varied display of fossils, paintings, instruments, costumes and textiles which give an interesting glimpse in to life in the desert.

⁝ On a camel's back

Camel safaris draw many to Jaisalmer. They give an insight into otherwise inaccessible desert interiors and a chance to see rural life, desert flora and wildlife. The 'safari' is not a major expedition in the middle of nowhere. Instead, it is often along tracks, stopping off for sightseeing at temples and villages along the way. The camel driver/owner usually drives the camel or rides alongside (avoid one sharing your camel), usually for two hours in the morning and three hours in the afternoon, with a long lunch stop in between. There is usually jeep or camel cart backup with tents and 'kitchen' close by, though thankfully out of sight. It can be fun, especially if you are with companions and have a knowledgeable camel driver.

They vary greatly in quality with prices ranging from around Rs 350 per night for the simplest (sleeping in the open, vegetarian meals) to those costing Rs 4,500 (deluxe double-bedded tents, attached western baths). Bear in mind that it is practically impossible for any safari organiser to cover his costs at anything less than Rs350 – if you're offered cheaper tours, assume they'll be planning to get their money back by other means, ie shopping/drug selling along the way. Safaris charging Rs 500-1,000

can be adequate (tents, mattresses, linen, cook, jeep support, but no toilets). It is very important to ascertain what is included in the price and what are extras.

The popular 'Around Jaisalmer' route includes Bada Bagh, Ramkunda, Moolsagar, Sam dunes, Lodurva and Amar Sagar with three nights in the desert. Some routes now include Kuldhara's medieval ruins and the colourful Kahla village, as well as Deda, Jaseri lake (good birdlife) and Khaba ruins with a permit. Most visitors prefer to take a two days/one night or three days/two nights camel safari, with jeep transfer back to Jaisalmer. A more comfortable alternative is to be jeeped to a tented/hut camp in the desert as a base for a night and enjoy a camel trek during the day without losing out on the evening's entertainment under the stars. A short camel ride in town up to Sunset Point (or at Sam/Khuri) is one alternative to a 'safari' before deciding on a long haul, and offers great views of upper levels of havelis too! – watch out for low slung electric wires. Pre-paid camel rides have now been introduced – Rs80 for a half hour ride. For some, "half an hour is enough on a tick-ridden animal". For a selection of tour operators offering camel safaris, see page 209.

see page 209

Western Rajasthan Jaisalmer

Folklore Museum ⓘ *on the way to Gadi Sagar Lake, Rs 10*, was established by the same enterprising gentleman as the Cultural Centre. This is a rather neglected display of interesting old documents, photographs and puppets.

Gadi Sagar tank

The Gadi Sagar (Gadisar or Gharisar) tank, southeast of the city walls, was the oasis which led Prince Jaisal to settle here. Now connected by a pipe to the Indira Gandhi Canal, it has water all year. It attracts migratory birds and has many small shrines around it and is well worth visiting, especially in the late afternoon. The delightful archway is said to have been built by a distinguished courtesan who built a temple on top to prevent the king destroying the gate. Boats are available for trips round the lake from Rs50 for half an hour on a pedalo made for two.

● Sleeping

Jaisalmer *p201, map p202 and p204*
Some hotels close in Apr-Jun. Very low room prices may be conditional on taking the hotel's camel safari (check beforehand); refusal may mean having to move out. There are several budget hotels around the fort and near Amar Sagar Pol – check rooms first. Some allow travellers to sleep on the roof for Rs 30-50. The tourist office has a Paying Guest accommodation list. Avoid **Himalayan Guest House**.

A Fort Rajwada, 1 Hotel Complex, Jodhpur Rd, T02992-253 533, www.fortrajwada. 65 (26 more on the way) top class, central a/c rooms and 4 suites conceived by an opera set designer, in a modern luxury hotel, deceptively old-looking from the outside, built in strict accordance to the principles of vaastu, India's answer to feng shui. Architectural features have been recovered from crumbling local *havelis* and incorporated in to the stylish interior, which houses all the expected mod cons, of which the exsquisite bar is particularly worthy of mention. Friendly management and eager staff. Recommended.

A Heritage Inn, 4 Hotel Complex, Sam Rd, T02992-250 901, www.carnivalhotel.com. 15 uninspired rooms plus 40 far superior cottages, single-storey sandstone desert architecture, restaurant, bar, pleasant interior, garden, pool, well-managed.

A Jawahar Niwas, Bada Bagh Rd, T02992-252 208, www.jawaharniwas palace.com. 22 period furnished rooms in small but attractive carved *haveli*. Larger rooms in main palace, cheaper rooms in annexe, unimaginative dining hall but lovely pool, and superb views. Whole place could use a lick of paint, however, and staff seem slightly aloof.

A Rawal-Kot (Taj), Jodhpur Rd, T02992-252 638, www.tajhotels.com. 32 large, comfortable, a/c rooms, attractively furnished, good restaurants, modern yet medieval atmosphere, good views of fort from beautiful pool, friendly.

A-B Rang Mahal, 5 Hotel Complex, Sam Rd, T02992-250 907, www.hotelrangmahal.com. 53 spacious but slightly sterile rooms, desert architecture, pleasant gardens featuring wide range of plants, pool free to restaurant guests, book ahead for a 20 per cent discount.

A-C Mandir Palace, T02992-252 788, mandirpalace@hotmail.com. 27 well-maintained, a/c rooms in exclusive location inside royal palace. Not particularly well run but quite an experience.

B Dhola Maru, Jethwai Rd, T02992-252 863, www.hoteldholamaru.com. 42 a/c, 'ethnic style', slightly musty rooms in attractive sandstone building but standards slipping and mixed reports of unhelpful staff, informative lectures by owner though, okay pool and a wacky bar.

B Gorbandh Palace (HRH),1 Hotel Complex, Sam Rd, T02992-253 801, www.hrhindia. com. 67 unremarkable rooms around court-yard in plush hotel, traditional decor, central a/c, also luxury tents, good but pricey set meals, noisy entertainment, pleasant pool, book/ handicrafts shop, airport, station transfer.

B Himmatgarh Palace, 1 Ramgarh Rd, 2½ km from town, T02992-252 002, HimmatGH@sanchar.net.in. 40 a/c rooms and cottages (slow to cool) in attractive, slightly quirky sandstone building, great fort views from garden and pool

B Jaisal Castle, in fort, T02992-252 362, nnpjsm@sancharnet.in. 11 quirky rooms in rambling, characterful old *haveli*. Under-going extensive renovation, should be impressive when finished.

B Killa Bhawan, Kotri Para, T02992-251 204, www.killabhawan.com. 6 rooms, 2 a/c, in characterful old building, beautiful interiors, classiest place in fort by some margin.

B Mahadev Palace, Jethwai Rd, T02992-253 789, www.mahadevpalace.com. 31 a/c rooms in modern sandstone building, interiors slightly uninspired but clean and friendly, pleasant gardens and pool, depressing restaurant.

B Narayan Niwas Palace, opposite Jain Temple, Malka Rd, T02992-252 408, www. narayanniwas.com. A converted caravanserai with 43 disappointing a/c rooms; rest of property is far more impressive and could be amazing if better maintained. Pillared indoor pool is remarkable, and views from rooftop restaurant exceptional. Good reports on entertainment provided.

B-C Nachana Haveli, Gandhi Chowk, T02992-251 910, nachana_haveli@yahoo.com. 9

rooms, 6 more coming, in converted 18th-century Rajput *haveli* with carved balconies and period artefacts. Extensive renovation underway. Rooms are stylishly done with great bathrooms, particularly upstairs suites. Rooftop restaurant in the season, has very authentic feel overall.

C-D Jaisal Palace, near Gandhi Chowk, behind SBI, T02992-252 717, www.hotel jaisalpalace.com. 14 clean, simple rooms with bath, 6 a/c, 8 air cooled, 1st floor balconies with views, Rajasthani food on roof terrace in season, train/bus bookings.

C-D Moomal (RTDC), Amar Sagar Rd, T02992-252 342. 60 rooms, 17 a/c, better than RTDC average but still has institutional air, rooms could be cleaner, mediocre restaurant, bar, tours, friendly and helpful.

C-E Desert Boy's Guest House, Vyasa Para in fort, T02992-253 091, desert_p@yahoo. com. 14 jauntily furnished rooms in attractive property, great phots everywhere, good Italian rooftop restaurant.

D-E Fifu Guest House, opposite Nagarpalika (1 km out of town), T02992-254 317, www.rajasthan-desert-tour.com. 8 well decorated rooms in modern building with excellent rooftop views. Location slightly inconvenient but hosts are charming and free bicycles available for guests.Ring ahead for free pick up.

D-E Rawal, Salim Singh-ki Haveli Marg, Dibba Para, T02992-252 570. 20 clean, wallpapered rooms, all with attached bathrooms, Indian restaurant, good views from rooftop, pleasant, relaxed.

D-E Shahi Palace, near Government Bus Stand, T02992-255 920, shahipalace@yahoo. co.in. 9 tasteful rooms (7 more coming) in classy new establishment built almost entirely from sandstone. Outstanding bath- rooms, likeable manager. Recommended.

D-E Simla, Kund Para, T02992-253 061, simlahaveli@yahoo.co.in. 5 clean rooms in thoughtfully renovated 550-year-old *haveli*, attractive wall hangings, 1 large with bath, others minute with bath downstairs, no safari pressure, friendly management, a cut above the norm.

D-E Suraj, behind Jain Temple, T02992-251 623, hotelsurajjaisalmer@hotmail.com.

5 basic but clean rooms with bath (some large, painted) in beautiful 530-year-old *haveli*, some with view, atmospheric. Also 7 more rooms in annexe opposite, standard equally high.

D-F The Desert Haveli, near Jain Temple, T02992-251 555, desert_haveli@yahoo.com. 7 characterful rooms in charming, 400-year-old *haveli*, honest, friendly owner. Recommended.

D-F Paradise, opposite Royal Palace, T02992-252674, hotelparadise_gsm2001 @yahoo.co.in. 24 basic rooms, best **C** with hot showers, most with balcony and views, camping on roof terrace, safe lockers, limited room-service, long-established but some reports of being hassled.

E Swastika, Chainpura St, T02992-252483. 9 clean, well-kept rooms, all with bath, okay view, free tea and pick-ups, charming owner.

E-F Deepak, behind Jain temples, T02992-252 665. 25 rooms (most with hot showers, western toilets), some better value than others so check first, good vegetarian food but lacking in atmosphere overall.

E-F Golden City, Dibba Para, T02992-251 664, hotelgoldencity@hotmail.com. Clean comfortable air cooled rooms with hot shower, 3 **D** a/c, rooftop restaurant with good views, free station transfer, exchange, internet, family atmosphere plus a lovely new swimming pool, outstanding value.

E-F Hotel Victoria, Kund Para in fort, T02992-252 150, hotelvictoria@rediffmail. com. 6 quirky rooms in family home, owner amiably eccentric, good home-cooked veg meals, a little bit deifferent.

E-F Laxmi Niwas, T52758, in Fort (sign-posted). 6 simple but clean rooms with bath in newer section at east end of fort, better upstairs, with good views from terrace, good breakfast; also cheaper 5 basic, homely rooms with common bath in older section (west of fort), warm welcome.

E-F Moti Palace, Chogun Para, T02992-254 693, kailash_bissa@yahoo.co.uk. 5 clean, modern rooms, interesting location above main entrance to fort, great views from roof.

E-F Temple View, next to Jain Temple, T02992-252 832, jaisalmertempleview@hot mail.com. 7 well decorated rooms, 3 with

For an explanation of sleeping and eating price codes used in this guide, see inside the front cover. Other relevant information is found in Essentials, see pages 40-45.

attached bath, attention to detail, great view of temples from roof, entertaining owner.

F Hotel Ashoka, opposite Railway station, T02992-256 021. 20 cleanish rooms in quiet location, good option if you want to be close to the station.

F Hotel Pleasure, Gandhi Chowk, T02992-252 323, hotelpleasure@rediffmail.com. 5 clean rooms in homely establishment with innovative facilities including free washing machine and filtered drinking water.

F Rajdhani, near Patwon-ki Haveli, T02992-252746. 7 clean rooms with hot shower, great view from rooftop, friendly staff, calm atmosphere.

F Residency Centre Point, near Patwan ki Haveli, T02992-252 883. 5 basic but characterful rooms in quiet, family run hotel, good views from roof.

F Samrat, south of Salim Singh-ki-Haveli, T02992-251 498. 10 average rooms, some with bath and balcony, rooftop restaurant, helpful, family run, slightly downtrodden feel.

● Eating

Jaisalmer *p201, map p202 and p204*

¶¶ 8th July, just inside fort (another opposite Fort Gate). Vegetarian. Pleasant rooftop seating – popular for breakfast, pizzas, food average, pleasant for evening drink, mixed reports on service.

¶¶ Kalpana, outside fort gate. Good selection, great people-watching spot. Service can be slow but all the food comes at the same time. Also serves beer.

¶¶ La Purezza, Vyas Para. Excellent salads, Italian cheese veggies and other unusual offerings. Has another outlet in Manali.

¶¶ Little Tibet, beyond the palace chowk. Momos and much more of travellers' choice, generous, hygienic, enthusiastic staff, popular.

¶¶ Natraj, next to Salim Singh-ki-Haveli. Mixed. Spacious rooftop with good views and a/c room, beer bar, wide choice (meat dishes Rs 80-100), average Indian and Chinese, clean toilet, pleasant spot.

¶¶ Surya, near Laxmi Niwas. Mixed. Good food, colourful, atmospheric, sit on cushions overlooking the city, outstanding views. Recommended.

¶¶ Sky, Gandhi Chowk, mainly Indian, 'English' breakfasts and some Italian. On

rooftop, Rajasthani dancers and musicians, colourful and noisy!

¶¶ Top Deck, Gandhi Chowk, good meat dishes (lamb steaks, southern fried chicken, Rs 60), staff very cool.

¶¶ Trio, Gandhi Chowk, partly open-air, tented restaurant with small terrace, choice of cushions or chairs, excellent 'proper' tea, good atmosphere and creative food (try safari soup), musicians at dinner expect tips, view of Mandir Palace and fort illuminated, usually crowded, mixed reports on food and service, perhaps becoming a victim of its own success.

¶ Palace View Restaurant, Gandhi Chowk, near Jain Temples. Varied selection but main attraction is the home made apple pie.

¶ Ringo Rooftop (separate from hotel), Gandhi Chowk, good north Indian including meat dishes. Superb views of fort.

¶ Vyas, Fort. Simple, good veg *thalis* (Rs 20-30), pleasant staff.

Snacks and drinks

Chai stalls at **Gopa Chowk** make good 'Indian' tea before 1730. Hot and crisp kachoris and samosas opposite Jain temples near **Narayan Niwas**, are great for breakfast or high tea.

Dhanraj Bhatia, scrumptious Indian sweets including Jaisalmeri delights (try *godwa*).

Doodh bhandars in Hanuman Chauraya sell a delicious mix of creamy milk, cardamom and sugar, whipped up with a flourish, between sunset and mid-night.

Kanchan Shree, Gopa Chowk, 250 m from Salim Singh ki Haveli. Still among the best for drinks. *Lassis* (19 varieties) and ice cream floats, as well as cheap, tasty *thalis*.

Mohan Juice Centre, near *Sunil Bhatia Rest House*. Delicious lassis, good breakfasts.

● Bars and clubs

Jaisalmer *p201, map p202 and p204*

Gorbandh Palace has a well stocked bar, **Jawahar Niwas**, **Naryan Niwas** and other **B**'s.

● Entertainment

Jaisalmer *p201, map p202 and p204*

Desert Cultural Centre, Gadisar Circle. Two puppet shows every evening, at 1830 and 1930, Rs30 entry, Rs20 camera, Rs50 video.

☸ Festivals and events

Jaisalmer *p201, map p202 and p204*
Feb/Mar Holi is especially colourful but gets riotous. See also p212 for details of the festival at the Sam Dunes nearby.

☉ Shopping

Jaisalmer *p201, map p202 and p204*
Shops open 1000-1330 and 1500-1900. Jaisalmer is famous for its handicrafts – stone-carved statues, leather ware, brass enamel engraving, shawls, tie-and-dye work, embroidered and block printed fabrics, but garments are often poorly finished. Traders are more relaxed and welcoming here, and expect you to bargain. Look in **Siré Bazar**, **Sonaron-ka-Bas** and the narrow lanes of the old city including **Kamal Handicrafts**, **Ganpati Art Home**, and **Damodar** in the Fort. In Gandhi Chowk: **Rajasthali**, closed Tue; the good, fairly-priced selection at **Khadi Emporium** at the end of the courtyard just above **Narayan Niwas Hotel**. **Jaisalmer Art Export**, behind Patwon-ki Haveli has high-quality textiles.

Books
Bhatia News Agency, Court Rd. Good selection including travel guides; second-hand books bought and sold.

Tailors
Mr Durga, small shop near fort entrance (between **New Tourist** and **Srilekha Hotels**). Excellent western-style tailoring. Shirts made to measure, around Rs 200.
Nagpur, Koba Chowk. Western-style tailoring.
Raju, Kachari Rd, outside Amar Sagar Pol. Western-style tailoring.

▲ Activities and tours

Jaisalmer *p201, map p202 and p204*
Camel safaris
Thar Safaris, T02992 252722, charges Rs 950); **Safari Tours**, T02992 251058, has Rawla Kanoi with 10 'desert huts' with shared facilities and 10 tents with private bathrooms, about 8 km from Sam; **Royal Desert Safaris**, T02992 252538 has 85 Swiss-cottage tents with attached toilets near the dunes charges Rs 4500 per night.

Sahara Travels, **Comfort Tours** (Gorbandh Palace), **Aravalli Safaris**, **Travel Plan**, also offer reliable safaris. Less upmarket, but still reliable options include those from **Shahi Palace**, **Fifu Guesthouse** and **Desert Haveli**.

Cooking
Learn Indian cookery with Karuna at Ishar palace, in the fort near the Laxminath Temple, T02992-253 062, karunaacharya@ yahoo.com. Courses of any length can be arranged, and come highly recommended.

Music
Anyone interested in learning to play a Rajasthani musical instrument, or to hear a performance, should contact Kamru Deen on T02992-254 181, arbamusic@yahoo.co.in.

Paragliding
SPSKaushik, T94143 05121, offers paragliding in the desert, with participants being towed behind a jeep for Rs750 a go. A unique way to see the desert!

Sightseeing tours
Aravali Safari, near Patwon-ki Gali, T02992-252 632. Professional. Recommended.
Forts & Palaces, Nachna Haveli, Gandhi Chowk, T02992-252 538, jaipur@palaces -tours.com. Experienced, efficient.
Rajasthan Tourism, T02992-252 406. City sightseeing: half day, 0900-1200. Fort, *havelis*, Gadisagar Lake. Sam sand dunes: half day, 1500-1900.
Sahara Travels, Gopa Chowk, right of the 1st Fort gate, T52609. Mr (Desert) Bissa's reliable camel safaris with good food.
Thar Safari, Gandhi Chowk, near **Trio**, T52722, F53214. Reliable tours.
   Other camel safaris which have been recommended to us are those from **Shahi Palace Hotel**, "too much food!", **Desert Haveli** and **Fifu Hotel**.
Avoid Adventure Travel, near Fort 1st Gate; Travellers Agency (of Puskhar Palace), near Skyroom restaurant; Adventure Tours, at New Tourist Hotel, and safaris offered by Himalayan Guesthouse.

Swimming
Gorbandh Palace (non-residents Rs 350); also **Heritage Inn** (meal plus swim deals) and **Fort Rajwada**.

⊕ Transport

Jaisalmer *p201, map p202 and p204*
Jaisalmer is on NH15 (Pathankot- Samakhiali).
Transport to town from train and bus station
is by autorickshaws or jeeps; police are on
duty so less harassment.

Air
No flights from the nearest airport at
Jodhpur. **Alliance Air** from Delhi, 1030, via
Jaipur; to Delhi, 1330. Check with **Crown
Travels**, Sam Rd, T02992-252 632

Bus
Be aware that touts may board buses outside
town to press you to take their jeep; it is
better to walk 10-15 mins from Amar Sagar
Pol and choose a hotel.
    State (Roadways) buses, from near the
station, T02992-251 541 and near Amar
Sagar Pol. Services to **Ajmer**, **Barmer**,
Bikaner (330 km on good road, 7 hrs,
Rs 104), **Jaipur** (638 km); Abu Rd for
Mount Abu. **Jodhpur** (285 km) hourly
service, 5 hrs, Rs 70, RTDC coach, depart
Jaisalmer, 1400 (depart Jodhpur 0630).
Udaipur: (663 km), tiring 14 hrs. Private
deluxe coaches from outside Amar Sagar
Pol, to Jodhpur and Bikaner. Operators:
Marudhara Travels, Station Rd, T02992-
252 351. **National Tours**, Hanuman
Choraha, T02992-252 348.

Train
Foreign Tourist Bureau with waiting room,
T02992-252 354, booking office T02992-251
301. **Jodhpur**: *Jaisalmer Jodhpur Exp, 4609,
4809 Exp*, 2225, 7 hrs, sleeper, Rs 510. Can get
very cold (and dusty) so take sleeping bag, or
book bedding. (From Jodhpur, *4810*, depart
2315, 6½ hrs).

⊕ Directory

Jaisalmer *p201, map p202 and p204*
Banks Open 1030-1430, Mon-Fri,
1030-1230, Sat, closed Sun. On Gandhi
Chowk: **Bank of Baroda** and **SBBJ**, TCs and
cash against credit cards; **State of Bank of
India**, Nachna Haveli, currency only. There is
also an ATM which accepts international
cards close to Hanuman Chowk on the road
which leads to Sam.
Hospital S J Hospital, Gandhi Marg,
T02992-252 343.
Internet Joshi Travel, opposite PO,
Central Market, Gopa Chowk, T/F50455
joshitravel@hotmail.com. Cyber café,
modern equipment, also STD, fax etc. **Desert
Cyber Inn**, inside fort close to Little Tibet
restaurant.Others may have problems
connecting.
Post The GPO is near Police Station,
T02992-252 407. With Poste Restante.
Useful addresses Fire: T02992-252 352.
Police: T02992-252 668.

Around Jaisalmer

*Many of the settlements close to Jaisalmer have become well used to tourists, so it's
worth venturing a little further out to get an idea of life in the desert. Highlights include
the remarkable ghost city of Khuldera, and of course the chance to take it all in from on
top of a camel.* ▶▶ *For Sleeping, Eating and other listings, see page 212.*

Bada (Barra) Bagh
ⓘ *Rs 10 entry, auto-rickshaws Rs 40 return.* Some 6 km north of Jaisalmer, Bada Bagh
is an attractive oasis with mango trees and other vegetation not normally seen in the
desert. The reservoir and systems of sanitary drainage may interest some but the
cenotaphs are unexciting. There is a viewpoint from the royal *chhatris* (memorials)
here but the intrusive tall army watch posts spoil sunset views.

Amar Sagar and Lodurva
The pleasant **Amar Sagar** ⓘ *free, Rs 10 foreigners, camera Rs 50, video Rs 100,* 5 km
northwest, was once a formal garden with a pleasure palace of Amar Singh

(1661-1703) on the bank of a lake which dries up during the hot season. The Jain temple there has been restored.

A further 10 km away is **Lodurva** ① *0630-1930, free, Rs 10 foreigners, camera Rs 50, video Rs100*. It contains a number of Jain temples that are the only remains of a once flourishing Marwar capital. Rising honey-coloured out of the desert, they are beautifully carved with *jali* outside and are well maintained. Worth visiting. The road beyond Lodurva is unsealed.

Khuldera

This is a fascinating ghost town, and well worth stopping at on the way to Sam. The story goes that 400 or so years ago, Salim Singh, the then prime minister of Jaisalmer, took a distinct shine to a Paliwal girl from this village. The rest of the Paliwal people did not want this beautiful girl taken away from them, and so after intense pressure from the PM decided to abandon the village one night, with everyone dispersing in different directions, never to return. It is remarkably well preserved, and best visited with a guide who can point out the most interesting buildings from the many still standing. **Khabha**, just south of here, is also recommended.

Sam dunes (Sain)

① *Rs 2, car Rs 10 (camera fees may be introduced), camel rates usually start at Rs 50 per hr but can be bargained down.*

Sam dunes, 40 km west of Jaisalmer, is popular for sunset camel rides. It is not really a remote spot in the middle of the desert but the only real large stretch of sand near town; the dunes proper only covering a small area, yet quite impressive. Right in the middle of the dunes, **Sunset view** is like a fairground, slightly tacky with lots of day-trippers – as many as 500 in the high season; the only escape from this and the camel men is to walk quite a way away!

Khuri

① *Rs 3 (may be increased in line with Desert National Park), car Rs 10, buses from Jaisalmer take 1½ hrs, jeep for 4, Rs 450 for sunset tour.*

Khuri, 40 km southwest of Jaisalmer, is a small picturesque desert village of decorated mud thatched buildings which was ruled by the Sodha clan for four centuries. Visitors are attracted by shifting sand dunes, some 80 m high, but the peace of the village has been spoilt by the growing number of huts, tents and guesthouses which have opened along the road and near the dunes. Persistent hotel and camel agents board all buses bound for Khuri. The best months to visit are from November to February.

Thar Desert National Park

① *T02992-252 489, Rs 200 per person. Permission to enter the park is needed from the Collector as well as the Director.*

The Desert National Park is near Khuri, the core being about 60 km from Jaisalmer (the road between Sam and Khuri is motorable with a high clearance vehicle). The park was created to protect 3,000 sq km of the Thar Desert, the habitat for drought resistant, endangered and rare species which have adjusted to the unique and inhospitable conditions of extreme temperatures. The desert has undulating dunes and vast expanses of flat land where the trees are leafless, thorny and have long roots. Fascinating for birdwatching, it is one of the few places in India where the **Great Indian bustard** is proliferating (it can weigh up to 14 kg and reach a height of 40 cm). In winter it also attracts the migratory **houbara bustard**. You can see imperial black-bellied and common Indian sand grouse, five species of vultures, six of eagle, falcons, and flocks of larks at Sudasari, in the core of the park, 60 km from Jaisalmer.

Chinkaras are a common sight, as are Desert and Indian foxes. Blackbuck and Desert cat can be seen at times. Closer to sunset, you can spot desert hare in the bushes.

While most hotels will try to sell you a tour by four-wheel drive vehicle, this is no longer necessary. You can hire any jeep or high clearance car (Ambassador, Sumo) for the trip to the park. Off-the-road journeys are by camel or camel cart (park tour Rs 50 and Rs 150 respectively).

Barmer

This dusty desert town, 153 km south of Jaisalmer, is surrounded by sand dunes and scrublands. It is a major centre for wood carving, *durrie* rug weaving, embroidery and block printing (you can watch printers in Khatriyon ki galli). The 10th- to 11th-century Kiradu temples, though badly damaged, are interesting. **Someshvara** (1020), the most intact, has some intricate carving but the dome and the tower have collapsed. The town itself is surprisingly industrial and not especially charming; those interested in seeking out handicrafts are well advised to locate **Gulla**, the town's only guide. He can normally be contacted at the **KK Hotel**, see below, or emailed in advance on gulla_guide@yahoo.com. The small number of visitors to Barmer means that he doesn't get too many opportunities to practice his profession; be sure to explain exactly what you would like to see, and try to fix a price before starting the tour.

Dhorimmana

The area further south of Barmer has some of the most colourful and traditional Bishnoi villages and a large population of *chinkaras* and desert fauna. The village women wear a lot of attractive jewellery but may be reluctant to be photographed so it is best to ask first. **PWD Rest house** has clean and comfortable rooms.

● Sleeping

Bada Bagh *p210*
C Suman Motel has rooms and vegetarian restaurant nearby.

Sam dunes *p211*
D Samdhani (RTDC), T02992-252 392.
8 huts facing the dunes, very busy in late afternoon and sunset but very pleasant at night and early morning.

Khuri *p211*
D-E Khuri Guest House, T03104-274 044.
Simple rooms or huts, friendly management. Recommended.
D-E Mama's, T01304-274 023. Cool, thatched huts, tasty meals, recommended.

Thar Desert National Park *p211*
E Rest Huts, facing the park, are adequate, contact Park Director on T02992-252 489

Barmer *p212*
D-E KK Hotel, Station Rd, T02982-230 038.
24 okay rooms, some a/c, very similar to Krishna nearby.
D-E Krishna, Station Rd, a few mins' walk

from station, T02982-220 785. The biggest and best in town with 32 decent rooms, some a/c, but no restaurant.

✹ Festivals and events

Sam dunes *p211*
Feb 3-day Desert Festival (21-23 Feb 2005, 10-12 Feb 2006, 31 Jan-2 Feb) with *Son et Lumière* amid the sand dunes at Sam, folk dancing, puppet shows and camel races, camel polo and camel acrobatics, Mr Desert competition. You can also watch craftsmen at work. Rail and hotel reservations can be difficult.

Barmer *p212*
Thar Festival in Mar highlights desert culture and handicrafts.

● Transport

Barmer *p212*
From **Barmer**, the hot and dusty bus journey to Jaisalmer takes 4 hrs; Mt Abu, 6 hrs.

Eastern Rajasthan

Alwar, Sariska and around	216
Delhi Jaipur Road	217
Alwar	217
Alwar to Sariska	218
Sariska Tiger Reserve	218
Listings	219
Deeg, Bharatpur and around	220
Bhandarej to Bharatpur	222
Bharatpur	222
Keoladeo Ghana National Park	223
Listings	225
Ranthambhore National Park	227
Listings	230
Ajmer and Pushkar	232
From Jaipur to Ajmer	233
Ajmer	234
Pushkar	238
Listings	239

⁑ Footprint features

Don't miss	211
The Pragmatic Prakratik Society	229
A saint of the people	233
The pull of the cattle and camels	237

Introduction

This is one of the most visited regions of Rajasthan, lying as it does on the well-trodden '**Golden Triangle**' route of Delhi-Agra-Jaipur, but retains some hidden treasures and surprisingly untouched towns. Primary among these are some delightful, sensitively restored heritage hotels, essentially ex-maharaja's palaces, including those in **Neemrana** and **Kesroli**, and the quirky charms of **Bhanwar Vilas Palace** in **Karauli**.

All within easy range of Delhi, the towns and villages of Eastern Rajasthan – from the bustly pilgrimage centre of **Ajmer** in the south, and its laid-back neighbour, **Pushkar**, renowned for its holy lake and extraordinary November camel fair, to the utterly unspoilt towns of **Alwar** and **Deeg** in the north, there's an amazing variety of human habitats to choose from.

They are also surrounded by a natural world in which wild animals and birds continue to find a protected home in sanctuaries and wildlife parks, including the magnificent **Bharatpur-Keoladeo Ghana National Park**, home to the rare Siberian Crane during its migratory season and a great place for a cycle, and the incomparable **Ranthambhore National Park**, one of the world's top venues for tiger spotting, but also a beautiful landscape to explore even when the tigers don't show.

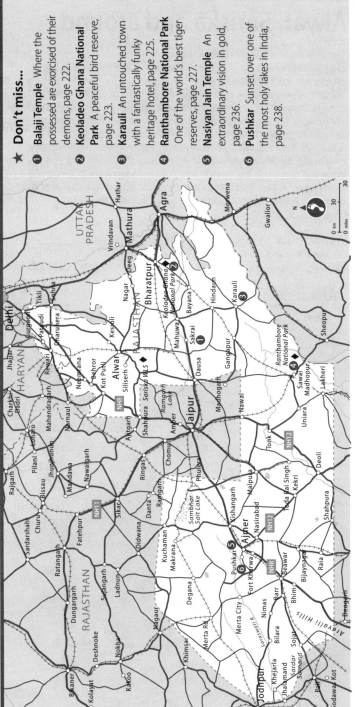

★ **Don't miss...**

❶ **Balaji Temple** Where the possessed are exorcised of their demons, page 222.

❷ **Keoladeo Ghana National Park** A peaceful bird reserve, page 223.

❸ **Karauli** An untouched town with a fantastically funky heritage hotel, page 225.

❹ **Ranthambore National Park** One of the world's best tiger reserves, page 227.

❺ **Nasiyan Jain Temple** An extraordinary vision in gold, page 236.

❻ **Pushkar** Sunset over one of the most holy lakes in India, page 238.

Eastern Rajasthan

Alwar, Sariska and around

Alwar has fascinating monuments including the Bala Quilla fort overlooking the town and the Moti Doongri fort in a garden. The former, which was never taken by direct assault, has relics of the early Rajput rulers who had their capital near Alwar, the founders of the fort. Over the centuries it was home to the Khanzadas, Mughals, Pathans, Jats and finally the Rajputs. There are also palaces, and colonial period parks and gardens. The town itself is very untouristy and spread over a large area, making navigation difficult at times, but is generally very welcoming.

The 480 sq km Sariska sanctuary is a dry deciduous forest set in a valley surrounded by the barren Aravalli hills. The princely shooting reserve of the Maharajah of Alwar in the Aravallis was declared a sanctuary in 1955 and is a tiger reserve under Project Tiger. Although the chances of spotting a tiger here are not as good as at Ranthambore, it still has a rugged appeal. ▸▸ For Sleeping, Eating and other listings, see pages 219-220.

Ins and outs

Getting there and around Alwar is well connected to both Delhi and Jaipur by bus and train, and is only a three-hour drive from Delhi, or 1½ hours from Jaipur. Sariska is

Alwar

Sleeping
Alka 1
Alwar 8
Ankur 2
Aravali 3
Ashoka 4
Atlantic 5
Kothi Rao 9
Meenal 10
New Tourist 6
Railway Retiring Rooms 7

Eating
Baba 1
Imperial 2
Narulas 3

Tourist information Alwar **Rajasthan** ① *Tourist Reception Centre, Nehru Marg, opposite railway station, T0144-234 7348, closed weekends.*

Background

As Mughal power crumbled Rao Pratap Singhji of Macheri founded Alwar as his capital in 1771. He shook off Jat power over the region and rebelled against Jaipur suzerainty making Alwar an independent state. His successors lent military assistance to the British in their battles against the Marathas in AD 1803, and in consequence gained the support of the colonial power. The Alwar royals were flamboyant and kept a fleet of custom-made cars (including a throne car and a golden limousine), and collected solid silver furniture and attractive walking sticks.

Delhi Jaipur Road

The NH8 is the main route between Delhi and Jaipur but although it is very busy there are some attractive stops en route, notably at Neemrana, which allows an overnight stay between Delhi and Jaipur.

Tikli, 8 km off the Sonah road (turn off at Badshapur), about an hour's drive from Delhi towards the Aravalli hills, is a gem of a rural escape lovingly conceived by an English couple who have architecturally combined the best of East and West, following Lutyens. The exclusive 'farmhouse' stands in a flower and bird filled garden, has an inviting pool and is a place to spoil yourself. Ask for Manender Farm, Gairatpur Bass village. **Rewari**, 83 km from Delhi, was founded in 1000 AD by Raja Rawat but there are the ruins of a still older town east of the 'modern' walls. It has been a prosperous centre for the manufacture of iron and brass vessels. On a rocky outcrop just above an unspoilt village, is the beautiful **Neemrana Fort**, built in 1464 by Prithvi Raj Chauhan III and converted into an exceptional hotel. The village with a step well, and the fort ruins above, are worth exploring.

Alwar → *Phone code: 0144. Colour map 3, grid C1. Population: 211,000.*

Alwar is protected by the hilltop **Bala Quilla** which has the remains of palaces, temples and 10 tanks built by the first rulers of Alwar. It stands 308 m above the town, to the northwest, and is reached by a steep four-wheel drive track (with permission from the police station). There are splendid views.

The **Vinai Vilas Mahal,** the City Palace (1840) ① *1000-1630, free, museum Rs 3,* with intricate *jali* work, ornate *jarokha* balconies and courtyards, houses government offices on the ground floor, and a fine museum upstairs. The palace is impressive but is poorly maintained, with dusty galleries (you may find children playing cricket in the courtyard). The Darbar Room is closed, and the throne, miniatures and gilt edged mirrors can only be viewed through the glass doors and windows or by prior permission of the royal family (which is not easily obtained). The museum is interesting, housing local miniature paintings, as well as some of the Mughal, Bundi and other schools, an array of swords, shields, daggers, guns and armour, sandalwood carvings, ivory objects, jade art, musical instruments and princely relics. There are over 7,000 manuscripts in various Asian languages (part housed in the Oriental Research Institute, also in the Palace). Next to the city palace are the lake and royal cenotaphs. On the south side of the tank is the Cenotaph of Maharaja Bakhtawar Singh (1781-1815) which is of marble on a red sandstone base. The gardens are alive with peacocks and other birds. To the right of the main entrance to the palace is a two-storey processional elephant carriage designed to carry 50 people and be pulled by four elephants.

The **Yeshwant Niwas**, built by Maharaja Jai Singh in the Italianate style, is also worth seeing. Apparently on its completion he disliked it and never lived in it. Instead he built the **Vijay Mandir** in 1918, a 105-room palace beside Vijay Sagar, 10 km from Alwar. Part of it is open to the public with prior permission from the royal family or their secretary but is worth seeing it from the road, with its façade resembling an anchored ship. When not in Delhi, the royal family now live in Phool Bagh, a small 1960s mansion opposite the New Stadium.

Alwar to Sariska

At **Siliserh**, 15 km to the west, runs an aqueduct which supplies the city with water. The lake, a local picnic spot, has boats for hire. **Kesroli**, 10 km northeast, has a seven-turreted 16th-century fort atop a rocky hillock, now sympathetically (though more modestly) restored into a hotel by the owners of Neemrana (see above). It is a three-hours' drive from Delhi and convenient for an overnight halt. Turn left off NH8 at Dharuhera for Alwar Road and you will find it **Kushalgarh Fort** is en route to Sariska. Near Kushalgarh is the temple complex of **Talbraksha** (or Talvriksh) with a large population of rhesus macaque monkeys. Guides report panthers having been seen near the **Cafeteria Taal** here, probably on the prowl for monkeys near the canteen.

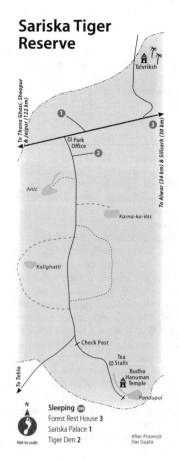

Sariska Tiger Reserve

Sleeping
Forest Rest House 3
Sariska Palace 1
Tiger Den 2

Not to scale

After Prosenjit Das Gupta

Sariska Tiger Reserve

→ *Phone code: 0144. Colour map 3, grid C1.*

ⓘ *Rs 25, free on Sat, foreigners Rs 200 every day including still camera, video Rs 200; vehicle Rs 125 per trip. Early morning jeep trips from Sariska Palace Hotel or Tiger Den go into the park as far as the Monkey Temple, where you can get a cup of tea and watch monkeys and peacocks. Jeep-hire for non-standard trips in the reserve, Rs 700 for 3 hrs, excluding entry fees. Further information from Wildlife Warden, Sariska, T0144- 233 2348.*

The main rhesus monkey population live at Talvriksh near Kushalgarh (see above), whilst at Bhartri-Hari you will see many langurs. The chowsingha, or **four-horned antelope**, is found at Sariska. Other deer include chital and sambar. You may see nilgai, wild boar, jackals, hyenas, hares and porcupines, though tigers and leopards are more rarely seen, since the reserve is closed at night to visitors. During the monsoons the place is alive with birds but many animals move to higher ground. There are ground birds such as peafowl, jungle fowl, spur fowl and the grey partridge. Babblers, bulbuls and tree pies are common round the lodges.

The **Kankwari Fort** (20 km), where Emperor Aurangzeb is believed to have imprisoned his brother **Dara Shikoh**, the rightful heir to the Mughal throne, is within the park. The old **Bhartrihari** temple (6 km) has a fair and six hour dance-drama in September to October. **Neelkanth** (33 km) has a complex of sixth- to 10th-century carved temples. **Bhangarh** (55 km), on the outskirts of the reserve, is a deserted city of some 10,000 dwellings established in 1631. It was abandoned 300 years ago, supposedly after it was cursed by a magician. **Sariska**, the gateway for the Sariska National Park, is a pleasant, quiet place to stay and relax. Excursions by jeep are possible to forts and temples nearby.

The park is open all year round. During the monsoon travel through the forest may be difficult. The best season to visit is between November and April. In the dry season, when the streams disappear, the animals become dependant on man-made water holes at Kalighatti, Salopka and Pandhupol.

● Sleeping

Delhi Jaipur Road *p217*
AL Tikli Bottom, Tikli, T011-2335 1272, www.tiklibottom.com. Four immaculate, uniquely furnished guest bedrooms, promises imaginative cuisine (own garden produce) and a peaceful place to unwind outside Delhi in the middle or at the end of an Indian tour. A memorable en-famille experience. Advance reservations only.
AL-A Neemrana Fort Palace, T01494-246007, www.neemranahotels.com. There are 45 rooms quiet and peaceful (occasional loud chanting from village below!), full of character and beautifully furnished with collectors' pieces (particularly recommended: Baag, Dakshin, Jharoka, Surya Mahals), though some (eg Moonga) are a testing climb up to the seventh level. Superb Rajasthani and French cuisine (non-residents Rs 650 which allows looking around), other visitors must pay Rs 100, magical atmosphere, part-day rates, reservations essential. Highly recommended.

Alwar *p217, map p216*
B-C Alwar, 26 Manu Marg, T0144-2700012, www.hotelalwar.com. Set back from the main road with an attractive garden, 16 rooms, 7 in impressive new block (some a/c) with attached baths (hot showers), TV, refrigerator and phone, restaurant (closed on Mon), arrangements for swimming and tennis at nearby club, efficient service, popular.
B-C Kothi Rao, 31 Moti Dungri, T0144-270 0741, kothirao@yahoo.com. 9 a/c rooms in extremely homely hotel, reminiscent of an English B&B, run by polite, welcoming family.
B-E Aravali, Nehru Marg, near the station, T0144-233 2883. 30 rooms of widely ranging styles and standards, from suites to dorms, plus a restaurant and bar. There's a pool, but even guests have to pay to use it! 50 per cent discount to YHA members.
C-E Ankur, Manu Marg, T0144-2333025. Same hotel occupies two buildings on opposite sides of square. The 27 rooms (10 a/c) in the motel-style block closest to the 'Imperial' are significantly better than the 19 rooms opposite, and probably the pick of all the nearby options.
C-E New Tourist, 2 Manu Marg, T0144-270 0897. 20 rooms of a higher standard than most in Alwar, keen and friendly management, beer bar, "fully homely comfort". Recommended.
C-F Ashoka, Manu Marg, T0144-234 6780. 30 rooms, clean and comfortable, deluxe rooms have TV, running hot water and western toilets, cheaper rooms have Indian toilets and hot water in buckets, restaurant (Rs 35 *thalis*), good value.
D Meenal (RTDC), near Circuit House, T0144-234 7352. 6 rooms with bath (2 a/c), restaurant, bar, quiet location.
D-E Atlantic, Manu Marg, T0144-234 3181. 15 rooms with attached baths, only **D** a/c and deluxe rooms have Western toilets.
E Alka, Mangal Marg, T332796. Basic rooms.
E Saroop Vilas Palace, near Moti Doongri, T0144-233 1218. Renovated royal mansion

● *For an explanation of sleeping and eating price codes used in this guide, see inside the*
● *front cover. Other relevant information is found in Essentials, see pages 40-45.*

taken over by private entrepreneur, 4 rooms with attached baths (western toilets), vegetarian restaurant serving reasonable Chinese and South Indian fare.

Alwar to Sariska *p218*
B Hill Fort Kesroli (Heritage Hotel), Alwar Rd, Kesroli, T01468-289352, www.neem ranahotels.com. Around a courtyard are 22 comfortable, if eccentric, airy rooms, reasonable restaurant and service, relaxing, and in a lovely isolated rural location.
C-D Lake Palace (RTDC), Siliserh, T0144-2886322. 10 rooms, 5 a/c, restaurant, modest but superb location.

Sariska *p218, map p218*
A Sariska Palace, 40 km from Alwar railway, T0144-284 1322, www.sariska.com. 72 refurbished a/c rooms, (annexe lacks the charm of the lodge), restaurant and bar (generally only open for residents), gym, pool, new ayurvedic and yoga centre, tours, enormous converted royal hunting lodge, built in 1898, full of photographs and stuffed tigers, set in expansive and well-maintained gardens. Rs 500 entry fee for non-residents, off set against restaurant bill.
C Baba Resorts, T0144-288 5231, next door to Sariska Tiger Camp, is similar to its neigh-bour. Both are good options for the price.
C Sariska Tiger Camp, 19 km towards Alwar on main road, T0144-288 5311. 8 mud-walled but classy rooms in pleasant surroundings, plus 20 luxury tents during the winter season. Looks better from inside than out.
C-D Tiger Den (RTDC), in the sanctuary, T0144-284 1342. Superbly located tourist bungalow with views of hill and park, 30 rooms with attached baths (hot showers) but shabby and dirty public areas, vegetarian restaurant (Indian buffets Rs 130-150), bar (no snacks, carry your own to have with beer/drinks) shop sells cards and souvenirs,

nice garden, friendly management.
D Forest Rest House, Main Rd, opposite turning to Kushalgarh. 3 simple rooms, only open during the winter season.

ⓓ Eating

Alwar *p217, map p216*
Ⓨ Narulas, Kashiram Circle, T0144-233 3966. Indian/Chinese/Continental. A/c restaurant, popular for Punjabi non veg and veg dishes, "best in town".
Ⓨ Baba, Hope Circle. Popular for 'milk cake' (*kalakand*) and other Rajasthani sweets.
Ⓨ Imperial Guest House, 1 Manu Marg, T0144-270 1730. Rooms disappointing but South Indian restaurant is popular and good value.
Ⓨ Moti Doongri Park has a number of stalls selling cheap south Indian snacks in the evening. You can also get inexpensive Chinese and north Indian.

ⓔ Transport

Alwar *p217, map p216*
Bus There are regular buses to/from **Delhi** (4½-5 hrs) and **Jaipur**. Frequent service to **Bharatpur** (2½ hrs), **Deeg** (1½ hrs) and **Sariska** (1 hr).
Train **New Delhi**: *Shatabdi Exp, 2016*, not Sun, 1941, 2½ hrs. **Delhi**: *Jodhpur Delhi Exp, 4860*, 0835, 3 hrs; *Jaipur-Delhi Exp, 2414*, 1845, 3 hrs.

Sariska *p218, map p218*
Air Nearest airport at Jaipur (110 km).
Train Nearest at Alwar (36 km), with buses to the sanctuary.

ⓘ Directory

Alwar *p217, map p216*
Internet Near the bus and railway station and on Manu Marg.

Deeg, Bharatpur and around

For a typical dusty and hot north Indian market town, Deeg gained the somewhat surprising reputation as the summer resort of the Raja of Bharatpur. Located on the plains just northwest of Agra, the Raja decided to develop his palace to take full advantage of the monsoon rains. The fort and the 'Monsoon' pleasure palace have

ingenious fountains and are of major architectural importance, their serenity in stark
contrast to the barely controlled chaos of the rest of the town.

The road which connects Agra to Jaipur, forming the southern side of the 'Golden Triangle', sees huge volumes of tourist traffic, but relatively few visitors stop along the way. There are, however, some really worthwhile sights just off the road, known as the NH11. Balaji temple is particularly remarkable. One of the most popular halting places on the 'Golden Triangle', Bharatpur, at the confluence of the Ruparel and Banganga rivers, is best known for its Keoladeo Ghana Bird Sanctuary. Once the hunting estate of the Maharajas of Bharatpur, with daily shoots recorded of up to 4,000 birds, the 29-sq km piece of marshland, with over 360 species, is one of the finest bird sanctuaries in the world. ►► For Sleeping, Eating and other listings, see pages 225-227.*

Ins and outs

There are regular bus services from both Mathura and Bharatpur to Deeg, with the road from Bharatpur being by far the smoother of the two. Bharatpur, 40 km south of Deeg, has good bus and train connections from Agra, Jaipur and Delhi. Keoladeo Ghana National Park is 4 km south of Bharatpur town.

History

Badan Singh (1722-1756), a Sinsini Jat, began the development of Deeg as capital of his newly founded Jat Kingdom. The central citadel was built by his son **Suraj Mal** in 1730. In the late 18th century the town reverted to the Raja of Bharatpur. The British stormed the fort in December 1804, after which the fortifications were dismantled.

The Bharatpur ruling family was Jat and constantly harassed the later Mughals. Under Badan Singh they controlled a large tract between Delhi and Agra, then led by Suraj Mal they seized Agra and marched on to Delhi in 1763.

Deeg → *Phone code: 05641. Colour map 3, grid C2. Population: 38,000.*

The rubble and mud walls of the square **fort** are strengthened by 12 bastions and a wide, shallow moat. It has a run-down *haveli* within, but is otherwise largely abandoned. The entrance is over a narrow bridge across the moat, through a gate studded with anti-elephant spikes. Negotiating the thorny undergrowth, you can climb the ramparts which rise 20 m above the moat; some large cannons are still in place on their rusty carriages. You can walk right around along the wide path on top of the walls and climb the stairs to the roof of the citadel for good views all round.

The **palaces**, directly opposite the fort, are flanked by two reservoirs, Gopal (west) and Rup Sagar (east), and set around a beautifully proportioned central formal garden in the style of a Mughal *char bagh*. The main entrance is from the north, through the ornamental, though unfinished, Singh (Lion) Pol; the other gates are Suraj (Sun) Pol (southwest) and Nanga Pol (northeast). The impressive main palace **Gopal Bhavan** (1763), bordering Gopal Sagar, is flanked by Sawon and Bhadon pavilions (1760) named after the monsoon months (mid-July to mid-September). Water was directed over the roof lines to create the effect of sheets of monsoon rain. The palace still retains many of the original furnishings, including scent and cigarette cases made from elephant's feet and even a dartboard. There are two separate veg and non-veg dining rooms, the former particularly elegant, with floor seating around a low-slung horseshoe-shaped marble table. Outside, overlooking the formal garden, is a beautiful white marble *hindola* (swing) which was brought as booty with two marble thrones (black and white) after Suraj Mal attacked Delhi.

To the south, bordering the central garden, is the single-storey marble **Suraj Bhavan** (circa 1760), a temple and **Kishan Bhavan** with its decorated façade, five arches and fountains. The water reservoir to its west was built at a height to operate the fountains and cascades effectively; it held enough water to work all the fountains for a few hours though it took a week to fill from four wells with bullocks drawing water up in leather buckets. Now, the 500 or so fountains are turned on once a year for the **Monsoon festival** in August. All these are gravity fed from huge holding tanks on the Palace roof, with each fountain jet having its own numbered pipe leading from the tank. Coloured dyes are inserted into individual pipes to create a spectacular effect. The (old) **Purana Mahal** beyond, with a curved roof and some fine architectural points was begun by Badan Singh in 1722. It now houses government offices but the wall paintings in the entrance chamber of the inner court, though simple, are worth seeing.

Keshav Bhavan, a *baradari* or garden pavilion, stands between the central garden and Rup Sagar with the **Sheesh Mahal** (Mirror Palace, 1725) in the southeast corner. **Nand Bhavan** (circa 1760), north of the central garden, is a large hall 45 m long, 24 m wide and 6 m high, raised on a terrace and enclosed by an arcade of seven arches. There are frescoes inside but it has a deserted feel. The pavilion took the monsoon theme further; the double-roof was ingeniously used to create the effect of thunder above-water channelled through hollow pillars rotated heavy stone balls which made the sound! On a sunny day the fountains are believed to have produced a rainbow.

The **'Monsoon' Pleasure Palaces** ① *0930-1730, closed Fri, Rs 5, foreigners Rs 100*, to the west of the fort were begun by Suraj Mal.

Bhandarej to Bharatpur

Bhandarej, 62 km from Jaipur, south of NH11 after Dausa, is a relaxing place to stop for the night, see below.

The NH11 then goes through a series of small towns and villages to **Sakrai** (77 km) where there is a good road side RTDC restaurant. Some 15 km after Sakrai is the turning for Balaji, home to the really extraordinary **Balaji Temple**. This is where people come who believe themselves to have been possessed by devils, and who want the evil spirits exorcised. The scenes on the first floor in particular are not for the faint-hearted; methods of restraining the worst afflicted include chaining them to the walls and placing them under large rocks. Most exorcisms take place on Tuesdays and Saturdays, when there are long queues to get in. From **Mahuwa** a road south leads through Hindaun to Karauli (64 km).

Noted for its pale red sandstone, widely used for building, **Karauli**, founded in 1348, was the seat of a small princely state which played a prominent part in support of the Mughal Emperors. The impressive **City Palace** has some fine wall paintings, stone carvings and a fine Darbar Hall. Fairs are held at nearby temples lasting a week to a fortnight, see below Mahavirji, associated with the 24th Tirthankar Mahavir, is an important Jain pilgrimage centre.

Bharatpur → *Phone code: 05644. Colour map 3, grid C3. Population: 157,000.*

Built by Suraj Mal, the **Lohagarh Fort** appears impregnable. The British, initially repulsed in 1803, took it in 1825. There are double ramparts, a 46 m wide moat and an inner moat around the palace. Much of the wall has been demolished but there are the remains of some of the gateways. Inside the fort are three palaces (circa 1730) and Jewel House and Court to their north. The **museum** ① *1000-1630, closed Fri, Rs 3*, in the Kachhari Kalan exhibits archaeological finds from villages nearby, dating from the first to 19th centuries as well as paintings and artefacts; the armoury is upstairs.

Peharsar ① *Rs 30 to 'headman' secures a tour*, 23 km from centre, with a carpet weaving community, makes a very interesting excursion from Bharatpur.

Keoladeo Ghana National Park

ⓘ Rs 25, Rs200 foreigners, payable each time you enter, professional video camera Rs 1,500, amateur video Rs 200, car Rs 50. Café provides good lunch stop.

The late Maharaja Brajendra Singh converted his hunting estate into a bird sanctuary in 1956 and devoted many of his retired years to establishing it. He had inherited both his title and an interest in wildlife from his deposed father, Kishan Singh, who grossly overspent his budget – 30 Rolls Royces, private jazz band and extremely costly wild animals including "dozens of lions, elephants, leopards and tigers" – for Bharatpur's jungles. It has been designated a World Heritage site, and can only be entered by bicycle or cycle rickshaw, thus maintaining the peaceful calm of the park's interior.

Ins and outs

Getting around Good naturalist guides cost Rs 100 per hour per group or Rs 50 per hour per person at entrance, or contact Nature Bureau *ⓘ Haveli SVP Shastri, Neemda Gate, T/F05644-225498*. Official cycle-rickshaws at the entrance are numbered and work in rotation, Rs 50 per hour for two (drivers may be reluctant to take more than one). Well worthwhile as some rickshaw-wallahs are very knowledgeable and can help identify birds (and know their location): a small tip is appropriate. The narrower paths are not recommended as the rough surface make them too noisy. It is equally feasible to just walk or hire a bike. A boat ride is highly recommended for viewing; boatmen are equally knowledgeable; hire one from the Rest House near jetty.

> ‼ *Allow a full day, though you can spot many species in just two hours. It is best to carry your own pair of binoculars.*

Tourist information Tourist offices **Rajasthan** *ⓘ Hotel Saras, T05644-22542*, and **Wildlife office** *ⓘ Forest Rest House, T05644-22777*. Guides available. For tours

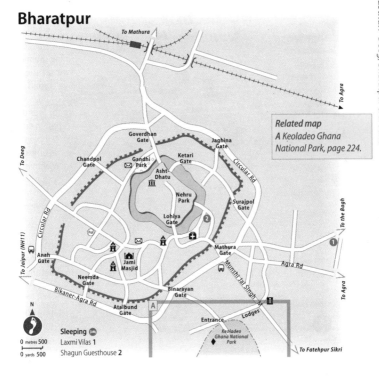

Bharatpur

To Mathura

To Deeg

To Agra

Related map
A Keoladeo Ghana National Park, page 224.

Goverdhan Gate
Jaghina Gate
Chandpol Gate
Gandhi Park
Ketari Gate
Asht-Dhatu
Circular Rd
Nehru Park
Surajpol Gate
Lohiya Gate
To the Bagh
Circular Rd
To Jaipur (NH11)
Anah Gate
Jami Masjid
Mathura Gate
Agra Rd
To Agra
Neemda Gate
Bikaner-Agra Rd
Binarayan Gate
Munshi Jai Singh
Atalbund Gate
Entrance
Lodges
To Fatehpur Sikri
Keoladeo Ghana National Park

N

0 metres 500
0 yards 500

Sleeping 🛏
Laxmi Vilas **1**
Shagun Guesthouse **2**

contact **GTA** ⓘ *near Tourist Lodge, Gol Bagh Rd, T05644-28188, vfauzdar@yahoo. com.* Knowledgeable English speaking guides, Rs 300 for 2 hrs. It is worth buying the **Collins Handguide to the Birds of the Indian Sub-continent** (available at the Reserve and in booksellers in Delhi, Agra, Jaipur etc), well illustrated. Also **Pictorial Guide to the birds of the Indian Sub-Continent** by Salim Ali and S Dillon, Ripley and **Bharatpur: Bird Paradise** by Martin Ewans, Lustre Press, Delhi, are also extremely good.

Keoladeo Ghana National Park

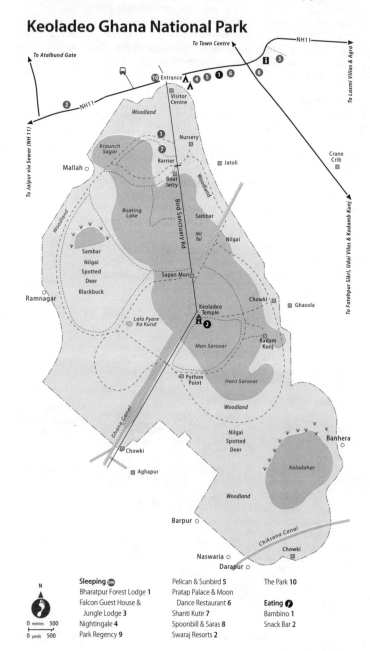

Sleeping 🛏
Bharatpur Forest Lodge **1**
Falcon Guest House &
  Jungle Lodge **3**
Nightingale **4**
Park Regency **9**

Pelican & Sunbird **5**
Pratap Palace & Moon
  Dance Restaurant **6**
Shanti Kutir **7**
Spoonbill & Saras **8**
Swaraj Resorts **2**

The Park **10**

Eating 🍴
Bambino **1**
Snack Bar **2**

Best time to visit Winters can be very cold and foggy, especially in the early morning. It is especially good November-February when it is frequented by Northern hemisphere migratory birds.

Sights

A handful of rare Siberian Crane visit annually. The ancient migratory system, some 1,500 years old, is in danger of being lost since young cranes must learn the route from older birds (it is not instinctive). These cranes are disappearing – eaten by Afghans and sometimes employed as fashionable 'guards' to protect Pakistani homes (they call out when strangers approach). September to October is the breeding season but it's worth visiting any time of the year.

Among other birds to be seen are egrets, ducks, coots, storks, kingfishers, spoonbills, Sarus cranes, birds of prey including Laggar falcon, greater spotted eagle, marsh harrier, Scops owl and Pallas' eagle. Shortage of water may result in migrants failing to arrive. There are also chital deer, sambar, nilgai, feral cattle, wild cats, hyenas, wild boar and monitor lizards, whilst near Python Point, there are usually some very large rock pythons.

Birds can be watched from a short distance from the road between the boat jetty and Keoladeo temple, especially Sapan Mori crossing, since they have got accustomed to visitors. Dawn (which can be very cold) and dusk are the best times; trees around Keoladeo temple are favoured by birds for sleeping in, so are particularly rewarding at dawn. Midday may prove too hot so take a book and find a shady spot. Carry a sun hat, binoculars and plenty of drinking water.

● Sleeping

Deeg *p221*
Avoid spending a night here but if you have to there are a couple of very basic options close to the bus station.

Bhandarej to Bharatpur *p222*
B Bhadrawati Palace, Bhandarej, T01427-283 351, www.bhadrawatipalace.com. 35 adequate rooms arranged around a central lawn in converted palace, extensive gardens, pool, wide choice in beautiful restaurant; also orchard with camping, 5 km from palace.
B Bhanwar Vilas Palace (Heritage Hotel), Karauli, T07464-220024, www.karauli.com. 29 comfortable rooms, including 4 a/c suites in converted palace, most air-cooled (cheaper in cottage), restaurant (Indian, Rajasthani), pool, tours, camping, amazingly ornate lounge and dining halls, real air of authenticity. Recommended.
C-D Manglam Inn, next to the Balaji turn off on the NH11, Balaji, T01420-247 393. This is the closest accommodation option, has 10 clean, good-sized rooms, 3 a/c, and friendly owners.
E Motel (RTDC), Mahuwa, T07461-33210. With 5 simple rooms, a fast food restaurant, toilets, basic motor repair facilities

Bharatpur *p222, map p223*
Most of Bharatpur's accommodation is located outside town, close to the entrance to the bird sanctuary. However, there is a great budget choice in the old city.
F Shagun Guest House, just inside Mathura Gate, T05644-232 455. 6 basic rooms, 1 with attached bathroom, all under Rs100, plus bicycle and binocular hire. Friendly, welcoming and knowledgeable manager.
C Chandra Mahal, Peharsar, Jaipur-Agra Rd, Nadbai, Peharsar, T05643-243238. 23 rooms in simply furnished, 19th-century Shia Muslim *haveli* with character, quality set meals (from Rs 250), jeep hire andgood service

Keoladeo Ghana National Park
p223, map p224
Some budget hotels have tented accommodation.
Inside the park **B Bharatpur Forest Lodge** (Ashok), 2½ km from gate, T05644-222 760, 8 km from railway and bus stand, book in advance. 17 comfortable a/c rooms with balconies, pricey restaurant and bar, very friendly staff, peaceful, boats for bird watching, animals (eg wild boar)

wander into the compound. Entry fee each time you enter park.

E Shanti Kutir Rest House, near boat jetty. 5 clean rooms in old hunting lodge, mostly used by guests of the Park Director.

Outside the park AL-A The Bagh, Agra Rd, 4 km from town, T05644-228 333, www.thebagh.com. 14 classy, well decorated, centrally a/c rooms with outstanding bathrooms in upmarket garden retreat. Attractive dining room, swimming pool and coffee shop planned, beautiful 200-year-old gardens, some may find facilities rather spread out.

A Swaraj Resorts, opposite park, T05644-233 250, swarajresorts@hotmail.com. 12 modern, well-equipped rooms plus extensive facilities including restaurant, gym, pool, billiards and table tennis. Not good value.

A Udai Vilas, Fatehpur Sikri Rd, 3 km from park, T05644-233 161, www.udaivilaspalace.com. 24 contemporary styled rooms in impressively run hotel, excellent restaurant, pleasant gardens, generally a cut above. Recommended.

A-B Laxmi Vilas Palace (Heritage Hotel), Kakaji ki Kothi, Agra Rd, 2½ km from town (auto-rickshaws outside), T05644-223 523, www.laxmivilas.com. 30 elegant, a/c rooms around a lovely central courtyard, good food and service, attractive 19th-century hunting lodge decorated in period style (jackals spotted), pleasantly old fashioned, welcoming friendly staff, "took good care of children when we went birding", exceptional pool and Jacuzzi. Recommended.

B Kadamb Kunj, Fatehpur Sikri Rd, 3 km from park, T05644-220 122, www.kadamb kunj.com. 16 modern, a/c rooms plus well-kept lawns, a good gift shop and restaurant.

B-C Park Regency, opposite park, T05644-224 232, hotelparkregency@yahoo.co.uk. 8 large, modern, clean rooms, 24-hour room service, pleasant lawns, friendly management, good value.

B-E Crane Crib, Fatehpur Sikri Rd, 3 km from park, T05644-222 224. Attractive sandstone building contains 25 rooms of wide-ranging standards and tariffs, but all reasonable value. Added attractions include a small cinema where wildlife shows are filmed nightly, bonfires on the lawn every night during winter and the welcoming attitude of the staff. Recommended.

C The Park, opposite Park gate, T05644-233 192, bansal39@sancharnet.in. 10 large, clean rooms plus an atypically light restaurant and well maintained lawn.

C Sunbird, near Park gate, T05644-225 701, www.hotelsunbird.com. Clean rooms with hot shower, better on 1st floor, very pleasant restaurant, friendly staff, bike hire, good value, well maintained. Highly recommended.

C-D Pratap Palace, near Park Gate, T05644-224 245, www.hotelpratap palace.net. 30 rooms (10 a/c) with bath, whole place feels slightly run down, mediocre restaurant but helpful management, good value.

C-D Saras (RTDC), Fatehpur Sikri Rd, T05644-223 722. 25 simple clean rooms, some a/c (limited hot water), dorm (Rs 50), restaurant (indifferent food), lawns, tourist information, camping, rather dull.

D-E Falcon Guest House, near Saras, T05644-223 815. 10 clean, well-kept rooms, some a/c with bath, owned by naturalist, good information, bike hire, quiet, very helpful, warm welcome, off-season discount.

D-F Nightingale and Tented Camp, near Park gate, T05644-227 022. Deluxe 2-bed tents with bath, others with shared bath, good food, open only during the winter season.

E Jungle Lodge, Shankar Colony (next to Falcon), T05644-225 622. 8 basic but clean rooms, excellent meals for residents (huge portions, cheap), quiet, friendly family, 'no Indians' policy, motorbike hire.

E-F Kiran Guest House, 364 Rajendra Nagar, 300 m from park gate, T05644-223 845. 5 clean rooms, excellent meals in rooftop restaurant, peaceful, safe, homely, helpful and knowledgeable family, free station pick ups. Recommended.

E-F Pelican, near Park gate, T05644-224 221. 9 clean rooms with fan, best No 8 with hot (salty!) shower (ask for towel), quite modern with tiny balcony, restaurant, friendly, bike hire (Rs 40 per day), good info.

E-F Spoonbill, near Saras, T05644-223 571, hotelspoonbill@rediffmail.com. Good value rooms with shared facility (hot water in buckets), dorm (Rs 60), run by charming ex-Army officer, courteous and friendly service, good food, bike hire, also 4 more good-size rooms in 'New Spoonbill' down the road.

Eating

Keoladeo Ghana National Park
p223, map p224
Inside the park ▝▝▝ **Forest Lodge**, over-priced buffets feeding the many tour groups.
Snack Bar, dirty, serving only drinks and biscuits.
Outside the park All restaurants offer some Indian and Western dishes.
▝▝▝ **Laxmi Vilas**, wide choice but some find it disappointing ("standard fare doled out to Westerners").
▝▝▝ **Eagle's Nest**, new 100-seater restaurant with the promise of a/c to come.
▝▝▝ **Moon Dance** tent, near **Pratap Palace**. Good food, lively atmosphere, beer.
▝ **Bambino**, open-air dining in a garden.
▝ **Pelican**, good choice, chicken, vegetarian, Israeli dishes, 'westernized'.
▝ **Spoonbill**, good food obliging (beer and special *kheer* on request). Recommended.

Festivals and events

Bhandarej to Bharatpur *p222*
In Karauli, **Sivaratri** (**26 Feb 2005**, 10 Feb 2006, 7 Feb 2007), **Kaila Devi** (**6 Apr 2005**, 26 Mar 2006, 16 Mar 2007).

Bharatpur *p222, map p223*
Brij Festival, a few days before Holi, honours lord Krishna with folk dances and drama relating the love story of Radha-Krishna. **21-23 Mar 2005**, 10-12 Mar 2006, 27 Feb-1 Mar 2007.

Transport

Bhandarej to Bharatpur *p222*
All trains except *Rajdhani Express* stop at Gangapur City, 30 km from Karauli.

Bharatpur *p222, map p223*
The nearest airport is at Agra (55 km).
The buses to Bharatpur tend to get very crowded but give an insight into Indian rural life. From **Agra** (55 km, 1½ hrs, Rs 12), **Deeg** Rs 15; **Delhi** (185 km, 6 hrs, Rs 70) and **Jaipur** (175 km, 5 hrs, Rs 60) arrive at Anah Gate just off NH11 (east of town).
Train from: **Delhi (ND)**: *Paschim Exp, 2925*, 0630, 4 hrs; *Golden Temple Mail, 2903*, 1540, 3½ hrs; *Mumbai-Firozepur Janata Exp, 9023*, 0800, 5½ hrs. **Sawai Madhopur**: *Paschim Exp, 2926*, 1955, 2½ hrs; *Golden Temple Mail, 2904*, 1055, 2½ hrs.
An auto-rickshaw from train station (6 km) to park Rs 50; from bus stand (4 km), Rs 20.

Keoladeo Ghana National Park *p223, map p224*
There are bikes for hire near **Saras** or ask your hotel; Rs 40 per day; hire on previous evening for an early start next day.

Directory

Bharatpur *p222, map p223*
Banks SBBJ, near Binarayan Gate, may ask to see proof of purchase, or refuse to change Tcs.

Ranthambhore National Park

→ *Phone code: 07462. Colour map 5, grid A4.*

The park is one of the finest tiger reserves in the country; most visitors spending a couple of nights here are likely to spot one of these wonderful animals. Once the private tiger reserve of the Maharaja of Jaipur, in 1972 the sanctuary came under the Project Tiger scheme. It covers 410 sq km and runs from the easternmost spur of the Aravallis to the Vindhya range. It has both the old fort and the wildlife sanctuary, also known as Sawai Madhopur, after the nearby town, which has some Jain temples with gilded paintings. Set in dry deciduous forest, the area covers rocky hills and open valleys dotted with small pools and fruit trees. The fort dominates the landscape. The path to it zigzags up the steep outcrop in a series of ramps and through two impressive gateways. ▸▸ For Sleeping, Eating and other listings, see pages 230-231.

Getting there and around The national park is 10 km east of Sawai Madhopur, with the approach along a narrow valley; the main gate is 4 km from the boundary.

> ⚡ *Avoid weekends when there are larger numbers of noisy visitors.*

The park has good roads and tracks. Entry is by park jeep or open bus (Canter) on three-hour tours; 18 jeeps (or Gypsys) and 20 Canters are allowed in at any one time to minimize disturbance. Jeeps are better but can be difficult to get in the peak season so request one at the time of booking your lodge. Visitors are picked up from their hotels. The park is open 1 October-30 June. Tours: winter 0700-1000, 1500-1800; summer 0630-0930, 1430-1730. Jeep hire: Rs 750 for up to five passengers; jeep entry Rs 125; guide Rs 150; plus individual entry fee Rs 25 (Indians), Rs 200 (foreigners). Camera free, video Rs 200. Seat in a Canter, Rs 200. Bookings start at 0600 and 1330 for same day tours; advance bookings from1000-1330. Forest Department Project Tiger Office, T07462-220 223, is behind the railway station.

Best time to visit From November to April. The vegetation dies down in April exposing tigers. Temperatures range from 49-28°C. It can be very cold at dawn in winter so go prepared.

Wildlife

Tiger sightings are reported almost daily, usually in the early morning, especially from November to April. Travellers see them "totally unconcerned, amble past only 30 ft (10 m) away"! Sadly, poaching is prevalent, and the tiger population has been depleted to around 30. The lakeside woods and grassland provide an ideal habitat

Ranthambhore National Park

To Delhi
To Tonk & Jauputi
Banas River
ANANTPURA
SIMLI
LAKARDA
Padam Talao
Raj Bagh
Sawai Madhopur
To Jaipur
Jogi Mahal
Khandar Fort
Ranthambhore Fort
LAHPUR
To Mumbai
To Kota, Mumbai & Sawai Madhopur City
KAILASHPURI
Chambal River

N

0 km (approx) 5
0 miles (approx) 5

Sleeping
Aman-i-Khas **2**
Aranya Resorts **11**
Castle Jhoomar Baori **3**
Hill View **12**
Hammir **4**
Pugmark **13**

Tiger Den **14**
Tiger Safari **1**
Vanya Vilas **5**
Ranthambhore Bagh **6**
Regency **7**
Sawai Madhopur
Lodge **8**

Sher Bagh &
The White House **9**
Tiger Moon Resort **10**
Vinayak **15**

Eating
Mountain View **1**

The Pragmatic Prakratik Society

Much of the credit for Ranthambhore's present position as one of the world's leading wildlife resorts goes to India's most famous "tiger man", Mr Fateh Singh Rathore. His enthusiasm for all things wild has been passed on to his son, Dr Goverdhan Singh Rathore, who set up the Prakratik Society in 1994. This charitable foundation was formed in response to the increasing human encroachment on the tiger's natural forest habitat; in 1973 there were 70,000 people living around Ranthambhore Park, a figure which has now increased to 200,000.

The human population's rapidly rising firewood requirements were leading to ever-more damaging deforestation, and the founders of the Prakratik Society soon realized that something needed to be done. Their solution was as brilliant as it was simple; enter the "biogas digester". This intriguingly named device, of which 225 have so far been installed, uses cow dung as a raw material, and produces both gas for cooking, negating the need for firewood, and organic fertilizer, which has seen crop yields increase by 25 per cent.

The overwhelming success of this venture was recognized in June 2004, when the Prakratik Society was presented with the prestigious Ashden Award for Sustainable Energy in London.

for herds of chital and sambar deer and sounders of wild boar. Nilgai antelope and chinkara gazelles prefer the drier areas of the park. Langur monkeys, mongoose and hare are prolific. There are also sloth bear, a few leopards, and the occasional rare caracal. Crocodiles bask by the lakes, and some rocky ponds have fresh water turtles. Extensive birdlife includes spurfowl, jungle fowl, partridges, quails, crested serpent eagle, woodpeckers, flycatchers etc. There are also water birds like storks, ducks and geese at the lakes and waterholes. Padam Talao by the Jogi Mahal is the park's favourite water source; there are also water holes at Raj Bagh and Milak.

Ranthambhore fort

ⓘ *Free. The entrance to the fort is before the gate to the park. Open dawn to dusk, though the Park Interpretation Centre near the small car park may not be open.*

There is believed to have been a settlement here in the eighth century. The earliest historic record is of it being wrested by the Chauhans in the 10th century. In the 11th century, after Ajmer was lost to Ghori, the Chauhans made it their capital. Hamir Chauhan, the ruler of Ranthambhore in the 14th century gave shelter to enemies of the Delhi sultanate, resulting in a massive siege and the Afghan conquest of the fort. The fort was later surrendered to Emperor Akbar in the 16th century when Ranthambhore's commander saw resistance was useless, finally passing to the rulers of Jaipur. The forests of Ranthambhore historically guarded the fort from invasions but with peace under the Raj they became a hunting preserve of the Jaipur royal family. The fort wall runs round the summit and has a number of semi-circular bastions, some with sheer drops of over 65 m and stunning views. Inside the fort you can see a Siva temple – where Rana Hamir beheaded himself rather than face being humiliated by the conquering Delhi army – ruined palaces, pavilions and tanks. Mineral water, tea and soft drinks are sold at the foot of the climb to the fort and next to the Ganesh temple near the tanks.

● Sleeping

Ranthambhore National Park
p227, maps p228 and p230

Book well ahead. Hotels tend to be overpriced – rooms can be dusty and electricity erratic. Carry a torch. Most down to **B** category are geared for tour groups so may neglect independent travellers. In Sawai Madhopur, the small hotels in the noisy market areas are rather seedy.

LL Aman-i-Khas, close to park, T07462-252 052, www.amanresorts.com. 6 super luxury a/c tents in beautiful surroundings, minimum 3 night stay on all-inclusive basis (US$2,250).

LL Vanyavilas (Oberoi), T07462-223 999, www.oberoihotels.com. 20 acre, very upmarket garden resort set around a re-created *haveli* with fantastic frescoes. 25 unbelievably luxurious a/c tents (wood floor, TV, marble baths), pool, billiards, elephant rides, nightly wildlife lectures, dance shows in open-air auditorium, "fabulous spa", friendly and professional staff. Exceptional.

LL-L The Pugmark, Khilchipur, T07462-252 205, www.thepugmark.net. 22 luxury a/c cottages, including one with its own pool, in an entertainingly over the top resort. Defining feature is the "imaginatively landscaped" garden, replete with all manner of waterways, plastic rocks and illuminations.

L Sawai Madhopur Lodge (Taj), Ranthamb-hore Rd, T07462-220 541, www.tajhotels.com. 20-min drive from park, 32 a/c rooms (6 tents Oct-Mar), dated hunting lodge but comfortable, good buffet in stately wood-panelled dining hall watched over by tigers' heads, pool, tennis front desk lacks sparkle, park tour by jeep Rs 1420 each.

L Sherbagh Tented Camp, Sherpur-Khiljipur, T07462-252 120, www.sherbagh.com. 12 luxury tents with hot showers, award winning eco-camp, bar, dinner around fire, lake trips for birders, jungle ambience, well organized. Open 1 Oct-30 Mar, tariff includes all meals.

AL-A The Whitehouse, close to Sher Bagh, T07462-252 099. www.ranthambhore.co.uk. 3 very comfortable rooms in charming period property set in peaceful gardens. Common leopard sightings at nearby waterhole. All meals included. Owned by the Singh Rathore family, see box.

A Ranthambhore Regency, T07462-223 456, www.ranthambhor.com. 39 a/c rooms in cottages in swanky modern surroundings. Very clean pool and huge, 100 cover dining hall, plus evening folk performances and slide shows.

A Tiger Den Resort, Khilchipur, Ranthambhore Rd, T07462-252 070, www.tigerdenresort.com. 40 simple but pleasant a/c rooms in brick cottages around a well-kept lawn, evening meals (Indian buffet) seated around braziers, surrounded by farmland near guava groves, 6 km from park. All meals included.

A Tiger Moon Resort, near Sherpur on the edge of the park, 12 km from railway, T07462-252 042, www.indianadventures.com. 32 stone (25 a/c), and 5 simple bamboo

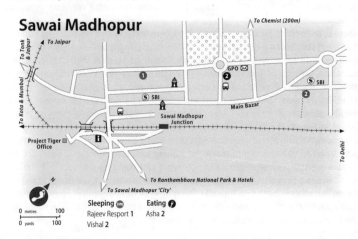

Sawai Madhopur

To Chemist (200m)
To Jaipur
To Tonk & Jaipur
To Kota & Mumbai
GPO
SBI
SBI
Main Bazar
Sawai Madhopur Junction
To Delhi
Project Tiger Office
To Ranthambhore National Park & Hotels
To Sawai Madhopur 'City'

N

0 metres 100
0 yards 100

Sleeping ●   Eating ●
Rajeev Ressort 1   Asha 2
Vishal 2

'cottages', all with modern fittings, hot water, some tents are added in the peak season, buffet meals, bar, library, pool, pleasant "jungle ambience". All meals and two safaris included.

B-C Aranya Resorts, Ranthambore Rd, T07462-221 121, aranyaresort@rediffmail. com. 10 clean, modern rooms in convenient location for park, reasonably priced veg food.

B-C Hill View, Ranthambhore Rd, T07462-222 173, hillviewholidayresort@rediffmail.com. Attractive, large garden complex set in hills with great views, 17 cottage rooms (8 a/c), attached baths, fixed meals, great lawns.

B-C Ranthambore Bagh, Ranthambhore Rd, T07462-221 728, www.ranthambhore.com. 12 luxury tents and 12 simple but attractive rooms in this pleasantly laid back property. Family run, pride has been taken in every detail; the publis areas and dining hall are particularly well done. Highly recommended.

C Hammir, T07462-220 562. One of Ranthambore's oldest hotels, it was undergoing much-needed renovation at the time of writing. There are 20 rooms, 8 a/c, plus a new swimming pool and a friendly, cheerful manager.

C Jhoomar Baori (RTDC), Ranthombore Rd, T07462-220 495. Set high on a hillside, and so something of an effort to get to, this former hunting lodge is an interesting building, and offers fantastic views of the area. There are 12 rooms, some bigger than others, but all quirkily arranged, plus a small bar and okay restaurant. Good value.

C-D Vinayak (RTDC), Ranthambhore Rd, close to park, T07462-221 333. 14 adequate rooms, including 5 a/c, plus pleasant lawns in a good location, and a gloomy restaurant which serves fantastic veg *thalis*.

D-E Tiger Safari, T07462-221 137, www.tigersafariresort.com. 14 cosy rooms, plus 4 attractive a/c cottages, very clean baths (hot shower), quiet, arranges park jeep/bus, very helpful manager, good value. Recommended.

E-F Rajeev Resort, 16 Indira Colony, Civil Lines, Sawai Madhopur, T07462-221 413. 12 fairly decent rooms, 2 a/c (some with western toilets), and larger 4-bedded rooms, simple meals to order.

F Vishal, Main Bazar, opposite SBI, Sawai Madhopur, T07462-220 695. 7 passable rooms some with bath (hot water in buckets).

❼ Eating

Ranthambhore National Park
p227, maps p228 and p230
As well as these options, try hotels.

🍴 **Mountain View Restaurant**, Ranthambhore Rd. Standard menu but pleasant lawns to sit out on and a friendly welcome.

🍴 **Asha**, next to bus stand, T07462-220 803. Don't be put off by uninviting exterior, this is a great little eatery, friendly, fast service and cheap, scrumptious food.

▲▲ Activities and tours

Ranthambhore National Park
p227, maps p228 and p230
Forts & Palaces, Sawai Madhopur, T07462-234 042, www.palaces-tours.com.

❺ Transport

Ranthambhore National Park
p227, maps p228 and p230
Bus
Bus Stand is 500 m from railway station. Road from Sawai Madhopur to Bundi via **Lakheri** is not nearly as bad as it was.

To **Sawai Madhopur** from Kota and Jaipur are slow (4 hrs); trains are better.

Train
Sawai Madhopur Junction, T07462-220 222. It is on the main Delhi-Mumbai line. From **Jaipur**: *Jaipur-Mumbai, 2956,* 1350, 2 hrs. **Jaipur**: *Mumbai-Jaipur Exp, 2955,* 1035, 2 hrs. **Jodhpur**: *Sawai Madhopur-Jodhpur Intercity Exp, 2465,* 1710. **Kota**: *Golden Temple Mail, 2904,* 1320, 1¼ hrs; *Mumbai Exp, 2956,* 1550, 1½ hrs. **Mumbai**: *Jaipur Mumbai Exp, 2956,* 1550, 16 hrs; *Paschim Exp, 2926,* 2220, 17¼ hrs; *Golden Temple Mail, 2904,* 1320, 15 hrs. **New Delhi** (via Bharatpur and Mathura) *Golden Temple Mail, 2903,* 1300, 6 hrs; *Dehra Dun Exp, 9019,* 2140, 8 hrs.

❶ Directory

Ranthambhore National Park
p227, maps p228 and p230
Internet Cyber Café on Ranthambhore Rd near entrance to **Ankur Resort** entrance. **Useful numbers** Tiger Watch, T07463-220811.

Ajmer and Pushkar

Although geographically close, these towns could hardly be more different. Situated in a basin at the foot of Taragarh Hill (870 m), Ajmer is surrounded by a stone wall with five gateways. Renowned throughout the Muslim world as the burial place of Mu'inuddin Chishti, who claimed descent from the son-in-law of Mohammad, seven pilgrimages to Ajmer are believed to equal one to Mecca. Every year, especially at the annual Islamic festivals of Id and Muharram, thousands of pilgrims converge on this ancient town on the banks of Ana Sagar Lake. Many visitors are discouraged by the frantic hustle of Ajmer on first arrival, but it's worth taking time to explore this underrated city.

Pushkar lies in a narrow dry valley overshadowed by impressive rocky hills which offer spectacular views of the desert at sunset. The lake at its heart, almost magically beautiful in the really early morning or late evening light, is one of India's most sacred. The once peaceful lakeside village on the edge of the desert has been markedly changed in recent years by the year-round presence of large numbers of foreigners who were originally drawn by the Pushkar fair. There are now many hotels, restaurants, cafés and shops catering to Western tastes and many travellers find it hard to drag themselves away from such a feast of creature comforts. The village is transformed once again during the celebrated camel fair into a colourful week of heightened activity. ▸▸ *For Sleeping, Eating and other listings, see pages 239-244.*

Ins and outs

Getting there There are trains and buses to Ajmer from the surrounding main towns and cities. Ajmer is the main transport hub for Pushkar although there are some direct bus services. Buses for Pushkar from Ajmer use the stand nearby the railway station; the main State and Private Bus Stands are chaotic and dirty, and are about 2 km away. Most visitors arrive in Pushkar by bus which heads for the Central (Marwar) Bus Stand overrun by aggressive hotel touts and porters, but you can ask to be dropped before hand on entering the town from Ajmer.

Getting around The main sights and congested bazaars of Ajmer, which can be seen in a day at a pinch, are within 15-20-minutes walk of the railway station but you'll need a rickshaw to get to Ana Sagar. Shuttle buses run between the main bus stand and the railway station. Pushkar is small enough to explore on foot. Hire a bike to venture further. ▸▸ *See Transport, page 244, for further details.*

Tourist information In Ajmer, there is a tourist office alongside **Khadim Hotel**, ① *T0145-52426, 0800-1800, closed Sun and second Sat of month.* Very helpful. Approved guide (four to eight hours, about Rs 250-400) and tourist taxi hire. Counter at railway station open seven days a week 0700-1800, near first-class main gate, entrance on right from car park.

History

According to tradition, Ajmer was founded in AD 145 by Raja Ajaipal, one of the Chauhan kings. In the 11th and 12th centuries it was attacked by Mahmud of Ghazni and Muhammad Ghuri. Born in Afghanistan, Mu'inuddin Chishti visited Ajmer in 1192 and died here in 1235. His tomb became a place of pilgrimage.

The houses of Mewar, Malwa and Jodhpur each ruled for a time until Akbar annexed it in 1556 and made the dargah a place of pilgrimage. He built a palace, later occupied by Jahangir who laid out the beautiful Daulat Bagh garden by the artificial

⁝ A saint of the people

Khwaja Mu'inuddin Chishti probably came to India before the Turkish conquests which brought Islam sweeping across northern India. A sufi, unlike the Muslim invaders, he came in peace. He devoted his life to the poor people of Ajmer and its region. He was strongly influenced by the *Upanishads*; some reports claim that he married the daughter of a Hindu raja.

His influence during his lifetime was enormous, but continued through the establishment of the Chishti school or *silsila*, which flourished 'because it produced respected spiritualists and propounded catholic doctrines'. Hindus were attracted to the movement but did not have to renounce their faith, and *Sufi khanqah* (a form of hospice) were accessible to all.

Almost immediately after his death Khwaja Mu'innuddin Chishti's followers carried on his mission. The present structure was built by Ghiyasuddin Khalji of Malwa, but the embellishment of the shrine to its present ornate character is still seen as far less important than the spiritual nature of the Saint it commemorates.

lake Ana Sagar which dates from circa 1135. Jahangir also received the first British ambassador from King James I in the Daulat Bagh in 1616. Shah Jahan, Aurangzeb's successor, embellished the garden with five fine marble pavilions.

After the Mughals, Ajmer returned to the House of Jodhpur and later to the Marathas. The British annexed it in 1818 and brought it under their direct rule.

From Jaipur to Ajmer

The drive along the NH8 from Jaipur to Ajmer is worth taking. After crossing relatively low lying land to Kishangarh the road enters the Aravalli hills. The direct railway line from Jaipur to Jodhpur passes by the Sambhar salt lake, a site of special wetland interest identified by the Slimbridge Waterfowl Trust, and Makrana, where the white marble used in the Taj Mahal was quarried.

Sambhar Lake

The salt lake, one of the largest of its kind in India, until recently attracted thousands of flamingoes and an abundance of cranes, pelicans, ducks and other waterfowl. About 120 species of birds have been checklisted. However, the poor monsoons of recent years have caused the lake to dry up leaving only a few marshy patches. Visitors have returned seeing less than 100 flamingoes, a few other species of waterfowl, and some ground birds like the Syke's Crested lark. It is a good idea to check the situation before visiting. Nilgai, fox and hare are spotted in the lake environs. The saline marshes are used for production of salt. The **Sakambari Temple** nearby, dedicated to the ancestral deity of the Chauhans, is believed to date from the sixth century.

Kuchaman

Kuchaman is a large village with temples and relics. Many visitors stop here for tea and snacks between Shekhawati and Ajmer. If you do stop, make time for a visit to the fort; it is a unique experience. Before the eighth century, Kuchaman lay on the highly profitable Central Asian caravan route. Here Gurjar Pratiharas built the massive clifftop fort with 10 gates leading up from the Meena bazaar in the village to the royal living quarters. The Chauhans drove the Pratiharas out of the area and for some time it was ruled by the Gaurs. From 1400, it has been in the hands of the Rathores who embellished it with mirrors, mural and gold work in superb palaces and pavilions such as the golden Sunheri Burj and the mirrored Sheesh Mahal, both in sharp contrast to the fort's exterior austerity. The Sariska Palace Group have taken over the fort, and restored and renovated the property at an enormous cost. Cars have to be parked in the courtyard after the first couple of gates, and four-wheel drive jeeps take guests to their rooms after checking in at the reception. You can visit the Krishna temple with a 2,000-year-old image, and the Kalimata ka Mandir which has an eighth-century black stone deity, shop in the Meena Bazar or watch local village crafts people.

Kishangarh → *Population: 22,000.*

Kishangarh was a small princely state, founded by Kishan Singh in 1603 as an independent state with a fort facing Lake Gundalao. Local artists known for their depiction of the Krishna legend and other Hindu themes were given refuge here by the royal family during the reign of the Mughal emperor, Aurangzeb, who, turning his back on the liberal views of earlier emperors, pursued an increasingly zealous Islamic purity. Under their patronage the artists reached a high standard of excellence and they continue the tradition of painting Kishangarh miniatures here which are noted for sharp facial features and elongated almond-shaped eyes. Most of those available are cheap copies on old paper using water colours instead of the mineral pigments of the originals. Today the town has retained some bustly charm, and is an interesting place to have a wander around. Powerloom weaving is a major industry, together with marble carving and polishing (India's best marble is quarried at nearby Makrana).

The fort palace stands on the shores of Lake Gundalao. Its Hathi Pol (Elephant Gate) has walls decorated with fine murals, and, though partly in ruins, you can see battlements, courtyards with gardens, shady balconies, brass doors and windows with coloured panes of glass. The temple has a fine collection of miniatures.

Roopangarh

About 20 km from Kishangarh, Roopangarh was an important fort of the Kishangarh rulers founded in AD 1649 on the old caravan route along the Sambhar Lake. The fort stands above the centre of the village which is a centre for craft industries – leather embroidery, block printing, pottery and handloom weaving can all be seen. The Sunday market features at least 100 cobblers making and repairing *mojdi* footwear. Some 12 km away is the old town of **Salemabad** with a stepped kund (tank) and Nimbarak Tirth temple which attract Hindu pilgrims.

Ajmer → *Phone code: 0145. Colour map 5, grid A2. Population: 490,000. Altitude: 486 m.*

The **Dargah of Khwaja Mu'inuddin Chishti** (1143-1235) is the tomb of the Sufi saint (also called 'The Sun of the Realm') which was begun by Iltutmish and completed by Humayun. Set in the heart of the old town, the entrance is through the bazar. Access to the main gate is on foot or by tonga or auto. The Emperor Akbar first made a pilgrimage to the shrine to give thanks for conquering Chittor in 1567, and the second for the birth of his son Prince Salim. From 1570 to 1580 Akbar made almost annual pilgrimages to Ajmer on foot from Agra, and the *kos minars* (brick marking pillars at about two-mile intervals) along the road from Agra are witness of the popularity of the pilgrimage route. It is considered the second holiest site after Mecca. On their first visit, rich Muslims pay for a feast of rice, ghee, sugar, almonds, raisins and spices to be cooked in one of the huge pots in the courtyard inside the high gateway. These are still in regular use. On the right is the Akbar Masjid (circa 1570), to the left, an assembly hall for the poor. In the inner courtyard is the white marble Shah Jahan Masjid (circa 1650), 33 m long with 11 arches and a carved balustrade on three sides. In the inner court is the Dargah (tomb), also white marble, square with a domed roof and two entrances. The ceiling is gold-embosse velvet, and silver rails and gates enclose the tomb. At festival times the tomb is packed with pilgrims, many coming from abroad, and the crush of people can be overpowering.

From Station Road, a walk through the bazars, either to Dargah/Masjid area or to Akbar's Palace/Nasiyan Temple area, is interesting.

The whole complex has a unique atmosphere. The areas around the tomb have a real feeling of community; there is a hospital and a school on the grounds, as well as numerous shops. As you approach the tomb the feeling of religious fervour increases, often heightened by the music being played

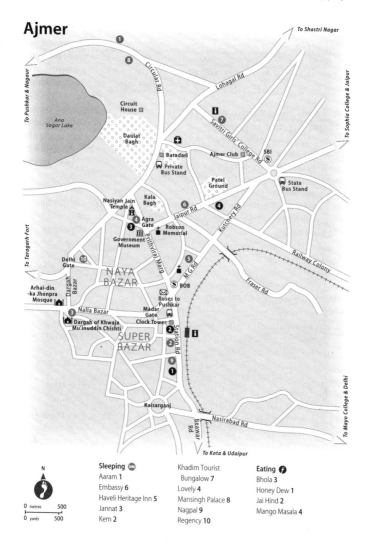

Ajmer

Eastern Rajasthan Ajmer & Pushkar

N

0 metres 500
0 yards 500

Sleeping
Aaram 1
Embassy 6
Haveli Heritage Inn 5
Jannat 3
Kem 2

Khadim Tourist
 Bungalow 7
Lovely 4
Mansingh Palace 8
Nagpal 9
Regency 10

Eating
Bhola 3
Honey Dew 1
Jai Hind 2
Mango Masala 4

66 99 As you approach the tomb the feeling of religious fervour increases, often heightened by the music being played. For many visitors, stepping in to the tomb itself is the culmination of a lifetime's ambition...

outside the tomb's ornate entrance. For many visitors, stepping in to the tomb itself is the culmination of a lifetime's ambition, reflected in the ardour of their offerings.

Nearby is the **Mazar** (tomb) of Bibi Hafiz Jamal, daughter of the saint, a small enclosure with marble latticework. Close by is that of Chimni Begum, daughter of Shah Jahan. She never married, refusing to leave her father during the seven years he was held captive by Aurangzeb in Agra Fort. She spent her last days in Ajmer, as did another daughter who probably died of tuberculosis. At the south end of the Dargah is the **Jhalra** (tank).

The **Arhai-din-ka Jhonpra Mosque** ('The Hut of two and a half days') lies beyond the Dargah in a narrow valley. Originally a Jain college built in 1153, it was partially destroyed by Muhammad of Ghori in 1192, and in 1210 turned into a mosque by **Qutb-ud-din-Aibak** who built a massive screen of seven arches in front of the pillared halls, allegedly in two and a half days (hence its name). The temple pillars which were incorporated in the building are all different. The mosque measures 79 x 17 m with 10 domes supported by 124 columns and incorporates older Hindu and Jain masonry. Much of it is in ruins though restoration work was undertaken at the turn of the century; only part of the 67 m screen and the Jain prayer hall remain.

Akbar's Palace, built in 1570 and restored in 1905, is in the city centre near the east wall. It is a large rectangular building with a fine gate. Today it houses the **Government museum** ① *1000-1630, closed Fri, Rs 3, No photography*, which has a dimly presented collection of fine sculpture from sixth to 17th centuries, paintings and old Rajput and Mughal armour and coins.

The ornate **Nasiyan Jain Temple** (Red Temple) ① *Prithviraj Marg, 0800-1700, Rs 5*, has a remarkable museum alongside the Jain shrine, which itself is open only to Jains. It is well worth visiting. Ajmer has a large Jain population (about 25 per cent of the city's total). The Shri Siddhkut Chaityalaya was founded in 1864 in honour of the first Jain Tirthankar, Rishabdeo, by a Jain diamond merchant, Raj Bahadur Seth Moolchand Nemichand Soni (hence its alternative name, the Soni temple). The opening was celebrated in 1895. Behind a wholly unimposing exterior, on its first floor the Svarna Nagari Hall houses an astonishing reconstruction of the Jain conception of the Universe, with gold plated replicas of every Jain shrine in India. Over 1,000 kg of gold is estimated to have been used, and at one end of the gallery diamonds have also been placed behind decorative coloured glass to give an appearance of backlighting. It took twenty people 30 years to build. Encased in a huge room behind glass panels, the whole of the reconstruction can be seen from different external galleries. The holy mountain, Sumeru, is at the centre of the continent, and around it are such holy sites as Ayodhya, the birthplace of the Tirthankar, recreated in gold plate, and a remarkable collection of model temples. Suspended from the ceiling are *vimanas* – airships of the gods – and silver balls. On the ground floor, beneath the model, are the various items taken on procession around the town on the Jain festival day of 23 November each year. The trustees of

The pull of the cattle and camels

The huge *Mela* is Pushkar's biggest draw. Over 200,000 visitors and pilgrims and hordes of cattle and camels with their semi-nomadic tribal drivers, crowd into the town. Farmers, breeders and camel traders buy and sell. Sales in leather whips, shoes, embroidered animal covers soar while women bargain over clay pots, bangles, necklaces and printed cloth.

Events begin four to five days before the full moon in November. There are horse and camel races and betting is heavy. In the *Ladhu Umt* race teams of up to 10 men cling to camels, and one another, in a hilarious and often chaotic spectacle. The Tug-of-War between Rajasthanis and foreigners is usually won by the local favourites. There are also sideshows with jugglers, acrobats, magicians and folk dancers. At nightfall there is music and dancing outside the tents, around friendly fires – an unforgettable experience despite its increasingly touristy nature – the 2003 edition even featured a laser show!. the cattle trading itself actually takes place during the week before the fair; some travellers have reported arriving during the fair and there being no animals left!

the temple are continuing to maintain and embellish it. The walls and ceilings of the main hall have been completely re-painted in traditional style, and the surrounding galleries are undergoing a similar programme of renovation. Copies of Mughal miniature paintings on silk are available outside.

Excursions

Mayo College (1873), only 4 km from the centre, was founded to provide young Indian princes with a liberal education, one of two genuinely Indo-Saracenic buildings designed by De Fabeck in Ajmer, the other being the **Mayo Hospital** (1870). The College was known as the 'Eton' of Rajputana and was run along the lines of an English Public School. Access is no longer restricted to Rajput princes.

Ana Sagar, an artificial lake (circa 1150) was further enhanced by Emperors Jahangir and Shah Jahan who added the baradari and pavilions. The **Foy Sagar**, 5 km away, another artificial lake was a famine relief project.

Taragarh (Star Fort), built by Ajaipal Chauhan in 1100 with massive 4½ m thick walls, stands on the hilltop overlooking the town. There are great views of the city but the walk up the winding bridle path, tiring. A jeepable road, however, has reduced the climb on foot and made access easier. Jeeps charge Rs 500 for the trip. Tea and snacks are sold in stalls at viewpoints. Along the way is a graveyard of Muslim 'martyrs' who died storming the fort.

Leaving Ajmer

The NH8 south of Ajmer towards Udaipur is relatively quiet. After 38 km, you come across **Fort Kharwa**, which is an interesting place to stay, but has no telephone number so is difficult to book. Built in 1568, the fort overlooks a lake with good birdlife. Good value. The road continues south through dry rocky hills, with occasional date palms and open savanna or agricultural land. Just south of **Bhim** the **Hotel Vijay** is modest but quite clean.

Leaving Ajmer for Pushkar, the road passes the village of **Nausar** and a striking 2-km long pass through the **Nag Pahar** (Snake Hill) which divides Pushkar from Ajmer.

Pushkar Lake is one of India's most sacred lakes. It is believed to mark the spot where a lotus thrown by Brahma landed.

Pushkar → *Phone code: 0145. Colour map 5, grid A2. Population: 15,000.*

Fa Hien, the Chinese traveller who visited Pushkar in the fifth century AD, commented on the number of pilgrims and although several of the older temples were subsequently destroyed by Aurangzeb, many remain. Ghats lead down to the water to enable pilgrims to bathe.

The **Brahma temple** ① *0600-1330, 1500-2100 (changes seasonally)*, at the far end of the lake, is a particularly holy shrine and draws pilgrims throughout the year.

> ❢ *There are dozens of temples here, most of which are open 0500-1200, 1600-2200.*

Although it isn't the only Brahma temple in India, as people claim, it is the only major pilgrim place for followers of the Hindu God of Creation. It is said that when Brahma needed a marital partner for a ritual, and his consort Saraswati (Savitri) took a long time to come, he married a cow-girl, Gayatri, after giving her the powers of a goddess (Gayatri because she was purified by the mouth of a cow or gau). His wife learnt of this and put a curse on him – that he would only be worshipped in Pushkar.

There are 52 ghats around the lake, of which the Brahma Ghat, Gan Ghat and Varah Ghat are the most sacred. The medieval **Varah temple** is dedicated to the boar incarnation of Vishnu. It is said the idol was broken by Emperor Jahangir as it resembled a pig. The **Mahadev Temple** is said to date from 12th century while the **Julelal Temple** is modern and jazzy. Interestingly enough the two wives of Brahma

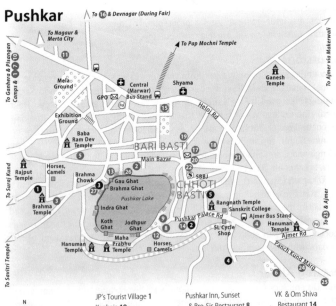

Pushkar

Sleeping 🛏
Bharatpur Palace 13
Chandra Lake 26
Colonel's Camp 10
Inn Seventh Heaven 21
Jagat Palace 23

JP's Tourist Village 1
Kanhaia 19
Lake View 2
Navratan Palace 3
New Park 25
Oasis 4
Paramount 5
Peacock Holiday
  Resort 6
Peacock International
  Camp 16
Purple Garden 18

Pushkar Inn, Sunset
  & Bro-Sis Restaurant 8
Pushkar Palace 9
Pushkar Resorts 7
Pushkar Villas Resort 24
Rainbow 27
RTDC Tourist Village 11
Sarovar 12
Shanti Palace 20
Shiva Guest House
  & Sri Savitri 17
Shyam Krishna 22

VK & Om Shiva
  Restaurant 14
White House &
  Raghav Resort 15

Eating 🍴
Juice Centre 1
Little Italy Pizzería 4
Moondance 2
Rainbow 3
Venus 5

Ghat (steps) ≡

have hilltop temples on either side of the lake, with the Brahma temple in the valley. A steep 3-km climb up the hill which leads to the **Savitri Temple** (dedicated to Brahma's first wife), offers excellent views of the town and surrounding desert.

The **Main (Sadar) Bazar** is full of shops selling typical tourist, as well as pilgrim knick-knacks and is usually very busy. At full moon, noisy religious celebrations last all night so you may need your ear plugs here.

Excursions

Merta City, the fortified town west of Persistan Pushkar, is associated with Mira Bai of Chittaurgarh, who was renowned as a poet. The station is at Merta Road. **Khejarla**, a small village south, is another convenient place to break your journey. The massive turreted fort gives good views over the surrounding arid countryside. Nearby is a small shrine on a large rock with a Surya-Naka stone with a small 'D' shaped hole – those who can wriggle through it prove they have no sin! There is an unfinished step well which a mystic abandoned having built single-handed over just two nights.

⊜ Sleeping

Jaipur to Ajmer *p233*
AL Kuchaman Fort (Heritage Hotel), Kuchaman, T01586-220 882, www.thekuchamanfort.com. 35 distinctive a/c rooms in a part of the fort, attractively furnished, restaurant, bar, jacuzzi, gym, luxurious pools (including a 200-year old cavernous one underground), camel/horse riding, royal hospitality, superb views and interesting tour around the largely unrestored fort.
B Phool Mahal Old City, Kishangarh, T01463-247 405, www.royalkishangarh.com, superbly located at the base of Kishangarh Fort on the banks of Gundalao lake (dries up in summer). This 1870 garden palace has 16 well maintained a/c rooms, as well as an elegant lounge and dining room, all with period furnishings and marble floors. There's also a chance to see the owner's exquisite collection of miniature paintings
B Roopangarh Fort (Heritage Hotel), Roopangarh, T01497-220 217, www.royalkishangarh.com. 20 large, high-ceilinged rooms, rich in character although some of the furnishing is quite basic, Queen's Suite is really special. Marwar decor and cuisine, 18th-century miniatures, free village safaris plus excursions to Makrana and Sambhar salt lake, good sunrise and sunset views, friendly staff.
D Sambhar Lake Resorts, Sambhar Lake, T01425-224 034. 6 cottage rooms, bath with hot showers (but need improving), friendly staff, camel rides and jeep safaris across the saline marshes and sand dunes, also arranges short rail journey on diesel locomotive driven trolleys that carry salt from the pans to the towns. Rs1150 includes meals and safaris. Day visit (Rs 500) includes veg lunch, tea and a tour of the salt marshes by camel cart or rail trolley.

Ajmer *p234, map p235*
Prices rise sharply, as much as 10 times, during the week of the Pushkar mela. Many hotels are booked well in advance. The tourist office, T52426, has a list of Paying Guest accommodation.
A Mansingh Palace, Ana Sagar Circular Rd, Vaishali Nagar, T0145-242 5702, www.mansinghhotels.com. 60 rooms in attractive sandstone building modern and the most comfortable in town. Pleasant restaurant, comfortable bar and clean pool.
B-C Hotel Embassy, opposite City Power House, Jaipur Rd, T0145-262 3859, hotel embassy@hotmail.com. 31 smart a/c rooms in building undergoing renovation to 3-star standard. Enthusiastic, professional staff, elegant restaurant.
C-D Aaram, off Ana Sagar Circular Rd, opposite Mansingh, T0145-242 5250. 22 slightly grubby rooms, some a/c, restaurant, small garden, friendly manager.
C-D Hotel Ajmeru, Khailand Market, near Akbar Fort, T0145-243 1103, www.hotel ajmeru.com. 12 very clean, light, modern rooms, 8 a/c, in relatively quiet location.
C-D Hotel Jannat, very close to Durgah, T0145-243 2494, www.ajmerhoteljannat. 36 clean, modern rooms in great location, friendly staff, a/c restaurant, all mod cons.

C-D Khadim (RTDC), Savitri Girls' College Rd, near bus station, T0145-262 7490. 55 rooms, some a/c (**C** suites), best are the uncarpeted rooms which have been recently renovated to a good standard, dorm (Rs 50), gloomy restaurant, bar, Tourist Information, car hire, pleasant setting, usual RTDC service.

C-D Regency, Delhi Gate, near Dargah, T0145-262 2439, www.bahubalugroup.com. 24 ordinary rooms, some a/c, off unloved corridors. Lobby has feel of unfilled pool, a/c restaurant, bar, travel, in very crowded area but set back from road, genial management.

C-E Nagpal, opposite railway station, T0145-262 7427. 19 rooms, 3 a/c, sizes vary widely but all well maintained, rooms at rear less noisy.

D Fort Khejarla, Khejarla, T02930-8311. Simple rooms in the old part, meals (Rs 180), excursions to Raika and Bishnoi tribal villages. Contact Curvet India, Delhi T011-2684 0037.

D Haveli Heritage Inn, Kutchery Rd, T0145-262 1607. 8 good-sized, clean, comfortable rooms in homely 125 year old building. Family run, good home cooking, located on busy main road but set back with a pleasant courtyard, very charming owner.

D Raj Palace Motel, Merta Rd, T1590-220 202, 25 clean rooms with bath, 6 a/c, friendly family. Recommended.

E Hotel Lovely, opposite Sabji Mandi, Agra Gate, T0145-262 2191. 8 okay rooms in modern building, friendly, hard-working owner.

E-F KEM, Station Rd, T0145-242 9936. 45 rooms in period building near the railway station, 1st class rooms are clean and acceptable, 2nd class less so. Service practically non-existant. Attached bath.

Pushkar *p238, map p238*

The town suffers from early morning temple bells. During the fair, hotel charges can be 10 times the normal rate. Booking in advance is essential for the better places. Some budget hotels offer views of the lake from communal rooftops; to escape the noise of the Main Bazar, choose one in a back street of Bari Basti or near Ajmer Bus Stand.

L-A Pushkar Palace (WelcomHeritage), on lakeside, T0145-277 2001, pushkarpalace.com. 52 tasteful, well-appointed rooms, including 25 suites overlooking the lake, in beautifully renovated old palace. The dining room and lakeside terrace are outstanding, gardens also lovely. Common areas are well-maintained, helpful staff. Recommended.

A Jagat Palace (WelcomHeritage), Ajmer Rd, T0145-277 2001, www.pushkarpalace.com. 36 a/c rooms in new building made to resemble a Rajput fort, colourful, naturally-lit interiors, attractive vegetarian restaurant, beautiful pool and gardens, room sizes vary.

A Pushkar Resorts, Ganhera Village, Motisar Rd, 5 km out of town, T0145-277 2944, www.pushkarresorts.com. Pushkar's most upmarket resort, 40 individual a/c cottages decorated in European style, extensive gardens, delicious meals (home-grown produce), beautiful pool, sports (putting green, golf practice tees), book/handicraft shop, unique camel kafila (caravan) tours, desert jeep safaris, quite an oasis.

C Pushkar Villas Resort, Panch Kund Rd, T0145-277 2689, arajoria@hotmail.com. Newish place which feels a little unfinished, very popular with tourist taxi drivers. 13 good-sized rooms (7 a/c) around pleasant gardens and a well-maintained pool.

C-D New Park, Panch Kund Rd, T0145-277 2464, www.newparkpushkar.com. Some distance from town but set in a peaceful location surrounded by fields. 24 adequate if pricey rooms (14 a/c), lovely gardens, pool.

C-E JP's Tourist Village Resort, Ganhera, 2 km from town, T0145-277 2067, www.pushkarhotelbooking.com. 30 very rustic, basic rooms built in traditional style, with mud walls, thatched roofs, hand painted decorations and too basic bathrooms. Whole place has pleasantly quirky feel, great gardens, dusty pool, terrific treehouses, definitely different.

C-F Sarovar (RTDC), on lakeside, T0145-277 2040. 38 clean rooms (best with lake view, in old part), some a/c with bath, cheap 6-bed dorm, set around courtyard in former lakeside palace, indifferent vegetarian restaurant, attractive gardens.

D-E Bharatpur Palace, lakeside, T0145-277 2320. 18 unusually decorated rooms, with clean bathrooms and exceptional views of the ghats.

D-E Chandra Lake, on Chandra Ghat, T0145-277 2896. 6 to 8 very basic rooms and bathrooms but what a view! If you can do without your creature comforts, it's a hugely authentic experience.

D-E Inn Seventh Heaven, next to Mali ka Mandir, T0145-510 5455, www.inn-sev enth-heaven.com. 8 beautiful rooms in a fantastically well restored 100-year-old *haveli*. Very friendly, informal atmosphere, particularly in excellent rooftop restaurant, charming owner. Highly recommended.

D-E Navratan Palace, near Brahma temple, T0145-277 2981, F277 2225. 33 clean rooms, some a/c with hot showers (Rs 300-600), comfortable though not particularly attractive, clean pool, small garden with views. Well maintained but some have found management unfriendly.

D-E Peacock Holiday Resort, 1 km from centre, near Ajmer Bus Stand, T0145-277 2093, arajoria@hotmail.com. 30 rooms, some a/c, pleasant shady courtyard and small clean pool, rooms vary in size but are all a reasonable standard, laid-back staff.

D-E Sunset, on the lake, T0145-277 2382, hotelsunset@hotmail.com. 20 plain, clean rooms, 3 a/c, around attractive garden. Well located close to lake, plus access to Sunset Café (see below). There are 6 more similar rooms in **Pushkar Inn** on same grounds.

D-F Oasis, near Ajmer Bus Stand, T0145-277 2100, www.hoteloasispushkar.com. 34 clean rooms with bath, some a/c, in motel-style arrangement, garden, well maintained pool.

D-F Paramount Palace, Bari Basti, T0145-277 2428, hotelparamountpalace@hot mail.com. 16 clean, basic rooms, some with bath, best with balcony elevated site with splendid views from rooftop.

E-F Kanhaia, near Mali Mandir, T0145-277 2146. 14 rooms, best has sofa, with good bathrooms and friendly staff, good value.

E-F Lake View, on lake, T0145-277 2106, www.lakeviewpushkar.com. Great views of lake make up for very average rooms, views from rooftop superb.

E-F Raghav Resort, Panday Nursery Farm, T0145-277 2207, www.lakeviewpushkar.com. 14 reasonable rooms surrounded by beautiful nursery gardens, attractive outdoor restaurant, a peaceful retreat.

E-F VK, near Pushkar Palace, T0145-277 2174. 13 clean, basic rooms, some with bath and 24-hr hot water (power shower!), **Om Shiva** garden restaurant nearby, has that slightly unfinished feel.

E-F White House, in narrow alley near Marwar Bus Stand, T0145-277 2147,

hotelwhitehouse@hotmail.com. 10 very clean, impressively white rooms in well maintained building overlooking nursery gardens. Good views from pleasant rooftop restaurant, free mango tea. Recommended.

F Mona Lisa, near Ram Ghat, T0145-277 2356. 10 rooms with common bath, pleasant atmosphere, hot showers, friendly.

F Purple Garden, near Gautam Ashram, Choti Basti, T0145-277 2920, purplegardenhotel@yahoo.co.in. 7 basic but well-maintained rooms with attached bathrooms, plus 4 with common facilities, and some nice touches added by the owner's New Zealand wife. Central garden is indeed purple and looks especially pleasant from the small rooftop café. Recommended. Camel safaris also arranged, see below.

F Rainbow, Mahadev Chowk, T0145-277 3309. 11 rooms with bath and hot water, rooftop restaurant with pool table and good views but noisy area.

F Shanti Palace, near Varah temple, Y0145-277 2422, shantipalace@hotmail.com. 12 basic rooms in very peaceful surroundings, plus a pleasant owner and good views of town from the roof.

F Shiva Guest house, near market post office, T0145-277 2120. Basic but clean rooms in calm environment enhanced by presence of 7 tortoises in central courtyard.

F Shubham Palace, near Sub Tahseal, T0145-277 3695, vandanagupta280@ yahoo.com. 10 basic rooms in very homely and relaxing homestay, with plenty of shaded outdoor seating.

F Shyam Krishna Guest House, Chhoti Basti, T0145-277 2461. Part of 200-year old temple complex with 25 rooms around a courtyard, some with *jali* work on upper floor, run by friendly Brahmin family.

F Sri Savitri, near market post office, T0145-277 2327. 7 slightly ramshackle but characterful rooms, comes highly recommended by frequent visitors, not least for the friendly owner.

During the fair

It is best to visit early in this week when toilets are still reasonably clean.

Tourist Village is erected by RTDC. A remarkable feat, it accommodates 100,000 people. Conveniently placed with deluxe/ super deluxe tents (Rs 5-6,000 with meals), ordinary/dorm tents (Rs 200 per bed), 30 'cottages', some deluxe (Rs 4000; Rs 350-850 off-season). Beds and blankets, some running water, Indian toilets are standard. Meals are served in a separate tent (or eat delicious cheap, local food at the tribal tented villages near the show ground). Reservation with payment, essential (open 12 months ahead); contact RTDC, Chandralok Building, 36 Jan Path, New Delhi 110001, or at Jaipur.

Others, privately run charge about US$ 150-250 including meals for Regular and 'Swiss' double tent (US$15 extra bed). Some private camps are some distance from fair ground and may lack security:

Colonel's Camp, Motisar Rd, Ghanera, T0141-220 2034, www.meghniwas.com. 120 Deluxe tents with toilet and shower in attractive gardens.

Peacock International Camp Resort, T0145-277 2689. 25 tents with common facilities among orchards with pool at Devnagar (2 km from Mela Ground), free transport.

Pushkar Palace (see above). Sets up 50 'Swiss' tents and 50 Deluxe.

Royal Tents Camp (WelcomHeritage) comfortable tents with verandah, flush toilet, hot water in buckets or shower of sorts, Rajasthani cuisine, very well organized. Reserve through WelcomHeritage or T0291-251 0101.

Wanderlust Desert Camp, T011-2467 9059, www.wanderlustindia.cim. 120 Swiss tents with bath, electricity, varied meals.

⊙ Eating

Ajmer *p234, map p235*
Son halwa, a local sweet speciality, is sold near the dargah and at the market near Station Road (try **Azad**).

♥♥♥ **Mansingh Palace**, Ana Sagar Circular Rd. International. Pricey, unexciting food.

♥♥ **Mango Masala**, Sandar Patel Marg, T0145-242 2100. American Diner-styled place with wide-ranging menu including pizzas, sizzlers, Indian and sundaes. Standard is high, portions large and service outstanding.

♥♥ **Silver Leaf**, in Embassy Hotel (see above). Good range of multi-cuisine choices in sophisticated surroundings.

♥ **Bhola**, Agra Gate, good vegetarian food, no nonsense service.

♥ **Honey Dew**, Station Rd. Indian, Continental. Pleasant shady garden, good Indian snacks all day, disappointing Western.

♥ **Jai Hind**, in alley by clock tower, opposite railway station. Best for Indian vegetarian. Delicious, cheap meals.

♥ **Madeen**, opposite station. Simple but tasty.

♥ **Tandoor**, Jaipur Rd, 1 km from bus station. Dinner in the garden with log fires, a/c section for lunch, good food (try paneer butter masala and tandoori chicken), cake shop, icecreams, also snacks to takeaway, cyber café. Recommended.

Pushkar *p238, map p238*
No meat, fish or eggs are served in this temple town. Alcohol and 'narcotics' are banned. Take special care during the fair: eat only freshly cooked food and drink bottled water. Long-stay budget travellers have encouraged western and Israeli favourites like falafel and apple pie, while Nepali and Tibetan immigrants have brought their own specialities. Roadside vendors offer a variety of cheap, filling *thalis*, such as 'Govinda' close to Ajmer bus stand. Non-vegetarian dishes are sold only out of town.

♥♥ **Honey & Spice Café**, in alleyway of Laxmi Market, old Rangji Temple Complex, fantastic coffee, cakes and light meals, superb.

♥♥ **Little Italy Pizzeria**, Panch Kund Rd, high quality Italian dishes supervised by ex-pat Italian chef, plus Israeli and Indian specialities.

♥♥ **Moondance**, just by the turning to Pushkar Palace. Western. Run by friendly Nepalese, service can be slow. Recommended.

♥♥ **Pushkar Palace**, recommended for evening buffet in luxurious surroundings with great view over the lake. Inn Seventh Heaven (see above) great food, great atmosphere.

♥ **Halwai ki gali** and other sweet shops sell malpura (syrupy pancake), as well as usual Rajasthani/Bengali sweets.

♥ **Karmima**, and other small places opposite Ashish-Manish Riding, offer home cooked *thalis* (Rs 15/20) and excellent fresh, pure orange/sweet lime juice.

♥ **Om Shiva**, 20 m from **VK Hotel** in a garden. Good breakfasts (brown bread, garlic cheese, pancakes, fruit), buffets (Rs 45) or à la carte, well presented and hygienic. Another branch, opposite State Bank of Bikaner & Jaipur, is inferior.

¶ **RS**, near Brahma Temple. Good Indian, some Chinese and western (Rs 40-50).

¶ **Rainbow** (above Krishna), Brahma Chowk. Wide choice (pizzas, jacket potatoes, enchiladas, humus, falafel, Indian dishes), fruit crumble with choc sauce and ice cream.

¶ **Sunset Café** by Pushkar Palace overlooking lake. Particularly atmospheric in the evening when crowds gather to listen to music and watch sunset, very extensive menu. Recommended.

¶ **Venus**, Ajmer Rd. Mixed menu. A la carte (good sizzlers) in the garden, also *thalis* (Rs 40), on the attractive rooftop.

⊛ Festivals and events

Ajmer *p234, map p235*
The **Urs Festival** commemorating Khwaja Mu'inuddin Chishti's death in 1235 is celebrated with 6 days of almost continuous music, and devotees from all over India and the Middle East make the pilgrimage. Qawwalis and other Urdu music developed in the courts of rulers can be heard. Roses cover the tomb. The festival starts on sighting the new moon in Rajab, the 7th month of the Islamic year. The peak is reached on the night between the 5th and 6th days when tens of thousands of pilgrims pack the shrine. At 1100 on the last morning, pilgrims and visitors are banned from the dargah, as the khadims, who are responsible through the year for the main-tenance of worship at the shrine, dressed in their best clothes, approach the shrine with flowers and sweets. On the final day, women wash the tomb with their hair, then squeeze the rose water into bottles as medicine for the sick.

Pushkar *p238, map p238*
Kartik Purnima is marked by a vast **cattle and camel fair** (12-15 Nov 2005, 2-5 Nov 2006, 21-24 Nov 2007'), see box. Pilgrims bathe in the lake, the night of the full moon being the most auspicious time, and float 'boats' of marigold and rose petals in the moonlight. Camel traders often arrive a few days early to engage in the serious business of buying and selling and most of the animals disappear before the official starting

date. Arrive 3 days ahead if you don't want to miss this part of the fair. The all-night drumming and singing in the Tent City can get very tiring, but the fair is a unique spectacle. Travellers warn of pickpockets.

○ Shopping

Ajmer *p234, map p235*
Fine local silver jewellery, tie-and-dye textiles and camel hide articles are best buys. The shopping areas are Madar Gate, Station Rd, Purani Mandi, Naya Bazar and Kaisarganj. Some of the alleys in the old town have good shopping.
Arts and Art's, Bhojan Shala, near Jain Temple.

Pushkar *p238, map p238*
There is plenty to attract the western eye; check quality and bargain hard.

Cloth
Essar, shop 6, Sadar Bazar, opposite Narad Kunj. Excellent **tailoring** (jacket Rs 250-300 including fabric).
Harish, Brahma Temple Rd, for light weight razai quilts, bedsheets, cloth bags.

Didgeridoos
Niru's Didg Shop, near PNB Bank, make your own, have some lessons, all things didgeridoo.

Hairdressing and massage
Many hotels now offer health clubs, barbers, massages, yoga.
Shri Ram Janta, Chhoti Basti Ghat, No 12. Offers "bone crack", with "turbo-powered hands"! (Rs 50) – also henna, haircuts, hand painting.

Paintings
Miniatures on silk and old paper are everywhere.
JP Dhabai's, opposite Shiva Cloth Store near Payal Guest House, Main Bazar. Offers fine quality (painted with a single squirrel hair!) at a price. Recommended.

▲ Activities and tours

Pushkar *p238, map p238*
Horses Rs 150-200 per hr, camel Rs 30-50 per hr, at most hotels and near Brahma temple.

Lessons: Rs 150 per hr (minimum 10 hr over 5 days) from **Ashish- Manish**, opposite Brahma Temple, or **Shannu's Riding School**, owned by a French Canadian, Panch Kund Rd, T0145-277 2043. For camel safaris that come well recommended contact **Purple Garden** hotel on T0145-277 2920.
For swimming pools: **Sarovar**, **Oasis**, **Peacock hotels**, non-residents pay Rs 40-50. At Pushkar Palace Hotel, **Pushkar Travels**, offer tours, excellent service, good buses, ticketing Rs 50. Avoid Shiva Travel Agents.

⊖ Transport

Jaipur to Ajmer *p233*
For **Sambhar Lake** take the train to **Phulera**, 7 km from Sambhar village, 9 km from the lake. Jeeps charge Rs 50 for the transfer.

Kishangarh is an important railway junction between **Jaipur** and **Ajmer**, with regular trains from both places.

Ajmer *p234, map p235*
Auto rickshaw
To **Pushkar**, Rs 60 after bargaining.

Bus
Enquiries, T0145-242 9398. Buses every 30 mins to **Agra**, rs157, 9 hrs, **Delhi**, rs177, 9 hrs, **Jaipur**, rs56, 2½ hrs, **Jodhpur**, rs89, 5 hrs; **Bikaner**, rs116, 7 hrs; **Chittaurgarh** rs 79, 5hrs **Udaipur** rs120, 7hrs via Chittaurgarh, **Kota** via Bundi. Buses for **Pushkar** (Rs 10) which leave from near the station, are very crowded.

Jeep
Good option to get to **Pushkar** but difficult to get.

Train
Ajmer Station is seemingly overrun with rats and is not a great place to wait for a night train. Mansingh Palace Hotel allows short-stay rates, useful if you have a wait of several hours.

Reservations, T0145-243 1965, 0830-1330, 1400-1630, enquiries, T131/132. Adequate station restaurant. **Ahmadabad**: *Aravali Exp, 9708*, 1005, 11½ hrs; *Ahmadabad Mail, 9106*, 0735, 10 hrs; *Ashram Exp, 2916*, 2325, 8½ hrs, last 3 via Beawar, 1 hr; **Chittaurgarh**: *Ahmadabad Exp, 9943*, 0750, 5 hrs; *Chetak Exp,*

9615, 0150, 4½ hrs. **Jaipur**: *AjmerJaipur Exp, 9652*, 0640, 3 hrs. *Aravali Exp, 9707*, 1733, 2½ hrs; *Shatabdi Exp, 2016*, 1530, not Sun, 2 hrs. **Delhi**: *Ahmadabad Delhi Mail, 9105*, 2033, 9 hrs; *Shatabdi Exp, 2016* not Sun, 1530, 6½ hrs; (OD) *Ashram Exp, 2915*, 0215, 8 hrs; **Jaipur**: *Aravali Exp, 9707*, 1735, 2½ hrs. **Jodhpur**: *Jodhpur Mail, 4893*, 0545, 6 hrs. **Udaipur**: *Ahmadabad Exp, 9943*, 0750, 8½ hrs.

Pushkar *p238, map p238*
Auto-rickshaw
To **Ajmer** Rs 60 after bargaining.

Bicycle/motorbike
Rs 10 entry 'tax' per vehicle. Hire: **Michael Cycle SL Cycles**, Ajmer Bus Stand Rd, very helpful, Rs 3 per hr, Rs 25 per day; also from the market. **Hotel Oasis** has Vespa scooters, Rs 300 per day. Enfield Ashram, near **Hotel Oasis**, Rs 400 per day for an Enfield.

Bus
Frequent service to/from **Ajmer** Rs10. Direct buses to **Jodhpur** via Merta (8 hrs) but it is quicker to return to Ajmer and take an express bus (4-5 hrs) from there ('First class' passengers travel on the roof!). Pushkar Travels, good minibuses; avoid Shrinath Travels, overcrowded, often late, charges last minute premiums.

Car
Rs 10 entry 'tax' per vehicle. **Delhi**, 8 hrs; **Jaipur**, 3 hrs.

⊙ Directory

Ajmer *p234, map p235*
Banks Bank of Baroda, opposite GPO, accepts Visa, Mastercard; State Bank of India near Bus Stand, changes cash, TCs. SBI, near bus stand. Also government approved money changers in Kavandas Pura main market.

Pushkar *p238, map p238*
Banks SBBJ changes TCs; Hotels Peacock and Oasis offer exchange for a small commission.
Internet Near Oasis Hotel, Ajmer Bus Stand, and now all over town.
Hospitals Shyama, Heloj Rd, T72087.
Post One at the Chowk with a very helpful Postmaster, east end of Main Bazar.

Northern Rajasthan

Bikaner and around	248
Bikaner	249
Around Bikaner	250
Listings	252
Shekhawati	256
Sights	257
Listings	262

⚇ Footprint features

Don't miss	245
Life after the rains	254
Fit for a merchant	258
The love story of Dhola and Maru	260

Introduction

This is one of the less-visited regions of Rajasthan, but is well worth passing through on your way to the better known areas. **Bikaner**, perhaps the least touristy big city in Rajasthan, has until now been somewhat overshadowed by the state's other cities, but is gaining popularity both as an interesting place to visit in its own right, and as a place to go for a camel safari; as scenic as Jaisalmer but far less commercial. Even further off the beaten track, desert villages such as **Kakoo** offer an accessible insight in to rural desert life, while wildlife enthusiasts will find plenty of interest in both **Gajner National Park** and **Tal Chappar Wildlife Sanctuary**.

Shekawati has its own quirky charm; still largely undeveloped, its outdoor treasures sit as silent testimony to an illustrious past, strangely at odds with the day to day bustle on their doorsteps. The region's boom days, when the indigenous Marwari businessmen were trading with the four corners of the globe, constantly vying to out do each other in the elaborateness of their *haveli* homes, are long gone. Marwari traders still enjoy a reputation as astute businessmen, but today operate in India's major business centres, many of their *havelis* having fallen in to disrepair but still intact enough to give a fascinating glimpse of a time gone by. It's an area which should be experienced rather than glimpsed at; the numerous horse, camel and bicycle safaris on offer represent the perfect pace of travel in this unrushed region.

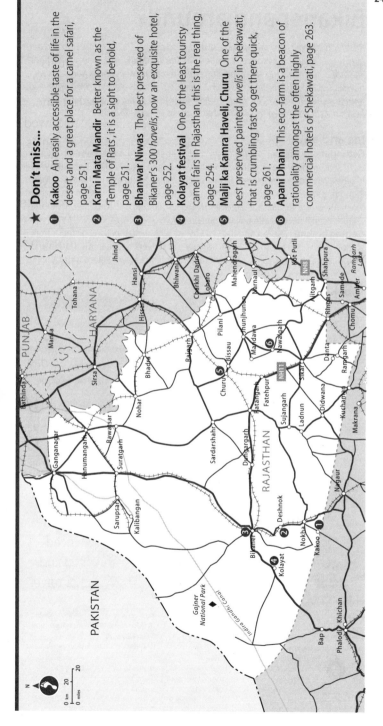

★ Don't miss...

① **Kakoo** An easily accessible taste of life in the desert, and a great place for a camel safari, page 251.

② **Karni Mata Mandir** Better known as the 'Temple of Rats', it is a sight to behold, page 251.

③ **Bhanwar Niwas** The best preserved of Bikaner's 300 *havelis*, now an exquisite hotel, page 252.

④ **Kolayat festival** One of the least touristy camel fairs in Rajasthan, this is the real thing, page 254.

⑤ **Malji ka Kamra Haveli, Churu** One of the best preserved painted *havelis* in Shekawati, that is crumbling fast so get there quick, page 261.

⑥ **Apani Dhani** This eco-farm is a beacon of rationality amongst the often highly commercial hotels of Shekawati, page 263.

Bikaner and around

Bikaner is an oasis town among scrub and sand dunes. The rocky outcrop in a barren landscape provides a dramatic setting for the Junagarh Fort, one of the finest in western Rajasthan. The old walled city retains a medieval air, and is home to over 300 havelis, while outside the walls some stunning palaces survive. Well off the usual tourist route, Bikaner is en route to Jaisalmer from Jaipur or Shekhawati, and well worth a visit. ▶▶ *For Sleeping, Eating and other listings see pages 252-256.*

Ins and outs

Getting there Bikaner is a full day's drive from Jaipur so it may be worth stopping a night in Samode or the Shekhawati region (see pages 135 and 256). The railway station is central and has services from Delhi (Sarai Rohilla), Jaipur and Jodhpur. The New Bus Stand is 3 km to the north but if coming from the south you can ask to be dropped in town. There are regular bus services to Desnok, but to get to Gajner, Kakoo or Tal Chappar you'll need to hire private transport. ▶▶ *See Transport, page 255, for further details.*

Getting around The fort and the Old City are within easy walking distance from the station. Autos and cycle-rickshaws transfer passengers between the station and the New Bus Stand. Taxis can be difficult to get from the Lalgarh Palace area at night.

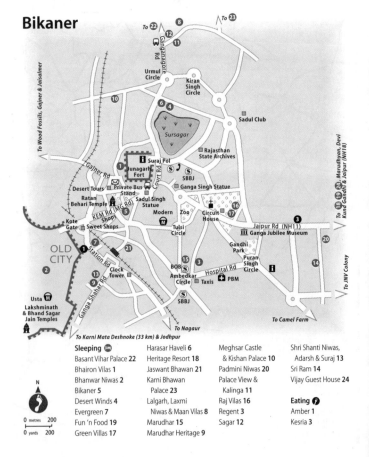

Bikaner

Sleeping			
Basant Vihar Palace 22	Harasar Haveli 6	Meghsar Castle	Shri Shanti Niwas,
Bhairon Vilas 1	Heritage Resort 18	& Kishan Palace 10	Adarsh & Suraj 13
Bhanwar Niwas 2	Jaswant Bhawan 21	Padmini Niwas 20	Sri Ram 14
Bikaner 5	Karni Bhawan	Palace View &	Vijay Guest House 24
Desert Winds 4	Palace 23	Kalinga 11	
Evergreen 7	Lalgarh, Laxmi	Raj Vilas 16	**Eating**
Fun 'n Food 19	Niwas & Maan Vilas 8	Regent 3	Amber 1
Green Villas 17	Marudhar 15	Sagar 12	Kesria 3
	Marudhar Heritage 9		

N

0 metres 200
0 yards 200

Bikaner→ *Phone code: 0151. Colour map 2, grid B3. Population: 530,000.*

Bikaner is an oasis town among scrub and sand dunes. The rocky outcrop in a barren landscape provides a dramatic setting for the Junagarh Fort, one of the finest in western Rajasthan. The old walled city retains a medieval air, and is home to over 300 *havelis*, while outside the walls some stunning palaces survive. Well off the usual tourist route, Bikaner is en route to Jaisalmer from Jaipur or Shekhawati, and well worth a visit The area around Bikaner also has some notable diversions; the infamous 'rat temple' at Deshnok and nearby Kakoo to the south, and the wildlife sanctuaries of Gajner and tal Chappar to the east and west.

Background
Bikaner was set up as an independent kingdom in 1488 by Rao Bikaji, the younger son of Jodhpur's founder, Rao Jodha. Protected by the harsh desert countryside and by the military rulers who even humbled Aurangzeb's powerful Mughal army, it developed as a major centre in the cross-desert caravan trade. Even today, Bikaner's Marwari traders are noted throughout North India for their business acumen.

Like other desert trading cities, Bikaner would have decayed into a small town of little significance with the development of the sea ports but for the foresight of the still highly revered **Maharajah Ganga Singhji** who introduced wide ranging economic reforms which ensured the survival of the city. Among his greatest achievements was the 1927-1928 **Bikaner Gang Canal** which turned 285,000 ha of arid scrub into cultivable land.

Sights
Junagarh Fort ⓘ *1000-1630 (last entry), Rs 50, Indians Rs 10; camera Rs 30, video Rs 100 (limited permission), guided tours in Hindi and English, private guides near the gate offer better 'in-depth' tours; Rs 100 for 4, 2 hrs,* is one of the finest examples in Rajasthan of the paradox between medieval military architecture and beautiful interior decoration. Started in 1588 by Raja Rai Singh (1571-1611), a strong ally of the Mughal Empire, who led Akbar's army in numerous battles, it had palaces added for the next three centuries.

You enter the superbly preserved fort by the yellow sandstone **Suraj Prole** (Sun Gate, 1593) to the east. The pale red sandstone perimeter wall is surrounded by a moat (the lake no longer exists) while the Chowks have beautifully designed palaces with balconies, kiosks and fine *jali* screens. The interiors are beautifully decorated with shell-work, lime plaster, mirror-and-glass inlays, gold leaf, carving, carpets and lacquer work. The ramparts offer good views of the elephant and horse stables and temples, the old city with the desert beyond, and the relatively more recent city areas around the medieval walls.

The walls of the **Lal Niwas**, which are the oldest, are elaborately decorated in red and gold. Karan Singh commemorated a victory over Aurangzeb by building the **Karan Mahal** (1631-1639) across the Chowk. Successive rulers added the **Gaj Mandir** (1745-1787) with its mirrored Shish Mahal, and the **Chattra Niwas** (1872-1887) with its pitched roof and English 'field sport' plates decorating the walls.

The magnificent **Coronation Hall**, adorned with plaster work, lacquer, mirror and glass, is in Maharaja Surat Singh's **Anup Mahal** (1788-1828). The decorative façades around the Anup Mahal Chowk, though painted white, are in fact of stone. The fort also includes the **Chetar Mahal** and **Chini Burj** of Dungar Singh (1872-1887) and **Ganga Niwas** of Ganga Singh (1898-1943), who did much to modernize his state and also built the Lalgarh Palace to the north. Mirror work, carving and marble decorate the ornate **Chandra Mahal** (Moon Palace) and the **Phul Mahal** (Flower Palace), built by Maharaja Gaj Singh. These last two are shown to foreigners at the end as a 'special tour' when the guide expects an extra tip! The royal chamber in the Chandra Mahal has strategically placed mirrors so that any intruder entering could be seen by the maharaja from his bed.

The fort **museum** has Sanskrit and Persian manuscripts, miniature paintings, jewels, enamelware, silver, weapons, palanquins, howdahs, and war drums. During the Second World War, Ganga Singhji was a signatory to the Versailles treaty, and pictures of his life and rule, the bi-plane he received as a war memento, and other princely relics of the period can be seen in the fort. **Har Mandir**, the royal temple where birth and wedding ceremonies were celebrated, is still used for Gangaur and other festivities. The well nearby is reputedly over 130 m deep.

Prachina Museum ① *0900-1800, Rs 25 (guided tour), Rs10 Indians, shop, small clean café outside is open air but shady*, in the grounds, exhibits beautifully crafted costumes, carpets and ornamental objects.

Lalgarh Palace ① *palace closed Wed, museum closed Sun, 1000-1700, Rs 40 (museum extra Rs 20).* The red sandstone palace stands in huge grounds to the north of the city, surrounded by rocks and sand dunes. Designed by Sir Swinton Jacob in 1902, the palace complex, with extensions over the next few decades, has attractive courtyards overlooked by intricate *zenana* screen windows and *jarokha* balconies, columned corridors and period furnishings. The banquet hall is full of hunting trophies and photographs. His Highness Doctor Karni Singh of Bikaner was well known for his shooting expertise – both with a camera and with a gun. The bougainvillaea, parakeets and peacocks add to the attraction of the gardens in which the Bikaner State Railway Carriage is preserved. The Lalgarh complex now has several hotels (see Sleeping page 252). You can visit Lalgarh for a meal and to see the **Sri Sadul Museum** which houses old maps, some superb photos and royal memorabilia. Plenty of interest and well displayed.

Rampuria Street and the Purana Bazar There are some exquisite *havelis* in Bikaner belonging to the Rampuria, Kothari, Vaid and Daga merchant families. The sandstone carvings combine traditional Rajasthani *haveli* architecture with colonial influence. Around Rampuria Street and the Purana Bazar you can wander through lanes lined with fine façades. Among them is **Bhanwar Niwas** which has been converted into a heritage hotel.

Ganga Golden Jubilee Museum ① *Public Park, 1000-1630, Rs 3*, has a fine small collection of pottery, massive paintings, stuffed tigers, carpets, costumes and weapons. There are also some excellent examples of Bikaner miniature paintings which are specially prized because of their very fine quality. You can also see petrified wood fossils from the desert.

Around Bikaner

Bhand Sagar
① *Free but caretakers may charge Rs 10 for cameras.*
Some 5 km southwest, Bhand Sagar has a group of Hindu and Jain temples which are believed to be the oldest extant structures of Bikaner, dating from the days when it was just a desert trading out-post of Jodhpur. The white-painted sandstone **Bandeshwar Temple** with a towering *shikhara* roof and painted sculptures, murals, mirrorwork inside, is the most interesting. The **Sandeshwar Temple**, dedicated to

Neminath, has gold leaf painting, *meenakari* work and marble sculptures. They are hard to find and difficult to approach by car but rickshaw wallahs know the way. There are numerous steps but wonderful views. A longer excursion to Kalibangan to the north, is described below.

Gajner National Park

Now a part of a palace hotel, Gajner National Park, 30 km west of Bikaner, used to ba a private preserve which once provided the royal family of Bikaner with game. The park is a birder's paradise surrounded by 13,000 ha of scrub forest which also harbours large colonies of nilgai, chinkara, blackbuck, wild boar and desert reptiles. Throughout the day, a train of antelope, gazelle and pigs can be seen arriving to drink at the lake. Winter migratory birds include the Imperial black-bellied sand grouse, cranes and migratory ducks. Some visitors have spotted Great Indian bustard at the water's edge. There is a picnic spot by the lake from where visitors can view the birds. It is worth stopping for an hour's mini-safari if you are in the vicinity.

Kolayat

Some 50 km southwest via Gajner road, Kolayat is regarded as one of the 58 most Hindu important pilgrimage centres. It is situated around a sacred lake with 52 ghats and a group of five temples built by Ganga Singhji (none of which is architecturally significant). The oasis village comes alive at the November full moon when a three-day festival draws thousands of pilgrims who take part in ritual bathing.

Karni Mata Mandir

ⓘ *Closed 1200-1600, free, camera Rs 40.*

This 17th-century temple, 33 km south of Bikaner at Deshnoke, has massive silver gates and beautiful white marble carvings on the façade. These were added by Ganga Singh (1898-1943) who dedicated the temple to a 15th-century female mystic Karniji, worshipped as an incarnation of Durga. A gallery describes her life. Mice and rats, revered and fed with sweets and milk in the belief that they are reincarnated saints, swarm over the temple around your feet; spotting the white rat is supposed to bring good luck. Take socks as the floor is dirty, but note that the rats are far less widespread than they are made out to be. Sensationalized accounts give the impression of a sea of rats through which the visitor is obliged to walk barefoot, whereas in reality, while there are a good number of rats, they generally scurry around the outskirts of the temple courtyard – you're very unlikely to tread on one! The temple itself is beautiful, and would be well worth visiting even without the novelty of the rats.

Kakoo

This picturesque village, 75 km south of Bikaner, with attractive huts and surrounded by sand dunes, is the starting point for desert camel safaris costing Rs 1500 per day with tented facilities. Staying here makes a fantastic introduction to the practicalities of life in the desert; this is probably the most authentic desert settlement in this area that can be easily reached by road.

Camel Research Farm

ⓘ *closed Sun, 1430-1700 (not all the camels are there until 1600), Rs5, Rs10 camera.*

A pleasant cycle ride along a very quiet road, or hire a rickshaw, 9 km southeast, claims to be the only one in Asia. Home to over 300 camels, but slightly disorienting without a guide who are available for Rs100. It's worth having a look round the museum first. Rides can be arranged but there are no refreshments. Good views from the top of the tower.

One of North India's most important early settlement regions stretches from the Shimla hills down past the important Harappan sites of **Hanumangarh** and **Kalibangan**, north of Bikaner. Late Harappan sites have been explored by archaeologists, notably A Ghosh, since 1962. They were identified in the upper part of the valley, the easternmost region of the Indus Valley civilization. Across the border in Pakistan are the premier sites of Harappa (200 km) and Moenjo Daro (450 km). Here, the most impressive of the sites today is that of **Kalibangan** (west off the NH15 at Suratgarh). On the south bank of the Ghaggar River it was a heavily fortified citadel mound, rising about 10 m above the level of the plain. There were several pre-Harappan phases. Allchin and Allchin record that the bricks of the early phase were already standardized, though not to the same size as later Harappan bricks. The ramparts were made of mud brick and a range of pottery and ornaments have been found. The early pottery is especially interesting, predominantly red or pink with black painting.

● Sleeping

Bikaner p249, map p248
Budget hotel rooms usually have shared bath; often serve Indian veg food only. Tourist office has list of Paying Guest hotels.
AL-A Laxmi Niwas, Lalgarh Palace Complex, T0151-220 2777, www.laxminiwaspalace.com. 42 large, tastefully furnished rooms and suites with fabulous carvings and beautifully painted ceilings, all arranged around the stunningly ornate courtyard. Superb bar, restaurant and lounge, discreet but attentive service, absolutely unique. Recommended.
A Heritage Resort, along the Jaipur highway, '9 Km' post, T0151-752 393, www.carnival-hotels.com. 36 modern, well-appointed cottage rooms in a pleasant location. Attractive gardens, outdoor coffee shop, pool, 3-hole golf course, friendly management.
A Lalgarh Palace, 3 km from the railway, T0151-254 0201, lallgarhpalace@realbikaner.com. 38 large a/c rooms in beautiful and authentic surroundings (see Sights p249), magnificent indoor pool, atmospheric dining hall, mixed reports on food but quite an experience.
A Raj Vilas, Public Park, T0151-252 5901, www.rajvilaspalace.com. Large, modern hotel with 55 uninspired but functional central a/c rooms, 2 restaurants and a cramped pool.
A-B Bhanwar Niwas, Rampuria St, Old City (500 m from Kote Gate), ask for Rampuria Haveli, T0151-2 52 9323, www.bhanwarniwas.com. 26 beautifully decorated rooms (all different) around a fantastic courtyard in an exquisite early 20th-century *haveli*. Original decor has been painstakingly restored to

stunning effect, the last word in style, great service. Highly recommended
B Karni Bhawan Palace (HRH), Gandhi Colony behind Lalgarh Palace, T0151-252 4701, www.hrhindia.com. 12 comfortable a/c rooms and spacious suites in completely original art deco mansion. Elegant furniture, modern fittings, good restaurant, large garden, peaceful, attentive service, feels like the original inhabitants have just stepped out for a while.
C Basant Vihar Palace, Ganganagar Rd, T0151-225 0675, www.basantviharpalace.com. Rooms in attractive early-20th century palatial sandstone mansion built by Maharajah Ganga Sinhji, magnificent darbar hall, pool, large gardens, old lily ponds.
C Bhairon Vilas, near fort, T0151-254 4751, www.hotelbaironvilas.tripod.com. Restored 1800s aristocratic *haveli*, great atmosphere, 18 eclectic rooms decorated with flair, excellent rooftop restaurant (musicians, dancers), good views, lawn, a carnival of kitsch but mixed reports about the service.
C Fun 'n Food, NH11 8 km from town, T0151-752 589, www.realbikaner.com. Good option for families; reasonable rooms plus 2 swimming pools, fairground rides and a boating lake.
C Sagar, next to Lalgarh Palace, T0151-520 677, www.sagarhotelbikaner.com. 42 reasonable rooms in modern building, half with a/c, plus 6 round huts, popular restaurant, expensive exchange, reports of poor service, strong commercial bias.
C-D Padmini Niwas, 148 Sadul Ganj, T0151-252 2794, padmini_hotel@rediffmail.com.

8 (4 more planned) clean, basic, comfy rooms (some a/c) in laid back bungalow in quiet location. Swimming pool under construction, pleasant lawn. Recommended.
C-D Palace View, near Lalgarh Palace, T0151-527 072. 15 clean, comfortable rooms (some a/c), good views of palace and gardens, food to order, small garden, courteous, hospitable family.
C-E Marudhar Heritage, Bhagwan Mahaveer Marg, near Station Rd, T0151-252 2524, hmheritage20000@yahoo.co.in. 27 variable rooms, aircooled or a/c, bath with hot showers (am), TV, clean and comfortable, generous *thalis* (Rs 50), friendly owner.
C-E Meghsar Castle, 9 Gajner Rd, T0151-527 315, www.hotelmeghsarcastle.com. 16 aircooled rooms in modern hotel built in traditional Rajput sandstone style, attractive garden, friendly manager.
C-F Harasar Haveli, opposite Karni Singh Stadium, T0151-220 9891, www.hotelharasar haveli.com. Notorious for paying hefty commissions to rickshaw drivers; often full when others are empty. Otherwise a nice enough place; 24 rooms (8 more plus swimming pool planned) in converted mansion, some with verandahs and good views, dining room with period memorabilia, plus great rooftop restaurant, garden, exchange, internet, clean and friendly.
D Hotel Bikaner, off KEM Rd, T0151-252 6516, hotlbkn@yahoo.com. Classic modern Indian-style hotel, clean and friendly, a/c rooms not bad value, a/c bar and restaurant.
D Jaswant Bhawan, Alakh Sagar Rd, near railway station, T0151-521 834. 12 rooms in a charming old building, quiet location, restaurant, lawn, good value. Recommended.
D Marudhar, Ambedkar Circle, T0151-204 853, hotelmarudhar@yahoo.com. 26 clean, well-maintained rooms, 9 a/c, friendly staff. Better than **Thar** and **Ashoka** next door.
D-E Desert Winds, opposite Karni Stadium, next to Harasar Haveli, T0151-254 2202. 6 clean, comfortable rooms, good food, pleasant balcony and garden, friendly family. Run by knowledgable ex-tourist officer.
D-E Hotel Regent, Sadul Colony, near PBM Hospital, T0151-254 1598, bituharisingh @yahoo.com. 11 modern, clean, comfortable

rooms, 4 a/c, in quiet area. Excellent home-cooked meals, owner Hari is a most hospitable and knowledgeable host, good value, recommended. Camel safaris also arranged.
D-E Sri Ram, A-228, Sadul Ganj, T0151-252 2651, www.hotelsriram. A hotel, guest house and youth hostel all in one building! 20 rooms, all clean and well-maintained, some a/c, run by hugely knowledgable and entertaining ex-army man and his family, ring ahead for free pick up. Recommended.
D-E Suraj Hotel, near Railway Station, Rani Bazar, T0151-2521 902, surajhotel@vsnl.com. 20 rooms in modern building, well run, slightly shabby but good value. Attached veg restaurant recommended.
D-F Shri Shanti Niwas, GS Rd, near Railway Station, T0151-542 320, shrishanti@vsnl.com. Wide range of rooms incl. some a/c, well maintained, friendly staff.
E Kalinga, Lallgarh Palace Complex, T0151-209 751. 9 clean, adequate rooms, a/c particularly good value.
E-F Evergreen, Station Rd, T0151-254 2061. Clean, professionally run and maintained to a high standard. Easily the best of the budget options in this area; consider nearby Delight and Deluxe only if this is full.
E-F Green Villas, behind Raj Vilas, T0151-252 1877. 4 simple, clean rooms in a friendly homestay, home-cooked meals great value.
E-F Vijay Guest House, opposite Sophia School, Jaipur Rd, T0151-223 1244, www.camelman.com. 6 clean rooms with attached bathrooms, plus 2 with common bath. Slightly distant location compensated for by free use of bicycles or scooter, free pick-ups from bus/train, and even free rickshaw rides to town. Delicious home cooked meals, pleasant garden, quiet, very hospitable (free tea and rum plus evening parties on lawn), knowledgeable host, great value. Recommended. Vijay's camel safaris also highly recommended.
E-F Vinayak Guest House, near Mataji Temple, Old Ginani, T0151-220 2634. Friendly homestay run by manager of URMUL shop, single women and couples preferred.
F Adarsh Guest House, GS Road, near the train station, T0151-206 731. 8 basic rooms set back from road, not bad for the money.

● For an explanation of sleeping and eating price codes used in this guide, see inside the
● front cover. Other relevant information is found in Essentials, see pages 40-45.

⠇ Life after the rains

When in Bikaner, try to spare the time to drop in at URMUL's showroom, Abhiviyakyi, opposite the new bus stand. A fair trade NGO, URMUL works with the marginalized tribespeople of the Thar desert. The droughts of the 1980s made farming, the traditional source of livelihood for the majority of these people, no longer a viable option. URMUL was formed in 1991 with the aim to teach these people new skills which could bring them the income that the absent rains had taken away. As the range of products on offer testifies, the project has been a huge success. All the items on sale, including clothing, tablecloths, bed linen, shoes and bags, have been made by the projects participants, and are of a quality previously unseen in the often all too amateur 'craft' sector.

F **Railway Retiring Rooms** and dorm are good value, reservations T524660.

Around Bikaner *p250*
A **Gajner Palace**, Gajner National Park, T01534-255 061, www.hrhindia.com. 44 a/c rooms in the elegantpalace and its wings, set by a beautiful lake., Rooms in main building full of character (Edwardian Raj nostalgia), those in wings well maintained but very middle England, a festival of flock. Sumptuous lounge bar and restaurant overlooking lake, magnificent gardens, boating, good walking (great views from Shabnam Cottage on a hilltop), pleasantly unfrequented and atmospheric, friendly manager and staff, no pool Visitors are welcome from 0800 to 1730, Rs 100.
E **Dr Karni Singh's Rest House**, adjoining the home of his forefathers, Kakoo, T01532-253 006. Has 6 simple rooms and 4 rustic huts with attached baths, hot water in buckets for overnight stay, only place in town but a great experience. Good camel safaris arranged, with the advantage of getting straight in to the desert rather than having to get out of town first as in Jaisalmer/Bikaner.
F **Yatri Niwas**, near Karni Mata Mandir, has simple rooms.

⊙ Eating

Bikaner *p249, map p248*
Veg restaurants on Station Rd. You can dine in style at the first 4 hotels listed.
♈♈ **Amber**, Indian, some western dishes. Most popular, and the veg *thali* is exceptional but some reports of falling standards.

♈♈ **Bhairon Vilas**'s breezy rooftop for Rajasthani meals, atmospheric, order ahead.
♈♈ **Bhanwar Niwas**, amazingly ornate dining hall, good way of having a look around if you're not staying there.
♈♈ **Kesria**, Jaipur Rd. Pleasant countryside location, popular on breezy summer evenings but disappointing food.
♈ **Niroj**, near government bus stand. Popular for Indian-Chinese-Continental food, bar.
♈ **Teja Garden**, Jaipur Rd. Pleasant outdoor garden restaurant, average food.
♈ **Vijay Guest House**, delicious home-cooked veg *thalis*, non-veg set menu (Rs 60-100).

Fast food
Try the local specialities – *Bikaneri bhujia/ sev/namkeen* – savoury snacks made from dough. Sweets (including Rajasthani *ghevar* and Bengali *rasgulla*) are best at **Bikharam Chandiram**, **Aggarwal**, **Girdharalal** and **Haldiram**, all in Station Rd, Kote Gate area. **Chhotu Motoo** at Joshi. Fresh Rajasthani sweets and snacks. Visit Purana Bazar for ice-cold lassis by day, hot milk (milk, sugar, cream, whipped up with a flourish) at night.

⊛ Festivals and events

Bikaner *p249, map p248*
Camel Fair (**Jan** 24-25 in 2005, 13-14 2006, 2-3 2007) and Diwali (**Oct/Nov**) are especially spectacular in Junagarh Fort, in the Old City near Kote Gate and some smaller palaces.

Around Bikaner *p250*
In Kolayat, the **Cattle and Camel Fair** (12-21 Nov 2005, 1-9 Nov 2006) is very colourful

and authentic but it can get quite riotous after dark. Since facilities are minimal, it is best to arrive before the festival to find a local family with space to spare, or ask a travel agent in Bikaner.

Shopping

Bikaner *p249, map p248*
Bikaner is famous for *Usta* work which includes footwear, purses and cushions. You can also get local carpets and woodwork. The main shopping centres are on KEM (MG) Rd (from near the fort) and around Kote Gate in the Old City, Modern Market.
Abhivyakti, URMUL Desert Craft, Sri Ganganagar Rd, next to new bus stand, T0151-252 2139. Run by the URMUL trust, a charitable foundation which works to improve the livelihoods of the poorest desert communities. The shop sells a good selection of locally produced household linen, soft furnishing and clothing, and operates a fair trade policy. Recommended.
Cottage Industries Institute, Junagarh Fort.
Kalakar Arts, Sardar Hall, Lalgarh Palace Rd, T0151-220 4477. Good selection of silver jewellery and other artefacts.

Activities and tours

Bikaner *p249, map p248*
The main tour here is a camel safari. You have to arrange these through private operators; the 4 below are recommended.
Aravalli Tours, opposite Municipal Council Hall, Junagarh Rd, T571124. Rs 1600 per person (toilet tent between 5 2-person tents) for upmarket experience. Other tours too.
Camel Man, Vijay Guest House, Jaipur Rd, T0151-223 1244, www.camelman.com. Offers good value, reliable, friendly and professional safaris, jeep tours, cycling. Light weight 'igloo' tents, clean mattresses, sheets, good food and guidance. Safaris to see antelopes, colourful villages and potters at work; vary from 1-2 hr rides to those lasting 5 days; Rs 500-800 per person per day.
Thar Desert Safari, Ganganagar Rd, behind new bus stand, T0151-252 1661, www.thar desertsafari.com. Honest, unpretentious outfit offering simple, no frills camel tours.
Vino Desert Safari, Gangashahar, T0151-227 0445, www.vinodesertsafari.com. Runs good

value, low-key safaris, including some longer distance 'inter-city' treks, eg Bikaner-Osian, 12 days.

Transport

Bikaner *p249, map p248*
From **Delhi** (435 km); **Jaipur** (330 km); **Jodhpur** (250 km); **Jaisalmer** (320 km); **Ajmer** (280 km); **Mumbai** (1,250 km).

Bus
The New Bus Stand is 3 km north of town. Private buses leave from south of the Fort. **Rajasthan Roadways**, enquiries, T0151-252 3800; daily deluxe buses to **Ajmer, Jodhpur, Jaisalmer** (8 hrs), **Udaipur**. 2 daily to **Delhi** via Hissar (12 hrs).

Rickshaw/taxi
Autos between station and Bus Stand or Lalgarh Palace, Rs 25. Taxis are unmetered. Found at train station, bus stand or hotels.

Train
Enquiries, T0151-220 0131, reservations, 0800-1400, 1415-2000, Sun 0800-1400. For tourist quota (when trains are full) apply to Manager's Office by Radio Tower near Jaswant Bhawan Hotel. **Delhi**: *Bikaner-DSR Exp, 4790,* 0830, 10 ½ hrs; *Bikaner-DSRi Mail, 4792,* 1945, 10 hrs. From Delhi (SR), the overnight train (*DSR Bikaner Mail, 4791,* 2125, best 2nd Class sleeper), gives very good sunrise views. **Jaipur**: *Intercity Exp, 2466,* 0540, 5 hrs. **Jodhpur**: *KJC Exp, 4667,* 1230, 5½ hrs; *Ranakpur Exp, 4707,* 0935, 5½ hrs (continues to Ahmadabad, further 10 hrs) and Mumbai (Bandra), another 10½ hrs.

Around Bikaner *p250*
For **Karni Mata Mandir** the train leaves Bikaner at 1000, returns 1230, buses from Bikaner New Bus Stand or Ganga Shahar Rd, hourly, Rs 7 (share auto-rickshaw from Station Rd to Bus, Rs 3), on return journey, for Station Rd, get off at **Thar Hotel** and walk or take auto-rickshaw, taxi about Rs 200 return.
For **Kalibangan** catch the bus from **Suratgarh**, which can be reached by bus from Bikaner, Hanumangarh, Sirsa (Haryana) or Mandi Dabwali (Punjab). Alternatively, the broad gauge train line connects Suratgarh with **Anupgarh**, about 15 km from the

Pakistan border, where it terminates. Kalibangan is about half way to Anupgarh. The nearest station is Raghunathgarh, but travel from there to Kalibangan is difficult (check at Suratgarh or Anupgarh). From Suratgarh to Anupgarh: Passenger, 0755, 2¼ hrs. Trains from **Suratgarh**: **Bikaner** (Lalgarh Junction): *Chandigarh Exp, 4887*, 0835, 3¼ hrs. **Bhatinda**: *Chandigarh Exp, 4888*, 1955, 3¼ hrs.

⦿ Directory

Bikaner *p249, map p248*
Banks Bank of Baroda, Ambedkar Circle,

cash against Visa; **State Bank of Bikaner & Jaipur**, Ambedkar Circle; also near fort's Suraj Pol. Changes TCs but may charge up to 10 per cent commission! **Harasar Haveli Hotel** charges 1 per cent.
Hospital **PBM Hospital**, Hospital Rd, T0151-524175, or T0151-252 5312.
Internet Meghsar Castle, Hotel Sagar and Harasar Haveli, Rs 2 per min; others at Sadulganj, Sagar Rd, Jaipur Rd and Gajner Rd, and near the fort.
Post GPO: behind Junagarh Fort.
Useful addresses Police: T100/ T0151-252 2225.

Shekhawati

Covering an area of about 300 sq km on the often arid and rock-studded plains to the northwest of the Aravalli mountain range, Shekhawati is the homeland of the Marwari community. The area is particularly rich in painted havelis; *Sikar district in the southwest and Jhunjhunun in the northeast form an 'open-air art gallery' of paintings dating from the mid-19th century. Although a day trip gives you an idea of its treasures, it is better to spend two or three nights in Shekhawati to see some good examples of temples, frescoed forts,* chhatris *and step-wells at leisure. There are other diversions laid on such as horse or camel safaris and treks into the hills, for visitors who can spare a little more time. Shekhawati sees far fewer visitors than the better-known areas of Rajasthan, and as such retains something of a 'one pen/rupee' attitude to tourists. This is generally quite innocent and should not be a deterrent to potential visitors.* ⮕ *For Sleeping, Eating and other listings, see pages 262-264.*

Ins and outs

Getting there You can get to the principal Shekhawati towns by train but road access is easier. A car comes in handy to see the area, though there are crowded buses from Delhi, Jaipur and Bikaner to some towns. Buses leave every 30 minutes from 0500-2000 from Jaipur's Main Bus Station and take about three hours. You can get from one Shekhawati town to another by local bus which run every 15 to 20 minites, and take about an hour. ⮕ *See Transport, page 264, for further details.*
Getting around Roads between the towns have been much improved recently, although there is still some work left to be done. Within each town it is best to enlist the help of a local person (possibly from the hotels listed below) to direct you to the best *havelis*, as it can be very difficult to find your way around. See below for unusual alternative safaris.
Tourist information Recommended reading includes *The painted towns of Shekhawati* by Ilay Cooper, a great Shekhawati enthusiast (Mapin, Allahabad, 1994), with numerous colour photos and maps. *Shekhawati: Rajsthan's painted houses* by P Rakesh and K Lewis is also well illustrated.

History

The 'garden of Shekha' was named after Rao Shekhaji of Amarsar (1433-1488) who challenged the Kachhawahas, refusing to pay tribute to the rulers at Amber. These Rajput barons made inroads into Muslim territory even during Mughal rule, and declared Shekhawati independent from the Jaipur suzerainty until 1738. During this period the merchants lavishly decorated their houses with paintings on religious, folk and historical themes. As Mughal power collapsed Shekhawati became a region of lawless banditry. In the early 19th century the British East India Company brought it under their control, bringing peace but also imposing taxes and tolls on trade which the Marwaris resented. Many of the merchants migrated to other parts of the country to seek their fortune and those who flourished returned their wealth to their homeland and took over as patrons of the artists.

> ❗ *Avoid visiting bazars alone: tourists have been harassed. Women alone may find young men's behaviour aggressive.*

Sights

Ramgarh has the highest concentration of painted *havelis*, though they are not as well maintained as those of Nawalgarh which has the second largest selection. It is easier to visit *havelis* in towns that have hotels, such as Nawalgarh, Mandawa, Dundlod, Mukundgarh, Mahansar, Fatehpur, Baggar and Jhunjunun, and where the caretakers are used to visitors. though towns like Bissau, Alsisar, Malsisar and Churu have attractive *havelis* as well.

The *havelis* are often occupied by the family or retainers who will happily show you around but many charge a fee of about Rs 20. Many *havelis* are in a poor state of repair with fading paintings which may appear monotonously alike to some. Some visitors find towns like Fatehpur and Mandawa very dirty, unkempt and disappointing.

Shekhawati (Jhunjhunun & Sikar districts)

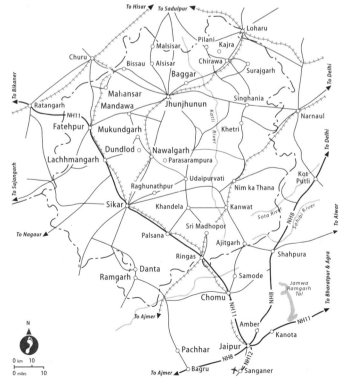

Fit for a merchant

The *havelis* in Shekhawati were usually built around two courtyards – one for general use, and the other a *zenana* courtyard for the women. The latter was also used for laundry and so often had a well and occasionally a play area for children. Security was a prime concern so a haveli was typically entered by a solid gate with a smaller door in it for regular use by residents. Watchmen had rooms on either side of the entrance. The *baithak* (reception room) had mattresses and bolsters for sitting on the floor while others were set aside for sleeping or storage. The *havelis* were enlarged as the families grew larger or wealthier, and with the onset of peaceful times, they became more palatial and lavished with decoration.

The *haveli* was made from brick or local stone. It was plastered in two layers with decorations on the second layer – a polished lime plaster finish often set with agate and other semi-precious stones. Murals were either painted on dry surfaces or on wet plaster. Mineral colours were derived from indigo, ochre, lead, copper, lapis lazuli, lime and even gold. Synthetic blue was imported and only the wealthiest could afford strong blue tones on their *havelis*. Some of the finest frescoes were near the door separating the courtyard from the main chambers and these were often restored or repainted during weddings and festivals. The subject of the paintings varied. The 10 avatars of Vishnu were popular, especially scenes from *Krishna Lila* and the *Ramayana*. The *Mahabharata*, the *Ragamala* (depicting musical modes of different seasons), folk tales, historic events, daily life in Shekhawati and floral and faunal themes were also popular, together with a fascination for portraying the British and their curious ways.

Sikar District

Occupying the southwestern flank of the Shekhawati region, Sikar district has a number of picturesque forts, towns and villages.

Sikar The late 17th-century fort was built when Sikar was an important trading centre and the wealthiest *thikana* (feudatory) under Jaipur. It now has a population of 148,000. You can visit the old quarter and see the Wedgwood blue 'Biyani' (1920) and 'Mahal' (1845), Murarka and Somani *havelis* and murals and carvings in Gopinath, Raghunath and Madan Mohan temples. From Jaipur take the NH11 to Ringas (63 km) and Sikar (48 km).

Laksmangarh Founded early 19th century, the town plan was based on Jaipur's model; this can be seen by climbing up to the imposing old fort which has now been renovated by the Jhunjhunwala family. The fine *havelis* include one of the area's grandest – Ganeriwala with char chowks (four courtyards) – the 'Rathi' *haveli* near the Clock Tower in the market, and others in the Chowkhani.

Fatehpur Fatehpur, founded in the mid-15th century by a Kayamkhani Nawab, has very attractive *havelis* along the Churu-Sikar road. Visit in particular the Devra (1885), Singhania (circa 1880), Goenka (circa 1880) and Saraogi. Later amusing frescoes showing European influence can be seen in the Jalan and white Bharthia (1929) *havelis*. The area called 'Chamria Colony' to the north of town is also interesting for its art deco architecture. Good tie-and-dye fabrics can be bought here.

Pachar This is a little town west of Jaipur in the middle of the sand dunes with the golden sandstone castle scenically situated on a lakeshore. A road north from Bagru on the NH8, also gives access. The place is pleasantly free from 'give me pen, give me rupees' children.

259

Ramgarh Ramgarh was settled by the Poddars in the late 18th century. In addition to their many *havelis* and that of the Ruias, visit the *chhatris* with painted entrances near the bus stand, the temples to Shani (with mirror decoration) and to Ganga. Ramgarh has the highest concentration of painted *havelis*, though they are not as well maintained as those of Nawalgarh which has the second largest selection. Town has a pleasantly laid back feel.Look for handicrafts here.

Danta Danta, originally a part of Marwar, was given to Thakur Amar Singhji in the mid-17th century. It is well off the beaten track and as such is completely unspoilt. Two empty *kilas* (forts) and the residential wing (early 18th-century) combine Mughal and Rajput art and architectural styles.

Jhunjhunun District
Mandawa At Fatehpur, a country road to the east takes you to Mandawa (22 km), a small, rather dirty bustling town. The *havelis* here are past their prime but can be interesting. Founded in the mid-18th century, it has interesting murals in the large rugged fort (circa 1755) built by Thakur Nawal Singh, which is now a hotel. The Goenka havelis – Ladhuram Tarkesvar (1878) and Dedraj Turmal (1898); the Ladia havelis – Gulab Rai (1870) and Sneh Ram (1906), Nandlal Murmuria (1935), Bansidhar Newatia (1910) and the Mohanlal Saraf (1870) havelis are interesting. The Siva temple here has a rock crystal lingam. The Mandawa Haveli near Sonthaliya Gate (northeast of town) displays local crafts, 0600-2200 daily. If you stay overnight in Mandawa you can visit the Harlalka *baoli* (a working step well) early in the morning to watch oxen at work on the ramp to raise water.

Mukundgarh Mukundgarh is the market for textiles and brass betel cutters. The town lies 10 km south of Jh.injhunun and 14 km from Mandawa. The Ganeriwala havelis (1860s and 1870s) are worth visiting as well as the Jhunjhunwala (1859) haveli with Krishna stories and Sukhdev haveli (circa 1880).

Nawalgarh Nawalgarh, some 25 km southeast of Mandawa, was founded in 1737 by Thakur Nawal Singh. There are numerous fine *havelis* worth visiting here. The town has a colourful bazar – though lone tourists have been harassed in the bazar – and two forts (circa 1730). **Nawalgarh fort** has fine examples of maps and plans of Shekhawati and Jaipur. The **Bala Kila** which has a kiosk with beautiful ceiling paintings is approached via the fruit market in the town centre and entered through the **Hotel Radha**. It also has the **Roop Niwas Palace** (now a hotel) and some 18th-century temples with 19th- and early-20th-century paintings. There are other interesting temples in town including Ganga Mai near Nansa Gate.

The **Anandilal Poddar Haveli**, now converted to the **Poddar Haveli Museum** ① *Rs 70 (foreigners) includes camera and guide*, is perhaps the best restored *haveli* of Shekhawati. The 1920s *haveli* has around 700 frescoes including a Gangaur procession, scenes from the Mahabharata, trains, cars, the avatars of Vishnu, bathing scenes and British characters, some of the best frame the doors leading from the courtyard to the rooms. The upper storey of the *haveli* is now a school but the ground floor has been opened as a museum. The photo-gallery records the life of Congressman and freedom fighter Anandilal Poddar, and the merchant-turned-industrialist Poddar family. There is a diorama of costumes of various Rajasthani tribes and communities, special bridal attires, a gallery of musical instruments, the

Northern Rajasthan Shekhawati

● The love story of Dhola and Maru

There are numerous versions of this romantic legend of the separation of a young couple and their subsequent reunion. The story which originated in northwestern Rajasthan, is the subject of many paintings.

Dhola, or Salhakumar, prince of Narvar, is married in infancy to Princess Maruni (Maru) of Pugal in Marwar, after their families meet by chance in Pushkar. However, the child bride returns home with her parents and only wakens to a longing for her husband when she reaches adolescence. The parents seeing their heartbroken daughter pining for her absent love, send minstrels to the court of Narvar but without luck. They learn that Prince Dhola has remarried and his new bride, Malvani of Malwa, has intercepted the messengers before they could reach Dhola. Although, the prince longs to find his first wife, Malvani uses every means to hold him back. However, at long last, Dhola escapes when his second wife falls asleep, having found a camel that will speed him to Pugal within a single day. He surmounts the many obstacles that are conjured up by the unscrupulous Malvani, and the couple are reunited. On the return journey, Maru is bitten by a venomous snake but Dhola remains with his dead wife. His prayers are answered when a passer-by performs a miracle and brings her back to life and the young couple are taken by the remarkable, fleet-footed camel back to the kingdom of Narvar. The tale ends happily – Maru assumes her rightful place and is adored by the people of Narvar, while Malvani emerges bitterly defeated by the gentle princess from the harsh and arid deserts of Marwar.

frescoes in the courtyard, which have been remarkably restored, are worth seeing. Among the remarkable Murarka *havelis* are the 19th-century **Kesardev Murarka** which has a finely painted façade and the Radheshyam Murarka which was built in the early-20th century. The latter portrays processions, scenes from folk tales, Hindu and Christian religious paintings, sometimes interspersed with mirrorwork. Other fine *havelis* are those of the Bhagat, Chokhani, Goenka, Patodia, Kedwal, Sangerneria, Saraogi, Jhunujhunwala, Saha and Chhauchuria families. The paintings here depict anything from European women having a bath (Aath – 'eight' – Haveli complex) to Hindu religious themes and Jesus Christ. Some of the *havelis* are complexes of several buildings which include a temple, dharamshala, cenotaph and a well). ① *Most charge Rs 15-20 for viewing.*

Parasarampura About 12 km southeast of Nawalgarh, Parasarampura has a decorated *chhatri* to Sardul Singh (1750) and the adjacent Gopinath temple (1742); these are the earliest examples of Shekhawati frescoes painted with natural pigments (caretaker has keys, and will point things out with a peacock feather).

Dundlod West of Nawalgarh, the best murals are in the **castle** (1750) ① *Darbar Hall Rs 20 for non-residents*, now a Heritage Hotel. You enter the moated castle by the Suraj Pol and proceed through the Bichla Darwaza and Uttar Pol (north) before arriving at the courtyard. Steps lead up to the majestic Diwan Khana furnished with period furniture, portraits and hangings; there is a library with a collection of rare books of Indian history and the *duchatta* above, which allowed the ladies in *purdah* to watch court ceremonies unobserved. Ask for the key to the painted family *chhatris* nearby. The Goenka haveli near the fort has three painted courtyards, and the

Satyanarayan temple has religious paintings but both these may be closed in the low season. The interesting deep step well now has an electric pump. The Polo Centre provides an opportunity to see camel, horse and bicycle polo, tent pegging etc. Mukundgarh is the nearest station where you can get jeeps and taxis.

Jhunjhunun Jhunjhunun was a stronghold of the Kayamkhani Nawabs until defeated by the Hindu Sardul Singh in 1730. The Mohanlal Iswardas Modi (1896), Tibriwala (1883) and the Muslim Nuruddin Farooqi Haveli (which is devoid of figures) and the *maqbara* are all worth seeing. The *Chhe* (6) Haveli complex, Khetri Mahal (1760) and the Biharilal temple (1776), which has attractive frescoes (closed during lunch time), are also interesting. The Rani Sati temple commemorates Narayana Devi who is believed to have become a sati; her stone is venerated by many of the wealthy *bania* community and an annual Marwari fair is held (protesting women's groups feel it glorifies the practice of *sati*). Since 1947, 29 cases of *sati* have been recorded in the Sikar and its two neighbouring districts.

Baggar The grand *haveli* of the Makharias, 10 km north east of Jhunjhunun, has rooms along open corridors around grassy courtyards and wall paintings of gods and angels being transported in motor cars!

Mahansar Founded in the mid-18th century, the town, 30 km northeast of Jhunjhunun, has a distinctly medieval feel. It has the Poddar haveli of Son Chand, the Rama Temple (ask for the key to the Golden Room; expensive at rs100 but very well preserved and the large Raghunath Temple with some of the finest paintings of the region. The fort (1768) has palaces and a baradari which were added later.

Churu Set in semi-desert countryside, Churu, northwest of Baggar, was believed to have been a Jat stronghold in the 16th century. In the 18th century it was an important town of Bikaner state and has an 18th-century fort. The town thrived during the days of overland desert trade. The local Rajputs barons revolted only to be crushed by the royals of Bikaner. The town has some interesting 1870s Oswal Jain *havelis* like those of the Kotharis and the Suranas. **Banthia** (early-20th century), **Bagla** (1880), **Khemka** (1800s). There are also the Bajranglal mantri haveli and the Poddar haveli and numerous towers, temples, wells and reservoirs which are interesting. The main attraction, however, is the extraordinary **'Malji-ka-Kamra'**, a crumbling, colonnaded *haveli* which houses some amazing interior scenes, get there before it's too late.

Tal Chappar A possible day excursion from one of the castle hotels is a visit to **Tal Chappar Wildlife Sanctuary** near Sujjangarh covering 71 sq km of desert scrubland with ponds and salt flats. It has some of the largest herds of Blackbuck antelope in India (easily seen at the watering point near the park gate itself during the dry season), besides chinkara gazelle, desert cat, desert fox and other dryland wildlife. Huge flocks of demoiselle and common cranes can be seen at nearby lakes and wetlands during the winter months (September-March) where they feed on tubers and ground vegetation. Some 175 different species of bird visit the park over the course of a year, including sandgrouse, quails, bar headed geese and cream coloured desert courser. The best time to visit is just after the rainy season, generally August and September The enthusiastic and charming forest guard, Brij Dansamor, is a good guide to the area. A local NGO, Krishna Mirg, is active in tree plantation and in fund-raising for the eco-development of Tal Chappar, providing support fodder during dry months to blackbuck and cranes. **Forest Department Rest House** has five basic but adequate rooms at Rs 300 per double. To book ahead call the head office in Churu on T01562 250938. Try **Hanuman** tea stall for delicious *chai* and the local sweet, malai laddoo. the drive to Tal Chappar can be long and tiring. If you are travelling between

Bikaner and Shekhawati in a jeep, it is worth making a detour. **Riaskhan, To1425-24391**, has a fleet of open, convertible and hardtop (closed) jeeps for visiting Tal Chappar from Kuchaman, Sambhar or Roopangarh, at Rs 1200-1500.

⊜ Sleeping

Sikar District *p258*

B Castle Pachar, Pachar, T01576-264 611. 16 very well-decorated rooms in a fascinating old property, good collection of portraits, paintings and weaponry, delicious if very rich food, charming hosts, swimming pool under construction. Recommended.

C Ashirwad Palace, Churu Bypass, NH11, 2 km from Fatehpur, T01571-222 635. 12 clean, modern, slightly overpriced rooms around a small lawn.

C Dera, off the high street, Danta, T01577-270 041. Open 1 Oct to 31 Mar. 14 large, characterful rooms in residential wing below the 2 old forts, good restaurant (meals Rs 160), peacocks at dawn, camel rides (Rs 250 per hr, Rs 550 per 3 hrs), horse safaris (see above), Jeep safaris (minimum 4 persons), Rs 1,200 each per day, unique.

C-D Hotel Niros, Station Rd, Sikar, T01572-255 815. 31 rooms in upmarket establishment including an a/c restaurant boasting some unusual water features.

D Haveli (RTDC), Sikar Rd, 500 m south of bus stand, Fatehpur, T01571-230 293. 8 clean rooms, some a/c with bath, pleasant building, dull restaurant, best bet in town.

E Aravalli Resort NH11, Sikar. Two air-cooled rooms with bath (simple, shabby), inexpensive Indian restaurant, gift shop, popular tourist stop to pick up mineral water.

E Shekhaji Resort, opposite Asirwad Palace, Fatehpur, T01571-222 078. 4 basic rooms plus an airy restaurant, pool planned.

Jhunjhunun District *p259*

B Castle Mandawa , Mandawa, T01592-223 124, www.mandawahotels.com. Huge castle with lots of character but parts rather run-down. 68 a/c rooms, some in tower, complete with swing, most with 4-posters and period trappings but rooms vary so select with care ("cheerless, cold, hard beds"), excellent views, atmospheric but a bit overpriced, mixed reports, some disappointed with meals (Rs 450-500).

B Desert Resort, Mandawa, T01592-223 151, 1 km south, www.mandawahotels.com. 60 rooms in 3 wings including a *haveli*, modern amenities, pricey restaurant (Rs 250-500 and only buffets for tour groups), pool, shady garden, good views of countryside, camel rides. Again lacks warmth, very business-like.

B Dundlod Fort, Heritage Hotel, in village centre, Dundlod, T01594-252519, www.dun lod.com. 42 rooms, but only 11 open at time of writing. Upgraded rooms particularly good, others mediocre with poor bathrooms, good state rooms with period furniture, **A** suites with terraces, good food (Rs 180-220), power cuts can be a problem but full of atmosphere and interesting murals, pool, library, tours, horse safaris a speciality, warm welcome, very hospitable and helpful. Recommended

B Mukundgarh Fort (Heritage Hotel), Mukundgarh, T11-3094 1192, pleasure hotels@rediff mail.com. 45 rooms in converted mid-18th-century fort) with frescoes along wide corridors, slightly musty but authentic interiors, modern bathrooms, restaurant, bar and pool, friendly management, slightly rundown

B Piramal Haveli, Baggar, T0159-222 220, www.neemranahotels.com. 100-year-old home, restored sensitively, excellent vegetarian meals and attentive service, quirky original frescoes, simple but overpriced, not as much atmosphere as at castle hotels.

B Roop Niwas Palace, Nawalgarh, T01594-222 008, www.roopniwaspalace. com. 1 km north of town. 37 rooms (older ones are large, air-cooled and simply furnished with old fashioned Western bathrooms, the newer are a/c but smaller), most are in 3 storeys around courtyards and a few in garden-side annexe. Good food, large gardens (peacocks), pool, horse safaris a speciality, qualified guides, attractive, small 90-year old palacebut service disappointing.

C Heritage Mandawa, off Mukundgarh Rd, Mandawa, T01592-223 742, www.hotelheri

---

🌓 *For an explanation of sleeping and eating price codes used in this guide, see inside the*
⬤ *front cover. Other relevant information is found in Essentials, see pages 40-45.*

tagemandawa.com, 200 m from the main bazar street and the bus stand. 13 rooms with local 'ethnic' furnishings in an old *haveli*, attached baths, dining hall, clean and pleasant, manager and staff very friendly and accommodating (good discounts in the low-season), camel rides, guides, taxis. Camping possible in grounds.

C Jamuna Resort, Baggar Rd, Jhunjhunun, T0159-2232 871, www.shivshekawati.com. 4 a/c cottage rooms with attractive mirror work and murals, 'Golden Room' with painted ceiling "like a jewel box", frescos, open-air Rajasthani veg/non-vegetarian restaurant serves delicious food, gardens, pool (open to hotel/restaurant guests only), local guided tours. Recommended.

C Mandawa Haveli, near Sonthaliya Gate, Mandawa, T01592-223 088, http://hotel mandawa.free.fr. 7 rooms with modernized baths in a 3-storeyed, characterful *haveli* with original 19th-century frescoes in court-yard, Rajasthani meals, museum and library. Friendly staff, authentic feel. Recommended.

C Narayan Niwas Castle, near bus stand, Mahansar, T01562-264 322. 16 rooms open of a total of 500 in fort, no's 1 and 5 really exceptional, poor bathrooms, attractive wall paintings, pleasingly unspoilt, converted by Thakur Tejpal Singh, delicious meals (cooked by his wife), homemade liquers, charming owners, a "Fawlty Towers" experience.

C-D Hotel Shekawati Heritage, off Station Rd, Jhunjhunun, T01592-237 134, www. hotelshekhawatiheritage.com. 22 rooms, 10 a/c, certainly not heritage but clean and friendly, quiet location.

C-D Natraj Hotel, Churu, T01562-257 245. 28 clean, modern rooms, best bet in town.

C-D Shiv Shekhawati, Muni Ashram, Khemi Sati Rd, Jhunjhunun, T0159-2232 651, www.shivshekawati.com. 20 simple clean rooms, 8 a/c, all with bath and hot water, good veg restaurant, tourist office (guides). Same owner of both, LK Jangid, is friendly and very knowledgeable.

D Apani Dhani, Jhunjhunu Rd, 1 km from railway station, 500 m north of Bus Stand, Nawalgarh, T01594-222 239, www.apani dhani.com. 8 environmentally friendly huts on an ecological farm run by the charming and authoritative Ramesh Jangid. Attractive, comfortable, solar-lit thatched cottages traditionally built using mud and straw,

modern bathrooms (some with "footprint" toilets), home-grown veg, immaculately presented, relaxing atmosphere. Accommodation and education in one enticing package. Recommended.

D Hotel Shekawati, off Mukandgarh Rd, Mandawa, T01592-223 036. Simple, basic rooms, only budget place in town, adequate.

D-E Hotel Aman, near railway station, Jhunjhunun, T01592-231 090. 10 rooms, 4 a/c, reasonable restaurant, 24 hour checkout.

D-F Neelam, opposite Khetan Hospital, Jhunjhunun, T0159-238415. 24 rooms, a/c and air-cooled, economical rooms with shared facilities, restaurant serving snacks, slightly shabby.

E Shekawati Guest House, near Roop Niwas, Nawalgarh, T01594-224 658, www.shekawatirestaurant.com. 6 clean, well presented rooms and an attractive thatched restaurant run by the friendly and refreshingly female Kalpana Singh. She is a qualified cook; the food here is exceptional and cooking classes can be arranged, as can local tours, recommended. The DS Bungalow next door is a poor imitation.

E Tourist Pension, behind Maur hospital, Nawalgarh, T01594-224 060, www.apani dhani.com. 8 rooms in modern house run by Ramesh's brother, Rajesh (see above). Lacks the charm of apani dhani but is clean, well priced and welcoming.

E-F Sangam, near bus stand, Jhunjhunun, T0159-232 544. Clean rooms, better with bath at rear, veg meals, best budget option.

🍴 Eating

Sikar District *p258*

🍴 **Natraj Restaurant**, Main Rd, Sikar. Does good meals and snacks, clean, reasonable.
🍴 **Paradise**, inexpensive Indian food.

Jhunjhunun District *p259*

🍴🍴 **Roop Niwas**, Nawalgarh, for heritage experience (and unreliable service).
🍴 **Shekawati Guest House**, Nawalgarh, for delicious, hygienically prepared fare.

✡ Festivals and events

Jhunjhunun District *p259*

If you are in Mandawa in **Oct** or **Nov** you might catch the **Desert Music Festival**.

○ Shopping

Jhunjhunun District *p259*
In Mandawa there are some reasonably priced, good quality miniatures on 'silk' at the **Mandawa Art School** at the castle gate, and fabrics and carpets at **CM Souvenirs**, Main Market.

▲ Activities and tours

Camel safaris
Roop Niwas Palace, Apani Dhani (Nawalgarh), Dundlod and Mandawa offer these. On a 5-day safari, you might cover Nawalgarh-Mukundgarh-Mandawa-Mahansar-Churu, crossing some of the finest sand dunes in Shekhawati; Nawalgarh to Fatehpur for 3-day safaris, and 1 week country safaris to Tal Chappar Wildlife Sanctuary. The cost depends on the number in the group and the facilities provided ranging from Rs 800-1,500 per day. 1-day safaris arranged by the heritage hotels cost about Rs 800 with packed lunch and mineral water.

Horse safaris
Dundlod Fort and Roop Niwas at Nawalgarh offer 1-week safaris with nights in royal tents (occasionally in castles or heritage hotels) to cover the attractions of the region. The most popular take in the Pushkar or Tilwara fairs. You can expect folk music concerts, camp-fires, guest speakers, masseurs, and some-times even a barber, all with jeep support. You ride 3 hrs in the morning and 2 hrs in the afternoon, and spend time visiting eco-farms, rural communities and *havelis* en route.

Trekking
There are some interesting treks in the Aravalli hills near Nawalgarh starting from Lohargal (34 km), a temple with sacred pools. Local people claim that this is the place recorded in the *Mahabharata* where Bhim's mace is said to have been crafted. A 4- to 5-day trek would take in the Bankhandi peak (1,052 m), Krishna temple in Kirori Valley, Kot Reservoir, Shakambari mata temple, Nag Kund (a natural spring) and Raghunathgarh fort. The cost depends on

the size of the group and the facilities provided. **Apani Dhani** arranges highly recommended treks with stays at the temple guest houses and villages for US$ 50 per person per day for minimum of 2 persons.

⊖ Transport

Bicycle
Apani Dhani, **Nawalgarh**, arranges cycle tours in Shekhawati.

Bus
To **Nawalgarh** from Delhi, best from ISBT daily at 0800, 2200 and 2300, 8 hrs. From **Jaipur** frequent buses from 0630-1830 (Express in the morning), 3½ hrs. Also to **Sikar** from Jaipur and Bikaner.

Jeep
For hire in **Nawalgarh**, **Mandawa** and **Dundlod**, about Rs 1,200 per day.

Taxi
From **Jaipur**, diesel Ambassador, Rs 1,200 for day tour of parts of Shekhawati; with detours (eg Samode), up to Rs 1,500; Rs 1,700 including 1 night. A/c cars can be twice as much. Local hire is possible in **Mandawa**, **Mukundgarh** and **Nawalgarh**.

Train
From **Jaipur**, 3 trains run daily to stations to Shekhawati. *Shekhawati Exp* (Delhi-Jaipur): To **Mukundgarh** from Delhi, 2315, 7½ hrs; from Jaipur, 1015, 1330, 1805, 4 hrs. To **Nawalgarh** from Delhi, 2230, 8½ hrs. To **Jhunjhunun** from Delhi, departs 2315, 7½ hrs, arriving in Sikar after 2 hrs; from Jaipur, departs 1805, 5 hrs, continues to Delhi, 6 hrs. To **Sikar** from Bikaner, dep 2025, 7 hrs.

❶ Directory

Jhunjhunun District *p259*
Banks SBBJ and Bank of Baroda, Mandawa. In Nawalgarh, SBBJ changes currency and TCs, but poor rate. **Roop Niwas** can sometimes help get better rates. **UCO Bank** changes currency in Dundlod.

Background

History	266
Modern Rajasthan	277
Economy	279
Culture	280
Religion	292
Land and environment	305
Books	316

❋ Footprint features

Gandhi	275
Elopement marriages	291
An eye to the future	296
Tiger, tiger	311
Blackbuck and bishnois	312

History

Settlement and early history

Rajasthan was among the first regions of South Asia to be settled. Similarities between hand axes and cleavers discovered in the Chittaurgarh region of southeastern Rajasthan and those found in the Olduvai gorge in Africa have led archaeologists to suggest a slow diffusion from Africa to India, the Indian tools being much more recent. Rajasthan is particularly rich in Middle Palaeolithic artefacts, dating from between 17,000 and 40,000 years before the present, probably during a considerably wetter period than at present. The settlers made use of even apparently inhospitable environments. In the Marwar region of Rajasthan, sand dunes often encloses shallow lakes which were the source of aquatic food for the inhabitants, while the dunes themselves were covered in thick scrub which supported a rich fauna, a source of food for hunters.

The first settlers

By 3500 BC agriculture had spread throughout the Indus Plains and had reached northwestern India. Between 3000 BC and 2500 BC many new settlements sprang up in the heartland of what from 2500 BC became the Harappan or Indus Valley civilization, including cities such as Kalibangan in Rajasthan. Numerous townships of this Harappan period (2500-1500 BC) have been excavated in Rajasthan, most of them along rivers, near the sea coast, or in hills suitable for stone quarrying. In northwestern Rajasthan Kalibangan was a major town and there are many other sites in the now dried up river beds of the Ghaggar and Sarasvati rivers.

The Indus Valley Civilization was entirely home grown. What stimulated its origins however remains unclear, but its emergence as a distinct culture seems to have been sudden. Speculation continues to surround the nature of its language, which is still untranslated. It may well have been an early form of the Dravidian languages which today are found largely in South India, though as even the most basic characteristics such as whether the script should be read from left to right or right to left have not been conclusively demonstrated the questions far outnumber the reliable answers.

India from 2000 BC to the Mauryas

By 1700 BC the entire Indus Valley civilization had disintegrated. The causes remain uncertain. Sir Mortimer Wheeler's early explanation that the violent arrival of new waves of Aryan immigrants was responsible has now been discarded. Increasing desertification of the already semi-arid landscape, a shift in the course of the Indus as the result of an earthquake such as that which created the so-called "Allah's Bund" in Kachchh in 1819, and internal political decay have each been suggested as instrumental in its downfall. Whatever the causes in Rajasthan, some features of Indus Valley culture were carried on by succeeding generations.

Possibly a little before 1500 BC northern India entered the Vedic period. Aryan settlers moved southeast towards the Ganga valley. Classes of rulers *(rajas)* and priests *(brahmins)* began to emerge. Conflict was common. In one battle of this period a confederacy of tribes known as the Bharatas defeated another grouping of 10 tribes. They gave their name to the region to the east of the Indus which is the official name for India today – Bharat.

The centre of population shifted east from the banks of the Indus to the land between the rivers Yamuna and Ganga, the *doab* (pronounced *doe-ahb*, literally 'two waters'). This region became the heart of emerging Aryan culture, which, from 1500 BC onwards, laid the literary and religious foundations of what ultimately became Hinduism. Little is known of developments in Rajasthan at this time, but the centre of gravity of the emerging Hindu culture was clearly to the north and east. 267

The first fruit of this development was the **Rig Veda**, the first of four Vedas (literally knowledge), composed, collected and passed on orally by Brahmin priests from 1300 BC to about 1000 BC. The later Vedas show that the Indo-Aryans developed a clear sense of the Ganga-Yamuna *doab* as 'their' territory. Later texts extended the core region from the Himalaya to the Vindhyans and to the Bay of Bengal in the east. Beyond lay the land of mixed peoples and then of barbarians, outside the pale of Aryan society.

The Mauryas

Chandragupta Maurya Within a year of the retreat of Alexander the Great from the Indus in 326 BC, Chandragupta Maurya established the first indigenous empire to exercise control over much of the subcontinent. Under his successors that control was extended to all but the extreme south of peninsular India.

Asoka The greatest of the Mauryan emperors, Asoka took power in 272 BC. He inherited a full blown empire, but extended it from Afghanistan to Assam and from the Himalaya to Mysore.

Asoka (described on the edicts as 'the Beloved of the Gods, of Gracious Countenance') left a series of inscriptions on pillars and rocks were written in *Prakrit*, using the *Brahmi* script, although in the northwest they were in Greek using the *Kharoshti* script. They were unintelligible for over 2,000 years after the decline of the Mauryan empire until James Prinsep deciphered the Brahmi script in 1837. Although Buddhist influence was never as strong in Rajasthan as in some parts of India, Asoka left an engraved rock at Girnar near Junagadh in modern Gujarat with 14 of his edicts, indicating that Kathiawad was an important Mauryan stronghold on the west coast of the Indian peninsula.

Through the edicts, Asoka urged all people to follow the code of *dhamma* or *dharma* – translated by the Indian historian Romila Thapar as 'morality, piety, virtue and social order'.

Sakas The Sakas or Scythians, and other Central Asian tribes, entered from the northwest. They set up rule in Rajasthan before the Christian era. Colonel Tod, in his 'Annals of Mewar', suggests that the Kathi royal families of Kathiawadi states like Jasdan, Jetpur, Bhilkha are direct descendants of the Sakas. Rudraman, one of their major rulers, left edicts which can be seen in suburban Junagadh, Gujarat.

Classical Period – the Gupta Empire AD 319-467

Although the political power of Chandra Gupta and his successors never approached that of his unrelated namesake, nearly 650 years before him, the Gupta Empire produced developments in every field of Indian culture. Their influence has been felt profoundly across South Asia to the present. Many Gupta period terracottas and artefacts have been found in Rajasthan; and are displayed in the state's museums.

Geographically the Guptas originated in the same Magadhan region that had given rise to the Mauryan Empire. Extending their power by strategic marriage alliances, Chandra Gupta's empire of Magadh was extended by his son, Samudra Gupta, who took power in AD 335, across North India. He also marched as far south as Kanchipuram in modern Tamil Nadu, but the heartland of the Gupta Empire remained the plains of the Ganga. Chandra Gupta II reigned for 39 years from AD 376 and was a great patron of the arts. Trade with Southeast Asia, Arabia and China all added to royal wealth.

Throughout the Gupta period, the Brahmins, Hinduism's priestly caste, were in the key position to mediate change. They refocused earlier literature to give shape to the emerging religious philosophy. In their hands the *Mahabharata* and the *Ramayana* were transformed from secular epics to religious stories. The excellence of contemporary sculpture both reflected and contributed to an increase in image worship and the growing role of temples as centres of devotion.

Eventually the Gupta Empire crumbled in the face of repeated attacks from the northwest, this time by the Huns. By the end of the sixth century Punjab and Kashmir had been prised from Gupta control and the last great Hindu empire to embrace the whole of North India and part of the peninsula was at an end.

Regional kingdoms and cultures

The collapse of Gupta power opened the way for successive smaller kingdoms to assert themselves. After the comparatively brief reign of **Harsha** in the mid-seventh century, which recaptured something both of the territory and the glory of the Guptas, the Gangetic plains were constantly fought over by rival groups.

The Rajputs The political instability and rivalry that resulted from the ending of Gupta power opened the way for new waves of immigrants from the northwest and for new groups and clans to seize power. The most significant of these were the Rajputs (meaning 'sons of kings').

Rajput clans trace their origins to one of three mythical sources. The *Suryavanshi* Sisodias (Guhilot) dynasties claim direct descent from the Sun God. They had their capital at Vallabhi in Kathiawad before moving to Nagda and Chittaurgarh in the seventh century, and ultimately to Udaipur after the Mughal conquest of Chittaurgarh. Further north the Kachhawahas, who also claim descent from the sun, took over the Amber region in AD 967. The *Krishnavanshi* Bhatti Rajputs, like the Jadeja Rajputs of Kachchh-Kathiawad, claim descent from the Moon God and Lord Krishna. They migrated to the western desert in the early 11th century and established Jaisalmer in 1156. According to the legend recorded by Chanda Bardai in his epic *Prithviraja Raso*, written for the Rajput King Prithviraj III of Delhi between 1178-1192, a third myth suggests that the four original Rajput warriors were created out of the sacrificial fire-pit – the *agni kula* – of sage Vashista on Mount Abu. The *rishis* – ascetic sages – called them into being to oppose the *rishis'* enemies. By the sixth century the four clans which claim descent from the sacrificial fire, the Paramaras (Pawar), Parihar (Pratihara), Chauhan (Chahamma) and Chalukya (Solanki or Vaghela) clans, came to control large areas of the Deccan and Malwa.

The chief criterion for inclusion in the lists of Rajput clans was the scale of their estates. New colonization in the medieval period turned previously tribal, and 'untamed', territory into the domain of agriculture, trade and the Hindu mainstream. But alongside the colonization process ran an equally important strand of widening social inclusion into the 'Kshatriya' ranks. Chattophadhyaya illustrates the point by reference to the according of Kshatriya status to formerly tribal groups such as the Medas and Hunas.

Each of the major dynasties established control over specific territories. The Chalukyans (Solankis) took Anhilwara (present day Patan) in 961 AD and became sovereign in the Gujarat region stretching from Mount Abu to Malwa. This period saw the rise of western India's finest Hindu and Jain temples, including those of Modhera, Dilwara, Girnar, Taranga, Kumbhariyaji, Somnath, Osian, Menal, Jhalawar and Bardoli. The Solankis introduced important water harvesting systems while the Chauhans built impressive defence structures such as the hill forts at Ranthambhore and Nagaur in Rajasthan. There were two Chauhan lines, the Sambhar dynasty from Ajmer, which became a national power under Raja Prithviraj, and the Kheechi line which ultimately set up a kingdom at Pawagadh.

Rajput chivalry Through their myths of an essential Rajput identity, the Rajputs fostered a reputation for chivalry, valour and honour in battle and their attitude to women. In the commonly presented idealized view of Rajputs they strove against all odds to preserve the civilization of their ancestors, although they were successively forced to accept the suzerainty of first the Mughals and then the British. Death was preferable to dishonour, and before their greatest battles, when certain defeat was anticipated, their queens and princesses committed mass suicide (*jauhar*) to save themselves from being touched by enemy hands, the men then marching naked to the battlefield. See page 175.

The spread of Islamic power
The Delhi Sultanate From about AD 1000 the external attacks which inflicted most damage on Rajput wealth and power came increasingly from the Arabs and Turks. Mahmud of Ghazni raided the Punjab, Rajasthan and ultimately Gujarat virtually every year between 1000 and 1026, attracted both by the agricultural surpluses and the wealth of India's temples. By launching annual raids during the harvest season, Mahmud financed his struggles in Central Asia and his attacks on the profitable trade conducted along the Silk Road between China and the Mediterranean. The enormous wealth in cash, golden images and jewellery of North India's temples drew him back every year and his hunger for gold, used to re-monetize the economy of the remarkable Ghaznavid Sultanate of Afghanistan, was insatiable. He sacked many wealthy centres in the northwest until his death in 1030.

Muslim political power was heralded by the raids of Mu'izzu'd Din and his defeat of massive Rajput forces at the Second Battle of Tarain in 1192. He made further successful raids inflicting crushing defeats on Hindu opponents from Gwalior to Varanasi. The foundations were then laid for the first extended period of Muslim power, which came under the Delhi sultans.

Qutb u'd Din Aibak took Lahore in 1206, although it was his lieutenant **Iltutmish** who really established control from Delhi in 1211. Qutb ud din Aibak converted the old Hindu stronghold of Qila Rai Pithora in Delhi into his capital and began several magnificent building projects, including the Quwwat-ul-Islam mosque and the Qutb Minar, a victory tower. Iltutmish was a Turkish slave – a *Mamluk* – and the Sultanate continued to look west for its leadership and inspiration. However, the possibility of continuing control from outside India was destroyed by the crushing raids of **Genghis Khan** through Central Asia and from 1222 Iltutmish ruled from Delhi completely independently of outside authority.

In 1290 the first dynasty was succeeded by the Khaljis, which in turn gave way to the Tughluqs in 1320. Despite its periodic brutality, this period marked a turning point in Muslim government in India, as Turkish Mamluks gave way to government by Indian Muslims and their Hindu allies. The Delhi sultans were open to local influences and employed Hindus in their administration. In the mid-14th century their capital, Delhi, was one of the leading cities of the contemporary world but in 1398 their control came to an abrupt end with the arrival of the Mongol Timur. .

Timur's limp caused him to be called Timur-i-leng (Timur the Lame, known to the west as Tamburlaine). This self-styled 'Scourge of God' was illiterate, a devout Muslim, an outstanding chess player and a patron of the arts. He cut a bloody swathe through to Delhi. He is believed to have been responsible for five million deaths. Famine followed the destruction caused by his troops and plague resulted from the corpses left behind. It was a carnage which however offered temporary political opportunity to opponents of Sultanate rule to the south. In 1398 the Tomar Rajput Bir Singh Deo recaptured Gwalior from the Muslims and became Raja of Gwalior, establishing a dynasty which was to leave a profound impression on the development of Rajput architecture.

The period of Empire

The Mughal Empire

The descendants of conquerors, with the blood of Timur (Tamburlaine) and Genghis Khan in their veins, the Mughals came to dominate Indian politics from Babur's victory near Delhi in 1526 to Aurangzeb's death in 1707. Their legacy was not only some of the most magnificent architecture in the world, but a profound impact on the culture, society and future politics of South Asia.

Babur (the tiger) Founder of the Mughal Dynasty, Babur was born in Russian Turkestan on 15 February 1483, the fifth direct descendant on the male side of Timur and 13th on the female side from Genghis Khan. He established the Mughal Empire by leading his cavalry and artillery forces to a stupendous victory over the combined armies of Ibrahim Lodi, last ruler of the Delhi Sultanate and the Rajput Raja of Gwalior, at **Panipat**, 80 km north of Delhi, in 1526. When he died four years later, the Empire was still far from secured, but not only had he laid the foundations of political and military power but he'd also begun to establish courtly traditions of poetry, literature and art which became the hallmark of subsequent Mughal rulers. Babur was charismatic. He ruled by keeping the loyalty of his military chiefs, giving them control of large areas of territory.

Humayun The strength of Babur's military commanders proved a mixed blessing for Humayun, his successor. Almost immediately after Babur's death Humayun was forced to retreat from Delhi by two of his brothers and one of his father's lieutenants, the Afghan **Sher Shah Suri**. Humayun's son Akbar, who was to become the greatest of the Mughal emperors, was born at Umarkot in Sindh, modern Pakistan, during this period of exile, on 23 November 1542.

Humayun found the artistic skills of the Iranian court stunningly beautiful and he surrounded himself with his own group of Iranian artists and scholars. Planning his move back into India proper, Humayun urged his group of artists to join him and between 1548 and his return to power in Delhi in 1555, he was surrounded by this highly influential entourage.

Akbar One year after his final return to Delhi, Humayun died from the effects of a fall on the stairs of his library in the Purana Qila in Delhi. Akbar 'the Builder of Empire' was therefore only 13 when he took the throne in 1556. The next 44 years were one of the most remarkable periods of South Asian history, paralleled by the Elizabethan period in England, where Queen Elizabeth I ruled from 1558 to 1603. Although Akbar inherited the throne, it was he who really created the empire. At the age of 15 he had conquered Ajmer and large areas of Central India. Chittaurgarh and Ranthambhore fell to him in 1567-1568, bringing most of what is now Rajasthan under his control.

Through his marriage to a Hindu princess he ensured that Hindus were given honoured positions in government, as well as respect for their religious beliefs and practices. He sustained a passionate interest in art and literature, matched by a determination to create monuments to his empire's political power and he laid the foundations for an artistic and architectural tradition which developed a totally distinctive Indian style. This emerged from the separate elements of Iranian and Indian traditions by a constant process of blending and originality of which he was the chief patron.

Akbar deliberately widened his power base by incorporating Rajput princes into the administrative structure and giving them extensive rights in the revenue from land. He abolished the hated tax on non-Muslims (*jizya*) – ultimately reinstated by his

66 99 The descendants of conquerors, with the blood of Timur and Genghis Khan in their veins, the Mughals came to dominate Indian politics...

strictly orthodox great grandson Aurangzeb – ceased levying taxes on Hindus who went on pilgrimage and ended the practice of forcible conversion to Islam.

Artistic treasures abound from Akbar's court – paintings, jewellery, weapons – often bringing together material and skills from across the known world. Emeralds were particularly popular, with the religious significance which attaches to the colour green in mystic Islam adding to their attraction. Some came from as far afield as Colombia. Akbar's intellectual interests were extraordinarily catholic. He met the Portuguese Jesuits in 1572 and welcomed them to his court in Fatehpur Sikri, along with Buddhists, Hindus and Zoroastrians, every year between 1575 and 1582.

Akbar's eclecticism had a political purpose, for he was trying to build a focus of loyalty beyond that of caste, social group, region or religion. Like Roman emperors before him, he deliberately cultivated a new religion in which the emperor himself attained divinity, hoping thereby to give the empire a legitimacy which would last. While his religion disappeared with his death, the legitimacy of the Mughals survived another 200 years, long after their real power had almost disappeared.

Jahangir Akbar died of a stomach illness in 1605. He was succeeded by his son, Prince Salim, who inherited the throne as Emperor Jahangir ('*world seizer*'). He commissioned works of art and literature, many of which directly recorded life in the Mughal court. Hunting scenes were not just romanticized accounts of rural life, but conveyed the real dangers of hunting lions or tigers; implements, furniture, tools and weapons were made with lavish care and often exquisite design.

Nur Jahan Jahangir's favourite wife, Nur Jahan, brought her own artistic gifts. Born the daughter of an Iranian nobleman, she had been brought to the Mughal court along with her family as a child and moved to Bengal as the wife of Sher Afghan. She made rapid progress after her first husband's accidental death in 1607, which caused her to move from Bengal to be a lady in waiting for one of Akbar's widows.

At the Mughal court in 1611 she met Jahangir. Mutually enraptured, they were married in May. Jahangir gave her the title Nur Mahal (Light of the Palace), soon increased to Nur Jahan (Light of the World).

By 1622 Nur Jahan effectively controlled the empire. She commissioned and supervized the building in Agra of one of the Mughal world's most beautiful buildings, the **I'timad ud-Daula** ('Pillar of government'), as a tomb for her father and mother. Her father, **Ghiyas Beg,** had risen to become one of Jahangir's most trusted advisers and Nur Jahan was determined to ensure that their memory was adequately honoured. She was less successful in her wish to deny the succession after Jahangir's death at the age of 58 to Prince Khurram. Acceding to the throne in 1628, he took the title of Shah Jahan (*Ruler of the World*) and in the following 30 years his reign represented the height of Mughal power.

● *Despite their artistic achievements, Mughal politics was cruel and violent. Akbar ordered*
● *that the beautiful Anarkali, a member of his harem, should be buried alive when he suspected she was having an affair with his son Jahangir.*

Background History

Shah Jahan The Mughal Empire was under attack in the Deccan and the northwest when Shah Jahan became Emperor. He tried to re-establish and extend Mughal authority in both regions by a combination of military campaigns and skilled diplomacy and most of the Deccan was brought firmly under Mughal control.

He also commissioned art, literature and, above all, architectural monuments, on an unparalleled scale. The Taj Mahal may be the most famous of these, but a succession of brilliant achievements can be attributed to his reign. From miniature paintings and manuscripts, which had been central features of Mughal artistic development from Babur onwards, to massive fortifications such as the Red Fort in Delhi, Shah Jahan added to the already great body of outstanding Mughal art.

Throughout this period Rajput rulers adjusted in varying degrees to the dominance of the Mughal emperors. Seeking to maximise their own remaining authority without risking punitive raids which would have destroyed what control they had, many of the clan leaders made direct arrangements with successive emperors which gave them continued effective control over their own territories. Sometimes clan leaders took sides in the internal feuding within the Mughal court. Udai Singh of Udaipur for example gave the young Prince Khurram, the future Emperor Shah Jahan, shelter in his Jag Mandir palace in Lake Pichola when he was fleeing his father Jahangir's wrath, and it is striking that both Jahangir and Shah Jahan had Rajput mothers.

Aurangzeb All this changed with the ascension of Aurangzeb ('The jewel in the throne') to the throne. He needed all his political and military skills to hold on to an unwieldy empire that was in permanent danger of collapse from its own size.

Aurangzeb realized that the resources of the territory he inherited from Shah Jahan were not enough to sustain the empire's power. One response was to push south, while maintaining his hold on the east and north. Initially he maintained his alliances with the Rajputs in the west, which had been a crucial element in Mughal strategy. However, in 1678 he claimed absolute rights over Jodhpur and went to war with the Rajput clans, at the same time embarking on a policy of outright Islamisation. For the remaining 29 years of his reign he was forced to struggle continuously to sustain his power.

The Maratha challenge

A great threat to Mughal and Rajput control of Rajasthan through the 18th century was that of the **Maratha confederacy**. The Marathas were unique in India in uniting different castes and classes in a nationalist fervour for the region of Maharashtra. When the Mughals ceded the central district of Malwa, the Marathas were able to pour through the gap created between the Nizam of Hyderabad's territories in the south and the area remaining under Mughal control in the north.

By 1750 they had reached the gates of Delhi. When Delhi collapsed to Afghan invaders in 1756-1757 the Mughal minister called on the Marathas for help. Yet again Panipat proved to be a decisive battlefield, the Marathas being heavily defeated by the Afghan forces of Ahmad Shah on 13 January 1761. However Ahmad Shah was forced to retreat to Afghanistan by his own rebellious troops demanding two years arrears of pay, leaving a power vacuum. The Maratha confederacy dissolved into five independent powers, with whom the incoming British were able to deal separately. For them, the door to the north was open.

The decline of Muslim power

Aurangzeb never fully came to terms with the rising power of the Marathas, though he did end their ambitions to form an empire of their own. Nor was Aurangzeb able to create any wide sense of identity with the Mughals as a legitimate popular power. Instead, under the influence of Sunni Muslim theologians, he retreated into insistence on Islamic purity. He imposed Islamic law, the *Sharia*, promoted only Muslims to positions of power and authority, tried to replace Hindu administrators and revenue collectors with Muslims and reimposed the *jizya* tax on all non-Muslims. By the time of his death in 1707 the empire no longer had either the broadness of spirit or the physical means to survive.

East India Company and the rise of British power

The British were unique among the foreign rulers of India in coming by sea rather than through the northwest and in coming first for trade rather than for military conquest. The ports that they established – Madras (Chennai), Bombay (Mumbai) and Calcutta (Kolkata) – became completely new centres of political, economic and social activity. Before them Indian empires had controlled their territories from the land. The British dictated the emerging shape of the economy by controlling sea-borne trade.

In its first 90 years of contact with South Asia after the Company set up its first trading post at Masulipatnam, on the east coast of India, it had depended almost entirely on trade for its profits. In 1608 it established its warehouse on the west coast at Surat, already an important port, and it remained their headquarters until it moved to Bombay in 1674. The Company was accepted and sometimes welcomed, partly because it offered to bolster the inadequate revenues of the Mughals by exchanging silver bullion for the cloth it bought.

Alliances In the century and a half that followed the death of Aurangzeb, the British East India Company extended its economic and political influence into the heart of India. As the Mughal Empire lost its power India fell into many smaller states. The Company undertook to protect the rulers of several of these states from external attack by stationing British troops in their territory. In exchange for this service the rulers paid subsidies to the Company. As the British historian Christopher Bayly has pointed out, the cure was usually worse than the disease and the cost of the payments to the Company crippled the local ruler. The British extended their territory through the 18th century as successive regional powers were annexed and brought under direct Company rule.

Progress to direct British control was uneven and often opposed. The Sikhs in Punjab, the Marathas in the west and the Mysore sultans in the south, fiercely contested British advances. The Marathas were not defeated until the war of 1816-1818, a defeat which had to wait until Napoleon was defeated in Europe and the British could turn their wholehearted attention once again to the Indian scene. Even then the defeat owed as much to internal faction fighting as to the power of the British-led army.

In 1818 India's economy was in ruins and its political structures destroyed. Irrigation works and road systems had fallen into decay and gangs terrorized the countryside. Thugs and dacoits controlled much of the open countryside in Central India and often robbed and murdered even on the outskirts of towns. The peace and stability of the Mughal period had long since passed. Between 1818 and 1857 there was a succession of local and uncoordinated revolts in different parts of India. Some were bought off, some put down by military force.

A period of reforms

While existing political systems were collapsing, the first half of the 19th century was also a period of radical social change in the territories governed by the East India Company. **Lord William Bentinck** became Governor-General at a time when England itself was entering a period of major reform. In 1828 he banned the burning of widows on the funeral pyres of their husbands (*sati*) and then moved to suppress the ritual murder and robbery carried out in the name of the goddess Kali (*thuggee*). But his most far reaching change was to introduce education in English.

From the late 1830s massive new engineering projects began to be taken up; first canals, then railways. However, it was in eastern India that British control was most directly imposed and the consequent changes were most sharply felt. Although much of modern Gujarat was also brought under direct British control, under the governance of Bombay, most Rajput areas remained under their subordinate authority as Rajputana.

British-led innovations stimulated change and change contributed to the growing unease with the British presence, particularly under the Governor-Generalship of the Marquess of Dalhousie (1848-1856). The development of the telegraph, railways and new roads, three universities and the extension of massive new canal irrigation projects in North India seemed to threaten traditional society, a risk increased by the annexation of Indian states to bring them under direct British rule. The most important of these was Oudh.

The Rebellion

Out of the growing discontent and widespread economic difficulties came the Rebellion or 'Mutiny' of 1857 (now widely known as the First War of Independence). Although it had little support among the Rajput rulers and Rajputana remained seemingly uninvolved, no part of India was unaffected. The 1857 rebellion marked the end not only of the Mughal Empire but also of the East India Company, for the British Government in London took overall control in 1858. After the establishment of the British Indian Empire, the Rajput Princely States gained in the appearance and show of power just as they lost its reality.

Pomp and circumstance The British awarded gun salutes on the basis of importance. Rajasthan had 19 'gun salute' states, 17 of them ruled by various Rajput clans, Bharatpur by a Jat dynasty and Tonk by a Muslim Nawab, with countless non salute chieftains. The princes maintained huge fleets of European and American cars, stables of elephants and horses, chariots and horse-drawn carriages, and travelled in their own royal rail saloon carriages which could be attached to regular trains for their journeys across the subcontinent. Some even had private aircraft. This was a period of grand darbars, parties, banquets, weddings, processions, polo and cricket matches and royal hunting camps. A strict order of precedence was maintained according to gun salutes awarded to each state. The Maharajah of Baroda was entitled to 21 gun salutes, the Maharana of Udaipur to 19 gun salutes, the Maharajahs of Jaipur, Jodhpur, Bundi, Bikaner, Kachchh, Kota, Karauli and Bharatpur to 17 gun salutes and so on.

While the show of power was far from reality, for these maharajahs came under the British Raj, the princes were given considerable freedom of rule and many of them proved to be capable rulers. Their highness Ganga Singh of Bikaner was one of a few ruler whom introduced wide-ranging reforms that are landmarks in administration in India. British political agents, collectors and other residents were appointed to look into affairs of state, and when a crown prince inherited the throne as a minor a British representative was selected to handle the state on his behalf. Ajmer was a seat of British administrators, and during the summer months Mount Abu was a popular retreat for British and royal residents of Rajasthan to escape the heat of the plains.

Yet within 30 years a movement for self-government had begun and there were the first signs of a demand that political rights be awarded to match the sense of Indian national identity. This took varied forms. In Udaipur the Maharishi Dayanand wrote the *Satyarath Prakash* which was a call to restore Hinduism to its 'pure' form, and the founding in 1875 of the Arya Samaj on the basis of these principles placed the emphasis on a return to Vedic Hinduism at the core of its view of Indian national identity, a view which is still a powerful influence through the recently deposed BJP party.

⁝ Gandhi

Gandhi was asked by a journalist when he was on a visit to Europe what he thought of Western civilization. He paused and then replied: "It would be very nice, wouldn't it". The answer illustrated just one facet of his extraordinarily complex character. A westernized, English educated lawyer, who had lived outside India from his youth to middle age, he preached the general acceptance of some of the doctrines he had grown to respect in his childhood, which stemmed from deep Indian traditions – notably ahimsa, or non-violence. From 1921 he gave up his Western style of dress and adopted the hand spun dhoti worn by poor Indian villagers, giving rise to Churchill's jibe that he was a 'naked fakir' (holy man). Yet if he was a thorn in the British flesh, he was also fiercely critical of many aspects of traditional Hindu society. He preached against the discrimination of the caste system which still dominated life for the overwhelming majority of Hindus. Through the 1920s much of his work was based on writing for the weekly newspaper Young India, which became The Harijan in 1932. The change in name symbolized his commitment to improving the status of the outcastes, Harijan (person of God) being coined to replace the term outcaste. Often despised by the British in India he succeeded in gaining the reluctant respect and ultimately outright admiration of many. His death at the hands of an extreme Hindu chauvinist in January 1948 was a final testimony to the ambiguity of his achievements: successful in contributing so much to achieving India's Independence, yet failing to resolve some of the bitter communal legacies which he gave his life to overcome.

Indian National Congress The movement for independence went through a series of steps. The creation of the Indian National Congress in 1885 was the first all-India political institution and was to become the key vehicle of demands for independence. However, the educated Muslim élite of what is now Uttar Pradesh saw a threat to Muslim rights, power and identity in the emergence of democratic institutions which gave Hindus, with their built-in natural majority, significant advantages. Sir Sayyid Ahmad Khan, who had founded a Muslim University at Aligarh in 1877, advised Muslims against joining the Congress, seeing it as a vehicle for Hindu and especially Bengali, nationalism.

Muslim League The educated Muslim community of North India remained deeply suspicious of the Congress, making up less than eight percent of those attending its conferences between 1900-1920. Muslims from Uttar Pradesh created the All-India Muslim League in 1906. However, the demands of the Muslim League were not always opposed to those of the Congress. In 1916 it concluded the Lucknow Pact with the Congress, in which the Congress won Muslim support for self-government, in exchange for the recognition that there would be separate constituencies for Muslims. The nature of the future Independent India was still far from clear, however. The British conceded the principle of self-government in 1918, but however radical the reforms would have seemed five years earlier they already fell far short of heightened Indian expectations.

Mahatma Gandhi Into a tense atmosphere Mohandas Karamchand Gandhi returned to India in 1915 after 20 years practising as a lawyer in South Africa. On his return the Bengali Nobel Laureate poet, Rabindranath Tagore, had dubbed him 'Mahatma' – Great Soul. The name became his. He arrived as the government of India was being given new powers by the British parliament to try political cases without a jury and to give provincial governments the right to imprison politicians without trial. In opposition to this legislation Gandhi proposed to call a *hartal*, when all activity would cease for a day, a form of protest still in widespread use. Such protests took place across India, often accompanied by riots.

The thrust for Independence Through the 1920s Gandhi developed concepts and political programmes that were to become the hallmark of India's Independence struggle. Rejecting the 1919 reforms Gandhi preached the doctrine of *swaraj*, or self rule, developing an idea he first published in a leaflet in 1909. He saw *swaraj* not just as political independence from a foreign ruler but, in Judith Brown's words, as made up of three elements: "It was a state of being that had to be created from the roots upwards, by the regeneration of individuals and their realization of their true spiritual being… unity among all religions; the eradication of Untouchability; and the practice of *swadeshi*." Swadeshi was not simply dependence on Indian products rather than foreign imports, but a deliberate move to a simple lifestyle, hence his emphasis on hand spinning as a daily routine.

Ultimately political Independence was to be achieved not by violent rebellion but by *satyagraha* – a 'truth force' which implied a willingness to suffer through non-violent resistance to injustice. This gave birth to Gandhi's advocacy of 'non-cooperation' as a key political weapon and brought together Gandhi's commitment to matching political goals and moral means. Although the political achievements of Gandhi's programme continue to be strongly debated the struggles of the 1920s established his position as a key figure in the Independence movement.

By the end of the Second World War the positions of the Muslim League, now under the leadership of **Mohammad Ali Jinnah** and the Congress led by Jawaharlal Nehru, were irreconcilable. While major questions of the definition of separate territories for a Muslim and non-Muslim state remained to be answered, it was clear to General Wavell, the British Viceroy through the last years of the War, that there was no alternative but to accept that independence would have to be given on the basis of separate states.

The transition to Independence and Partition

On 20 February 1947, the British Labour Government announced its decision to replace Lord Wavell as Viceroy with Lord Mountbatten, who was to oversee the transfer of power to new independent governments. It set a deadline of June 1948 for British withdrawal. The announcement of a firm date made the Indian politicians even less willing to compromise and the resulting division satisfied no one.

When Independence arrived – on 15 August for India and the 14 August for Pakistan because Indian astrologers deemed the 15th to be the most auspicious moment – many questions remained unanswered. Several key Princely States had still not decided firmly to which country they would accede. The Muslim Nawab of Junagadh exercized his right to accede to Pakistan, but the Indian Government, arguing that Junagadh had a predominantly Hindu population and lay surrounded by Hindus, insisted on organizing a plebiscite under Indian government supervision, and the Nawab was forced to flee into exile. Equally the future accession of Kashmir remained unclear with results that have lasted to the present day.

The end of the Princely States At Independence the 216 smallest states were abolished and merged into neighbouring provinces. Some 275 Princely states across India, including Rajasthan, had either acceded to the Indian union or signed standstill agreements with the new government while permanent arrangements were agreed. They were integrated initially into five new unions, each with its provincial governor or *Rajpramukh*. A further 61 states were brought under direct central government control. These arrangements, intended as temporary, were shortlived. The first stage of transition was completed in 1950 when they all became part of the Indian Union under an agreement in which the Princes retained their titles and government subsidies, known as their privy purses. The region's 18 princely states were ultimately absorbed into the new state of Rajasthan on 1 November 1956. In 1971 Mrs Gandhi abolished the remaining rights of the maharajahs and took away their privy purses.

The successors of royal families have lost power but still retain wide respect and considerable political influence. The palaces, many of them converted to hotels with varying degrees of success, maintain the memory of princely India.

Modern Rajasthan

Rajasthan is among India's least densely populated states, though population growth rates continue to be relatively high at over 1.5 per cent a year. India, with over one billion people in 2001, is the second most populated country in the world after China. That population size reflects the long history of human occupation and the fact that an astonishingly high proportion of India's land is relatively fertile. Some 60% of India's surface area is cultivated today, compared with about 10% in China and 20% in the United States.

Although the birth rate has fallen steadily over the last 40 years, initially death rates fell faster and the rate of population increase has continued to be about two percent – or 18 million – a year. Today nearly 30% of the population lives in towns and cities have grown dramatically. In 1971, 109 million people lived in towns and cities. The figure grew to over 300 million in 2001.

India's constitution and political institutions

In the years since independence, India has recorded some striking political achievements. With the two year exception of 1975-1977, when Mrs Gandhi imposed a state of emergency in which all political activity was banned, India has sustained a democratic system in the face of tremendous pressures. The general elections of May 2004, which involved an electorate of over 400 million and saw the use of electronic vote-counting machines for the first time, were the country's 14th.

The constitution Establishing itself as a sovereign democratic republic, the Indian parliament accepted Nehru's advocacy of a secular constitution. The President is formally vested with all executive powers exercised under the authority of the Prime Minister. Effective power lies with the Prime Minister and Cabinet, following the British model. In practice there have been long periods when the Prime Minister has been completely dominant. In principle parliament chooses the Prime Minister. The Parliament has a lower house (the *Lok Sabha*, or 'house of the people') and an upper house (the *Rajya Sabha* – Council of States). The former is made up of directly elected representatives from the 543 parliamentary constituencies (plus two nominated members from the Anglo-Indian community), the latter of a mixture of members elected by an electoral college and of nominated members. Constitutional amendments require a two-thirds majority in both houses.

India's federal constitution devolves certain powers to elected state assemblies. Each state has a Governor who acts as its official head. Many states also have two chambers, the upper generally called the Rajya Sabha and the lower (often called the Vidhan Sabha) being of directly elected representatives. In practice many of the state assemblies have had a totally different political complexion from that of the Lok Sabha. Regional parties have played a far more prominent role, though in many states central government has effectively dictated both the leadership and policy of state assemblies.

Secularism One of the key features of India's constitution is its secular principle. This is not based on the absence of religious belief, but on the commitment to guarantee freedom of religious belief and practice to all groups in Indian society. Some see the commitment to a secular constitution as under increasing challenge, especially from the Hindu nationalism of the Bharatiya Janata Party, the BJP. The BJP persuaded a number of minor regional parties to join it in government after the 1998 elections, appearing to move away from its narrowly defined conception of a Hindu state. In the 1999 elections the BJP achieved a compromise between the narrowly defined Hindu beliefs of its core support and the electoral demands of an enormously varied population, and ran its full electoral term of five years in government before being defeated by Sonia Gandhi's Congress Party in May 2004.

The judiciary India's Supreme Court has similar but somewhat weaker powers to those of the United States. The judiciary has remained effectively independent of the government except under the Emergency between 1975-1977. In recent years it has played an increasingly prominent role in public interest cases, defining legal principles in matters such as environmental protection and human rights which have often been both independent and well ahead of the political parties.

The police India's police service is divided into a series of groups, numbering nearly one million. While the top ranks of the Indian Police Service are comparable to the Indian Administration Service (IAS), lower levels are extremely poorly trained and very low paid. In addition to the domestic police force there are special groups: the Border Security Force, Central Reserve Police and others. They may be armed with modern weapons and are called in for special duties.

The armed forces Unlike its immediate neighbours India has never had military rule. It has approximately one million men in the army – one of the largest armed forces in the world. Although they have remained out of politics the armed services have been used increasingly frequently to put down civil unrest especially in Kashmir, where there are currently at least 400,000 troops.

Party politics For over 40 years Indian national politics was dominated by the **Congress Party**. Its strength in the Lok Sabha often overstated the volume of its support in the country, however and state governments have frequently been formed by parties – and interests – only weakly represented at the centre. The Congress built its broad based support partly by championing the causes of the poor, the backward castes and the minorities. Yet in 1998 its popular support completely disappeared in some regions and fell below 30 per cent nationally. Currently under the leadership of Sonia Gandhi, Rajiv Gandhi's Italian born widow, it returned to power in the general elections of May 2004.

The Non-Congress Parties Political activity outside the Congress can seem bewilderingly complex. There are no genuinely national parties. The only alternative governments to the Congress have been formed by coalitions of regional and ideologically based parties. Parties of the left – Communist and Socialist – have never broken out of their narrow regional bases in West Bengal and Kerala.

The most organized political force outside the Congress, the Jan Sangh, merged with the **Janata Party** for the elections of 1977. After the collapse of that government it re-formed itself as the **Bharatiya Janata Party (BJP)**. In 1990-1991 it developed a powerful campaign focusing on reviving Hindu identity against the minorities. In the decade that followed it became the most powerful opponent of the Congress across northern India and established a series of footholds and alliances in the South, enabling it to become the most important national alternative to the Congress.

Recent developments The May 2004 national elections in India saw the Congress Party return as the largest single party, though without an overall majority. This time however they were able to forge some previously impossible alliances with regional parties and they formed the new government under the Prime Ministership not of the party's leader, Sonia Gandhi, but of ex-finance minister, Manmohan Singh.

In the 1998 Lok Sabha elections in Rajasthan the BJP retained only five of the 25 seats, 18 of the remainder going to the Congress, and the BJP also lost power in the state assembly elections at the end of 1998.

Economy

Rajasthan has always been known for its mercantile achievers, from the days when the desert cities of Jaisalmer, Jodhpur and Bikaner were on important overland trade routes of merchant caravans travelling between the near east and the Far East.

Although the people of Marwar and Shekhawati are well known for their business acumen, Rajasthan does not have a strong commercial or industrial base and remains one of India's poorer states. Tourism, gems and jewellery, handicrafts and mineral mining make the major contribution to the regional economy in a state that has always been primarily agricultural and pastoral with most of the Rajasthani business houses preferring to set up industry at Mumbai, Ahmadabad, Delhi, Kolkata, Coimbatore, Chennai, Bangalore and Hyderabad.

Agriculture Rajasthan's low and erratic rainfall puts irrigation at a premium, but most of the crops are rainfed: wheat, hardy *bajra* (pearl millet) in the more arid areas; *jowar* (sorghum), maize and pulses (peas, beans and lentils) elsewhere. Cotton is important in the north and south of the state. Rajasthan shares waters from the Bhakra Dam project with Punjab, and the Chambal Valley project with Madhya Pradesh. With improved management techniques over 30 per cent of the sown area could be brought under irrigation. The enormously ambitious Rajasthan canal is working much less efficiently than had originally been planned. Rajasthan has a very large livestock population and is the largest wool producing state. It also breeds camels.

Minerals Rajasthan accounts for India's entire output of zinc concentrates, emeralds and garnets, 94 per cent of its gypsum, 76 per cent of silver ore, 84 per cent of asbestos, 68 per cent of feldspar and 12 per cent of mica. It has rich salt deposits at Sambhar and elsewhere, and copper mines at Khetri and Dariba. The white marble favoured by the Mughal builders is mined at Makrana, north of Ajmer. The famous Makrana white marble is mined near Ajmer. The Aravalli hills north of Udaipur are the mining zone for dolomite based marble in white and other colours. Kesriyaji (Rishabdeo) to the south of Udaipur is known for its serpentine based green marble, popular for cladding, Mount Abu for its black and panther spotted marble. The hills of Jalor, Barmer and Sirohi districts are have extensive granite, while Jaisalmer, Barmer, Bikaner and Jodhpur districts have sandstone, gypsum, lignite, silica sand and China clay. Other important minerals are limestone in the Kota-Jhalawar-Baran triangle (the famous Kota stone slabs are used as bathroom and kitchen counters in many houses, and for flooring), copper, lead, zinc, silver, limestone, mica and soap-stone in Ajmer, Alwar, Dungarpur, Chittaurgarh and Banswara districts. Gypsum, quartz and other stones are exploited in Bharatpur, and slate at Dhaulpur.

Industries The main large scale industries are textiles, the manufacture of rugs and woollen goods, vegetable oil and dyes. Heavy industry includes the construction of railway rolling stock, copper and zinc smelting. The chemical industry also produces caustic soda, calcium carbides and sulphuric acid, fertilizer, pesticides and insecticides. There is a rapidly expanding light industry which includes precision instrument manufacture at Kota and television assembly. The principal industrial complexes are at Jaipur, Kota, Udaipur and Bhilwara. Traditional handicrafts such as pottery, jewellery, marble work, embossed brass, block printing, embroidery and decorative painting are now very good foreign exchange earners.

Culture

Language

Rajasthan has its own distinct language, Rajasthani. It is an Indo-Aryan language – the easternmost group of the Indo-European family – among which Hindi is predominant. Sir William Jones, the great 19th-century scholar, discovered the close links between Sanskrit (the basis of nearly all North Indian languages) German and Greek. He showed that they all must have originated in the common heartland of Central Asia, being carried west, south and east by the nomadic tribes who shaped so much of the subsequent history of both Europe and Asia.

Sanskrit As the pastoralists from Central Asia moved into South Asia from 2000 BC onwards, the Indo-Aryan languages they spoke were gradually modified. Sanskrit developed from this process, emerging as the dominant classical language of India by the sixth century BC, when it was classified in the grammar of **Panini**. It remained the language of the educated until about AD 1000. The Muslims brought Persian into South Asia as the language of the rulers.

Hindi and Urdu The most striking example of Muslim influence on the earlier Indo-European languages is that of the two most important languages of India and Pakistan, Hindi and Urdu respectively. Most of the modern North Indian languages were not written until the 16th century or after. Hindi developed into the language of the heartland of Hindu culture, stretching from Punjab to Bihar and from the foothills of the Himalaya to the marchlands of central India, while Urdu became as the language of urban Muslims.

Rajasthani In Rajasthan, the principal language is Rajasthani, while the four most important dialects are *Marwari* in the west, *Jaipuri* in the east, *Malwi* in the southeast and *Mewati* in the northeast. Hindi is rapidly replacing Rajasthani as the lingua franca.

Scripts The earliest ancestor of scripts used in India today was **Brahmi**, in which Asoka's famous inscriptions were written in the third century BC. Written from left to right, a separate symbol represented each different sound. For about 1,000 years the major script of northern India has been the Nagari or Devanagari, which means literally the script of the 'city of the gods', though Gujarati has its own running script which developed as part of Gujarat's mercantile tradition.

Numerals Many of the Indian alphabets have their own notation for numerals. This is not without irony, for what in the western world are called 'Arabic' numerals are in fact of Indian origin. Local numerical symbols are still in use, but by and large you will find that the Arabic number symbols familiar in Europe and the West are common.

The role of English English now plays an important role across India. It is widely spoken in towns and cities and even in quite remote villages it is usually not difficult to find someone who speaks at least a little English. Other European languages are almost completely unknown. The accent in which English is spoken is often affected strongly by the mother tongue of the speaker and there have been changes in common grammar which sometimes make it sound unusual. Many of these changes have become standard Indian English usage, as valid as any other varieties of English used around the world.

Literature

Rajasthan has a long tradition of vernacular poetry in local dialects, but its literature has been profoundly influenced by the wider traditions of literature in India. Sanskrit was the first all-India language. Its early literature was memorized and recited. The hymns of the Rig Veda probably did not reach their final form until about the sixth century BC, but the earliest may go back as far as 1300 BC.

The Vedas The Rig Veda is a collection of 1,028 hymns, not all directly religious. Its main function was to provide orders of worship for priests responsible for the sacrifices which were central to the religion of the Indo-Aryans. Two later texts, the Yajurveda and the Samaveda, served the same purpose. A fourth, the Atharvaveda, is largely a collection of magic spells.

At some time after 1000 BC a second category of Vedic literature, **the Brahmanas**, began to take shape. Story telling developed as a means to interpret the significance of sacrifice. The most famous and the most important of these were the *Upanishads*, probably written at some time between the seventh and fifth centuries BC. The Brahmanas gave their name to the religion emerging between the eighth and sixth centuries BC, Brahmanism, the ancestor of Hinduism. Two of its texts remain the best known and most widely revered epic compositions in South Asia, the *Mahabharata* and the *Ramayana*.

The details of the great battle recounted in **the Mahabharata** are unclear. Tradition puts its date at precisely 3102 BC, the start of the present era and names the author of the poem as a sage, Vyasa. Evidence suggests however that the battle was fought around 800 BC at **Kurukshetra**. It was another 400 years before priests began to write the stories down, a process which was not complete until AD 400. The original version was about 3,000 stanzas long, but it now contains over 100,000 – eight times as long as Homer's Iliad and the Odyssey put together. The battle was seen as a war of the forces of good and evil, the **Pandavas** being interpreted as gods and the **Kauravas** as devils. The arguments were elaborated and expanded until about the fourth century AD. A comparatively late addition to the *Mahabharata*, the *Bhagavad-Gita* is the most widely read and revered text among Hindus in South Asia today.

Valmiki is thought of in India as the author of the second great Indian epic, **the Ramayana**, though no more is known of his identity than is known of Homer's. Like the *Mahabharata*, it underwent several stages of development before it reached its final version of 48,000 lines.

Sanskrit literature Sanskrit was always the language of the court and the élite. Other languages replaced it in common speech by the third century BC, but it remained in restricted use for over 1,000 years after that period. The remarkable Sanskrit grammar of Panini helped to establish grammar as one of the six disciplines essential to understanding the Vedas properly and to conducting Vedic rituals. The other five were phonetics, etymology, meter, ritual practice and astronomy. Sanskrit literature continued to be written in the courts until the Muslims replaced it with Persian, long after it had ceased to be a language of spoken communication. One of India's greatest poets, **Kalidasa**, contributed to the development of Sanskrit as the language of learning and the arts.

Literally 'stories of ancient times', the *Puranas* are about Brahma, Vishnu and Siva. Although some of the stories may relate to real events that occurred as early as 1500 BC, they were not compiled until the fifth century AD. Margaret and James Stutley record the belief that "during the destruction of the world at the end of the age, Hayagriva is said to have saved the *Puranas*. A summary of the original work is now preserved in Heaven!".

The stories are often the only source of information about the period immediately following the early Vedas. Each *Purana* was intended to deal with five themes: "the creation of the world (*sarga*); its destruction and recreation (*pratisarga*); the genealogy of gods and patriarchs (*vamsa*); the reigns and periods of the Manus (*manvantaras*); and the history of the solar and lunar dynasties".

Muslim influence For considerable periods between the 13th and 18th century, **Persian** became the language of the courts. Classical Persian was the dominant influence, with Iran as its country of origin and Shiraz its main cultural centre, but India developed its own Persian-based style. Two poets stood out at the end of the 13th century AD, when Muslim rulers had established a sultanate in Delhi, Amir Khusrau, who lived from 1253 to 1325 and the mystic Amir Hasan, who died about AD 1328.

The Mughal emperor Babur left one of the most remarkable political autobiographies of any generation, the *Babur-nama* (History of Babur), written in **Turki** and translated into Persian. His grandson Akbar commissioned a biography, the *Akbar-nama*, which reflected his interest in all the world's religions. His son Jahangir left his memoirs, the *Tuzuk-i Jahangiri*, in Persian. They have been described as intimate and spontaneous and showing an insatiable interest in things, events and people.

Colonial period The use of Persian was already in decline during the reign of the last great Muslim Emperor, **Aurangzeb** and as the British extended their political power so the role of English grew. There is now a very wide range of Indian literature accessible in English, which has thus become the latest of the languages to be used across the whole of South Asia.

In the 19th century English became a vehicle for developing nationalist ideals. However, notably in the work of **Rabindranath Tagore**, it became a medium for religious and philosophical prose and for a developing poetry. Tagore himself won the Nobel Prize for Literature in 1913 for his translation into English of his own work, *Gitanjali*.

Science

Calendar By about 500 BC Indian texts illustrated the calculation of the calendar, although the system itself almost certainly goes back to the eighth or ninth century BC. The year was divided into 27 *nakshatras*, or fortnights, years being calculated on a mixture of lunar and solar counting. See page 300.

Views of the universe Early Indian views of the universe were based on the square and the cube. The earth was seen as a square, one corner pointing south, rising like a pyramid in a series of square terraces with its peak, the mythical Mount Meru. The sun moved round the top of Mount Meru in a square orbit and the square orbits of the planets were at successive planes above the orbit of the sun. These were seen therefore as forming a second pyramid of planetary movement. Mount Meru was central to all early Indian schools of thought, Hindu, Buddhist and Jain.

However, about 200 BC the Jains transformed the view of the universe based on squares by replacing the idea of square orbits with that of the circle. The earth was shown as a circular disc, with Mount Meru rising from its centre and the Pole Star directly above it. These views have not completely lost their currency among some Jains today.

Mathematics Conceptions of the universe and the mathematical and geometrical ideas that accompanied them were comparatively advanced in South Asia by the time of the Mauryan Empire and were put to use in the rules developed for building temple altars. Indians were using the concept of zero and decimal points in the Gupta period. Furthermore in AD 499, just after the demise of the Gupta Empire, the astronomer Aryabhatta calculated Pi as 3.1416 and the length of the solar year as 365.358 days. He also postulated that the earth was a sphere rotating on its own axis and revolving around the sun and that the shadow of the earth falling on the moon caused lunar eclipses.

Art and architecture

Both have developed with a remarkable continuity through successive regional and religious influences and styles. Rajasthan has its own distinctive regional styles of both religious and secular building which have continued to evolve right up to the present day.

The Buddhist stylistic influence on early Hindu architecture was profound. The first Hindu religious buildings to have survived into the modern period were constructed in south and east India from the sixth century AD. The early Muslims destroyed much that was in their path. Yet the flowering of Islamic architecture which followed was not simply a transplant from another country or region, but grew out of India's own traditions. That continuity reflected many forces, not least the use made by the great Mughal emperors of local skilled craftsmen and builders. The first Emperor, Babur, expressed his admiration for the magnificence of the Rajput palace at Gwalior, and successive emperors tried to emulate and exceed the sumptuousness of Rajput forts and palaces while incorporating key elements from Muslim traditions.

Painting, sculpture, inlay work, all blended skills from a variety of sources and craftsmen – even occasionally from Europe. What emerged was another stepping stone in a tradition of Indian architecture, which wove the threads of Hindu tradition into new forms. The Taj Mahal was the ultimate product of this extraordinary process. Yet regional styles developed their own special feature and the main thrust of Hindu and Muslim religious buildings remains fundamentally different.

Architecture
Hindu temple buildings The principles of religious building were laid down by priests in the *sastras*. Every aspect of Hindu, Jain and Buddhist religious building is identified with conceptions of the structure of the universe. This applies as much to the process of building – the timing of which must be undertaken at astrologically propitious times – as to the formal layout of the buildings. The cardinal directions of north, south, east and west are the basic fix on which buildings are planned. In addition to the cardinal directions, number is also critical to the design, the ultimate

scale of the building is being derived from the measurements of the sanctuary at its heart.

Indian temples were nearly always built to a design based on philosophical understandings of the universe. This cosmology of an infinite number of universes, isolated from each other in space, proceeds by imagining various possibilities as to its nature. Its centre is seen as dominated by **Mount Meru** which keeps earth and heaven apart. The concept of separation is crucial to Hindu thought and social practice. Continents, rivers and oceans occupy concentric rings around the mountain, while the stars encircle the mountain in another plane. Humans live on the continent of **Jambudvipa** characterized by the rose apple tree (*jambu*).

The *sastras* show plans of this continent, organized in concentric rings and entered at the cardinal points. This type of diagram was known as a **mandala**. The centre of the *mandala* would be the seat of the major god. *Mandalas* provided the ground rules for the building of stupas and temples across India and gave the key to the symbolic meaning attached to every aspect of religious buildings.

The focal point of the temple, its sanctuary, was the home of the presiding deity, the 'womb-chamber' (*garbhagriha*). A series of doorways, in large temples leading through a succession of buildings, allowed the worshipper to move towards the final encounter with the deity to obtain *darshan* – a sight of the god. Both Buddhist and Hindu worship encourage the worshipper to walk clockwise around the shrine, performing *pradakshina*.

The elevations are symbolic representations of the home of the gods. Mountain peaks such as Kailasa are common names for the most prominent of the towers. In North and East Indian temples the tallest of these towers rises above the *garbagriha* itself, symbolizing the meeting of earth and heaven in the person of the enshrined deity. The basic structure is usually richly embellished with sculpture. When first built this would usually have been plastered and painted and often covered in gems. In contrast to the extraordinary profusion of colour and life on the outside, the interior is dark and cramped but here it is believed, lies the true centre of divine power.

Rajput architecture The Rajputs expressed their power in a variety of architectural forms. Although they were great patrons of Hindu religious art and worship, their most significant architectural legacy has been secular, paying particular attention to the construction of massive forts and lavish palaces. Merchants under Rajput protection also developed superb domestic architecture in their *havelis*. The main period of Rajput building dates from the mid-15th to the mid-18th centuries. It is no accident that this coincides with the period of Mughal dominance in north India, for it was a period during which the Rajputs had a relatively secure hold on power within their own territories, guaranteed in many cases by the superior force of the Mughals with whom for long periods they had close, protected relationships. The Rajput city capitals became the sites of the most extravagant palace building extravaganza in India.

In his book *The Rajput Palaces* Tillotson observed that "A Rajput palace was a symbol of dynasty, and each raja sought to outdo his neighbours and his predecessors in the splendour of his building projects". Palaces were sometimes doubled up as fortresses, others were designed and occupied for periods of peace. The standard features included a division into men's and women's quarters (*mardana* and *zenana*), the creation of large open courtyards as public space and much more confined rooms for private residence. The function of the palace was to demonstrate power, wealth and status, and thus the halls of public audience (*diwan-i-am*) played a prominent role and were often richly decorated. The hall of private audience (*diwan-i-khas*) was contained within the private quarters and was on a much smaller scale. Many Rajput palaces include a picture gallery – the *chitra shali* – and a bedroom with inlay mirror work, the *sheesh mahal,* while there would also be armouries and treasuries. The *zenana*, always less prolifically decorated, nonetheless would often have wonderfully constructed *jali* screens of pierced or latticed stone work, through which the women could watch proceedings outside without being seen.

The similarity of some of these features to those of Islamic building in India tempted early scholars to infer that Rajput architecture was simply derivative of Islamic, and in particular Mughal, traditions. Tillotson has argued that this view is mistaken, and points to the clear existence of a distinct Rajput palace complex style in the earliest remaining Rajput capital site of Chittaurgarh which existed well before the Mughals became supreme. A wealth of detail from later palaces, Tillotson argues, can be attributed to earlier Hindu temple models: the use of "square based columns, the *jarokha*, or cradle balcony; the *chajja* or deep eave; the *jali* or pieced stone screen; coloured tile decoration; the lotus rosette, and the first tentative use of the cusped arch."

It is clear that Rajput secular architecture borrowed from the tradition of religious architecture, a tradition of great antiquity. The Solanki, Parmara, Chauhan, Jetwa and Parihar rulers of eighth-13th century AD followed an architectural lay-out which is better known as the Chalukyan style. The Hindu and Jain temples of this period had a multi-columned portico entered through *torana* archways, an assembly hall called a *Sabha mandapam* and a shrine room. The outer walls and inside pillars were decorated with exquisite panels of sculpture depicting gods, goddesses, human and animal figures. Some of them portrayed voluptuous women and erotic friezes. The interior domes were corbelled and carved in detail, some of them had panels of carvings in concentric circles leading to the apex of the dome, superimposed by carved brackets. The interiors of the sanctum were usually plain and rarely had any carvings, certainly no erotica. Some temples like the Sun temple at Modhera had a 'kund' where devotees could have a bath before entering the portico of the temple for their worship. Temples such as those at Dilwara and Osian follow this layout and made extensive use of marble and other stones.

This period also saw the building of one of the region's most distinctive features, the highly decorated step-well (*baoli* or *vav*). The early works were simple but later in Gujarat more elaborate structures came into existence like the seven storeyed Rani-ki-Vav stepwell of Patan believed to date from AD 1052, the Vikia Vav at Ghumli near Porbandar probably dating to the 12th century and the five storeyed *vav* at Adalaj near Gandhinagar dating from the late 15th century. These stepwells had landings between flights of steps, exquisite carvings along the walls and pavilions/galleries/chambers cooled by air wafting off the water surface. It is believed these galleries may have doubled as caravanserais or as royal chambers for the ruling family to retreat from the heat of the summer sun.

Haveli architecture Rajasthan has a style of domestic residential architecture which reflected the needs and aspirations of the rich and powerful merchant class, the *haveli*, built around a courtyard and ornately decorated. In Rajasthan these *havelis* were built from local stone. The sandstone *havelis* of Jaisalmer, Bikaner, Jodhpur here are masterpieces of stone carving. The Shekhawati mansions had their courtyards decorated with wall paintings, and have been referred to as open-air art galleries. See also page 258.

Minor architectural features Rajput princes also characteristically built commemorative pavilions (*chattris* or *devals*), to mark royal cremation sites. The style of such *chattris* is often replicated in external features on both Rajput and Mughal buildings, including on the Taj Mahal.

Muslim religious architecture Although the Muslims adapted many Hindu features, they also brought totally new forms. Dominating the architecture of many

North Indian cities are the mosques and tomb complexes (*dargah*). The use of brickwork was widespread and they brought with them from Persia the principle of constructing the true arch and succeeded in producing a variety of domed structures, often incorporating distinctively Hindu features such as the surmounting finial. By the end of the great period of Muslim building in 1707, the Muslims had added magnificent forts and palaces to their religious structures, a statement of power as well as of aesthetic taste.

European buildings Nearly two centuries of architectural stagnation and decline followed the demise of Mughal power. The Portuguese built a series of remarkable churches in their territories that owed nothing to local traditions and everything to Baroque developments in Europe. Not until the end of the Victorian period, when British imperial ambitions were at their height, did the British colonial impact on public rather than domestic architecture begin to be felt. Fierce arguments divided British architects as to the merits of indigenous design. The ultimate plan for New Delhi was carried out by men who had little time for Hindu architecture and believed themselves to be on a civilizing mission. Others at the end of the 19th century wanted to recapture and enhance a tradition for which they had great respect. They have left a series of buildings, both in formerly British ruled territory and in the Princely States, notably in Rajasthan, which illustrate this concern through the development of what became known as the Indo-Saracenic style. The princes themselves often demonstrated highly eclectic tastes, importing such contrasting styles as Venetian-Gothic, Greek Doric and other Europeans styles for their new palaces and mansions. British architects like Sir Samuel Swinton Jacob, William Emerson, and Charles Mant, as well as local state architects and Parsi architects/builders, blended European and Indian features. Victorian, art deco and other European furnishings appointed the palaces, besides traditional arts, crafts, furniture and utensils of the region.

Art
Painting Rajasthan is well known for its wall paintings. Murals were painted on forts, temples, palaces and other historic buildings for centuries, but the fresco technique of Italy (painting on wet plaster) arrived with the Muslims to India. Mudwall painting is popular in Rajasthan, most of these paintings being done on hut walls by women during festivals and family celebrations. High quality *pichhwais* (temple paintings) are produced in Nathdwara, Udaipur and Bhilwara.

Miniature paintings The early miniature paintings in Western India are believed to originate from the classical murals of the Buddhist caves and ancient Jain art. In the 11th century, miniature paintings adorned palm leaf and cloth bound manuscripts, principally those of the Jains of Rajasthan and Gujarat. In the 16th century, the Mughals in India introduced Persian and West Asian techniques which strongly influenced the Rajasthani schools.

The Rajasthan princely states were important patrons of medieval miniature painting and various schools developed in different areas, drawing from local traditions and combining them with Mughal art. While Indian paintings had specialized in full frontal and three-quarter portraits, the Islamic painters introduced profiles. The Rajasthani painters depicted nature with bold colours and emphasized human forms while the Mughals introduced royal, courtly painting. Soon, flamboyant Rajput court culture began to appear as a popular theme but this was tempered by Hindu and Jain elements, local traditions and folk lore. Popular tales portrayed by the miniaturists were those from epics like the Ramayana and Mahabharata, Sanskrit writings like the Puranas and Shringara, iconography of the seasons (*Barah masa* or 12 months), and music (the Ragamala). Rajasthani ballads (love stories of

Dhola-Maru, Sohni-Mahival, Nala-Damyanti etc), festivals, historical events, battles and hunts, sports like polo and pig sticking, all found a place, while the painters looked at dunes, hills, forests, orchards and historic buildings for their backdrops.

Miniature paintings were usually done on paper, sheets being bound together to make a firm surface. Mineral and organic colours were applied using squirrel hair and featherquill brushes and adhesives like gum arabic were used for fixing. Terracotta was sometimes brushed over the subject to give the raised effect, enhanced by gold leaf or powder work. Rare and expensive ivory lent itself as a suitable base for prized miniaturist art which were done with transparent colours so that the base of ivory was visible. This was favoured by affluent Jains and royalty who commissioned paintings of religious subjects, portraits and courtly scenes.

Weaving Kota in eastern Rajasthan is known for its Doria saris with hundreds of weavers in the village of Khaitoon working to produce fine silk and cotton textiles with embroidered zari borders. Often the warp and weft threads are dyed in different colours to create a shot effect in Kota. Weavers of Jaisalmer, Jodhpur and other districts work on pit-looms to produce *durrie* rugs, carpets, woollen cloth and other fabrics. Weaving of traditional woollen *durries* also became associated with Bikaner, Jaipur (and Ahmadabad) jails but today attractive *durries* in pastel colours cater to the modern taste. Floor coverings called *jajams* are produced in Chittaurgarh. Handloom weaving on cradle looms is practised throughout Rajasthan.

Printing Hand-held wood blocks are carefully cut to enable patterns in different colours to be printed; up to five blocks may be used for an elaborate design. Children apprenticed to block makers and printers, master the craft by the age of 14 or 15. Traditionally colours were based on vegetable pigments though now many use chemical dyes. Printing is done in a long shed and after the block printing is complete, the fabric is boiled to make the dye fast. Good examples can be seen in the City Museum in Jaipur. Sanganer, just south of the city, is still well known for block-printing. Delightfully unspoilt, a trip there is worthwhile, see page 133.

Tie-and-dye *Bandhani* tie-dye is another intricate process and ancient technique common throughout Rajasthan. The fabric is pinched together in selected places, tied round with twine or thread and then dyed. Afterwards, the threads are removed to reveal a pattern in the original or preceding colour. The process is often repeated, the dyeing sequence going from light to dark colours. Jaipur, Jodhpur and Udaipur districts are well known for their *bandhani*. Another form of dyeing is the *lehariya* of eastern Rajasthan which leaves long lines or bands running diagonally on the fabric surface.

Jewellery Uncut gemstones are strung or set in typical Rajasthani jewellery, Jaipur being particularly famous for its gems and jewellery. Typical items are nose rings, ear ornaments, bangles and necklaces. *Kundan* work specializes in setting stones in gold; sometimes *meenakari* (enamelling) complements the setting on the reverse side of the pendant, locket or earring.

Pottery The best known pottery in Rajasthan is the 'Jaipur Blue'. This uses a coarse grey clay that is quite brittle even when fired. It is then decorated with floral and geometric patterns along Persian lines utilizing rich ultramarines, turquoise and lapis colours on a plain off-white/grey background. In the villages, the common pot is made from a combination of earth, water and dung. The coarse pots are thrown on a simple stone wheel, partially dried, then finished with a hammer before being simply decorated, glazed and fired.

Terracotta is one of the world's oldest media of artistic expression. Tribes still pray at shrines of terracotta horses and other animistic figures, made in villages like

Bhenswara in the Jalor Bhil belt and Chotta Udepur in eastern Rajasthan, among others. Pottery for water storage, ornamental plants and other utilities are made by Kumhars in most cities, towns and villages. Clay plaques for wall decor are available at Molela near Nathdwara. Pokharan produces attractive red pottery, while Merta near Ajmer is known for its delicate Kagazi pottery.

Embroidery Barmer, Jaisalmer and other districts of the western desert in Rajasthan are well known for their embroidered fabrics set with mirrors and other ornamentation. Leather embroidery is a well known craft Jalor, Barmer and Jodhpur districts. The most popular article of production is footwear called *mojdi*, with bold embroidery patterns, with Bhinmal in Jalor district being specially well known for its embroidered shoes. Camel leather work is done by the Ustas of Bikaner though this is losing popularity because of the high prices of each product.

Wood carving Barmer is known for its woodwork – surprising given the town's location in the desert – perhaps because of its tradition of wood block printing and the camel saddle market. Fancy wood crafts and furnishings are produced for domestic and export markets, sometimes with brass and other metal inlaid patterns. Udaipur is well known for its wooden toys and lacquered wood, Bassi near Chittaurgarh for wooden figures, Jaipur in recent times for wooden furniture. Jodhpur and Sawai Madhopur districts are also well known for their attractive furniture.

Metalware Jaipur city and various districts of Rajasthan are famous for their silver ornaments, utensils and artefacts. Jaipur is particularly well known for its engraved brassware with floral motifs or lacquered effect patterns. Zinc water bags/bottles are made in the desert cities and towns of Rajasthan. Gaduliya Lohars are nomadic smiths in Rajasthan. The swordsmiths of Sirohi, Udaipur and Alwar specialize in metal inlays.

Stone carving The Silavats and other artisans of Rajasthan excel in carving marble, sandstone and other material into beautiful *jali*-work (lattice), utensils and ornamental pieces. Outdoor furniture made from carved marble and other stones are made in Sirohi, Kishangarh and other districts of Rajasthan.

Other crafts Other crafts practised in Rajasthan include *khari* (embossed printing using gold and silver), engraving and lacquering brassware and embroidering camel skin. Papermaking is important in the Jaipur-Bagru-Sanganer triangle, zari embroidery at Surat, Jamnagar and Jaipur, and the making of marble bangles or grass tribal jewellery.

Music and dance

Music Indian music can trace its origins to the metrical hymns and chants of the Vedas, in which the production of sound according to strict rules was understood to be vital to the continuing order of the Universe. Through more than 3,000 years of development and a range of regional schools, India's musical tradition has been handed on almost entirely by ear. The chants of the **Rig Veda** developed into songs in the **Sama Veda** and music found expression in every sphere of life, reflecting the cycle of seasons and the rhythm of work.

Over the centuries the original three notes, which were sung strictly in descending order, were extended to five and then seven and developed to allow freedom to move up and down the scale. The scale increased to 12 with the addition of flats and sharps and finally to 22 with the further subdivision of semitones. Books of musical rules go back at least as far as the third century AD. Classical music was totally intertwined with dance and drama, an interweaving reflected in the term *sangita*.

At some point after the Muslim influence made itself felt in the north, north and south Indian styles diverged, to become Carnatic (Karnatak) music in the south and Hindustani music in the north. However, they still share important common features: *svara* (pitch), *raga* (the melodic structure) and *tala* (rhythm).

Hindustani music probably originated in the Delhi Sultanate during the 13th century, when the most widely known of North Indian musical instruments, the *sitar*, was believed to have been invented. **Amir Khusrau** is also believed to have invented the small drums, the *tabla*. Hindustani music is held to have reached its peak under *Tansen*, a court musician of Akbar. The other important northern instruments are the stringed *sarod*, the reed instrument *shahnai* and the wooden flute. Most Hindustani compositions have devotional texts, though they encompass a great emotional and thematic range. A common classical form of vocal performance is the *dhrupad*, a four-part composition.

The essential structure of a melody is known as a *raga* which usually has five to seven notes and can have as many as nine (or even 12 in mixed *ragas*). The music is improvised by the performer within certain governing rules and although theoretically thousands of *ragas* are possible, only around 100 are commonly performed. *Ragas* have become associated with particular moods and specific times of the day. Music festivals often include all night sessions to allow performers a wider choice of repertoire.

Dance The rules for classical dance were laid down in the Natya shastra in the second century BC, which is still one of the bases for modern dance forms. The most common sources for Indian dance are the epics, but there are three essential aspects of the dance itself, *Nritta* (pure dance), *Nrittya* (emotional expression) and *Natya* (drama). The religious influence in dance was exemplified by the tradition of temple dancers, *devadasis*, girls and women who were dedicated to the deity in major temples. India is also rich in folk dance traditions which are widely performed during festivals.

Folk dance Typical community folk dances of the Rajasthan region are based on the *Rasa* tradition of dancing in circles, clapping hands or striking sticks in unison to set the rhythm. The *Ghoomer* of Rajasthan is generally for women, who clap their hands or strike small sticks to the simple rhythm. The *Ger* of Rajasthan is a dance for men using larger sticks. Combination dances, for both men and women, are also performed. The best period to witness these dances Holi, Gangaur, Navratri and other festivals of Rajasthan.

Kachchhi Ghodi is a dance performed by men riding hobby-horses and sporting swords. The dances are accompanied by songs that recite tales of the Bavaria outlaws of Shekhawati, the Robin Hoods of Rajasthan.

Sidh Naths of Bikaner are deservedly famous for their fire dances. The performers dance on the fire as if it did not exist, and even put burning coals in their mouths, to the beat and rhythm of pipes and drums. The Dholis of Jalore district are known for their drum dance which is a sword, stick and scarf dance performed to powerful beats of five or more drums, as well as cymbals and other percussion instruments.

One of the most colourful dancing communities is the Kalbelia (generally snake charmers and nomadic workers by profession). The women wear embroidered veils called *odhnis*, skirts called *gaghras*, blouses called *cholis* and artistic jewellery, while men wear red turbans. A vigorous dance is the *Terah Tal* of Ramdeora near Pokaran, which has now become a popular dance throughout Rajasthan.

Bhavai is a dance drama, the folk theatre of Gujarat. In Rajasthan tribal dancers recite the tale of the mystic Pabhuji, unravelling a long narrative painting of the hero's life. Langas and Manganiars of western Rajasthan are professional singers whose haunting melodies recall the feel of the desert. Mirasis are professional musicians, usually employed for weddings and celebrations, sometimes accompanied by dancers, while the Naths of Rajasthan are acrobats who perform spell-binding acts to the tune of singing and music.

The pastoral communities of Rajasthan have dances based on the Dandia, Garba, Ger and Ghoomer formations. During Holi in Rajasthan, Bhils perform the Ger-Ghoomar which begins with men in an outer circle and women in the inner circle, but as the dance progresses both sexes get together.

The people

The population of Rajasthan is almost wholly of Indo-Aryan stock. However, they have a much higher percentage of scheduled tribes than the national average.

Tribal peoples

The tribal population of Rajasthan constitutes about 12 per cent of the state's population, nearly double the national average. The Bhils and Minas are the largest groups, but the less well known Sahariyas, Damariyas, Garasias and Gaduliya Lohars are all important. The tribes share many common traits but differences in their costumes and jewellery, their gods, fairs and festivals also set them apart from one another.

Bhils The Bhils comprise nearly 40 per cent of Rajasthan's tribal population with their stronghold in Baneshwar. *Bil* (bow) describes their original talent and strength. Today, the accepted head of all the Rajput clans of Rajasthan – the Maharana of Udaipur – is crowned by anointing his forehead with blood drawn from the palm of a Bhil chieftain, affirming the alliance and the loyalty of his tribe. Rajput rulers came to value the guerrilla tactics of the Bhils, and Muslim and Maratha attacks could not have been repelled without their active support. Furthermore, they always remained a minority and offered no real threat to the city-dwelling princes and their armies. Physically, the Bhils are short, stocky and dark with broad noses and thick lips. They once lived off roots, leaves and fruits of the forest and the increasingly scarce game. Most now farm land and keep cattle, goats and sheep, while those who live near towns often work on daily wages. Thousands congregate near the confluence of the Mahi and Som rivers in Dungarpur district for the Baneshwar fair in January and February.

Minas The Minas are Rajasthan's most widely spread tribal group. They may have been the original inhabitants of the Indus Valley civilization, mentioned in the *Vedas* and the *Mahabharata*, who were finally dispersed into the Aravallis by the Kachhawaha Rajputs. The Minas are tall, with an athletic build, light brown complexion and sharp features. The men wear a loincloth round the waist, a waistcoat and a brightly coloured turban while the women wear a long gathered skirt (*ghaghra*), a small blouse (*kurti-kanchali*) and a large scarf. Most Minas are cultivators who measure their wealth in cattle and other livestock. They worship Siva in temples decorated with stone carvings, and also Sheeta Mata (Shitala), the goddess of smallpox. Like other tribal groups they have a tradition of giving grain, clothes, animals and jewellery to the needy. The forest dwellings, *Mewas*, comprise a cluster of huts or *pals*. Though their marriage ceremony, performed round a fire, is similar to a Hindu one, divorce is not uncommon or particularly difficult. A man wanting a divorce tears a piece of his clothes and gives this to his wife, who then leaves the home carrying two pitchers of water. Whoever helps her unload the

Elopement marriages

The Garasias (under 3% of Rajasthan's tribals), have an interesting custom of marriage through elopement, which usually takes place at the annual Gaur fair in March. After the elopement, which can be spontaneous or pre-arranged, a bride price is paid to the bride's father. Once the couple have 'disappeared' they have to remain hidden in the jungle for three days while the rest of the tribe hunts for them. If caught during that period they are severely beaten and forcibly separated. However, if they have proved their skills in survival and in remaining hidden, their marriage is recognized and they return to live with the rest of the tribe. Should the arrangement not work out, the woman returns home. Widows are obliged to remarry, since their children – and not they – are given a share in the husband's property.

pitchers becomes her new husband! Of the tribes of Rajasthan the Minas have progressed the most and only in a few pockets do they follow traditional practices.

Gaduliya Lohars The Gaduliya Lohars, named after their beautiful bullock carts (*gadis*), are nomadic blacksmiths, said to have wandered from their homeland of Mewar because of their promise to their 'lord' Maharana Pratap who was ousted from Chittaurgarh by Akbar. This clan of warring Rajputs vowed to re-enter the city only with a victorious Maharana Pratap. Unfortunately the Maharana was killed on the battlefield, so even today many of them prefer a nomadic life.

Sahariyas The Sahariyas are jungle dwellers, their name possibly deriving from the Persian *sehr* (jungle). They are regarded as the most backward tribe in Rajasthan and eke out a living as shifting cultivators and by hunting and fishing. More recently they have also undertaken menial and manual work on daily wages. In most respects their rituals are those of Hindus. One difference is that polygamy and widow marriage (*nata*) are permitted, though only to a widower or divorcee.

Bishnois With the growing recent interest in environmental conservation the Bishnois of Rajasthan's desert districts have come into prominence. For centuries, they have protected wildlife and vegetation with a religious passion inspired by their medieval leader Jamboji. Jalore, Barmer, Nagaur, Jodhpur and Bikaner district have large groups of Bishnois. Their hamlets, called *dhannis*, comprise picturesque huts with thatch roofing and mud walls. Each *dhanni* is surrounded by vegetation. Antelope and gazelle feel safe in Bishnoi areas and are less shy than anywhere else.

Garasias One of the most colourful tribal communities is the Garasia adivasi, inhabitants of the Aravalli foothills of Sabarkanta and Banaskanta districts in north Gujarat, and Udaipur, Sirohi and Pali districts of Rajasthan. Garasia adivasis claim descent from Rajput men who married Bhil women (*Garasia* = landowner, *adivasi* = original inhabitant) and consider themselves superior to other tribes of the Aravalli foothills. They still own cultivable land and work on fields, the reason for the importance of the spring harvest in the life of this tribal community. Garasia homes are typically made from mud and bamboo decorated during festivals with line art and wall paintings. The women dress in colourful clothes, sport facial tattoos and wear artistic silver and grass jewellery. The men wear turbans of different colours, *kurtas* and ear ornaments, and pride themselves on being skilful archers. Potters make terracotta horses and other figurines for the animistic worship. The community can be seen at their colourful best during tribal fairs in March and April like the Gaur fair near Mount Abu and Chitra Vichitra fair near Poshina. These fairs feature ancestor mourning, music, dancing, revelry and match-making (elopement is not uncommon!).

Rathwas Like the Garasia Adivasis of northern Gujarat, the Rathwa of eastern Gujarat love music, dancing, colourful clothes and attractive ornaments, and are skilled archers. The Rathwas usually live in picturesque village houses, made of mud and roofed with intricately thatched straw, leaves, timber or locally made clay tiles. The interiors of these houses are embellished with a profusion of faunal figures called *pithoras*. The tribes worship at shrines comprising terracotta horses and other animistic clay figures and are strong believers in ghosts, spirits, ancestor worship and the Hindu pantheon. The *pithora* paintings are believed to be magical and ward away evil spirits.

The beautiful villages are often surrounded by agricultural fields, and may be set next to palm groves that the tribes tap for toddy, or in the heart of wooded hill country. Today, many of these tribal people have taken employment as mine workers, farm labourers and watchmen, but traditional handicrafts like wood carving, basket weaving and arrow crafting continue in this tribal belt, and the men still carry bows, arrows and guns when they travel. Ephemeral village markets (*haats*) are a daily event in the Rathwa tribal belt, with one of the largest being the Saturday bazaar at Chotta Udepur. The area comes alive with music, dancing, acrobatics and a showcase of colourful tribal dress during the fairs of Dasara and Holi. The Kawant fair offers an interesting insight into the tribes of this region, their clothing, ornaments, music and dancing.

Rabaris The Rabari (also called **Raika** in Rajasthan), the best known of the semi-nomadic herders, are widespread with many distinct subgroups. They have attractive houses in their villages, but travel with camels and cattle in search of pasture seasonally.

Siddis The Siddis live either side of the Rajasthan-Gujarat border, and are believed to have originally come from Africa in the 13th century. Employed by the Gujarat sultanate as mercenary warriors or slaves, some rose to become generals, working to protect important ports like Daman and Diu from Portuguese naval invasions. The Siddis of Gir live in hamlets that would not be out of place in the African bush, and retain many of their traditions and beliefs handed down through generations. Among their many Africans inheritances is the natural sense of rhythm reflected in their drumming and dance performances. They also retain some elements of African dress and custom such as breaking coconuts with their heads and fire-walking.

Jats and Ahirs The Jats inhabit Kachchh and the northwestern arid zone from Gujarat and Rajasthan to the North Western Frontier Province of Pakistan. Their turbans and dress are reminiscent of the days when camel caravans plied from the Near East to the Far East across the desert areas of western India. The Ahirs are an agricultural community of Kachchh. Their women are known for their colourful embroidery.

Religion

It is impossible to write briefly about religion in India without greatly oversimplifying. Over 80 per cent of Indians are Hindu, but there are significant minorities. Muslims number about 120 million and there are over 20 million Christians, 18 million Sikhs, six million Buddhists, two million Jains and a number of other religious groups.

Although nearly all these groups are represented in Rajasthan, the balance varies. Buddhism is barely represented, and there are only small communities of Sikhs and Christians. While Hinduism is dominant, there is a significant Muslim minority, and the greatest concentration of Jains in India.

One of the most persistent features of Indian religious and social life is the caste system. This has undergone substantial changes since Independence, especially in towns and cities, but most people in India are still clearly identified as a member of a particular caste group. The government has introduced measures to help the backward, or 'scheduled' castes – the *dalits*, meaning 'oppressed' – though in recent years this has produced a major political backlash.

Hinduism

It has always been easier to define Hinduism by what it is not than by what it is. Indeed, the name 'Hindu' was given by foreigners to the peoples of the subcontinent who did not profess the other major faiths, such as Muslims or Christians. The beliefs and practices of modern Hinduism began to take shape in the centuries on either side of the birth of Christ. But while some aspects of modern Hinduism can be traced back more than 2,000 years before that, other features are recent.

Key ideas

Some Hindu scholars and philosophers talk of Hinduism as one religious and cultural tradition. Yet there is no Hindu organization, like a church, with the authority to define belief or establish official practice. There are spiritual leaders who are widely revered and there is an enormous range of literature that is treated as sacred. In view of these characteristics, many authorities argue that it is misleading to think of Hinduism as a religion at all. Be that as it may, the evidence of the living importance of Hinduism is visible across India. Hindu philosophy and practice has also touched many of those who belong to other religious traditions, particularly in terms of social institutions such as caste.

Darshan One of Hinduism's recurring themes is 'vision', 'sight' or 'view' – *darshan*. Applied to the different philosophical systems themselves, such as *yoga* or *vedanta*, *darshan* is also used to describe the sight of the deity that worshippers hope to gain when they visit a temple or shrine hoping for the sight of a 'guru' (teacher). Equally it may apply to the religious insight gained through meditation or prayer.

The four human goals Many Hindus also accept that there are four major human goals; material prosperity (*artha*), the satisfaction of desires (*kama*) and performing the duties laid down according to your position in life (*dharma*). Beyond those is the goal of achieving liberation from the endless cycle of rebirths into which everyone is locked (*moksha*). It is to the search for liberation that the major schools of Indian philosophy have devoted most attention. Together with *dharma*, it is basic to Hindu thought.

The Mahabharata lists 10 embodiments of *dharma*: good name, truth, self-control, cleanness of mind and body, simplicity, endurance, resoluteness of character, giving and sharing, austerities and continence. In *dharmic* thinking these are inseparable from five patterns of behaviour: non-violence, an attitude of equality, peace and tranquillity, lack of aggression and cruelty and absence of envy. Dharma, an essentially secular concept, represents the order inherent in human life.

The great majority of Hindu homes will have a shrine to one of the gods of the Hindu pantheon.

Karma The idea of *karma*, 'the effect of former actions', is central to achieving liberation. As C Rajagopalachari put it: "Every act has its appointed effect, whether the act be thought, word or deed. The cause holds the effect, so to say, in its womb. If we reflect deeply and objectively, the entire world will be found to obey unalterable laws. That is the doctrine of karma".

Rebirth The belief in the transmigration of souls (*samsara*) in a never-ending cycle of rebirth has been Hinduism's most distinctive and important contribution to Indian culture. The earliest reference to the belief is found in one of the Upanishads, around the seventh century BC, at about the same time as the doctrine of karma made its first appearance. By the late Upanishads it was universally accepted and in Buddhism and Jainism it is never questioned.

Ahimsa AL Basham pointed out that belief in transmigration must have encouraged a further distinctive doctrine, that of non-violence or non-injury – *ahimsa*. The belief in rebirth meant that all living things and creatures of the spirit – people, devils, gods, animals, even worms – possessed the same essential soul. It was an idea that became particularly important for the Jains.

Schools of philosophy

It is common now to talk of six major schools of Hindu philosophy. *Nyaya, Vaisheshika, Sankhya, Yoga, Purvamimansa* and *Vedanta*.

Yoga Yoga, can be traced back to at least the third century AD. It seeks a synthesis of the spirit, the soul and the flesh and is concerned with systems of meditation and self denial that lead to the realization of the Divine within oneself and can ultimately release one from the cycle of rebirth.

Vedanta These are literally the final parts of the Vedic literature, the *Upanishads*. The basic texts also include the *Brahmasutra of Badrayana*, written about the first century AD and the most important of all, the *Bhagavad-Gita*, which is a part of the epic the *Mahabharata*. There are many interpretations of these basic texts.

Worship

Puja For most Hindus today worship ('performing puja') is an integral part of their faith. Acts of devotion are often aimed at the granting of favours and the meeting of urgent needs for this life – good health, finding a suitable wife or husband, the birth of a son, prosperity and good fortune. Puja involves making an offering to God and *darshan* (having a view of the deity). Hindu worship is generally, though not always, an act performed by individuals. Thus Hindu temples may be little more than a shrine in the middle of the street, tended by a priest and visited at special times when a *darshan* of the resident God can be obtained. When it has been consecrated, the image, if exactly made, becomes the channel for the godhead to work.

Rituals and festivals The temple rituals often follow through the cycle of day and night, as well as yearly lifecycles. The priests may wake the deity from sleep, bathe, clothe and feed it. Worshippers will be invited to share in this process by bringing offerings of clothes and food. Gifts of money will usually be made and in some temples there is a charge levied for taking up positions in front of the deity in order to obtain a *darshan* at the appropriate times.

Hindu deities

Today three Gods are widely seen as all-powerful: Brahma, Vishnu and Siva. While Brahma is regarded as the ultimate source of creation, Siva also has a creative role

66 99 Every aspect of Hindu, Jain and Buddhist religious building is identified with conceptions of the structure of the universe...

alongside his function as destroyer. Vishnu in contrast is seen as the preserver or protector of the universe. Vishnu and Siva are widely represented in sculpture and art (where Brahma is not) and have come to be seen as the most powerful and important. Their followers are referred to as Vaishnavites and Shaivites respectively and numerically they form the two largest sects in India.

Brahma In the literal sense the name Brahma is the masculine and personalized form of the neuther word Brahman. Popularly Brahma is recognised as the Creator. In the early Vedic writing, Brahman represented the universal and impersonal principle which governed the Universe. Gradually, as Vedic philosophy moved towards a monotheistic interpretation of the universe and its origins, this impersonal power was increasingly personalized. In the Upanishads, Brahman was seen as a universal and elemental creative spirit.

By the fourth and fifth centuries AD, the height of the classical period of Hinduism, Brahma was seen as one of the trinity of Gods – *Trimurti* – in which Vishnu, Siva and Brahma represented three forms of the unmanifested supreme being. It is from Brahma that Hindu cosmology takes its structure. The basic cycle through which the whole cosmos passes is described as one day in the life of Brahma – the *kalpa*. It equals 4,320 million years, with an equally long night. One year of Brahma's life – a cosmic year – lasts 360 days and nights. The universe is expected to last for 100 years of Brahma's life, who is currently believed to be 51 years old.

By the sixth century AD Brahma worship had effectively ceased (before the great period of temple building), which accounts for the fact that there are remarkably few temples dedicated to Brahma. Nonetheless images of Brahma are found in most temples. Characteristically he is shown with four faces, a fifth having been destroyed by the fire from Siva's third eye. In his four arms he usually holds a copy of the Vedas, a sceptre and a water jug or a bow. He is accompanied by the goose, symbolizing knowledge.

Sarasvati Seen by some Hindus as the 'active power' of Brahma, popularly thought of as his consort, Sarasvati, the goddess of education and learning, is worshipped in schools and colleges with gifts of fruit, flowers and incense. The development of her identity represented the rebirth of the concept of a mother goddess, which had been strong in the Indus Valley Civilization over 1,000 years before and which may have been continued in popular ideas through the worship of female spirits.

In addition to her role as Brahma's wife, Sarasvati is also variously seen as the wife of Vishnu and Manu or as Daksha's daughter, among other interpretations. Normally white coloured, riding on a swan and carrying a book, she is often shown playing a *vina*. She may have many arms and heads, representing her role as patron of all the sciences and arts.

Vishnu Vishnu is seen as the God with the human face. From the second century a new and passionate devotional worship of Vishnu's incarnation as Krishna developed in the South. By 1,000 AD Vaishnavism had spread across South India and it became closely associated with the devotional form of Hinduism preached by

An eye to the future

According to the doctrine of karma, every person, animal or god has a being or 'self' which has existed without beginning. Every action, except those that are done without any consideration of the results, leaves an indelible mark on that 'self', carried forward into the next life.

The overall character of the imprint on each person's 'self' determines three features of the next life: the nature of his next birth (animal, human or god), the kind of

family he will be born into if human and the length of the next life. Finally, it controls the good or bad experiences that the self will experience. However, it does not imply a fatalistic belief that the nature of action in this life is unimportant. Rather, it suggests that the path followed by the individual in the present life is vital to the nature of its next life and ultimately to the chance of gaining release from this world.

Ramanuja, whose followers spread the worship of Vishnu and his 10 successive incarnations in animal and human form. For Vaishnavites, God took these different forms in order to save the world from impending disaster. AL Basham has summarized the 10 incarnations (see Table).

Rama and Krishna By far the most influential incarnations of Vishnu are those in which he was believed to take recognizable human form, especially as Rama (twice) and Krishna. As the Prince of Ayodhya, history and myth blend, for Rama was probably a chief who lived in the eighth or seventh century BC.

Although Rama (or Ram – pronounced to rhyme with *calm*) is now seen as an earlier incarnation of Vishnu than Krishna, he came to be regarded as divine very late, probably after the Muslim invasions of the 12th century AD. The story has become part of the cultures of Southeast Asia.

Krishna is worshipped extremely widely as perhaps the most human of the gods. Often shown in pictures as blue in colour and playing the flute, he is the playful child stealing butter or the amorous young man teasing the young women looking after the cattle. His advice on the battlefield of the Mahabharata is one of the major sources of guidance for the rules of daily living for many Hindus today.

Lakshmi Commonly represented as Vishnu's wife, Lakshmi is widely worshipped as the goddess of wealth. Earlier representations of Vishnu's consorts portrayed her as Sridevi, often shown in statues on Vishnu's right, while Bhudevi, also known as Prithvi, who represented the earth, was on his left. Lakshmi is popularly shown in her own right as standing on a lotus flower, although eight forms of Lakshmi are recognized.

Hanuman The Ramayana tells how Hanuman, Rama's faithful monkey servant, went across India and finally into the demon Ravana's forest home of Lanka at the head of his monkey army in search of the abducted Sita. He used his powers to jump the sea channel separating India from Sri Lanka and managed after a series of heroic and magical feats to find and rescue his master's wife. Whatever form he is shown in, he remains almost instantly recognizable.

Siva Siva is interpreted as both creator and destroyer, the power through whom the universe evolves. He lives on Mount Kailasa with his wife **Parvati** (also known as **Uma, Sati, Kali** and **Durga**) and two sons, the elephant-headed Ganesh and the six-headed

Karttikeya. To many contemporary Hindus they form a model of sorts for family life. In sculptural representations Siva is normally accompanied by his 'vehicle', the bull (*nandi* or *nandin*).

Siva is also represented in Shaivite temples throughout India by the linga, literally meaning 'sign' or 'mark', but referring in this context to the sign of gender or phallus and *yoni*. On the one hand a symbol of energy, fertility and potency, as Siva's symbol it also represents the yogic power of sexual abstinence and penance. The linga has become the most important symbol of the cult of Siva.

A wide variety of myths appeared to explain the origin of linga worship. The myths surrounding the 12 *jyotirlinga* (linga of light) found at centres like Somnath in Gujarat go back to the second century BC and were developed in order to explain and justify linga worship.

Siva's alternative names Although Siva is not seen as having a series of rebirths, like Vishnu, he nonetheless appears in very many forms representing different aspects of his varied powers. Some of the more common are:

Chandrasekhara The moon (*chandra*) symbolizes the powers of creation and destruction.

Mahadeva The representation of Siva as the god of supreme power, which came relatively late into Hindu thought, shown as the linga in combination with the *yoni*, or female genitalia.

Nataraja, the Lord of the Cosmic Dance The story is based on a legend in which Siva and Vishnu went to the forest to overcome 10,000 heretics. In their anger the heretics attacked Siva first by sending a tiger, then a snake and thirdly a fierce black dwarf with a club. Siva killed the tiger, tamed the snake and wore it like a garland and then put his foot on the dwarf and performed a dance of such power that the dwarf and the heretics acknowledged Siva as the Lord.

Rudra Siva's early prototype, who may date back to the Indus Valley Civilization.

Virabhadra Siva created Virabhadra to avenge himself on his wife Sati's father, Daksha, who had insulted Siva by not inviting him to a special sacrifice. Sati attended the ceremony against Siva's wishes and when she heard her father grossly abusing Siva she committed suicide by jumping into the sacrificial fire. This act gave rise to the term *sati* (*suttee*, a word which simply means a good or virtuous woman). Recorded in the *Vedas*, the self immolation of a woman on her husband's funeral pyre probably did not become accepted practice until the early centuries BC. Even then it was mainly restricted to those of the Kshatriya caste.

Nandi Siva's vehicle, the bull, one of the most widespread of sacred symbols of the ancient world, may represent a link with Rudra who was sometimes represented as a bull in pre-Hindu India. Strength and virility are key attributes and pilgrims to Siva temples will often touch the Nandi's testicles on their way into the shrine.

Ganesh Ganesh, one of Hinduism's most popular gods, is seen as the great clearer of obstacles. Shown at gateways and on door lintels with his elephant head and pot belly, his image is revered across India. Meetings, functions and special family gatherings will often start with prayers to Ganesh and any new venture, from the opening of a building to inaugurating a company, will not be deemed complete without a Ganesh puja.

Shakti, The Mother Goddess Shakti is a female divinity often worshipped in the form of Siva's wife Durga or Kali. As Durga she agreed to do battle with Mahish, an *asura* (demon) who threatened to dethrone the gods. Many sculptures and paintings illustrate the story in which, during the terrifying struggle which ensued, the demon changed into a buffalo, an elephant and a giant with 1,000 arms. Durga, clutching weapons in each of her 10 hands, eventually emerges victorious. As Kali ('black') the mother goddess takes on her most fearsome form and character. Fighting with the chief of the demons, she was forced to use every weapon in her armoury, but every drop of blood that she drew became 1,000 new giants just as strong as he. The only way she could win was by drinking the blood of all her enemies. Having succeeded she was so elated that her dance of triumph threatened the earth. Ignoring the pleas of the gods to stop, she even threw her husband Siva to the ground and trampled over him, until she realized to her shame what she had done. She is always shown with a sword in one hand, the severed head of the giant in another, two corpses for earrings and a necklace of human skulls. She is often shown standing with one foot on the body and the other on the leg of Siva.

Gods of the warrior caste Modern Hinduism has brought into its pantheon over many generations gods who were worshipped by the earlier pre-Hindu Aryan civilizations. The most important is **Indra**, often shown as the god of rain, thunder and lightning. To the early Aryans, Indra destroyed demons in battle, the most important being his victory over Vritra, 'the Obstructor'. By this victory Indra released waters from the clouds, allowing the earth to become fertile. To the early Vedic writers the clouds of the southwest monsoon were seen as hostile, determined to keep their precious treasure of water to themselves and only releasing it when forced to by a greater power. Indra, carrying a bow in one hand, a thunderbolt in another and lances in the others and riding on his vehicle Airavata, the elephant, is thus the Lord of Heaven.

Mitra and **Varuna** have the power both of gods and demons. Their role is to sustain order, Mitra taking responsibility for friendship and Varuna for oaths and as they have to keep watch for 24 hours a day Mitra has become the god of the day or the sun, Varuna the god of the moon.

Soma The juice of the soma plant, the nectar of the gods guaranteeing eternal life, Soma is also a deity taking many forms. Born from the churning of the ocean of milk in later stories Soma was identified with the moon. The golden haired and golden skinned god **Savitri** is an intermediary with the great power to forgive sin and as king of heaven he gives the gods their immortality. **Surya**, the god of the sun, fittingly of overpowering splendour, is often described as being dark red, sitting on a red lotus or riding a chariot pulled by the seven horses of the dawn (representing the days of the week). **Usha**, sometimes referred to as Surya's wife, is the goddess of the dawn, daughter of Heaven and sister of the night. She rides in a chariot drawn by cows or horses.

Devas and Asuras In Hindu popular mythology the world is also populated by innumerable gods and demons, with a somewhat uncertain dividing line between them. Both have great power and moral character and there are frequent conflicts and battles between them.

The **Nagas** and **Naginis** The multiple-hooded cobra head often seen in sculptures represents the fabulous snake gods the Nagas, though they may often be shown in other forms, even human. Worshipped throughout India, in Rajasthan the naga – or sesa – is widely revered. The thousand-headed cosmic serpent is seen as the God Vishnu in the form of the snake. **Sesa** has the power to destroy the world at the end of every age by his fiery breath.

Hindu society

Dharma is seen as the most important of the objectives of individual and social life. Hindu law givers laid down rules of family conduct and social obligations related to the institutions of caste and jati which were beginning to take shape at the same time.

Caste Although the word caste was given by the Portuguese in the 15th century AD,
the main feature of the system emerged at the end of the Vedic period. Two terms –
varna and *jati* – are used in India itself and have come to be used interchangeably
and confusingly with the word caste.

Varna This literally means colour, had a fourfold division. By 600 BC this had
become a standard means of classifying the population. The fair-skinned Aryans
distinguished themselves from the darker skinned earlier inhabitants. The priestly
varna, the Brahmins, were seen as coming from the mouth of Brahma; the Kshatriyas
(or Rajputs as they are commonly called in Northwest India) were warriors, coming
from Brahma's arms; the Vaishyas, a trading community, came from Brahma's thighs
and the Sudras, classified as agriculturalists, from his feet. Relegated beyond the
pale of civilized Hindu society were the untouchables or outcastes, who were left with
the jobs which were regarded as impure.

Jati Many Brahmins and Rajputs are conscious of their *varna* status, but the great
majority of Indians do not put themselves into one of the four *varna* categories, but
into a *jati* group. There are thousands of different *jatis* across the country. While
individuals found it impossible to change caste or to move up the social scale, groups
would sometimes try to gain recognition as higher caste by adopting practices of the
Brahmins such as becoming vegetarians. Many used to be identified with particular
activities and occupations used to be hereditary. Caste membership is decided
simply by birth. Although you can be evicted from your caste by your fellow members
you cannot join another caste and technically you become an outcaste. Right up until
Independence in 1947 such punishment was a drastic penalty for disobeying one's
dharmic duty. In many areas all avenues into normal life could be blocked, families
would disregard outcaste members and it could even be impossible for the outcaste
to continue to work within the locality.

The Dalits Gandhi spearheaded his campaign for independence from British
colonial rule with a powerful campaign to abolish the disabilities imposed by the
caste system. Coining the term *harijan* (meaning 'person of God') Gandhi demanded
that discrimination be outlawed. Lists – or 'schedules' – of backward castes were
drawn up during the early part of this century in order to provide positive help to such
groups. The term *harijan* has been rejected by many former outcastes as paternalistic
and as implying an adherence to Hindu beliefs which some explicitly reject. Many
argue passionately for the use of the secular term 'dalits' – the 'oppressed'.

Affirmative action Since 1947 the Indian government has extended its positive
discrimination (a form of affirmative action) to scheduled castes and scheduled
tribes, particularly through reserving up to 50% of jobs in government-run institutions
and in further education, leading to professional qualifications for these groups.
Members of the scheduled castes are now found in important positions throughout
the economy. Most of the obvious forms of social discrimination have disappeared.
Yet caste remains an explosive political issue. Attempts to improve the social and
economic position of dalits and what are termed 'other backward castes' (OBCs)
continues to cause sometimes violent conflict.

Marriage Even in cities, where traditional means of arranging marriages have often
broken down and where many people resort to advertising for marriage partners in
the columns of the Sunday newspapers, caste is frequently stated as a requirement.
Marriage is generally seen as an alliance between two families. Great efforts are made
to match caste, social status and economic position, although the rules which govern
eligibility vary from region to region. In some groups marriage between even first

cousins is common, while among others marriage between any branch of the same clan is strictly prohibited.

Hindu reform movements

Hinduism today is a more self-conscious religious and political force than it was even at Independence in 1947. Reform movements of modern Hinduism can be traced back at least to the early years of the 19th century. These movements were unique in Hinduism's history in putting the importance of political ideas on the same level as strictly religious thinking and in interrelating them.

The **Arya Samaj**, founded in 1875 at Ajmer by Dayanand Sarasvati, was established to restore India to its Vedic Aryan religious roots. Particularly strong in Rajasthan and northwestern India, the Arya Samaj held that the Vedas contain all knowledge and truth. In its extreme form this has led to claims that references to everything ever invented can be found in the Vedas, including space travel and nuclear weapons, but the Arya Samaj also had a significant social reforming dimension.

The Hindu calendar While for its secular life India follows the Gregorian calendar, for Hindus, much of religious and personal life follows the Hindu calendar. This is based on the lunar cycle of 29½ days, but the clever bit comes in the way it is synchronized with the 365 day Gregorian solar calendar of the west by the addition of an 'extra month' (*adhik maas*), every 2½ to three years.

Hindus follow two distinct eras. The *Vikrama Samvat* which began in 57 BC and the *Salivahan Saka* which dates from 78 AD and has been the official Indian calendar since 1957. The *Saka* new year starts on 22 March and has the same length as the Gregorian calendar. In North India the New Year is celebrated in the second month of *Vaisakh*.

The year itself is divided into two, the first six solar months being when the sun 'moves' north, known as the *Makar Sankranti* (which is marked by special festivals), and the second half when it moves south, the *Karka Sankranti*. The first begins in January and the second in June. The 29½ day lunar month with its 'dark' (*Krishna*) and 'bright' (*Shukla*) halves based on the new (*Amavasya*) and full moons (*Purnima*), are named after the 12 constellations, and total a 354 day year. The day itself is divided into eight *praharas* of three hours each and the year into six seasons: *Vasant* (spring), *Grishha* (summer), *Varsha* (rains), *Sharat* (early autumn), *Hemanta* (late autumn), *Shishir* (winter).

Hindu, and corresponding Gregorian, calendar months

Chaitra	March-April	*Ashwin*	September-October
Vaishakh	April-May	*Kartik*	October-November
Jyeshtha	May-June	*Margashirsha*	November-December
Aashadh	June-July	*Poush*	December-January
Shravan	July -August	*Magh*	January-February
Bhadra	August-September	*Phalgun*	February-March

Islam

Islam is a highly visible presence in India today. Even after partition in 1947 over 40 million Muslims remained in India and today there are just over 120 million. It is the most recent of imported religions. From the creation of the Delhi Sultanate in 1206, by Turkish rather than Arab power, Islam became a permanent living religion in India.

The victory of the Turkish ruler of Ghazni over the Rajputs in AD 1192 established a 500-year period of Muslim power in India. The contact between the courts of the new rulers and the indigenous Hindu populations produced innovative developments in art and architecture, language and literature. Hindus and Hindu culture were profoundly affected by the spread and exercise of Muslim political power, but Islam too underwent major modifications in response to the new social and religious context in which the Muslim rulers found themselves.

From the middle of the 13th century, when the Mongols crushed the Arab caliphate, the Delhi sultans were left on their own to exercise Islamic authority in India. From then onwards the main external influences were from Persia. Small numbers of migrants, mainly the skilled and the educated, continued to flow into the Indian courts.

Muslim populations Muslims only became a majority of the South Asian population in the plains of the Indus and west Punjab and in parts of Bengal. Elsewhere they formed important minorities, notably in the towns of the central heartland such as Lucknow. In the central plains there was already a densely populated, Hindu region, where little attempt was made to achieve converts.

The **Mughals** wanted to expand their territory and their economic base. To pursue this they made enormous grants of land to those who had served the empire, and new land was brought into cultivation. At the same time, shrines were established to Sufi saints who attracted peasant farmers. By the 18th century many Muslims had joined the **Sunni** sect of Islam.

In some areas Muslim society shared many of the characteristic features of the Hindu society from which the majority of them came. Many of the Muslim migrants from Iran or Turkey, the élite **Ashraf** communities, continued to identify with the Islamic élites from which they traced their descent. They held high military and civil posts in imperial service. In sharp contrast, many of the non-Ashraf Muslim communities in the towns and cities were organized in social groups very much like the *jatis* of their neighbouring Hindu communities. While the élites followed Islamic practices close to those based on the Qur'an as interpreted by scholars, the poorer, less literate communities followed devotional and pietistic forms of Islam. The distinction is still very clear today and the importance of veneration of the saints can be seen at tombs and shrines in Rajasthan and Gujarat.

Muslim beliefs The beliefs of Islam (which means 'submission to God') could apparently scarcely be more different from those of Hinduism. Islam, often described as having 'five pillars' of faith has a fundamental creed; 'There is no God but God; and Mohammad is the Prophet of God' (*La Illaha illa 'llah Mohammad Rasulu 'llah*). One book, the Qur'an, is the supreme authority on Islamic teaching and faith. Islam preaches the belief in bodily resurrection after death and in the reality of heaven and hell.

The idea of heaven as paradise is pre-Islamic. Alexander the Great is believed to have brought the word into Greek from Persia, where he used it to describe the walled Persian gardens that were found even three centuries before the birth of Christ. For Muslims, Paradise is believed to be filled with sensuous delights and pleasures, while hell is a place of eternal terror and torture, which is the certain fate of all who deny the unity of God.

Islam has no priesthood. The authority of Imams derives from social custom and from their authority to interpret the scriptures, rather than from a defined status within the Islamic community. Islam also prohibits any distinction on the basis of race or colour and most Muslims believe it is wrong to represent the human figure. It is often thought, inaccurately, that this ban stems from the Qur'an itself. In fact it probably has its origins in the belief of Mohammad that images were likely to be turned into idols.

Muslim sects During the first century after Mohammad's death Islam split in to two sects which were divided on political and religious grounds, the Shi'is and Sunni's.

The **Sunnis** – always the majority in South Asia – believe that Mohammad did not appoint a successor and that Abu Bak'r, Omar and Othman were the first three caliphs (or vice-regents) after Mohammad's death. Ali, whom the Sunni's count as the fourth caliph, is regarded as the first legitimate caliph by the Shi'is, who consider Abu Bak'r and Omar to be usurpers. While the Sunni's believe in the principle of election of caliphs, Shi'is believe that although Mohammad is the last prophet there is a continuing need for intermediaries between God and man. Such intermediaries are termed *Imams* and they base both their law and religious practice on the teaching of the *Imams*.

The Islamic Calendar The calendar begins on 16 July 622 AD, the date of the Prophet's migration from Mecca to Medina, the Hijra, hence AH (Anno Hejirae). The Muslim year is divided into 12 lunar months, totalling 354 or 355 days, hence Islamic festivals usually move 11 days earlier each year according to the solar (Gregorian) calendar. The first month of the year is *Moharram,* followed by *Safar, Rabi-ul-Awwal, Rabi-ul-Sani, Jumada-ul- Awwal, Jumada-ul-Sani, Rajab, Shaban, Ramadan, Shawwal, Ziquad* and *Zilhaj.*

Jainism

Like Buddhism, Jainism started as a reform movement of the Brahmanic religious beliefs of the sixth century BC. Its founder was a widely revered saint and ascetic, Vardhamma, who became known as **Mahavir** – 'great hero'. Mahavir was born in the same border region of India and Nepal as the Buddha, just 50 km north of modern Patna, probably in 599 BC. Thus he was about 35 years older than the Buddha. His family, also royal, were followers of an ascetic saint, Parsvanatha, who according to Jain tradition had lived 200 years previously.

Mahavir's life story is embellished with legends, but there is no doubt that he left his royal home for a life of the strict ascetic. He is believed to have received enlightenment after 12 years of rigorous hardship, penance and meditation. Afterwards he travelled and preached for 30 years, stopping only in the rainy season. He died aged 72 in 527 BC. His death was commemorated by a special lamp festival in the region of Bihar, which Jains claim is the basis of the now-common Hindu festival of lights, Diwali.

Some Jain ideas, such as vegetarianism and reverence for all life, are widely recognized by Hindus as highly commendable, even by those who do not share other Jain beliefs. The value Jains place on non-violence has contributed to their importance in business and commerce, as they regard nearly all occupations except banking and commerce as violent.

Jain beliefs Jains (from the word Jina, literally meaning 'descendants of conquerors') believe that there are two fundamental principles, the living (*jiva*) and the non-living (*ajiva*). The essence of Jain belief is that all life is sacred and that every living entity, even the smallest insect, has within it an indestructible and immortal soul. Jains developed the view of *ahimsa* – often translated as 'non-violence', but better perhaps as 'non-harming'. *Ahimsa* was the basis for the entire scheme of Jain values and ethics and alternative codes of practice were defined for householders and for ascetics.

The five vows may be taken both by monks and by lay people. A Jain must not to kill any living being for food, sport or pleasure but the use of force is permissible in defending one's country, society, family or property. Jains practise strict vegetarianism – and even some vegetables, such as potatoes and onions, are believed to have microscopic souls. Where injury to life is unavoidable, a Jain is required to reduce this to a minimum by taking all precautions. The other vows require a Jain to speak the truth, not to steal (or cheat or use dishonest means in acquiring material wealth), to abstain from sexual relations (except with one's spouse for the lay people) and to set a limit on acquiring possessions and to use any surplus for the common good. The essence of all the rules is to avoid intentional injury, which is the worst of all sins.

Like Hindus, the Jains believe in *karma*, by which the evil effects of earlier deeds leave an indelible impurity on the soul. This impurity will remain through endless rebirths unless burned off by extreme penances.

Jains also regard the manner of dying as extremely important. Although suicide is deeply opposed, vows of fasting to death voluntarily may be regarded as earning merit in the proper context. Mahavir himself is believed to have died of self-starvation, near Rajgir in modern Bihar.

Jain sects Jains have two main sects, whose origins can be traced back to the fourth century BC. The more numerous **Svetambaras** – the 'white clad' – concentrated more in eastern and western India, wear only two or three unsewn white garments. The **Digambaras** – or 'sky-clad' – among whom the male monks go naked.

Unlike Buddhists, Jains accept the idea of God, but not as a creator of the universe. They see him in the lives of the 24 **Tirthankaras** (prophets, or literally 'makers of fords' – a reference to their role in building crossing points for the spiritual journey over the river of life), the 24 leaders of Jainism, whose lives are recounted in the Kalpsutra – the third century BC book of ritual for the Svetambaras. **Vardhamana Mahavir** (599-527 BC) who followed **Parsvanatha** (877-777 BC), is regarded as the last of these great spiritual leaders. The first and most revered of the Tirthankaras, **Adinatha Rishabdeva**, who lived in pre-historic times, is widely represented in Jain temples.

Gujarat is one of the modern strongholds of Jainism. Jains devote great attention to the care of sick animals and birds and run a number of special animal hospitals. Note the '*parabdis*', special feeding places for birds, in the town.

Buddhism

India was the home of Buddhism, which had its roots in the early Hinduism, or Brahmanism, of its time. Siddharta Gautama, who came to be given the title of the Buddha – or *enlightened one* – was born a prince into the kshatriya caste about 563 BC. By the time he died the Buddha had established a small band of monks and nuns known as the *sangha* , and had followers across northern India. During the early centuries BC and AD Buddhist caves mushroomed across Saurashtra. Buddhist relics can be seen at Talaja near Bhavnagar, Junagadh and surrounds, and at Khambilida near Gondal. Today however Buddhism is practised only on the margins of the subcontinent, from Ladakh, Nepal and Bhutan in the north to Sri Lanka in the south, where it is the religion of the majority Sinhalese community. Most are very recent converts, the last adherents of the early schools of Buddhism having been killed or converted by the Muslim invaders of the 13th century.

Sikhism

Guru Nanak, the founder of the religion, was born just west of Lahore and grew up in what is now the Pakistani town of Sultanpur. His followers, the Sikhs, (derived from the Sanskrit word for 'disciples') form perhaps one of India's most recognizable groups. Beards and turbans give them a very distinctive presence and although they represent less than two percent of the total population of India – and a far smaller proportion in Rajasthan and Gujarat – they are both politically and economically significant.

Sikh beliefs The first Guru, accepted the ideas of *samsara* – the cycle of rebirths – and *karma* (see page 294) from Hinduism. However, Sikhism is unequivocal in its belief in the oneness of God, rejecting idolatry and any worship of objects or images. Guru Nanak believed that God is One, formless, eternal and beyond description.

Guru Nanak also fiercely opposed discrimination on the grounds of caste. He saw God as present everywhere, visible to anyone who cared to look and as essentially full of grace and compassion. One of the many stories about his travels tells of how he was rebuked on his visit to Mecca for sleeping with his feet pointing towards the Qa'aba, an act Muslims would consider sacrilegious. Apologizing profusely, he had replied "If you can show me in which direction I may lie so that my feet do not point towards God, I will do so". His contact with Muslim families when still young prompted him to organize community hymn singing when both Hindus and Muslims were welcomed. Along with a Muslim servant, he also organized a common kitchen where Hindus of all castes and Muslims could eat together, thereby deliberately breaking one of the strictest of caste rules.

Guru Nanak preached that salvation depended on accepting the nature of God. If man recognized the true harmony of the divine order (*hookam*) and brought himself into line with that harmony he would be saved. Rejecting the prevailing Hindu belief that such harmony could be achieved by ascetic practices, he emphasized three actions; meditating on and repeating God's name (*naam*), 'giving', or charity (*daan*) and bathing (*isnaan*).

Many of the features now associated with Sikhism can be attributed to **Guru Gobind Singh**, who on 15 April 1699, started the new brotherhood called the *Khalsa* (meaning 'the pure', from the Persian word *khales*), an inner core of the faithful, accepted by baptism (*amrit*). The 'five ks' date from this period: *kesh* (uncut hair), the most important, followed by *kangha* (comb, usually of wood), *kirpan* (dagger or short sword), *kara* (steel bangle) and *kachh* (similar to 'boxer' shorts). The dagger and the shorts reflect military influence.

In addition to the compulsory 'five ks', the new code prohibited smoking, eating *halal* meat and sexual intercourse with Muslim women. These date from the 18th century, when the Sikhs were often in conflict with the Muslims. Other strict prohibitions include: idolatry, caste discrimination, hypocrisy and pilgrimage to Hindu sacred places. The *Khalsa* also explicitly forbade the seclusion of women, one of the common practices of Islam. It was only under the warrior king Ranjit Singh (1799-1838) that the idea of the Guru's presence in meetings of the Sikh community (the *Panth*) gave way to the now universally held belief in the total authority of the **Guru Granth**, the recorded words of the Guru in the scripture.

Christianity

There are about 23 million Christians in India. Christianity ranks third in terms of religious affiliation after Hinduism and Islam and there are Christian congregations in all the major towns of India.

The great majority of the Protestant Christians in India are now members of the Church of South India, formed from the major Protestant denominations in 1947, or the Church of North India, which followed suit in 1970. Together they account for approximately half the total number of Christians. Roman Catholics make up the active centres of Christian worship.

Origins Some of the churches owe their origin either to the modern missionary movement of the late 18th century onwards, or to the colonial presence of the European powers. However, Christians probably arrived in India during the first century after the birth of Christ. There is evidence that one of Christ's Apostles, **Thomas**, reached India in 52 AD, only 20 years after Christ was crucified. He settled in Malabar and then expanded his missionary work to China. It is widely believed that he was martyred in Tamil Nadu on his return to India in 72 AD and is buried in Mylapore, in the suburbs of modern Chennai. St Thomas' Mount, a small rocky hill just north of Madras airport, takes its name from him. Today there is still a church of Thomas Christians in Kerala. In north India the influence of Christian missions in education and medical work was greater than as a proselytizing force. Education in Christian schools stimulated reform movements in Hinduism itself and mission hospitals supplemented government-run hospitals, particularly in remote rural areas.

Land and environment

Geography

Rajasthan lies on the northwestern edge of the Indian Peninsula, the southernmost of India's three major geological regions. To its north are the alluvial plains of the Ganges and Indus rivers, and to their north again the great mountain chain of the Himalaya.

The origins of India's landscapes Only 100 million years ago the Indian Peninsula was still attached to the great land mass of what geologists call 'Pangaea' alongside South Africa, Australia and Antarctica. Then as the great plates on which the earth's southern continents stood broke up, the Indian Plate started its dramatic shift northwards. About 55 million years ago the northernmost tip of the peninsula collided with the Asian plate, in the next 20 million years bringing the first Himalayan uplift in what are now the western Himalaya. From 36 to five million years ago the peninsula continued its northward movement under the Asian plate but also rotated in an anticlockwise direction, pushing up a succession of parallel mountain ranges from Himachal Pradesh eastwards through Nepal to the eastern Himalaya. The Indian Plate is still moving north under the Tibetan Plateau at a rate of up to 2½ cms a year. This movement continues to have major effects on the landscapes of the entire region. The Himalaya are still rising, in places by several millimetres a year, and along the faulted junctions of the Indian and the Asian plates are some of the world's most active earthquake zones. The western borders of Rajasthan are particularly affected by this seismic activity.

The ancient rocks of the peninsula have also been disturbed by its continuing thrust under the Asian plate, the ancient sandstones of the Vindhyan ranges in southeastern Rajasthan and the Aravallis showing evidence of the buckling power of the impact.

The crystalline rocks of the Peninsula are some of the oldest in the world, some being over 3,100 million years old. Over 60 million years ago a mass of volcanic lava welled up through cracks in the earth's surface and covered some 500,000 sq km of southern Gujarat, Rajasthan, and Madhya Pradesh, while stretching south to Maharashtra and northern Karnataka.

Rajasthani landscape Running like a spine through Rajasthan the **Aravalli Hills** are one of the oldest mountain systems in the world. They form a series of jagged, heavily folded ranges, stretching from **Mount Abu** in the southwest (1,720 m) to Kota and Bundi in the east. Mount Abu is granite but the range has a mixture of ancient sedimentary and metamorphic rocks, and Rajasthan is the source of the glittering white **Makrana marble** used in the Taj Mahal. The ancient sandstones of the Vindhyan mountain system of Madhya Pradesh extend northwards into southeastern Rajasthan, eroded in places to form great cliff-topped scarps overlooking the often fertile alluvial plains below, as at Ranthambhore and Bundi.

The watershed between the eastward draining Chambal river system, which ultimately flows into the Bay of Bengal, and the Luni which flows into the Arabian Sea, runs along the crest line of the Aravallis from Udaipur in the southeast to Jaipur in the northwest.

To the west of this line is the arid and forbidding **Thar Desert**, with its shifting sand dunes and crushingly high summer temperatures. Carol Henderson has written that James Tod, the first British emissary to the region, was constantly reminded that the names for the region – *Marwar, Maroosthali*, or *Maru-desh*, mean 'the land of death'. Before Partition from Pakistan Jaisalmer and Bikaner dominated the overland routes to the west. However, the Great Indian desert is not completely barren but covered with shrubs and trees, interspersed with farmland, and fed by rivers like the Luni. Sand dunes rise over 70 m in Jaisalmer, Jodhpur, Bikaner and Barmer districts. The Indira Canal and other projects have greened vast stretches of the desert, making them suitable for cultivation and plantation, though they have not entirely achieved what was envisaged. Salt lakes like Sambhar and Tal Chapper, and dry beds of rivers like the Luni, are frequently seen in the desert and arid stretches of the Aravallis.

Jodhpur lies on the edge of this arid tract, the link between the true desert and the semi arid but cultivable regions to the east. To the southeast of the Aravalli divide are the wetter and more fertile river basins of the Chambal and its tributaries, though even here there are some outstandingly barren rocky hills and plateaus.

Around Jaipur and Bharatpur, cultivated land is interspersed with rocky outcrops such as those at Amber. In the south the average elevation is higher (330-1,150 m). Around Bharatpur the landscape forms part of the nearly flat Yamuna drainage basin. Mewar, the southeast region of modern Rajasthan, with Udaipur and Chittaurgarh as two of the region's former capitals, is hilly, and drains northeastwards into the only perennial river of southern Rajasthan, the Chambal. The surface geology of the southeast has been modified greatly by the great volcanic lava flows which have weathered to give rich black soils, especially fertile when irrigated and well drained.

Climate

The Tropic of Cancer runs through northern Gujarat and the southernmost tip of Rajasthan, and the climate of the region reflects this tropical position at the northwestern corner of the Indian subcontinent.

The monsoon In common with the rest of India, the climate of Rajasthan is dominated by the monsoon. What makes the Indian monsoon quite exceptional is not its regularity but the depth of moist air which passes over the subcontinent. Over India, for example, the highly unstable moist airflow is over 6,000 m thick compared with only 2,000 m over Japan, giving rise to the bursts of torrential rain which mark out

Monsoon is an Arabic word meaning 'season'. The term monsoon refers to the wind reversal which replaces the dry northeasterlies, characteristic of winter and spring, with the very warm and wet southwesterlies of the summer.

the wet season. However, most of Rajasthan is to the north of the main rainbearing
southwesterlies, and rainfall decreases sharply from the southeast to the northwest,
which is true desert. Rajasthan's location on the margins of pure desert has made
much of it particularly susceptible to climatic change throughout settlement history,
and fossil sand dunes found as far east as Delhi testify to the advance and retreat of
the desert over the last 5,000 years.

The wet season The monsoon season in Rajasthan lasts approximately three
months. It brings an enveloping dampness which makes it very difficult to keep
things dry. However, nowhere receives more than 1,000 mm a year, and the rain
comes mainly in the form of heavy isolated showers. Rainfall generally decreases
towards the northwest, Rajasthan merging imperceptibly into genuine desert.

Winter In winter high pressure builds up over Central Asia. Most of India is protected
from the cold northeast monsoon winds that result by the massive bulk of the
Himalaya and daytime temperatures rise sharply in the sun. In winter the daily
maximum in most low lying areas is 22-28°C and the minimum 8-14°C, but the air is
often almost bitingly dry. The sharp drop in temperature on winter nights makes warm
clothing essential between late November and mid February. To the south the winter
temperatures increase having minima of around 20°C. Despite the night-time cold,
Rajasthan often has beautiful weather from November through to March.

Summer From April onwards northwestern India becomes almost unbearably hot.
Except in the hills the summer maxima exceed 46°C and the average from May to
August is 38°C. In winter the daily maximum in most low lying areas is 22-28°C and
the minimum 8-14°C. The Aravallis, notably Mount Abu, offer welcome relief in the hot
season and are noticeably colder in winter.

At the end of May the upper air westerly jet stream, which controls the
atmospheric system over the Indo-Gangetic plains through the winter, suddenly
breaks down. It re-forms to the north of Tibet, thus allowing very moist southwesterlies to sweep across South India and the Bay of Bengal. They then double back
northwestwards, bringing rain across the Indo-Gangetic Plains to northwest India.

Vegetation

The dry tropical monsoon climate gives Rajasthan a quite distinctive natural
vegetation. Dry deciduous woodland is the most common cover in the wetter areas,
shading to desert vegetation in the arid west. Today forest cover has been greatly
reduced as elsewhere in India, mainly as a result of the need for agricultural land.

Deciduous forest Neither of the two types of deciduous tree dominant elsewhere in
India, **Sal** (*Shorea robusta*) and **teak** (*Tectona grandis*), are common in Rajasthan,
teak only being found in the Aravallis and sal absent altogether.

Western Rajasthan has distinct desert vegetation like the Sewan grasslands near
Jaisalmer, Phog which grows on sand dunes, capparis, a cactus-like *euphorbia*, aak
or *calotropis*, all three of which are fairly succulent and sustain life in the desert.
Kharjal (*Salvadora persica*) and the thorny khejra (*Prosopis cineraria*) are trees of the
desert. The second is often used for a dish called Ker-Sangri that is part of the Marwar
diet, while rohira, a truly desert tree, is used by wood carvers of Barmer and other
desert towns.

Flowering trees Many Indian trees are planted along roadsides to provide shade
and they often also produce beautiful flowers. The **silk cotton tree** (*Bombax ceiba*), up

to 25 m in height, is one of the most dramatic. The pale greyish bark of this buttressed tree usually bears conical spines. It has wide spreading branches and keeps its leaves for most of the year. The flowers, which appear when the tree is leafless, are cup-shaped, with curling, rather fleshy red petals up to 12 cm long while the fruit produce the fine, silky cotton which gives it its name.

Other common trees with red or orange flowers include the dhak, the gulmohur and the Indian coral tree. The smallish (6 m) deciduous **dhak** (*Butea monosperma*) has light grey bark and a gnarled, twisted trunk and thick, leathery leaves. The large, bright orange and sweet pea-shaped flowers appear on leafless branches from late March to May. The 8-9 m high umbrella-shaped **gulmohur** (*Delonix regia*), a native of Madagascar, is grown as a shade tree in towns. The fiery coloured flowers make a magnificent display after the tree has shed its feathery leaves. The scarlet flowers of the **Indian coral tree** (*Erythrina indica*) also appear when its branches with thorny bark are leafless.

Often seen along roadsides the **jacaranda** (*Jacaranda mimosaefolia*) has attractive feathery foliage and purple-blue thimble-shaped flowers up to 40 mm long. When not in flower it resembles a gulmohur, but differs in its general shape. The valuable **tamarind** (*Tamarindus indica*) has a short straight trunk and a spreading crown. An evergreen with feathery leaves, it bears small clusters of yellow and red flowers. The noticeable fruit pods are long, curved and swollen at intervals. In parts of India, the rights to the fruit are auctioned off annually for up to Rs 4,000 (US$100) per tree.

Fruit trees The large, spreading **mango** (*Mangifera indica*) bears the delicious, distinctively shaped fruit that comes in hundreds of varieties. The **banana** plant (*Musa*), actually a gigantic herb (up to 5 m high) arising from an underground stem has very large leaves which grow directly off the trunk. Each large purplish flower produces bunches of up to 100 bananas. The **papaya** (*Carica papaya*) grows to about 4 m with the large hand-shaped leaves clustered near the top. Only the female tree bears the fruit, which hang down close to the trunk just below the leaves.

Of all Indian trees the **banyan** (*Ficus benghalensis*) is probably the best known. It is planted by temples, in villages and along roads. The seeds often germinate in the cracks of old walls, the growing roots splitting the wall apart. If it grows in the bark of another tree, it sends down roots towards the ground. As it grows, more roots appear from the branches, until the original host tree is surrounded by a 'cage' which eventually strangles it.

Related to the banyan, the **pipal** or **peepul** (*Ficus religiosa*), also cracks open walls and strangles other trees with its roots. With a smooth grey bark, it too is commonly found near temples and shrines. You can distinguish it from the banyan by the absence of aerial roots and its large, heart shaped leaf with a point tapering into a pronounced 'tail'. It bears abundant 'figs' of a purplish tinge which are about a centimetre across.

Acacia trees with their feathery leaves are fairly common in the drier parts of India. The best known is the **babul** (*Acacia arabica*) with a rough, dark bark. The leaves have long silvery white thorns at the base and consist of many leaflets while the flowers grow in golden balls about 1 cm across.

The **eucalyptus** or **gum tree** (*Eucalyptus grandis*), introduced from Australia in the 19th century, is now widespread and is planted near villages to provide both shade and firewood. There are various forms but all may be readily recognized by their height, their characteristic long, thin leaves which have a pleasant fresh smell and the colourful peeling bark.

The wispy **casuarina** (*Casuarina*) grows in poor sandy soil, especially on the coast and on village waste land. It has the typical leaves of a pine tree and the cones are small and prickly to walk on. It is said to attract lightning during a thunder storm.

Bamboo (*Bambusa*) strictly speaking is a grass which can vary in size from small ornamental clumps to the enormous wild plant whose stems are so strong and thick that they are used for construction and for scaffolding and as pipes in rural irrigation schemes.

Flowering plants Many other flowering plants are cultivated in parks, gardens and roadside verges. The attractive **frangipani** (*Plumeria acutifolia*) has a rather crooked trunk and stubby branches, which if broken give out a white milky juice which can be irritating to the skin. The big, leathery leaves taper to a point at each end and have noticeable parallel veins. The sweetly scented waxy flowers are white, pale yellow or pink. The **Bougainvillea** grows as a dense bush or climber with small oval leaves and rather long thorns. The brightly coloured part which appears like a flower, is formed by large papery bracts, not by the petals, which are quite magnificent.

The **hibiscus** has an unusual trumpet shaped flower as much as 7 or 8 cm across, has a very long 'tongue' growing out from the centre and varies in colour from scarlet to yellow or white. The leaves are somewhat oval or heart-shaped with jagged edges.

On many ponds and tanks the floating plants of the **lotus** (*Nelumbo nucifera*) and the **water hyacinth** (*Eichornia crassipes*) are seen. Lotus flowers which rise on stalks above the water can be white, pink or a deep red and up to 25 cm across. The very large leaves either float on the surface or rise above the water. The rather fleshy leaves and lilac flowers of the water hyacinth float to form a dense carpet, often clogging the waterways.

Crops Rajasthan may have been the original home of millet cultivation in South Asia. The semi-arid climate means that millets, wheat and barley remain the staple cereal crops, though rice is grown on some irrigated land. There are many different sorts of **millet**, but the ones most often seen are finger millet, pearl millet (*bajra*) and sorghum (*jowar*). **Sugar cane** (*Saccharum*) is another commercially important crop. This looks like a large grass which stands up to 3 m tall. The crude brown sugar is sold as jaggery and has a flavour of molasses. **Cotton** (*Gossypium*) is important especially in Gujarat. The cotton bush is a small knee-high bush and the cotton boll appears after the flower has withered. This splits when ripe to show the white cotton lint inside. The Malwa region of southeastern Rajasthan and the neighbouring districts of Madhya Pradesh have been centres of cultivation of the **opium poppy** (*Papaver somniferum*) for at least 500 years. It is grown on tiny plots under strict government supervision, but provides a highly distinctive white patchwork character to the landscape. See page 178.

Wildlife

India has an extremely rich and varied wildlife, though many species only survive in very restricted environments.

Conservation

Alarmed by diminishing numbers of wild animals and the rapid loss of wildlife habitat the Indian Government established the first conservation measures in 1972, followed by the setting up of national parks and reserves. Some 25,000 sq km were set aside in 1973 for Project Tiger. Tigers have been reported to be increasing steadily in several of the game reserves, but threats to their survival continue, notably through poaching. The same is true of other, less well known species. Their natural habitat has been destroyed both by people and by domesticated animals (there are some 250 million cattle and 50 million sheep and goats). Rajasthan has some of India's best known parks, including Ranthambhore and Bharatpur. The Indian Government has defined national parks as areas in which no human activity is allowed, whereas in wildlife parks some grazing and minor forest produce collection can be permitted. The entry fee for foreigners and vehicle charges at some parks have been raised dramatically in recent years.

The cat family

The **tiger** (*Panthera tigris*), which prefers to live in fairly dense cover, is most likely to be glimpsed as it lies in long grass or in dappled shadow. Unlike the lion, it leads a quite solitary life. It is more nocturnal and depends on cover for hunting, the reason it is more difficult to spot. Rajasthan has two tiger reserves. Ranthambhore offers better chances of spotting a tiger over a two or three day visit than Sariska, the other tiger reserve. The tiger is a magnificent animal, richly coloured with bold stripes, up to 10 ft long and weighing about 200 kg. Females are smaller and weigh 20 per cent less than the males. You will often hear of tiger sightings in the hills of Rajasthan and south Gujarat but you are unlikely to see one outside the two tiger reserves.

The **leopard** or **panther** as it is often called in India (*Panthera pardus*), is far more numerous and widespread than the tiger, but is even more elusive. The hills of Rajasthan have a sizeable panther population but they are not often seen, being nocturnal and shy. Panthers average 7 ft in length, females being shorter. The typical colour is dull yellow with black rosette markings that become solid black spots on the head, neck, limbs and belly, and a whitish underside. Panther sightings are not uncommon in the Kachida valley of Ranthambhore National Park and they are also seen in the arid hills of Pali and Jalore district as the cats here have turned on livestock following the decimation of their natural prey like the gazelle. They often visit villages and waterholes. The panthers in these arid areas, close to the desert, are paler in colour than those of the hilly forest tracts, and sometimes also smaller.

The colour and markings of the **leopard cat** make it look like a miniature panther. They are seen in forest areas. The jungle cat is more common, having adapted to a variety of habitats from grasslands, thorn scrub, forests, agricultural areas, surrounds of wetlands and even proximity to towns and villages. Its longer legs and shorter tail distinguish the jungle cat from the domestic and other lesser wild cats. The jungle cat varies in colour from sandy grey in the arid areas to a brighter yellowish grey in greener areas. The **fishing cat** hunts at the marshes of the Keoladeo Ghana Sanctuary of Bharatpur, Rajasthan. Besides being adept at fishing with a blow of its paw and feeding on molluscs, it also hunts mammals and birds. Fishing cats do not enter the water but grab fish or mollusc from rocks and other vantage points on the shores of the marshlands. The desert zone is home to the **desert cat**, which has greyish yellow fur marked with black spots, striped cheek and a black ring on its tail.

The **caracal** is an agile, medium sized cat with pointed, tufted ears, and a short tail. They are rarely seen though present in many scrub jungles of the Gujarat-Rajasthan belt.

The dog family

The **Indian wolf** has become an endangered species, not least because it tends to turn on livestock, making it a target for pastoral communities. The scrublands of Kumbhalgarh Sanctuary have shown a proliferating population of wolves. Wolves have different methods of hunting depending on the habitat. In the desert the wolf hunts by chasing its prey at a steady pace waiting for it's quarry to get tired, while in areas that are more vegetated the strategy is to hunt by surprise. Wolves grow to about 75 cm at shoulder, and 95 cm in length. Holes in rocks and ground are their favoured homes in drylands. In the desert they may dig burrows on the dunes, while in the forests they will find shelter in bushes.

⁞ Tiger, tiger

At one time the tiger roamed freely throughout the sub-continent and at the beginning of this century the estimated population was 40,000 animals. Gradually, due mainly to increased pressure on its habitat by human encroachment and resulting destruction of the habitat, the numbers of this beautiful animal dwindled to fewer than 2,000 in 1972. This was the low point and alarmed at the approaching extinction of the tiger, concerned individuals with the backing of the Government and the World Wildlife Fund, set up Project Tiger in 1973. Initially nine parks were set up to protect the tiger and this was expanded over the years. However, despite encouraging signs in the first decade the latest tiger census suggests that there are still fewer than 2,500.

The **jackal** (*Canis aureus*), a lone scavenger in towns and villages, looks like a cross between a dog and a fox and varies in colour from shades of brown through to black. They feed on carcasses and the prey of larger carnivores but they will hunt smaller game and when in large packs even bring down deer, antelope and gazelle. The bushy tail has a dark tip. It is a common sight while driving through Rajasthan after dark. Their howling is often heard at dawn, dusk and sometimes at night.

There are two kinds of **fox** found in this region. The Indian fox is common in the plains and is grey in colour. The white footed desert fox is distinguished from the Indian fox by its white tipped tail as opposed to the black tipped tail of the latter and black markings on its ears. The habitats of the desert and Indian fox overlap in the western Rajasthani desert.

The dreaded **wild dog** or **dhole** has been sighted at Sariska and Ranthambhore national parks as recently as January 2001, though they had previously been thought to have become extinct in Rajasthan.

Other carnivores

The **sloth bear** (*Melursus ursinus*), about 75 cm at the shoulder, lives in broken forest, but may be seen on a lead accompanying a street entertainer who makes it 'dance' to music as a part of an act. They have a long snout, a pendulous lower lip and a shaggy black coat with a yellowish V-shaped mark on the chest. The sloth bear is present in many wildlife parks of the Aravallis including Ranthambhore and Kumbhalgarh in Rajasthan, but are not easily seen as they are active after dusk and shy of human presence. Being short sighted they are known to be nervous and attack human visitors to their habitat. Bears are omnivores. They will hunt other animals, feed on termites and other invertebrate, and climb trees for fruits, berries and flowers.

The **common mongoose** (*Herpestes edwardsi*) lives in scrub and open jungle. It kills snakes, but will also take rats, mice and chicken. Tawny coloured with a grey grizzled tinge, it is about 90 cm in length, of which half is pale-tipped tail. The **ratel or honey badger** is seen at Sariska.

Deer, antelope, oxen and their relatives

Once widespread, these animals are now largely confined to the reserves. The deer, unlike the antelopes that inhabit the grass and scrub, are animals of the forests and are rarely seen outside the wildlife sanctuaries.

The largest **deer** and one of the most widespread, is the magnificent **sambhar** (*Cervus unicolor*) which can be up to 150 cm at the shoulder. It has a noticeably shaggy coat, which varies in colour from brown with a yellowish or grey tinge through to dark, almost black, in the older stags. The sambhar is often found on wooded

Background Land & environment

⁞ Blackbuck and bishnois

The blackbuck is one of the handsomest antelopes with its elegant carriage and striking colour combination. Fleet footed, it often resorts to a bounding run across the countryside – the preferred habitat is grassland. The mature bucks are a deep brownish black with contrasting white underparts, and have spiralling horns, while juvenile males are brown and white. Does are fawn brown with white underparts, and are completely hornless. During the rutting season the bucks attain a remarkable sheen and they strut with heads raised and horns swept along their backs in a challenging stance. The rutting season varies locally but is generally around October and February-March.

Velavadhar National Park has one of the largest blackbuck populations among Indian sanctuaries. Gajner near Bikaner, the Sambhar Salt Lake, Tal Chappar in Shekhawati and Keoladeo Ghana National Park at Bharatpur are other good reserves for sightings. Blackbucks are held sacred by the Bishnois, the reason for their good numbers near Guda Bishnoi village of Jodhpur district.

hillsides and lives in groups of up to 10 or so, though solitary individuals are also seen. The sambhar is common in Ranthambhore, Sariska, and Bharatpur national parks. The small **chital** or **spotted deer** (*Axis axis*), only about 90 cm tall, are seen in herds of 20 or so, in grassy areas. The bright rufous coat spotted with white is unmistakable; the stags carry antlers with three tines. It is seen in good numbers at Ranthambhore, Sariska, and Bharatpur.

Antelopes live in open grasslands, never too far from water. The beautiful **blackbuck** or Indian antelope (*Antilope cervicapra*), up to 80 cm at the shoulder, occurs in large herds. The distinctive colouring and the long spiralling horns make the stag easy to identify. The larger and heavier nilgai or blue bull (*Boselaphus tragocamelus*), like the blackbuck and chowsingha, is one of a kind in its genus. The largest antelope in India, the Nilgai has a very small cone shaped horn in ratio to its height of 130 cm. The mature bull is iron grey in colour, the juveniles are tawny. The females are tawny and hornless. They are often seen in sparsely wooded hills and fields in batches of four to ten. The very graceful **chinkara** or Indian Gazelle (*Gazella gazella*) is only 65 cm at the shoulder. The light russet colour of the body has a distinct line along the side where the paler underparts start. Both sexes carry slightly S-shaped horns. Chinkara live in the desert and can thrive on minimal vegetation and obtain water from succulent leaves. Fleet footed and graceful, the chinkaras can be seen widely and in good numbers in the Desert National Park of Jaisalmer district and in the surrounds of Bishnoi villages of Jodhpur, Nagaur, Jalore, Barmer and Bikaner districts. The **chowsingha** or four horned antelope is the only animal in the world with two pairs of horns. Unlike the blackbuck they prefer forests to grasslands. Being diminutive in size and favouring the woodlands they are difficult to spot though they are present in good numbers at Sariska and Ranthambhore national parks, and sanctuaries like Kumbhalgarh and Sitamata.

The commonest member of the **oxen** group is the **Asiatic wild buffalo** or water buffalo (*Bubalus bubalis*). About 170 cm at the shoulder, the wild buffalo, which can be aggressive, occurs in herds on grassy plains and swamps near rivers and lakes. The black coat and wide-spreading curved horns, carried by both sexes, are distinctive. The **Indian bison** or **gaur** (*Bos gaurus*) can be up to 200 cm at the shoulder with a heavy muscular ridge across it. Both sexes carry curved horns. The young gaur is a light sandy colour, which darkens with age, the old bulls being nearly black with pale sandy coloured 'socks' and a pale forehead.

The **wild boar** (*Sus scrofa*) has mainly black body and a pig-like head, the hairs thicken down the spine to form a sort of mane. A mature male stands 90 cm at the shoulder and, unlike the female, bears tusks. The young are striped. Quite widespread, they often cause great destruction among crops.

One of the most important scavengers of the open countryside, the **striped hyena** (*Hyena hyena*) usually comes out at night. It is about 90 cm at the shoulder with a large head with a noticeable crest of hairs along its sloping back.

Monkeys

The **common langur** (*Presbytis entellus*), 75 cm, is a long-tailed monkey with a distinctive black face, hands and feet. It is the main primate of the Rajasthan region and is common at Sariska National Park, Sitamata sanctuary and other wildlife reserves. They are adaptable and are frequently seen in gardens of large cities and around Hanuman temples where they are fed. The **rhesus macaque** (*Macaca mulatta*), 60 cm, is more solid looking with shorter limbs and a shorter tail. It can be distinguished by the orange-red fur on its rump and flanks.

Squirrels

Palm squirrels are very common. The five-striped (*Funambulus pennanti*) and the three-striped palm squirrel (*Funambulus palmarum*) are 30 cm long (about half of which is tail). The five-striped is usually seen in towns. **Flying squirrel** is reported from Sitamata sanctuary but are rarely seen. The **common giant flying squirrel** (*Petaurista petaurista*) are common in the larger forests of India. The body can be 45 cm long and the tail another 50 cm. They glide from tree to tree using a membrane stretching from front leg to back leg which acts like a parachute.

Bats

The two bats most commonly seen in towns differ enormously in size. The larger so-called **flying fox** (*Pteropus giganteus*) has a wing span of 120 cm. These fruit-eating bats roost in large noisy colonies where they look like folded umbrellas hanging from the trees. In the evening they can be seen leaving the roost with slow measured wing beats. The much smaller **Indian pipistrelle** (*Pipistrellus coromandra*), with a wing span of about 15 cm, is an insect eater. It comes into the house at dusk to roost under eaves and has a fast, erratic flight.

Birds

Rajasthan is one of the most prolific birding areas in India. During the winter birds gather in large assemblages at lakes and parks, including those in towns, cities and villages, and while travelling between destinations a birder will find a fabulous variety of birds.

Dry land and desert birds The endangered **great Indian bustard** is often sighted in the Desert National Park of Jaisalmer district and in the scrub and grass of Bikaner, and have spectacular breeding displays. The **houbara bustard** is a winter visitor to western Rajasthan.

The **blackbellied** or **imperial sandgrouse** is another winter visitor, flocking in large numbers at Gajner lake and waterholes in the Thar desert national park for their daily drink. **Spotted sandgrouse** is frequently seen during the winter months in the drylands. The **common Indian sandgrouse** breeds in the arid belt of western Rajasthan. **Painted sandgrouse** frequent the wooded areas and taller grasses.

The **grey francolin** or partridge is a common sight in the countryside of both states, and their challenging cries can be heard almost everywhere. Painted francolin frequents forested areas like Kumbalgarh and Ranthambhore.

Water and waterside birds The *jheels* (marshes or swamps) of Rajasthan form one of the richest bird habitats in India. The magnificent **sarus crane** (*Grus antigone*, 150 cm) is one of India's tallest birds. The bare red head and long red legs and grey plumage make it easy to identify. **Demoiselle cranes** are seen in good numbers near Jodhpur, specially at Khichan where they are fed by the villagers. **Siberian cranes** visit Bharatpur but are becoming very rare as they are often lured to traps on their way south each winter. There are also large stork heronries at Bharatpur.

The **openbill stork** (*Anastomus oscitans*, 80 cm) and the **painted stork** (*Ibis leucocephalus*, 100 cm) are common too and are spotted breeding in large colonies. The former is white with black wing feathers and a curiously shaped bill. The latter mainly white, has a pinkish tinge on the back and dark marks on the wings and a broken black band on the lower chest. The bare yellow face and yellow down-curved bill are conspicuous.

Rosy, spotbilled and other **pelicans** are frequent visitors to many lakes including Sardar Sammand and Keoladeo Ghana National Park. White, black and glossy ibises, spoonbill and various **herons** including the little and cattle egrets and grey heron are frequently seen in Rajasthan's wetlands. Greater and Lesser **flamingos** are occasionally seen in Rajasthan. These long necked rosy white birds, with heavy bills, are graceful and attractive. When seen in flight, lesser flamingos can be distinguished by their shorter trailing legs. Alaniya dam near Kota, and the river Luni in western Rajasthan attract flamingos in good numbers.

By almost every swamp, ditch or rice paddy up to about 1,200 m you will see the **paddy bird** (*Ardeola grayii*, 45 cm). An inconspicuous, buff-coloured bird, it is easily overlooked as it stands hunched up by the waterside.

The commonest and most widespread of the Indian kingfishers is the jewel-like **common kingfisher** (*Alcedo atthis*, 18 cm). With its brilliant blue upper parts and orange breast it is usually seen perched on a twig or a reed beside the water.

Birds of open grassland, light woodland and cultivated land The **cattle egret** (*Bubulcus ibis*, 50 cm), a small white heron, is usually seen near herds of cattle, frequently perched on the backs of the animals.

The **rose-ringed parakeet** (*Psittacula krameri*, 40 cm) is found throughout India up to about 1,500 m while the **pied myna** (*Sturnus contra*, 23 cm) is restricted to northern and central India. The rose-ringed parakeet often forms huge flocks, an impressive sight coming in to roost. They can be very destructive to crops, but are attractive birds which are frequently kept as pets. The pied myna, with its smart black and white plumage is conspicuous, usually in small flocks in grazing land or cultivation. The all black **drongo** (*Dicrurus adsimilis*, 30 cm) is almost invariably seen perched on telegraph wires or bare branches. Its distinctively forked tail makes it easy to identify.

Weaver birds are a family of mainly yellow birds, all remarkable for the intricate nests they build. The most widespread is the **baya weaver** (*Ploceus philippinus*, 15cm) which nest in large colonies, often near villages. The male in the breeding season combines a black face and throat with a contrasting yellow top of the head and the yellow breast band. In the non-breeding season both sexes are brownish sparrow-like birds.

India's national bird, the magnificent **peafowl** (*Pavo cristatus*, male 210 cm, female 100 cm), is more commonly known as the peacock. Semi-domesticated birds are commonly seen and heard around towns and villages. In the wild it favours hilly jungles and dense scrub.

Reptiles and amphibians

Snakes India is famous for its reptiles, especially its snakes which feature in many stories and legends. In reality, snakes keep out of the way of people. Four main species of venomous snakes are seen in Rajasthan, the Indian **cobra**, both spectacled black, is the best known. The **common krait** has the most toxic venom but is less aggressive than the cobra and also more nocturnal and shy. **Saw scaled viper** is common in the plains, rocks and desert areas of Rajasthan. The saw scaled viper uses a locomotion called side winding to negotiate the hot sands of the desert dunes. **Russel's viper**, with its chain like markings, inhabits forests like Ranthambhore.

A large snake favoured by street entertainers is the cobras. The various species all have a hood which is spread when the snake draws itself up to strike. They are all highly venomous and the snake charmers prudently de-fang them to render them harmless. The best known is probably the **spectacled cobra** (*Naja naja*), which has a mark like a pair of spectacles on the back of its hood. The largest venomous snake in the world is the **king cobra** (*Ophiophagus hannah*) which is five metres in length. It is usually brown, but can vary from cream to black and lacks the spectacle marks of the other. In their natural state cobras are generally inhabitants of forest regions.

Equally venomous, but much smaller, the **common krait** (*Bungarus caeruleus*) is just over 1 m in length. The slender, shiny, blue-black snake has thin white bands which can sometimes be almost indiscernible.

The **Indian rock python** (*Python molurus*), about 4 m in length, is a 'constrictor' which kills it's prey by suffocation. The python point at Bharatpur is a good place to see them.

Lizards In houses everywhere you cannot fail to see the **gecko** (*Hemidactylus*). This small harmless, primitive lizard is active after dark. It lives in houses behind pictures and curtain rails and at night emerges to run across the walls and ceilings to hunt the night flying insects which form its main prey. It is not usually more than about 14 cm long, with a curiously transparent, pale yellowish brown body. At the other end of the scale is the **monitor lizard** (*Varanus*), which can grow to 2 m in length. They can vary from a colourful black and yellow, to plain or speckled brown. They live in different habitats from cultivation and scrub to waterside places and desert.

The desert areas of western Rajasthan are home to **spiny tailed lizard**, an omnivore that feeds on desert succulent vegetation, as well as termites and other insects, but their numbers are declining as they are sought after by 'medicine men' for their so-called aphrodisiac qualities.

Crocodiles The most widespread crocodile is the freshwater **mugger** or **marsh crocodile** (*Crocodilus palustris*) which grows to 3-4 m length. Muggers are often seen at reservoirs like, Sitamata and Kumbalgarh sanctuary lakes, Jaisammand Lake, and Ranthambhore National Park. The only similar fresh water species is the **gharial** (*Gavialis gangeticus*) which lives in large, fast flowing rivers. Up to twice the length of the mugger, it is a fish-eating crocodile with a long thin snout and, in the case of the male, an extraordinary bulbous growth on the end of the snout. They are found along the River Chambal in eastern Rajasthan.

Others

Two subspecies of **Indian hare** are present – the *blacknaped* is usually seen in the more wooded area, and the *desert* in western Rajasthan and other arid areas. The **pale hedgehog** is common, the long-eared species being seen in the desert, while **gerbils** are typical rodents of the desert, their bounding movement reminiscent of a miniature kangaroo. The **Indian elephant** (*Elephas maximus*) has been domesticated for centuries and today it is still used as a beast of burden. There are no wild elephants in Rajasthan.

Books

The literature on India is as huge and varied as the subcontinent itself. India is a good place to buy English language books as foreign books are often much cheaper than the published price. There are also cheap Indian editions and occasionally reprints of out-of-print books. There are excellent bookshops in all the major Indian cities.

Art and architecture

Burton, T Richard *Hindu Art*, British Museum PA. Well illustrated paperback; a broad view of art and religion.

Desai, VN *Life at court: Art for India's rulers, 16th-19th centuries*, Boston, Museum of Fine Arts, 1985.

Fass, V *The Forts of India*, London, 1986.

Gupta, ML *Frescoes and Wall paintings of Rajasthan*, Jaipur, 1965.

Jain, J and M *Mud architecture of the Indian desert*, Ahmadabad, AADI, 1992. New Delhi, Abhinav, 1994.

Michell, George *The Hindu Temple*, Univ of Chicago Press, 1988. An authoritative account of Hindu architectural development.

Michell, G & Martinelli, A *Royal Palaces of India*, Thames & Hudson, 1994.

Pramar VS *Haveli*, Ahmadabad, Mapin, 1989.

Sterlin, Henri *Hindu India*, Köln, Taschen, 1998. Traces the development from early rock-cut shrines, detailing famous examples; clearly written, well illustrated.

Tillotson, Giles *The Rajput Palaces*, Yale, 1987; *Mughal architecture*, London, Viking, 1990; *The tradition of Indian architecture*, Yale 1989. Superbly clear writing on development of Indian architecture under Rajputs, Mughals and the British.

Welch, SC *Indian Art and culture 1300-1900*, New York, Metropolitan Museum of Art, 1985.

Current affairs and politics

French, Patrick *Liberty or Death*, Harper Collins, 1997. Well researched and serious yet reads like a story.

Khilnani, Sunil *The idea of India*, Penguin, 1997. Excellent introduction to contemporary India, described by the Nobel prize winner Amartya Sen as "spirited, combative and insight-filled, a rich synthesis of contemporary India".

Manor, James (ed) *Nehru to the Nineties: the changing office of Prime Minister in India*, Hurst, 1994. An excellent collection of essays giving an insider's view of the functioning of Indian democracy.

Tully, Mark *No full stops in India*, Viking, 1991. An often superbly observed but controversially interpreted view of contemporary India.

History

Pre-history and early history
Allchin, Bridget and Raymond *Origins of a civilisation*, Viking, Penguin Books, 1997. The most authoritative up to date survey of the origins of Indian civilizations.

Basham, AL *The Wonder that was India*, London, Sidgwick & Jackson, 1985. Still one of the most comprehensive and readable accounts of the development of India's culture.

History

Medieval and modern
Edwardes, Michael *The Myth of the Mahatma*. Presents Gandhi in a whole new light.

Gandhi, Mohandas K *An Autobiography*, London, 1982.

Gascoigne, Bamber *The Great Moghuls*, London, Cape, 1987.

Keay, John *India: a History*, Harper Collins, 2000. A major new popular history of the subcontinent.

Nehru, Jawaharlal *The discovery of India*, New Delhi, ICCR, 1976.

Lt Col AF Pinhey *History of Mewar* has interesting comments on Tod's authenticity, 1909 (reprinted 1996, Rs 300).

Robinson, Francis (ed) *Cambridge Encyclopaedia of India*, Cambridge, 1989. An introduction to many aspects of South

Asian society.

Schomer, K et al eds *The Idea of Rajasthan: explorations in regional identity.* 2 vols. Delhi, American Inst of Indian Studies, 1994, Rs 750.

Sharma, GN *Social life in medieval Rajasthan,* Agra, 1968.

Spear, Percival & Thapar, Romila *A history of India,* 2 vols, Penguin, 1978.

Tod, J *Annals and antiquities of Rajasthan.* Two volumes. London, 1829-32 (reprinted 1994 in three volumes, Rs 600).

Wolpert, Stanley *A new history of India,* OUP, 1990.

Language

Snell, Rupert and Weightman, Simon *Teach Yourself Hindi.* An excellent, accessible, authoritative teaching guide with a cassette tape.

Yule, H and Burnell, AC (eds) *Hobson-Jobson,* 1886. New paperback edition, 1986. A delightful insight into Anglo-Indian words and phrases.

Literature

Chatterjee, Upamanyu *English August,* London, Faber, 1988. A wry account of a modern Indian Civil Servant's year spent in a rural posting.

Chaudhuri, Nirad Four books give vivid, witty and often sharply critical accounts of India across the 20th century: *The autobiography of an unknown Indian,* Macmillan, London; *Thy Hand, Great Anarch!,* London, Chatto & Windus, 1987.

Holmstrom, Lakshmi *The Inner Courtyard.* A series of short stories by Indian women, translated into English, Rupa, 1992.

Granta 57 *India! The Golden Jubilee.* A diverse collection on a wide range of topics.

Mehta, Gita *Raj,* Delhi, Penguin, 1990.

Naipaul, VS *A million mutinies now,* Penguin, 1992. Naipaul's 'revisionist' account of India turns away from the despondency of his earlier two India books (*An Area of darkness* and *India: a wounded civilisation*) to see grounds for optimism at India's capacity for regeneration.

Rushdie, Salman *Midnight's children,* London, Picador, 1981. A novel of India since Independence. At the same time funny and bitterly sharp critiques of South Asian life in the 1980s.

Rushdie, Salman and West, Elizabeth *The Vintage book of Indian writing,* Random House, 1997.

Scott, Paul *The Raj Quartet,* London, Panther, 1973 and *Staying on,* Longmans, 1985. Outstandingly perceptive novels of the end of the Raj.

Seth, Vikram *A Suitable Boy,* Phoenix House London 1993. Prize winning novel of modern Indian life.

Weightman, Simon (ed) *Travellers Literary Companion: the Indian Sub-continent.* An invaluable introduction to the diversity of Indian writing.

People and places

Bomiller, Elizabeth *May you be the mother of 100 sons,* Penguin, 1991. An American woman journalists' account of coming to understand the issues that face India's women today.

Jain, KC *Ancient cities and towns of Rajasthan,* Delhi, 1976.

Lord, J *The Maharajahs,* London, 1971.

Patnaik, N *A desert Kingdom: the Rajputs of Bikaner,* London, Weidenfeld & Nicholson,1990.

Robinson, A *Maharaja: the spectacular heritage of Princely India.* London, Thames & Hudson,1988. Photographs by S Uchiyama.

Singhvi, AK & Kar, A *Thar Desert in Rajasthan: land, man and environment,* Bangalore, Geological Society of India, 1991.

Religion

Doniger O'Flaherty, Wendy *Hindu Myths,* London, Penguin, 1974. A sourcebook translated from the Sanskrit.

Jain, JP *Religion and Culture of the Jains.* 3rd ed. New Delhi, Bharatiya Jnanapith, 1981.

Qureshi, IH *The Muslim Community of the Indo-Pakistan Sub-Continent 610-1947,* OUP, Karachi, 1977.

Theodore de Bary, W (ed) *Sources of Indian Tradition: Vol 1,* Columbia UP. Traces the origins of India's major religions through illustrative texts.

Vaudeville, C *Myths, saints and legends in Medieval India.* Delhi, OUP, 1996.

Zaehner, RC *Hinduism,* OUP.

Travel

Dalrymple, William *City of Djinns*, Indus/Harper Collins 1993, paperback. Superb account of Delhi based on a year living in the city.

Davidson, R *Desert places*, Viking, 1996. Crossing the desert on a camel's back with nomadic herders.

Hatt, John *The tropical traveller: the essential guide to travel in hot countries*, Penguin, 3rd ed 1992. Excellent, wide ranging and clearly written common sense, based on experience and research.

Keay, John *Into India*, London, John Murray, 1999. A seasoned traveller's introduction to understanding and enjoying India; with a new foreword.

Wildlife and vegetation

Ali, Salim and Dillon Ripley, S *Handbook of the birds of India & Pakistan* (compact ed); also in 5 volumes.

Cowen *Flowering Trees and Shrubs in India*.

Hawkins, RE *Encyclopaedia of Indian Natural History*, Bombay Natural History Soc/OUP.

Kazmierczak, Krys & Singh, Raj *A bird-watcher's guide to India*. Prion, 1998, Sandy, Beds, UK. Well researched and carrying lots of practical information for all birders.

Nair, SM *Endangered animals of India*, New Delhi, NBT, 1992.

Prater, SH *The Book of Indian Animals*.

Woodcock, Martin *Handguide to Birds of the Indian Sub-Continent*, Collins.

India on film

The Indian film industry is one of the largest in the world, each region having its own regional language films. The Hindi film industry is based in Mumbai, specialising in robust song and dance fantasies, all characterized as 'Bollywood' movies.

In a wholly different wold as the films by producers such as **Satyajit Ray** (Apu trilogy and many others), **Shyam Benegal** and **Aparna Roy**. Mira Nair's **Salaam Bombay** captured something of the social injustices of modern urban India. India has been the focus for many foreign and overseas based Indian film makers. Some have focused on the big political stories – **Richard Attenborough's**, **Gandhi**, or on video, the brilliant TV drama the **Jewel in the Crown**, evoking India at the end of the British period.

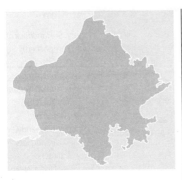

Language	320
Eating and drinking	323
Glossary	328
Index	336
Map index	339
Advertisers' index	339
Acknowledgements	340
Credits	341
Complete listings	340
Map symbols	343
Colour maps	344

Language

Hindi words and phrases

Pronunciation
a as in ah
o as in oh
nasalized vowels are shown as **an un** etc

i as in bee
u as oo in book

Basics
Hello, good morning, goodbye
Thank you/no thank you
Excuse me, sorry
Yes/no
nevermind/that's all right

namaste
dhanyava**d** or shukriya/nah**i**n shukriya
ma**f** k**i**jiye
j**i** ha**n**/ji nah**i**n
koi ba**t** nah**i**n

Questions
What is your name?
My name is...
Pardon?
How are you?
I am well, thanks, and you?
Not very well
Where is the...?
Who is...?
What is this...?

apka nam ky**a** hai?
mer**a** na**m**... hai
phir bat**a**iye?
ky**a** ha**l** hai?
ma**i**n th**i**k hun, aur **a**p?
ma**i**n th**i**k nah**i**n h**u**n
kah**a**n hai...?
kaun hai...?
yeh ky**a** hai...?

Shopping
How much?
That makes (20) rupees
That is very expensive!
Make it a bit cheaper!

Kitn**a**?
(b**i**s) rupaye
bahut mahanga hai!
thor**a** kam k**i**jiye!

The hotel
What is the room charge?
Please show the room
Is there an air-conditioned room?
Is there hot water?
... a bathroom/fan/mosquito net
Is there a large room?
It's not clean
Please clean it
Are there clean sheets/blanket?
This is OK
Bill please

kir**a**ya kitn**a** hai?
kamr**a** dikh**a**iye
ky**a** a/c kamr**a** hai?
garam p**a**ni hai?
... bathroom/pankh**a**/machhar d**a**ni
bar**a** kamr**a** hai?
sa**f** nah**i**n hai
sa**f** karw**a** d**i**jiye
sa**f** cha**d**aren/kambal hai**n**?
yah th**i**k hai
bill d**i**jiye

Travel
Where's the railway station?
How much is the ticket to Agra?
When does the Agra bus leave?
How much?

railway station kah**a**n hai?
Agra k**a** ticket kitne k**a** hai?
Agra bus kab j**a**egi?
kitn**a**?

left/right	baien/dahina
go straight on	sidha chaliye
nearby	nazdik
Please wait here	yahan thahariye
Please come at 8	ath bajai ana
quickly	jaldi
stop	rukiye

Restaurants → *For more information see Eating on page 42 and Eating and drinking, over the page.*

Please show the menu	menu dikhaiye
No chillis please	mirch nahin dalna
.sugar/milk/ice	.ch ini/doodh/baraf
A bottle of water please	ek botal pani dijiye
sweet/savoury	mitha/namkin
spoon, fork, knife	chamach, kanta, chhuri

Time and days

right now	abhi
morning	suba
afternoon	dopahar
evening	sham
night	rat
today	aj
tomorrow/yesterday	kal/kal
day	din
week	hafta
month	mahina
year	sal
Sunday	ravivar
Monday	somvar
Tuesday	mangalvar
Wednesday	budhvar
Thursday	virvar
Friday	shukravar
Saturday	shanivar
1	ek
2	do
3	tin
4	char
5	panch
6	chhai
7	sat
8	ath
9	nau
10	das
11	gyara
12	barah
13	terah
14	chaudah
15	pandrah
16	solah
17	satrah

18	atharah
19	unnis
20	bis
100/200	sau/do sau
1000/2000	hazar/do hazar
100,000	lakh

Words such as airport, bank, bathroom, bus, doctor, embassy, ferry, hotel, hospital, juice, police, restaurant, station, stamp, taxi, ticket, train are used locally though often pronounced differently eg daktar, haspatal.

and	aur
big	bara
café/food stall	dhaba/hotel
chemist	dawai ki dukan
clean	saf
closed	band
cold	thanda
day	din
dirty	ganda
English	angrezi
excellent	bahut achha
food/to eat	khana
hot (spicy)	jhal, masaledar
hot (temp)	garam
luggage	saman
medicine	dawai
newspaper	akhbar
of course, sure	zaroor
open	khula
police station	thana
road	rasta
room	kamra
shop	dukan
sick (ill)	bimar
silk	reshmi/silk
small	chhota
that	woh
this	yeh
town	shahar
water	pani
what	kya
when	kab
where	kahan/kidhar
which/who	kaun
why	kiun
with	ke sathh

Eating and drinking

Meat

gosht, mas	meat, usually mutton (sheep)
jhinga	prawns
macchli	fish
murgh	chicken

Vegetables (sabzi)

aloo	potato
bain gan	aubergine
band go bi	cabbage
bhindi	okra, ladies' fingers
gajar	carrots
khumbhi	mushroom
matar	peas
piaz	onion
phool gobi	cauliflower
sag	spinach

Fruit (phal)

amb	mango
ananas	pineapple
dab	green coconut
kela	banana
lichi	lychee
nariyal	coconut
nimbu	lemon
santra	orange
seb	apple

Pulses

masoor dal	pink, round split lentils
chana dal	chick pea
rajma	red kidney beans
urhad dal	small black beans

Spices and herbs

adrak (ada)	ginger
dal chini	cinnamon
dhaniya	coriander
elaichi	cardamom
garam masala	aromatic mixture of 'hot' spices, whole or ground (cardamom, cinnamon, cloves, cumin, black peppercorn etc)
haldi	turmeric
imli	tamarind
jira (zeera)	cumin
kari patta	'curry' leaf
kalonji	onion seed
laung	clove

mirch	chilli
pudina	mint
sarson	(rai) mustard
saunf	fennel
tej patta	bay leaf
til	sesame
zafran/kesar	saffron

Styles of cooking

Many items on restaurant menus are named according to methods of preparation, roughly equivalent to terms such as 'Provençal' or 'sauté'.

bhoona in a thick, fairly spicy sauce

chops minced meat, fish or vegetables, covered with mashed potato,crumbed and fried

cutlet minced meat, fish, vegetables formed into flat rounds or ovals, crumbed and fried (eg prawn cutlet, flattened king prawn)

do piaza with onions (added twice during cooking)

dumphuk steam baked

jhal frazi spicy, hot sauce with tomatoes and chillies

Kashmiri cooked with mild spices, ground almonds and yoghurt, often with fruit

kebab skewered (or minced and shaped) meat or fish; a dry spicy dish cooked on a fire

kima minced meat (usually 'mutton')

kofta minced meat or vegetable balls

korma in fairly mild rich sauce using cream/yoghurt

masala marinated in spices (fairly hot)

Madras hot

makhani in butter rich sauce

moli South Indian dishes cooked in coconut milk and green chilli sauce

Mughlai rich North Indian style

Nargisi dish using boiled eggs

navratan curry ('nine jewels') colourful mixed vegetables and fruit in mild sauce

Peshwari rich with dried fruit and nuts (Northwest Indian)

tandoori baked in a tandoor (special clay oven) or one imitating it

tikka marinated meat pieces, baked quite dry

vindaloo hot and sour Goan meat dish using vinegar

Typical dishes

aloo gosht potato and mutton stew

aloo gobi dry potato and cauliflower with cumin

aloo, matar, kumbhi potato, peas, mushrooms in a dryish mildly spicy sauce

bharela baigan aubergine stuffed with herbs and spices

bharela bhindi okra stuffed with herbs and spices

bhindi bhaji lady's fingers fried with onions and mild spices

boti kebab marinated pieces of meat, skewered and cooked over a fire

chakki ki sabji gram flour shaped into rectangles and cooked in a spicy gravy

dahi bat ete nu Shak potatoes marinated in a curd mixture and cooked in ghee

dal makhani lentils cooked with butter

dum aloo potato curry with a spicy yoghurt, tomato and onion sauce

ganthia nu shaak fried dough dumplings cooked in spicy gravy

gatte ki sabj gram flour dumplings in a spicy gravy

jungli maas/murg sheep/goat meat or chicken cooked in spices

ker sangri locally grown ker and sangri pods popular in the arid Marwar region of Rajasthan
kima mattar mince meat with peas
lal maas sheep and goat meat in a spicy gravy flavoured with tomatoes and onion
matar panir curd cheese cubes with peas and spices (and often tomatoes)
murgh massallam chicken in rich creamy marinade of yoghurt, spices and herbs with nuts
nargisi kofta boiled eggs covered in minced lamb, cooked in a thick sauce
pasinda/tikka/suley Rajasthani kebabs
ringana nu shak aubergine curry
rogan josh rich, mutton/beef pieces in creamy, red sauce
sag gosht mutton and spinach
sag panir drained curd (panir) sautéd with chopped spinach in mild spices
sev tameta tomato curry with gram flour vermicelli
undhiya seasonal winter vegetables made into a spicy stew
valore shak bean curry

Rice and millets
bhat/sada chawal plain boiled rice
biriyani partially cooked rice layered over meat and baked with saffron
daal baati wheat dumplings in the shape of rounds (*baati*) served with lentil soup (*daal*) often with a powdery dessert (*churma*)
Kheechada/bajra ki khichdi millet porridge flavoured with daal and salt served hot with ghee or milk or cold with yogurt
khichdi rice and lentils cooked with turmeric and other spices
masala baati wheat dumplings in the shape of rounds (*baati*) stuffed with peas spices and vegetables
masala puris puris friend with spices
missi raati gram flour dumplings
pulao/pilau fried (and then boiled) rice cooked with spices (cloves, cardamom, cinnamon) with dried fruit, nuts or vegetables. Sometimes cooked with meat, like a biriyani
wagharela bhaat rice seasoned with spices and mustard

Roti – breads
Bakhri stiffer version of chapati
besan parathas made from gram flour
chapati (roti) thin, plain, wholemeal unleavened bread cooked on a tawa (griddle), usually made from ata (wheat flour). Makkaikiroti is with maize flour. Soft, thicker version of poori, made with white flour
nan oven baked (traditionally in a tandoor) white flour leavened bread often large and triangular; sometimes stuffed with almonds and dried fruit
paratha fried bread layered with ghi (sometimes cooked with egg or stuffed with potatoes)
thepla spicy roti
poori thin deepfried, puffed rounds of flour

Accompaniments
achar pickles (usually spicy and preserved in oil)
chutni often fruit or tomato, freshly prepared, sweet and mildly spiced
dahi plain yoghurt
namak salt
papad, pappadom deep fried, pulse flour wafer rounds

raita yoghurt with shredded cucumber, pinapple or other fruit, or bundi, tiny batter balls

Sweets
These are often made with reduced/thickened milk, drained curd cheese or powdered lentils and nuts. They are sometimes covered with a flimsy sheet of decorative, edible silver leaf.

barfi fudgelike rectangles/diamonds
gajar halwa dry sweet made with thickened milk, carrots and spice
gor paapdi jaggery candi
gulab jamun dark fried spongy balls, soaked in syrup
gulabpak cashew and rose petal based dessert
halwa rich sweet made from cereal, fruit, vegetable, nuts and sugar
khir, payasam, paesh thickened milk rice/vermicelli pudding
kopra pak coconut flavoured dessert
kulfi coneshaped Indian ice cream with pistachhios/almonds, uneven in texture
jalebi spirals of fried batter soaked in syrup
laddoo lentil based batter 'grains' shaped into rounds
malpooda/malpuva pancakes fried in a sweet syrup
mohantal a gram flour fudge like dessert cut into squares or rectangles
rabdi/rabari a thickened and extremely sweet kheer
rasgulla (roshgulla) balls of curd in clear syrup
rasmalai spongy curd rounds, soaked in sweetened cream and garnished with pistachio nuts
sandesh dry sweet made of curd cheese
seera wheat flour roasted in ghee with sugar and cardamom
shahi tukra pieces of fried bread soaked in syrup and creamy thickened milk then sprinkled with nuts
srikhand West Indian sweet made with curds, sometimes eaten with fried puris
suji ladoo semolina-based batter grains shaped into rounds
thabdi milk-based *halwa*

Snacks
batata vaada batter fried potato dumplings
bhaji, pakora vegetable fritters (onions, potatoes, cauliflower, aubergine etc) deep-fried in batter
chat sweet and sour cubed fruit and vegetables flavoured with tama rind paste and chillis
chana choor, chioora ('Bombay mix') lentil and flattened rice snacks mixed with nuts and dried fruit
daal dhokli *dhokla* in lentil sauce
dosai South Indian pancake made with rice and lentil flour; served with a mild potato and onion filling (masala dosai) or without (ravai or plain dosai)
ganthia crunchy snack made of gram flour seasoned with chilli and turmeric powder
haandva a savoury cake made from different grain flour and baked with vegetables and spices
idli steamed South Indian rice cakes, a bland breakfast food given flavour by its spiced accompaniments
kachori fried pastry rounds stuffed with spiced lentil/ peas/potato filling
khandvi chick peas served as rolls with mustard seeds and spices
methi vaada/methi gota batter fried fenugreek dumplings

muthia a papad like wheat snack

namkin savoury pastry bits

pakoda/bhajia deep batter fried fritters

samosa cooked vegetable or meat wrapped in a pastry circle into 'triangles' and deep fried

sabudana vaada made from semolina dough

utthappam thick South Indian rice and lentil flour pancake cooked with spices/onions/tomatoes

vadai deep fried, small savoury lentil 'doughnut' rings. Dahi vada are similar rounds in yoghurt

Drinks

aam ras rich mango juice/milkshake served as an accompaniment with rice/khichdi

chai tea boiled with milk and sugar

doodh milk

kafi ground fresh coffee boiled with milk and sugar

kairi pani raw mango juice

lassi cool drink made with yoghurt and water, salted or sweetened

nimboo pani refreshing drink made with fresh lime and water, chilled bottled water, added salt or sugar syrup but avoid ice. Also, fresh lime soda

pani water

Glossary

A

aarti (arati) Hindu worship with lamps

abacus square or rectangular table resting on top of a pillar

acanthus thick-leaved plant, common decoration on pillars, esp Greek

acharya religious teacher

Adi Granth Guru Granth Sahib, holy book of the Sikhs

Adinatha first of the 24 Tirthankaras, distinguished by his bull mount

agarbathi incense

Agastya legendary sage who brought the Vedas to South India

Agni Vedic fire divinity, intermediary between gods and men; guardian of the Southeast

ahimsa non-harming, non-violence

akhand path unbroken reading of the Guru Granth Sahib

alinda verandah

ambulatory processional path

amla/amalaka circular ribbed pattern (based on a gourd) at the top of a temple tower

amrita ambrosia; drink of immortality

ananda joy

Ananda the Buddha's chief disciple

Ananta a huge snake on whose coils Vishnu rests

anda literally 'egg', spherical part of the stupa

Andhaka demon killed by Siva

Annapurna Goddess of abundance; one aspect of Devi

antarala vestibule, chamber in front of shrine or cella

antechamber chamber in front of the sanctuary

apsara celestial nymph

apse semi-circular plan, as in apse of a church

arabesque ornamental decoration with intertwining lines

aram pleasure garden

architrave horizontal beam across posts or gateways

ardha mandapam chamber in front of main hall of temple

Ardhanarisvara Siva represented as half-male and half-female

Arjuna hero of the Mahabharata, to whom Krishna delivered the Bhagavad Gita

arrack alcoholic spirit fermented from potatoes or grain

Aruna charioteer of Surya, the Sun God; Red

Aryans literally 'noble' (Sanskrit); prehistoric peoples who settled in Persia and North India

asana a seat or throne (Buddha's) pose

ashram hermitage or retreat

Ashta Matrikas The eight mother goddesses who attended on Siva or Skanda

astanah threshold

atman philosophical concept of universal soul or spirit

atrium court open to the sky in the centre In modern architecture, enclosed in glass

Avalokiteshwara Lord who looks down; Bodhisattva, the Compassionate

avatara 'descent'; incarnation of a divinity

ayah nursemaid, especially for children

B

baba old man

babu clerk

bada cubical portion of a temple up to the roof or spire

badgir rooftop structure to channel cool breeze into the house (mainly North and West India)

badlands eroded landscape

bagh garden

bahadur title, meaning 'the brave'

baksheesh tip 'bribe'

Balabhadra Balarama, elder brother of Krishna

baluster a small column supporting a handrail

bandh a strike

bandhani tie dyeing (West India)

bania merchant caste

banian vest

baoli or vav rectangular well surrounded by steps

baradari literally 'twelve pillared', a pavilion with columns

barrel-vault semi-cylindrical shaped roof or ceiling

bas-relief carving of low projection

basement lower part of walls, usually with decorated mouldings

basti Jain temple

batter slope of a wall, especially in a fort

bazar market

bedi (vedi) altar/platform for reading holy texts

begum Muslim princess/woman's courtesy title

beki circular stone below the amla in the finial of a roof

belvedere summer house; small room on a house roof

bhadra flat face of the sikhara (tower)

Bhadrakali Tantric goddess and consort of Bhairav

Bhagavad-Gita Song of the Lord; section of the Mahabharata

Bhagiratha the king who prayed to Ganga to descend to earth

bhai brother

Bhairava Siva, the Fearful

bhakti adoration of a deity

bhang Indian hemp

Bharata half-brother of Rama

bhavan building or house

bhikku Buddhist monk

Bhima Pandava hero of the Mahabharata, famous for his strength

Bhimsen Deity worshipped for his strength and courage

bhisti a water-carrier

bhogamandapa the refectory hall of a temple

bhumi literally earth; a horizontal moulding of a sikhara

bidi (beedi) tobacco leaf cigarette

bigha measure of land – normally about one-third of an acre

Bo-tree (or Bodhi) *Ficus religiosa*, pipal tree associated with the Buddha

Bodhisattva Enlightened One, destined to become Buddha

bodi tuft of hair on back of the shaven head (also *tikki*)

Brahma Universal self-existing power; Creator in the Hindu Triad

Brahmachari religious student, accepting rigorous discipline (eg chastity)

Brahman (Brahmin) Highest Hindu (and Jain) caste of priests

Brahmanism ancient Indian religion, precursor of modern Hinduism

Buddha The Enlightened One; founder of Buddhism

bund an embankment

bundh (literally closed) a strike

burj tower or bastion

burqa (burkha) over-dress worn by Muslim women observing purdah

bustee slum

C

cantonment planned military or civil area in town

capital upper part of a column

caryatid sculptured human female figure used as a support for columns

catamaran log raft, logs (*maram*) tied (*kattu*) together (Tamil)

cave temple rock-cut shrine or monastery

cella small chamber, compartment for the image of a deity

cenotaph commemorative monument, usually an open domed pavilion

chaam Himalayan Buddhist masked dance

chadar sheet worn as clothing

chai tea

chaitya large arched opening in the façade of a hall or Buddhist temple

chajja overhanging cornice or eaves

chakra sacred Buddhist wheel of the law; also Vishnu's discus

chala Bengali curved roof

Chamunda terrifying form of the goddess Durga

Chandra Moon; a planetary deity

Chandrasila step before a shrine, moonstone

chankramana place of the promenade of the Buddha at Bodh Gaya

chapatti unleavened Indian bread cooked on a griddle

chaprassi messenger or orderly usually wearing a badge

char sand-bank or island in a river

char bagh formal Mughal garden, divided into quarters

charka spinning wheel

charpai 'four legs' – wooden frame string bed

chauki recessed space between pillars: entrance

chaukidar (chowkidar) night-watchman; guard

chaultri (choultry) travellers' rest house (Telugu)

chaumukha Jain sanctuary with a quadruple image, approached through four doorways

chauri fly-whisk, symbol for royalty

chauth 25 per cent tax raised for revenue by Marathas

chhang strong mountain beer of fermented barley maize rye or millet or rice

chhatri umbrella shaped dome or pavilion

chhetri (kshatriya) Hindu warrior caste

chikan shadow embroidery on fine cotton (especially in Lucknow)

chitrakar picture maker

chlorite soft greenish stone that hardens on exposure

choli blouse

chowk (chauk) a block; open place in a city where the market is held

chunam lime plaster or stucco made from burnt seashells

circumambulation clockwise movement around a shrine

clerestory upper section of the walls of a building which allows light in

cloister passage usually around an open square

coir fibre from coconut husk

corbel horizontal block supporting a vertical structure or covering an opening

cornice horizontal band at the top of a wall

crenellated having battlements

crewel work chain stitching

crore 10 million

cupola small dome

curvilinear gently curving shape, generally of a tower

cusp, cusped projecting point between small sections of an arch

D

daal lentils, pulses

dacoit bandit

dada (dadu) grandfather; elder brother

dado part of a pedestal between its base and cornice

dahi yoghurt

dais raised platform

dak bungalow resthouse for officials

dak post

dakini sorceress

Dakshineshvara Lord of the South; name of Siva

dan gift

dandi wooden 'seat' carried by bearers

darbar (durbar) a royal gathering

dargah a Muslim tomb complex

darshan (darshana) viewing of a deity

darwaza gateway, door

Dasara (dassara/dussehra/dassehra) 10 day festival (Sep-Oct)

Dasaratha King of Ayodhya and father of Rama

Dattatraya syncretistic deity; an incarnation of Vishnu, a teacher of Siva, or a cousin of the Buddha

daulat khana treasury

dentil small block used as part of a cornice

dervish member of Muslim brotherhood, committed to poverty

deval memorial pavilion built to mark royal funeral pyre

devala temple or shrine (Buddhist or Hindu)

devasthanam temple trust

Devi Goddess; later, the Supreme Goddess

dhaba roadside restaurant (mainly North India) truck drivers' stop

dharmshala (dharamsala) pilgrims' rest-house

dharma moral and religious duty

dharmachakra wheel of 'moral' law (Buddhist)

dhobi washerman

dhol drums

dholi (dhooli) swinging chair on a pole, carried by bearers

dhoti loose loincloth worn by Indian men

dhyana meditation

digambara literally 'sky-clad' Jain sect in which the monks go naked

dikka raised platform around ablution tank

dikpala guardian of one of the cardinal directions mostly appearing in a group of eight

dikshitar person who makes oblations or offerings

dipdan lamp pillar

distributary river that flows away from main channel

divan (diwan) smoking room; also a chief minister

Diwali festival of lights (Oct-Nov)

diwan-i-am hall of public audience

diwan-i-khas hall of private audience

diwan chief financial minister

doab interfluve, land between two rivers

dokra tribal name for lost wax metal casting (cire perdu)

dosai (dosa) thin pancake

double dome composed of an inner and outer shell of masonry

Draupadi wife-in-common of the five Pandava brothers in the Mahabharata

dry masonry stones laid without mortar

duar (dwar) door, gateway

dun valley

durg fort

Durga principal goddess of the Shakti cult

durrie (dhurrie) thick handloom rug

durwan watchman

dvarpala doorkeeper

dvipa lamp-column, generally of stone or brass-covered wood

E

eave overhang that shelters a porch or verandah

ek the number 1, a symbol of unity

ekka one horse carriage

epigraph carved inscription

F

faience coloured tilework, earthenware or porcelain

fakir Muslim religious mendicant

fan-light fan-shaped window over door

fenestration with windows or openings

filigree ornamental work or delicate tracery

finial emblem at the summit of a stupa, tower, dome, or at the end of a parapet

firman edict or grant issued by a sovereign

foliation ornamental design derived from foliage

frieze horizontal band of figures or decorative designs

G

gable end of an angled roof

gadba woollen blanket (Kashmir)

gaddi throne

gadi/gari car, cart, train

gali (galli) lane; an alley

gana child figures in art

Gandharva semi-divine flying figure; celestial musician

Ganesh (Ganapati) elephant-headed son of Siva and Parvati

Ganga goddess personifying the Ganga river

ganj market

ganja Indian hemp

gaon village

garbhagriha literally 'womb-chamber'; a temple sanctuary

garh fort

Garuda Mythical eagle, half-human Vishnu's vehicle

Gauri 'Fair One'; Parvati

Gaurishankara Siva with Parvati

ghagra (ghongra) long flared skirt

ghanta bell

ghat hill range, hill road; landing place; steps on the river bank

ghee clarified butter for cooking

gherao industrial action, surrounding home or office of politician or industrial manager

giri hill

Gita Govinda Jayadeva's poem of the Krishnalila

godown warehouse

gola conical-shaped storehouse

Gopala (Govinda) cowherd; a name of Krishna

Gopis cowherd girls; milk maids who played with Krishna

Gorakhnath historically, an 11th-century yogi who founded a Saivite cult; an incarnation of Siva

gosain monk or devotee (Hindi)

gram chick pea, pulse

gram village; gramadan, gift of village

gumbaz (gumbad) dome

gumpha monastery, cave temple

gur palm sugar

guru teacher; spiritual leader, Sikh religious leader

gurudwara (literally 'entrance to the house of God'); Sikh religious complex

H

Haj (Hajj) annual Muslim pilgrimage to Mecca

hakim judge; a physician (usually Muslim)

halwa a special sweet meat

hammam Turkish bath

Hanuman Monkey devotee of Rama; bringer of success to armies

Hara (Hara Siddhi) Siva

harem women's quarters (Muslim), from 'haram', Arabic for 'forbidden by law'

Hari Vishnu Harihara, Vishnu- Siva as a single divinity

Hariti goddess of prosperity and patroness of children, consort of Kubera

harmika the finial of a stupa in the form of a pedestal where the shaft of the honorific umbrella was set

hartal general strike

Hasan the murdered eldest son of Ali, commemorated at Muharram

hat (haat) market

hathi pol elephant gate

hathi (hati) elephant

hauz tank or reservoir

haveli a merchant's house usually in Rajasthan

havildar army sergeant

hawa mahal palace of the winds

Hidimba Devi Durga worshipped at Manali

hindola swing

hippogryph fabulous griffin-like creature with body of a horse

Hiranyakashipu Demon king killed by Narasimha

hiti a water channel; a bath or tank with water spouts

Holi spring festival (Feb-Mar)

howdah seat on elephant's back, sometimes canopied

hundi temple offering

Hussain the second murdered son of Ali, commemorated at Muharram

huzra a Muslim tomb chamber

hypostyle hall with pillars

I

lat pillar, column

icon statue or image of worship

Id principal Muslim festivals

Idgah open space for the Id prayers

ikat 'resist-dyed' woven fabric

imam Muslim religious leader

imambara tomb of a Shiite Muslim holy man; focus of Muharram procession

Indra King of the gods; God of rain; guardian of the East

Ishvara Lord; Siva

iwan main arch in mosque

J

jadu magic

Jagadambi literally Mother of the World; Parvati

Jagannath literally Lord of the World; particularly, Krishna worshipped at Puri

jagati railed parapet

jaggery brown sugar, made from palm sap

jahaz building in form of ship

jala durga water fort

jali literally 'net'; any lattice or perforated pattern

jamb vertical side slab of doorway

Jambudvipa Continent of the Rose-Apple Tree; the earth

Jami masjid (Jama, Jumma) Friday mosque

Jamuna Hindu goddess who rides a tortoise; river

Janaka Father of Sita

jangha broad band of sculpture on the outside of the temple wall

jarokha balcony

jataka stories accounts of the previous lives of the Buddha

jauhar mass suicide by fire of women, particularly in Rajasthan, to avoid capture

jawab literally 'answer,' a building which duplicates another to provide symmetry

jawan army recruit, soldier

jaya stambha victory tower

jheel (jhil) lake; a marsh; a swamp

jhilmil projecting canopy over a window or door opening

-ji (jee) honorific suffix added to names out of reverence and/or politeness; also abbreviated 'yes' (Hindi/Urdu)

jihad striving in the way of god; holy war by Muslims against non-believers

Jina literally 'victor'; spiritual conqueror or Tirthankara, after whom Jainism is named

Jogini mystical goddess

Jyotirlinga luminous energy of Siva manifested at 12 holy places, miraculously formed lingams

K

kabigan folk debate in verse

kachcha man's 'under-shorts' (one of five Sikh symbols)

kacheri (kutchery) a court; an office for public business

Kailasa mountain home of Siva

kalamkari special painted cotton hanging from Andhra

kalasha pot-like finial of a tower

Kali literally 'black'; terrifying form of the goddess Durga, wearing a necklace of skulls/heads

Kalki future incarnation of Vishnu on horseback

kalyanamandapa marriage hall

kameez women's shirt

kanga comb (one of five Sikh symbols)

kankar limestone pieces, used for road making

kantha Bengali quilting

kapok the silk cotton tree

kara steel bracelet (one of five Sikh symbols)

karma impurity resulting from past misdeeds

Kartikkeya (Kartik) Son of Siva, God of war

kashi-work special kind of glazed tiling, probably derived from Kashan in Persia

kati-roll Muslim snack of meat rolled in a 'paratha' bread

keep tower of a fort, stronghold

keystone central wedge-shaped block in a masonry arch

khadi woven cotton cloth made from home-spun cotton (or silk) yarn

khal creek; a canal

khana suffix for room/office/place; also food or meal

khanqah Muslim (Sufi) hospice

kharif monsoon season crop

khave khana tea shop

kheda enclosure in which wild elephants are caught; elephant depot

khet field

khondalite crudely grained basalt

khukri traditional curved Gurkha weapon

kirpan sabre, dagger (one of five Sikh symbols)

kirti-stambha 'pillar of fame,' free standing pillar in front of temple

kohl antimony, used as eye shadow

konda hill (Telugu)

kos minars Mughal 'mile' stones

kot (kota/kottai/kotte) fort

kothi house

kotla citadel
kovil (koil) temple (Tamil)
Krishna Eighth incarnation of Vishnu
Kubera Chief yaksha; keeper of the treasures of the earth, Guardian of the North
kumar a young man
Kumari Virgin; Durga
kumbha a vase-like motif, pot
Kumbhayog auspicious time for bathing to wash away sins
kumhar (kumar) potter
kund lake, well or pool
kundan jewellery setting of uncut gems (Rajasthan)
kurta Punjabi shirt
kurti-kanchali small blouse
kutcha (cutcha/kacha) raw; crude; unpaved; built with sun-dried bricks
kwabgah bedroom; literally 'palace of dreams'

L

lakh 100,000
Lakshmana younger brother of Rama
Lakshmi Goddess of wealth and good fortune, consort of Vishnu
Lakulisha founder of the Pashupata sect, believed to be an incarnation of Siva
lassi iced yoghurt drink
lath monolithic pillar
lathi bamboo stick with metal bindings, used by police
lena cave, usually a rock-cut sanctuary
lingam (linga) Siva as the phallic emblem
Lingaraja Siva worshipped at Bhubaneswar
lintel horizontal beam over doorway
liwan cloisters of a mosque
Lokeshwar 'Lord of the World', Avalokiteshwara to Buddhists and form of Siva to Hindus
lunette semicircular window opening
lungi wrapped-around loin cloth, normally checked

M

madrassa Islamic theological school or college
mahamandapam large enclosed hall in front of main shrine
maha great
Mahabharata Sanskrit epic about the battle between the Pandavas and Kauravas
Mahabodhi Great Enlightenment of Buddha
Mahadeva literally 'Great Lord'; Siva
mahal palace, grand building
mahalla (mohulla) division of a town; quarter; ward
mahant head of a monastery
maharaja great king
maharana Rajput clan head
maharani great queen
maharishi (Maharshi) literally 'great teacher'
Mahavira literally 'Great Hero'; last of the 24 Tirthankaras, founder of Jainism
Mahesha (Maheshvara) Great Lord; Siva
Mahisha Buffalo demon killed by Durga
mahout elephant driver/keeper

mahseer large freshwater fish found especially in Himalayan rivers
maidan large open grassy area in a town
Maitreya the future Buddha
makara crocodile-shaped mythical creature symbolizing the river Ganga
makhan butter
mali gardener
Manasa Snake goddess; Sakti
manastambha free-standing pillar in front of temple
mandala geometric diagram symbolizing the structure of the Universe
mandapa columned hall preceding the temple sanctuary
mandi market
mandir temple
mani (mani wall) stones with sacred inscriptions at Buddhist sites
mantra chant for meditation by Hindus and Buddhists
maqbara chamber of a Muslim tomb
Mara Tempter, who sent his daughters (and soldiers) to disturb the Buddha's meditation
marg wide roadway
masjid literally 'place of prostration'; mosque
mata mother
math Hindu or Jain monastery
maulana scholar (Muslim)
maulvi religious teacher (Muslim)
maund measure of weight about 20 kilos
mausoleum large tomb building
maya illusion
medallion circle or part-circle framing a figure or decorative motif
meena enamel work
mela festival or fair, usually Hindu
memsahib married European woman, term used mainly before Independence
Meru mountain supporting the heavens
mihrab niche in the western wall of a mosque
mimbar pulpit in mosque
Minakshi literally 'fish-eyed'; Parvati
minar (minaret) slender tower of a mosque
mitthai Indian sweets
mithuna couple in sexual embrace
mofussil the country as distinct from the town
Mohammad 'the praised'; The Prophet; founder of Islam
moksha salvation, enlightenment; literally 'release'
monolith single block of stone shaped into a pillar
moonstone the semi circular stone step before a shrine (also chandrasila)
mouza (mowza) village; a parcel of land having a separate name in the revenue records
mridangam barrel-shaped drum (musical)
muballigh second prayer leader
mudra symbolic hand gesture
muezzin mosque official who calls the faithful to prayer
Muharram period of mourning in remembrance of Hasan and Hussain, two murdered sons of Ali
mukha mandapa, hall for shrine
mullah religious teacher (Muslim)
muqarna Muslim stalactite design

mural wall decoration

musalla prayer mat

muthi measure equal to 'a handful'

N

nadi river

Naga (nagi/nagini) Snake deity; associated with fertility and protection

nagara city, sometimes capital

nakkar khana (naggar or naubat khana) drum house; arched structure or gateway for musicians

nal staircase

nal mandapa porch over a staircase

nallah (nullah) ditch, channel

namaaz Muslim prayers, worship

namaste common Hindu greeting (with joined palms) translated as: 'I salute all divine qualities in you'

namda rug

Nandi a bull, Siva's vehicle and a symbol of fertility

nara durg large fort built on a flat plain

Narayana Vishnu as the creator of life

nata mandapa (nat-mandir; nritya sala) dancing hall in a temple

Nataraja Siva, Lord of the cosmic dance

nath literally 'place' eg Amarnath

natya the art of dance

nautch display by dancing girls

navagraha nine planets, represented usually on the lintel or architrave of the front door of a temple

navaranga central hall of temple

navaratri literally '9 nights'; name of the Dasara festival

nawab prince, wealthy Muslim, sometimes used as a title

niche wall recess containing a sculpted image or emblem, mostly framed by a pair of pilasters

Nihang literally 'crocodile': followers of Guru Gobind Singh (Sikh)

nirvana enlightenment; literally 'extinguished'

niwas small palace

nritya pure dance

O

obelisk tapering and usually monolithic stone shaft

ogee form of moulding or arch comprising a double curved line made up of a concave and convex part

oriel projecting window

P

pada foot or base

padam dance which tells a story

padma lotus flower, Padmasana, lotus seat; posture of meditating figures

pagoda tall structure in several stories

pahar hill

paisa (poisa) one hundredth of a rupee

palanquin covered carrier on poles for one

pali language of Buddhist scriptures

palli village

pan leaf of the betel vine; sliced areca nut, lime and other ingredients wrapped in leaf for chewing

panchayat a 'council of five'; a government system of elected councils

pandal marquee made of bamboo and cloth

pandas temple priests

pandit teacher or wise man; a Sanskrit scholar

pankah (punkha) fan, formerly pulled by a cord

parapet wall extending above the roof

pargana sub-division of a district usually comprising many villages; a fiscal unit

Parinirvana the Buddha's state prior to nirvana, shown usually as a reclining figure

parishads political division of group of villages

Parsi (Parsee) Zoroastrians who fled from Iran to West India in the eighth century to avoid persecution

Parvati daughter of the Mountain; Siva's consort

pashmina fine wool from a mountain goat

Pashupati literally Lord of the Beasts; Siva

pata painted hanging scroll

patan town or city (Sanskrit)

patel village headman

paya soup

pediment mouldings, often in a triangular formation above an opening or niche

pendant hanging, a motif depicted upside down

peon servant, messenger (from Portuguese *peao*)

peristyle range of columns surrounding a court or temple

Persian wheel well irrigation system using bucket lift

pettah suburbs, outskirts of town

pice (old form) 1/100th of a rupee

pida (pitha) basement

pietra dura inlaid mosaic of hard, semi-precious stones

pilaster ornamental small column, with capital and bracket

pinjra lattice work

pipal Ficus religiosa, the Bodhi tree

pir Muslim holy man

pitha base, pedestal

pithasthana place of pilgrimage

podium stone bench; low pedestal wall

pol fortified gateway

porch covered entrance to a shrine or hall, generally open and with columns

portico space enclosed between columns

Pradakshina patha processional passage

prakaram open courtyard

pralaya the end of the world

prasadam consecrated temple food

prayag confluence considered sacred by Hindus

puja ritual offerings to the gods; worship (Hindu)

pujari worshipper; one who performs puja (Hindu)

pukka literally 'ripe' or 'finished'; reliable; solidly built

punya merit earned through actions and religious devotion (Buddhist)

Puranas literally 'the old' Sanskrit sacred poems

purdah seclusion of Muslim women from public view (literally curtains)

pushkarani sacred pool or tank

Q

qabr Muslim grave

qibla direction for Muslim prayer

Footnotes Glossary

qila fort
Quran holy Muslim scriptures
qutb axis or pivot

R

rabi winter/spring season crop
Radha Krishna's favourite consort
raj rule or government
raja king, ruler (variations include rao, rawal)
rajbari palaces of a small kingdom
Rajput dynasties of western and central India
Rakshakas Earth spirits
Rama Seventh incarnation of Vishnu
Ramayana Sanskrit epic – the story of Rama
Ramazan (Ramadan) Muslim month of fasting
rangamandapa painted hall or theatre
rani queen
rath chariot or temple car
Ravana Demon king of Lanka; kidnapper of Sita
rawal head priest
rekha curvilinear portion of a spire or sikhara
reredos screen behind an altar
rickshaw 3-wheeled bicycle-powered (or 2-wheeled hand-powered) vehicle
Rig (Rg) Veda oldest and most sacred of the Vedas
Rimpoche blessed incarnation; abbot of a Tibetan Buddhist monastery (gompa)
rishi 'seer'; inspired poet, philosopher
rupee unit of currency in India
ryot (rayat/raiyat) a subject; a cultivator; a farmer

S

sabha columned hall (sabha mandapa, assembly hall)
sabzi vegetables, vegetable curry
sadar (sadr/saddar) chief, main especially Sikh
sadhu ascetic; religious mendicant, holy man
sagar lake; reservoir
sahib title of address, like 'sir'
sahn open courtyard of a mosque
Saiva (Shaiva) the cult of Siva
salaam literally 'peace'; greeting (Muslim)
salwar loose trousers
samadh(i) literally concentrated thought, meditation; a funerary memorial
samsara transmigration of the soul
samudra large tank or inland sea
sangam junction of rivers
sangarama monastery
sangha ascetic order founded by Buddha
sangrahalaya rest-house for Jain pilgrims
sankha the conch shell (symbolically held by Vishnu)
sanyasi wandering ascetic; final stage in the ideal life of a man
sarai caravansarai, halting place
saranghi small four-stringed viola shaped from a single piece of wood
Saraswati wife of Brahma and goddess of knowledge
sarkar the government; state; a writer; an accountant
sarod Indian stringed musical instrument
sarvodaya uplift, improvement of all

sati (suttee) a virtuous woman; act of self-immolation on a husband's funeral pyre
Sati wife of Siva who destroyed herself by fire
satyagraha 'truth force'; passive resistance
sayid title (Muslim)
schist grey or green finely grained stone
seer (ser) weight (about 1 kg)
sepoy (sepai) Indian soldier, private
seth merchant, businessman
seva voluntary service
Shakti Energy; female divinity often associated with Siva
shala barrel-vaulted roof
shalagrama stone containing fossils worshipped as a form of Vishnu
shaman doctor/priest, using magic, exorcist
shamiana cloth canopy
Shankara Siva
sharia corpus of Muslim theological law
shastras ancient texts defining temple architecture
shastri religious title (Hindu)
sheesh mahal palace apartment with mirror work
shehnai (shahnai) Indian wind instrument like an oboe
sherwani knee-length coat for men
Shesha (Sesha) serpent who supports Vishnu
shikar hunting
shisham a valuable building timber
sikhara (shikhara) curved temple tower or spire
shloka (sloka) Sanskrit sacred verse
sileh khana armoury
sindur vermilion powder used in temple ritual
singh (sinha) lion; Rajput caste name adopted by Sikhs
sinha stambha lion pillar
Sita Rama's wife, heroine of the Ramayana epic
sitar classical stringed musical instrument with a gourd for soundbox
Siva (Shiva) The Destroyer in the Hindu triad of Gods
Sivaratri literally 'Siva's night'; a festival (Feb-Mar)
Skanda the Hindu god of war; Kartikkeya
soma sacred drink mentioned in the Vedas
spandrel triangular space between the curve of an arch and the square enclosing it
squinch arch across an interior angle
sri (shri) honorific title, often used for 'Mr'; repeated as sign of great respect
sridhara pillar with octagonal shaft and square base
stalactite system of vaulting, remotely resembling stalactite formations in a cave
stambha free-standing column or pillar, often for a lamp or figure
stele upright, inscribed slab used as a gravestone
sthan place (suffix)
stucco plasterwork
stupa hemispheric Buddhist funerary mound
stylobate base on which a colonnade is placed
subahdar (subedar) the governor of a province; viceroy under the Mughals
Subrahmanya Skanda, one of Siva's sons
sudra lowest of the Hindu castes
sufi Muslim mystic; sufism, Muslim mystic worship
sultan Muslim prince (sultana, wife of sultan)

Surya Sun; Sun God

svami (swami) holy man; a suffix for temple deities

svastika (swastika) auspicious Hindu/ Buddhist cross-like sign

swadeshi home-made goods

swaraj home rule

swatantra freedom

syce groom, attendant who follows a horseman

T

tabla a pair of drums

tahr wild goat

tahsildar revenue collector

taikhana underground apartments

takht throne

talao (tal, talar) water tank

taluk administrative subdivision of a district

tamasha spectacle; festive celebration

tandava (dance) of Siva

tank lake dug for irrigation; a masonry-lined temple pool with stepped sides

tapas (tapasya) ascetic meditative self-denial

Tara literally 'star'; a goddess

tatties cane or grass screens used for shade

Teej Hindu festival

tehsil subdivision of a district (North India)

tempera distemper; method of mural painting by means of a 'body,' such as white pigment

tempo three-wheeler vehicle

terracotta burnt clay used as building material

thali South and West Indian vegetarian meal

thana a police jurisdiction; police station

thug professional robber/murderer (Central India)

tiffin snack, light meal

tika (tilak) vermilion powder, auspicious mark on the forehead; often decorative

tikka tender pieces of meat, marinated and barbecued

tillana abstract dance

tirtha ford, bathing place, holy spot (Sanskrit)

Tirthankara literally 'ford-maker'; title given to 24 religious 'teachers', worshipped by Jains

tonga two-wheeled horse carriage

topi (topee) pith helmet

torana gateway; two posts with an architrave

tribhanga triple-bended pose for standing figures

Trimurti the Hindu Triad, Brahma, Vishnu and Siva

tripolia triple gateway

trisul the trident chief symbol of the god Siva

triveni triple-braided

tuk fortified enclosure containing Jain shrines

tulsi sacred basil plant

tykhana underground room for use in hot weather (North India)

tympanum triangular space within cornices

U

Uma Siva's consort in one of her many forms

untouchable 'outcastes', with whom contact of any kind was believed by high caste Hindus to be defiling

Upanishads ancient Sanskrit philosophical texts, part of the Vedas

usta painted camel leather goods

ustad master

uttarayana northwards

V

vahana 'vehicle' of the deity

vaisya the 'middle-class' caste of merchants and farmers

Valmiki sage, author of the Ramayana epic

Vamana dwarf incarnation of Vishnu

vana grove, forest

Varaha boar incarnation of Vishnu

varna 'colour'; social division of Hindus into Brahmin, Kshatriya, Vaishya and Sudra

Varuna Guardian of the West, accompanied by Makara (see above)

Vayu Wind god; Guardian of the northwest

Veda (Vedic) oldest known Hindu religious texts

vedi (bedi) altar, also a wall or screen

verandah enlarged porch in front of a hall

vihara Buddhist or Jain monastery with cells around a courtyard

vilas house or pleasure palace

vimana towered sanctuary containing the cell in which the deity is enshrined

vina plucked stringed instrument, relative of sitar

Vishnu a principal Hindu deity; the Preserver (and Creator)

vyala (yali) leogryph, mythical lion-like sculpture

W

-wallah suffix often used with a occupational name, eg rickshaw-wallah

wazir chief minister of a raja (from Turkish 'vizier')

Y

yagya (yajna) major ceremonial sacrifice

Yaksha (Yakshi) a demi-god, associated with nature

yali see vyala

Yama God of death, judge of the living

yantra magical diagram used in meditation; instrument

yatra pilgrimage

yoga school of philosophy stressing mental and physical disciplines; yogi

yoni a hole symbolising female sexuality; vagina

Z

zamindar a landlord granted income under the Mughals

zari silver and gold thread used in weaving or embroidery

zarih cenotaph in a Muslim tomb

zenana segregated women's apartments

ziarat holy Muslim tomb

zilla (zillah) district

Index

A

accommodation 40
Achalgarh 167
Adinatha Temple 160
Agra 101
Agra Fort 103
ahimsa 294, 302
Ahirs 292
AIDS 54
air 24
airports 26
Ajmer 234
Akbar 270
Ala-ud-din Khalji 175
alcohol 44
Alwar 217
Amar Sagar 210
Ambaji 165
Amber 131
Amer 131
Ana Sagar 237
Anarkali 271
animals 309
Anupgarh 255
architecture 283
art 286
Aryabhatta 283
Asoka 267
Aurangzeb 114, 272
auto rickshaws 38

B

Babur 270
Bada Bagh 210
Baggar 261
Bagru 134
Baha'i Temple, Delhi 83
Bahadur Shah of
  Gujarat 175
Bakr-Id 48
Bal Samand Lake 193
Balaji Temple 222
Balotra 200
Bambora 154
banks 22
Bardoli 178
Bari Lake 146
Barmer 212
Bassi 176
begging 29
Bera 168
Bhakra Dam 279
Bhand Sagar 250
Bhandarej 222
Bharatiya Janata Party
  (BJP) 278
Bharatpur 222

Bharatpur-Keoladeo
  Ghana National
  Park 223
Bhenswada 168
Bhils 290
Bhim 237
Bhinmal 168
Bijaipur 176
Bikaner 248
bird watching 51
birds 313
Bishnoi 192
Bishnois 192, 291
bites 55
books 316
border crossings 26
Bose, Nandalal 72
Brahma 238, 295
Brahmanas 281
Brahmins 268
Buddha Jayanti 92
Buddhism 303
Bundi 178
buses 35

C

calendar 282, 300
camel fair, Pushkar 243
Camel Research Farm,
  Bikaner 251
camel safaris 50, 205
camera 21
camping 40
car 36
car hire 36
carpets 49
caste 299
Chandrabhaga Fair 184
Chandrasekhara 297
Chandrawati 181
charities 29
children, travelling with
  18, 54
Chittaurgarh 173
Choki Dhani 134
Christianity 304
Churu 261
cinema 46
City Palace, Jaipur 118
climate 13, 306
clothes 21
communications 59
conduct 27
Connaught Place 76
conservation 309
Constitution 277
costs 23

credit cards 22
cricket 52
crocodile 168
crops 309
cuisine 42
currency 22
customs 27
cycling 38, 51

D

dacoits 273
dak bungalows 42
Dalits 299
dance 289
Danta 259
darshan 293
Dasara 48, 92
Daspan 168
Deeg 221
Delhi 64
  activities 95
  directory 100
  eating 88
  entertainment 91
  festivals 91
  history 65
  markets 94
  nightlife 91
  shopping 92
  sights 65
  sleeping 83
  tours 95
  transport 64, 96
Delhi Jaipur Road 217
Delhi Sultanate 269
Deo Somnath 155
Deogarh 156
departure tax 26
Deshnoke 251
devadasis 289
dharamshalas 42
dharma 267
Dhorimmana 212
dhurries 49
diarrhoea 57
Digambaras 303
Dilwara Temples 164
disabled travellers 17
Diwali 48, 302
doab 266
drink 42
driving 36
drugs 30
Dundlod 260
Dungarpur 154
duty-free 20

E

East India Company 273
eating 27
economy 279
Eklingji 155
electricity 27
email 59
embassies 19
encashment
  certificate 23
entertainment 45
etiquette 27
eucalyptus 308
exchange 22
exports 20

F

Fairy Queen 32
Fateh Sagar 145
Fatehpur 258
festivals 13, 46
film 46, 318
first aid kit 53
flights 24
food 42
football 52
Fort Kharwa 237
forts 40
fruit 308

G

Gadi Sagar tank 205
Gaduliya Lohars 291
Gaitore 133
Gajner National Park 251
Gandhi 275
Gandhi Museum 75
Ganesh 297
Ganesh Chaturthi 48
Gangaur Fair 126
Garasias 291
gay travel 18
geography 305
Ghanerao 159
Gobind Singh, Guru 304
Granth, Guru 304
Guda 192
guesthouses 41
Gupta Empire 267
Gurudwara Bangla
  Sahib 77

H

handicrafts 292
Hanuman 296
Hanumangarh 252

Harappan Civilization 266
Harappan sites 252
Harijans 275
Hauz Khas 79
Havala 146
havelis 40, 285
Hawa Mahal 115
health 53
Hindi 17
Hindu deities 294
Hinduism 293
history 266
hitchhiking 39
Holi 46
holidays 46
horse safaris 50
horse safaris, Raj 161, 264
hotels 40
Humayun's Tomb 79

I
I'timad-ud-Daulah 106
Id-ul-Fitr 48
Id-ul-Zuha 48
Iltutmish Tomb 82
imports 20
Independence 276
Independence Day 47
Indian National
    Congress 275
Indra 298
Indrail Pass 33
Indus Valley
    Civilization 266
inoculations 53
Islam 300
itineries 12

J
Jacob, Sir SS 169
Jagannath 142
Jagat Singh I 142
Jahangir 271
Jai Singh II, Maharaja 77
Jaigarh Fort 133
Jainism 302
Jaipur 114
    eating 126
    sights 115
    sleeping 123
    transport 129
Jaisalmer 201
Jaisamand Lake 154
Jal Mahal 133
Jalor 168
Jama Masjid, Delhi 71
Jamwa Sanctuary 134
Janmashtami 48
Janpath 72
Jantar Mantar 77
Jaswant Singh 190

Jaswant Thada 192
jati 299
Jats 292
Jawai Dam 168
jewellery 49, 128
Jhalamand 192
Jhalarapatan 181
Jhalawar 181
Jhunjhunun 261
Jhunjhunun District 259
Jodhpur 188
jodhpurs 195
Junagarh Fort 249
jyotirlinga 297

K
Kakoo 251
Kali 298
Kalibangan 252
Kalidasa 282
Kanana 200
Kankroli 156
Karauli 222
karma 294
Karni Mata temple 251
Karttikeya 297
Kelwara 159
Keoladeo Ghana National
    Park 223
Kesroli 218
Khabha 211
Khaitoon 178
khalsa 304
khari 288
Khejarali 192
Khejarla 239
Khempur 155
Khetolai 199
Khichan 198
KhimsarOn 198
Khuldera 211
Khuri 211
Kishangarh 234
kite flying 127
kos minars 234
Kota 176
Krishna 296
Kuchaman 233
Kumbhalgarh 158
Kumbhalgarh Fort 158
Kumbhalgarh Wildlife
    Sanctuary 159
Kushalgarh 218

L
Lachhmangarh 258
Lake Pichola 145
Lakshmi 296
Lakshmi Narayan
    Mandir 77
Lal Qila 66

Lalgarh Palace 250
language 17, 280
lesbian travel 18
linga 297
liquor permits 21
literature 281
lodges 40
Lodi Gardens 78
Lodurva 210
Lohagarh Fort 222
Lotus Temple, Delhi 83
Luni 199

M
Madhogarh 135
Mahabharata 281
Mahadeva 297
Mahansar 261
Mahatma Gandhi 275
Mahavir 302
Mahisharsura 297
Mahuwa 222
Makar Sankranti 127
malaria 57
mandala 284
Mandawa 259
Mandore 192
maps 39
Marathas 272
marriage 299
mathematics 283
Mauryas 267
Mayo College 237
Medd, H 76
meditation 51
Meherangarh 190
Memorial Ghats 77
Menal 180
Merta City 239
Minas 290
miniature paintings 286
Mitra 298
money 22
monsoon 306
motorbike tours 52
motorcycling 39
Mount Abu 163
Mughal Empire 270
Mughals 301
Muharram 48
music 288
Muslim League 275
Mutiny 274

N
Nag Pahar 237
Nag Panchami 195
Nagas 298
Nagaur 198
Nagda 155
Nakoda 200

Nanak, Guru 303
Nandi 297
Nataraja 297
Nathdwara 156
National Gallery of
    Modern Art 72
National Museum 72
Nauchoki Bund 156
Nausar 237
Navratri 48
Nawalgarh 259
Neemrana Fort 217
Nehru Memorial
    Museum 73
New Delhi 72
New Year's Day 46
newspapers 60
Nimaj 199
non-cooperation 276
nuclear test 199
Nur Jahan 271

O
Old Delhi 66
opening hours 27
Osian 198

P
Pachhar 259
Padmini 175
painting 286
paintings 49
Palace of the Winds 115
Palace on Wheels 32
palaces 40
panther 168
Parasarampura 260
parcel post 59
Parliament House 75
Partition 276
Parvati 296
Peharsar 222
photography 21, 29
pithoras 292
planning 12
Pokaran 198
police 30
post 59
poste restante 59
Project Tiger 216, 227
Protestant 304
puja 294
Pushkar 238

Q
Qutb Minar Complex 80

R
Rabaris 292
radio 60
raga 289

rail 32
Rajpath 72
Rajputs 268
Rajsamand Lake 156
Raksha bandhan 47
Rama 296
Ramadan 48
Ramanuja 296
Ramayana 281
Ramdeora 199
Ramgarh 259
Ramgarh Lake 134
Ramlila 48, 92
Ranakpur 160
Ranthambhore National
    Park 227
Rashtrapati Bhavan 73
Rathwas 292
Rawla Narlai 160
reading list 316
rebirth 294
Red Fort 66
registration 21
religion 292
Republic Day parade 91
Rewari 217
rickshaws 38
Rig Veda 288
Rishabdeo 154
Rohet 199
Roopangarh 234
Round-the-World
    tickets 24
Roy, Jamini 72
Rudra 297
Rupees 22
Russell, RT 73

S
safaris 50
safety 30
Sahariyas 291
Sain 211
Sakas 267
Salawas 192, 199
Salemabad 234
Sam dunes 211
Sama Veda 288
Sambhar Lake 233

Samode 135
samsara 294
Sanganer 133
Sanskrit 280
Sarasvati 295
Sardar Samand 199
Sariska Tiger Reserve 218
sarod 289
sati 261, 273, 297
Savitri 298
Sawai Madhopur 227
science 282
scripts 280
seasons 46, 300
Secretariats 73
Secularism 278
security 30
Sesha 195
Shah Jahan 271
shahnai 289
Shakti 297
Shekhawati 256
shellfish 56
Sheoganj 167
Shergill, A 72
Shi'is Muslims 302
Shilipgram 146
shopping 49
Shukla, YD 72
Siberian Crane 225
Siddis 292
Sikandra 106
Sikar 258
Sikhism 303
Siliserh 218
Siri, Delhi 79
Sitamata Wildlife
    Sanctuary 154
sitar 289
Siva 296
sleeping 40
soccer 52
Soma 298
South Delhi 78
Spiritual University
    movement 167
sport 50
stings 55
stop-overs 24

student travellers 18
Sunni Muslims 302
Suratgarh 255
Surya 298
suttee 297
Svetambaras 303
swadeshi 276
swaraj 276

T
tabla 289
Tagore, Abanin-
    dranath 72
Tagore, Rabin
    -dranath 72, 282
Taj Mahal 101
Tal Chappar 261
Taragarh (Star Fort) 237
taxis 38
teak 307
telephones 60
television 60
thali 43
Thar Desert National
    Park 211
theft 30
thuggee 273
tiger 227
Tikli 217
Tilwara 200
time zone 27
tipping 29
Tirthankaras 303
tour operators 13
tourist offices 15
trains 32
transport
    air 24, 31
    bicycle 38
    bus 35
    car 36
    motorcycling 39
    rickshaws 38
    road 35
    taxi 38
    train 32
travellers' cheques 22
trees 307

trekking 52
tribal people 290
Tughluqabad 82

U
Udaipur 140
    City Palace 142
Uma 296
Umaid Bhawan
    Palace 189
Umed Bhawan 177
Usha 298

V
vaccinations 53
varna 299
Varuna 298
Vedanta 294
Vedas 267, 281
vegetation 307
Vidyadhar Bagh 134
Virabhadra 297
visas 19
Vishnu 295
volunteering 19, 29

W
water 43
weather 13, 60
websites 17
what to take 21
wildlife 154, 159, 218
women travellers 18, 30
work permits 21
working 19

Y
yoga 51, 294
yoni 297
youth hostels 42

Z
zari 178

Map index

A
Agra 104
  Taj Mahal and Taj Ganj 108
Ajmer 235
Alwar 216
Amber Palace 132

B
Bharatpur 223
Bikaner 248
Bundi 179

C
Chittaurgarh 174

D
Delhi
  Connaught Place 76
  New Delhi 74
  Old Delhi 68
  Paharganj 86

J
Jaipur 116
  City Palace 118

Jaisalmer 202
Jodhpur 189

K
Keoladeo Ghana National Park 224
Kota 177

M
Mount Abu 163
Mount Abu centre 164

P
Pushkar 238

R
Ranthambore National Park 228

S
Sariska Tiger Reserve 218
Sawai Madhopur 230
Shekhawati 257

U
Udaipur 141

Advertisers' index

Explore, UK   14
Forts & Palaces Tours, India   129
Ibex Expeditions, India   95
Indiatourism, London   352
M.V. Spices, India   196
Myths & Mountains, USA   32
Paradise Holidays, India   16
Parul Tours & Travels, India   16
Royal Expeditions Pvt Ltd, India   15
Steppes East, UK   16
Trans Indus, UK   15
Wanderlust, India   96

Acknowledgements

First and foremost grateful thanks to Robert and Roma Bradnock for the enormous amount of work they put in to compiling the first edition of this book.

I would also like to thank the following for their help and support:
The Martin family, Delhi
Judith Kent & Peter Holland
Tutu at Diggi Palace, Jaipur
Gazi at Hotel Golden City, Jaisalmer
Roberto
Rajesh at Maya, Agra
Thomas Verstraeten
Petra & Mustapha, somewhere in their van
Roberto & Karen, Jodphur
Hari at Regent Hotel, Bikaner
Melany Marker at URMUL
Alison Barrett, wife extraordinaire

Finally thanks to Dr David Snashall, Dr Martin Taylor, Dr Anthony Bryceson for Health and www.indianest.com and Suniti Chandra Mishra for allowing us to use his words at the beginning of this guide.

Credits

Footprint credits
Editor: Stephanie Lambe
Production assistant: Emma Bryers
Map editor: Sarah Sorensen
Picture editor: Claire Benison

Publisher: Patrick Dawson
Editorial: Alan Murphy, Sophie Blacksell, Sarah Thorowgood, Claire Boobbyer, Felicity Laughton, Laura Dixon, Nicola Jones
Cartography: Robert Lunn, Claire Benison, Kevin Feeney, Angus Dawson
Series development: Rachel Fielding
Design: Mytton Williams and Rosemary Dawson (brand)
Advertising: Debbie Wylde
Finance and administration: Sharon Hughes, Elizabeth Taylor

Photography credits
Front cover: Photo Library (Traditionally dressed woman in archway)
Back cover: POWERSTOCK (Pushkar Camel Fair)
Inside colour section: Alamy; POWERSTOCK; Impact; Image State; Robert Harding

Print
Manufactured in Italy by LegoPrint
Pulp from sustainable forests

Footprint feedback
We try as hard as we can to make each Footprint guide as up to date as possible but, of course, things always change. If you want to let us know about your experiences – good, bad or ugly – then don't delay, go to **www.footprintbooks.com** and send in your comments.

Publishing information
Footprint Rajasthan
2nd edition
© Footprint Handbooks Ltd
December 2004

ISBN 1 904777 23 6
CIP DATA: A catalogue record for this book is available from the British Library

® Footprint Handbooks and the Footprint mark are a registered trademark of Footprint Handbooks Ltd

Published by Footprint
6 Riverside Court
Lower Bristol Road
Bath BA2 3DZ, UK
T +44 (0)1225 469141
F +44 (0)1225 469461
discover@footprintbooks.com
www.footprintbooks.com

Distributed in the USA by
Publishers Group West

Complete title listings

Footprint publishes travel guides to over 150 destinations worldwide. Each guide is packed with practical concise and colourful information for everybody from first-time traveller to travel aficionados. The list is growing fast and current titles are noted below.

Available from all good book shops and online

www.footprintbooks.com

(P) Denotes pocket guide

Latin America & Caribbean
Argentina
Barbados (P)
Bolivia
Brazil
Caribbean Islands
Central America & Mexico
Chile
Colombia
Costa Rica
Cuba
Cusco & the Inca Trail
Dominican Republic (P)
Ecuador & Galápagos
Guatemala
Havana (P)
Leewards (P)
Mexico
Nicaragua
Peru
Rio de Janeiro (P)
St Lucia (P)
South American Handbook
Venezuela

North America
Vancouver (P)
New York (P)
Western Canada

Africa
Cape Town (P)
East Africa
Egypt
Libya
Marrakech (P)
Morocco
Namibia
South Africa
Tunisia
Uganda

Middle East
Dubai (P)
Israel
Jordan
Syria & Lebanon

Asia
Bali
Bangkok & the Beaches
Cambodia

Goa
Hong Kong (P)
India
Indian Himalaya
Indonesia
Laos
Malaysia
Myanmar (Burma)
Nepal
Northern Pakistan
Pakistan
Rajasthan & Gujarat
Singapore
South India
Sri Lanka
Sumatra
Thailand
Tibet
Vietnam

Australasia

Australia
East Coast Australia
New Zealand
Sydney (P)
West Coast Australia

Europe

Andalucía
Barcelona (P)
Berlin (P)
Bilbao (P)
Bologna (P)
Britain
Cardiff (P)
Copenhagen (P)
Croatia
Dublin (P)
Edinburgh (P)
England
Glasgow (P)
Ireland
Lisbon (P)
London
London (P)
Madrid (P)
Naples (P)
Northern Spain
Paris (P)
Reykjavík (P)
Scotland
Scotland Highlands
  & Islands
Seville
Spain
Tallin (P)
Turin (P)
Turkey
Valencia (P)
Verona (P)

Map symbols

Administration

- □ Capital city
- ○ Other city/town
- ⌇⌇ International border
- ⌇⌇ Regional border
- ⌇⌇ Disputed border

Roads and travel

- —— National highway, motorway
- —— Main road
- —— Minor road
- ---- Track
- ······ Footpath
- ⊢■ Railway with station
- ✈ Airport
- 🚍 Bus station
- Ⓜ Metro station
- ---- Cable car
- ++++ Funicular
- ⛴ Ferry

Water features

- ≈ River, canal
- ◯ Lake, ocean
- ⌄⌄⌄ Seasonal marshland
- ░ Beach, sand bank
- ⑅ Waterfall

Topographical features

- ◯ Contours (approx)
- ⋔ Mountain
- △ Volcano
- ⇆ Mountain pass
- ⏧ Escarpment
- ⊓⊓ Gorge
- ⌒ Glacier
- ▦ Salt flat
- ⊛ Rocks

Cities and towns

- ═══ Main through route
- ═══ Main street
- ═══ Minor street

- ⌁ Pedestrianized street
- Σ ⊂ Tunnel
- → One way street
- ▥▥▥ Steps
- ⊨ Bridge
- ⊥⊥⊥ Fortified wall
- ▦ Park, garden, stadium
- ⊜ Sleeping
- ❷ Eating
- ❶ Bars & clubs
- ⊚ Entertainment
- ▭ Building
- ▪ Sight
- ⊞ ⊦ Cathedral, church
- ⛩ Chinese temple
- 🛕 Hindu temple
- ⋏ Meru
- ⌂ Mosque
- △ Stupa
- ✡ Synagogue
- ⓘ Tourist office
- ⏛ Museum
- ✉ Post office
- ⓟ Police
- Ⓢ Bank
- @ Internet
- ♪ Telephone
- ⊕ Market
- ✚ Hospital
- ⓟ Parking
- ⛽ Petrol
- ⛳ Golf
- Ⓐ Detail map
- ◁Ⓐ Related map

Other symbols

- ∴ Archaeological site
- ♦ National park, wildlife reserve
- ☘ Viewing point
- ▲ Campsite
- ⌂ Refuge, lodge
- 🏰 Castle
- ⌇ Diving
- ⇞⇞⇞ Deciduous/coniferous/palm trees
- ⌂ Hide
- ⌇ Vineyard
- ⚗ Distillery
- ⌇ Shipwreck
- ✕ Historic battlefield

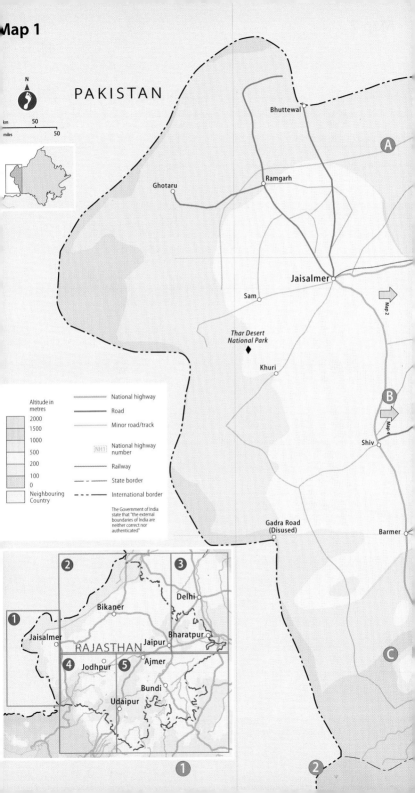

Map 2

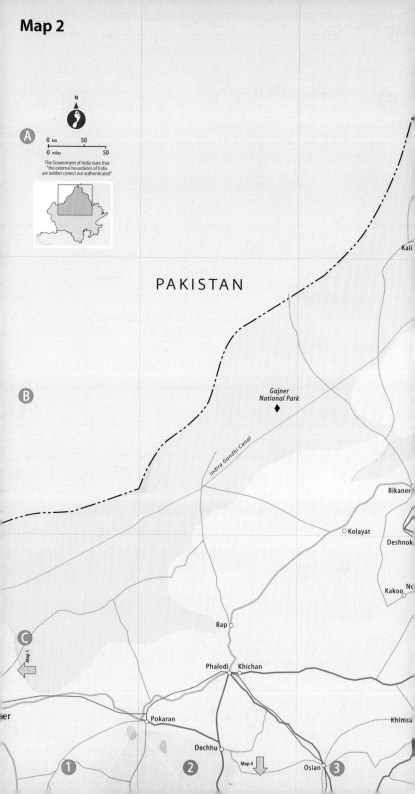

N

0 km 50
0 miles 50

The Government of India state that "the external boundaries of India are neither correct nor authenticated"

A

PAKISTAN

Kali

B

Gajner National Park

Indira Gandhi Canal

Bikaner

Kolayat

Deshnok

Kakoo   No

C

Map 1

Bap

Phalodi   Khichan

Khimsa

er

Pokaran

① ② ③

Dechhu

Map 4

Osian

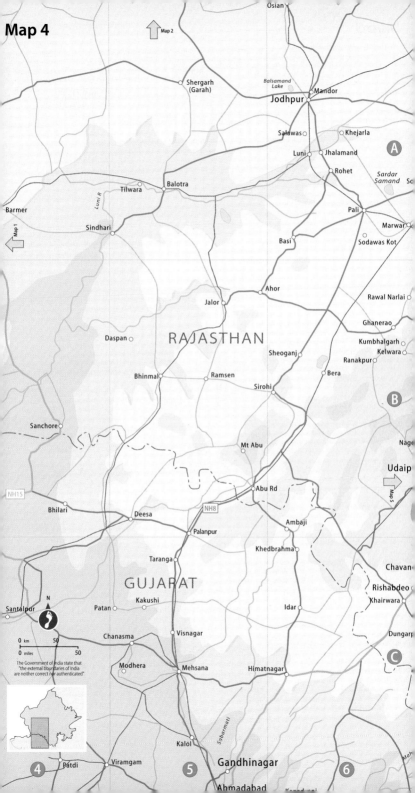

Map 4

Osian

Map 2

Balsamand
Lake

Shergarh
(Garah)

Mandor

Jodhpur

Salawas

Khejarla

A

Luni

Jhalamand

Rohet

Sardar
Samand

Sc

Luni R

Tilwara

Balotra

Barmer

Map 1

Sindhari

Pali

Marwar

Basi

Sodawas Kot

Ahor

Rawal Narlai

Jalor

Ghanerao

Daspan

RAJASTHAN

Kumbhalgarh

Kelwara

Sheoganj

Ranakpur

Bhinmal

Ramsen

Bera

Sirohi

B

Sanchore

Mt Abu

Nage

NH15

Udaip

Map 5

Bhilari

Deesa

Abu Rd

NH8

Palanpur

Ambaji

Khedbrahma

Taranga

Chavan

GUJARAT

Rishabdeo

Santalpur

N

Kakushi

Idar

Khairwara

Patan

Dungar

Chanasma

Visnagar

C

Modhera

Mehsana

Himatnagar

0 km   50

0 miles   50

The Government of India state that
"the external boundaries of India
are neither correct nor authenticated"

Sabarmati

Kalol

4 Patdi

Viramgam

5 Gandhinagar

6

Ahmadabad

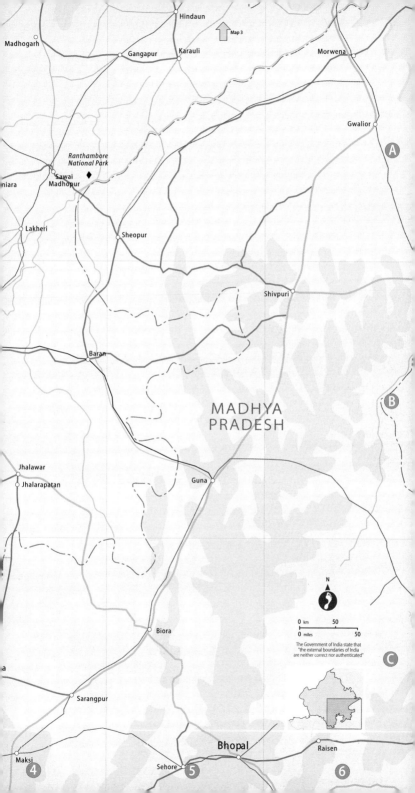

BRIGHTNESS

- ◀ ▶ +

This is a land where nothing is ever black and w
A land of lights and darks, cool marble palaces a
warm golden sands.

This is a land where thousands of years of histo
rubs shoulders with 21st century luxury.
When will you let India leave its technicolour
fingerprint on you?

For a brochure call 08700 102 183.
Phone the India Tourist Office on 020 7437 3677
or email info@indiatouristoffice.org quoting HJo
www.incredibleindia.org

Incredible Ind